Road to
DIVORCE

Road to
DIVORCE

ENGLAND
1530–1987

BY

LAWRENCE STONE

OXFORD UNIVERSITY PRESS
1990

Oxford University Press, Walton Street, Oxford OX2 6DP

Oxford New York Toronto
Delhi Bombay Calcutta Madras Karachi
Petaling Jaya Singapore Hong Kong Tokyo
Nairobi Dar es Salaam Cape Town
Melbourne Auckland

and associated companies in
Berlin Ibadan

Oxford is a trade mark of Oxford University Press

British Library Cataloguing in Publication Data
Stone, Lawrence
Road to divorce: England 1530–1987.
1. England. Divorce, history
I. Title 306.890942
ISBN 0–19–822651–9

Library of Congress Cataloging in Publication Data
Stone, Lawrence.
Road to divorce: England 1530–1987 / by Lawrence Stone.
p. cm.
1. Divorce—England—History. 2. Divorce—Law and legislation—
Great Britain—History. I. Title.
HQ876.S73 1990 306.89'0942—dc20 90–32565
ISBN 0–19–822651–9

Typeset by Wyvern Typesetting Limited, Bristol
Printed and bound in Great Britain by
Biddles Ltd, Guildford and King's Lynn

To
the Fellows, Speakers, and Discussants
at the Seminar of the Shelby Cullom Davis Center
for Historical Studies,
1969–1989
from whom I have learnt so much about so much

Acknowledgements

Any book published today on the subject of marriage, separation, and divorce in early modern and modern England is inevitably constructed on the solid foundations of a large body of earlier work, mostly published in the last twenty years. This book would never have been written if some fifteen years ago Dr E. G. W. Bill, Librarian of Lambeth Palace Library, had not asked me to try to put together a consortium of American libraries to provide funds for a period of years, in order to microfilm the Process Books from the records of the Court of Arches. This was done, and microfiches of this enormous, invaluable, and hitherto inaccessible body of archival records, now augmented by microfilms of the bulk of the other records of the court, are deposited at the National Research Library and can be obtained on loan. For about eight years I was therefore able to consult these materials at leisure at Princeton. I am also indebted to Dr Bill and Miss Barber for their generous assistance while I was working on original records of the court in Lambeth Palace Library.

For a systematic survey of the records of some seven Consistory Courts, I am indebted to my research assistant, Dr Timothy Wales. Under my supervision, he spent two years examining selected samples of surviving records, tabulating matrimonial suits for statistical purposes, briefly noting all cases, and xeroxing or microfilming materials which he considered important. I am deeply grateful to him for his devotion to the task, and for the intelligence and historical imagination he exercised.

I am also very grateful to Mr Geoffrey Clark. For two summers he combed the microfilm records of the Old Bailey for materials concerning bigamy, infanticide, rape and similar problems related to marriage, separation, and sexual relations. He also listed all the cases of Parliamentary divorce in the *Journals of the House of Lords*, and carried out statistical analyses of the cases in the Court of Arches.

My third invaluable helper has been my wife, Jeanne C. Fawtier Stone, who interrupted her own research in order to help me complete this book. She has put into the computer and edited all my handwritten drafts of this volume and most of the two companion volumes still in preparation, has commented extensively on the text, and has spent many weeks on the thankless and dreary tasks of checking footnotes and compiling the index.

The fourth person upon whom I have relied heavily for assistance has been my long-suffering secretary, Mrs Joan Daviduk, who typed my almost illegible drafts of many of the case studies, some of the best of which have been used in the two ancillary volumes, and who also typed the

vi

Acknowledgements

flow of correspondence about the book as it took shape over the past nine years.

For financial support of this project I am indebted to the Rockefeller Foundation (G. A. Hum. 8116) and to the National Endowment of the Humanities (Grant R. O.–20220–82). I am also grateful for two semesters of paid leave from Princeton University, for a Rollins Research Grant from Princeton History Department, and for another grant from the Humanities Research Committee of Princeton University.

Among the staff of the many libraries and record offices visited for this project, all of whom were extremely helpful, I should like to single out those of the Bodleian Library, the Oxford University Law Library, and the British Library. For facilitating several days of intensive work on the extremely rich collection of printed pamphlet trial records in the Royal Irish Academy in Dublin, I am very grateful to Ms Brigid Dolan. I have been greatly helped by the staff of the Country Record Offices of Buckinghamshire, Devon, Dorset, East Sussex, Hertfordshire, Huntingdonshire, Lincolnshire, Norfolk, Nottinghamshire, Somerset, Suffolk, and Warwickshire. Several groups and individuals have read or heard drafts of two chapters. I am grateful to the members of the Shelby Cullom Davis Seminar and to the members of the History, English, and Law Departments of the University of California at Berkeley for some very helpful criticism of Chapter IX on Criminal Conversation. Thanks to them I was stimulated into making considerable revisions of the argument. An early draft of the General Introduction was severely (and rightly) criticized by a group of friends at the Institute for Advanced Study (including Susan Amussen, Greg Denning, Donna Merwick, Miri Rabin, and David Underdown), thanks to which I entirely rewrote the whole of the first, theoretical section.

The number of individuals who have helped me along the way are legion. Professor Owen Fiss kindly read Chapter IX and made a number of very helpful criticisms. Dr John Haskey of the Office of Population Census and Surveys in London was kind enough to supply me with much statistical data about current trends in divorce. Mrs Annette Lawson provided helpful comments about adultery. Professor Mary Poovey allowed me to see an advance copy of the section of her book concerning Caroline Norton and the 1857 Divorce Act. Professor Susan Watkins not only gave me useful advice about modern statistics and guided me to the relevant literature in the field, but also read Chapter XIII for me and pointed out many errors of fact and logic. Others who have helped with advice, xeroxes of original materials or footnote references include Professor Charles Donahue, Jr; Professor Clint Francis, who supplied me with materials from his work on the Common Pleas records; Robin Harcourt Williams of Hatfield House; Professor Douglas Hay; Dr David Hayton; Professor S. N. Katz; Dr R. J. B. Knight of the National Maritime

Acknowledgements

Museum; Dr John Looney; A. P. W. Malcolmson of the Public Record Office of Northern Ireland, for supply of advice and references from manuscripts in the National Library of Ireland and elsewhere; Dr Simon Newman; Professor James C. Oldham, who supplied me with lists of crim. con. cases from his forthcoming edition of Lord Mansfield's Trial Notes; Professor Mary Lyndon Shanley; Professor David Sugarman; Naomi Tadmore; and Rachel Weil. Finally, I am indebted to Connie Wilsack for her copy-editing of the manuscript.

L.S.

Princeton, New Jersey
September 1989

Contents

Contents

VIII Judicial Separation

Contents

Contents

List of Plates

xvii

List of Plates

List of Figures

List of Figures

List of Tables

List of Tables

Abbreviations

Adultery Anatomised	Anon., *Adultery Anatomised*, 2 vols. (London, 1761)
Alleman	G. S. Alleman, *Matrimonial Law and the Materials of the Restoration Drama* (Wallingford, Penn., 1942)
Anderson	S. Anderson, 'Legislative Divorce: Law for the Aristocracy?', in G. R. Rubin and D. Sugarman (eds.), *Law and Society 1750–1914: Essays in the History of English Law* (Abingdon, 1984), 412–40
Baron & Feme	Anon., *Baron & Feme: A Treatise of Law and Equity concerning Husbands and Wives*, 3rd edn. (London, 1738).
Biggs	J. M. Biggs, *The Concept of Matrimonial Cruelty* (London, 1962)
Bill Preventing Clandestine Marriages	*A Bill for the More Effectual Preventing of Clandestine Marriages* (London, 1740), (BL 375. c8)
Bon Ton Mag.	*Bon Ton Magazine*, 3 vols. (London, 1791–3)
Bright	J. E. Bright, *A Treatise of the Law of Husband and Wife respecting Property* (London, 1849)
Bristol and Glos. Arch. Soc. Trans:	*Bristol and Gloucestershire Archaeological Society Transactions*
J. S. Burn	J. S. Burn, *History of the Fleet Marriages, with some account of the Wardens of the Prison, the Parsons and their Registers* ... (London, 1834)
R. Burn	R. Burn, *The Ecclesiastical Law* (London, 5th edn. 1788; 9th edn. 1842)
Camden Misc.	Camden Miscellany, Camden Soc.
Campbell, *Lives of the Chief Justices*	J. Lord Campbell, *Lives of the Chief Justices of England*, 2 vols. (London, 1848–9)
CC:	Consistory Court
Clancy	J. Clancy, *A Treatise on the Rights, Duties, and Liabilities of Husband and Wife at Law and Equity* (London, 1827)
Clifford	A. Clifford, *A History of Private Bill Legislation* (London, 1885)

Collection of Trials	Anon., *A Collection of the most Remarkable and Interesting Trials* (London, 1756)
Conjugium Languens	Anon., ['Castamore'], *Conjugium Languens, or the Natural, Civil and Religious Mischiefs Arising from Conjugal Infidelity and Impurity* (London, 1700)
Crim. Con. A & T.	Anon., *Crim. Con. Actions and Trials* (London, n.d.)
Crim. Con. Gaz.	*Crim. Con. Gazette*, 2 vols. (London, 1838–9)
Dibdin and Healey	Sir Lewis Dibdin and Sir Charles E. H. Chadwyck Healey, *English Church Law and Divorce* (London, 1912)
DNB	*Dictionary of National Biography* (Oxford)
DRO	Diocesan Record Office
Eng. Rep.	*English Reports*, 187 vols. [1220–1865] (London, 1900–30)
Evans	W. D. Evans, *A General View of the Decisions of Lord Mansfield in Civil Cases* (London, 1803)
Feme Coverts	Anon., *A Treatise of Feme Coverts* (London, 1732)
Gally	H. Gally, *Some Considerations upon Clandestine Marriages* (London, 1750)
Gent's Mag.	*Gentleman's Magazine*
Gillis	J. R. Gillis, *For Better for Worse: British Marriages to the Present* (New York, 1985)
GLRO	Greater London Record Office
Godolphin	J. Godolphin, *Repertorium Canonicum or Abridgement of the Ecclesiastical Laws of the Realm* (London, 1880)
Hansard	T. C. Hansard, *Parliamentary History*, Series 1–
Hardships of Laws on Wives	Anon., *The Hardships of English Laws in relation to Wives* (London, 1735)
Helmholtz	R. H. Helmholtz, *Marriage Litigation in Medieval England* (Cambridge, 1974)
HMC	Historical Manuscripts Commission
Holcombe	L. Holcombe, *Wives and Property: Reform of the Married Women's Property Law in Nineteenth Century England* (Toronto, 1983)
Houlbrooke, *Church Courts*	R. A. Houlbrooke, *Church Courts and the People during the English Reformation* (Oxford, 1979)
Howard	G. E. Howard, *A History of Matrimonial Institutions*, 3 vols. (London, 1904)

HWRO	Hereford and Worcester County Record Office
Ingram, *Church Courts, Sex and Marriage*	M. Ingram, *Church Courts, Sex, and Marriage in England 1570–1640* (Cambridge, 1987)
JH Commons	*Journal of the House of Commons*
JH Lords	*Journal of the House of Lords*
Laws Respecting Women	Anon., *The Laws Respecting Women* (London, 1737)
Letter to the Public	Anon. [Marsh], *A Letter to the Public . . . upon the Subject of the Act of Parliament for the Better Preventing of Clandestine Marriages* (London, 1753), (BL, 518 h 12 (1))
Lewis	J. Lewis, *In the Family Way: Child-bearing in the British Aristocracy, 1760–1860* (New Brunswick, 1986)
Lincs. CCAO	Lincolnshire County Council Archives Office
Lichfield JRO, LCC	Lichfield Joint Record Office, Lichfield Consistory Court
Lond. Chron.	*London Chronicle*
LPCA	Lambeth Palace, Court of Arches MSS
Luttrell	N. Luttrell, *A Brief Historical Relation of State Affairs*, 6 vols. (Oxford, 1857)
MacQueen, *House of Lords.*	J. F. MacQueen, *A Practical Treatise on the Appellate Jurisdiction of the House of Lords and the Privy Council, together with the Practice of Parliamentary Divorce* (London, 1842)
MacQueen, *Rights and Liabilities*	J. F. MacQueen, *The Rights and Liabilities of Husband and Wife* (London, 1849)
MacQueen, *Marriage, Divorce, and Legitimacy*	J. F. MacQueen, *A Practical Treatise on the Law of Marriage, Divorce, and Legitimacy* (London, 1860)
MacQueen, *Scotch Appeals.*	J. F. MacQueen, *Reports of Scotch Appeals and Writs of Error in the House of Lords* (Edinburgh, 1855)
Marchant	R. A. Marchant, *The Church under the Law, Justice, Administration and Discipline in the Diocese of York, 1560–1640* (Cambridge, 1969)
Marriage & Soc.	R. B. Outhwaite (ed.), *Marriage and Society: Studies in the Social History of Marriage* (New York, 1981)
Menafee	S. P. Menafee, *Wives for Sale* (Oxford, 1981)

NC Trials for Adultery (1797)	Anon. *A New Collection of Trials for Adultery: or a General View of Modern Gallantry and Divorce from the year 1780 to the middle of the year 1797*, 3 vols. (London, 1796 [sic])
NCC Trials for Adultery (1780):	*A New and Complete Collection of Trials for Adultery*, 2 vols. (London, 1780)
OB Proc.:	*Old Bailey Proceedings* (London, 1714–1834)
5 *Parl. Debates: Commons*	*Parliamentary Debates*, 5th Series, *House of Commons*
5 *Parl. Debates: Lords*	*Parliamentary Debates*, 5th Series, *House of Lords*
Parl. Hist.	W. Cobbett, *Parliamentary History of England*, 36 vols. (London, 1806–20)
Peerage	G. E. Cokayne, *Complete Peerage of England*, 14 vols. (London, 1910–65)
Philogamus	Philogamus, *The Present State of Matrimony* (London, 1739)
Plowden	F. Plowden, *Crim. Con. Biography*, 2 vols. (London, 1838–9)
Poynter	T. Poynter, *A Concise View of the Doctrine and Practice of the Ecclesiastical Courts in Doctors Commons on Marriage and Divorce* (London, 1824)
PP	*Parliamentary Papers*
Preventing Marriages, founded on adultery	Anon., *Thoughts on the Propriety of Preventing Marriages Founded on Adultery* (London, 1800)
Report on the Ecclesiastical Courts	*Report from the Commissioners relating to the Ecclesiastical Courts (PP* Eng. 1831–2), vol. 24
RIA/HP	Royal Irish Academy, Haliday Pamphlets
RIA/HT	Royal Irish Academy, Haliday Tracts
Roberts	J. Roberts, *Divorce Bills in the Imperial Parliament* (Dublin, 1906)
Roper	R. S. Dennison Roper, *A Treatise on the Law of Property arising from the Relations between Husband and Wife* (London, 1820)
Rowntree and Carrier	G. Rowntree and N. H. Carrier, 'The Resort to Divorce in England and Wales, 1858–1957', *Population Studies*, 11 (1957–8)
Roy. Com. Divorce 1853 [1–3]:	*Report of the Royal Commission on Divorce and Matrimonial Causes, 1853 (Parliamentary Papers*, 1852–3, vols. 40–2)
Roy. Com. Divorce 1912 [1–3]:	*Report of the Royal Commission on Divorce and Matrimonial Causes, 1912 (Parliamentary Papers*, 1912–13, vols. 18–20)

Roy. Com. Divorce 1956	Report of the Royal Commission on Marriage and Divorce, *1956* (*Parliamentary Papers*, 1955–6, vol. 23)
Roy. Com. Marriage 1868	Report of the Royal Commission on the Laws of Marriage, *1868* (*Parliamentary Papers*, 1867–8)
Salmon	J. Salmon, *A Critical Essay concerning Marriage* (London, 1724)
Salop RO	Shropshire Record Office
Shelford	L. Shelford, *A Practical Treatise of the Law of Marriage and Divorce* (London, 1841)
Sibbit	J. Sibbit, *Thoughts on the Frequency of Divorces in Modern Times* (London, 1800)
State Trials	W. Cobbett, *Complete Collection of State Trials*, ed. W. B. Howell (London, 1809–28)
Stone, *Broken Lives*	L. Stone, *Broken Lives* (Oxford, forthcoming)
Stone, *FSM*	L. Stone, *Family, Sex, and Marriage in England 1500–1800* (London, 1977)
Stone, *Uncertain Unions*	L. Stone, *Uncertain Unions* (Oxford, forthcoming)
Swinburne	H. Swinburne, *A Treatise of Spousals or Matrimonial Contracts* (London, 1686)
T & C Mag.	*Town and Country Magazine* (London, 1769–93)
Till	B. D. Till, 'The Administrative System in the Ecclesiastical Courts in the Diocese and Province of York. Part III, 1660–1883': A Study in Decline (unpublished typescript deposited in the Borthwick Institute, York)
Trials for Adultery at Doctors Commons	*Trials for Adultery or the History of Divorces, being Select Trials at Doctors Commons ... from the year 1760 to the present time*, 7 vols. (London, 1779–80)
Trumbach	R. Trumbach, *The Rise of the Egalitarian Family: Aristocratic Kinship and Domestic Relations in Eighteenth-Century England* (New York, 1978)
Walpole's Correspondence	*Horace Walpole's Correspondence*, ed. W. S. Lewis *et al.*, 48 vols. (New Haven, 1937–80)
Warws RO	Warwickshire Record Office
Wharton	J. J. S. Wharton, *An Exposition of the Laws relating to the Women of England* (London, 1853)
Wolfram	S. Wolfram, 'Divorce in England 1700–1857', *Oxford Journal of Legal Studies*, 5 (1987), 155–86

General Introduction

There is no one branch of the law more important, in any point of view, to the great interests of society, and to the personal comforts of its members, than that which regulates the formation and the dissolution of the nuptial contract. No institution indeed more nearly concerns the very foundations of society, or more distinctly marks by its existence the transition from a rude to a civilized state, than that of marriage.

Speeches of Henry Brougham (Philadelphia, 1841), 2: 289

The history of the passions is curious and important. They undergo rapid revolutions; and to understand their various appearances, we must study the civil and religious constitutions which have influenced their direction.

Anon., *Letters On Love, Marriage and Adultery* (London, 1789), 89

In the momentary meeting of men, brought about by the requirements of law, the historian may grasp the forces and purposes of a system.

J. T. Noonan, Jun., *Power to Dissolve: Lawyers and Marriages in the Courts of the Roman Curia* (Cambridge, Mass., 1972), 181

1. The Background: A Non-Separating and Non-Divorcing Society

A few years ago, Professor Bernard Bailyn observed that 'to write essential ... narratives—dominated by a sense of movement through time, incorporating the technical studies, and devoted to showing how the present world was shaped by its emergence from a very different past ... seems to me to be the great challenge of modern historical scholarship'.[1]

Eight hundred years ago, in the Christian West, the highly restrictive moral code of the medieval canon law made divorce virtually impossible, except for the very rich and powerful who could lobby and bribe their way to annulments from Rome. By way of contrast, a few years ago a

---

[1] B. Bailyn, 'The Challenge of Modern Historiography', *American Historical Review*, 87 (1982), 7.

judge in America casually granted one woman no fewer than sixteen divorces in eleven years. In England, today, divorce has in practice become an administrative rather than a judicial procedure, and because of the huge numbers involved it is inevitably processed with conveyor-belt speed and impersonality. It is estimated that a third of all marriages in England (and a half of all those in America) will end in the divorce court.[2]

Divorce is thus now as central to our culture and experience as death and taxes. How did we get this way? How and when did this situation evolve from a medieval one in which divorce was absolutely forbidden? How did English lawyers and laity devise ways to get around the letter of the law in the long centuries before divorce was first officially legalized in 1857? How is it that the justification of marital separation, which once was limited to wifely adultery, now embraces a wide range of marital shortcomings by both parties, including mere temperamental incompatibility? How did formal marital breakdown change from a scandalous rarity to a morally neutral commonplace?

It must never be forgotten that England in the early modern period was neither a separating nor a divorcing society: death was virtually the sole agent for dissolving marriage. There is little reason to suppose that there were proportionately fewer unhappy marriages than there are today; indeed there may well have been more. But there were a number of very powerful forces at work to keep together even the most miserable and most bitterly quarrelling of couples. First there were a set of intern-alized values, inculcated from the earliest age by religion and education. Both sexes were told that marriage was a sanctified and indissoluble contract, and women were taught that it was God's will that they should obey their husbands. As late as 1808 a popular magazine catering to middle- and upper-class women was urging them to 'read frequently and with close attention the matrimonial service, and take care in doing it not to overlook the word OBEY'.[3] There can be little doubt that this advice more closely reflected the sentiments of the great majority of married women than the handful of feminist tracts of the period which are so widely read today.

These internalized controls were reinforced by powerful external pressures, thanks to the watchful and persistent supervision of the marriage by parents, kin, 'friends', and neighbours. These groups outside the nuclear household rarely hesitated to intervene, to arbitrate, to advise, and even to impose reconciliation upon any couple threatening to separ-

---

[2] See below, Table 13.9.
[3] *La Belle Assemblée* (London, 1808), 4: 82.

ate. This practice of close neighbourly and kinship surveillance of domestic relations before and during marriage had long roots in the past, going back at least to the Middle Ages.[4] Those who broke the code of the village concerning sexual or power relations within the family were liable to be held up to ignominy by noisy public shame punishments called 'rough music', 'Skimmingtons', or 'charivaris'. Thus a husband-beating wife, a passively hen-pecked husband, a couple married despite gross disparities in age, a cuckold, an adulterous wife, or, by the eighteenth century, an excessively brutal husband, were all liable to be treated to these humiliating demonstrations of public disapproval.[5]

Just as the reconciliation of quarrelling spouses and the arrangement of private separations by deeds were negotiated by family and friends, so in upper-class circles the formal expulsion of a wife from house and home on grounds of adultery was usually the result of a solemn family conclave, which often turned into a kind of private trial attended by the family solicitor.[6] Close kin and often neighbours were thus nearly always deeply involved in a failing marriage at all the critical stages of its disintegration, beginning with attempts to shore it up and ending in mediation to see fair play at a separation and to keep the scandal of the break-up out of the courts. For example in 1781, after a separation of beds had been followed by a total breach between the couple, 'the families and friends of Matthew Lewis and Fanny Maria Lewis tried to arbitrate their differences, and endeavoured to prevail on Fanny to conform to the wishes of her husband with respect to her behaviour and the company she should keep'. Only when this effort to make the marriage conform to the contemporary norms of marital peace through wifely obedience had failed to produce the desired results, were 'articles of separation' reluctantly agreed upon 'through the means of their friends'.[7]

Sometimes attempts by family friends to interfere and patch up a marriage only succeeded in alienating one or both parties. For example, in 1774 the marriage of Richard and Elizabeth Lytton of Knebworth in Hertfordshire was breaking up because of his conviction that the

---

[4] S. Amussen, 'Féminin/masculin: Le Genre dans l'Angleterre de l'époque moderne', *Annales: Economies, sociétés, civilisations* (Mar.–Apr. 1985), 270–7.

[5] E. P. Thompson, ' "Rough Music": Le Charivari anglais', ibid. 27 (1972), 185–312; N. Z. Davis, 'The Reasons of Misrule: Youth Groups and Charivaris in Sixteenth-Century France', *Past and Present*, 50 (1971); M. Ingram, 'Ridings, Rough Music and the "Reform of Popular Culture" in Early Modern England', ibid. 105 (1984); G. R. Quaife, *Wanton Wenches and Wayward Wives, Peasants and Illicit Sex in Early Seventeenth-Century England* (London, 1979), 200.

[6] E.g. the Middleton case in Stone, *Broken Lives*, and the Clavering case, below, 207; see also the Halford case in *JH Lords*, 52: 165.

[7] GLRO, London CC, DL/C/179.

3

'continued and invariable settled aversion and contempt with which you have always thought proper to treat me' had now developed into 'causeless hatred to me, risen to an unaccountable pitch'. Elizabeth was only too anxious for a reconciliation, and family and friends rushed in with their advice. Elizabeth's brother wrote to Richard telling him of his wife's continued 'warm affection' and urging 'a meeting between each party and their friends which may fortunately be productive of an accommodation'. He also reminded Richard of the dangers of adverse publicity, telling him 'how harsh was the construction that the world put upon your residing for so long a time last year from your family at Bath'. He therefore urged a meeting, to avoid 'the same disagreeable reflections' and 'insinuations'.

But this did nothing to alter Richard's resolve never to see his wife again, and the intervention of a family friend, John Paradine, merely made things worse. Paradine had unexpectedly called on Richard on a Sunday night to urge him to a reconciliation, but apparently had received a very frosty welcome. He later wrote to Richard to explain that he had been motivated only by the best intentions: 'having always looked upon a separation to be attended with very fatal consequences, especially where there are children, I sincerely wished that a reconciliation might be affected if possible'. He admitted that he had interfered in a delicate private matter, 'and thereby subject myself to the imputation of an officious intruder'. His effort had clearly been a disaster.[8] But even when the ultimate outcome was a separation and not a reconciliation, as occurred with the Lewises and the Lyttons, the details were normally worked out by 'friends and relatives' on both sides, as frequently attested in the preamble to the actual separation deed.[9]

In addition to these internal and external constraints upon the breakup of a marriage, there were the harsh facts that it was virtually impossible for all but a handful of the very rich to obtain a full divorce with permission to remarry, and that a separated wife faced exceptionally severe penalties. Unless she was protected by a private deed of separation, she was in practice virtually an outlaw. All the income from her real estate was retained by her husband, as well as all future legacies which might come to her. All her personal property, including her future earnings from a trade and her business stock and tools, were liable to seizure by her husband at any moment. She was unable to enter into a legal contract, to use credit to borrow money, or to buy or sell property. All her savings belonged to her husband. And finally all her children were con-

[8] Lytton and Lytton (1774), Herts RO, 574, 83 B.
[9] See e.g. Hurt and Hurt (1766), Lincs RO, 1 W D 2.

trolled entirely by their father, who was free to dispose of them as he wished, and to deprive their mother of any opportunity ever to speak to them again. These were conditions which tended to make marital breakdown at the insistence of the wife a rarity, unless her interests had been protected by a carefully drawn up deed of separation.

Another reason why private separations were rare before 1640 is that throughout the sixteenth and early seventeenth centuries, the church authorities made every effort to force middling and lower-status couples to stay together. Episcopal and archdeaconal visitation enquiries always included an item asking the churchwardens for the names of married couples from the village who were living separately, and up to 1640 this information flowed in. For example, some thirty couples were reported over a seven-year period in the archdeaconry of Chichester, in Sussex. Many of them were poor people who had remarried and then found it impossible to live together because of quarrels over the management of children by earlier marriages. Thus, an entry for 1626 runs:

We present John Brookes and Ellen his wife for keeping house apart, by reason that their children which he had by a former wife, and she by a former husband, cannot well agree, making debate between them; therefore for a more quiet and contented living, keep two several houses, and come and go one to another when they think well.

Others were more obviously cases of desertion, such as the two couples reported in the same year

whom we present for that they have not kept company with their wives for the space of half a year, the former leaving her without necessary maintenance, the latter left his with 3 small children upon the parish.[10]

Clearly, what bothered the churchwardens was that the burden of maintenance in these cases of separation fell on the parish. Examples of such presentments for living separately are still to be found in the 1660s, but thereafter they fade away as moral attitudes towards separation changed for good, and as church control of sexual and marital behaviour began to collapse.

As a result, there is little evidence that variations in the strictness of divorce laws in any way influenced the degree of marital breakdown or adultery in a given society. The classic example is Scotland: divorce has been permitted ever since the mid-sixteenth century for adultery or desertion, with remarriage for the innocent party, but until the twentieth century the divorce rate remained almost negligible. When the option of

---

[10] *Churchwardens' Presentments*, ed. H. Johnstone, *Sussex Rec. Soc.* 49 (1947–8), 120, 62.

divorce for reasons of adultery by either party was first made available in England in 1857, it too, after an initial spurt, had little real effect on the incidence of divorce until the First World War. In 1911 the number of divorces was still below 1,000 a year, out of a population of 6.6 million married couples.

The writing of a long book about a process which before the twentieth century was experienced by only a tiny minority of the population may be thought to require some justification. The answer is that divorce is an event which in its symbolic significance to society is comparable only to capital punishment: they are both socially approved, accepted, and irrevocable terminations, whether of a marriage or a life. Both carry a heavy baggage of passionately felt moral principles and symbolic meaning. This explains why legislative change to cut back or abolish the one, or to permit or facilitate the other, has been so extremely rare in the last three centuries, and so bitterly fought over whenever it occurred—at least before the middle of the twentieth century. Hence, divorce provides a means of recapturing the history of changes in *mentalités* in England in the early modern and modern period, how these changes have affected and been affected by legislation, and how the public have contrived to twist the law for their own purposes. This may be thus a story about the private lives of a minority, but it is one which offers a privileged, indeed almost unique, insight into the interaction of the public spheres of morality, religion, and the law.

Since divorce is an outcome of marriage, its evolution is inextricably bound up with that of the latter. Marriage was generally regarded as the normal outlet for a woman's energies, although in practice the proportion of spinsters in England was very high in the sixteenth and seventeenth centuries, running at well over 10 per cent. In the past, just as today, marriage was the individual union of two spouses for affective or procreative purposes, and companionship, love, and lust certainly helped to bind it. But well into the seventeenth century these were all secondary considerations. As an institution, marriage created an economic partnership in which each spouse contributed his or her own specialized function. A marriage also created an alliance between families and kin groups, building social, economic, and political ties of crucial importance to large numbers of persons. Finally, marriage acted as the most important vehicle for the transfer of property, far more important than purchase and sale. Small wonder that it was extremely difficult to disentangle this complex web of impersonal ties, and that few even wanted to do so, however indifferent or even hostile its affective base might be.

The outer terminal dates of this study are set at the Reformation, which first reintroduced legalized divorce into Europe (but not into England), and the late twentieth century, which has seen a revolution in behaviour, values, and the law, and the rise of divorce from a statistically insignificant oddity to a commonplace event. The inner core of this study, however, lies between the Restoration of the Anglican church and its canon law jurisdiction in 1660 and the passage of the first divorce law in 1857. These dates impose themselves as years when symbolic events marked the beginning and end of the prehistory of divorce in England. Between these dates, forces were set in motion which were to prepare the way for the dramatic changes of the last hundred years. The strange convolutions of law and custom that evolved during these two centuries were all attempts to circumvent or modify the harsh fact that, largely for accidental reasons, England was the only Protestant country in Europe in which the medieval Catholic ban on divorce remained entirely unchanged.

Before the early twentieth century, it is by and large true to say that virtually the only causes for separation or divorce in the West were adultery, or desertion for seven years or more. But adultery was perceived very differently, depending on the sex of the actor. Even a single act of adultery by a wife was an unpardonable breach of the law of property and the idea of hereditary descent, since it presented a threat to the orderly transmission of property and status by the possible introduction of spurious offspring. It was also seen as a breach of the moral order, since it involved an invasion of a husband's property rights on his wife's body. Adultery by the husband, on the other hand, was generally regarded as a regrettable but understandable foible, rather than a serious threat to a marriage, and therefore was something best ignored by a prudent wife. Hence the double sexual standard. In these days when the ideology of sexual equality is paramount, this distinction seems barbaric, and a typical example of male injustice to women. In fact, however, it made good sense in the days before contraception and genetic coding. In the first place, in a society in which birth defined status and in which property and title were transferred from father to children, it was of critical importance that the inheritors should be the genetic offspring of their legal fathers. But as the Roman jurist Gaius observed, 'maternity is a fact, paternity is a matter of opinion', which is why there were such constant fears of a wife imposing a bastard upon the family as heir to its property and title.

Secondly, there is evidence to suggest that in men, the extreme if brief intensity of the purely physical pleasure of sex makes it easier to achieve with little or no emotional commitment. This perhaps explains why the

7

ancient profession of prostitution has been exclusively devoted to satisfying the sexual needs of men. But since the beginning of time there has been no such simple solution to the sexual needs of women. Until the last few decades, the lack of reliable methods of contraception and the universally low standards of health and hygiene kept all women of child-bearing age in a state of constant anxiety about their bodies. They worried about whether they were pregnant, and if so whether the child would come to term, about their own chances of surviving the ordeal of labour without anaesthesia, and whether they could feed the child, supposing that it was not still-born. Those who were barren were no better off, since their failure to produce children was likely to create a sense of guilt and inadequacy, to cause friction within the marriage, and to deny them the compensatory satisfactions of motherhood.

Thirdly, men have had a widespread tendency to be intensely jealous of any rival for the sexual favours of their wives, especially since adultery by a wife was commonly regarded as casting doubts on her husband's virility. It is this sense of a traumatic psychological blow to masculine self-identity that has made suspicion of a wife's adultery a staple theme of novels and plays from Shakespeare's *Othello* to Harold Pinter's *Betrayal*. For the adulterous wife, moreover, to cuckold an unloved husband could be a way of exercising power in an otherwise powerless situation.[11]

2. The Historiography: Family History

Family history in the last thirty years has followed three tracks, all useful in their own way, but all limited if taken in isolation (as has usually happened). The best-known track is the demographic one, which has demonstrated for the early modern period a unique North-Western European pattern of late marriage at 25 to 27; relatively low nuptiality (10 to 20 per cent of the population not marrying at all); and a cyclical pattern of rise and fall of pre-marital and extra-marital conceptions.[12] Demographic statistics are the numerical consequences of certain modes of behaviour, but they throw little light on just what that behaviour was, and none at all on the motives and sentiments that caused it. For example, there is an air of implausibility about recent attempts to tie the observed changes in fertility to economic calculations about the future, based on

[11] A. Lawson, *Adultery: An Analysis of Love and Betrayal* (New York, 1988), 25, 31.

[12] J. Hajnal, 'European Marriage Patterns in Perspective', in D. V. Glass and D. E. C. Eversley (eds.), *Population in History* (London, 1965); P. Laslett, K. Oosterveen, and R. Smith (eds.), *Bastardy and its Comparative History* (Cambridge, Mass., 1980), 18, 23–4.

changes in real wages some forty years before.[13] Statistics can tell us little about what was in the minds of people when they delayed marriage, or went through a clandestine marriage, or conceived a child out of wedlock, or broke up a marriage. It is certain that these acts bore a different moral significance at different times and among different classes of people, but what those meanings were can only rarely be extracted from the statistics.

A second approach to family history has been through the study of the size and composition of the household.[14] It is certainly important to know that as far back as the sixteenth century most households in England were nuclear, and that relatively few contained grandparents, relatives, or siblings. But the bare fact that the mean household size across time and class was about 4.75 persons is one of those statistics thrown up by the computer which is almost entirely devoid of meaning. A household varied in size not only from class to class, but also from stage to stage in the life cycle of its members. It comprised parents, children, relatives, hired servants, and lodgers, some of the servants and the lodgers possibly also being relatives. The mere fact that this disparate group lived together under one roof tells us absolutely nothing about the ties of power, mutual economic aid, affect, love, hate, or indifference which may have bound them together. Nor can these data tell us whether or not the relatives or patrons who were really influential in an individual's life—usually referred to as 'friends'—lived elsewhere down the street or in some other village. One cannot deduce much about human relationships from a household census.[15]

A third type of family study has focused on sentiments and affect: the shift of emotional relationships, mutual expectations, attitudes to sexuality, perceptions of moral duty, concepts of honour and shame, virtue and vice, salvation and sin. These matters are all intimately connected with shifts in religious dogma, attitudes towards the body's sexual appetites, and ideas about the relationship between the self and parents, kin, and neighbours. They are also closely connected to economic needs, especially concerning inheritance of real and personal property, and the labour requirements of the family.

---

[13] E. A. Wrigley, 'The Growth of Population in Eighteenth-Century England: A Conundrum Resolved', *Past and Present*, 98 (1983), 136–43, 148.

[14] P. Laslett and R. Wall, *Household and Family in Past Time* (Cambridge, 1972), 132.

[15] L. K. Berkner, 'The Use and Misuse of Census Data for Historical Analysis of Family Structure', *Journal of Interdisciplinary History*, 5 (1975); M. Chaytor, 'Household and Kinship: Ryton in the Late Sixteenth and Early Seventeenth Centuries', *History Workshop Journal*, 10 (1980); and review of Laslett and Wall, *Household and Family*, by P. M. G. Harris in *Journal of European Economic History*, 3 (1974), 765–7.

Between 1660 and 1800, there took place a major shift in attitudes towards the role of parents and friends in the choice of marriage partners, and in the appropriate motives for that choice. Children were allowed more freedom to choose their own spouses, naturally with a good deal of advice from parents and others, and the socially acceptable criterion for the choice came gradually to lay greater emphasis on the affective bonding of the couple.[16] Paradoxically, this led in the late eighteenth century to an apparent rise in the amount of marital unhappiness, leading to adultery and marital breakdown. This was caused partly by the fact that the reality of day-to-day cohabitation could never match the expectations aroused by notions of love disseminated in the popular romances of the age, and partly because emotions are in any case more ephemeral and volatile than interests. Contemporaries were well aware of the connection between romantic love and marital unhappiness, and eighteenth-century parents were continually, but vainly, warning their daughters not to read novels lest they derive from them totally unrealistic notions about the joys of the married state.

Since this book is primarily concerned with changing moral attitudes, it builds mainly on early studies of human emotional relationships. To achieve its object, however, it must add another component, namely the law, the neglect of which has been one of the worst deficiencies in historiography in all fields of enquiry over the last forty years. A careful study must be made of legal statutes and prescriptions, but without taking them as evidence of actual behaviour. Indeed, special attention must be given to the marked difference between the ostensible and the latent functions of the law, a difference created by the success of the clients in manipulating the court system for their own purposes.

The relationship of the law to public opinion is far from straightforward. On the one hand the law is directly influenced by society, since the legislators who make the law are themselves inevitably affected by the values of their time. On the other hand once enacted, the statute law itself moulds public opinion and behaviour. The lines of influence therefore travel two ways, up from the public to the lawyers and judges, as well as down from the law through the interpretations of the lawyers and judges back to the public. There is a reciprocal relationship between the enacted law, current theories of justice, and the social, economic, and cultural background.[17]

In the last decade, several young English historians have investigated

---

[16] Stone, *FSM*, ch. 7; see also below, ch. II/2.

[17] See C. W. Francis, 'The Structure of Judicial Administration, and the Development of Contract Law in Seventeenth Century England', *Columbia Law Review*, 83 (1983).

the legal records of the ecclesiastical courts for evidence of marital litigation from the late fourteenth to the mid-seventeenth centuries and have come up with a large amount of new and more reliable information over that long period. It should be noted, however, that there is no consensus in sight about just what conclusions should be drawn from the evidence uncovered.[18]

3. The Objectives

The first problem is to elucidate the ways of making a marriage, which turn out to have been extremely complicated and varied. In Catholic countries, the laws of marriage were fundamentally changed in 1563 at the Council of Trent, in order to bring them under the tight control of the church. Protestant England left the medieval laws of marriage unchanged except briefly during the Interregnum from 1640 to 1660, when the Protectorate placed the performance and registration of marriage in secular hands, an arrangement which had long been adopted by the Puritans in New England. As a result, ecclesiastical and common law governing the making of marriage in England before the act of 1753 was so obscure and contradictory, and the discrepancy between canon law and popular custom was so great, that there were large numbers of persons who were quite uncertain whether or not they were properly married, and what were the personal and property rights to which they were entitled. It is fair to say that before 1753, marriage was to a considerable extent out of the control of either church or state, in spite of half-hearted attempts by both to hang on to the reins. If the laws about the making of marriage were in practice too obscure, the laws about the breaking of marriage were in theory all too clear. For most of the early modern period, England thus endured the worst of all worlds, largely lacking either formal controls over marriage or satisfactory legal means of breaking it.

The first purpose of this book is therefore to identify and explain the extraordinary laxity and ambiguity of the English laws of marriage which

[18] Ingram, *Church Courts, Sex, and Marriage*; E. R. C. Brinkworth, *Shakespeare and the Bawdy Court of Stratford* (London, 1972); C. B. Herrup, 'Law and Morality in Seventeenth-Century England', *Past and Present*, 106 (1985); E. S. Hockaday, 'The Consistory Court of the Diocese of Gloucester', *Bristol and Glos. Arch. Soc. Trans.* 46 (1924); Houlbrooke, *Church Courts*; id., *The English Family, 1450–1700* (London, 1984); B. Lenman, 'The Limits of Godly Discipline in the Early Modern Period', in K. von Greyarz (ed.), *Religion and Society in Early Modern Europe 1500–1800* (London, 1984); Marchant, *Marriage and Soc.*; G. R. Quaife, *Wanton Wenches and Wayward Wives* (London, 1979); J. A. Sharpe, *Defamation and Sexual Slander in Early Modern England*, Borthwick Papers 58 (York, 1980); S. D. Amussen, *An Ordered Society: Gender and Class in Early Modern England* (Oxford, 1988); J. Addy, *Sin and Society in the Sixteenth Century* (London, 1989).

endured up to 1753, and the equally extraordinary strictness of the laws of separation and divorce which lasted until 1857. At first sight both seem wholly dysfunctional in terms of human needs and legal efficiency, a matter which calls out for both analysis and explanation. More interesting, and largely unknown, are the various and wholly unanticipated ways by which the public succeeded in exploiting the ambiguities of the marriage laws and in undermining the rigidity of the separation and divorce laws. Under a surface façade of a law which never changed, many things were happening to bring it more into conformity with the demands of clients.

The last chapter of this book traces the story of the divorce revolution of the last hundred years from the first breach in the barrier in 1857 to the situation today. This too has a perplexing and unexpected history, as changing social mores came into conflict with resisting legislative conservatism and wavering theological beliefs, the end result being a purely administrative process which is today churning out 150,000 divorces a year.

To illustrate in detail the way both marriage and divorce operated in practice, and the ways by which men and women managed to achieve their ends of legitimizing or breaking marriage by twisting the law to suit themselves, two ancillary volumes will contain a series of selected case-studies. The first volume, *Uncertain Unions*, tells stories about the making of marriage before 1753; and the second, *Broken Lives*, tells stories about the breaking of marriage before 1857.

The second and parallel objective of this book is to trace the slow, irregular, and tentative evolution of moral values concerning relations between the sexes in England, and the consequent shift from concepts of patriarchy to those of sexual equality.[19] In the sixteenth and seventeenth centuries, England stood out from continental Europe in two respects, the first of which was the extraordinary personal and sexual freedom enjoyed by unmarried girls—at any rate those from the poor and the middling sorts. The second was the extreme powers granted to and sometimes exercised by husbands over wives right up to the late seventeenth century. Such a system of near-complete dependence of wives was functional to the society in which it evolved. It suited an arrangement designed to secure an alliance between two kin groups, and to transfer and transmit property in the male primogenitural line. It also suited a

---

[19] I prefer the old-fashioned word 'sex' to the more fashionable 'gender' since it carries less ideological baggage and is thus a more useful category of historical analysis. For a lucid argument on the other side, see J. W. Scott, 'Gender: A Useful Category of Historical Analysis', *American Historical Review*, 91 (1986).

society in which dominance and submission was the only known way of preserving order, whether in a household or in a state. Two-and-a-half centuries later, this near-absolute control of husbands over wives had virtually disappeared, certainly from the law and largely from the minds of most men.

The full significance of this mental and behavioural revolution is today very hard for us to grasp. It is easy to forget that under the patriarchal system of values, as expressed in the enacted law as it endured until the nineteenth century, a married woman was the nearest approximation in a free society to a slave. Her person, her property both real and personal, her earnings, and her children all passed on marriage into the absolute control of her husband. The latter could use her sexually as and when he wished, and beat her (within reason) or confine her for disobedience to any orders. The children were entirely at the disposal of the father, who was legally empowered to remove them, put them to work, or marry them, just as he though fit, without consulting the wishes of his wife. He could even debar his wife from ever setting eyes on them or writing to them. As women historians have been pointing out, the subsequent revolution in marriage was mainly a long battle for the liberation of wives from this position of total legal subordination.

The reality of marital relations, of course, was in many, perhaps most, cases far less harsh and one-sided than the law prescribed. Personal affection or strength of character could and often did override both customs and laws. Contemporaries realized only too well that wives could often turn the tables on their husbands and get their way by tact, finesse, and pretended obedience, as was pointed out by Lord Halifax in a widely read letter to his daughter published in 1688.[20] Thus, in practice, patriarchy was usually by no means as brutal as it now sounds, since its full rigours were often softened by human understanding. But if things went wrong between husband and wife, then the full force of the law could be brought to bear, with devastating consequences to the latter.

When legal change took place in the nineteenth century, it occurred above all as a result of changes in the minds of men in positions of power. They were slowly persuaded that this absolute authority was no longer justified by theology or by the practical necessities of family life. They therefore took slow, hesitant, but in the end irreversible steps to create the legal and psychological equality within marriage which exists today. Just how and why this remarkable transformation has occurred is still not

[20] Marquis of Halifax, *The Lady's New Year's Gift or Advice to a Daughter*, in H. C. Foxcroft, *The Life and Letters of Sir George Savile, Bart., First Marquis of Halifax* (London, 1898), 2: 393–408.

entirely clear, especially since it was only in the mid-nineteenth century that agitation by middle-class women began to have any significant effect on male attitudes or statutory law. Feminists of the late seventeenth and eighteenth centuries who are widely read today, such as Mary Astell or Mary Wollstonecraft, seem to have had no practical effect at all except to alienate many men. It is only in the 1830s, 1840s, and 1850s, when well-born, well-connected, and intelligent but carefully unthreatening elite women like Caroline Norton and Barbara Leigh Smith Bodichon began to lobby influencial legislators and law lords, that one can begin to see significant changes in both male attitudes and statute law.

The third purpose of this project, which is central to the two volumes of case-studies, is to try to penetrate into the hearts and minds of persons in the past. This objective is in full conformity with Marc Bloch's definition of his quarry as a historian: 'ma proie, c'est l'homme'. It has been argued that 'voyeurism is one of the preconditions of the novel' in the eighteenth century.[21] A similar invasion of the privacy of the dead by the historian requires no defence: voyeurism is indeed one of the social historian's essential methods. In the case-studies in *Uncertain Unions* and *Broken Lives*, the dead rise up from their graves and speak to us in their own words about what they saw, heard, felt, and thought. The readers of this material do indeed become historical voyeurs, peering through key-holes, cracks in deal partitions, or holes deliberately drilled for the purpose, or listening with ears against the wall. What they hear are conversations around the fire in the kitchen, soft cries and whispers, the normal hubbub of life in a household; occasionally also the screams of battered wives or the sounds of adulterous intercourse.

It is undeniable that this highly personal approach to the past runs the danger of over-interpretation, neglect of analysis, and disregard for the structural forces in history. To avoid these weaknesses, this book is designed to provide the structural and analytical framework within which the case-studies in the other two can be set. The latter will attempt to answer the question 'what was it like to live in the past?'. How different was the historical other from us in his or her religious beliefs and practices, moral convictions, marital and sexual behaviour, style of life, and concept of the self?

Few data can begin to answer these questions more vividly and directly than case-studies drawn from the records of litigation in the ecclesiastical courts, if only because so much of the drama of marital conflict was played out in open court, and so much of the testimony of principals and witnesses was written down.

---

[21] L. C. Davis, *Factual Fictions: The Origins of the English Novel* (New York, 1983), 188.

One of the first tasks of the historian is to identify the obstacles which for so long stood in the way of change in the laws of marriage, separation, and divorce. One formidable enemy of any change was the fear of grave social and political side-effects. Any tampering with the law appeared to threaten a change not only in interpersonal relationships but in economic property transfers, the power of the church, and even, symbolically, the security of the state. After all, did not Gibbon ascribe at least a part of the responsibility for the decline of Rome to the liberal divorce laws of the Imperial aristocracy? Did not the English associate the worst excesses of the French Revolution with the short-lived experiment in liberal divorce laws in France? Ever since Aristotle, the family had been regarded as the paradigm and the building block of all other social institutions. Undermine it, and who knew what chaos would follow?[22] As a result, the law of marriage in England was not significantly altered from the twelfth century until 1753, and then not touched again before the institution of civil registration in 1836. The law of marriage today remains virtually unchanged from what it was at that time.

As for divorce, there was no legal change before 1857, and not much change in practice until the twentieth century, when the ideology of individualism finally triumphed over the ideology of social responsibility, and when secularism not only almost completely eroded the ancient power of the church but also created theological and moral doubt and conflict among the clergy. As a result, in the last twenty years the divorce laws have been rapidly eased, even in most Catholic countries, and by now no-fault divorce laws have become common. Even so, each reform has generated an enormous amount of conflict and political friction; change has not come easily. It is no accident that no government since that of Palmerston in 1857 has dared to take the initiative over so explosively controversial a topic: all twentieth-century bills on divorce have been introduced by private members.

Legislation concerning marriage and divorce was peculiarly resistant to change, often over centuries, not only because of ideology but also because there were powerful groups with an interest in its perpetuation. One was the professional lawyers, especially those practising in the church courts. Any institution tends to build up a corporate identity and personality, and over time it develops its own ways of thinking about and understanding the world around it and the functions which it performs.[23]

---

[22] G. J. Schochet, *The Authoritarian Family and Political Attitudes in Seventeenth-Century England: Patriarchalism in Political Thought* (New Brunswick, 1988); M. Shanley, 'Marriage Contract and Social Contract in Seventeenth-Century English Political Thought', *Western Political Quarterly*, 32 (1979).

[23] M. T. Douglas, *How Institutions Think* (Syracuse, 1986).

This was particularly true of so ancient and barnacled an institution as the English ecclesiastical courts, which up to 1857 continued to administer a system of canon law concerning marital break-down and separation which had not been changed since the fourteenth century. Ancient rules shaped the rigid categories and classifications into which the canon lawyers crammed the disorderly behaviour of spouses, thus creating a 'thought style' which became part of the collective ethos of the group. A striking example of this was the defence, well into the nineteenth century, of the medieval legal remedy of separation from bed and board by an ecclesiastical court, without permission to remarry. This separation from bed and board was defended despite the well-known fact that such a solution to a broken marriage was merely an invitation to illicit cohabitation and bastardy. Moreover, the lawyers and petty bureaucrats who administered the church courts had a strong economic and professional interest in protecting their legal turf. They were the major beneficiaries from the disorder and uncertainty in the laws of marriage, separation, and divorce.

There were two other influential social groups who were strongly opposed to any change in the marriage or divorce law. The first was the Church of England clergy who, while denying marriage was a sacrament and conceding that it was a civil contract, nevertheless also regarded it as sacred and indissoluble, in accordance with the words of Christ. The most powerful of this group were the bishops, the great majority of whom right up to the 1960s were the most inflexible defenders of the traditional laws which sanctioned separation from bed and board and prohibited divorce. For centuries, the vociferous opposition of these bishops, who were well entrenched in the House of Lords, made legislative change over divorce extremely difficult to achieve.

Another interest group of opponents of change were women, especially from the elite and middle class, who were fearful that any relaxation of the divorce laws might encourage their husbands to desert them. For women, divorce has always tended to involve serious financial loss, especially because of their lack of training or opportunities for a career, the extreme difficulty of enforcing alimony payments from a reluctant or impoverished ex-spouse, and the burden of child-support. These women were politically weak, but the absence of any strong support from within their ranks, and indeed the presence of a good deal of active opposition, inevitably made the task of divorce reformers more difficult.

A further reason why the laws remained unchanged for so long is that large elements of the male elite laity were quite content with the *status quo*. Thus the younger sons, the small gentry, and the new men struggling for money and status in the House of Commons were satisfied with the chaotic condition of the laws of marriage before 1753, since it offered them the chance to marry a great landed heiress without the permission of her parents.

Similarly, the richest men in England were satisfied by the ban on divorce with remarriage, since their wealth and status gave them various options. One was to obtain a separation and keep a mistress, which could be done openly without social derogation. Alternatively, by mutual consent with their wives to collusion and occasional perjury, they could always contrive to obtain a Parliamentary divorce. Only the moralists among the laity, who objected to all this sordid dissimulation, were strong advocates of reform. Equally, the elite were content with the law's provision for a husband to make a claim against a wife's lover for damages because of her adultery—an action known as 'criminal conversation', or 'crim. con.'.[24] During its early years the action increased their control over their wives' sexuality and reinforced their monopoly over that particular piece of property; and in its later years it reinforced their claims for a Parliamentary divorce.

Given all this conservative opposition, one may well ask a second and more difficult question, which is why change in the law happened at all. The advocates of radical change, such as John Milton, were always a tiny and unrepresentative minority who spoke only for themselves. As has been seen, pressure from women for change in the law of divorce was very rare before the early nineteenth century. The reason for this was partly that most women meekly accepted the patriarchal or paternal model of society and family, and partly that they had little to gain by any change. But on rare occasions, one or two did speak out in protest against the injustice of their almost helpless legal position as wives. Thus in 1663, the law lords were extremely shocked when faced with a wife claiming the enforcement of a pre-marital contract with her husband which stated 'that she shall not be subject to him'. They angrily declared it 'void and contrary to the law of God and Nature, and public honesty'.[25] Thirty years later, many Whigs would reluctantly espouse Locke's contract theory of the state but resolutely deny its applicability to the family.

Although hardly any women issued overt challenges to the laws of marriage and divorce, a few, like Mary Astell and Mary Chudleigh, wrote pamphlets asking why contract theory should not apply to them. Others asked for greater equality before the law, rights over their own property, a share in rights over child custody, and the right to be treated with

---

[24] See below, ch. IX.
[25] *Manby and Richardson* v. *Scot* (1663), *Eng. Rep.* 83: 1065.

17

something better than brutality or neglect. But this tiny handful of female protesters had absolutely no effect. After the Glorious Revolution of 1688, English wives would remain for another two hundred years in the paradoxical situation of being the legal chattels of husbands who were constantly boasting that they lived in a society unique in the world for its devotion to the principles of liberty.

In the last chapter of this book, which deals with the period after 1857, another set of questions is asked. The first is why divorce grew only very slowly after the Divorce Act of 1857, so that the numbers were still negligible in 1914. The second is why, after 1914 and especially after 1960, was there an unprecedented growth in the numbers of divorces, accompanied by an equally unprecedented weakening of moral controls over adultery by either sex.

4. A Model of Legal Change

Any theory of change in the laws of marriage, separation, and divorce must build upon a series of assumptions. The first is the familiar one that there are very few ideas without an interest lurking behind them, and no interests without ideas to support them. The second is that any cultural change has to be initiated by a specific group of actors, whose motives can then be examined in the twin perspectives of interests and ideology. The third is that the results, although subject to capricious spurts and lags due to the personal influence of powerful individuals such as monarchs, archbishops, or law lords, cannot be altogether random. Any model has to be constructed on the assumption that social policy in the long run satisfies the wishes of the propertied laity, and of members of powerful institutions, especially the church, Parliament, and the law. Public policy, as expressed in enacted law, has somehow to reflect the values, beliefs, and interests these groups represent. The fourth, and perhaps the most important assumption, is that that latent function of litigation—especially matrimonial litigation—often bore little or no relation to its ostensible function. The influential laity were constantly finding ways to use the law for their own purposes, if only to save face and avoid scandal.

All the available examples prove that changes in the laws of marriage and divorce took place in three stages. The first impetus for change came from the clients themselves, as they started putting pressure on the existing law to satisfy their changing aspirations. This revealed a gap between the current values of the laity and the existing law. Attempts were then made to bridge this in two ways. Since the law provides a template to which petitions for separation or divorce must conform if they are to succeed, clients increasingly found ways to comply with the rules by resorting to connivance, collusion, and the witholding of evidence. At times they even resorted to the invention of evidence by open perjury. They thus contrived to conform to the letter of the law while totally violating its spirit.

As a result, the law of separation and divorce often seems like a mere fiction, a fig-leaf inadequately covering the very different reality of human behaviour. For whole centuries, some men and women were indeed trapped in the machinery of the law: Henry VIII is perhaps the most famous example. But others, who lacked Henry's power to change the law to suit himself, contrived to make or break their marriages by means of subterfuge, deception, perjury and concealment. In most of these activities they were aided and abetted by skilful conveyancers, so-licitors, proctors, and other legal functionaries, all of whom knew quite well that they were participating in systematic fraud against the letter of the law. Very often the judges knew it too, and the whole court-room scene was no more than a hollow charade, not infrequently bordering on low farce.

Private correspondence on such matters between husband and wife, and between both spouses and their lawyers, in those rare cases when it survives, offers an illuminating and sobering glimpse behind the scenes. Through such material it is possible to observe the client and his or her lawyer deciding on strategy and tactics, and the two spouses negotiating with each other behind the scenes, either for an out-of-court settlement or a collusive suit. It frequently turns out that the public litigation was nothing but a smoke-screen: either it was designed to facilitate a compromise agreement which had already been arranged privately, or else it was a blackmail tactic to force the defendant into such a settlement.

The next stage was reached when the lawyers and judges attempted to narrow the widening gap between legal theory and human practice by modifying the law, whether by inventing legal fictions or by brazenly changing the law by judicial reinterpretation. Common law, with its respect for case precedents, lent itself fairly easily to such manipulation and reinterpretation by powerful and innovative judges. The changing definitions of legal cruelty, on which basis a separation could be justified, is a classic example of such a process.[26]

The third and last stage was reached when the level of duplicity and

---

[26] For comments along these lines, see R. Chester and J. Streather, 'Cruelty in English Divorce: Some Empirical Findings', *Journal of Marriage and the Family*, 34 (1972), 706–7.

hypocrisy became intolerable to law lords and legislators alike. Only then was the law finally changed in order to bring it more into line with current social practice and moral attitudes. Critically important for this last stage was the lead given by influential law lords, who became exasperated by daily exposure to blatant connivance and collusion in their courts. For example, it was the virtually unanimous desire of the law lords to stop the scandal of collusion in Parliamentary divorce cases which generated the political momentum needed to pass the first Divorce Reform Act of 1857. Such a battle usually ended in a compromise, which was invariably described by its supporters as a reform and by its opponents as the high road to moral and political disintegration. At the very least, when the change occurred it brought the law a little more in line with human behaviour.

A good example of this three-stage process at work is the events leading up to the Marriage Act of 1753. By 1740, clandestine marriage had turned the ostensible function of the law into a mere false charade, and the lawyers and judges knew it. In order to remedy the situation, the only solution was to change the law so as to eliminate altogether both contract marriages and clandestine marriages. This was achieved, after a prolonged and bitter struggle, in 1753. Another example is the invention in about 1700 of the anomaly of divorce by a private act of Parliament in a society in which divorce was legally prohibited. The invention was followed by its perversion through collusion by about 1770, and finally by its abolition in 1857. There was always a long time-lag, usually at least half a century, between the second stage—the unanimous perception that the law was being systematically evaded—and the third stage, the enactment of statutory reform. This time-lag still operated even in the early twentieth century, so that the substantial reforms of the divorce law recommended by a royal commission in 1912 were not turned into statute law until twenty-five years later, in 1937.

As usual in political history, the action of powerful personalities played a critical role in each lurch forward in law reform. It was the skilful stage-management of Lord Hardwicke which was chiefly responsible for the passage of the 1753 Marriage Act. It was Palmerston's iron determination to keep Parliament sitting through the broiling heat of August which railroaded through the first Divorce Reform Act of 1857. It was A. P. Herbert's tireless public agitation and adept buying off of interest groups which made possible the Divorce Reform Act of 1937. And it was L. Abse's devotion to the cause of divorce law reform which made possible the even more revolutionary Divorce Reform Act of 1969.

The decision-makers in the changes of the law regarding marriage and

divorce belonged exclusively to the top third of society. The middling
sort were largely trapped by the law; they were neither rich enough nor
unscrupulous enough to buy their way out, like the elite, nor incon-
spicuous enough to be able to ignore the law with impunity. The poor, in
contrast, were without property, so they had little or nothing to lose by
ignoring the law altogether. It was far too expensive for them to contem-
plate its use, and instead they contrived their own quasi-legal or illegal
means of self-divorce—such as desertion, elopement, private separation,
or the occasional wife-sale. So long as both parties were satisfied, the
illegality of the procedure was irrelevant, and any subsequent act of
bigamy carried few serious risks of discovery or of serious punishment if
exposed. Marriage, separation, and divorce, therefore, were amorphous
and changing institutions that carried different meanings for different
groups within the society.

The model does not suggest or imply that the growth of marital breakdown and the rise of divorce were linear processes moving steadily
forward over time. They were clearly nothing of the sort, at any rate
before 1923. In so far as numerical counts mean anything, both seem to
have moved in fits and starts, even during the explosive growth phase in
the last half of the twentieth century.

5. Morals

The model of change here put forward clearly depends heavily upon
shifts in what today are called *mentalités*. But these in turn are naturally
dependent upon changes in social structure, especially the rise of the
upper middling and the professional men, groups which possessed a
more individualistic and secular set of values. It is true that the rise in the
divorce rate after 1860 seems to have been a compensatory mechanism
for the decline in adult mortality, and the consequent prolongation of the
duration of marriage. But it was changing moral attitudes, themselves the
outcome of a variety of social, economic, and cultural influences, and
differing from group to group within the society, which mainly governed
behaviour in such intimate and critically important affairs, both to the
individual and to the society, as the making and the breaking of marriage.
Burke observed in 1782 that the constitution of a country 'is made by the
peculiar circumstances, occasions, tempers, dispositions, and moral,
civil, and social habitudes of the people, which disclose themselves only
in a long space of time'.[27] The same applies to the nature of pre-marital

[27] Quoted by J. G. A. Pocock in his *Politics, Language, and Time: Essays on Political Thought
and History* (New York, 1971), 226.

or pre-contract sexual relations; the use of verbal and written contracts or clandestine marriages as substitutes for regular marriage in church by a clergyman; the socially acceptable amount of physical or mental cruelty by the husband towards his wife; the significance attached to male adultery; the propriety of litigation for damages for female adultery; and the acceptability of connivance, collusion, condonation, deception, concealment, or outright lying in court in order to win a separation or divorce.

Moral values loom so large in the language used by the players in this drama that, unless one is prepared to assume that they were all hypocrites, considerable weight has to be given to them. But few historical topics are harder to handle with clarity, sensitivity, and accuracy than shifts in the sensibilities, mental structures, or moral codes which govern human behaviour. In the first place, one is usually dealing—certainly in the West since the sixteenth century—in moods and systems of value which appear to be prevalent at certain times but are never universally held, and are always in unstable competition with others. Second, each social grouping tends to live in its own mental world, which is sometimes quite similar to those of other groups, but perhaps more often strikingly different. Third, there is a constant flow of ideas between different groups, sometimes only one way—say, from the top down—but perhaps more often in both directions. Thus, elite culture, middling-sort culture, and popular culture are never clearly distinct and are for ever either pulling apart or coming together. Fourth, while the historian interested in this type of change can locate sometimes subtle, sometimes very obvious shifts in perceptions, sensibilities, and codes, there are at all times pioneers and laggards, innovators and hold-overs, so that the picture is never a clear-cut one, and the date of a shift from one code to another can never be established with any precision.

For example, at some point after 1660, European societies moved away from deep religious faith among the elite accompanied by total acceptance of the moral propriety and political necessity of persecuting even to death anyone who clung to another faith or none at all. At some point after 1660, the members of the political nation everywhere gradually adopted an easy-going deism, came to regard God as a remote divine watch-maker, and accepted a belief in the moral rightness and practical necessity of religious toleration. But this was a process which in most of Europe took anything up to two centuries to accomplish, and each society moved at its own pace.[28] Similarly, the shift among the elite from a men-

---

[28] For a good summary of the contraction in England from the 16th to the 18th century of the areas of life dominated or controlled by religion, see J. C. Sommerville, 'The Destruction of

tal world based on concepts of patriarchy, hierarchy, honour, and shame to one based more on the commercial values of the market-place and individualistic ideas about freedom of choice also took one or two centuries to take hold, even in the single society of England.[29] Some changes in these areas took legal form and were quite dramatic in their apparent significance, but the timing of their general acceptance and use is another matter. The slow evolution of the idea of possessive individualism is a good example.

Some of the changes involved a prolonged tug-of-war over several centuries between old values and new ones, for example between honour and money, or between the duty of obedience to parents and the right of individual choice over the selection of a spouse. Nor were the trends always moving in the same direction: they often ebbed and flowed erratically. Moreover, at all periods passionate beliefs are usually held only by small, well-organized minorities, the majority being carried along in their wake, unable to do much more than moderate the oscillations of the current stirred up by the radicals. As historians, we are therefore perforce dealing with minority mind-sets, which only slowly became those of the majority.

Since the change in moral codes was so slow, hesitant, and irregular, its social, geographical, and even psychological spread so limited, and any privileged code so constantly under challenge from others, it is extremely difficult to demonstrate that a significant change did actually take place. It is only with the benefit of hindsight that, through changes in the use or meaning of words and symbolic acts, the full significance of some of these shifts can be perceived.

Finally, the historian of moral codes and mental worlds faces the intractable problem of the interpretation of texts, all of which have their drawbacks. The most reliable are clearly memoirs, correspondence, and autobiographies, even if they are intrinsically self-serving. Equally valuable are the depositions of witnesses and pleadings of legal counsel in court cases: the former reveal the moral codes of the people, and the rhetoric of the latter what they believed would appeal to judges and juries. Imaginative literature, such as widely read novels, plays, or poetry, offers useful guides to public opinion, since the mere fact of their success suggests that they may be moulding and reinforcing, as well as mirroring, certain values.

Religious Culture in Pre-Industrial England', *Journal of Religious History*, 15 (1988); for the 19th century see Owen Chadwick, *The Secularization of the European Mind in the Nineteenth Century: The Gifford Lectures in the University of Edinburgh for 1973–4* (Cambridge, 1975).

[29] E. P. Thompson, *Whigs and Hunters: The Origin of the Black Act* (London, 1975); C. B. MacPherson, *The Political Theory of Possessive Individualism: Hobbes to Locke* (Oxford, 1962).

Prescriptive texts, however, which deal with ideal morality and behaviour, such as political speeches and pamphlets, works of political economy, and the sermons of prominent theologians, are unreliable guides to actual behaviour. The first drawback is that it is hard to tell whether they were widely read and admired, or largely ignored; indeed, in some cases the modern historian often has an uneasy feeling that he may well be the first to take them seriously. Second, there is always a very wide gap between theory and practice, between uplifting moral sentiments and crass day-to-day behaviour.

The record is sufficiently clear to indicate that the Gramscian idea of cultural hegemony is not much help in studying the family, since ideas about appropriate behaviour seem to well up from below or from a rival segment of the elite, and finally to overcome the official value system set out by the theologians, the moralists, and the ecclesiastical lawyers. It is only long after this shift in values and behaviour has taken place that the legislature slowly moves to alter the law.[30]

6. The Legal System

When examining eighteenth-century legal records, it must always be remembered that most cases of litigation between individuals were intended merely to force the defendant to arbitration. For a majority of litigants in the early modern period, going to law was a tactical manoeuvre, part blackmail and part bluff, the object being to obtain an out-of-court settlement, and thus the restoration of order. As a result, only about a fifth to a half of all cases which were initiated in most eighteenth-century ecclesiastical and civil courts ever came to sentence, the rest being either settled out of court or dropped.[31] What does survive, however, from the minority of cases fought to a finish, is a wealth of detailed testimony by several thousand individuals, providing evidence such as can be obtained from no other source.

The legal situation in England was peculiarly complicated by the fact that there were three different legal systems—canon law, equity law, and common law—which were applied by three different groups of lawyers and judges, serving three different sets of courts, working according to three different rules of evidence, and applying three different codes of

---

[30] For a persuasive reassessment of the concept of cultural hegemony, see J. T. Jackson Lears, 'The Concept of Cultural Hegemony', *American Historical Review*, 90 (1985).

[31] J. A. Sharpe, ' "Such Disagreement betwyxt Neighbours": Litigation and Human Relations in Early Modern England', in J. Bossy (ed.), *Disputes and Settlements: Law and Human Relations* (Cambridge, 1983), 182–7.

law. Since all three had some claims to authority over the laws of marriage, separation, and divorce, these three groups of lawyers were in uneasy competition for business, and the jockeying for power and perquisites between them forms an important subplot until the final defeat of the canon lawyers in 1857.

The canon law determined the rules of marriage, which were revised and restated in the canons of 1604. The common law was deeply involved, since marriage was probably the most important single method for the transmission of property. Since common law also had jurisdiction over questions of debt and credit, and since a husband was responsible for his wife's debts, the common law courts inevitably found themselves drawn into deciding upon the validity of a marriage.

Once such case occurred in 1710, when Master of the Rolls Sir John Trevor decided that by common law Henry Elmes was not the husband of Anne Ordway, and therefore not liable for her debts. A year later, however, the ecclesiastical Court of Arches decided that according to canon law Henry Elmes was indeed her husband—even if she was only married by a Fleet parson in a distiller's house—and was therefore by common law responsible for her debts.[32]

Moreover, the capacity of common law to award monetary damages for injury—originally restricted to cases of financial loss and physical assault—was extended to cover injured feelings. In the late seventeenth century, it took steps to offer legal actions to deal with the problems of three types of seduced women: to provide compensation to the unmarried and uncontracted pregnant girl, through a seduction suit brought by her father against her seducer; to provide compensation to the unmarried but semi-contracted pregnant girl through a suit brought by her against her seducer for breach of promise; and to provide compensation to the husband of a married woman seduced into adultery, through a crim. con. suit by her husband against her lover. The case of a woman who had a provable claim to a binding contract which was later denied by the man remained within the jurisdiction of the ecclesiastical courts; on proof of the contract the man would be ordered to marry the woman, on pain of excommunication.

The equity law of Chancery took cognizance of trusts—including those made by married women to keep their property at their own disposal—and also decisions about and enforcement of alimony. Since Chancery also exercised wardship over orphans and lunatics, it insisted upon its consent being obtained for their marriage. Finally, the local

---

[32] *Elmes* v. *Elmes* (1711), LPCA, D.677; Eee.10, fos. 342–4; B.14/205.

manorial courts decided upon rights of widows and children to inherit copyhold estates.

Another example of how a single quarrel could spawn a host of lawsuits in different legal systems is a case in 1671, in which Miss Bragg sued Mr Elkin, claiming a marriage contract. Choosing to fight by canon law, she started in the London Consistory Court; when she lost there, she appealed to the Court of Arches. Meanwhile her father, turning to common law, had stepped up the pressure on Mr Elkin by having him arrested by King's Bench on an action for £3,000 damages for breach of promise of marriage. Mr Elkin fought back by suing Mr Bragg at common law for trespass and assault for beating him, for which he won £9 damages, and also sued in the equity court of Chancery to be relieved of prosecution by reason of Bragg's frivolous suits. Thus in the end all three branches of the English law—canon, common, and equity—were drawn into the affair.[33]

Another problem with the laws governing marriage and divorce is that the principle of unexpected consequences, the wide gap between intentions and results, is peculiarly applicable to them. When in the twelfth century the pope decreed that free mutual consent of both spouses, duly witnessed, was the only necessary prerequisite for a binding life-long marriage, he could not have dreamed of the flood of litigation which this would unleash upon the church courts of Europe in the late Middle Ages, and later still in England. Nor could he have anticipated the perversion of his decree so as to facilitate male seduction of young unmarried girls.

Similarly, the original object of the crim. con. action had been to punish the seducers of married women and to compensate the latter's cuckolded husbands. By 1800, however, the great majority of actions were collusive, and their true, latent function was to provide a legal smoke-screen under which both husband and wife could obtain an undefended Parliamentary divorce and remarry. Current usage in the early nineteenth century is thus a most misleading guide to original intentions.

Many other examples can be offered to demonstrate that the principle of unintended consequences reigns supreme over all the laws of marriage and divorce in England during the last five hundred years. Powerful pressures to make the law serve the community often forced the former into strange mutations of its parts to purposes other than those for which they were intended. Stephen Jay Gould's remarks about the revolution-

---

[33] *Bragg* v. *Elkin* (1671), LPCA, Eee. 4, fos. 608, 612.

ary adaptation of the body seem to be equally applicable to the matrimonial law: 'legs were fins, ear-bones were jaw-bones, and jaw-bones were gill-bones'. Things are not what they seem, and certainly not what they set out to be.[34]

The eighteenth-century legal system—if system it can be called—was a world which is almost entirely alien to modern ways of thought, despite the fact that it was strewn with institutions bearing deceptively familiar names, such as King's Bench, Chancery, JPs, and so on. So clear, so lucid, so eminently reasonable in the calm exposition of Blackstone, the great eighteenth-century legal writer, closer inspection reveals it to be a dense, complex, and bewildering jungle, full of contradictions, anomalies, legal fictions, and downright foolishness. Natural justice seems even more remote from the law than is usually the case. To enter the eighteenth-century machinery of the law is to penetrate the heart of darkness.

It is impossible for even the most enthusiastic of teleologists to make the tortuous and morally very ambivalent story of marital breakdown and legal divorce fit the Procrustean bed of any concept of 'Progress', in either ethical or pragmatic terms. There is no sequence of unambiguous moral improvements which all lead towards the greater happiness of the greatest number.

Nor does there exist any single model of change which can explain the history of marital breakdown and divorce in a single country for all periods of time and for all classes of society.[35] Any historian who claims that either the law has always shaped marital practices or that marital practices have always shaped the law, or that the causes of change were at bottom either legal, or economic and social, or cultural and moral, or intellectual, is offering a simplistic solution which is unsupported by the evidence. History is messier than that.

7. The Evidence

A. THE USE OF LEGAL RECORDS

i. *Advantages*

Perhaps the richest discovery by historians in recent years is the enormous wealth of archival material hidden away in the largely uncatalogued

---

[34] S. J. Gould, 'Cardboard Darwinism', *New York Review of Books*, 33/14 (1986), 54.

[35] See e.g. the very cautious conclusions of R. Phillips, *Putting Asunder: A History of Divorce in Western Society* (Cambridge, 1988), 630–40.

records of the ecclesiastical courts. The value of these records stems from the fact that the officials who compiled them followed the Roman law practice of writing down all the evidence. Every accusation, every answer, every deposition of every witness, every interrogatory, was carefully recorded for posterity. It is this treasure chest of intimately revealing material which has been looted for the case-studies which make up the two satellite volumes, *Uncertain Unions* for the making of marriage, and *Broken Lives* for its unravelling.

What is missing from the court records are the lawyers' arguments, or the judges' directions to the jury, or the reasons for their sentences. These only survive in any quantity from the eighteenth century, when stenographers began to abstract and publish them for the information of the legal profession. A second drawback is that court records register only stories of the rare marriages which failed, not the vast majority which somehow survived, or at least stayed out of court.

In order to probe the secret world of marital behaviour, the historian has little option but to use what he has, which is legal evidence drawn from exceptional cases of divorce and separation in what was basically a non-divorcing and non-separating society. For it must never be forgotton that the whole period up to 1857 belongs to the prehistory not only of divorce, but also of marital breakdowns.

It is also possible that there was some difference between the very small numbers of cases of separation and divorce which ended up in a court of law, and the much larger number settled out of court. Those which came to court were those in which private arbitration and agreement had failed; and both parties were so embittered that they were prepared to spend large amounts of time, energy and money on litigation. These litigated cases are thus the tip of an iceberg of unknown dimensions.

It might seem that the evidence is biased towards the pathology of social deviance and moral failure. But it is not only disastrous marriages which appear in court records, since many had started exceptionally well, or were entirely uneventful until a crisis had been triggered by a wholly unexpected act of adultery. In any case, the bias has its positive compensations, for it is only at times of crisis, such as revolutions in society and marital breakdowns in families, that the innermost workings of a social system and the values which support it are exposed to the historian's gaze. Moments of crisis and rupture reveal secrets which in normal times remain hidden since they are taken for granted.

The second justification for using matrimonial litigation is that it provides a unique window into the hearts and minds not merely of the middling groups and the elite but also of the poor who served and supported them, spied on them, gossiped about them, and gave testimony for or against them. Only these sources can supply detailed information about why and how people chose their spouses, how they got along together within a marriage, and what role, if any, was played by kin, neighbours, and friends.

These records, then, can tell us how and why marriages finally broke down, even if they cannot tell us how many. This is not to claim that court records tell us all, for much is deliberately left out, as we shall see. But combined with other data, and used with discretion, they allow us to peer closer into the human condition in the past than any other records which have survived, except for a handful of exceptionally intimate, and therefore perhaps untypical, diaries such as those of Pepys and Boswell.

Finally, the use of this legal material has the immense advantage of providing the historian with a check on the perceptions and precepts of moralists and theologians, whose opinions about what ought to be may bear little relation to what was. Through legal records, first-hand information can be obtained about the values and the behaviour in real life of actors in situations involving heavily charged conflict.

ii. Limitations

It must be admitted, however, that legal records have some serious drawbacks. None of this evidence is altogether straightforward and unambiguous. For example, different modes of argument are used in different forms of communication. A pronouncement by a judge from the bench, a sermon by a theologian from a pulpit, an article in a newspaper or periodical, a speech in the House of Lords or the Commons, the testimony of a litigant or witness in a court, private correspondence between spouses, discussion between a litigant and his or her lawyer—all are evidence. But not only do different actors speak in different voices, but the same people may express themselves differently at different times in different company.

Moreover, the law speaks in a language of its own, one which does not always reveal what the historian wants to know. Its professional practitioners possess their own values, modes of expression, and logic, while barristers are obliged to fashion their rhetoric to persuade a group of jurymen.[36] The adversarial structure of the litigation process affects what is said, what is left unsaid, and the way the evidence is produced and interpreted. The forms of pleadings were constantly being adjusted to fit

---

[36] T. A. Green, *Verdict According to Conscience: Perspectives on the English Criminal Trial Jury, 1200–1800* (Chicago, 1985).

the law, so that public litigation about 'adultery', 'desertion', or 'cruelty' often bore little relation to what was going on behind the scenes. Litigation, in short, has a culture of its own, which shapes the nature of the evidence it produces.

Marital litigation has always been a theatrical display in which the actors have been striving to win the case, not to investigate and reveal the full truth of the causes of the marital breakdown. The prime object of the litigants, their lawyers, and their witnesses was to tell one side of the story and to conceal the other, in the process creating opposite fictions. The majority of witnesses probably did their best to tell the truth under oath. But since marital disputes are usually intensely emotional conflicts, many witnesses were caught up in the drama and were biased by feelings of loyalty, hatred, or a desire for revenge. For example, in any marital break-up, women servants tended to side with their mistresses, and men servants with their masters.

Beyond this, however, servants—who were invariably the key witnesses—were also often motivated by greed as well as passion, for they were poor and the protagonists for whom they testified were usually rich and powerful. Bribery, either to give false testimony or not to appear in court at all, was inevitably a common occurrence in a situation in which the reward could easily amount to a year's wages. Some of the witnesses were drawn from the London underworld, persons who were ready to sell false testimony to the highest bidder, and were always prepared to switch their story if they could get a better offer from the other side. It is also worth noting that the Old Bailey records prove that few perjurers in a law-suit were ever put on trial, and fewer still were convicted and put in the pillory, at any rate before the early nineteenth century (Plate 1). Perjurers in the witness box were therefore fairly safe.[37] On the other hand, they were usually fairly easy to identify, and their duplicity more commonly took the prudent form of denials of what was true, or false professions of ignorance, rather than barefaced lies.

Another problem is the reliability of memory. Many witnesses described in minute detail quite long conversations which had taken place several years before, but it is questionable how far such testimony is to be relied upon. In most cases, however, it seems unlikely that the conversation was entirely invented, and the details are sometimes supported by the testimony of other witnesses. Furthermore, one may assume that members of a predominantly oral culture, such as the labouring poor in the seventeenth and eighteenth centuries, had more retentive memories

[37] For an exception to this generalization, see the Westmeath case in Stone, *Broken Lives*.

than do those of a literate culture, who are largely reliant upon written—or now perhaps visual—records. On the other hand, some of the conversations or details of events sound almost too good to be true, and one clearly has to allow room for imaginative embroidery or even pure invention.

Another reason to question the evidence of a minority of witnesses is that they had clearly been coached by a lawyer. What gives the game away is when a string of witnesses use exactly the same adjectives to describe a character, or exactly the same words to express admiration or dislike.

Quite apart from the potential unreliability of some witnesses, many of the procedures applied in the various courts of law in some way or another tended to conceal or withold certain vital pieces of evidence. The written interrogatories used for cross-examination by the ecclesiastical courts were much criticized for their incapacity to reveal the truth. In 1777, a critic complained about 'the imperfect and wretched manner in which cross examination is managed on paper'. Sixty years later, in 1836, while commenting on a lost opportunity for an independent enquiry by two arbitrators into a charge of marital cruelty, two distinguished lawyers, Sir John Campbell and Sir William Follett, concluded that 'it would have had the advantage also that all parties would have been examined, an advantage which is seldom attainable in legal proceedings'.[38]

In the common law courts, the strict rules of evidence also hindered the truth. To give but one striking example, in common law a wife had no legal personality since it was subsumed in that of her husband. She was therefore unable to testify, either in person or through her counsel, or even to produce witnesses in her defence, in a civil suit for damages brought by her husband against her alleged lover. As a result, Lord Erskine, who for decades had been the barrister most actively engaged in 'crim. con.' litigation against the lovers of adulterous wives, commented at the end of his life in the 1850s that in nineteen cases out of twenty the original fault lay not with the wives but with their neglectful or adulterous husbands—but none of the evidence against the husbands was produced in court. This was often as a result of willing collusion, but sometimes because the wives were not permitted to testify on their own behalf.

In addition to the obstacles raised by inefficient methods of interrogation and strict rules of evidence, it has to be remembered that the undefended cases—which were the large majority—were undoubtedly collusive, and in others the defence was perfunctory and deliberately misleading. This drawback is offset, however, by the fact that the most

---

[38] *Laws Respecting Women* 344 n. ff. Notts RO, STM 217 (Moore case, 1836).

revealing cases, which are those used in this study, are that minority which were hotly contested. Here the lies, evasions, and distortions of the witnesses tended to cancel each other out, and from the fog of confusing testimony there usually emerges something which at least has the appearance of truth, both to the contemporary judge and to the twentieth-century historian. A more serious defect in the court records is that the reasoning behind the judges' sentences have only survived in the published law reports, most of which only mention cases which made legal history by setting new precedents. Thus, for one reason or another, vital pieces of evidence are often missing. It would be a mistake, however, to exaggerate the unreliability of the evidence taken from these transcripts of court trials. They are not only the best evidence we have; they are also astonishing in their completeness and intimate detail.

iii. Fact or Fiction

The late seventeenth and early eighteenth centuries was a period in which the distinction between fact and fiction, between historical truth and the work of the imagination, was still badly blurred. Many of the stories, both in this book and especially in its two companion volumes of case histories, *Uncertain Unions* and *Broken Lives*, are in many ways very similar to those found in the works of Defoe, Fielding, and Richardson. All three of these authors wrote fiction which they presented as if it were the unvarnished truth. *The Journal of the Plague Year, Robinson Crusoe, Roxana, Moll Flanders, Amelia*, and *Pamela* are all cases in point.[39] These early works of the imagination modelled themselves on a series of different genres, many of which also provide the raw data of this study. One is the newsletters or pamphlets recounting a particular sex or murder trial; another is journalistic reports in the newspapers of sensational trials or events; a third is short-hand reporting of court cases; and a fourth is short-hand notes of speeches by famous barristers such as Thomas Erskine, or instructions to juries by famous common law judges such as Mansfield and Kenyon, or judical sentences by famous civil law judges such as Sir William Scott.

Many of these eighteenth-century novelists were deeply concerned with the making and breaking of marriage. Like real persons in a real court-room, their creations were obsessed with problems of money, love, and sexual transgression, as well as criminality of one sort or another. The reader needs to remember that the case-studies recounted in *Uncertain Unions* and *Broken Lives* are not one but two steps away from

[39] Davis, *Factual Fictions*; M. McKeon, *The Origins of the English Novel* (Baltimore, 1987), esp. ch. 6 and Conclusion.

that mythical beast 'the Truth', as embedded in the records. Firstly, the huge mass of raw data—in some cases the records amount to a quarter of a million words, and in one case to half a million words—has necessarily been compressed so as to present a more or less coherent story. Secondly, the contradictions have been sorted out, the repetitions have been eliminated, the chronology has been reconstructed, and a new narrative has been created, albeit one which makes careful mention of inconsistencies in the record. Unfortunately, almost all these stories offer only faint traces of a beginning, and usually no end at all. The actors emerge from the fog of a past only dimly sketched in by the testimony of witnesses, and after the trial ends and sentence is pronounced they usually abruptly fade back into the darkness from which they sprang, leaving no trace in the historical record of what happened to them thereafter. The two volumes of case-studies therefore contain a set of narratives which appear to the author (and usually also to the contemporary judge), to be the most plausible interpretation of the records.[40]

B. THE COURT OF ARCHES

Situated in the headquarters of the civil lawyers at Doctors' Commons in London, the Court of Arches (Plate 2) was the appeal court for cases before all the ecclesiastical courts in the Province of Canterbury, that is, an area south of a line running roughly from the Mersey to the Humber. Before the industrial revolution in Lancashire and Yorkshire, it contained about three-quarters of the population of England and Wales. In addition, the court acted as a court of first instance in a limited number of special cases, for example from 'Peculiars'—churches which, because of some quirk of history, were not subject to any bishop, and nor, therefore, to the jurisdiction of his court.

The archives of the Court of Arches are virtually complete after 1660, and it is these which have supplied most of the case-studies in the two ancillary volumes. It is sheer luck that they survived the virtual demise of the court in 1857, when, according to one account, they were thrown down a well at St Paul's Cathedral.[41] Like all the other ecclesiastical courts, immediately after its restoration in 1660 the Court of Arches was swamped with a huge backlog of cases from the years during the Inter-

---

[40] The safeguard against any twisting of the evidence is that the Court of Arches material is readily available on microform in both England and America; transcripts of many of the more sensational trials in other courts are also easily available in the seven volumes of *Trials for Adultery at Doctors' Commons*, recently reprinted by Garland Press, New York.

[41] M. D. Slatter, 'The Records of the Court of Arches', *Journal of Ecclesiastical History*, 4 (1953), 139–53.

regnum when the church courts had been suppressed. Although most of them were settled out of court, the total number of cases of all kinds appealed to the court in the 1660s was as high as 2,400 per decade. After 1680, however, so great was the decline of business in all the Consistory Courts that by the 1700s appeals to the Court of Arches were down to about two hundred per decade, a figure which was maintained until the court was legislated out of existence in 1857 (Fig. 1.1, Table 1.1).

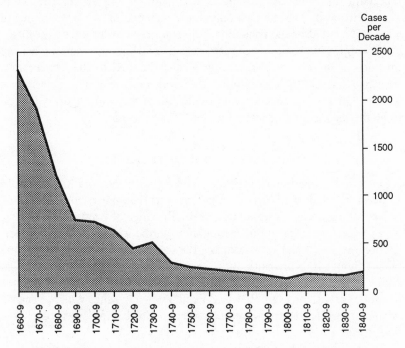

FIGURE 1.1   Court of Arches: All Cases 1660–1849 [Table 1.1]

In the late seventeenth century, matrimonial cases, either to prove a marriage or to break one, formed only a relatively small part of the total volume of business of the court, which included disputes over tithes and the probate of wills, and defamation cases. As a proportion of all suits brought before the court, matrimonial cases only amounted to about 10 per cent during the century from the 1660s to the 1760s—a period which witnessed a massive overall decline in the court's activity. After the 1760s, however, whereas other business continued to decline, matrimonial business picked up, so much so that during the first half of

34

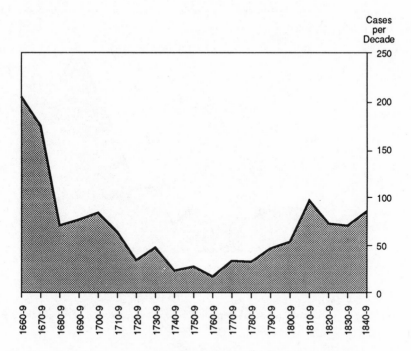

Cases
per
Decade

FIGURE 1.2   Court of Arches: All Matrimonial Cases 1660–1849
[Table 1.1]

the nineteenth century after 1810 it represented almost half of all the cases coming before the court (Figs. 1.2 and 1.3, Table 1.1).

There were two types of matrimonial cases, according to whether their prime purpose was to prove a disputed marriage or to break one up. The bulk of the cases which occurred in the late seventeenth century belonged to the first category, and were based on claims of a pre-contract or a prior clandestine marriage, both of which were difficult to prove (Fig. 1.4, Table 1.3).

As has been explained, the geographical catchment area for the Court of Arches was the ecclesiastical Province of Canterbury, containing twenty-two bishoprics, each with its own Consistory Court. By far the most active court for matrimonial cases was that of London, which between 1700 and 1810 supplied between a quarter and a half.[42]

---

[42] For all the above statistical calculations of cases in the Court of Arches, I am indebted to the skill and care of my research assistant Geoffrey Clark. His work was based on J. Houston (ed.), *Index of Cases in the Records of the Court of Arches at Lambeth Palace Library 1660–1913*, British Record Society (London, 1972), 85.

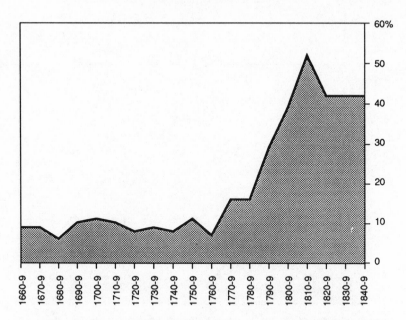

FIGURE 1.3   Court of Arches: Matrimonial Cases as a Proportion of All Cases 1660–1849 [Table 1.1]

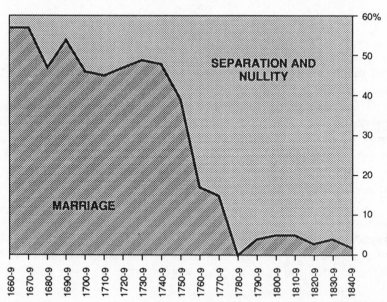

FIGURE 1.4   Court of Arches: Types of Cases: Marriage or Separation 1660–1849 [Table 1.3]

Fortunately for the modern historian, in a substantial proportion of the fully contested cases appealed from a bishop's court to the Court of Arches during the eighteenth century, all the various documents relating to the original case were collected together, copied into compact books called Process Books, and sent to London. In other cases, the original documents were sent loose in a package to London, and were eventually scattered and refiled under their respective categories. After 1800 a new system was adopted, by which all the loose documents in a case were filed together.

It has always to be remembered that litigation was as much blackmail as war, and as a result about 60 per cent of all matrimonial cases in the Court of Arches were settled out of court and never reached sentence (Table 1.2). As a result, there are only 321 usable Process Books, comprising about a quarter of all the matrimonial cases and a third of all separation cases entered in the Act Books of the Court between 1710 and 1800. But for the decades before 1710 and after 1800, the proportion of separation cases with Process Books falls to well below 10 per cent (Fig. 1.5, Table 1.4). The data-base between 1660 and 1710 was therefore filled out by examining some of the better-documented separa-

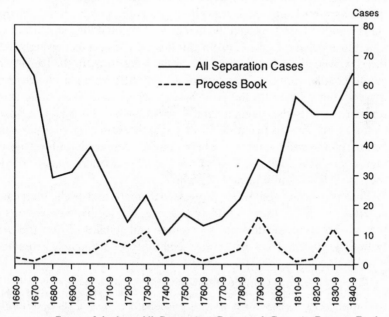

FIGURE 1.5   Court of Arches: All Separation Cases and Cases in Process Books
1660–1849 [Table 1.4]

37

tion cases, the records of which were scattered under different categories.

The next question is whether the cases appealed to the Court of Arches form a reasonable sample of all the cases generated by the Consistory Courts. To test this, investigation was made of the surviving records of seven Consistory Courts: of the Archdeaconry of Chester (which was part of the Province of York), and of the dioceses of Exeter, Gloucester, Lichfield, Norwich, Worcester, and London. Together, these supplied about half of all the cases appealed to the Court of Arches, and thus comprise a reasonably large representative sample of the whole, well distributed between the east and the west of southern and midlands England, as well as the great capital city of London (Fig. 1.6).[43]

The first discovery was that the matrimonial cases in which appeal was made to the Court of Arches omit almost all the 'office cases', that is, cases brought by court officials rather than private litigants. These flourished in the last half of the seventeenth century, two-thirds of them involving clergy performing, and couples undertaking, clandestine marriages. These cases were not appealed by the defendants since they realized that they could not win (Fig. 1.7, Table 1.5).

The class composition of litigants varied considerably over time. Sizeable numbers of quite humble people continued to sue one another in the Consistory Courts well into the eighteenth century, although they slowly tended to be replaced by members of the middling sort. But over time the appellants to the Court of Arches were drawn increasingly from the rich, who alone could afford the rising legal costs. In the late seventeenth century, some 12 per cent of all plaintiffs were still drawn from the very poor; by 1780, the poor had vanished altogether, while small tradesmen, artisans, yeomen, and husbandmen, who had comprised about 13 per cent of plaintiffs up to 1780, thereafter fell to 4 per cent. From 1660 to 1780, clerical workers, semi-professionals and well-to-do men of business comprised over a third of all petitioners, but after 1780 they too fell away to a fifth of the whole.

The proportion of solid professional men and rich merchants remained fairly stable at around 15 per cent, but the big increase was in the 'quality': the wealthy landed squires and nobility. From the very beginning in 1660, they had always been disproportionately prominent

[43] The Archdeaconry of Chester covered all of Cheshire, and Lancashire south of the Ribble. I am deeply grateful to my research assistant Timothy Wales, who over a period of three years undertook the monumental task of sampling these materials, tabulating them, xeroxing the most promising items, and drawing up statistical analyses of all surviving records of matrimonial cases in these seven Consistory Courts.

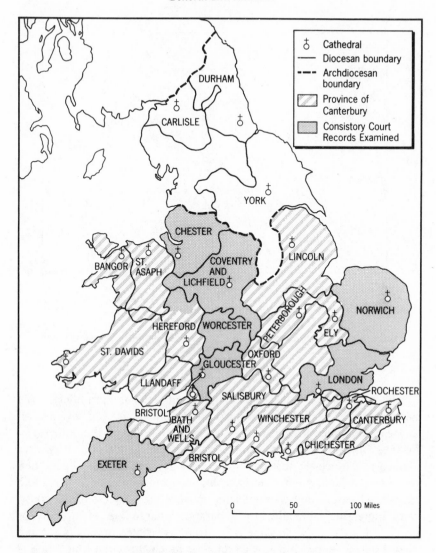

FIGURE 1.6   Map of English Dioceses

among petitioners relative to their numbers in the population, amounting to just under a third of the total. But between 1780 and 1820 their hold on the court became so great that they comprised well over a half of all petitioners. There was thus a remorseless drift to greater and greater elitism in the ranks of the petitioners, as rising legal costs increasingly excluded first the poor, and then the lower middling sorts (Table 1.6).

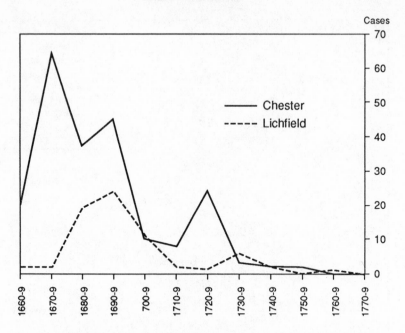

FIGURE 1.7   Office Prosecutions in Chester and Lichfield Consistory Courts
1660–1779 [Table 1.5]

The most surprising discovery about the quantity of matrimonial business in the Court of Arches was not its decline in the late seventeenth
and early eighteenth centuries, which merely reflected the collapse of
business in the Consistory Courts, but the resurgence of activity after
about 1780, especially in separation cases (Figs. 1.1 and 1.2). From then
to 1840 the landed elites and the higher professional and mercantile
classes, who were now monopolizing most of the business of the court,
were increasingly litigating for separation on grounds of adultery or
cruelty. Since exactly the same rising trend is visible not only in Puritan
New England but also in Switzerland at much the same time[44] one is
forced to conclude that there was some deep shift of mood and morals in
Protestant areas in the late eighteenth century which made legal separation and divorce much more acceptable solutions to marital disharmony

---

[44] S. S. Cohen, ' "To Parts of the Worlds Unknown": The Circumstances of Divorce in
Connecticut, 1750–1797', *Canadian Review of American Studies*, 11 (1980), 287; N. Cott,
'Divorce and the Changing Status of Women in Eighteenth-Century Massachusetts', William
and Mary Quarterly, 33 (1976), 587–92; J. R. Watt, 'Divorce in Early Modern Neuchatel 1547–
1806', *Journal of Family History*, 14 (1989), 147.

than they had been earlier. It is also possible that the amount of adultery was increasing.

C. PROVINCIAL CONSISTORY COURTS

Throughout the Middle Ages and the early modern period, provincial Consistory Courts (Plate 3), one for each bishopric, had controlled matrimonial affairs, including separations, as well as sexual morals, sexual defamation, Sabbath-breaking, tithe payments and the probate of wills. Although these courts were still active and busy up to 1640, they were becoming more and more unpopular because of their gross corruption and their use to persecute not only Catholics but also Puritans.[45]

During the Interregnum they were either ineffective or legally abolished by the Puritans, but by 1660 they were re-established in full force and resumed their activities as before. Suits before these courts were of two kinds. Some were official suits brought by officers of the court to punish offenders, and the rest, which constituted by far the largest part, were private suits between litigants. For about twenty years these courts were extremely active, clearing up the backlog from the Interregnum and resuming the persecution of religious dissidents and the regulation of sexual morals—a function which throughout the seventeenth century they shared with the Quarter Sessions run by JPs.[46]

After about 1680, however, the amount of business connected with matrimonial or sexual morals coming before all these provincial courts began to decline steeply (Fig. 1.8, Table 1.7). One reason was the drift of more and more cases to the Consistory Court of London, whose business grew with the rapid growth of this huge metropolis and the transfer of local legal business to the place of residence of the most skilled lawyers and judges. But there were deeper reasons for the collapse of the provincial courts between 1680 and 1720. In the first place, suits brought by court officials against offenders almost entirely disappeared as the laity's resentment against this kind of moral police intensified in an age of rational religion and hostility to religious or moral enthusiasm. There was also, however, a second general reason for the collapse. The growing secularization of society undermined the self-confidence and moral integrity of the officials of the courts, and between 1680 and 1720 they slid easily from acting out of religious and moral conviction to acting out of a desire to pocket fees.

[45] Ingram, *Church Courts, Sex, and Marriage*, ch. 12; C. Hill, 'The Bawdy Courts', in his *Society and Puritanism in Pre-Revolutionary England* (London, 1964).
[46] A. Fletcher, *Reform in the Provinces: The Government of Stuart England* (New Haven, 1986), 229–82.

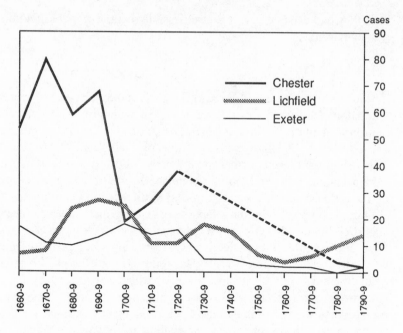

FIGURE 1.8   Matrimonial Cases in Chester, Lichfield, and Exeter Consistory Courts
1660–1799 [Table 1.7]

This drift was accentuated by political and religious developments. The refusal of Parliament in 1660 to revive the High Commission, with broad powers to punish offenders, in the long run had a devastating effect on the disciplinary powers of the church courts, whose penalties were now confined to excommunication and penance. Even these were becoming unenforceable, since a writ for arrest from Chancery was usually too expensive to be worthwhile. The policy of James II of issuing Declarations of Indulgence for Papists and Dissenters caused the suspension of much of the activities of the courts in enforcing religious conformity. After the Act of Toleration of 1689, court officials hesitated to prosecute for moral or religious offences, for fear of driving their potential victims to register as Dissenters. Thus after the 1689 act, the punishment of Sabbath-breaking became almost impossible as the public interpreted the act as a licence to frequent the alehouse rather than the church on a Sunday morning. When the court officials did take action, their sole instrument of punishment, namely excommunication, was undermined by the regular issue of general pardons which wiped the slate clean, as happened in 1672, 1689, 1694, and 1708. It was this vacuum of moral authority which between 1690 and 1730 the Societies for the Reformation of Manners tried desperately, but ultimately vainly, to fill.[47]

The troubles of these courts increased in the 1690s, as the common law courts were increasingly emboldened to steal business from them. After 1696, an act removed jurisdiction over small tithes from the courts to the JPs. To make matters worse, the Stamp Acts of the 1690s raised the cost of paper, and therefore especially the costs of litigation in church courts, which relied entirely on written records.

The result of this combination of factors, part structural and part conjunctural, was a sharp decline of business, which severely reduced the income of advocates, proctors, and other court officials. In an effort to counter the effects of this decline, their attention was ever more sharply focused on maximizing their fees, and further augmenting their income through bribes. The inevitable result was more corruption, and additional decline in morale, efficiency, and the quality of the legal process.[48]

So low had the courts sunk by 1740 that they had all but abandoned the filing of inventories attached to wills, and after 1770 virtually no inventories at all were being registered.[49] After about 1740, ecclesiastical court officials lived almost entirely on two sources: the profits of selling marriage licences, and fees from the remaining litigants. The sale of marriage licences contributed no less than half the income of these courts in the eighteenth century, which explains the corrupt way in which the court officials handled this business.[50] These conclusions, drawn from the manuscript records of these six provincial Consistory Courts in the south of England, are confirmed by an unpublished study of the Consistory Court of York after 1660.[51] The increasingly mercenary aspect of the court is shown in the way litigation by proctors against their clients to recover their fees rose from 5 per cent of all cases in the early 1660s to 15 per cent by the 1690s.[52]

D. THE LONDON CONSISTORY COURT

By far the largest canon law court in the south of England, and one whose dominance of matrimonial business became increasingly over-

---

[47] R. Houlbrook, 'The Decline in Ecclesiastical Jurisdiction', in R. O'Day and F. Heal (eds.), *Continuity and Change* (Leicester, 1976); T. Isaacs, 'The Anglican Church and the Reformation of Manners', *Journal of Ecclesiastical History*, 33 (1982).

[48] M. G. Smith, *Pastoral Discipline and the Church Courts: The Hexham Court 1680–1730*, Borthwick Papers, 62 (York, 1982), 2–3.

[49] P. Lindert, 'Unequal English Wealth since 1670', *Journal of Political Economy*, 94 (1986), 1132. [50] See ch. IV. [51] Till, 63, 69. [52] Ibid. 61, 65, 171.

whelming by the late eighteenth and early nineteenth centuries, was the Consistory Court of London which sat, together with the Court of Arches, in Doctors' Commons (Table 1.8). It was therefore generally known as Doctors' Commons (Plate 4).

Cases of separation constituted most of the increase in matrimonial litigation, which doubled in numbers between the 1750s and 1820s. The role of adultery was critical in this increase. In the late seventeenth century, only a quarter of all matrimonial litigation had involved adultery, or adultery with cruelty, but between the 1770s and the 1840s the proportion was as high as 69 per cent, while the sheer numbers rose from about twenty per decade to over seventy. These figures perfectly match the rise in the number of cases of crim. con. in King's Bench and the number of petitions for Parliamentary divorces. The London Consistory Court was now the main conduit for matrimonial breakdown in the country, as clients—mainly husbands—poured in to take advantage of short residential requirements and the high legal expertise available in the capital in order to sue their wives for separation on grounds of adultery.

E. OTHER RECORDS

The intensive study of these records of ecclesiastical litigation has been combined with examination of contemporary legal handbooks; of published transcripts of trials in the secular courts; and, in a few cases, of very illuminating unpublished private correspondence as well as some lengthy published or manuscript accounts of litigants' own sides of the story.[53]

Other vital information came from contemporary pamphlets. Whenever changes in the statute law were under discussion in Parliament, pamphleteers weighed in on both sides to influence the legislators, while Parliamentary debates were faithfully followed and reported. The *Journal of the House of Lords* provides much detail about the evidence in support of petitions for Parliamentary divorces. Details of adultery revealed by witnesses in 'crim. con.' actions became the soft-core pornography of the late eighteenth century, and there was a flourishing trade, especially between 1760 and 1860, in pamphlets and collections of pamphlets about the most scandalous and titillating of these cases. One of the motives behind the passage of the 1857 Divorce Act was to try to put a stop to the revelation in court proceedings and subsequent publications of the more scabrous details of adulterous behaviour.

---

[53] See Con Phillips's account of herself in Stone, *Broken Lives*.

In addition, the *Old Bailey Proceedings* (the published records of the criminal court for the London area) have been combed from 1716 to 1834 for trials for bigamy; pamphlets describing breach of promise trials and 'crim. con.' trials have been scanned. These printed trials have one great advantage over the official court records, which is that they set out at length the arguments of the lawyers on both sides and the directions to the jury by the judge, which provide invaluable information about the rhetoric of lawyers and the moral attitudes of judges and juries. Numerous private deeds of separation and some collections of correspondence have been found in private family archives. Although few in number, these last have been of critical importance in making it possible to probe behind the public trials into the extensive negotiations and plea-bargaining which was often taking place behind the scenes.[54]

8. Some Definitions

The unfamiliar phrase 'the middling sort' is used to describe a specific group of persons in the seventeenth and eighteenth centuries, without suggesting that they already had any homogeneous collective consciousness or political or moral programme. It is used because this was how contemporaries described that large and growing amorphous mass of persons who belonged neither to the quality above them nor the manual labourers and the poor below them. Second, it avoids the loaded words 'middle class' or 'bourgeoisie', both of which are controversial in meaning and contaminated by Marxist economic ideology. The 'middling sort' embraced a wide variety of persons, from rich merchants and bankers to prosperous shop-keepers and yeomen down to farmers and small tradesmen and clerks. It was a group defined by culture, morals, leisure activities, and occupations as much as by wealth or status. Although this group was in the process of self-definition and self-awareness throughout the eighteenth century, it cannot properly be called a class, in the Marxist sense of the word, before about 1850.

There are also four common words which have undergone considerable changes in meaning since the eighteenth century, and the use of which is consequently liable to give rise to confusion unless clearly defined. These are 'family', 'friends', 'marriage', and 'divorce'.

Today we use 'family' almost entirely in its most restrictive use, that is, the nuclear group of parents and children. In the eighteenth century, 'family' certainly had that meaning, but more commonly it included all

---

[54] See Stone, *Broken Lives*, The Grafton case.

those residing under one roof, including relatives and domestic servants. It could also describe the total lineage, past, present, and future, a definition usually restricted to upper-class kin-groups of distinguished pedigree. In this book, the modern usage will be adopted, restricting the word 'family' to its nuclear core, and using the word 'household' to embrace all the residents, the word 'kin' to include members of the extended family, wherever they resided, and the word 'lineage' to describe ancestors.

The word 'friends' today describes persons of either sex to whom one is primarily bound by ties of affection. In the eighteenth century and earlier, in the plural it was normally used in an instrumental sense of persons, whether kin or not, who could be relied on to provide good-will, support, advice, and patronage, and from whom one might well have expectations of a handsome legacy. They were, in short, persons of power and influence, who in a world run by patronage rather than merit were granted respect, duty, and, whenever possible, obedience, and whose displeasure it would be very unwise to incur. These 'friends' were always closely concerned with a marriage, either arranging and promoting it, or disapproving and blocking it. In this work the word 'friends' will be used in its eighteenth-century, instrumental sense.[55]

'Marriage' is today a clearly defined legal situation, created by taking part in some public ritual, whether religious or secular, and by the signing of certain documents. No such clarity existed up to the early eighteenth century, when legally binding marriages could be made in two ways which were distinct from the public ceremony performed by a clergyman in a church according to the rules of the *Book of Common Prayer*. One was by a mere verbal exchange of promises before two witnesses; and the other was by a religious ritual performed at any time or place by someone in holy orders, regardless of whether the performance was in direct breach of the canon law. To clarify matters, eighteenth-century terminology will be used, the first of these irregular but legally valid unions being called a contract marriage, and the second a clandestine marriage.

Finally, there is the word 'divorce'. In the eighteenth century, 'divorce' could mean two things. One, known as *divortium a vinculo*, meant what it means today—that is full, legal severance of a marriage by a judicial body, allowing both spouses to marry again. This was something which before 1857 only Parliament could grant, as an anomalous exception to the rule prohibiting all divorce. The other, known as *divortium a mensa et*

---

[55] My ideas about these two definitions were clarified by an unpublished paper by Naomi Tadmor of The Hebrew University, to whom I am very grateful.

thoro, meant separation from bed and board by an ecclesiastical court, without permission to remarry. In the interests of clarity, this last is here called 'judicial separation', although technically this is an anachronism, since the phrase only began to be used for separations granted by the new secular High Court for Matrimonial Causes set up by the act of 1857.

It is important to remember that divorce is a legal condition. It is not to be confused with a *de facto* state of marital breakdown, which may lead to many illegal or legal results, the former of which can perhaps best be described as forms of self-divorce. The first cohort in which over 90 per cent of those whose marriages broke down were eventually divorced by a court of law was that which married in the 1960s.[56]

[56] M. J. Murphy, 'Demographic and Socio-Economic Influences in Recent British Marital Breakdown Patterns', *Population Studies*, 39 (1985), 442.

PART ONE

The Making of *Marriage*

For the love of God take an order for marriages here in England. For here is marriage for pleasure, and voluptuousness, and for goods, and so that they may join land to land, and possessions to possessions: they care for no more in England.

Hugh Latimer's 'Last Sermon before Edward VI', in *The Works of Hugh Latimer*, ed. G. E. Corrie for the Parker Society (1844–5), 1: 243

Few persons will believe that the present times are remarkable for chastity and conjugal fidelity, or that the marriage laws which have been bequeathed us by the Council of Trent have secured in an eminent degree the object they were intended to accomplish.

J. W. Morris, *Observations on the Marriage Law* (London, 1815), 391

❧ II ❧

The Law and Custom of Marriage

1. Introduction: The Law of Marriage

If marriage is regarded in social rather than legal terms, it is a complex and often lengthy process and not merely a formal public event. This has become evident in the last few years, when the Western world has become full of young couples in various stages of negotiation. Some are courting, often including a good deal of physical intimacy; some are temporarily or semi-permanently cohabiting; others are secretly becoming engaged or even married. If they marry, they do it at a Registry Office, or openly in a field, or wood, or private house, or formally and publicly in a grand ceremony in a church. Many produce children in or out of wedlock at any stage of these various proceedings. The traditional sequence of the chaste courtship, followed by the formal engagement announced in the newspapers, followed by the public wedding in a church, followed by consummation, followed by pregnancy, is now no longer the norm. All these are stages in the process of coming together, but there is now no standard for orderly progression from one stage to another, nor even a single socially accepted mode of formal bonding. In this respect we have, quite suddenly, and perhaps only temporarily, created a situation not dissimilar to that which prevailed in early modern England.

At that time, far more people and institutions had a vested interest in the process of marriage than merely the man and woman involved, their rivals and their competitors. There were also the 'friends', who often assumed the right of control or veto and were in a position to enforce their will by the granting or witholding of money, house, property, or patronage. And there were the neighbours, who had to be persuaded to accept the couple into their midst as a morally bonded domestic unit. If they disapproved, they could express their feelings by a noisy public demonstration, called 'rough music', or by denouncing the couple to the ecclesiastical authorities as legally suspect—something which happened not infrequently before about 1700.

The major institutions of the society were also involved in a marriage. The church was closely concerned, partly since it had for centuries

51

enjoyed sole legal control over matrimonial affairs, and partly since it was increasingly insisting upon active participation in the ceremony by the parish priest. The state was also concerned in a variety of ways. At the theoretical level, a host of writers in the seventeenth century tried to base the divine right of kings upon the patriarchal principle embedded in the family structure. At a more mundane level, the state became directly concerned in the 1690s when it tried first to raise money by putting a tax on marriages, and then imposed a heavy stamp duty on marriage licences and certificates. And in 1753 it radically changed the law of marriage by act of Parliament. At the local level, the JPs, churchwardens, and overseers of the poor were very anxious to prevent the birth of children out of wedlock or the desertion of a destitute family, since in both cases the financial responsibility for upkeep was transferred from the father to the community poor rate.

There is some uncertainty as to whether large numbers of persons living together as husband and wife at this time were in fact legally married. Neighbours and communities were on the whole prepared to regard stable cohabitation, the exchange in conversation of words such as 'husband' or 'wife,' the use of the same surname, and the baptism of children as creating a socially acceptable presumption of marriage. The records reveal no 'charivaris' or popular demonstrations of protest against persons living in these frequently fluid and ambiguous situations, and by the end of the seventeenth century, churchwardens had virtually ceased to report doubtful cases at ecclesiastical visitations so long as bastardy was not involved.

However, a customary practice which might perhaps be acceptable to the couple and to a village community or a city neighbourhood was not at all the same as a marriage that was valid in ecclesiastical law or the common law, each of which applied different criteria of proof. In the thirteenth century, Pope Innocent III, following the canon lawyer Gratian and Pope Gregory IX in the twelfth, had decreed that free consent of both spouses, not the formal solemnities by a priest or in a church, was the sole essence of marriage. Consequently, a valid and binding marriage was created by a mere verbal exchange of vows to this effect between a man and a woman over the age of consent (14 and 16, respectively), witnessed by two persons, and expressed in the present tense.[1]

The standard handbook on contracts or spousals written by a learned canon law judge in about 1600[2] lovingly described how in the late Middle

---

[1] A. Esmein, *Le Mariage en droit canonique* (Paris, 1891), 1: 95–137; C. Donahue, Jr. 'The Policy of Alexander the Third's Consent Theory of Marriage', *Proceedings of the Fourth International Congress of Medieval Canon Law* (The Vatican, 1976).

[2] H. Swinburne, *A Treatise of Spousals or Matrimonial Contracts* (London, 1686). For a

Ages, canon lawyers and commentators had refined the simple principle of voluntary mutual contract into a set of complex rules, which were not at all clearly understood by the laity. The Canon law distinguished between a contract *per verba de presenti*, that is, in the present tense, and a contract *per verba de futuro*, that is, in the future tense. If duly attested by two credible witnesses, the first was binding and the other revocable at will unless followed by consummation. Thus, the statement 'I take you for my wife/husband' was fully binding, but the statement 'I shall take you for my wife/husband' was not binding unless followed by sexual consummation, which was taken to imply present consent. The third and perhaps the most common type of contract was conditional: 'I do contract matrimony with thee, if thy father consent.'[3] If the parent or other party named in the contract, usually a 'friend', refused, this conditional contract was clearly not binding. Similarly, the conditional nature of the contract was unambiguous if it ran 'I will marry you if your brother will give me £200 with you.'[4] Thus, in church law, a contract duly performed in the present tense was complete in substance, if not in ceremony, and was indissoluble. It would also make any later marriage—even one performed in church—voidable by a court sentence as bigamous.

In the Middle Ages there were thus two culturally acceptable forms of marriage in England. There was the official mode practised by the ruling elite, which demanded a public and clerically supervised marriage, in a church, within canonical hours, after either putting up the banns three times or purchasing a licence. And there was also the popular mode of verbal contract or spousals, accompanied by folk rituals. To borrow for a moment from semiotics, the verbal contract was an element in a code which had meaning in the experience of a particular audience. In this case, the canon law in the Middle Ages had played a very unusual role. It had served partly as agent of the power elite to enforce compliance with the official code, but also partly as upholder of popular beliefs and practices which found expression in these rituals of spousals or verbal private marriage contracts.[5]

This acceptance by the church of verbal contract marriages was extraordinary for three reasons. First, it was impractical; as F. W. Maitland has pointed out, 'of all people in the world, lovers are the least likely to

biography of the author, see J. D. M. Derrett, *Henry Swinburne, 1551–1624*, Borthwick Papers 44 (York, 1973).
[3] Salmon, 188.   [4] *Baker* v. *Taylor* (1672), LPCA, Eee.4, fo. 597.
[5] See Helmholtz, 33–66; M. M. Sheehan, 'The Formation and Stability of Marriage in Fourteenth-Century England: Evidence of an Ely Register', *Mediaeval Studies*, 33 (1971); id., 'Marriage Theory and Practice in the Conciliar Legislation and Diocesan Statutes of Medieval England', ibid. 40 (1978).

distinguish precisely between the present and the future tenses'.[6] Second, it flew in the face of medieval secular practice, by which marriage in the propertied classes was settled by parents, guardians, and influential 'friends', the economic and political fortunes of the family being the prime consideration. Third, it went against the desire of the church to control marriage, to turn it into a sacrament, and to make central to its validity participation by a priest and the location of the ceremony in a church.

Nor was there much historical support for this position. The consent of the parties was basic to the Roman law of Justinian, but so also was the consent of parents or guardians. The pagan Germanic marriage depended on the payment of a bride price by the bride's family to that of the groom; consent was not recognized as relevant. The Eastern Orthodox Church had always insisted on the need for church ritual. By rejecting both any form of religious ceremony and any place for the interests of the family, the master, or the lord, the new policy of the twelfth-century canon lawyers ran contrary to the wishes and interests of two of the most powerful forces in the society, the church and the family.

In practice, of course, it did not work. Throughout the Middle Ages, secret contract marriages and clandestine marriages were indeed made in defiance of parental wishes. But in the long run the interests of kin and society prevailed, and financial arrangements or political influence continued to be paramount among all but the very poor. The state, and even the church, demanded publicity—the former in order to establish property rights, and the latter both to identify fornication and adultery and to enforce the concept of marriage as a sacrament symbolized by a church ritual. What may be called the Romeo and Juliet syndrome that had been made possible by the twelfth-century ruling was intolerable to all parties except the couple themselves.

As a result, three things happened in the late Middle Ages. The propertied laity ignored the laws and continued to arrange the marriages of their children; the number of litigated cases declined; and the church courts became more and more hostile to contract marriages, especially if they lacked adequate proof and if they were mere pre-contracts which were being used to break up a later church marriage.[7] For the most part, therefore, by the late Middle Ages the 'spousals' or contract had become merely a preliminary ritual of betrothal, to be followed by a public church ceremony of marriage. This European-wide medieval practice of

[6] F. Pollock and F. W. Maitland, *The History of English Law*, 2nd edn. (Cambridge, 1899), 2: 368–9.
[7] Helmholtz, 25, 66, 68–9, 186; Sheehan, 'The Formation and Stability of Marriage'; see also H. A. Kelly, 'Clandestine Marriage and Chaucer's "Troilus" ', *Viator*, 4 (1973), 435–49.

betrothal found its most famous visual expression a kind of 'pictorial marriage certificate', in the famous Arnolfini portrait by Jan van Eyck dated 1434. Even the two witnesses are visible in the mirror.[8]

At the Council of Trent in 1563, the Catholic church put an end to one part of this confusion by insisting that the validity of a marriage depended on a public ceremony before a priest and two or more witnesses, accompanied by a written entry in a parish register. The council failed at the last moment to rule that under-age children also had to obtain the permission of parents or guardians, but this omission was rectified by the secular laws of the state. Thus, in France, a royal ordinance of 1556, re-issued and strengthened in 1579 and 1639, made any marriage of a woman under 25 or a man under 30 invalid in civil law if performed without the consent of parent or guardian. In other words, such a marriage might be valid in canon law, but it would not carry with it any property rights. The object of these edicts was to protect the children of the elite from being seduced into marriage with persons of lower status, whether for money or for love. This principle was further reinforced by the penal law of 'rapt', which in France was taken to mean not merely rape or forcible abduction and marriage, but also the marriage of a woman without parental consent. Thus, in the eyes of the church, a man might marry his mistress by mutual agreement without parental consent, but by doing so he became liable to the death penalty on a charge of 'rapt' in the eyes of the secular courts.[9]

Such a situation has been rightly described as the product of a family–state compact, by which both sides gained.[10] Thanks to these royal edicts, elite families, especially those who became hereditary servants of the state thanks to the purchase of offices, could control the passing of their property and office through the blood-line down to posterity in ways of their own choosing. The state gained control over all marriages, which by analogy was seen as a buttress to its own control over society as a whole. In France, the Crown and the civil jurists thus decisively defeated the pope, the bishops, and the ecclesiastical lawyers. It should be pointed out that the French state also controlled reproduction, and all forms of marital separation, as well as having a role in the punishment of sexual delinquents, confining adulterous wives in nunneries, and wayward sons in the Bastille by *lettres de cachet* at the request of the families.

Thus, in France the monarchy felt itself to be so dependent on the

---

[8] E. Panofsky, 'Jan Van Eyck's Arnolfini Portrait', *Burlington Magazine*, 64 (1934), 124.

[9] C. E. Holmès, *L'Eloquence judiciare de 1620 à 1660: Reflet des problèmes sociaux, religieux et politiques de l'époque* (Paris, 1967), 72–7, 113.

[10] T. S. Hanley, 'Engendering the State: Family Formation and State Building in Early Modern France, *French Historical Studies*, 16 (1989).

patriarchal family as a model for its power that it went to extraordinary pains to support and reinforce the latter. This raises the question why similar controls were not also imposed by the state in England. Instead, the government in the late seventeenth and early eighteenth centuries abandoned most of such powers as they still possessed over reproductive behaviour, and before 1753 made few serious attempts to suppress either clandestine or contract marriages. The best explanation for this is the complicated legal situation in England, split between three rival systems: civil, equity, and common law; the relative internal weakness of the English state, which lacked a local bureaucracy; the absence of a systematic policy of the sale of hereditary offices; and after 1660, the development among wealthy families of a fairly effective system of primogeniture to govern the transmission of property. But this does not explain why it was not until 1753 that elite parents obtained through Parliament authority to prevent secret marriages by their rebellious teenage children. The story of the control of marriage in England is thus radically different from that in France, largely due to different state structures.

For a very complicated set of largely accidental reasons—related to the convoluted history of the rise of Protestantism in England—nothing was done at the Reformation to alter the law of marriage, so that although the study of canon law was forbidden, the pre-Tridentine canon law continued to be the law of the land until the Marriage Act of 1753. The only change was that marriage ceased to be regarded as a sacrament, although it remained a spiritual act and therefore indissoluble.

The common law, however, had long since rejected the canon law doctrine of contract marriages, and refused to confer property rights except to persons who had gone through a public ceremony, customarily at the door of the church. Without such a ceremony the husband had no enforcible legal claim on the property of his wife. In consequence she retained her legal personality, but on the death of her husband she had no claim to dower (one third of his property); and their children had no claim to inheritance as legitimate heirs. In the Middle Ages even this simple law had its exceptions. Thus, at Wakefield in 1286, a family successfully claimed inheritance according to local custom for the eldest son 'born after troth-plight' but before marriage in church.[11]

As late as 1732, a legal treatise repeated the traditional position of the church, although now it sounded a little hollow:

Nothing is more requisite to a complete marriage by the laws of England than a

---

[11] P. Hair, *Before the Bawdy Courts: Selections from Church, Court, and other Records relating to the Correction of Moral Offences in England, Scotland and New England* (New York, 1972), 114.

full, free, and mutual consent between parties ... for marriage is of divine institution, to which only the consent of the parties is necessary, though solemnizing of it is a civil right, regulated by the laws and customs of nations.[12]

As a result, during the sixteenth, seventeenth, and eighteenth centuries in England, there was a wide gap between the ideal and the real process of making a marriage, the gap being especially wide in the upper reaches of society. So far as the propertied laity was concerned, the ideal marriage began with the selection by the parents of the potential spouse, an agreement among both sets of parents upon the financial arrangements, and the acceptance of this choice by both parties, either voluntarily or under pressure. Once this was settled, it was increasingly common by the sixteenth century to procure a licence to dispense with the banns; then there took place the public ceremony in the church, or at its door, presided over by the priest, with the usual questions and answers and the accompanying ritual of the ring. Before the Reformation, this had been immediately followed by a nuptial mass. After all this came the wedding feast and the public bedding of the couple, who only then were left alone to consummate the marriage.

In reality, however, especially lower down the social scale, things often did not follow this sequence. The process began with a free courtship and exchange of gifts, culminating in a contract or spousals, sometimes carried out without the consent of parents and even without witnesses. This put the couple in a condition constantly referred to in the late seventeenth and eighteenth centuries as 'married in the eyes of God'.[13] In other words, a secret contract, or, later on, a clandestine marriage which was binding but illegal, both of them carried out without parental consent, were options very much open to young people in England. In many cases, it was a successful pre-emptive strike by the young couple, in order to secure their own choice of a spouse in defiance of their parents and the courts.

In that sense, nothing much had changed from the fourteenth to the early sixteenth centuries, except that whereas in the fourteenth century litigation over disputed contracts—and a few clandestine marriages—provided the bulk of the matrimonial business of the church courts, by the early sixteenth century the proportion had dwindled to less than half, mainly because the judges were adopting an increasingly rigid policy of rejecting wherever possible these tiresome and often scandalous unofficial unions. On the other hand, by the late seventeenth century the attitude of the church courts to consummation before the church ceremony had been modified. The offenders were no longer liable to punishment as forni-

[12] *Feme Coverts*, 25.   [13] *Eng. Rep.* 91: 381; *Feme Coverts*, 34.

cators, but only as violators of an edict of the church prohibiting bedding before the spousals had been ratified by an open church wedding.[14]

Even though it met with increasing hostility from the courts, the existence of the contract marriage from the Reformation to 1753 placed limits on the patriarchal authority of parents and guardians to dictate or forbid a marriage. Moreover, in Chancery the lawyers acted still further to limit the power of parents and guardians. In the first place, the court refused to enforce marriage brokage bonds. There were bonds made by aspiring suitors to pay sums of money to persons thought to have influence over a young woman (usually an heiress), to induce her to marry him, the money being payable on marriage out of the heiress's estate. In the mid-eighteenth century Lord Hardwicke declared that 'the Court has been extremely jealous of any contract of this kind, made with a guardian or servant, especially with a servant, in respect of the marriage of persons over whom they have an influence'. The court was equally careful to block any bequest in a will in restraint of marriage. It would allow a legacy conditional upon the recipient not marrying until 21; not marrying without the consent of friends; or not marrying a particular individual. But it would *not* allow a legacy on condition of no marriage at all (except in the case of widows), or of marrying a particular individual.[15]

In these ways, the powers of parents to dictate the marriage of their children was less than absolute. 'Patriarchy' may therefore be too strong a word to describe the parent–child relationship in England, at least by the early eighteenth century. 'Paternalism' is perhaps more appropriate to the still extensive, but by no means total, power exercised by parents over the marriage of their children, even in exalted circles. What parents did have at their disposal was the power of the purse, by which they could exercise considerable economic pressure not to marry without their consent. The Marriage Act of 1753 certainly strengthened parental power by nullifying any marriage made by a minor under 21 without the consent of parents or guardians, which was intended to be an effective deterrent to runaway juvenile marriages. But by then the ideology of affective individualism was beginning to influence the attitude of all but the most authoritarian of parents, persuading them that it was appropriate for them to offer advice and prevent grossly unsuitable matches, but improper to dictate the actual individuals their children should marry, or to impose a veto without good reason. They expected to exercise the right to advise and consent, but in most families that was all. It was usually, but not always, sufficient.

[14] Wharton, 219.   [15] Ibid. 220.

2. Courtship

There were three modes of courtship in early modern England, each of which was characteristic of, but not peculiar to, one of the three groupings into which contemporaries tended to divide the population.

Among the quality, courtship before the middle of the seventeenth century was usually a stilted and formal affair of short duration and limited significance. The procedure took two forms. The first was the selection of a possible spouse by the parents or friends, after careful examination of his or her economic prospects, and preliminary agreement with the other set of parents and friends about the terms of the financial settlement. The couple were then brought together, in order to discover whether or not they found each other personally obnoxious. If no strong negative feelings were aroused, the couple normally consented, the marriage settlement was signed, and the arrangement for a formal church wedding went forward. Alternatively, a man might meet or see a girl in a public place, in church, or at a ball or party. If he was attracted to her, he would approach her parents and friends and formally ask their permission to court her. If investigation proved that he was financially and personally suitable, permission was granted and courting went forward, with all the usual rituals of visits, conversation, gifts, and expressions of love and devotion (Plate 5).

These requests to parents or guardians for permission to pay court were normally made in person, but occasionally they were put in writing, which allows the historian a view of the formalities which surrounded such occasions. One such letter was written in 1755 by a relatively impecunious clergyman in Nottinghamshire to a Mrs Neville, seeking permission to offer marriage to her ward, Miss Snow. He explains that he has met Miss Snow thanks to 'my intimacy with Mrs Snow', and has come 'to admire in her an agreable person, an affable and engaging behaviour, joined to a fine understanding'. He goes on to declare that these

are charms too prevailing to pass without observation. Me, I own, they have fixed amongst the number of her most passionate admirers, and I have considered 'em so attentively that to be possessed of the lady who is mistress of such admirable and valuable qualifications is (however undeserving I may be of such an inestimable treasure) become necessary to my happiness. I should have subjected myself to the charge of acting improperly . . . had I paid my addresses to Miss Snow, . . . and her own prudence and good sense would have blamed me for offering to do it without your knowledge and approbation. You have been, and still are, to her in the place of a parent. . . . Knowing this, I should be unpardonable if I was to take any step toward the accomplishment of my hopes previous to that of having your sentiment upon the matter.

After this long-winded preamble, the Revd Knowles frankly conceded that he was not much of a financial catch. He had no private income, he lived entirely upon his two church livings, which brought in £120 a year, and he was still paying off debts owed by his late father. He stressed that his intention 'is not to lay my force upon the lady's inclinations, for I honestly declare to you I wouldn't marry the best woman in the three kingdoms unless I was as certain of her affections as I was of her hand'. He winds up with the request: 'Remember, dear madam, that the happiness of a man . . . is at present in your hands.'[16]

What is noticeable about this letter is, first, that in polite society in the mid-eighteenth century it was still expected that a would-be suitor should first request, in the most stilted and formal manner, the permission of the guardian; second, that the motives for the suit should be entirely based upon mutual affection—but with no hint of either romantic love or sexual passion; and third, that although there was a frank recognition that a difference in financial circumstances might raise an obstacle to the match, the suitor did not regard it as an insuperable one. We are already moving away from the world of Defoe, and even Fielding, and into the more ambiguous one of Jane Austen.

Occasionally, of course, and increasingly throughout the eighteenth century, unsupervised couples from propertied families would meet at court, or at Bath, or on the hunting-field, and conduct their own courtship in complete secrecy. Sooner or later, however, they were obliged to face up to the necessity of obtaining consent of parents or friends. Negotiations and haggling over the settlement now became the last step instead of the first, as the father of the bride decided upon the size of the marriage portion, and the father of the groom upon the appropriate current maintenance for the couple, as well as the jointure for the bride if she outlived the groom.

In the sixteenth and seventeenth centuries, the pressure of parents, friends, and kin in the highest circles of society was all but irresistible, especially because of the financial pressures which could be, and often were, brought to bear. By the eighteenth century, however, the concept of affective individualism had penetrated even these elevated circles, and thanks to the romantic movement, by the end of the century the tables had been entirely turned. By then, even in great aristocratic households, mutual affection was regarded as the essential prerequisite for matrimony, even if sometimes this led to disappointing results. Thus, in 1796, the parents and lawyers arranged the financial details of a match between the

---

[16] Notts RO, DD.231/9.

heir to the Duke of Leeds and a great heiress, Lady Gertrude Villiers. Once all this was satisfactorily settled, the couple were sent off to the seaside together to get to know each other. The result was not a success, and it was reported that the match was 'entirely off, after an ineffectual attempt to fall in love with each other at Weymouth and which was rather an awkward business for both'.[17] By this time, at the end of the eighteenth century, we have entered a new world in which, even in a social group for whom large estates and ancient titles were the stakes in the game, the complex calculations of scheming parents and artful lawyers took second place—and willingly so—to the dictates of the heart. Other elite couples were inspired to marry by more carnal ambitions. Few spelt it out more frankly than Frederick Mullins in 1747, when he complained that the trustees of his marriage settlement were unnecessarily delaying 'my taking possession of the charming Phoebe', adding by way of explanation that they were 'not so eager for a f--k as I am'.[18]

Below this level, among the propertied middling sort, arrangements were much more fluid, and depended to a considerable degree upon the personal characters of parents and children. Some parents were as authoritarian as dukes, others adopted a policy of affectionate and tolerant *laissez-faire*. What is clear, however, is that in general in this middling social class, English women as well as men enjoyed what was by European standards a quite exceptional freedom to select their own spouses and to conduct their own courtship rituals. The rituals included the usual meetings, talks, exchanges of presents, expressions of love and affection, and discussion of economic prospects. They tended to be prolonged, rarely lasting less than four months and sometimes continuing for one or two years.

There is now no doubt that British courting rituals normally involved the habit—unknown elsewhere outside Scandinavia and New England—of 'bundling', that is of staying up all night together in the woman's place of residence, after the old folks had gone to bed, either without their knowledge or with their tacit consent. This took place either in the kitchen beside the fire or in a bedroom, on or in the bed. Sometimes such all-night sessions occured at weekly intervals for months or years on end, and yet, at least in the seventeenth century—unlike the eighteenth—only in a tiny minority of cases did it result in pregnancy. Although the rules were never explicitly stated, one has to conclude that there were strong built-in conventions surrounding the practice of bundling which dictated that full

[17] The reference has unfortunately been mislaid.
[18] A. P. W. Malcolmson, *The Pursuit of the Heiress: Aristocratic Marriage in Ireland, 1750–1820* (Ulster Historical Foundation, 1982), 33.

intercourse should be avoided, although it is equally hard to escape the conclusion that there took place an exchange of most other forms of sexual gratification.

In 1668, for example, a Miss Lloyd admitted that she 'hath sat up several nights in company with him', but claimed they were never alone. She explained that the young people in the house used to assemble in her chamber at night, sometimes in their night-gowns, and that occasionally her suitor 'in a frolic in the presence of others did tumble me on the bed'.[19]

What is so surprising about these courting procedures in the seventeenth century, then, is that they involved three features which at first sight seem wholly incompatible, and indeed were to prove so in the eighteenth century. One was the delay of marriage to a decade after puberty (and for the poor after leaving home), that is to about 26 or 28 for men and 24 to 26 for women; the other was the all but universal practice among the lower and the middling sort of bundling; and the third was the very low level of both bastardy and pre-nuptial conceptions which resulted. England in the seventeenth century was sexually an extraordinarily restrained society. Inhibiting factors were the fear of pregnancy, probably leading to financial ruin, public disgrace, and a severely diminished chance of future marriage; the moral and religious teachings of the Puritan ministers about sin leading to damnation in the next world; and the strong disapproval of neighbours and kin. So alarming were these images and threats that remarkably little pregnancy resulted from bundling despite the fact that mechanical means of contraception were unknown to the poor at this time, and *coitus interruptus* known to some but perhaps not very commonly practised. Medical abortifacients were certainly widely known, especially the plant savin, but their efficiency is uncertain, and when mixed with heavy metals like mercury, as they often were, they could produce agonizing and lethal results.

Among the propertyless poor, who comprised perhaps the bottom third of the population, young people's freedom of courting was almost absolute, if only because the parents lacked the economic resources to exercise effective control. In any case, one or both sets of parents were often already dead by the time their children reached a decision to marry. Parental power was further reduced in this class by the fact that most young people had left home long before the time they became seriously interested in the opposite sex. At about 16 most poor girls left home to go into domestic service and most boys would go off to become living-in agricultural servants working the land on an annual contract, or apprentices serving a seven-year stint to learn a trade and qualify to set up in

[19] *Dove* v. *Lloyd* (1668), LPCA, Ee.3, fo. 328.

business. The reason for this massive export of children to serve in other people's houses is not at all clear. It was far more common in England than elsewhere in Europe, but the only explanation advanced at the time was that other people's children are easier to control than one's own. As a result, poor boys and girls were free to meet unchaperoned as fellow-servants in the same house, or at village fairs and festivals, dances, and church services. Thereafter they made their own arrangements for courting, subject only to the prurient curiosity and gossip of neighbours and other servants (Plate 6).

Whether their choice was based on love, lust, affection, or a prudent calculation of economic advantage was something which varied from individual to individual. There was no clear-cut correlation between freedom of choice and choice based on personal attraction, although this motive obviously tended to bulk larger in the minds of the potential bride and groom than it did in those of parents and 'friends'.

By the early eighteenth century, the breakdown of the sexually inhibiting ethical code of Puritanism had created a serious dilemma, especially for young girls. In the dessicated language of game theory, the courting process is a system of barter, in which the man's chief asset is the financial security he has to offer, and the woman's is monopoly access to her virgin body. The assumption underlying this model is that the male libido is more easily aroused than that of the female, especially among young girls not yet fully awakened to the pleasures of sex. This model is flawed by the fact that in eighteenth-century England a woman had a financial card to play as well as a physical one, since she usually brought with her to the marriage a 'portion', a cash contribution which might be relatively quite substantial. What made things particularly difficult for girls in the early eighteenth century was the problem of how far they could prudently go in advertising their physical attractions during 'bundling', now that the Puritan inhibitions upon display had been lifted. The result was an explosion of pre-nuptial pregnancies and bastardies, since there were few guidelines to steer a young girl betwen the Scylla of prudishness which would deter prospective suitors, and the Charybdis of too easy compliance which might lead to loss of virginity before a binding contract had been made. One way in which some girls tried to protect themselves in the eighteenth century was to conduct their courting, often including fairly heavy petting, in the presence of other women, usually their sisters, their maids, or sometimes their mothers, relying on these eye-witnesses to prevent things from going too far. All these aspects of the courting scene of eighteenth-century England are brought out by the story of the Harris girls.[20]

[20] See Stone, *Uncertain Unions*.

3. Customary Unions and Concubinage

Some scholars of the family now believe that in the early modern period, and more especially in the late eighteenth and nineteenth centuries, considerable numbers of English men and women lived in a condition of customary concubinage, illegal according to the law of church or state but recognized by the neighbourhood. The principal evidence for this theory is folklore recorded by late nineteenth-century antiquaries, much of it coming from Wales and the south-west of England.[21] If this were true on the scale that is claimed, it is surprising that such ceremonies as jumping over a broomstick hardly ever figure in any of the hundreds of cases of contract which turn up in court records of the eighteenth century. In the middle of the century, a commentator dismissed such ceremonies as foreign nonsense:

In some countries the same convention between males and females is accompanied with the ceremonial jumping over a stick; but if in England a couple were to interchange promises of perpetual fidelity, cohabitation, and good offices ratified by the like ceremony, and then going to bed together, were gravely to expect to be called husband and wife by their acquaintance, they would be looked upon as people out of their wits.[22]

It seems more than likely that, especially in remote areas such as Wales, where there were few resident landlords or educated clergymen to exercise control, such customs may have been generally accepted, and concubinage have been frequent. But just how frequent we have no idea. There is good reason to think that in most of England, especially the south and east, the all-important problem of legal property transfer was sufficient to restrict mere concubinage to the abject poor. Moreover, from the late sixteenth century to the late seventeenth century, there was combined pressure by community, church, and state, acting through churchwardens, constables, JPs, apparitors, and church courts, to regularize sexual and marital behaviour and punish deviants. This undoubtedly reduced the amount of bastardy and pre-nuptial conceptions to an astonishingly low level, and must have made concubinage by folk custom uncomfortable and fairly rare.

It is certainly quite possible that concubinage increased again after 1680, as the legal pressures from the church courts and the JPs eased off, the former going into sharp decline, and the latter focusing their energies upon trying to keep the rising bastardy rate in check in order to relieve the pressure on the poor rates. By the eighteenth century, the old moral

---

[21] Gillis, chs. 2, 3, 5, 7; esp. pp. 141–5.   [22] *Letter to the Public*, 37 (*recte* 45).

controls on bundling were clearly breaking down, the evidence being the rise in bastardy between 1690 and 1790 from 6 to 20 per cent of all first births, and the even more startling explosion of pre-nuptial conceptions.[23] By the late eighteenth century, consummation and conception normally preceded—and indeed precipitated—marriage, as shown by the fact that a third of all brides were pregnant on their wedding day, and over half of all first births were conceived out of wedlock. Contract marriages may have been legally dead, but these forms of 'marriages in the sight of God' were clearly accepted among the lower sort in the eighteenth century as a moral justification for starting sexual relations, on the assumption, usually justified, that the man would marry the woman if and when she became pregnant. Lord Brougham was therefore right when in 1849 he declared 'it is an exceedingly common contract of seduction . . . in all the counties of England, but particularly I am sorry to say in the northern counties, to make a bargain to live together, and only to marry if there is pregnancy. That is a very common case, no doubt, and common in Scotland too, I apprehend.'[24] But this temporary concubinage and pregnancy is not at all the same as living indefinitely in a state of concubinage without an official marriage, nor is it in any way incompatible with a high level of subsequent marital fidelity, which is indeed what mid-nineteenth-century commentators such as Gladstone and Bishop Wilberforce believed.[25]

The other piece of evidence against believing that outside the London area there were at any time large numbers of couples living in indefinite concubinage in early modern England is the absence of any obvious large deficit in the figures for marriages taken from parish registers. No one doubts that there were defects in the registers due to inefficiency, non-conformity, and clandestine marriage, especially in the London area, and that there was a lot of pre-nuptial sexual activity, but there appears to be no evidence of any large-scale practice of life-long concubinage blessed by folk custom.[26]

Everything suggests that after 1660 not cohabitation but quasi-official modes of making a marriage were adopted by most of those who, for one

[23] E. A. Wrigley, 'Marriage, Fertility, and Population Growth in Eighteenth-Century England', in *Marriage & Soc.*, 156–7, 162; Wrigley was the first to point out that by calculating the ratio of illegitimate births and pre-nuptial conceptions to all *first* births, it would be possible to calculate the number of first births conceived out of wedlock; P. Laslett, *Family Life and Illicit Love in Earlier Generations* (Cambridge, 1979), 115, 119, 132; P. E. Hair, 'Bridal Pregnancy in Earlier Rural England Further Examined', *Population Studies*, 24 (1970), 60. If urban areas, especially London, could be included, there is little doubt that both the proportions and the size of the rise in the 18th century would be much higher.

[24] *Select Committee on the Marriage Law (Scotland) 1849 (PP 1849)* 12: 18.

[25] See below, ch. XII.2.*d*.

[26] E. A. Wrigley and R. S. Schofield, *The Population History of England, 1541–1871* (London, 1981).

reason or another, chose to avoid the public ceremony performed by a clergyman in the church of their place of residence. There can be no doubt that the institutional chaos of the 1650s in matters of church administration and discipline had the most serious effects upon both marriage and separation. Officially, banns should have been called in church, and the marriage service carried out by a secular JP, a process many found unacceptable. As a result, verbal contracts, or 'spousals', as they were called, which had almost died out under legal pressure from the church courts before 1640, were revived during the Interregnum and had to be suppressed again by the church courts between 1660 and 1680. Clandestine marriages had also become very common during the Interregnum, when church weddings by the Book of Common Prayer were banned. From then to 1753, they became the most popular way of evading a formal church marriage by a qualified minister of the church of England.

At the Restoration in 1660, the Church of England officials of the revived ecclesiastical courts therefore found themselves confronted by the now recalcitrant poor, as well as by a large group of the better sort—ex-Puritans, now labelled Dissenters—who were no longer allies but rivals and enemies whom they were determined to persecute. They were also faced with a large-scale revival of contract and clandestine marriages and by a huge backlog of matrimonial litigation.

❧ III ❧

Contract Marriage

A present and perfect consent alone maketh matrimony, without either public solemnization or carnal copulation, for neither is the one nor the other the essence of matrimony, but consent only.

H. Swinburne, *A Treatise of Spousals, or Matrimonial Contracts* (London, 1686; written *c.*1600), 14

When two persons agree to have . . . commerce for the procreation and bringing up of children, and for such lasting cohabitation that, in a state of nature, would be a marriage, and in the absence of all civil and religious institutes, [it] might safely be presumed to be, as it is popularly called, a marriage in the sight of God.

Sir William Scott, in Lindo *v.* Belisario (1795), *Engl. Rep.* 161: 535

1. The First Suppression and the Revival, 1540–1660

The story of how the church courts operated to control sexuality and marriage in the century after the Reformation is now well known, even if there is still near total disagreement about their administrative efficiency and popularity.[1] The courts survived the Reformation intact, and made regular use of archdeacon's visitations to oblige village churchwardens to report any cases of suspected unmarried cohabitation, bastardy, adultery, separated couples, or contract or clandestine marriages. As a result, the church courts were reasonably successful in keeping the lid on the somewhat boisterous popular sexuality which has already been described. They were helped in this task by the secular authorities, who were increasingly anxious to suppress sin, although their chief concern

[1] Helmholtz; Marchant; A. P. Moore, 'Marriage Contracts in the Reign of Queen Elizabeth', *Associated Architectural Societies Reports*, 30 (1909); Ingram, *Church Courts, Sex, and Marriage*, 378–92 for a detailed bibliography; id., 'Spousals Litigation in English Ecclesiastical Courts, *c.*1350–1640', in *Marriage & Soc.*; id., 'The Reform of Popular Culture? Sex and Marriage in Seventeenth-Century England', in R. B. Reay (ed.), *Popular Culture in Seventeenth Century England* (London, 1985); C. Hill, *Society and Puritanism in Pre-Revolutionary England* (London, 1964), 298–343; G. R. Quaife, *Wanton Wenches and Wayward Wives: Peasants and Illicit Sex in Early Seventeenth-Century England* (London, 1979); C. B. Herrup, 'Law and Morality in Seventeenth-Century England', *Past and Present*, 106 (1985); Houlbrooke, *Church Courts*; id., 'The Making of Marriage in Mid-Tudor England', *Journal of Family History*, 10 (1985).

was of course to deter bastardy, which was liable to put a burden on the village poor rate.

The second concern of the church courts, especially after about 1580, was slowly to push more and more of the population into formal and public weddings in church presided over by a clergyman, as the Council of Trent had decreed for members of the Catholic church in 1563. This meant taking an increasingly sceptical attitude to cases of alleged contract, by which couples assured each other that they were 'married in the eyes of God'. At this point the parents and 'friends' were informed of what was going forward and asked for their advice, consent, and financial help. If a satisfactory financial arrangement could not be worked out, the couple frequently abandoned the whole affair, sometimes with great grief, sometimes with resignation. Detailed accounts of hundreds of such episodes show clearly that love and material interest were inextricably interwoven in the courting ritual in the minds of most participants. As the moment of decision came closer, 'interest' tended to loom larger. Sometimes the two issues became polar opposites, facing the couple with a hard choice between love or money. More often, however, the two remained closely interlocked, since the courting process involved not merely the choice of a congenial and sexually attractive companion but also a shrewd calculation of economic prospects. Even so, the potentiality for conflict certainly existed in the minds of the participants, especially if the girl became pregnant. The pressure from the man's parents and friends often intensified, and sometimes the man reluctantly, or cynically, went back on his alleged promise to marry. When one such son asked his father 'What would you have me do else [except to marry the pregnant girl]', his father crudely reported 'why, man, cannot . . . a man fall into a turd, but must bind him to his nose as long as . . . he liveth'.[2]

It is hardly surprising that the early Protestant reformers in the 1530s and 1540s denounced these private contracts, or that in the reign of Elizabeth the clergy were instructed to exhort their parishioners to avoid them.[3] Nor is it surprising that many of the laity continued to believe in the legal validity of a verbal contract, often without regard to the tense, at least up to about 1600. In 1585, an Essex man was so confident of his legal rights over a woman by a contract that when he changed his mind he agreed to sell those rights to a rival for ten shillings. When the rival put up the banns without paying the money, the man forbade them by

---

[2] Ingram, *Church Courts, Sex, and Marriage*, 203; for many examples of this scenario, see Moore, 'Marriage Contracts', and Stone, *Uncertain Unions*.
[3] J. C. Jeaffreson, *Brides and Bridals* (London, 1872), 82.

virtue of his pre-contract and took the matter to court, where of course he lost.[4]

Contracts crop up in Shakespeare's *Twelfth Night*, *Measure for Measure* and *The Winter's Tale*, and in several plays by Beaumont and Fletcher. Shakespeare's Claudio confesses to a friend that

> ... upon a true contract
> I got possession of Julietta's bed.
> You know the lady; she is fast my wife,
> Save that we do the denunciation lack
> Of outward order.

In this case the contract was kept secret until a dowry could be extracted from the lady's friends, but the lady became pregnant and Claudio ended up in prison.[5]

A contract might be valid and binding in canon law, but in common law, and therefore in all matters relating to property, it had no standing whatever. It gave the alleged husband no rights over his alleged wife's property. It imposed on her none of the disabilities of coverture, such as being unable to make contracts, or a will, or run up debts. It gave her no right to dower (a third of her husband's property after his death for her life). The children had no claim on their parents' property as legitimate heirs. Finally, a subsequent church marriage was recognized as valid unless proved otherwise in a church court.[6] Few of the lower sort, however, were aware of these serious drawbacks to a contract marriage, and if they were, some of them were so poor that these questions of property were of no concern to them.

In the face of a gross disharmony between the medieval canon law, the common law, the practices and beliefs of the laity, and the growing interest of the church in controlling marriage, the English ecclesiastical courts responded by slowly but surely tightening the rules of evidence on all contract litigation which came before them.[7]

As a result, the success rate of private suits to enforce contracts in the present tense fell from a half in the fourteenth century to a third in the early sixteenth, a fifth in the late sixteenth, and an even smaller proportion in the early seventeenth century. By adopting this policy, the courts were responding to the wishes and interests of propertied parents and kin

[4] Moore, 'Marriage Contracts', 265.

[5] W. Shakespeare, *Measure for Measure*, I/ii; see also *Twelfth Night*, v/i, and *The Winter's Tale*, IV/iii.

[6] MacQueen, *Marriage, Divorce, and Legitimacy*, 6–7; Shelford, 35; Salmon, 180.

[7] C. Donahue, Jr., 'The Canon Law on the Formation of Marriage and the Social Practices of the later Middle Ages', *Journal of Family History*, 8 (1983).

while also strengthening the control over marriage by the church. It was by no means an unpopular policy and it shifted a significant proportion of the population from being 'married in the eyes of God' to 'being married in the eyes of God and the Church'.[8]

In the sense that the ecclesiastical courts kept control of illicit sexuality and forced most of the population into public weddings in church, the operation of these courts between 1570 and 1640 can certainly be regarded as a success.[9] It is equally clear, however, that the officials who administered these courts, like those of most courts at this period, were extremely corrupt. After all, their vigilance in exposing sin resulted in official fees and encouraged offers of unofficial bribes to look the other way. The cost of all this litigation therefore pressed hard on the village authorities and on the poor victims. Sin did not come cheap in early Stuart England. It was this corruption, extortion, and bribery, as well as the tensions provoked by concurrent attempts to enforce an increase in tithes to keep pace with inflation, which caused Puritan polemicists so savagely to attack the church courts by giving them the derisive label of 'the bawdy courts'.[10] It was well known that court officials could be bought off for cash, that humiliating public penances could be converted into private confessions in return for money, and that those who refused to pay were liable to be harrassed by repeated summonses to some distant court, or exposed before the public as sexual delinquents. The Puritans were strongly in favour of the objectives of the courts: the punishment of illicit sexuality, the strengthening of marriage, and the elimination of dubiously authenticated contract and clandestine unions. What they objected to was the element of corruption which they believed undermined the efficiency and credibility of the system.

In one diocese, that of Gloucester, there is overwhelming evidence that accusations of widespread corruption were true.[11] Elsewhere hard evidence is lacking—but then courts do not keep records of the corruption of their officials. But the diatribes of the Puritans are supported by the open recognition of corruption expressed by so many enthusiastic supporters of the Church of England. Men such as Richard Hooker, Lord Burghley, archbishops Grindal, Parker and Whitgift, and bishops Bedell and Goodman all complained of illegal, corrupt, and unpopular exactions on the public.[12] These supporters of the church recognized

---

[8] Ingram, 'Spousals', 52; Houlbrooke, *Church Courts*, 64–5; id., 'The Making of Marriage', 341; Marchant, 61–2.

[9] This is the position strongly taken in Ingram, *Church Courts, Sex, and Marriage*, ch. 11.

[10] Hill, *Society and Puritanism*, ch. 8.

[11] F. D. Price, 'Elizabethan Apparitors in the Diocese of Gloucester', *Church Quarterly Review*, 134 (1942).

[12] Hill, *Society and Puritanism*, 316–29.

that such abuses undermined public confidence in it and played straight into the hands of its critics. Parliament protested again and again about these abuses and as Puritan radicalism grew in the 1630s, so did the volume of indignation.

When Parliament abolished the courts altogether in 1646, along with episcopacy, without stopping to think carefully about what was to be put in their place, the act reflected some seventy years of pent-up frustration. Undoubtedly, all contemporary courts were corrupt and unpopular; undoubtedly, friction over the collection of tithes was inevitable; and undoubtedly many common lawyers were merely jealous of the volume of litigation handled by the church courts. The latter were hated by the poor for punishing sexual sin with humiliating public shame punishments, from which the better sort could often buy their way out. They were hated by the Puritans for enforcing conformity in religious ceremonial. They were hated by the better sort in general for the corrupt, extortionate, and often slack way in which they ran their affairs.[13]

2. The Second Suppression, 1660–1753

The problem that faced the ecclesiastical courts after 1660 was how to deal with the massive revival during the late 1640s and 1650s of the practice of secret contracts, which had almost disappeared from court litigation before the war, and how to drive most of the population back again into regular public weddings in church.

A. THE AMBIGUITIES OF THE LAW

Some disputes about the validity of contracts were caused by genuine misunderstanding or failure to recall what was actually said; others, by wishful thinking on the part of pregnant girls; others by an unwillingness to recognize that the contract had always been conditional upon the consent of parents and 'friends'; still others by genuine changes of mind, either because of a slaking of sexual appetite, or a decline of love, or parental pressure. The majority of the disputed contracts seem to have been broken up by other people—parents, kin, 'friends', or, in the case of servants or apprentices, even masters.

Although it was usually the man who reneged on his alleged promise, often after getting the woman pregnant, sometimes it was the woman who backed out of the contract. In 1688 a Miss Lloyd and a Mr Dove

[13] For the opposite view, i.e. that the courts were a popular success and were only destroyed because of short-term political factors, see Ingram, *Church Courts, Sex, and Marriage*, 369–72.

first made a verbal contract, and a few days later signed a written contract before witnesses. They began to sleep together on the night of the signing, on the standard grounds that they were now 'husband and wife before God'. Thomas Dove was nothing if not boastful about his exploits, telling his sister that he had slept with Katherine Lloyd 156 times, 'several days or nights, four or five times a day or night and many nights or days three times a night or day, and never less than twice a night or day from the time of his being contracted until the time they fell out and parted (except for four or five nights and days).' Despite (or perhaps because of) these implausible sexual feats, the relationship ended badly, however, as Miss Lloyd's relatives bullied her into breaking off the engagement and marrying a knight instead. Mr Dove was later forced into signing a release to the contract, allegedly under threat of death by five armed men hired by Miss Lloyd. But as soon as he was released, he sued the men for assault, and Miss Lloyd to prove the validity of the contract. Although the Consistory Court sided with Miss Lloyd and rejected the contract, Mr Dove appealed to the Court of Arches, but he dropped the case before it came to sentence.[14]

B. THE PROBLEM OF PROOF

If both parties agreed that an unconditional contract had been made, the church courts ruled that their word was to be believed. But at an early stage the church courts had also ruled that 'faith in the way of marriage, pledged secretly and without witnesses, betwixt man and woman, be of no effect if either party do deny it'.[15]

In the case of conditional contracts, the condition was often expressed either not very explicitly or not at the same time as the contract. A man or woman might repeatedly have made it clear that he or she could not marry without the consent of 'friends', and then make a verbal contract in the present tense. In his or her eyes, the contract was conditional on the previously stated provision, whereas to the other party it seemed to be unqualified. The potentiality for misunderstanding was thus enormous, especially if one remembers the remark of Justice Oliver Wendell Holmes that 'you can always imply a condition in a contract'.[16]

In the case of unconditional contracts, it frequently occurred that one

---

[14] *Dove* v. *Lloyd* (1668), LPCA, Ee.3, fos. 328–437; see also *Clowes* v. *Leeke* (1719) in Stone, *Uncertain Unions*.

[15] J. T. Noonan, Jr., 'Power to Choose', *Viator*, 4 (1973); D. Whitelock *et al.*, *Councils and Synods* (London, 1981), vol. 1, pt. 2, p. 277.

[16] O. W. Holmes, *Harvard Law Review*, 10 (1898), 466 (quoted in J. T. Noonan, Jr., *Power to Dissolve: Lawyers and Marriage in the Courts of the Roman Curia* (Cambridge, Mass., 1972), 267).

of the two, usually the woman, did not listen too carefully to the exact tense of the verbs of the promises her lover was making in order to get her into bed. In any case, 'the vulgar frequently confound the tenses and take the future for the present', as a legal commentator remarked in 1724.[17]

Worse still was the fact that so many of these verbal contracts were made in private, without witnesses. Civil lawyers were embarrassed by this situation and fell back on the feeble argument that if it really happened, then it was valid in conscience and in the eyes of God; but it was unenforceable in law.[18] As always, 'promises of marriage have been the trite and known method of seduction of young women from virtue'. Not every girl had the calm good sense of a heroine of Beaumont and Fletcher, whose eager wooer declares:

> . . . I will instantly
> Before these testify my new alliance,
> Contract myself unto thee, then I hope
> We may be more private.

To which the cautious heroine retorts:

> . . . But thou shalt not, Sir,
> For so has many a maidenhead been lost,
> And many a bastard gotten.[19]

This particular contract points to the ambiguity of the word 'will' in the English language, which can mean either consent in the present or intent in the future. Thus 'I will take you to my wife/husband' may mean 'I am willing to take you as my wife/husband here and now in the present,' or 'I have every intention of taking you . . . some time in the future.' The one was binding in law, the other was not. These fine distinctions are not those to which a couple inflamed by the heat of passion, often illiterate, none too sure of grammatical niceties, and certainly ignorant of the subtleties of the law were likely to be giving much thought at the time, or to recollect very clearly afterwards.[20] As Lucy Locket remarked cynically, 'Sure men were born to lie, and women to believe them!'[21]

It is hard to know what to make of the surprisingly frequent seventeenth-century practice of mock contracts, carried out in drunken jest but in imitation of the real thing. The danger of such jokes was that if one

---

[17] Salmon 182.   [18] Ibid. 199.

[19] *Letter to the Public*, 40; F. Beaumont and J. Fletcher, *The Fair Maid of the Inn*, IV/i.

[20] H. Swinburne, *A Treatise of Spousals or Marriage Contracts* (London, 1686, but written c. 1600), 57–76, 84–5.

[21] J. Gay, *The Beggar's Opera* (London, 1728), II/xiii.

or both partners insisted upon it, the ceremony might well be declared by an ecclesiastical court to have fulfilled all the requirements for a legally valid and binding marriage by contract. One such event took place late one Saturday night in April 1670 in the village of Severn Stoke, Worcester. A drinking party had been in progress, towards the end of which 'a young fellow and a maid would needs be married together'. The party therefore adjourned to the house of another man who owned a ring to lend for the ceremony. Then 'another young fellow took the Book of Common Prayer and read a great part of the office of matrimony and joined them together'. On this occasion, neither party took the frolic seriously, and the parson of the village reported sadly that ' 'Tis made but a jest of, but for my part I relate it with grief of heart and 'tis no less trouble to many others to hear holy things thus made a mock of'.[22]

Even if the facts were clear, a church court had increasing difficulty in enforcing obedience to the law, since excommunication was the only penalty at its disposal. After forty days, however, it could ask the Court of Chancery for a writ of *significavit* to instruct the local sheriff to arrest the offender and hold him in gaol until he had agreed to comply with the court orders. In practice, however, this was a cumbersome and expensive procedure, which the church courts were extremely reluctant to put into motion because of its high cost. In the sixteenth century, the Consistory Court of Norwich obtained only about two writs a year, and the Consistory Court of Winchester only a little over one in every two years. In the nineteenth century, the numbers were even fewer.[23]

C. RITUAL EXCHANGES

The gap between the law and popular custom was widened by the latter's faith in rituals which had little or no validity in a court of law. One was a gift by a man to a woman of a ring, the acceptance of which was popularly believed to imply a formal contract. The legal status of such a gift, however, was more uncertain, as was shown by a case of 1652 which was fought up from court to court with differing verdicts. A man attempted to prove a marriage on the basis of the offer and acceptance of a gold ring set with a ruby and diamond and inscribed 'Quos Deus conjunxit, homo non separet,' and also, more ambiguously, 'Amor omnia vincit.' He claimed that when he gave the woman the ring he said: 'Take this ring in

---

[22] HWRO BA 2302/17/4116; for examples of 'jokes' with more serious consequences, see Stone, *Uncertain Unions*.

[23] Houlbrooke, *Church Courts*, 50; F. D. Price, 'The Abuses of Excommunication and the Decline of Ecclesiastical Discipline under Queen Elizabeth', *English Historical Review*, 57 (1942).

token of my constant love and affection towards you in the way of matrimony, and in case you consent thereunto keep the same, and think of the writings therein contained.' It is hardly surprising that the canon lawyers could not decide just what significance to give to this equivocal gift.[24]

Another very common ritual involving an exchange of significant tokens concerned either the gift of a bent or 'bowed' coin, or the breaking of a coin in two, each party keeping one half. Aphra Behn and Shadwell made considerable use in their plots of secret pre-contracts accompanied by the breaking of coins.[25] One of Farquhar's female characters confides to a friend: 'We're contracted,' in answer to which she receives the cynical comment: 'Contracted! alack a day, poor thing. What, you have changed rings or broken an old broad piece between you!'[26]

A rare written contract of 1684 runs as follows:

I do own and acknowledge the breaking of this gold to be a real and firm contract between us, so as hereby I do oblige myself never to marry any other man but yourself and do own myself your wife before almighty God, only wanting the ceremony of the church, which I do promise to perform whenever you command me.

Witness my hand

Elizabeth Beecher

Unfortunately Elizabeth failed to persuade her lover to sign the reciprocal contract, which he kept to himself unsigned until he died. Worse still, she also wrote another document on the same day, which ran:

I do hereby promise under my hand that if I am not with child by you in two years to make void the contract which is now between us.

Eliza Beecher

Worst of all, she became pregnant not within the stipulated two years, but first after four years, and again after six.[27]

What is interesting about this contract is not so much the very unusual condition attached to it, but first the stress on the symbolic significance of 'the breaking of this gold', which is repeated over and over again in similar cases (the metal is of course more usually silver), and second the constantly repeated concept of being 'your wife before almighty God'.

---

[24] G. I. O. Duncan, *The High Court of Delegates* (Cambridge, 1971), 158–9.

[25] A. Behn, *The False Count* (1682), I/ii, V/i; *The Lucky Chance* (1687), I/i; T. Shadwell, *The Squire of Alsatia* (1688), V/i; *The Volunteers* (1692), V/i.

[26] *Tatler*, 4/249 (1710), 268; Stone, *Uncertain Unions*; J. C. Jeaffreson, *Brides and Bridals* (London, 1872), I: 76; G. Farquhar, *The Inconstant* (1702), II/i.

[27] Bodl., Rawlinson MSS, B.382, fo. 105.

The symbolism of the broken coin is obvious, but exactly why the bent coin carried such heavy meaning in the seventeenth and early eighteenth century is not clear. But there is no doubt that it did, even in genteel circles. In 1710, the *Tatler* published a letter in which a shilling piece was made to speak and say: 'The wench bent me and gave me to her sweetheart,' and there is evidence that the same ritual was familiar even in aristocratic circles.[28]

Other gifts, predominantly from a man to a woman, were normal accompaniments to virtually every courtship of which we have record. Thus in 1668 Miss Lloyd's suitor gave her ribbons and a fan.[29] The regular citation of their gifts in the court-room to bolster an argument for a valid contract indicates that contemporaries regarded such gift exchanges as more than mere tokens of esteem. Both the gift and its acceptance constituted, it was believed, evidence certainly of a courtship relationship, and possibly a contractual one. The fact that when the woman wished to break off the engagement she nearly always scrupulously returned all the gifts she had received adds weight to this argument that even quite trivial presents of food and gloves had significance to contemporaries. The church courts, however, paid no attention to any gift apart from a ring.[30]

D. LEGAL POLICY

The hostility of the seventeenth-century church courts to verbal contracts and their reluctance to break up a public church marriage preceded by banns or a licence was well exemplified in a case in 1663, soon after the Restoration. In 1655, William Armitage and Mary Norcliffe were duly contracted in marriage before two witnesses, using the usual verbal formulae in the present tense. One of the two witnesses actually made a written memorandum of the event as a record. For the next five years the couple kept in touch and exchanged presents. Among other gifts of gloves and so forth, William sent Mary 'a gold and enamel ring with the posy " 'Twas God alone made us one" '—legally a somewhat ambiguous statement, but no doubt he thought it was obvious what he meant. In return she sent him gloves and stockings. According to strict church law, nothing should have been clearer than the validity of the 1655 contract. But in the next few years William Armitage was under

---

[28] *Tatler*, 4/249 (1710), 268; the Osborn case in Stone, *Uncertain Unions*.

[29] *Dove* v. *Lloyd* (1668), LPCA, Ee.3, fo. 407.

[30] See LPCA, *passim*, and P. Rushton, 'The Testament of Gifts: Marriage Tokens and Disputed Contracts in North-East England, 1560–1630', *Folk Life*, 24 (1985–6).

great pressure from his relatives to marry a rich woman, pressure which he steadily resisted. In the end it was Mary who weakened, clearly also under strong parental pressure, and in 1661 she was publicly married in church by licence to one Robert Cox. Two years later, however, she rebelled, went back to her former lover, and asked the court for a jactitation of her marriage to Cox—that is, a sentence prohibiting him from claiming marriage to her, on the grounds of her pre-contract to Mr Armitage six years before. As usual in such cases, the Consistory Court rejected the suit, and the Court of Arches did the same, despite the weight of the evidence in its favour.

The laity therefore continued, if in steadily diminishing numbers, to come to court with claims of ambiguous and unproven promises, of ritual exchanges of gifts, of public recognition in the neighbourhood as a married couple, and of calling each other 'husband' and 'wife'. Right up to the passage of the new Marriage Act of 1753, some lawyers and clergy continued to advance the theory that 'habit and repute, with cohabitation of man and wife, is in general good evidence that the parties at some time or other exchanged the matrimonial consent'. As late as 1754 a clergyman observed that 'there is not a countryman or country woman who, if they are thus contracted, will not tell you that they are *man and wife before God*'.[31]

In other words, after seven hundred years, the laity in England had not yet understood what did or did not constitute sufficient proof of a contract, and whether or not it could invalidate a later marriage and bastardize the children. But even by 1600, none of these pieces of evidence were accorded much respect by the canon lawyers who ran the church courts. The latter were looking for some certainty and proof in the morass of unverifiable claims, vague assumptions, and tokens with indeterminate meaning. They were increasingly exasperated by the claims of women driven into court by pregnancy caused by a faithless suitor. As a result, more and more rarely did these (mostly female) plaintiffs succeed. On the other hand those (mostly men) who were seeking 'jactitation of marriage', that is a court-ordered injunction to the defendant to cease all claims to a marriage based merely on a verbal contract, were increasingly successful.

In the early seventeenth century the moral theologian William Gouge frankly admitted his confusion, explaining that 'contracted persons are in a middle degree betwixt single persons and married persons; they are

[31] LPCA, B.6/17; E.1, 33–6, 407–10; Ee1/fos. 379–88, 423–32, 543–50; H. Stebbing, *An Enquiry into the Force and Operation of the Annulling Clauses in a late Act for the better preventing of Clandestine Marriages* (London, 1754), 19; *Roy. Com. Marriage, 1868*: 82.

neither simply single nor actually married'.[32] If this was the best a professional theologian could do, it was hardly surprising that the laity were
confused. During the late seventeenth century, canon lawyers and
theologians slowly tried to bring order out of chaos by establishing distinctions between three different modes of contract: secret exchanges of
vows witnessed by God alone; vows made before God and the church,
that is in the presence of a priest and witnesses; and vows made before
God, the church and the world, that is in a public ceremony at the church
door or before the altar in the presence of friends, relatives and neighbours. Only the last two were valid and binding.

In theory, the church courts in the early eighteenth century still clung
to the principle that a properly proven pre-contract must nullify a later
marriage, even one which had been carried out in church by a clergyman
and had resulted in children.[33] In practice, however, after 1660 the
courts went out of their way not to break up a marriage even if there was
good evidence of a prior contract. They also rejected all contract marriages unless supported by an unquestionable body of hard evidence,
including two plausible witnesses. In taking these positions, the canon
lawyers and judges were undoubtedly mainly concerned to reduce the
method of establishing a legally binding marriage to a church wedding
conducted by a qualified clergyman before a congregation of witnesses.
Another possible motive was the potentially explosive political implica-
tions of accepting conditional or breakable marriage contracts in a society
where the royalist assertions of the divine right of kings was based upon
the natural rights of a husband and father in his family. Most political
commentators, from Aristotle all the way to Filmer, regarded the family
as the basic building block of the society, and the model for the state
itself. But if the family was built on a breakable and conditional contract,
why not also the state?

In essence this was the position adopted by John Locke and Bishop
Hoadly in the late seventeenth and early eighteenth centuries. They
argued in favour of a notion of a contract between the governing elite or
the monarch and the mass of the governed. As Hoadly put it in 1708 'the
great end of government is the happiness of the governed society; . . .
[which] consists in the enjoyment of liberty, property, and the free
exercise of religion'.[34] This being the case, it is hardly surprising that the

---

[32] W. Gouge, *Of Domesticall Duties* (London, 1622), 199; Helmholtz, 28.

[33] Sir Robert Paine Case (1660), *Eng. Rep.* 82: 941; H. Conset, *The Practice of the Spiritual or Ecclesiastical Courts* (London, 1685), 254–6; P. F. Goyer, *The Proctor's Practice in the Ecclesiastical Courts* (London, 1744), 85.

[34] Quoted by J. Gascoigne, 'Anglican Latitudinarianism and Political Radicalism in the Late Eighteenth Century', *History*, 71 (1986), 23.

conservative canon lawyers who ran the church courts in the late seventeenth century were rejecting almost every suit to validate a contract marriage, unless the evidence for it was absolutely overwhelming. There must surely be some connection between the steady hardening of attitude by the courts to the contractual basis of marriage throughout the seventeenth century and the concurrent rise of ideas about divine right and passive obedience which were so much emphasized by those who wished to elevate the monarchy over its subjects.

E. THE END OF CONTRACT LITIGATION

In the 1660s and 1670s there was a revival of contract litigation in order to deal with the consequences of the legal chaos of the Interregnum. Thereafter, however, contract suits died away to almost nothing between 1680 and 1733, because of these hostile attitudes of the courts. It slowly became obvious to litigants that the canon lawyers once more were determined to suppress contract marriages, regardless of the canon law in their favour. In the early 1730s there were three bitterly contested and very expensive contract cases which were brought up through the ecclesiastical courts and fought to a finish. They seem to have made legal history as the last of their kind.[35] All three were cases of women who gave birth as a result of sexual relations entered into on the basis of an alleged contract with a suitor which was later repudiated.

The sentences in these cases show clearly how the courts were now twisting the canon law in order to invalidate contracts. On the other hand, the patent illegality of the sentences led to a public attack on the church courts and judges as 'a pack of knaves disguised with the robes of spiritual power'. It was argued that it was better 'to have three suits depending in Westminster Hall than one in the Arches or any other ecclesiastical Court'. Bishop Burnet was quoted as having declared the courts to be hopelessly corrupt; and to round out the indictment, they were described as 'now the only system of the worst and most unreformed popery'.[36]

As a result of the continued hostility of laymen in general, civil lawyers,

[35] *Goole* v. *Hudson* (1732); *Fitzmaurice* v. *Fitzmaurice* (1733); *Da Costa Villa Real* v. *Da Costa Villa Real* (1733). All three are mentioned by J. Johnstoun, *A Judicial Dissertation concerning the Scriptural Doctrine of Marriage Contracts* (London, 1734), (BL, 518 C.23 (4)), 32; for the first, see J. Goole, *The Contract Violated or the Hasty Marriage* (London, 1733); also LPCA Ee.10/4; Eee.13, fos. 413–19; documents concerning the third are in LPCA, while the second, which went to the Court of Delegates, was published. Self-serving accounts of the second were published at the time: Elizabeth Fitzmaurice, *Love and Artifice* (London, 1734); Anon., *Elizabeth Fitzmaurice and Lord William Fitzmaurice* (London, 1733), (BL, 518 C.23 (3)).

[36] Johnstoun, *Judicial Dissertation*, 32.

equity lawyers like Hardwicke, common lawyers like Mansfield, and also women seduced on promise of what proved to be unenforceable contracts, the legality of marriage contracts was abolished as part of the Hardwicke Marriage Act of 1753.[37]

F. INTERNATIONAL COMPARISONS

If the engagement process in seventeenth-century England is compared with that across the Channel in Normandy, the differences are more striking than the similarities.[38] In Normandy, as in England, the poor underwent a long process of courtship at fairs and other public gatherings; parental consent was then requested, and if it was forthcoming a public contract was followed by banns and a church wedding. But in Normandy there is no hint of any contract or engagement before the parents had given their consent; and there was only one form of marriage, which following the putting up of banns and was conducted by a priest in public in a church. This was introduced by the Council of Trent in 1563, and was generally applied, as were French royal edicts demanding parental consent for any marriage of a man under 30 or a woman under 25. The result was a striking divergence between the law and practice of marriage on the two sides of the Channel.

In Scotland, the law concerning contract marriages remained into the nineteenth century very much as it had been in England before 1753. The only difference was that a witnessed verbal contract in the present tense in Scotland was not only binding for life in ecclesiastical law, but also carried with it full property rights in civil law. In 1868 the Scottish judge Lord Neaves wrote a ditty to explain the situation to his bemused colleagues south of the border:

> This maxim itself might content ye,
> That marriage is made—by consent;
> Provided it's done *de presenti*,
> And marriage is really what's meant.
> Suppose that young Jocky and Jenny
> Say 'We two are husband and wife',
> The witnesses needn't be many—
> They're instantly buckled for life.[39]

This legal levity was all very well, but in fact the Scottish situation had

---

[37] *Laws Respecting Women*, 37.

[38] J. Gouesse, 'La Formation du couple en Basse-Normandie', *XVIIIᵉᵐᵉ siècle*, 102–3 (1974), 45–58.

[39] 'Claverhouse' [Meliora Smith], *Irregular Border Marriages* (London, 1934), quoted by T . C. Smout, 'Scottish Marriages, Regular and Irregular', in *Marriage & Soc.*, 204–5.

long caused great concern among lawyers. In 1772, twenty years after England had abolished contract marriages, the Scottish judge Lord Hailes remarked bitterly: 'What was the law of all Europe, while Europe was barbarous, is now the law of Scotland only, when Europe has become civilized.' It was said that in eighteenth-century Scotland, a third of all marriages were irregular.[40] What worried the Scottish judges was that

the consequence of these peculiarities in our marriage law is that there are at all times in Scotland a large number of individuals who cannot tell whether they are married or unmarried, and a still larger number of children as to whom no one can affirm whether they are legitimate or not.[41]

The English judges were equally discontented with this Scottish law of marriage, especially since it opened up the escape hatch of flight to Gretna Green for those seeking swift marriages without parental consent. In 1849, Lord Brougham complained that 'the promise is made secretly, in the course of the seduction, and is parcel of the act of seducing the female. Then the difficulty is for the female to prove it.' The distinguished civil lawyer Stephen Lushington summed up the general English opinion of the day: 'I do not know a greater evil, or one productive of more misery or more mischief, than the uncertainty of the constitution of the marriage tie; I speak now of uncertainty in the way of proof.'[42] Worse still was the fact that Scottish law and English law were running into conflict over marriage at just the time that they were also quarrelling over divorce.[43]

3. Legal Imperialism by the Common Law Judges

During the late seventeenth century, the common lawyers devised two new actions to allow individuals to sue for damages if they had been injured by unenforceable marriage contracts. The actions were also designed to help the victims of the tightening up of judicial decision-making in the church courts concerning contract.

The underlying moral principle behind both these actions, that for seduction and that for breach of promise, was one that only fully developed in the mid- to late eighteenth century, which is why both these actions took on new life at that time. The first was that young women were innocent and defenceless victims of the wiles and pressures of men, and were often

---

[40] *Roy. Com. Marriage, 1868*, 28: xxi.   [41] Ibid. xxii.
[42] *Select Committee on the Marriage Law (Scotland)*, (PP 1849), 12: 21.
[43] *Dalrymple* v. *Dalrymple* (1817), *Eng. Rep.* 161: 665–93.

duped by deceitful males into surrendering their chastity in return for vague, secret and unprovable promises of marriage. The second principle was that a woman's bargaining position in the marriage market was gravely damaged by the loss of chastity and giving birth to an illegitimate child, but that it could be compensated for by a monetary payment by the seducer to increase her marriage portion. Both these propositions were correct in the ambiguous half-romantic, half-calculating atmosphere in which, as has been seen, courtship was conducted in the late eighteenth and nineteenth centuries. As juries were well aware, the moral purpose of the law was to protect women from temptation, and to compensate them if they were deceived or if the marriage contract was not fulfilled.

There can be little doubt that a prime interest of the lawyers was to offer a remedy for any tort, but in the process they managed to expand the range of business in the common law courts, at a time when litigation in general was falling off. Two cases illustrate the legal thinking underlying these new actions. In 1745, the judges in the Court of Common Pleas were faced with an appeal of a case in which £3,000 damages had been awarded to a husband for the enticement away of his wife. It was objected by the defence that 'there is no precedent of any such action', but the reply by Lord Chief Justice Willes was that 'a special action on the case was introduced for this reason, that the law will never suffer an injury and a damage without a remedy'.[44] In another case on a quite different issue some years later, the same objection of novelty was angrily brushed aside on the same grounds by Chief Justice Pratt: 'this action is for a tort. Torts are infinitely various, not limited or confined; for there is nothing in nature but may be an instrument of mischief.'[45]

A further extension of this vision of the common law courts as being unfettered in their jurisdiction over torts was made in 1763 by Lord Mansfield, when faced with a case in which the master of a female apprentice had sold the girl for £200 to a rich debauchee to be his mistress. Objections were made that this might be a sin, but that neither party was guilty of an offence cognizable in a criminal court. Mansfield replied: 'this court has the superintendence of offences *contra bonos mores*, and a conspiracy to corrupt the innocence of a young female is an offence which may be subject to an information or indictment, and which we can visit with fine and imprisonment or infamous punishment.' He declared the crime to be a conspiracy, and thus an indictable misdemeanour.[46] It is clear

---

[44] *Winsmore v. Greenbank* (1745), *Eng. Rep. 125: 1331–2*.

[45] *Chapman v. Pickersgill* (1762), ibid. *95: 734*.

[46] *Rex v. Delaval, Bates and Fraine* (1763), ibid. *97: 913–16*; Campbell, *Lives of the Chief Justices*, 2: 424–5.

that in the eyes of all these eighteenth-century chief justices, the role of guardian of public morals had shifted decisively from the now-impotent ecclesiastical courts to the courts of common law.

4. Suits for the Seduction of a Daughter

The seduction suit was brought by a father demanding compensation for the loss of his daughter's domestic services by reason of her impregnation. This was something of a legal fiction, since in practice the action was intended to offer compensation for a seduced girl who did not have sufficient proof to launch a suit against her lover for breach of promise of marriage.[47]

The first known seduction action by a father came before Chief Justice Rolle in 1653, a time when the ecclesiastical courts were suspended. He was very unsure of his ground, and was very careful to exclude from any consideration the seduction and the pregnancy, declaring that only 'the loss of the service [of the daughter to her father] is the ground of the action'. Other suits followed in the common law courts in the 1660s, and by 1700 the action was fully established, although still limited to damages for loss of services.[48]

For a long while, however, this was not a very effective legal procedure. For one thing, the plaintiff could be non-suited, if it could be proved that his daughter had willingly allowed herself to be seduced.[49] Moreover the legal foundation for the action was dealt a crippling blow in 1766 when Lord Mansfield decided, logically enough, that a father could not sue for loss of his daughter's services if she had already left home to go into domestic service when the seduction and pregnancy occurred. Since this was the case of the overwhelming majority of pregnant girls in the eighteenth century, the action was now strictly confined to the well-to-do who could afford to keep their daughters at home. So long as this was the case, however, an action lay, even if the girl's mother had connived at the relationship to the extent of allowing the man into her daughter's bedroom for hours at a time.[50]

The action took on new life in the early years of the nineteenth century because of the new moralism inspired by Evangelical religion and a fear of French Revolutionary ideas. When a case came before Lord Eldon in

---

[47] W. S. Holdsworth, *A History of English Law* (London, 1902–42), 8: 428–9; S. Staves, 'British Seduced Maidens', *Eighteenth Century Studies*, 14 (1981), 127–9; Evans, 2: 177–80.
[48] *Norton* v. *Jason* (1653), *Eng. Rep.* 82: 809–10; *Sippora* v. *Basset* (1664), ibid. 1071; *Russell* v. *Corne* (1704), ibid. 92: 186.   [49] *T & C Mag.* 2 (1770), 571.
[50] *Postlethwaite* v. *Parkes* (1766), *Eng. Rep.* 97: 1147–9; *Satterthwaite* v. *Dewhurst* (1785), ibid. 99: 899–900; *Bennett* v. *Allcott* (1787), ibid. 100: 90.

1800, in which an elderly married man had twice run off with a 17-year-old girl with her knowledge and consent, the Chief Justice made an emotional appeal to the jury. He said that 'not only as a man but as a parent who had daughters nearly of the same age with the plaintiff's daughter', he would 'prefer the loss of even life itself to that of one of his daughters being debauched'. He pointed out that the issue before the jury was to assess damages not to the girl for her impregnation but to her widowed mother for loss of her services, and stressed that the mother had a right to such damages. Under the influence of these directions, the jury quickly assessed damages at the substantial sum of £400, a figure which bore no relation to the cost of the services lost.[51]

Thereafter the action became increasingly common, and over the next quarter of a century numerous very marginal cases were successfully brought, both in London and at the county assizes. For example, damages of £30 were awarded to the mother of a girl who was first made pregnant by one suitor and then hastily married to another.[52] Damages of £750 were awarded to the father of a girl who willingly went to the army barracks, spent three nights there in the lieutenant's room, and returned with £5 in her pocket, although no evidence was offered of compulsion or gang-rape.[53]

Under the pressure of the new morality, the pretence of loss of domestic services was now often abandoned, and one lawyer openly admitted that the suit was to uphold public morality as well as for compensation to the father because 'his hearth and household had been dishonoured'. For example, at the Leicester Assizes in 1826, Justice Garrow told the jury that the defendant would get off lightly if the only cost to him was payment for the delivery and maintenance of the child, and for the loss of services to the girl's father during her pregnancy. So slight a penalty, he argued, would 'sanction his debauchery'. He continued, with masterly evasion of the law: 'It would not become me to say that you are to erect yourselves into the guardians of public morals and to lash and scourge vice whenever she lifts her head. But you are to recollect that you are to compensate for a private injury.' Thus encouraged, the jury awarded damages of £200. Juries seem to have paid little attention to arguments for the defence that 'a girl who will so far forget herself as to anticipate the connubial rites, deserves little redress at the hands of the jury'.[54] The latter must have been only too well aware that almost half of all English brides were pregnant on the day of

---

[51] *Lond. Chron.* (1800), 195.

[52] *Leeds Mercury*, 22 Aug. 1809. I owe this reference to Dr J. J. Looney.

[53] *Creighton* v. *Townshend*, RIA/HP, 1102. For other cases of heavy damages to parents for the seduction of girls living at home, see Plowden, 2: 139, 158–60, 163–7, 185, 187, 249, 253–4, 257–9, 277–9, 296–7, 299, 304–5, 330, 343; *Crim. Con. Gaz.* 2 (1828), 275–6.

[54] Plowden, 2: 215, 253.

marriage. What they objected to, and punished severely, was not pre-nuptial sexual relations, which were normal, but the refusal of the man to marry the girl after she became pregnant.

In the early nineteenth century, the action thus threatened to turn into a suit for the protection of public morality. But this trend was stopped in its tracks in 1844, when in a test case before the Court of Common Pleas, Chief Justice Tindal surveyed the long history of the suit, reminded the court of the seventeenth- and eighteenth-century precedents concerning the need to prove the actual loss of domestic services, and dismissed the case.[55]

This is a classic instance of an action motivated at least in part by the institutional imperialism by the common law courts against the church courts, revived and twisted out of legal shape during the moral panic in the 1790s onward and finally brought back to its original limited purpose by a strict constructionist judge in 1844. In its heyday from 1790 to 1844, the action was stimulated by the acute anxiety about the seduced maiden which played such a central role in the plots of late eighteenth and early nineteenth-century novels. The ample damages awarded allowed the father to provide his debauched daughter with a dowry sufficiently large to make her attractive on the marriage market, so that in a perverse, class-limited, roundabout way, crude justice was done. But the absurdity of the action, its quality of legal fiction, and the whole concept that the daughter was her father's property and that injury to her entitled him to damages became more and more anachronistic in the nineteenth century as the concepts of individualism, gender egalitarianism, and legal rationality took increasing hold. Moreover, if compensation for loss of services was taken seriously, it was an action that was highly unjust in its social application: 'the quasi-fiction [loss of service] . . . affords protection to the rich man whose daughter occasionally makes his tea, and leaves without redress the poor man whose child . . . is sent unprotected to earn her bread among strangers'.[56] In 1885 seduction of girls under 16 was made a mis-demeanour, and thereafter the old action for loss of services fell into disuse, although it was not officially abolished until 1970.[57]

5. Suits for Breach of Promise

The poetry of love is now wedded to the trammels of the law. The offspring of this union is the action of breach of promise of marriage.

C. J. MacColla, *Breach of Promise* (London, 1879), 35

[55] *Grinnell* v. *Wells* (1844), *Eng. Rep.* 135: 422–4.
[56] Ibid. 424, n. *a*.
[57] Staves, 'British-seduced Maidens', 131–2.

In the end, the action for breach of promise was far more successful than the action for seduction in extracting monetary damages for injury during the courting process. Like the latter, it emerged out of the common practice of settling out of court a repudiation of a marriage contract by a monetary settlement. Odd cases are known from the late sixteenth century, but this did not become common until about the 1670s.[58] The action thus evolved very showly and tentatively before, through, and after the temporary suspension of the ecclesiastical courts during the Interregnum.

It was not until a test case in 1672 that the judges had an extended discussion of the legality of the action. The arguments used in favour of it were that 'we bring not the action to meddle with the marriage, but for the damages, that he hath not taken her according to his promise. . . . Marriage to a woman especially is an advancement or preferment', and therefore 'loss of matrimony is a temporal loss'. Chief Justice Vaughan, however, had his doubts, arguing that although a covenant to marry by a written deed was cognizable by common law, a mere verbal promise was subject only to ecclesiastical jurisdiction. He concluded that he was 'doubtful if any action could be maintained on mutual promises to marry'.[59]

But these doubts failed to stop the slow march of the common law courts into this new territory, as the ecclesiastical courts became increasingly reluctant to accept verbal contracts. The language used by the judges indicates that a desire to offer a common law remedy for an injury hitherto punishable only by canon law was an important motivating factor. Thus, in 1703 they ruled that since a marriage contract in the present tense was binding in ecclesiastical law, a suit for damages for breach of promise was sustainable in common law. By 1732 a legal writer could state flatly that 'on a promise of marriage, damages may be recovered on an action at law if either party refuses to marry'.[60]

There is one intriguing piece of evidence to suggest that in well-founded cases of contracts in the present tense, some ecclesiastical court judges in the early years of the eighteenth century attempted to fight off this incursion by the common lawyers into their territory by themselves offering compensation to the female victims of unfulfilled promises. The evidence comes from legal advice offered in about 1703 or 1704 to a

[58] *Baker* v. *Smith* (1651), *Eng. Rep.* 82: 722–3, 729–30; *Mills* v. *Middleton* (1670), ibid. 83: 1289; *Holcroft* v. *Dickenson* (1672), ibid. 124: 933–6.
[59] *Holcroft* v. *Dickenson* (1672), ibid. 933–6; MacQueen, *Rights and Liabilities*, 221; B. J. D. White, 'Breach of Promise of Marriage', *Law Quarterly Review*, 10 (1894), 135.
[60] *Jesson* v. *Collins* (1703), in Salmon, 204–5; *Feme Coverts*, 30.

Derbyshire woman who had been jilted and was suing to prove a contract. In this case there were reliable witnesses to the contract. But to strengthen the case, the lawyer advised the woman to produce evidence of courtship by the man before the contract; of her having rejected other desirable suitors shortly before or any time after the contract; of their secretly sleeping together after the contract; and if possible some evidence that the lover had tried to come to terms with her by offering her money to withdraw the suit.

The lawyer advised that since the judge had failed to order the man to marry her despite the strength of the evidence, he would probably award her not only full legal costs but also monetary compensation for breach of promise, the sum being appropriate to the relative circumstances of the two parties and the seriousness of the breach of faith. He cited two recent cases in which suits brought by women to enforce marriage contracts had been dismissed, but with the women awarded respectively £50 and £200 in compensation. The lawyer concluded 'I would add other like instances in causes of contracts by other judges. Neither of these mentioned were appealed as I remember.'[61]

What this letter reveals is that the ecclesiastical court judges were well aware of the hardships they were inflicting upon women by their draconian policy against contract marriages, and were themselves imposing damages for breach of promise upon the men. There seems to be no legal justification for this in canon law, and there is no mention of it in contemporary legal handbooks. So far as is known, these efforts by the church courts soon petered out, since the imposition of damages or fines clearly went beyond the legal authority of these courts.

Apart from jilted victims of poorly documented contracts in the present tense, there were also to be considered unsuspecting victims of contracts in the future tense, who had been unaware that they were not legally binding. In a test case in 1731, an ecclesiastical lawyer admitted that the church courts had virtually abandoned all attempts to enforce contracts in the future. The most the courts might do was to 'admonish' the couple to marry in church, but they would make no efforts to enforce the order.[62]

By the mid-eighteenth century, therefore, the breach of promise action was firmly established in common law and was filling an urgent need. It also fitted the mood of the times. It was no accident that the growth of the action coincided not only with the abolition of contract marriage by the Marriage Act of 1753, but also with the extraordinary emphasis in novels and public discussion upon the plight of respectable virgins seduced under

---

[61] *Webb* v. *Webb* (*c.*1702–3), HWRO, Lichfield CC, BA 2088/2, 6. 761–3.
[62] Holt and Ward (1731), *Eng. Rep.* 94: 707–8.

false pretences and left pregnant and unmarried (Plate 7). This wave of anxiety, exemplified by the enormous success of Richardson's *Pamela*, caused a massive rise in both the numbers of cases brought before the courts and in the size of the damages awarded by the juries. The plaintiffs in the numerous cases brought in the late eighteenth and early nineteenth centuries fell into three broad types. There was the woman who had allowed sexual intercourse to take place after exchanging promises of marriage which were repudiated after she became pregnant. Second, there was the woman who exchanged promises of marriage in the future with a young man struggling to make his way in the world, and who remained chaste and faithful to him for several years, sometimes as many as six, and then learned that her lover had married someone else, sometimes by his own choice, sometimes under pressure from his parents and 'friends'. The woman had rejected other suitors for many years and now found herself cast on the marriage market at a fairly late age, a disadvantage for which she sought compensation. Third, there was the woman, often a widow of mature age, who had entered into careful negotiations with a man, agreed to marry him, set a day, bought her clothes, and wound up her business affairs, only to find that the man backed out of the agreement at the very last moment, just before or on the wedding day. She sued for compensation for her hurt feelings and her blighted hopes of a husband.[63]

The moral to be drawn from a reading of this depressing evidence of duplicity, folly, and disappointment is that courting in the early modern period was often governed by the cut-throat principle of *caveat emptor*. Female plaintiffs in breach of promise actions had been exposed to seduction under promises which were later betrayed, and they now faced possible character assassination in court. On the other hand, there was also a small minority of male defendants who were the innocent victims of entrapment by scheming women whose sole object had always been suits for large damages.

Virtually none of the litigants were drawn either from the very poor or from the very rich. Among the latter group, family surveillance of daughters was careful, and most young girls had been trained to value their chastity too highly to let themselves be seduced before marriage. On the rare occasions when this occurred, the man presumably preferred to marry or settle out of court. This total immunity of rich noblemen from breach of promise suits continued until the late nineteenth and early twentieth centuries, when suits by chorus girls against wealthy aristocrats became an

[63] This typology is based on some 60 cases brought between 1780 and 1840. They mostly come from *Eng. Rep.*, *Gent's Mag.*, *Lond. Chron.*, RIA/HP, *Crim. Con. Gaz.* 2, and Plowden, 2.

occasional occurrence. It cannot be argued that this status group were immune to the charms of women from the stage in the eighteenth or early nineteenth centuries. Only a tiny handful actually married such women, but many took one or more as temporary mistresses.[64]

The litigants were therefore confined to a broad spectrum of the middling sort, the same group from which the juries and judges were mostly drawn. The damages awarded can therefore be taken to accord with the moral values of this group. In 1787, one ingenious lawyer made the argument that in such actions the largest damages should be awarded to female plaintiffs from just this middling sort:

In the higher ranks, if reputation is lost, they find shelter in the possession of goods of fortune. In the lower order of the people, the force of transactions of this nature is lost, through want of possessing the nicer feelings. But in the middle order, where the party is not independent, proper compensation should be made.[65]

In the eighteenth and early nineteenth centuries, judges stressed the public interest need to discourage males from seducing young women on promises of marriage and then abandoning them when they became pregnant. For this reason, judicial direction expanded the legal proofs of a promise to include mere tacit consent, backed by no more than circum-stantial evidence.[66] Among the personal considerations mentioned by the judges as important in assessing damages, emphasis was given to the moral reputation of the plaintiff—the lower the reputation the smaller being the damages; and the moral behaviour of the defendant—the more scandalous and exploitative, the greater being the damages. Thus a defendant who had merely broken his word, perhaps under pressure from parents and friends, was treated much less severely than one who had impregnated the woman and then repudiated her.

Among the few male plaintiffs there were adventurers who had been courting a woman merely for her money, and then sued her for breach of promise when she broke off the relationship. These men were always either non-suited or awarded a nominal one-shilling damages. For example in 1786, Lieutenant Charles Bourne sued the Countess of Crepy Canaple, an ugly, affected, but very rich widow. He had courted her merely for her money and had extracted a promise of marriage from her. But in a role-reversal she took him into her bed instead, and steadfastly

---

[64] For the mistresses of the rich see the 300 'Tête à Tête' articles in *T & C Mag.* 1–24 (1769–93). One of the earliest cases occurred in 1746, when one Mary Smith sued the 9th Earl Ferrers for £20,000, but the case was dismissed and she got nothing (*Peerage*, 5: 339 n. *c*.). For marriages of peers with women from the stage, see *Notes and Queries*, 10 Aug. 1935; J. M. Bulloch, 'Peers Who Have Married Players', quoted in *Peerage* 12: app. C.

[65] *Homans* v. *Johnson* (1787), RIA/HP, 524. 14.

[66] *Hutton* v. *Mansell*, *Eng. Rep.* 87: 928.

refused to marry him. The jury awarded him one shilling.[67] Another example occurred in 1826, when a young surgeon courted a rich young widow, who agreed to marry him. The day was set, the dress and wedding cake bought, but at the last minute the widow called the marriage off. Six months later, she married someone else, and the surgeon sued her for breach of promise. But the widow found witnesses to testify that before the marriage the surgeon had boasted that he was only marrying her for her money and had demanded that all her property be put into his hands. Later he told a friend: 'I do not care a damn for her, for I know I can get £200 damages.' He also said that she was in no position to marry anyone else, since she had allowed him 'to take indecent liberties with her'. But he was wrong, for the judge told the jury that 'the lady had loved not wisely but too well', and the jury brought in a verdict of acquittal.[68]

Information detrimental to the proposed marriage partner, revealed subsequently to the promise, was usually accepted as a valid defence. Physical disease was one possible reason. Information about an abscess on the breast of a 70-year old man allegedly caused a 60-year old woman to break off the match between them. When he sued her for breach of promise, the first jury awarded him the enormous sum of £4,000. But this verdict was overthrown, and there was a second trial, the matter being finally settled out of court with a grant by the woman to the man of a life annuity of £200.[69] A more bizarre case came up in 1858 when a man contracted to marry a woman, but subsequently fell ill with galloping tuberculosis. He called off the marriage on the grounds that in his condition sexual excitement might kill him, so that he was in no condition to fulfil the duties of marriage. The judges became hopelessly enmeshed in this case, which went to appeal. Some contended that the contract was to perform the ceremony of marriage, which the man was perfectly capable of doing. Others took the more pragmatic view that sexual intercourse was an integral part of marriage, and that the man was therefore within his rights to renege on his promise. In the end the latter view prevailed, but only after a long legal tussle.[70]

In the eighteenth and early nineteenth centuries, the weight of the argument in assessing the amount of the damages was generally the relative moral conduct of the two parties and their relative circumstances in life, and in particular the capacity of the defendant to pay the assessed damages. Unlike in crim. con. cases, even the puritanical Lord Chief

---

[67] *T & C Mag.* 18 (1786), 105–8.
[68] *Abbot* v. *Young* (1829); Plowden, 2: 335–7; *Crim. Con. Gaz.* 2: 300.
[69] *Atcheson* v. *Baker* (1796), *Eng. Rep.* 170: 209–10; *Lond. Chron.* (1797), 1: 431, 485.
[70] *Hall* v. *Wright* (1858), *Eng. Rep.* 120: 688–706.

Justice Kenyon went out of his way to urge jurors to award damages according to the capacity of the defendant to pay. In a case in 1790 he instructed the jury: 'You should always respect the situation in life of the person who is to pay those damages. . . . I do not say, always, that a man who cannot pay with his purse shall be called upon to pay in his person.' Fortunately for the defendant in this case, he had not seduced the plaintiff, so that the Chief Justice's moral indignation had not been aroused.[71] On the average, the damages awarded by juries in the eighteenth and early nineteenth centuries were therefore moderate in size, as befitted the financial position of the litigants. In the period 1790 to 1830, for which the evidence is particularly plentiful, the vast majority of the awards were between £100 and £500, although a few ambitious plaintiffs were asking for damages of £5,000, £7,000, and even £20,000.[72] But these demands were not really serious; in 1826, for example, a pregnant serving girl asked for £2,000 but settled out of court for £75.[73]

The only exceptions to this generalization of the award of modest damages was in cases where the defendant was known to be very rich and had behaved very badly. The largest award on record was £7,000, made in 1747 against a pluralist clergyman who was a prebendary, a canon, and a vicar. Letters were produced proving frequent exchanges of promises of marriage which were never fulfilled, as a result of which the lady 'had refused the addresses of a gentleman'.[74]

In another case in which large damages were given, the defendant was a major, a member of the elite, the heir of a nobleman and the son of a colonel, while the plaintiff was merely the daughter of a respectable minor gentleman. The major had courted the girl, and despite being warned off by her father had continued a secret exchange of love letters in which he had declared that 'I was ready to run all risks and marry you.' But in the end, the pressure on him by her father and his noble relatives was too great, and he courted and married a rich woman of his own social class. As a result, the defendant could look forward to a life of affluence and a future inheritance of a title and £20,000 a year, while the plaintiff was left with nothing, neither a husband nor a substantial marriage portion with which to attract one. Her lawyer argued that she had seen 'her happiness sacrificed to the pride of power and the pomp of heraldry'. The judge admonished the jury to ignore the cause of the defendant's breach of promise, that is the threats from his relatives: 'it is not his fault but her

---

[71] *Elizabeth Chapman* v. *William Shaw* (1790), in BL, 5176 g 10. 27–8.
[72] *Bond* v. *Oliver* (1798), *Lond. Chron.* (1798), 2: 539; *Foster* v. *Mellish* (1802), ibid. 91 (1802), 194–5.
[73] *Crim. Con. Gaz.* 2: 240.   [74] *Gent's Mag.* 17 (1747), 293.

wrong that you are to estimate'. The jury quickly assessed that wrong to be worth £4,000.[75] These huge damages were altogether exceptional, however, and were the subject of much public comment, as in 1824 when the respectable Miss Foote sued a rich Jew, Mr Hayne, and was awarded £3,000 damages (Plate 8).

Up to about 1850, therefore, the story of breach of promise is a fairly straightforward one of how the common law seized its chance in the late seventeenth century to capture some turf from the church courts; and how the consolidation and expansion of this legal territory took place in the late eighteenth and early nineteenth centuries, during the climax of romantic moralism about the plight of seduced and abandoned maidens from respectable homes. The only limit on the scope of the suit came as a result of the Marriage Act of 1753; this voided any contract made by a minor without parental consent, thus removing from the ranks of potential plaintiffs all those under the age of 21.[76] Before about 1850 there was no serious questioning of the ethical propriety of the action. Between the 1850s and 1880s, however, breach of promise came to be seriously criticized on the grounds of its mercenary character. In America, the action was attacked on the grounds that it was sustainable on the basis of minimal evidence; that it fostered a purely monetary concept of courtship; that it was against public policy, since it forced couples into unwanted and loveless unions; and, finally, because it was greatly biased in favour of women. In 1858, an English judge admitted: 'I am aware that many persons think that such an action should not be allowed.'[77]

The criticism of the mercenary character of the action continued. Between 1878 and 1890, seven attempts were made to introduce bills in the House of Commons either to abolish it or to limit damages strictly to out-of-pocket expenses and loss of value on the marriage market, rather than on vague and arbitrary notions of moral injury. All but one of these motions were not even debated or voted on, so small was the support for them.[78] It is no accident that it was soon after the legislature had secured the property rights of married women that it was also being urged by a minority to consider the abolition of the breach of promise action: the argument was that it was increasingly being used as a means of extortion by unscrupulous women, who first entrapped a rich man and then black-

[75] *Austen* v. *Vereker* (1815), RIA/HP, 1085.

[76] *Hemming* v. *Freemantle* (1761), *Gent's Mag.* 31 (1761), 536.

[77] M. Grossberg, *Governing the Hearth* (Chapel Hill, 1985), 51; *Hall* v. *Wright* (1758), *Eng. Rep.* 120: 704.

[78] 3 *Hansard*, 249, *passim*. For the one vote, see ibid. 245, Index *sub* 'Breach of Promise of Marriage'.

mailed him with a suit. Misogynist feelings rose, and one commentator observed:

Formerly marriage was a woman's sole aim . . . but now a woman has a wide field of action. Her first view is to engage a man's affections in order to entrap him into a marriage. If this fails, her second view, after inflaming his desires, is to yield to them, for which she is to be rewarded with a handsome portion.[79]

In 1868 the *Law Times* claimed, without any supporting evidence, that 'nine tenths of the actions for breach of promise are purely mercenary', the result of traps deliberately set by designing women.[80]

There seem to have been three reasons for the spread of this new attitude. The first was the belief that now that women were being accorded greater equality of economic opportunity they no longer needed the protection of the breach of promise suit. The second was the conclusion, drawn from a number of notorious cases, that unscrupulous gold-diggers were increasingly exploiting the action in order to entrap and blackmail rich and sometimes titled men, either the very young or the very old. In 1892, a judge went so far as to declare: 'love is not a necessary element in a breach of promise suit'.[81] To make matters worse, juries were now awarding these gold-diggers damages which judges and the educated public considered grossly in excess of what was justified. Damages assessed according to the degree of the moral wrong and the capacity of the defendant to pay gave way to damages assessed on a scale to satisfy the demand for punishment for alleged moral turpitude. Juries could not resist the demands for compensation of a tearful pretty girl of humble origin complaining of seduction on promise of marriage by a rich old lecher.

By the early twentieth century, a third argument was being developed in favour of abolition of the action. This was that 'there are numerous miserable marriages which take place under the compulsion of an action for breach of promise'.[82] The primacy of the quest for individual happiness was thus now introduced into the argument.

In 1886, on the other hand, the *Law Times* weighed in with a reasoned defence of the action. It noted its popularity, as measured by the number of cases, and the wide publicity in the newspapers to which they gave rise. It observed that members of the legal profession could hardly be in favour of killing the goose which laid so many rich golden eggs at their feet. It

---

[79] White, 'Breach of Promise', 139.

[80] R. J. Combs, ' "The Most Disgusting, Disgraceful, and Inequitous Proceeding in our Law": The Action for Breach of Promise of Marriage in Nineteenth-Century Ontario', *University of Toronto Law Journal*, 38 (1988), 81. I owe this reference to David Sugarman.

[81] White, 'Breach of Promise', 139.

[82] *Roy. Com. Divorce, 1912; Minutes of Evidence*, 1: 120.

argued that the real and only question was 'whether or not the right of action does or does not afford valuable protection to women'. It concluded that it did, in view of the fact that 'marriage is a woman's chief, perhaps only, opening in life', any delay in which 'leaves her permanently depreciated in the matrimonial market'. Secondly, it argued shrewdly that the breach of promise action was a necessary corollary to the extreme freedom from restraint allowed to young girls in England as compared with those on the Continent. Without the threat of a breach of promise suit, 'the English custom of "engagement" . . . would, for good or bad, disappear'. In proof of this contention, the *Law Times* referred to a wealthy male defendant's recent payment of an out-of-court settlement of £10,000 to a female plaintiff.[83]

In part because of the demise in 1857 both of the ecclesiastical courts' jurisdiction over marriage and of the crim. con. action, the years between 1850 and 1914 saw the action for breach of promise reach its peak in terms of the number of cases, the size of the damages awarded, and the degree of publicity given to these trials in the newspapers. Just like the crim. con. action before it, the breach of promise action reached its greatest popularity just as it faced growing criticism from certain influential quarters of the laity, clergy, and lawyers. And just like the crim. con. action, it offended Victorian sensibilities by mixing categories which according to contemporary cultural values should be socially distinct: men and women; love and commerce; public and private; in the breach of promise suit, all were blurred.[84]

Between 1850 and 1914, there took place a slow shift of public opinion from toleration or approval of the action as a necessary defence of respectable young women against predatory and deceitful seducers to condemnation of it as a public scandal, an open invitation to blackmail by scheming women (or men), and an example of arbitrary and irrational generosity on the part of juries awarding damages. As evidence of this irrationality, attention was drawn to the fact that the women whose chances on the marriage market were most seriously damaged were the ugly ones, who needed substantial dowries to move them off the shelf. It was to the pretty ones, however, that juries gave the largest damages, although they were the ones who needed the money least in order to find husbands.[85] As women gained a more secure place in society, with more guaranteed rights and protections, so the image of the passive, weak, sexless female exploited by predatory males gave way to the opposite image

---

[83] *Law Times*, 29 Nov. 1884: 77; I owe this reference to David Sugarman.
[84] Combs, 'Action for Breach of Promise', 67.
[85] *Law Quarterly Review*, 10 (1894), 141.

of innocent or gullible men enticed into promises of marriage by predatory women.[86] And as women increasingly obtained access to education and began to infiltrate, in however small numbers, and in the face of severe discrimination, into professional jobs, so the argument that a woman's sole career lay in marriage lost some of its force. By the First World War, the action was still at its apogee, but at the same time it was falling into increasing disrepute. As a result, in the first half of the twentieth century the numbers of suits and the publicity accorded to them gradually declined. The breach of promise action had served its social purpose, and in 1970 it was abolished.[87]

[86] Grossberg, *Governing the Hearth*, 54.
[87] I owe this information to Ms Ginger Foster.

IV

Clandestine Marriage

'Give every man his due, and learn the way of truth.' This advice cannot be taken by those that are concerned in the Fleet marriages; not so much as the priest can do the thing that is just and right there, unless he designs to starve. . . . The fear of the Lord is the beginning of wisdom. The marrying in the Fleet is the beginning of eternal woe.

Revd Walter Wyatt [Fleet parson], 1716 (J. S. Burn. 7)

A ceremony performed in a little room of an alehouse in the Fleet, and by a profligate clergyman . . . all in rags, swearing like a trooper and haggling about what he is to have for his trouble, and half-drunk perhaps at the very time he is performing the ceremony.

Speech by Lord Hillsborough in the House of Commons in 1753 (*Parl. Hist.* 15: 63)

Gretna Green, like the purgatory of Catholics, purifies sin.

P. Anchini, *A Few Remarks on the Present Laws of Adultery and Seduction in England* (London, 1835), 13

1. Definition and Development

A clandestine marriage was a legally binding marriage, but one conducted in a manner which broke canon law. It was binding since it was conducted by a man who at least purported to be a clergyman (although often one not holding a cure) and since it followed the ritual prescribed by the *Book of Common Prayer*. But it could be irregular in a number of ways, the central one being that it was done in secret rather than in public: it was a *clandestine* marriage. First, it was done without either the prior reading of banns or the procuring of a valid licence from a church official. Second, it took place anywhere but in the parish church of one of the spouses. It might be performed in a 'Peculiar'—one of those churches that, for historical reasons, were accidentally exempt from episcopal jurisdiction; or in a church in another diocese. But it could equally well take place in a private house, an alehouse, a coffee shop, a prison, or even a brothel. It could, and usually did, take place outside the canonical hours of 8.00 a.m. to 12.00 p.m., often in the middle of the night. It was usually not recorded in any official parish register, sometimes (though rarely) not even in a personal notebook or private register kept by the officiating clergyman.

After 1597, a clergyman conducting a clandestine marriage became liable to prosecution in an ecclesiastical court and to a sentence of suspension from all clerical functions for three years, thus forcing him into unemployment. The disadvantage of using this penalty against a clergyman with a cure of souls was that it left his congregation untended for three years. The only penalty for the bride and groom and witnesses was excommunication, but this had no teeth, and anyway seems only rarely to have been used, and hardly at all after about 1680.[1] Even so, during the first half of the seventeenth century, there can be little doubt that increasing numbers submitted to the standard procedure laid down in the canons of 1604 for a regular church marriage. This involved putting up banns three times or obtaining a licence,[2] followed by a marriage ceremony which was conducted in church before the communion table by a beneficed clergyman, in the parish of residence of the bride, and within canonical hours.

Despite the relative success of the church courts before 1640 in suppressing contract marriages, scattered evidence suggests that clandestine marriages were already becoming a serious problem. In Wiltshire, the number of official prosecutions of parsons rose to ten or more a year in the 1620s and 1630s, any one of which defendants may have married dozens of couples clandestinely. In the diocese of York, in 1632–3 alone there were thirty cases of parsons or curates prosecuted for conducting clandestine marriages.[3]

The restored church courts in the 1660s faced a far more difficult situation. Ever since 1653, Church of England weddings had been forbidden, so that it had been a pious duty for ejected Anglican clergymen to conduct clandestine marriages for the faithful in private houses. At the same time, the control of the church over marriage had been weakened by the creation of a system of secular marriages by JPs, and there had sprung up a substantial body of Dissenters who conducted marriage ceremonies in their own chapels, using their own rituals. Things continued for some while in a state of confusion, so that in 1661–2 the vicar of Aylesbury in Buckinghamshire was calling the banns in church in the usual manner and

---

[1] For a late case of the excommunication of witnesses, see *Robins* v. *Wolseley* (1754), LPCA, D 1768.

[2] For the figures for licences in 1854, see *Seventeenth Annual Report of the Registrar General for Births, Deaths and Marriages in England* (London, 1856).

[3] Ingram, *Church Courts, Sex, and Marriage*, 213–18, claims it was not serious, despite his own rather disturbing figures. For the villages, see K. D. M. Snell, 'Parish Registration and the Study of Labour Mobility', *Local Population Studies*, 33 (1984), 31 n. 6; Marchant, 219.

then marrying couples in private houses, just as had been prescribed during the Cromwellian regime.[4]

2. Demand from the Laity

A clandestine marriage performed by some sort of clergyman, using the words prescribed in the Book of Common Prayer, offered five great advantages over a mere contract marriage. The first was that the participating of a clergyman gave it the appearance of respectability. The second was that the ceremony, however sordid, was recognized by both canon law and common law as legally binding and as carrying with it full property rights. This was a by-product of the shift from marriage by consent to marriage by religious ceremony. The third was that it was easier to prove that the marriage had taken place, since there were witnesses, usually a written entry in a marriage register (even if a private one), and often a written certificate. The fourth was that it was considerably cheaper than an official church marriage service, which made it very attractive to the poor. On the other hand, it was more expensive than a contract, which cost nothing; it had some, but not all, of the same uncertainties about proof; and the behaviour of the officiating clergyman and the nature of the surroundings were both often extremely squalid.

The fifth and last advantage, which was perhaps the most important to the bride and groom, was that it provided secrecy. There were several very common practical reasons why couples from the middling sort should want such secrecy. The first was as a pre-emptive strike to thwart the known or feared oppositon to the marriage by parents, kin, and 'friends', usually because of a status or financial difference between the bride and groom. Many of these couples were minors under the age of 21, who wanted the marriage kept secret until they came of age. Others were couples in which one of the partners—usually the man—had or professed to have expectations from a wealthy but cantankerous parent or relative. On the grounds that this benefactor would cut him out of his or her will if it became known that he had married without consent, he insisted that the marriage be kept secret until this person should die. This was particularly true of wards in Chancery, as the Irish lord chancellor complained in 1804: 'my wards are continually carried off, and whether married or not I frequently find difficult to discover'.[5]

---

[4] *The Episcopal Visitation Book for the Archdeaconry of Buckingham, 1662*, ed. E. R. C. Brinkworth, *Bucks. Record Society*, 7 (1943), 31–2.

[5] A. P. W. Malcolmson, *The Pursuit of Heiresses: Aristocratic Marriage in Ireland* (Ulster Historical Foundation, 1982), 38.

Others had their own special reasons for secrecy. Some were maid-servants fearful of dismissal if their marriage became known. Some were apprentices who would be in breach of their articles if they married before their seven-year term was out, or college fellows who would be obliged to resign their fellowships. Others were widows who would lose the copy-holds or annuities which they enjoyed as jointures from their first husbands if it became known that they had remarried. Others were in a hurry to use a secret marriage in order to thwart contract litigation against them by a discarded lover.

A handful of men sought secrecy since they were incestuously marrying their deceased wife's sister or a niece. Others, who were committing bigamy after abandoning their first wife, were naturally anxious to keep the marriage as secret as possible, even if they felt reasonably secure from a prosecution for felony. Many, either voluntarily or under duress, were hastily marrying pregnant women to whom they were contracted, in order to legitimize their children; they needed secrecy to cover their shame. Others were incautious lovers who had impregnated young girls after vague promises, and had been given by a JP the option of either an immediate shot-gun marriage or else imprisonment until they could provide sureties to pay the parish for the maintenance of their unborn child. The case of these last two groups was complicated by the fact that in England, unlike Scotland, pre-nuptially conceived children had no right at common law to inherit their parents' property. Children whose parents married after their birth were legitimate by canon law, but illegitimate by common law, a situation known as 'special bastardy'.[6] Other couples among the very poor who wished to get married in secret were afraid of opposition from the parish authorities on the grounds that they had no visible means to support a family and were therefore likely to produce children who would be a burden on the parish poor rate.[7] Taken all together, these groups amounted to a sizeable number of couples from all walks of life and economic levels who had their own perfectly legitimate reasons for seeking secret marriages.

A minority, however, had evil intentions, and it was this minority that gave clandestine marriage such a bad name in the eighteenth century. Some, for example, were merely ruthless and scheming adventurers who had either kidnapped or obtained the love of rich heiresses, and now wanted to marry them for their money without the knowledge or consent of their parents or friends. One such episode occurred in 1719, when Miss Anne Leigh, heiress of £200 a year and £6,000 in cash, was abducted by a

[6] R. Burn, 1: 112, 117–19; Patrick Fraser, *A Treatise on the Law of Scotland relative to Parent and Child, Guardian and Ward* (Edinburgh, 1866), 45–64.   [7] Gillis, 88–9.

half-pay officer, married against her will in the Fleet, and so barbarously treated that 'she now lies speechless'.[8]

The forcible abduction of heiresses had long been a penal offence, however, and ambiguous episodes involving half-willing, half-drugged victims, mostly women but occasionally men, were more common. For example, in 1737, a man on a charge of bigamy testified in court that he had got horribly drunk one night and woken up the next morning to find himself in bed with a strange woman. ' "And who are you? How came you here", says I. "Oh my dear", says she, "we were married last night at the Fleet" '.[9]

In addition to all these groups with practical reasons to seek clandestine marriage, large numbers of others were motivated by sheer modesty. The most obvious evidence of this desire to avoid publicity in marriage was the growth in the numbers willing to pay the substantial fees for a licence rather than having banns called three times in the local church. By the eighteenth century, at least a fifth, and possibly a third, of the population were being married by licence.[10] Many of these were couples from the middling sort who were fearful of public gossip and ridicule if the banns were read in their home parish church and who therefore desired a private ceremony. In 1700, the parson of Myddle in Shropshire lamented this aversion to putting up the banns, observing that 'nowadays the proud foolish girls, though they have not money enough to pay for a licence, yet will scorn that ancient and commendable way of being asked in church'.[11] In 1753 it was pointed out that 'such is the delicacy of English women that in the country they will travel ten miles from their own parishes to be married in a place where they were not known'.[12] An MP explained that 'it shocks the modesty of a young girl to have it proclaimed through the parish that she is going to be married, and a young fellow does not like to be exposed beforehand to the jeers of his companions'.[13]

This modesty persisted well into the nineteenth century; as an arch-deacon, Sir George Prevost, Bt., told the Royal Commission on Marriage in 1867 'there is a very general feeling among the poor of wishing to keep their marriages private', the main reason being fear of ridicule and salacious gossip. A public wedding was said to be 'distasteful in many parts of the country'; some have sound reasons for concealment, he said, while

---

[8] *Original Weekly Journal*, 26 Sept. 1719, quoted by J. S. Burn, 7 n. 2.

[9] J. S. Burn, 82 n. 1; for other examples see the classic Muilman case, involving the notorious Con Phillips, in Stone, *Uncertain Unions*, or the story of Beau Fielding in the Calvert case in id., *Broken Lives*.

[10] D. J. Steel, *National Index of Parish Registers* (London, 1968), 1: 226–8.

[11] J. Gough, *The History of Myddle* (Firle, 1980), 51.

[12] *A Letter to the Public*, 28–9.

[13] *Parl. Hist.* 15: 19; see also ibid. 39: 60.

others 'are apprehensive of temporary annoyance from their neighbours'. In consequence, many of that large majority of marriages still preceded by banns were carried out through 'evasion, deceit, and fraud' in the safe anonymity of the churches of crowded cities. Even when the banns were called in the church of residence, the couple usually took care not to appear at the service that day, since 'they were afraid of being laughed at'.[14]

This long-standing and widespread aversion to the publicity involved in putting up the banns is probably to be explained by the unusual freedom of social contacts accorded to young people in England, which extended to some degree of sexual experimentation in the common 'bundling' procedure. It is understandable that a couple about to be married would not wish to expose their intention before a congregation with some of whom they had had previous sexual contacts. Moreover, a clandestine marriage or one performed by licence in an unknown church avoided the need to endure the often boisterous rituals of the guests at the wedding festivities, which included treating, feasting, practical jokes, and ribald songs culminating in public bedding and the throwing of the bride's stocking across the bed. Such rituals were not merely acutely embarrassing to the newlyweds but could also involve them in no small expense.[15]

Secrecy also avoided any danger of a charivari. This was the traditional noisy, riotous, often obscene, public street demonstration at the time of a wedding, not by the wedding guests but by the unmarried youth of the village, demanding to be paid off with money or drinks in return for the loss of two of their numbers to the ranks of the married.[16]

For some couples, the prime incentive was not privacy but speed. Sailors on a brief drunken binge before setting out on a long voyage were notoriously in a hurry, and a Fleet marriage could accommodate them within the hour. As a result, in 1710, at the height of the great war with France, sailors comprised a quarter of all the men marrying clandestinely in the Fleet.[17] Women in an advanced state of pregnancy were also in a hurry, as were runaway couples fearful of interference by parents.[18]

Last but not least, there were increasing numbers, running into thousands, who were seeking not so much secrecy or speed as economy. In

[14] *Roy. Com. Marriage, 1868*, 32, 165, 168, 72; see also ibid. 36, 38 and app: 1, 2, 7, 8, 15, 16, 71, 165.

[15] For a description of such traditional wedding customs see Gillis, 55–80, 135–9.

[16] E. P. Thompson, ' "Rough Music": Le Charivari anglais', *Annales: Économies, sociétés et civilisations*, 27 (1972); N. Z. Davis, 'The Reasons of Misrule: Youth Groups and Charivaris in Sixteenth-Century France', *Past and Present*, 50 (1971); A. Burguière, 'The Charivari and Religious Repression in France during the Ancien Regime', in R. Wheaton and T. K. Hareven (eds.), *Family and Sexuality in French History* (Philadelphia, 1980).

[17] R. L. Brown, 'The Rise and Fall of the Fleet Marriages', in *Marriage & Soc.* 126.

[18] J. S. Burn, 75 n. 1, 83 n. 1.

the first place, the fees for a clandestine marriage in the early eighteenth century—especially for a Fleet marriage—were only about a third of those charged by a qualified clergyman for a regular public church service. Even so, the fees usually came to 7s. 6d., or about a week's wages for the poor. More important was that secrecy made it possible to avoid the expense of giving a large wedding feast for kin and neighbours, although many Fleet marriages were in fact followed by drunken feasts (Plate 12).

As for the well-to-do, their strong aversion to banns was amply proved by their universal willingness to go to the expense of buying a licence instead. In their cases, the motive was apparently pride. As Horace Walpole once wrote to a friend, 'How would my Lady A—— have liked to be asked in a parish church for three Sundays running? I really believe she would have worn her [widow's] weeds for ever, rather than have passed through so impudent a ceremony!'[19]

From the late seventeenth to the late nineteenth century, there were thus important and persistent practical and psychological reasons why there was a very high and apparently increasing demand for secret marriage. It met a strongly felt need among all classes of society, from peer to pauper. Between 1660 and 1753, clandestine marriage served as a safety valve in the pressure-cooker system of legalized official church marriage, still largely controlled by parents and 'friends', regulated by church, state, and parish, and delayed a decade or more after sexual maturity. In so poorly policed a society as England the supply to meet the demand was not slow in springing up.

3. Supply by the Clergy

A. SURROGATES

A key group who catered to this demand were the surrogates, beneficed clergy scattered over the countryside who were authorized to issue marriage licences. The bishops' registrars sold them in blank to the surrogates, who resold them to the laity at a profit. For instance, in 1752 in the diocese of Worcester (very roughly coterminous with the county), in addition to the bishop's official in the city of Worcester itself, there were thirty-one surrogates.[20] With licences costing £1. 1s. 4d. each (including the 7s. 6d. stamp tax), surrogates had a very strong financial incentive to sell as many as possible, and not to enquire too closely about the truth of

---

[19] G. Harris, *Life of Lord Hardwicke* (London, 1847), 2: 486–7.
[20] HWRO, Worcester CC, BA 2088 (6) 13: 444; see also Borthwick Institute, York CC, HEX 2.

applicants' sworn statements concerning their age, consent of parents or guardians, or place of residence, nor to pay too much attention to the quality of the persons who acted as bondsmen that the statements were all true. Many of them insisted on marrying the couple themselves, to add to their profits, instead of filling in the licence for the performance of the marriage in the parish of residence. Some left the place of marriage blank, to be filled in by the purchaser. Indeed some of them were said to hold weekly 'markets' to drum up business.[21]

To give but one example of the sort of thing which went on, in 1691 a surrogate of Farnham, Surrey, by the name of Revd Thomas Parker, issued a marriage licence but left the woman's name blank. This was done at the request—no doubt accompanied by a bribe—of a clerical acquaintance. Parker also took a bond for the truth of the allegations made about the qualifications of both to marry, which also left the woman's name blank, and which even omitted the standard clause guaranteeing parental consent to the marriage of a minor. These documents permitted an impoverished young man to be clandestinely married to a rich young heiress without the knowledge or consent of her parents, guardians, or 'friends'.[22]

The surrogates were well aware that licences were often obtained from them by perjury—a sworn denial that there was any impediment to the marriage and a false statement about place of residence—but the financial temptations were larger than many of them could resist. Risks were small, since lying to obtain a licence was not perjury at common law, while the persons who went bond that the sworn statements were all true, 'are always infamous scoundrels and beggars, and the consequence of suing a beggar is too well known to need explaining'.[23]

Despite evidence of widespread corruption, the church did nothing to put its house in order. In 1661, 1689, and 1713, Convocation, the lower house of the church legislature, discussed the matter but failed to take action. In 1664 a distinguished civil lawyer, Sir Leoline Jenkins, suggested stopping the issue to surrogates of blank licences, which he rightly regarded as a prime cause of the corrupt traffic in licences for clandestine marriages. But too many high officials in the ecclesiastical courts drew too much income from this sleazy traffic to make abolition practical.[24]

---

[21] *Archbishop Herring's Visitation Returns, 1743*, vol. 1 (*Yorkshire Archaeological Society Record Series* 71 (1928), 18); H. Prideaux, 'The Case of Clandestine Marriages Stated' (1691), *Harleian Misc.* 1.

[22] *Salter v. Salter* (1692), GLRO, London CC, DL/C/146, fo. 186.

[23] *Archbishop Herring's Visitation Returns, 1743*, 19.

[24] Till, 179.

B. RURAL CLERGY

Once the licence had been procured from a surrogate, by whatever means, there were plenty of clergy living so close to the poverty line that they were willing to run the risk of a three-year suspension from office in order to conduct a clandestine ceremony in a far-away church, late at night or early in the morning when no one was around. No questions were asked, and the clerk and the sexton were often employed as witnesses in return for a tip of 6*d*. each. The safest church was a 'Peculiar', outside the jurisdiction of any bishop, and in the late seventeenth century such a place was known as 'a lawless church'. Many clergymen were even willing to run the risk of marrying couples without a licence; indeed, before the government put a stamp tax on licences in 1694 and fixed the penalty of not using stamped paper at a £100 fine, the majority of the poor seem to have dispensed with this expensive preliminary. In one list of clandestine marriages of 1668, only four couples out of twenty had licences. Some couples were allegedly so innocent as to believe the assurances of a clergyman 'who pretended a right to marry all people who came to him in that kind'.[25]

The frequency of these rural clandestine marriages in the late seventeenth and early eighteenth centuries wreaks havoc upon the data available to modern demographers attempting to reconstitute the vital records of village families. Thus, the proportion of missing marriages on family reconstitution forms between 1601–30 and 1661–90 rises at Terling, Essex, from 47 to 66 per cent; at Colyton, Devonshire, from 37 to 68 per cent; and at Shepshed, Leicestershire, from 46 to 58 per cent. The missing marriages were either recorded elsewhere or were not recorded at all.[26] It seems more than likely that the bulk of the increase must be due to clandestine marriages.

So common was clandestine marriage in the countryside after the Restoration in 1660 that church officials made every effort to stamp it out. No fewer than fifty-eight clergymen were prosecuted for this offence in the archdeaconry of Chester in the course of the twenty-three years from 1676 to 1699.[27] These prosecutions were the result of a general letter by the bishop in 1676, ordered to be read in every church, giving instructions to ferret out offenders, whom he claimed were causing 'the discomfort and unhappiness of many parents, the ruin of many young

---

[25] Exeter DRO, CC, 94; HWRO, 795.702 BA2305/15; for a revealing correspondence between a local surrogate and the diocesan registrar about the loss of income because of clandestine marriages in Hexham in the early 18th century, see Borthwick Institute, York CC, HEX 2.
[26] *Local Population Studies*, 33 (1984), 28 n. 6.   [27] Chester DRO, EDC 5, *passim*.

people, evil example to others, and great scandal to the Church and Government'.[28] A recent visitation had turned up twenty-three clergy in the archdeaconry who had conducted clandestine marriages in the last year or two, of whom several had conducted more than one, and five were clearly in the business on a professional scale. Most of these clandestine marriages were conducted in private houses or alehouses, a few were in church but without banns or licences, and at least one took place 'in the middle of a field'.[29] In Leicestershire between 1662 and 1714, a fifth of all clergy prosecuted in the church courts were accused of performing clandestine marriages.[30] In the diocese of York, prosecutions for clandestine marriage peaked in the 1670s and 1680s.[31]

By 1720, however, the ecclesiastical court system had virtually collapsed. Official prosecutions petered out, and churchwardens now routinely returned *omnia bene* at visitations. This meant that despite the increase of the statutory penalties, the chances of a clergyman operating a 'marriage shop' in the countryside being detected and punished was much smaller in the early eighteenth century than it had been in the 1670s and 1680s.

A classic example of a rural clandestine marriage business in the early eighteenth century which operated fairly openly is that carried on in the very small parish of Fledborough in Nottinghamshire. Between 1712 and 1730 only eleven marriages took place there, all of them between residents. In 1730, however, the incumbent, the Revd Amos Sweetaple, was made a surrogate. This was an authority which he interpreted as giving him the right to sell marriage licences and marry all comers, regardless of their place of residence. Between 1730 and 1754, when the new Marriage Act shut him down, he used his authority to marry 490 couples, all but 15 of whom came from outside the village. This was not a marriage shop on the scale of those in London, but the performance in this tiny village of twenty marriages a year could hardly have gone unnoticed by his superiors; presumably they were also sharing in the profits. To judge by the range of his clients, his activities were well known over a wide area.[32] The result was that England was full of people like Robert Davies of Northwich and Elizabeth Madson of Whitegate 'who say they are married together, but 'tis not known whether nor how nor when they were married'.[33]

---

[28] Ibid. EDC 5/1676, no. 31.   [29] Ibid. EDC 46.

[30] J. Pruett, *The Parish Clergy under the Later Stuarts*, (Urbana, 1978), 132.

[31] Till, 72.

[32] T. M. Blagg and G. P. Proctor, *Nottinghamshire Marriage Registers*, 20: 1915, quoted in J. D. Chambers, *The Vale of Trent 1670–1800 (Economic History Review*, Supplement 3), 50; for other examples see Gillis, 92–3.   [33] Chester DRO, EDC 46, fo. 29ᵛ.

There can be little doubt that in most instances it was poverty rather than greed which drove these rural clergymen into breaking the law. Rich laity often tempted them with large rewards, and some offered them bonds to save them from prosecution if there were any legal problems later—bonds which in fact always turned out to be worthless. One parson under extreme financial pressure put it bluntly in a letter of 1664 to the chancellor of the diocese of Worcester: 'necessity itself forced me to the undertaking of those things which have hitherto been done by me, only to preserve myself from starving in prison. Before I was confined 'twas never done by me.' A curate who in 1699 had likewise been jailed for performing clandestine marriages and for issuing a certificate with a blank for the couple 'to date it when they thought fit' was described by a court official as 'so miserable a creature that he can hardly be termed *compos mentis*, and almost eat up with lice'.[34] Prison for a poor man in seventeenth- or eighteenth-century England was a chamber of horrors, and many of the marrying clergy caught up in the legal machinery at this time were clearly penniless and fearful of imprisonment for debt. Suspension from office for three years for conducting a clandestine marriage service virtually forced the victim to repeat the offence, as the only way he could then earn a living. Thus, an Irish clergyman who had been already been suspended once argued that he only did it a second time from dire necessity. As a result of the first suspension he found himself 'incapacitated to get by the profession so much as ten shillings to clothe and feed my family and growing children; all the pains and expense of my education, and all the labour and study of my life rendered barren and useless to me'.[35]

C. LONDON CLERGY

In addition to these country parsons and curates busy adding to their income on the side, mostly in a small way, there also sprang up some very professional marrying shops in London, located either outside the reach of episcopal control in 'Peculiars' or in or around the Fleet and King's Bench prisons. In the late seventeenth century, the three 'Peculiar' churches most active in the London marriage business were St James's Duke's Place, The Holy Trinity Minories, and St James-on-the-Wall, commonly called Lamb's Chapel.[36] Not only were their incumbents

[34] HWRO, BA 2309/9, 59.
[35] M. Dudley, *A Short and True State of the Affair between the Right Reverend Jemmet Lord Bishop of Cork and Ross, and the Reverend Marmaduke Dudley* (Dublin, 1750), RIA/HP, 223.
[36] See J. S. Burn, 3–6; Stone, *Uncertain Unions*.

exempt from episcopal jurisdiction, but they were also authorized to issue marriage licences, a situation which was tantamount to a permit to print money. Over a period of years many thousands of marriages were performed in these churches, in total disregard of the law. An educated guess on the basis of the surviving registers is that in the late seventeenth century these three London churches were responsible for between 2,500 and 3,000 marriages a year, which was not far off the total of official marriages in all of London.[37]

As an example of the sort of thing that happened, take the case of an apprentice called Allen, who in 1703 decided on a clandestine marriage at Lamb's Chapel. It was carried out by the Revd J. Wilde, the 60-year old curate of St Clare, Silver Street, and Reader at the chapel. Under later cross-examination, Wilde admitted that he had been made a deacon twenty years before, but had never been ordained a clergyman empowered to conduct religious services. He also refused to swear that all marriages performed in Lamb's Chapel were entered in the register book of marriages. Allen had procured a licence by paying the sexton a guinea; there had been two witnesses to the marriage, and the subsequent ritual bedding had also been witnessed. Two years later, Allen repudiated the marriage and married another woman. When his first wife went to Mr Wilde to try to prove her marriage, she found him slippery, evasive, and greedy. He charged her 7s 6d. just to look at the register, (where there was no entry) and a shilling for a certificate of marriage, but flatly refused in court to swear to its accuracy. She won her case in the Consistory Court, but lost it when an appeal was brought to the Court of Arches.[38]

The other great centre for clandestine marriages in the late seventeenth century was inside the Fleet Prison; between 1700 and 1710 fifty to sixty couples were being married there every week. This was made possible because clergymen suspended for three years for performing a clandestine marriage, and imprisoned in county gaols for debt could get themselves transferred to the Fleet Prison by writs of habeas corpus. Once there, they were able to set up in the business of marrying all comers in the chapel of the prison, no questions asked, and before the new legislation in 1695 without licences.[39]

In addition to these semi-professional marriage shops, many London

---

[37] E. M. Tomlinson, *History of the Minories, London* (London, 1907), 228–74; W. P. R. Phillimore and G. E. Cockayne, *Registers of St James, Duke's Place* (London, 1900), 1: v; D. J. Steel, *National Index of Parish Registers* (Chichester, 1976), 1: 295–6.

[38] *Allen* v. *Allen* (1705), LPCA, Eee. 9, fos. 67–105; B. 14, fo. 82.

[39] For the Revd J. Vyse, see Stone, *Uncertain Unions*.

clergymen also added to their income by performing clandestine marriages of dubious validity. If things later went wrong with the marriage, such a hard-to-prove ceremony could create havoc in the courts and in the lives of those involved. Thus, in 1682, the maidservant Ellen Hughes sued in the London Consistory Court to prove her marriage to the apprentice James Lancaster. She could show they had cohabited for four years as man and wife, and she exhibited a certificate of marriage signed by the rector of All-Hallows-by-the-Wall. Under examination, however, the rector, who had held the office for twenty-one years, put up a very poor showing. He explained that he kept 'his own private book' for clandestine marriage entries, which did not appear in the parish register. He also admitted that he had married the couple by their first names only, leaving their surnames blank to be filled in afterwards. He claimed that six months later Ellen had come to him and asked for a certificate of marriage, and for the first time told him the surnames, which he then entered in his private book. He refused to admit that Ellen had merely bribed him to enter the names, but James Lancaster denied that any marriage had taken place, the court did not believe the clergyman, and Ellen lost her case because the proof was so uncertain.[40]

4. Parliamentary Legislation, 1666–1718

Between 1666 and 1718, no fewer than ten bills were introduced in Parliament to put a stop to the clandestine marriage business, but none of them received much support.[41] The reasons for the opposition are obscure, but to judge from later developments, the Lords took the side of the aggrieved parents of runaway children, while the Commons were anxious to protect the freedom of under-age heiresses to choose their own husbands—preferably themselves—despite the cost in corruption, fraud, perjury, bigamy, doubtful marriages, and children of uncertain legitimacy. One bill, first introduced in 1677 and still going the rounds eight years later, is of particular interest since it contained some of the main reform ideas which in modified form were finally put into force seventy-five years later, in 1753.[42] Minors (under the age of 18 for boys and 16 for girls) who married without the consent of their fathers or guardians were to be punished by the forfeiture of their claims to property. An officiating clergyman who forged a licence and/or performed a clandestine marriage

---

[40] GLRO, London CC, DL/C/195, fo. 73.

[41] *Law Review*, 2 (1845), 149, 152; *JH Lords*, 12: 358, 13: 90–156, 14: 11–60, 287–313, 322–415, 626–56; 15: 742–6; 16: 148–50, 175–82, 315–43; 28: 14–154, *passim*, 228; 31: 175; Gally, 26.

[42] HMC, *House of Lords MSS 1678–88*, 276–80.

was to be punished by death without benefit of clergy. This bill was clearly impractical, since very few landed squires and noblemen were going to vote for the total loss of hereditary claims to property, and very few bishops would vote for the execution of clergymen.[43]

In the 1690s, the need to find money to finance the wars with France drove the government first to place a tax in 1695 on all marriages, including clandestine ones (which largely failed), and then to impose a substantial stamp tax (5s. 0d.) on marriage licences and marriage certificates. This at once drew official attention to the loss of revenue to the Crown from the widespread practice of clandestine marriages. An act of 1695 forbade the conduct of marriages in churches or chapels exempt from episcopal jurisdiction unless a licence had been obtained. In 1696, another act forbade marriages by unbeneficed clergymen and imposed the criminal penalty of a £100 fine upon those who conducted such marriages without stamped licences or who issued certificates on non-stamped paper, and upon surrogates who sold licences without charging the stamp duty. Then, in 1712 a further act shut down altogether the Fleet Prison as a safe haven for clergymen conducting clandestine marriages by fining the gaoler £100 for every marriage he allowed in his prison.[44]

Even these acts left gaping loopholes, however; an undated bill of about 1712–20 was designed to plug them, but ultimately proved abortive.[45] The preamble explained that, despite the 1712 act, abuses continued since clandestine marriages simply moved outside the Fleet and King's Bench prisons and were performed in even larger numbers than before in taverns, alehouses, and other houses in the Rules. Second, the 1712 act had ordered the removal of imprisoned clergy from London to county gaols, but it failed to specify that they could not get themselves returned again to the Fleet or King's Bench by the use of a writ of habeas corpus. Furthermore, clergy convicted under the act could by a legal device continue performing clandestine marriages in the Fleet for up to eighteen months, during which time they could make five times the £100 fine imposed on them. Then, just before removal, they would run away and disappear. It was estimated that the loss of stamp duties from clandestine marriages still amounted to £4,000–£5,000 a year, since the duties on the affidavit to procure a licence, the bond for a licence, the licence itself, and

---

[43] BL, Add. MSS 35580, fo. 174; for another failed bill in 1692, see *A Representation of the Prejudices that may arise in Time from an intended Act concerning Marriages, etc.* (London, 1692), (Bodl. Pamph. 208).

[44] 6–7 W. III cap. 6; 7–8 W. III, cap. 35; 9–10 W. III, cap. 35; 10 Anne cap. 19; Brown, 'Rise and Fall', 120–1; *Laws Respecting Women*, 35; *PP, Accounts and Papers*, 35(1868–9), 902–3.

[45] *A Proposed Act to prevent the Loss of Stamp Duty arising from Clandestine Marriages* (BL 816 m. 6 (77)).

the marriage certificate totalled 12s. 6d. per marriage, all of which was lost on some 6,000–7,000 clandestine marriages.

In 1714–15, the lower clergy in Convocation made two attempts to put their house in order, but both failed for largely accidental reasons, such as the unexpected death of Queen Anne.[46] Their basic objective was to put teeth into the enforcement of the canons of 1603 by imposing fines on all transgressing clergy. These would have included parish clergy who allowed others to use their churches for clandestine marriages; parish clerks who failed to keep accurate marriage records; surrogates who issued licences for marriages in churches other than those in the place of residence of one of the couple, or otherwise issued licences without due precautions. It also proposed punishment by fine of any lay person who lied about their age or whether their parent or guardian had given consent, or who married in an unspecified place. If it could have been passed and enforced, the draft offered a fairly comprehensive net to catch most offenders. But the clergy were not enthusiastic about it, and in any case Convocation lacked powers to punish the laity. Thus one more reform effort failed.

In 1739 a bill to prevent clandestine marriages was introduced into the House of Lords and given a second reading, but died in committee.[47] A year later an attempt was made to put a stop to the runaway marriages of the under-age children of the rich—which was perhaps the main concern of the propertied classes—in a bill introduced into the House of Lords, but it too failed to pass.[48] The time was clearly not yet ripe.

5. Fleet Marriages, 1696–1753

As usual, these acts had both expected and unexpected consequences. Some, but not all, professional marriage shops in various 'Peculiars' in London were certainly closed down, such as St James's, Duke Place. The act of 1712 also stopped the performance of clandestine marriages inside the Fleet Prison. In the countryside, however, clandestine marriages continued to be performed despite the penalties, and false licences continued to be issued. Although the tax on official licences may have frightened off more respectable clergy, it also increased the financial incentive to fraud by the unscrupulous.

---

[46] Gally, 149–50; D. Wilkins, *Concilia Magnae Britanniae et Hiberniae, 1546–1717* (London, 1737), 4: 653–4, 659–60; Bodl., Tanner MSS 282, fo. 159.

[47] *JH Lords*, 25: 465, 471, 479.

[48] Bill Preventing Clandestine Marriages; see also the failed bill in the House of Commons in 1732–3, *JH Commons*, 22: 80, 125.

In London the trade simply moved elsewhere, and between 1710 and 1753 it expanded at a tremendous rate into the Rules of the Fleet Prison, a sanctuary area just outside the prison where clergymen imprisoned for debt could obtain licence to live.[49] As these parsons were already in prison for debt, they could not be imprisoned to force them to pay the £100 fine imposed on them, and as they held no cure or were already suspended from one, they could not be suspended again. Virtually immune from punishment, they could therefore marry customers freely and cheaply, at any time of day or night, anywhere within the Rules of the Fleet (Plate 9). Many provided a licence of some sort, mostly on unstamped paper, and issued official-looking certificates, also on unstamped paper (Plate 10).

Business in the Rules of the Fleet was so brisk that, as with twentieth-century massage-parlours, it led to the development of several ancillary occupations. There were the 'plyers' or 'runners'—touts who hung around the street urging passers-by to patronize their employers. Sundays were naturally the busiest days of the week, and by nine in the morning, 'Fleet parsons [are] at their stations on Ludgate Hill, looking out sharp for weddings from Whitechapel and Wapping', where the lower-class clientele of sailors were congregated[50] (Plate 11). There were the keepers of the marriage houses, most of them inns, brandy-shops, alehouses, or coffee-shops, of which about forty are known by name between 1710 and 1753, about twenty being in active business at any one time. Their owners were the entrepreneurs of the whole business, and they made a handsome profit from the subsequent, often very riotous, feasts (Plate 12). So highly developed had the operation become by 1723 that 'several of the brandy-shop men and victuallers keep clergymen in their houses at twenty shillings a week, hit or miss', and went to the trouble of fitting out an upstairs room called a 'chapel'.[51] The brides were often given away by the owners of the property, who, for a fee, also made the entries in the register. Men controlled all aspects of the trade, although the keepers of the registers were often women.

Between seventy and a hundred Fleet parsons were at work in the Rules between 1700 and 1753. Most of them were, or had once been, properly ordained clergymen, although a few of them were complete frauds. Often they were graduates of Oxford or Cambridge who had fallen upon hard

[49] J. S. Burn, *passim*; Brown, 'Rise and Fall', 121–2; Steel, *National Index*, 1: 296–313; J. C. Jeaffreson, *Brides and Bridals* (London, 1872), 2: 122–42; J. Ashton, *The Fleet, its River, Prison, and Marriages* (London, 1889); Gillis, 94–8.

[50] Anon., *Hell on Earth or the Town in an Uproar* (London, 1729), 3, 14.

[51] Brown, 'Rise and Fall', 127; MacQueen, *Marriage, Divorce, and Legitimacy*, 3; Jeaffreson, *Brides and Bridals*, 2: 139–43, 149.

times through drink or misfortune, or whose curacies were so miserably paid that they did not bring in enough to live on. But if conducted on a large enough scale, clandestine marriage was such a lucrative business that some of these Fleet parsons in the 1730s and 1740s were earning several hundred pounds a year; we know that at least one, the Revd John Mottram, enjoyed a princely income of over £2,000. Most, however, seem to have lived in squalor and to have spent most of their earnings on drink. Many were hardened scoundrels, and many others were broken-down alcholics. One, the Revd Walter Wyatt, confided to his pocket-book his guilty awareness that he was living off a scandalous and un-Christian trade—although this did not stop him from earning about £500 a year from chasing customers all over town, even in Piccadilly.[52]

Fraud was rampant in all aspects of Fleet marriages. For a fee, false entries could be inserted in the registers, genuine ones erased, and entries back-dated to cover a pregnancy and thereby 'to please their parents'. If it came to proving a marriage, perjured witnesses were easy to come by in those dingy lanes and courtyards, and the ecclesiastical courts, King's Bench, and Chancery were kept busy dealing with the frustrating legal consequences of this dubious trade. It was hardly surprising that one of the busiest of the Fleet parsons in the 1720s and 1730s was known as 'the Bishop of Hell'.[53]

The Revd Dare once back-dated a marriage from 1741 to 1723. The Revd Thomas Crawford tried to add to the credibility of his documentation by labelling his book of entries 'The Old and True Register'. Another tried to baffle his pursuers by keeping nine different registers, one for each of the various ale-houses and coffee-houses where he performed marriages. Some parsons even kept professional 'husbands' available who would marry any pregnant girl in a hurry, often two or three of them in a single year.[54] Others tried to drum up business by distributing hand-bills, or by putting advertisements in newspapers—evidence of the new power of the printing press to drive the machine of a consumer-oriented society. One such handbill of the 1740s reads as follows:

---

[52] For the lives of some these Fleet parsons, see J. S. Burn, 49–59, and Stone, *Uncertain Unions*; for the Revd Walter Wyatt, see the epigraph of this chapter and J. S. Burn, 53–4.

[53] *OB Proc.* (1735–6), 164, 208–9; (1736–7), 119–20, 138–9, 171–2; (1739–40), 63–9; (1743–4), 219–21; see also Stone, *Uncertain Unions*.

[54] J. S. Burn, 11, 55, 57–8, 82, 83, 90, 92; Jeaffreson, *Brides and Bridals*, 1: 151–7; see also O. Goldsmith, *The Vicar of Wakefield* (1766), ed. A. Friedman (London, 1974), 122; and the case of Con Phillips in Stone, *Uncertain Unions*.

G.R.
At the true Chapel at the Old Red Hand and Mitre,
three doors from Fleet Lane, and next door to the White Swan.
Marriages performed by authority
by the Reverend Mr Simpson
educated at the University of Cambridge,
and late chaplain to the Earl of Rothes.
N.B. Without imposition.[55]

Unfortunately for his image, in 1751 the Revd Simpson was involved in a bigamy case. Under questioning, he seemed unsure which bishop had ordained him, and admitted that he had never held a benefice, but only one or two petty curacies worth between £20 and £30 a year. He then added, implausibly: 'I don't do it for lucre or gain,' to which the judge replied tersely: 'You are a nuisance to the public.'[56]

Although the principle patrons of these corrupt Fleet parsons were the poor, especially sailors, the Rules of the Fleet were also being used by a few children of the elite as a place in which to be secretly married without the knowledge of their parents.[57] But its most scandalous aspects took other forms. At least one couple were evidently two lesbians, one disguised as a man;[58] many turned out to be bigamists; and others were the victims of force, fraud, alcohol, or drugs.[59]

During the first half of the eighteenth century, more than one enterprising clergyman still managed to carry on a lucrative trade outside the Rules of the Fleet, in spite of the new laws. One set up shop in the Savoy Chapel, the jurisdiction over which was claimed by two government bureaucracies, those of the Crown and of the Duchy of Lancaster. During the 1750s the minister sheltered himself by switching for protection sometimes to one and sometimes to the other, until in the end Lord Mansfield cut through the bureaucratic red tape, convicted him, and put him out of business. Mansfield declared that he 'used to marry about 1400 couples a year, 900 of whom were generally women with child'.[60]

An even more successful and longer-lasting clandestine marriage business was set up in 1730 by the Revd Alexander Keith in Mayfair Chapel off Piccadilly, where he 'constructed a very bishopric for revenue', as Horace Walpole put it.[61] He advertised widely in the newspapers, offering to marry all comers for a guinea, including a 5s. 0d. stamped

---

[55] J. S. Burn, 54.
[56] *The Humours of the Fleet*, pt. 2 (BL, 1163. h. 2; this collection contains many newspaper advertisements).
[57] J. S. Burn, 94–126.   [58] Ibid. 77, 90.   [59] See Stone, *Uncertain Unions*.
[60] Evans, 1: 100; for the quotation from Lord Mansfield, I am indebted to J. C. Oldham.
[61] H. Walpole, *Memoirs of the Reign of George II*, ed. Lord Holland (London, 1847), 1: 339.

licence and a certificate,[62] and was patronized by a far higher class of clientele than those who crowded into the Rules of the Fleet. In 1741 he was sued for officiating as a clergyman without an episcopal licence by the Rector of St George's Hanover Square (on whose revenue he was no doubt encroaching), and a year later he was formally excommunicated by the Bishop of London. A consummate showman, Keith riposted by solemnly excommunicating in his chapel the bishop, the judge of the Consistory Court who had found him guilty, and the rector of St George's Hanover Square, who had launched the prosecution. But these theatrical tricks did not save him, and in April 1743 the Court of Chancery incarcerated Keith in the Fleet Prison for defiance of excommunication.[63]

Keith stayed in the Fleet Prison until he died, but this did not prevent him from continuing to run a thriving business in a house in Mayfair which was fitted up as a chapel and serviced by four Fleet parsons acting as his deputies. In 1747 the business was in full swing, and the clerk described the procedure as follows: 'One Mr Walker marries and I carry the licences to Mr Keith, and he registers them.'[64] It thus seemed a very reputable operation in every regard except for its clandestine nature, and it attracted a very respectable clientele. In 1749 Keith's wife died, and he used this as an opportunity to pull off a publicity stunt: he had the body embalmed and exhibited in a shop in South Audley Street, declaring that it would remain there until such time as he was released and able to attend the funeral. As things turned out, although his business had been closed down by the Marriage Act of 1753, he was still in the Fleet when he died after fifteen years of prosperous confinement.

When the marriage bill was being debated he wrote a pamphlet against it, claiming that its prime purpose was to put him out of business. There may have been some truth in the allegation, since he had succeeded in frightening and outraging all elite parents by secretly marrying in his chapel of Mayfair a series of young aristocrats infatuated with wholly unsuitable girls: Henry Brydges Duke of Chandos in 1744, James Viscount Strange in 1746, James Duke of Hamilton in 1752, and Lord George Bentinck in 1753.[65]

The astonishing scale of the clandestine marriage business in London can be estimated by adding the number performed in the Rules of the Fleet to those which took place elsewhere in London. At its peak in the

---

[62] *Daily Advertiser*, 3 Mar. 1747.

[63] *Trebeck* v. *Keith, Eng. Rep.* 26: 700; G. Clinch, *Mayfair and Belgravia* (London, 1892), 56–8; Jeaffreson, *Brides and Bridals*, 2: 158–66.

[64] *OB Proc.* (1746–7), 233.

[65] *The Humours of the Fleet*, 59 (BL, 11633. h. 2); *DNB sub* Alexander Keith; A. Keith, *Observations on the Act for Preventing Clandestine Marriages* (London, 1753); J. S. Burn, 148–50.

1740s, as many as 6,600 marriages a year were being conducted within the Rules of the Fleet, out of a total in all England of about 47,000.[66] Most of the clients were of the lower middling sort from London and its suburbs. This means that in the first half of the eighteenth century, the great majority of Londoners, as well as a significant proportion of those from the Home Counties, were being clandestinely married in the Rules of the Fleet.[67] If one adds those married in Keith's Mayfair Chapel, the Savoy, and elsewhere, the total of clandestine marriages performed in London in the 1740s cannot have fallen far short of 8,000 a year, which amounts to 17 per cent of all the legal marriages performed in England. A reasonable guess would therefore be that between 15 and 20 per cent of all marriages in England in the middle of the eighteenth century were conducted in these clandestine ways.[68]

6. The Demand for Reform

In 1730, all the Fleet parsons were indicted for failing to issue their certificates on stamped paper, but since the certificates were not legal anyway this move to put a stop to clandestine marriages failed.[69] However, the growing number of complaints in the London newspapers showed that during the 1730s elite public opinion increasingly began to turn against the clandestine marriage system. An attempt in Parliament in 1739 to introduce legislation to put an end to clandestine marriages failed to reach a third reading.[70] But the laity were becoming increasingly exasperated by these scandalous marriage procedures, especially since they served occasionally to facilitate secret runaway marriages of upper-class heiresses. For example, in 1744 Henry Fox, future Lord Holland, used a clandestine marriage in a private house in the Fleet to run off with Lady Georgiana Lennox, daughter of the second Duke of Richmond, an event which converted him into a staunch opponent of any reform.

The courts were also exasperated by the unreliability of the evidence for clandestine marriages, and in the 1730s the lord chief justice and other criminal court judges at the Old Bailey began to reject Fleet registers as evidence for or against the frequent charges of bigamy in which they

---

[66] Brown, 'Rise and Fall', 123; E. A. Wrigley and R. Schofield, *The Population History of England, 1541–1871* (London, 1981), 499.

[67] Brown, 'Rise and Fall', 124–5.

[68] J. R. Gillis estimates that 20–30% of all marriages were clandestine or common law, but I regard this as too high. See id. 'Conjugal Settlements: Resort to Clandestine and Common Law Marriage in England and Wales 1650–1850', in J. Bossy (ed.), *Disputes and Settlements: Law and Human Relations in the West* (Cambridge, 1983), 264.

[69] J. S. Burn, 12–14; Jeaffreson, *Brides and Bridals*, 2: 150.

[70] *JH Lords*, 25: 465, 471, 479.

figured.[71] In the Court of Chancery Lord Hardwicke also regularly rejected an entry in a Fleet register as evidence. On one celebrated occasion he is said to have seized a register produced in court and torn it in pieces to show what he thought of it.[72]

These legal outbursts by the common law judges in the late 1730s and early 1740s did nothing to reduce the activity of the Fleet parsons, to deter their clientele, nor even to close the issue of the legal validity of Fleet registers. Although register books were twice again rejected by common law courts in 1776 and 1803, in 1781 a court accepted a Fleet certificate as proof of a marriage by Lord Saye and Sele. After some hesitation, in 1794 Lord Kenyon solemnly declared the registers to be 'private memoranda' which were 'a species of evidence totally inadmissible . . . the Books of the Fleet . . . are not in any case received as evidence of marriage'.[73] This was the end of the losing battle for the Fleet registers to achieve recognition in a court of law. Fortunately for the historian, however, in 1821 the state bought from the owners 'the old ale-soaked and tobacco-grimed registers and the filthy pocket-books of the public-house touters, recording secret unions'.[74]

By the 1740s, Lord Chancellor Hardwicke was also complaining publicly in court about the scandalous way surrogates filled in blanks on licences for any parish, or even for several parishes. The case that aroused his especial indignation was one in which a minor, Sophia Moore, a ward of the Court of Chancery, had run away from her guardian and entered into a clandestine marriage. Her prospective husband, John Peck, had gone to Doctors' Commons itself, the headquarters of the ecclesiastical bureaucracy of the Province of Canterbury, in order to procure a licence. The official asked: 'Is the woman of age?', to which Peck replied: 'By her looks she seems to be 24.' The official accepted this vague declaration, remarked 'then she may be of age', and issued the licence. But the licence itself was defective in that the place of marriage was not properly filled in with the parish of residence. It merely said: 'Bushey, Watford, Aldenham . . .' (all in Hertfordshire), leaving a blank space for other parishes to be added at will. The couple arranged to be married at Pinner by the usher of a school, who himself filled in the blank in the licence with the words 'or Pinner in the County of Middlesex'. He later explained to the court that it

---

[71] *Eng. Rep.* 163: 25–9.

[72] T. Peake, *Nisi Prius Cases* (London, 1795), 136; P. C. Yorke, *Life and Correspondence of Philip Yorke, Earl of Hardwicke* (Cambridge, 1913), 1: 123; 2: 447.

[73] *State Trials*, 14: 1367 n. *; *Read* v. *Passer* (*c.*1795), *Eng. Rep.* 170: 332–3. But in Chancery Lord Eldon in 1809 still refused to commit himself: *Lloyd* v. *Passingham* (1809), ibid. 33: 907–8; *Walker* v. *Wingfield* (1812), ibid. 34: 385.

[74] *Roy. Com. Marriage, 1868*, 32: 18. These documents are now in the PRO, RG 7.

was common to issue licences for marriage in several parishes and to leave a blank so that 'it might be filled up with the name of any other parish where the parties should be married'.

Hardwicke was infuriated, saying that the procedure carried out in this case included possible offences against both ecclesiastical and statute law, as well as constituting a contempt of Chancery by the secret marriage of a ward of the court. He observed: 'it is very surprising, considering the canons have laid down such particular rules in relation to marriages by licence, that clergymen should be so very careless in observing them'. Not only was it normal for the church authorities to issue blank licences and not seek proof of age of minors, but as a crowning absurdity and scandal, 'proctors sometimes stand at the door of the [Doctors'] Commons, and solicit persons to take out licences, just in the same manner as the runners to Fleet parsons do'.[75]

By 1740 there was thus little difference between the practices of the officials of the ecclesiastical courts and those of the Fleet parsons. In 1751 a commentator lamented: ' 'Tis pity that the ecclesiastical thunder is not suffered to break against these pests of society.'[76] But not a few of the 'pests' were now officials of the church itself: the church was part of the problem. Towards the end, moreover, the ecclesiastical courts were tending to accept the legality of clandestine marriages on the basis of evidence so flimsy that it would not have been accepted in any secular court. In 1752 the London Consistory Court declared valid a marriage allegedly performed twenty-three years before, despite the fact that there was only one witness, and the man had married another woman eight years before. In 1754 it again accepted a Fleet marriage allegedly made seven years before, although it was supported by only one witness and a certificate on unstamped paper, and although the man had subsequently married again—clandestinely at Mayfair Chapel—and had since died.[77]

It was this kind of arbitrary behaviour by the church courts which drove Lord Hardwicke to refuse to brook any interference by the church in lay affairs, even in punishing laity who were involved in clandestine marriages. In a test case in 1736, he declared that since the canons of 1604 had never been ratified by Parliament, they therefore gave the church courts powers to punish only the clergy.[78] This effectively made new Parliamentary legislation the only solution to the problems raised by the growth of Fleet marriages.

[75] *Eng. Rep.* 27: 697–9; 26: 499; see also Mr Herbert's case (1731), ibid. 24: 993.
[76] Anon., *Memoirs of the Life of M. De La Fontaine* (London, 1751), 44.
[77] *Walton* v. *Rider* (1752), *Eng. Rep.* 161: 7–12; *Plunkett/Sharp* v. *Sharp and Day* (1754), ibid. 255–7; see also *Grant* v. *Grant* (1754), ibid. 217–19.
[78] *Middleton* v. *Croft* (1736), *Eng. Rep.* 94: 549, 1059–97, 1098–105.

Protests by judges in the courts, especially Lord Chancellor Hardwicke, were supported by essays by moral reformers in the public press and by a barrage of satirical comment from novelists and playwrights. Clandestine marriage figures in over a third of the plots of plays from Wycherley and Vanbrugh in the late seventeenth century to Steele in the early eighteenth century. A survey of the plots of 241 comedies dating from 1660 to 1714 has shown that 91 of them involve a clandestine marriage, 70 of them false marriages or marriages performed by trickery and deception, and 26 mock or joke marriages. There can thus be no doubt that the system, and especially its abuses, were much on the mind of the upper-class London audiences of these comedies.[79]

Although many of the references in these plays to clandestine marriages of young couples were made without moral comment, others stressed the more scandalous aspects of the trade. Shadwell described a clergyman as 'a brave swinging orthodox and will marry any couple at any time; he defies licence and canonical hours and all those foolish ceremonies'. Congreve remarked of the growing marriage trade in London: 'there's such a coupling at [St] Pancras, that they stand behind one another, as 'twere in a country dance'.[80]

By the 1720s and 1730s the system was increasingly subject to satirical derision, and Fielding—as always, an acute social commentator—was relentless in his criticism. Someone seeking a speedy marriage was reassured: 'the person understands his business, he has ply'd several years at the Fleet'. In *The Wedding Day*, Millamour denounces Mrs Useful: 'Thou hast . . . sent more to bed together, without a licence, than any parson of the Fleet.'[81] In 1753, the year of the Marriage Act, Smollett made bigamy arising from a clandestine Fleet marriage the key to the plot of his novel *Ferdinand Count Fathom*.[82] Thus from 1720 onwards, the tide of social criticism of the clandestine marriage was rising as fast as was the business itself. It was its very success that generated the backlash which made possible the legislation of 1753, which was intended to abolish it once and for all.

A particularly well documented case of multiple Fleet marriages— widely publicized, thanks to a pamphlet war between the contending parties—was *Cresswell* v. *Cresswell*, which was used to great effect by Dr Henry Gally in an influential pamphlet of 1750.[83] Gally pointed out the

---

[79] W. Wycherley, *The Country Wife* (1675), IV/iii; J. Vanbrugh, *The Relapse* (1696), IV/iv; R. Steele, *The Funeral* (1702), V/iv; Alleman, 82.

[80] T. Shadwell, *The Squire of Alsatia* (1688), V/i; W. Congreve, *The Way of the World* (1700), I/i.

[81] H. Fielding, *Pasquin* (1736), III/i; *The Wedding Day* (1743), I/ii.

[82] Chs. 55, 56.   [83] Gally.

scale of human suffering under current conditions, in which the legality of marriage and the legitimacy of children were constantly being called into question. In the Cresswell case, an heiress, Miss Warneford, had married in good faith a young gentleman, Mr Cresswell, and had born him children. But a Miss Scrope sued for nullity on grounds of bigamy, claiming that a prior Fleet marriage had taken place between herself and Mr Cresswell. The Warneford marriage was therefore declared null and void, and the children were bastardized.

However, Miss Scrope soon found herself caught in the same trap, for as she was searching the Fleet registers for proof of her own marriage, she turned up a record of an even earlier marriage by Cresswell to a third woman who was still living. So both of Cresswell's last two marriages, to Miss Warneford and Miss Scrope, were in fact bigamous. The point rammed home by Dr Gally was that a person acting in all good faith could no longer have confidence that his or her marriage might not turn out to be bigamous, since the new spouse might have at some previous date contracted a clandestine Fleet marriage with another person. The trouble was that 'the proof of clandestine marriages is always precarious and sometimes impossible, owing to the unreliable quality of the registers and the venality of their keepers'. As a result, 'they are ready to be produced or concealed as a marriage is to be proved or disproved—all which management is at the command of the person that pays best'.[84]

7. Conclusion

The story of this extraordinary explosion of clandestine marriages between 1660 and 1753, first all over the country and then mainly in professional London marriage shops, reveals several things about the relationship between the law, law enforcement, and public opinion. Demand for secret private marriages was so intense among all classes of society that it flooded in like a rising tide, seeping into the cracks and crannies of the precarious sea-wall of legislation, ecclesiastical court prosecutions, and punishment. When one passage was blocked, another was soon found to accommodate the apparently almost insatiable demand. Although the problem existed in the early seventeenth century (when it was exacerbated by contract marriages), it was the events of the Interregnum which seem to have triggered the large-scale development of this

---

[84] Anon. [Lancelot Lee], *The Miserable Effects of Grasping at Riches* (London, 1749), (Bodl., Godwin Pamph. 812*(5)), first published in 1747 in the *General Evening Post*; T. E. Cresswell, *A Narrative of the Affair between Mr Cresswell and Miss Sc——e* (London, 1748), (Bodl., ibid. (6)); E. Scrope, *Miss Scrope's Answer to Mr Cresswell's Narrative* (London, 1749), (Bodl., 8° Art P 232(1)).

curious social phenomenon. The state was concerned after 1695 because clandestine marriage affected the revenue from stamp duties. The judges were exasperated by having to deal with cases of inheritance, bigamy, incest, etc., in which the evidence was nothing better than a grubby private marriage register kept by some down-at-heel clerk or shifty woman in an alehouse in the Rules of the Fleet, and full of false erasures, insertions, and back-dating. After a heroic effort to stamp out rural clandestine marriage in the decades from 1660 to 1690, the church more or less withdrew from the battle. So long as the country was full of half-starved curates, poverty drove many to augment their income by supplying the public demand for secret weddings. Indeed, the surrogates who issued the marriage licences themselves became some of the worst offenders, so that by the early eighteenth century the church had covertly come to live on the illegal profits from the clandestine marriage trade.

What is strange is why the repeated efforts in Parliament to pass a bill to put a stop to the trade failed again and again, sometime in the Lords, and always, before 1753, in the Commons. The abuses were obvious enough, but many thought that the remedy would be worse than the disease.

❧ V ❧

From the Marriage Act of 1753 to 1868

1. The Marriage Act of 1753

The opening salvo which started the campaign for a bill finally to suppress clandestine marriage was the lengthy pamphlet published in 1750 by one of the king's chaplains, the Revd Henry Gally, about the scandalous Cresswell case.[1] He began by stating that the Mayfair and Fleet marriage scandal was bad and getting worse, and had reached the stage of being 'a disgrace to any civilized nation'. But he saw at once what was one of the key problems, namely that any curbing of the system would be criticized as an attack on English freedom, for 'liberty, even mistaken liberty, is the darling of the people'. He ran down the now standard list of scandals and injustices associated with secret contracts and clandestine marriages, and pointed out that England was out of step with the whole Roman Catholic world, which had put its marriage laws in order at the Council of Trent in 1563, and also with most countries of Europe, which by secular law demanded parental consent for all marriage of minors.

He then faced up to the second critical issue, which was whether it was morally right to legislate to annul clandestine but otherwise canonically legal marriages. This turned on the principle that marriage was not a sacrament but a civil contract, which, although blessed by the church, was open to control by the secular authorities. He took care of the vested interest of the church officials, who for so long had profited from the sale of marriage licences, by assuring them that their income would probably rise rather than fall if all persons who had previously sought clandestine marriages were in future obliged to purchase a licence. On the other hand, he put much of the blame for the widespread practice of clandestine marriages in churches far from either of the couple's homes upon surrogates who filled in licences for marriage in churches other than those of the places of residence of one of the couple, in defiance of the canon law.

He denied that women would be harmfully affected by annulling

[1] Gally.

clandestine marriages, on the grounds that those whose marriages were annulled would be free to marry again (although he ignored the point that by then they would be damaged goods in the marriage market). And he denied that putting severe restrictions on cheap, easy, and secret marriages would drive many poor or impatient couples to fornication or cohabitation instead. After half a century of failed attempts at reform and the relentless growth in the problem he concluded that the only solution was for Parliament to pass a law 'absolutely to annul all clandestine marriage'.

The publication of Dr Gally's pamphlet was swiftly followed by two particularly scandalous cases—one being the marriage of a notorious courtesan Con Phillips, to protect herself from arrest for debt;[2] and the other a bigamous Scottish marriage which had just been appealed to the House of Lords. After the man's death, his thirty-year marriage had been declared null, leaving his widow penniless and their child bastardized, thanks to the successful claim by another woman of a clandestine precontract.[3] So disturbed was Lord Bath by this case that in January 1753 he introduced a motion to the House of Lords for a bill to abolish all contract and clandestine marriages. The twelve common law judges made an attempt to draft a bill, but it was so defective that the House of Lords rejected it.

Lord Chancellor Hardwicke (Plate 13), who had been waiting for twenty-five years to reform the marriage laws, seized the opportunity to take charge. He rewrote the bill and for the next six months personally master-minded its passage through both Houses of Parliament, in the face of some fierce opposition, by the use of rhetoric, logic, cajolery, and behind-the-scenes threats, deals, and lobbying. He bought off the peers by allowing the archbishops to retain the right to issue special licences for noblemen to be married how, where, and when they pleased.[4] He satisfied the middling sort by allowing the surrogates to continue to sell ordinary licences to dispense with banns, despite the fact that it was the corrupt distribution of these licences which had been no small cause of the clandestine marriage problem. He tried to satisfy the parish clergy by arguing that the suppression of clandestine marriages would drive the poor into getting married in church, thus augmenting clerical incomes generally. He bought off the Scots by omitting Scotland from the bill, leaving it to be taken care of by another bill prepared by the Scottish Lords in Sessions.[5] He bought the support of the squires by offering them the

[2] Stone, *Uncertain Unions.*

[3] *Cochran* v. *Campbell, JH Lords,* 28: 14.   [4] *Parl. Hist.* 15: 31 n. *.

[5] There is a draft of a bill to cover Scotland in Hardwicke's papers, possibly for consideration by the Court of Sessions. BL, Add. MSS 35880, fos. 84–91; *JH Lords,* 28: 98, 218.

one thing they really wanted, which was a legal veto power over the marriages of their children up to the age of 21. He kept all the lawyers in both Houses lined up solidly behind the bill, partly by persuasion, partly by exploiting their desire to clip the wings of the ecclesiastical courts, partly by appealing to their exasperation at the problems of legal proof of marriage raised by the existing situation. When all else failed, he made it clear that any opponent of the bill would be punished by being excluded from the lord chancellor's extensive patronage.

Thus Hardwicke contrived a most ingenious bill which had something in it for almost everybody. It was a triumph of cunning draftsmanship, and the editor of his papers called it 'one of the greatest legislative measures of Lord Hardwicke . . . this great measure which is one of the most extensive and general importance ever submitted to the legislature'.[6] It did indeed set the basic rules of marriage in England for nearly a century, and it is justly known to history as 'Hardwicke's Marriage Act'.

The battle over the bill was fought stage by stage, first through the House of Lords, then through the House of Commons (which made many amendments), then finally through the House of Lords again, the whole process lasting from January to June 1753. Its passage aroused intense passions inside Parliament, and split the government; one of the fiercest opponents of the bill was Henry Fox, secretary of state for war and himself the beneficiary of a run-away clandestine marriage.[7] Outside Parliament the bill also aroused intense popular feeling. Henry Fox's coach was dragged through the streets by cheering crowds, and handbills were distributed on both sides.[8] Public opinion was stirred up by a bitter pamphlet war, which raged for three years, from 1753 to 1755 and produced at least sixteen pamphlets, some of them as long as small books.[9]

Hardwicke's bill had five essential elements. He recognized that under existing conditions there was no way effectively to stop clandestine marriages, despite the fact that they were illegal according to the canon law of 1604. His solution was therefore to make null and void any marriage not preceded by banns or an official licence, not carried out publicly in a church or chapel by a regular clergyman in the prescribed daylight hours. The second problem was how to make the penalties so severe that they would drive the Fleet parsons to abandon their lucrative trade. Under the

[6] G. Harris, *The Life of Lord Chancellor Hardwicke* (London, 1847), 2: 484–5.
[7] The surviving records of the debates are to be found in H. Walpole, *Memoirs of the Reign of George II*, ed. Lord Holland (London, 1847), 1: 336–49; *Parl. Hist.* (1753–65), 15: 1–87; BL, Add. MSS 35880 (drafts of the bill by Lord Hardwicke at various stages) and 35877, fos. 121–4 (notes on the Lords' debate, 4 May 1753).   [8] J. S. Burn, 16.
[9] Since a full list of these pamphlets has never been assembled, all that have come to light are named in the Appendix. There are no doubt others.

bill, any minister who conducted such a marriage would in future be treated as guilty of a felony, without benefit of clergy. The first draft left open the possibility of death by hanging, but this was later softened to transportation for fourteen years.[10] This ferocious clause effectively put an abrupt end to the Mayfair and Fleet marriage problem.

Third, recent cases of highly unsuitable secret marriages by minors, some of them by daughters of men of rank and property to rapacious fortune-hunters, and others by their sons to pretty but penniless maidservants, had aroused alarm among many elite parents. To put a stop to this, the bill copied Continental practice in making null and void all marriages of any sort made by a boy or girl under the age of 21 without the consent of parent or guardian. Fourth, all marriages by mere verbal or written contract, in whatever tense, were made null and void, thus ending once and for all the system of contract marriages.

The fifth problem was that of proof of marriage that had so long bothered lawyers, especially in disputed cases of bigamy or inheritance. The difficulty was well described by Hardwicke in a speech in the Lords:

The proof of clandestine marriages as now celebrated is attended with insuperable difficulties. There is no register. The only evidence must be that of the parson, or pretended parson who married the parties. He may be dead. In the multiplicity of faces he may not remember. He will remember or not as he is paid by either side in the dispute. If he does remember, he is infamous and will not be credited in a court of justice. The inconveniences of this want of proof will be severely felt in the course of years if this practice goes on.[11]

The solution finally devised by the Commons was to add a clause stating that a marriage was null and void unless an entry was recorded in a parish register and signed by the bride, and groom, at least two witnesses, and the officiating clergyman. Parliament also reinforced the ecclesiastical procedure which dated back to 1600, by which a copy of each register was to be sent to the bishop annually for safe-keeping. This would act as a precaution against later alterations or deletions of the original record. In addition, tampering with, inserting, or destroying an entry was made a felony punishable by death. Hardwicke noted with satisfaction that this clause made an entry in a parish register 'almost irrefragible by any other evidence'.[12] In future the lawyers would have the hard evidence they needed.

The arguments for and against the bill ranged around a very limited number of issues, many of which were, or were alleged to be, of great import to religion, the constitution, the family, and society. They came up repeatedly in the debates in both Houses, and again in the subsequent

---

[10] BL., Add. MSS 35880, fos. 1–15.   [11] Ibid. fo. 75ᵛ.   [12] Ibid. fo. 73.

pamphlet war from 1753 to 1755. Those in favour of the bill urged the unquestioned need to close down the Mayfair and Fleet marriage business. They also emphasized the need to clarify what did or did not constitute a marriage, so as to settle once and for all legal cases of bigamy and legitimacy.

They claimed that marriage was a contract like any other, and that it was therefore within the powers of the secular legislature to regulate it and establish the circumstances under which it was null and void. The clause nullifying any marriage of a minor under 21 made without the consent of parents or guardians was defended as reasonable and necessary, in view of the alleged frequency of rash, foolish, and improvident marriages by eldest sons, and those of heiresses to purely mercenary adventurers. It would offer protection to rich parents, without unduly limiting the freedom of their children, who could always wait until they were 21 in order to marry the person of their choice. Supporters cited the example of most of the countries of Europe, such as France and Holland, where the parental veto applied to children as old as 25 or 30.

The objection that by this bill the legislature would nullify a sacred and indissoluble contract of marriage performed by a clergyman was brushed aside by Attorney-General Ryder with the characteristic Enlightenment comment: 'Thank God we have in this age got the better of this, as well as we have of a great many other, superstitious opinions.' He thanked the bishops for supporting the bill, thereby 'consenting to render Christianity consonant with common sense'. Ryder went on to let the cat out of the bag by observing, with reference to the clause about the need for parental consent if under 21 'If it were possible, I confess that a distinction should be made between the marriages of persons of rank and fortune, and those of the people we usually call the vulgar; but this it is impossible to do in this country.'[13] In short, the bill was really what the propertied classes wanted, but it would have to apply to the poor as well.

Opponents of the bill questioned the authority of Parliament to nullify a marriage which was still binding by canon law, raised frightening visions of the likely socio-political consequences of the bill, and fought bitterly against any increase of parental power over marriage. An early nineteenth-century writer on the law of marriage, Mr Jacob, wrote: 'An opinion was commonly entertained that matrimony ordained and regulated by the divine law, was not to be treated as a human institution, and was not a proper subject for the interference of the civil legislature.'[14] Some clergy

[13] *Parl. Hist.* 15: 6, 11.
[14] E. Jacob, quoted in Bright, 2: 369. This was the first objection of *Gent's. Mag.* (1753), 23: 400; (1768), 38: 361.

also protested that it was unfair to single out the clerical performers of clandestine marriage for the harsh punishment of transportation while allowing the bridegrooms to go scot-free.

More serious was the repeated allegation that the real purpose of the bill was to give parents of rank and fortune a veto power over the marriage of their children, a proposal which had been introduced frequently into Parliament since 1690 and always hitherto defeated. This continued to be a bone of contention, and as late as 1823 it was said that the act was passed 'for purpose of protecting patrimony against matrimony'.[15]

The main argument levelled against the proposal to nullify all clandestine marriages was that this would end a form of marriage which, however discreditable, was clearly extremely popular because it was quick, cheap, and easy. The argument ran that in future marriage would become more difficult, more embarrassing (because of the obligation to put up the banns), more expensive (because of the fees), and slower (thanks to the month's residence requirement and time for the banns to be read). The point was made that such an act might work perfectly well in countries such as France or Italy, where the young were kept carefully segregated. But 'in England, where the youth of both sexes are so often in company together, shutting up the way which leads to matrimony opens that which must tend to fornication'. A Tory, John Shebbeare, asked rhetorically: 'Can passion be restrained by law, and human hearts be governed like watches, turned to go faster or slower, as the bearer pleases?'[16] Shebbeare and others rejected the parental veto clause as not only a threat to liberty but as an unworkable restraint upon the twin irresistible passions of love and sexual desire. They prophesied widespread cohabitation, not an increase in church marriages.

A somewhat illogical deduction from the forecast of fewer marriages and more fornication and concubinage was that the result would be a serious population decline. Since a large population was needed as a labour force for a growing economy and as cannon-fodder to fight the endless wars with France, the bill would in the long run undermine the economic and military strength of England. Far-fetched as it may seem, this argument was very widely used, both in the Parliamentary debates and in the pamphlet war, and was repeated by Blackstone.[17]

[15] *Roy. Com. Marriage, PP 1867–8*, 32: 64.
[16] Shebbeare, *The Marriage Act*, 2: 47, 6.
[17] W. Blackstone, *Commentaries on the Laws of England* (Oxford, 1765–9), cited by P. C. Yorke, *The Life and Correspondence of Philip Yorke, Earl of Hardwicke* (Cambridge, 1913), 2: 61: this criticism did not appear in the first (1765) edition, which was published while Lord Hardwicke was still alive.

The parental veto on marriage under 21 was also seen as a great threat to the nation. It was feared that in consequence the landed elite would marry their sons to all the great heiresses of other members of the class, thus accumulating for themselves most of the landed property of the country. They would also monopolize the heiresses of great mercantile fortunes, thereby accumulating much of the liquid capital of the country as well. As a result of the former, opponents foresaw that in time a limited number of great nobles would come to own so much of the property of England that they could control a majority of Parliamentary elections, thus reducing the House of Commons (and the king) to political impotence. According to this paranoid vision, the emergence of an all-powerful and immensely wealthy Venetian oligarchy was inevitable.[18] It was also argued that the tying up of property and liquid capital in a few hands was a threat to a commercial society based on the free market and the circulation of capital. Some even defended the marriage of peers to serving maids on the principle of keeping wealth circulating in society.

In retrospect, few of these arguments against the bill seem very convincing, and it is hardly surprising that the Lords passed it by 100 to 11, the Commons (after many amendments, mostly minor) by 125 to 56, and that the Lords accepted the amended bill without a vote. But it should not be forgotten that the bill aroused strong passions, and that the debates were extremely long and bitter; one of the debates in the Commons over the nullity clause lasted until half past three in the morning.[19] Contemporaries were well aware of the enormous significance of what they were doing. What is remarkable, however, is that so much rather far-fetched opposition should have been mounted against a bill which most legislators clearly favoured. After all, there were many reasons why those represented in Parliament should have wanted to put a stop to all forms of clandestine marriages and secret contract marriages. Men of property were above all afraid of losing control over the marriage of their under-age children, who as things stood were in a position to defy their parents by slipping out of the house, hurrying with their lovers to Ludgate Hill, and getting themselves married within the hour. Lawyers and judges were tired of dealing with cases of bigamy dependent on unprovable allegations of Fleet marriages, based on unreliable testimony and the equally suspect Fleet Registers. The respectable parish clergy were anxious to recover for themselves the marriage fees of their parishioners, which in the London area were being largely siphoned off by the clandestine marriage trade.

[18] The same prognostication of constitutional disaster was voiced in 1762–3 in Oliver Goldsmith's *Vicar of Wakefield* (ed. A. Friedman (London, 1974), 97).

[19] Walpole, *Memoirs of George II*, 1: 336–49.

They also looked forward to forcing the Dissenters back to the Anglican church to obtain legally valid marriages. The state was anxious to stop the substantial loss of revenue from stamp duty on marriage licences and bonds. Finally, it was obvious to all that the whole Mayfair and Fleet marriage business was a scandal to 'the holy state of matrimony', and 'a reproach . . . upon our nation' in the eyes of foreigners.[20]

2. From 1753 to 1868

The passing of the Marriage Act of 1753 spelled the end of the thousands of squalid clandestine marriages carried out in the Rules of the Fleet. It put a damper on rural clandestine marriages conducted by impecunious clergy on the basis of licences obtained by perjury from venal surrogates, and it effectively destroyed any vestiges of contract marriages. Most of the Fleet parsons hastened to shut up shop, but not before gorging themselves with windfall profits from the rush of business in the last weeks before the act came into force. One rash but enterprising clergyman who tried to fill the gap was the incumbent of the Savoy Chapel, for which he claimed legal immunity on the grounds that it was under royal patronage. He married 353 couples in 1754 and no fewer than 1,190 in 1755. But in the following year he and another clergyman were tried and convicted at the Old Bailey on a charge of conducting clandestine marriages, and were duly sentenced to fourteen years' transportation to America. This effectively made the point that the ruling elite at last meant business.[21]

In fact, however, the English Parliament had been lagging way behind that in Ireland, which had been the first to make the conduct of a clandestine marriage a penal offence, largely in order to stop secret marriages of Protestants with Catholics.[22] Consequently, the first and last clergyman who suffered death for performing a clandestine marriage was one Sewell, who was executed in Dublin in 1740. In his speech from the scaffold he observed that 'the miserable provision made for the inferior clergy, still more miserable by their numbers and their generally ill-judged early marriages, throws them upon things which often endanger their bread and sometimes their lives, of which I am a wretched instance'.[23]

It would be foolish to suppose, however, that the Hardwicke Marriage Act of 1753 accomplished all that it set out to do. It is reasonable to assume that among the lower levels of the middling sort in the London area, who had been the principal patrons of the old clandestine marriage and contract system, most must at last have been obliged to conform to the

---

[20] Yorke, *Philip Yorke*, 2: 121.   [21] *OB Proc.* (1756), 47–53, 263–72; (1757), 351.
[22] 9 Geo II cap. 11; 19 Geo II cap. 13; quoted in Gally, 27.
[23] *The Last Speech of Mr Sewell* (London, 1740), (BL, 1890 e 5 (193)).

rules, while others relapsed into concubinage. Whether the act accomplished much more, however, is doubtful. In the first place, Parliament had no powers to change canon law, and in any case the act itself left many loopholes. Those from the upper middling sort and the quality now almost invariably sought privacy by marriage by licence, not always in their church of residence. This was made possible by what was later called 'the Lord Holland clause', which had been forced on Lord Hardwicke by the active lobbying of Henry Fox, later Lord Holland. Under this clause, a false statement of place of residence on a licence did not nullify a marriage. Taking advantage of this loophole, it was said that numbers of well-to-do couples lied about their place of residence when obtaining a licence from a surrogate. Other couples quietly rented rooms for a month in another parish so as legally to qualify for taking out a licence for marriage in that church, thus *de facto* carrying out a clandestine marriage in full legal fashion.[24]

As for the poor, they were as anxious as ever to avoid a public church wedding in their place of residence, because of their desire for privacy. Others deliberately wished to break the law of marriage, either to marry without parental consent or to commit incest or bigamy. After 1754, the easiest way for a poor young couple to get married legally while both evading the new system and thwarting the wishes of their parents was by visiting a crowded city parish and asking for the banns to be called. Thanks to the population explosion of the late eighteenth century, central-city parish clergy were marrying up to forty couples on a Sunday, so that it was absolutely impossible for them or their clerks to check on the ages or places of residence of all these prospective spouses. Nor was there much chance that news of the marriage would come to the knowledge of the couple's parents, friends, or neighbours back home in their village. Witnesses before the Royal Commission on Marriage of 1867–8 described the current situation in terms almost identical to those used by proponents of the act of 1753. In mid-Victorian England, 'nothing is so easy as to elude discovery of a marriage'.[25]

Whether or not the 1753 Marriage Act served to deter the lower classes from marriage and so encouraged large-scale alleged 'common-law marriage' still remains an open question. There can be no doubt that many contemporaries thought that numbers increased, and there is evidence to support it. The bastardy rate certainly rose sharply in the late eighteenth century, but so did the rate of pre-nuptial conceptions. If consensual unions in fact grew in the late eighteenth and early nineteenth centuries,

[24] Ralph Bigland, *Observations on Marriage* (London, 1764), 56.
[25] *Roy. Com. Marriage, 1868*, 30: 1, 2, 8, 14–15, 36–40, 48–9, 70–2, 165–7.

they seem to have been associated with the social traumas of mass migration, urbanization, and industrialization, or with economic and social backwardness, rather than with the working of the 1753 act.[26] In this context, the injudicious revelation by Attorney-General Ryder at the time that the framers of the bill would have preferred to limit the veto power to parents of rank and wealth takes on peculiar significance. If the poor were in fact driven out of church marriages by the act, it was the accidental result of the inability of the ruling classes openly to create two legal systems of marriage, one for the rich and one for the poor.

Failing England, there was always abroad for those who could afford it. In 1760 it was claimed that there were boats waiting at Southampton to carry run-aways—for a fee of five guineas—to Guernsey where clandestine marriages were still legal.[27] Whether or not this was true is not known, but Guernsey was soon far outstripped by Scotland as a place in which to get married in a hurry. The Scottish Court of Sessions failed to agree to overthrow the ancient Scottish marriage laws permitting contract and private marriages in order to bring that country into line with its neighbour to the south. The result was that a very serious gap opened up in the barrier erected by the 1753 act against such marriages. Those wishing to marry in a clandestine manner had only to cross the border into Scotland in order to do so quickly, and cheaply. This facility caused the rise of a brisk marriage business at Gretna Green, on the main West road as it crossed the border, where clergy stood ready to marry all comers at an instant's notice.[28]

The vast majority of the clients at Gretna Green were poor people who lived within easy walking or riding distance, and in the late eighteenth century, the trade tended to cater to the impulse buyer. For example, in 1792 a bombardier by the name of William James courted a Miss Goodfellow, a minor and an heiress, and they decided to run away to Gretna Green (Plate 14). He took along with him a friend, Richard Harrison, 'in case of a rescue being attempted'. They travelled north on two horses, James on one and Miss Longfellow behind Harrison on the other. The bridegroom stopped on the way to carouse with friends, while Harrison and the bride rode on together. James caught them up and reproached them for 'leaving him on the road'. Miss Goodfellow retorted that she resented his 'want of attention', and a quarrel developed. Harrison tried to intervene, and a fight started between the two men, stopped only by a constable. Miss Goodfellow then said she had decided not to marry James, but 'was resolved not to return home without a

---

[26] Gillis, 196–209, 219.   [27] *Gent's Mag.* (1760), 30: 30–1.
[28] 'Claverhouse' [Meliora Smith], *Irregular Border Marriages* (Edinburgh, 1934); *Gretna Green and its Traditions* (Paisley, 1905).

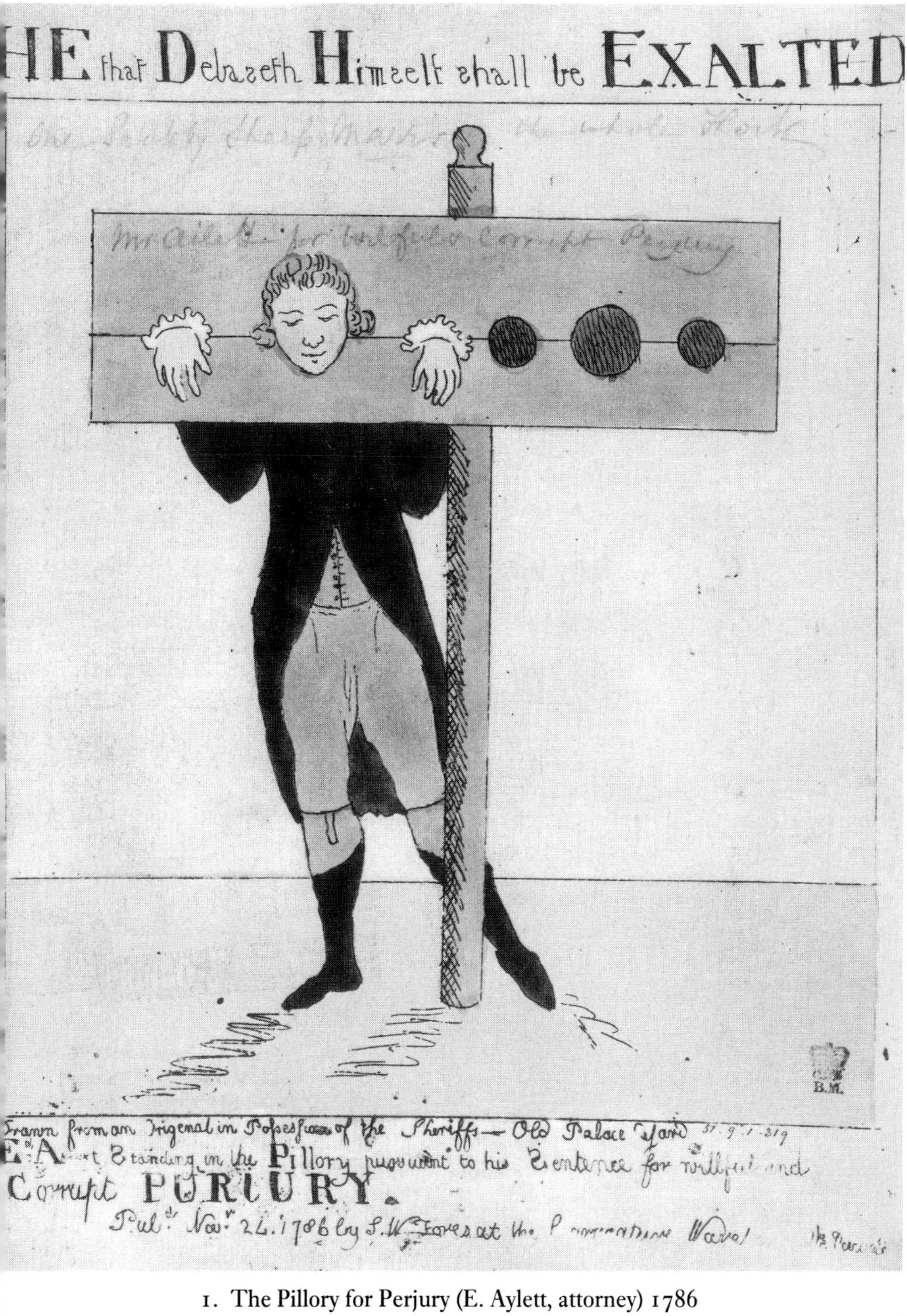

1. The Pillory for Perjury (E. Aylett, attorney) 1786

2. The Court of Arches, by T. Rowlandson, 1808

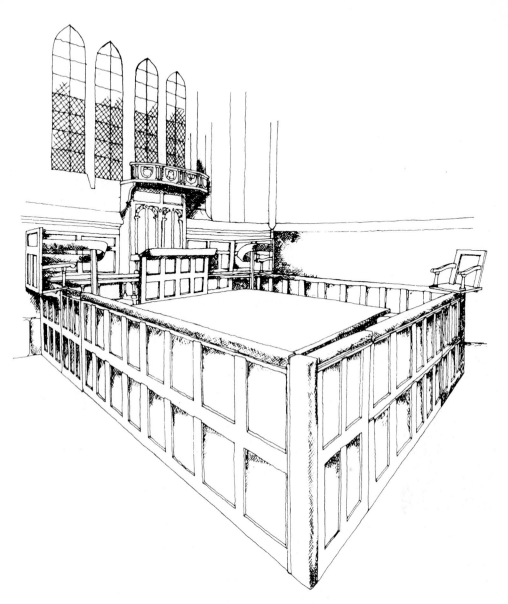

3. The Consistory Court of Chester, in Chester Cathedral

4. The London Consistory Court, Doctors' Commons, 1825: The Suit for Separation of Sir Wastel Brisco

A RECEIPT for COURTSHIP

Two or three dears, and two or three sweets;
Two or three balls, and two or three treats;
Two or three serenades, given as a lure;
Two or three oaths how much they endure;
Two or three messages sent in a day;
Two or three times led out from the play;
Two or three soft speeches made by the way;

Two or three tickets for two or three times;
Two or three love letters writ all in rhymes;
Two or three months keeping strict to these rules,
Can never fail making a couple of fools.

Published Dec'r 9, 1805,
by LAURIE & WHITTLE, 53,
Fleet Street, London.

5. Courtship in High Life, c.1800

6. Courtship in Low Life, by T. Rowlandson, 1785

7. Breach of Promise *c.* 1770

8. £3,000 Damages for Breach of Promise by Mr Hayne to Miss Maria Foote, 1824

9. A Fleet Marriage of an Adventurer to an Elderly Widow, *c.*1730

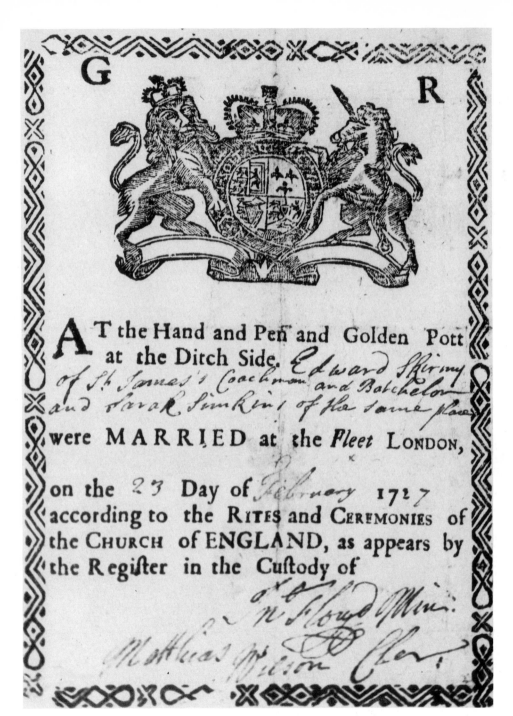

G R

AT the Hand and Pen and Golden Pott at the Ditch Side. *Edward Skirmy of St. James's Coachman and Batchelor and Sarah Simkins of the same place* were MARRIED at the *Fleet* LONDON,

on the *23* Day of *February* 172*7* according to the RITES and CEREMONIES of the CHURCH of ENGLAND, as appears by the Register in the Custody of

Wm. Lloyd Mini: Mathias Wilson Clerk:

10. A Fleet Marriage Certificate

Between a brisk young Sailor & his Landlady's Daughter at Rederiff.

Scarce had the Coach discharg'd its trusty Fare, Pray step this way—just to the Pen in Hand Th' alarmed Parsons quickly hear the Din.
But gaping Crouds surround th' amorous Pair: The Doctor's ready there at your Command: Th' experienc'd. Matron come an artful Guide,
The busy Fryers make a mighty Stir! This way! another cries! Sir I declare She led the way without regarding either.
And whispering cry, d'ye want the Parson, Sir? In this Confusion jostled to and fro, And the first Parson splic'd 'em both together.
  The true and ancient Register is Here: Th' inamour'd Couple know not where to go:

I I. A Street Scene near the Fleet, by W. Hogarth, 1747

12. A Fleet Wedding Feast, c.1747

Within the image: Philip Earl of Hardwicke Viscount Royston apointed Lord High Chancellor Of Great Britain 20 Feb: 1736

13. Lord Chancellor Hardwicke, by T. Hudson, 1736

14. Elopement to Gretna Green, 1789

15. Elopement of Georgiana Lady Astley with Lt Thomas Garth, 1826

16. Lord Eldon Depriving Mr Wellesley Pole of Child Custody, 1827

husband' and was willing to take Harrison instead. He agreed, they set off, and were married a few hours after they had met. Whether the marriage endured, history does not relate.[29]

In addition to catering for poor people from the local area, Gretna Green was also the resort of some members of the rich and titled from the south who wanted a quiet and secret marriage, usually to thwart parental or family control or to cover a pregnancy. For a while, flight to Gretna Green became quite fashionable as a mode of clandestine marriage in polite circles, and Sheridan in 1775 makes his heroine Lydia lament the collapse of her plans: 'There had I projected one of the most sentimental elopements!—so becoming a disguise—so amiable a ladder of ropes!— Conscious moon—four horses—Scotch parson—with such surprise to Mrs Malaprop—and such paragraphs in the newspapers! Oh! I shall die with disappointment.'[30] In 1835, Lord Brougham claimed, with doubtful accuracy, that 'it is well known that at one time the Archbishop of Canterbury, the Lord Chancellor and the Lord Privy Seal were all married at Gretna Green, and had issue after marriage contracted there'.[31]

The marriage-makers of Gretna Green were some of the greatest beneficiaries of the 1753 act, and thanks to improvements in communications by turnpike roads after 1777 the business continued to grow for a century. In its peak year of 1854, 731 couples were married there. This was a substantial number, but it did not approach the many thousands taken care of by the mass industry of the Fleet marriage market in the 1740s. But in the 1850s it was on the edge of a further explosive growth, thanks to the expansion of the railways.

By the end of the eighteenth century, it was clear that most of the arguments by the original opponents of the 1753 Marriage Bill were fallacious. There had been no striking concentration of wealth in the aristocracy, nor any gigantic explosion (so far as we can tell) of fornication and concubinage. But time had shown that there were serious defects in the 1753 act. The first was caused by the failure of the Scots to extend the provisions of the bill north of the border. This had provided a safe haven for clandestine marriages, but at least one which was some two hundred miles from London. Second, the act carefully excluded from its strict provisions marriages by Jews and Quakers, but no provision was made for those of Nonconformists and Catholics.

---

[29] *Lond. Chron.* (1792), 72/2: 500.

[30] R. B. Sheridan, *The Rivals* (1775), v/i; for a less romantic version of what really happened, involving sordid financial haggling with a drunken and semi-literate parson, see *Bon Ton Mag.* 1 (1791), 262–3.

[31] *Speeches of Lord Brougham* (Philadelphia, 1841), 2: 290–1; the Lord Chancellor referred to was clearly Lord Erskine, who was married at Gretna Green in 1820.

Another serious defect of the bill as drafted was that it made null and void any marriage in which there was the slightest mistake, however trivial or accidental, in the wording of the banns or licence with respect to age. It was therefore possible for either spouse, years or even decades later, to annul the marriage because of an error about age, possibly caused by a false statement by him or her self. In other words, the bill accidentally opened up a new avenue for self-divorce, which, it was claimed, was quite commonly used by both husbands and wives. One such case occurred in 1805, when a wife successfully annulled a marriage of eighteen years and in the process bastardized six children. The reason for the annulment was that she herself had deliberately overstated her age by a few weeks, as she was in fact still a minor. In another case, a marriage of twenty-seven years was annulled. Between 1810 and 1822 sixty marriages were annulled by these means in the Consistory Court of London and the Court of Arches. By 1820, however, Sir William Scott, who presided over the Court of Arches, was already working round the edges of the law so as to be able, whenever possible, to refuse to nullify marriages of long standing, despite the terms of the act. His grounds were that 'such an union is not to be dissolved unless by some pressing obligations of law'.[32] These cases occurred in dozens rather than hundreds, but they pushed up the number of nullities in the London Consistory Court and created scandal by giving the appearance of being the equivalent of divorces.[33] As a result of this evidence, in 1823 Parliament passed an act amending the 1753 Marriage Act so as to block this avenue to easy divorce.

Taking advantage of these defects in the working of the act, its old enemies made two attempts to abolish or drastically modify many of its main provisions, in 1765 and 1781. In 1765 it was proposed to abolish the parental veto clause but to retain the clauses enforcing marriage by banns or licence and fool-proof registration. The new bill was vigorously supported by the Duke of Bedford, an old opponent of the 1753 act, who argued that it had been 'calculated to prevent' inconvenient marriages in great families. But in order to save thousands, it has undone millions.' He claimed that there were now more clandestine marriages than ever. The bill barely passed in the Commons, which as usual disliked the parental veto clause, but it was defeated in the Lords thanks to the opposition of Lord Mansfield and the Archbishop of Canterbury, an alliance of the

---

[32] Joseph Phillimore, *The Substance of a Speech of Joseph Phillimore LL.D. in the House of Commons, on Wednesday March 27 1822 . . . on a Bill to Amend the Marriage Act* (London, 1822), 17–32, 43; *Select Committee on the Marriage Law (Scotland) 1849, (PP 1849)*, 12: 24; *Johnston* v. *Parker* (1819), *Eng. Rep.* 161: 1252; *Diddear* v. *Faucet* (1821), ibid. 1421.

[33] For example, there were 28 such nullities in London on grounds of minority in the five years 1813–17; GLRO, London CC, DC/C/627.

leaders of the law and the church. The second bill, introduced by Fox in 1781, passed the Commons by 90 to 27 but was also defeated in the Lords.[34]

Further change only came as a result of three quite different forces at work in early nineteenth-century England: the secularization of society, the demand for law reform in the 1840s and 1850s, and the concurrent idealization of middle-class morality and the domestic hearth. In 1836, the trend towards secularization resulted in the provision, for the first time in English history apart from a brief period in the 1650s, of purely secular marriage by a public registrar.[35] In practice, this set up a two-track system for marriage in England. One was conducted by a minister in holy orders in a church or chapel, and regarded as a sacred religious ceremony. The other was conducted by a state official in an office, and regarded as a purely secular contract. It was swift and cheap, and was intended to lure the poor back into matrimony.

Over the next 150 years, civil marriage gained recognition and popularity only very slowly. In 1844, six years after the act setting up the civil marriage procedure, the percentage of all first marriages by a registrar was under 3 per cent, and by 1904 it was still only 18 per cent. Growth continued at the same slow steady pace until 1962 when it reached 30 per cent.[36] Thus, up to 1962, church weddings were still holding their own to a remarkable extent, and it is only in this last twenty-five years that there has occurred an explosive growth of civil first marriages that reflects the collapse of regular church-going in late twentieth-century England (Table 5.1, Fig. 5.1).

Oddly enough, it took longer to reform the law by closing the loophole opened up by English couples marrying by clandestine contracts across the border at Gretna Green. For nearly a century, the English courts were unable to decide whether a Gretna Green marriage was legally valid in England, so as to legitimate the children and justify the transmission of property. Lord Mansfield first declared such marriages to be void in English law since they were performed in order to defraud the 1753 Marriage Act. Later, however, this view was challenged, and a long period of uncertainty followed.[37] Things got so confused that in the late eighteenth century the validity of a Gretna Green marriage was admitted

---

[34] BL, Add. MSS 35880, fos. 110, 163–7; see Poynter, 63–71.

[35] 6–7 W IV cap. 86.

[36] *Registrar General's Statistical Review of England and Wales for 1967*, P. iii (London, 1971), 15; J. Haskey, 'Trends in Marriages: Church, Chapel and Civil Ceremonies', *Great Britain Population Trends*, 22 (1980).

[37] Remarks by Lord Brougham in 1849 (*Select Committee on the Marriage Law (Scotland) 1849 (PP 1849)*, 12: 18).

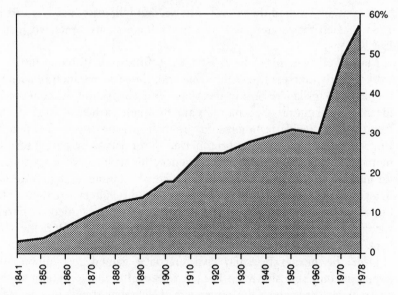

FIGURE 5.1   Proportion of First Marriages in Civil Registry Offices (England and Wales) 1841–1978 [Table 5.1]

by the ecclesiastical courts and the Court of Common Pleas, but denied by the Court of King's Bench.[38] As a result of these many anomalies, by 1844 the 1753 act was widely regarded as full of 'inconsistencies and inequities', and in its pre-1823 form as a disgrace to the statute book.[39]

Despite this state of confusion, when Lord Brougham introduced a bill in 1835 to prevent English runaways taking advantage of Gretna Green marriages it was defeated in Parliament. He only got his way twenty-one years later, in 1856, when he introduced a new bill which declared that a Gretna Green marriage of an English couple was not legally valid in England unless it had been preceded by three weeks' residence in Scotland. The main reason for the easy passage of the bill was the well-founded fear that the newly built railways would flood Gretna Green with swarms of fresh clients from all parts of England. For the poor the act made the enterprise too expensive and slow, while for the rich it provided time for family intervention in the affair before the marriage took place. As a result, the act effectively put a stop to the traffic.[40]

[38] *Eng. Rep.* 162: 331, 336–40.
[39] *Law Review* (1845), 152; J. Stoddart, *A Letter to Lord Brougham on the Opinions of the Judges in the Irish Marriage Cases* (London, 1844), 67.
[40] 3 *Hansard*, 142: 205–6; 19–20 Vict. cap. 96.

3. Conclusion

It is not too strong to say that the marriage law as it operated in practice in England from the fourteenth to the nineteenth centuries was a mess. The church asserted that mere verbal consent, freely given and duly witnessed, constituted a binding marriage. But common law denied the effect on the transmission of property of these private contracts. After wrestling with the problem of proof for centuries, the church courts slowly came to the conclusion that the problem was insoluble, and evaded the law by virtually denying all but fully proven contracts. Meanwhile the propertied laity refused to renounce control over the marriages of their children, or at the very least their authority to advise and consent.

Unlike in all other Protestant and Roman Catholic countries, nothing was done at the Reformation to change the situation. As the Church of England increased its authority in the late sixteenth and early seventeenth centuries, it forced or persuaded more and more of the population away from contract marriages and into open church ceremonies. But as a reaction to this pressure, and as a result of the collapse of the institutional structure of clerical marriage in the 1650s, there began to spread, with the complicity of venal surrogates and impoverished curates, the practice of the clandestine church marriage performed illegally by an ordained clergyman. Between 1696 and 1712, Parliament tried to shut down the clandestine marriage system because the state was losing revenue from the tax of marriages and the stamp duty on licences and certificates of marriage. But the legislation did little to suppress clandestine marriages in the countryside and it positively stimulated the explosion of a very large-scale clandestine marriage market in the Rules of the Fleet Prison and in a few privileged 'Peculiar' churches in London which had immunity from the law.

Lord Hardwicke's Marriage Act of 1753 certainly shut down the Fleet marriage market but it was quite unable to stop lower class concubinage supported by local custom, flight over the border to Gretna Green, and the widespread practice of having the banns published not in the parish church of residence but in the safe anonymity of big urban churches. Although the more scandalous practices of the Fleet parsons were certainly brought to an end, in 1868 the rules governing marriage were not much more strictly obeyed then than they had been before 1753. The reason for this was that the act flew directly in the face of a rising tide of demand, fuelled partly by individualism and romanticism but above all by a dogged desire for privacy, itself a product of the traditional freedom of pre-marital social relations and sexual experimentation among the English poor.

Moreover, the common law, equity law in Chancery, and ecclesiastical law continued to be at odds with one another over many aspects of marriage, while judges in the same courts continued to hold different views about the laws of evidence and the validity of marriage, thus leaving in a fog of uncertainty rights to property, dower, jointure, inheritance, and the legitimacy of children. There was no certainty concerning what did or did not constitute a marriage; the means for evasion of the law were easily available; and large numbers one way or another either contrived to be married in ways which defied the laws concerning incest, bigamy, or consent, or else were not legally married at all.

The root cause of the trouble was that there was no consensus within society at large about how a legally binding marriage should be carried out. Popular custom took one position, the church another, and the state and the propertied laity a third. After 1753, Scotland and Ireland were out of step with England.

In the eighteenth century, the JPs had no interest in taking up the control of sexuality where the church courts left off, except to try to curb the rising tide of illegitimacy because it represented a burden on the poor rate. Parliament was at odds within itself, the House of Commons and the House of Lords repeatedly taking different sides on proposals to reform the law of marriage. The Lords naturally favoured parental veto over marriage of minors, while the Commons, which contained many heiress-seeking younger sons and small gentry, naturally opposed it. Legal and clerical vested interests grew up to protect the *status quo*, however scandalous it might seem. As a result there was vociferous, if in fact minoritarian, opposition on religious, political, libertarian, and demographic grounds against the 1753 Marriage Act.

In any case, the English were at best a largely ungovernable people, and after about 1690 no one tried very hard to do more than tax them. The principle of liberty conflicted with the desire for order, while the pluralistic structures of the state, the church, and the courts of law prevented concerted action, and widespread revulsion against 'enthusiasm' stifled moral reform movements. 'Old Corruption' flourished in every nook and cranny of the state, the church, the law, and the universities, thus providing a solid vested interest against change. Not even the powerful practical need for the protection of dynastic inheritance and the powerful ideology surrounding property were sufficient to erect a legal system of marriage that offered comprehensive protection to those interests and ideas. Nothing serious was done before the act of 1753, and even this was a partial failure. In 1773 *The Lady's Magazine* argued that 'no law was ever made since the Revolution that has occasioned so many broken hearts, unhappy lives, and accumulated distresses as this has'.[41] After 1753 the law was in direct conflict with the principle of affective individualism with regard to the free choice of a spouse. Only the early Victorians were able partially to break the log-jam by extensive enquiry and legislation, but even they had little control over the swarming poor in the new industrial cities.

The result was a condition of moral and legal confusion which appeared to many thoughtful contemporaries from the sixteenth to the nineteenth centuries to maximize insecurity, misery, and disappointment. Except in terms of an endless confused conflict between deeply entrenched vested interests, it is impossible to advance a plausible functionalist interpretation of the twists and turns of the law of marriage in England from the sixteenth to the nineteenth centuries. It was the product of a complex historical evolution in which law, ethics, and social behaviour were continually at loggerheads. Reform moved at a snail's pace over the centuries, and the standard sequence of events was first a change in social attitudes and behaviour, then a change in judicial interpretation of the law, and finally, up to a century after the shift had begun, a change in statutory legislation. But the legislation itself was always something of a disappointment. It almost never achieved all that it set out to do, and it usually created unexpected and unwanted side-effects. The public almost always found a way to get around the law for their own purposes, but the cost in human misery was very high.

[41] *The Lady's Magazine* (1773), 4: 131.

PART TWO

The Breaking of Marriage

Many a man wants a wife, but more want to get rid of one.
H. Fielding, *Don Quixote In England* (1734), I/iv

❧ VI ❧

Desertion, Elopement, and Wife-sale

1. Modes of Marital Break-up

There were five distinct ways in which the break-up of a marriage could be achieved in England in the early modern period, only two of which involved litigation. The first of these was by suing in the church courts for separation from bed and board, without permission to remarry. This could be obtained on the two grounds of adultery and/or life-threatening cruelty. The second was by full divorce by act of Parliament, with permission to remarry. This could be obtained between 1690 and 1857, but only by the handful of husbands who could afford it, and whose wives had committed adultery.

The third method, which was confined to the middling and better sort, was by a 'private separation'. This was an agreement to part, negotiated between the two spouses and embodied in a deed of separation drawn up by a conveyancer. For the poor who possessed little or no property, the normal procedure was simply desertion or elopement. Husbands with a little property sometimes adopted a different strategy to achieve the same end. They either ejected their wives and locked them out of the house, or themselves set up a new household elsewhere with a mistress. Another, but much rarer, method of separation for those with a little property was by the ritual of wife-sale, a custom unique to Britain and New England, by which a husband publicly sold to another man not only his wife but also all legal responsibility for her and her upkeep.

2. Elopement and Desertion

For those with little or no property, the most obvious method of breaking a marriage was to leave home. Not a few wives were forced to leave in order to escape from repeated and possibly life-threatening cruelty. Most of this cruelty was a product of poverty, brutality, and alcohol; some of it was clearly the product of pure sadism; some of it was caused by the psychological frustration of the husband at being trapped for life in a household with a woman he had come to hate. But occasionally, cruelty was deliberately used to force the wife to supply more money: either by persuading her parents to give a larger marriage portion, or by inducing her to surrender control over property which had been secured to her by a trust deed before marriage.[1]

Some wives who were battered, mistreated, or merely neglected decided to carve out a new life for themselves and eloped with a lover, sometimes taking with them a considerable quantity of household goods. They were the ones who tended most often to end up in court, but they were probably also the ones with the most promising future ahead of them. These elopements (Plate 15) commonly occurred after ten to fifteen years of marriage, when either the wives could no longer endure their ill-treatment or had fallen in love with someone else. Often the two went together.

The options for men were more extensive. The simplest was just to desert—to walk out of the house one day and never come back. The financial results for a wife and children suddenly deprived of the main wage-earner could be catastrophic, and many ended up on the poor relief rolls. Among the poor it is impossible to quantify the scale of husbandly desertion. One indication of how widespread it was is that in the 1580s a census taken of the poor in the city of Norwich showed that deserted wives comprised nearly a tenth of all the women on relief, and a quarter of those on relief who lacked husbands.[2] Throughout the eighteenth century, around 6 per cent of all women in south-east England who applied for poor relief were abandoned wives, a proportion which rose after 1780 because of the number of husbands who left home to serve as soldiers in the wars. Among the poor, enlistment appears to have been 'the institutionally accepted form of family desertion'. These abandoned wives, over half of whom were left with children to support, seem to have survived for about two years before being forced to ask for relief. In the end, however, desertion by their husbands drove them down to the extreme depths of degradation, poverty, and despair.[3]

The majority of runaway husbands seem to have moved into another county and settled down to a new life with a new woman, living either in concubinage or tied by a verbal contract or by a bigamous clandestine or church marriage. One gets the strong impression that the number of bigamists in early modern England must have been quite large. Detection was difficult, and even when proved, the case could only come to trial if one or both of the two wives was sufficiently angered to launch a prosecution at her own expense.

---

[1] See Stone, *Broken Lives*.
[2] J. F. Pound, *The Norwich Census of the Poor, 1570*, Suffolk Record Soc. 40: 18.
[3] K. D. M. Snell, *Annals of the Labouring Poor: Social Change and Agrarian England, 1660–1900* (Cambridge, 1985), 2. 361–2, Table 7. 8.

In theory, bigamy was a penal offence carrying the death penalty, but in practice it was mitigated by benefit of clergy. Thus, throughout the eighteenth century there were only a few dozen trials for bigamy in the Old Bailey, which covered all London and Middlesex, and none of those convicted suffered death. After pleading benefit of clergy, they were sentenced to be burnt in the thumb with a hot iron, a relatively mild punishment, especially if the executioner was bribed to keep the iron not too hot and the time of contact with the skin not too long.[4] By the 1760s it was asserted in court that such burning was 'constantly and notoriously done in the face, and with the knowledge of the judges themselves, with a cold iron'.[5] In the 1790s, however, the penalty for bigamy was changed to transportation for seven years without benefit of clergy, and the number of convicted offenders went up sharply. The chances of being prosecuted for bigamy were still quite small in the early nineteenth century, but if it occurred, and the defendant was convicted, his chances of a sentence of transportation were high.

Instead of merely deserting, the husband sometimes closed down the house and sold the furniture, in order to deprive his wife of a roof over her head. The defect of such a procedure was that it rendered the husband liable to be sued by his wife in a church court for 'restitution of conjugal rights'.[6]

3. Wife-sale

Among the poor who could not afford to pay maintenance, amicable separations by mutual consent were presumably quite common, but the problem remained of how to annul all the legal and financial obligations of marriage. How could a husband be sure that he might not find himself liable to arrest for debts run up unbeknown to him by his separated wife? How could he be sure that after his death his wife would not suddenly reappear and put in a claim for a third of his estate as dower? On the other hand, how could a separated wife prevent her husband from intermittently raiding her home and seizing all her goods and earnings, which by law were still his? Moreover, how could she be certain that, if she started a new household, her ex-husband might not suddenly decide to sue her lover for 'criminal conversation', and levy crippling damages?

The best way was by a written deed of separation, accompanied by a bond to be forfeited if the terms of the deed were broken. Many, however, were too poor to afford such luxuries; they simply parted company and

---

[4] *OB Proc., passim.*   [5] *Rex* v. *Beardmore* (1759), *Eng. Rep.* 97: 565.
[6] See below, 194*d.*

hoped for the best. Another way, of which much has been made in recent years, was a kind of public self-divorce, namely wife-sale. The origins of such a practice go back to the late sixteenth and seventeenth centuries, when it was common practice to exchange money for rights over persons, including occasionally wives. A paradox of this story is that it was in pre-modern England that the bartered bride was common and the sale of a wife began, and that it was in modern England of the Victorian period that both practices became morally objectionable. The church courts of the sixteenth century were much opposed to such practices; they prosecuted offenders (on the very rare occasions on which they found them) and sentenced them to perform public penance.[7] But the practice lingered on, the church courts decayed, and the new rigour of the 1753 Marriage Act seems to have stimulated a rapid increase in the frequency, and a standardization of the procedure, of wife-sale all over southern England and the Midlands (Table 6.1, Fig. 6.1).[8]

The ritual employed is accurately described by a commentator in 1777:

Among the common people, a method is sometimes practised of dissolving a marriage, no less singular than compendious. When a husband and wife find themselves heartily tired of each other, and agree to part; if the man has a mind to authenticate the intended separation by making it a matter of public notoriety, thinking, with Petruchio, that his wife is his goods and chattels, he puts a halter about her neck, and thereby leads her to the next market place, and there puts her up to auction to be sold to the best bidder, as though she was a brood-mare or a milch-cow. A purchaser is generally provided beforehand on these occasions; for it can hardly be supposed, that the *delicate* female would submit to such public indignity unless she was sure of being purchased when brought to market. To the highest bidder, the husband, by delivering up the end of the halter, makes a formal and absolute surrender of his wife, and, as he imagines, at once absolves her and himself from all the obligations incident to marriage!—Although there are none so high as to be above the notice of the law; yet it should seem by this instance, there are some so low as to disregard its notice, thinking mutual consent law enough to set them free, little dreading remorse of conscience, and less the anathemas of the church.[9]

The key ingredient of the ritual was maximum publicity, obtained by its taking place on market day in a cattle market. This publicity guaranteed the active concurrence of the community in legitimizing the transfer. The

---

[7] Menafee, 211; Marchant, 241–2; R. W. Malcolmson, *Life and Labour in England* (London, 1981), 103–4; B. Hair, *Before the Bawdy Court: Selections from Church Court and Other Records relating to the Correction of Moral Offences in England, Scotland and New England, 1300–1800* (New York, 1972), 136.

[8] For the geographical distribution see Menafee, 33.

[9] *The Laws Respecting Women*, 55.

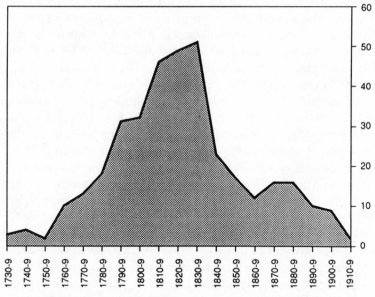

FIGURE 6.1   Recorded Wife-sales 1730–1919 [Table 6.1]

motive behind the sale was the pursuit of personal happiness, in that the husband wanted to be rid of his wife, she was already attracted to the purchaser, and the purchaser wanted her. The ritual always did no more than give public recognition to a pre-arranged agreement between all three parties.

The details of the ritual were designed to emphasize the final nature of the transfer of property, by imitating as closely as possible the sale of a cow or a sheep. A halter was used to lead the wife from her home to the market, and from the market to the house of the purchaser; money was paid in exchange for her; and the seller paid the clerk of the market a toll for his wife, just as he would have done if he had sold a cow. To make the parallel with a cattle sale closer still, some early sales even involved the nominal selling of the wife by her weight. After the sale, all three participants commonly went to an ale-house, where the seller spent some of the purchase money on drinks all round. The wife often removed and returned her wedding ring to the man who was in her eyes her now ex-husband.

All this elaborate symbolism had a very real purpose, which was to try to make the sale appear as legally binding as possible, especially with respect to any future financial responsibility by the husband for the wife. Every effort was made to transfer from the legal husband to the other man all obligations for support, debt payment, and dower, and where there was a change of residence to shift from one parish to another the possible burden on the poor rate of the wife and any future children. In the late eighteenth century, a few careful wife-sellers tried to reinforce the public ritual by a written deed of sale. In one, drawn up in 1766, the husband sold for six guineas 'all rights, property claim, services and demands whatsoever'. In another, drawn up in 1815, a Mr Osborn 'does agree to part with my wife Mary Osborn and child to Mr William Sergeant for the sum of one pound, consideration of giving up all claim whatever'.[10]

In practice, however, whenever a wife-sale was tested in the courts, it was declared invalid, illegal, and immoral. In 1699, a case came before the King's Bench in which a wife sued her first husband for dower. When her husband pleaded that she had eloped, she retorted that he had sold her to her lover. The court decided that the defence of a wife-sale, even if proven, was no bar to an action for dower, but that it would be important in mitigating damages if the husband attempted a suit for criminal conversation.[11] In 1763, Lord Mansfield, in King's Bench, cited a case in Chancery before Lord Chancellor Hardwicke in which the latter had ordered the seller prosecuted on the grounds that such a sale was 'notoriously and grossly against public decency and good manners'. But he refrained from saying anything about its legal consequences.[12]

Even as the number of recorded cases mushroomed in the late eighteenth century, so opposition to the procedure by the upper classes grew. Rightly or wrongly, it was seen as part of that web of popular customs, pastimes, sports, and manners, which the elite believed it was their duty to extirpate from a modernizing society.[13] Especially after the moral panic of the 1790s, the JPs in Quarter Sessions became much more active in punishing participants in these rituals, while some test cases in the central law courts left no doubt as to the illegality of the whole procedure.

For a long while, these legal assaults did nothing to stop wife-sales, reports of which rose from two per decade in the 1750s to a peak of fifty in the 1820s and 1830s (Fig. 6.1). By the 1790s, the comment was uniformly adverse whenever these sales were mentioned in the press. In 1799, for example, *The Times* reported a London sale in the following terms:

---

[10] C. Kenny, 'Wife-Selling in England', *Law Quarterly Review*, 45 (1929), 496; Gillis, 211.

[11] *Coot* v. *Berty* (1699), *Eng. Rep.* 88: 1283–4; for crim. con. see below, ch. IX.

[12] Lord Mansfield took the same severe line against parents trying to sell a daughter as a rich man's mistress; *Laws Respecting Women*, 56; *Rex* v. *Delaval* (1763), *Eng. Rep.* 97: 915; 1283–4.

[13] R. W. Malcolmson, *Life and Labour*.

On Friday a butcher exposed his wife to sale in Smithfield Market, near the Ram Inn, with a halter about her neck, and one about her waist, which tied her to a railing; when a hog-driver was the happy purchaser, who gave the husband three guineas and a crown for his departed rib. Pity it is there is no stop put to such depraved conduct in the lower order of people.[14]

If the graph in Fig. 6.1 is even roughly correct, what is surprising is that it took the magistrates so long to get a grip on this particular example of lower-class 'depravity'. Although by 1819 it was claimed that wife-sales were 'of late years punished with laudable severity',[15] it was not until the 1840s that the number of cases reported per decade dropped precipitously. This stamping out of the procedure allowed the embarassed judges of England, when reproached by their foreign colleagues, flatly to deny that Englishmen sold their wives like cattle in a cattle market.[16] By 1853 a legal handbook could dismiss the whole business as a popular myth: 'It is a vulgar error that a husband can get rid of his wife by selling her in the open market with a halter round her neck. Such an act on his part would be severely punished by the local magistrate.'[17]

A whole book has been written about wife-sales, and in recent years it has aroused considerable interest among historians of popular culture.[18] It is very doubtful, however, whether the use of the ritual of the cattle market was very ancient, and even whether the reported numbers are not seriously inflated by rumour, hearsay, and scandal. It is disturbing to note how many alleged cases in the boom period of the late eighteenth and early nineteenth centuries were reported in local newspapers across the country, but not in those in the region where they were supposed to have occurred.[19] It is possible, of course, that local sales were only news elsewhere, since everyone in the area knew about them. But many newspaper reports of punishments at Quarter Sessions also do not appear in the official records.[20]

It therefore seems very likely that a number of the newspaper reports and of stories told by old people to gullible late Victorian folklorists were based on fictional hearsay, told and retold for their sensational news value. In every case of which detailed accounts survive, it is clear that huge crowds collected to watch the proceedings. For example, in 1806, an attempted wife-sale in Hull had to be postponed 'owing to the crowd which such an extraordinary occurrence had gathered together'.[21] This

---

[14] *The Times*, 18 July 1797.   [15] Menafee, 233.   [16] See below, 291–2.
[17] Wharton, 312.   [18] Menafee, *passim*; Gillis, 211–19; Kenny, 'Wife-selling'.
[19] Menafee, items 88, 121, 142, 167, 184, 185, 195, 202.
[20] Ibid., items 155, 162, 163, 169.
[21] G. O. W. Mueller, 'An Enquiry into the State of a Divorceless Society', *University of Pittsburgh Law Review*, 18 (1956–7), 569.

strongly suggests that a wife-sale was in fact a very infrequent event, and that it was its extreme rarity, as well as its scandalous nature, which gave it a high publicity value for the expanding local newspapers of England.

We can be reasonably confident that fewer than three hundred cases of wife-sale occurred in all England during the peak seventy years from 1780 to 1850. Thus, wife-sales pale to insignificance compared with the thousands of unreported desertions and elopements which must have been taking place during this period. Magistrates' orders for maintenance issued in the late Victorian period prove that temporary desertions alone were by then running at tens of thousands a year.[22] It is impossible to believe that this was a wholly new development. Wife-sale, therefore, was no more than a very rare occurrence, which for about half a century attracted attention far beyond its true significance, largely because of its news value. The attention devoted to the procedure by historians in recent years is explicable by the current anthropological interest in symbolic ritual, of which wife-sale is a striking example.

[22] See below, Table 13.3.

❧ VII ☙

Private Separation

It is a constant practice to resort to separation by agreement.
Dr Stephen Lushington, LL.D. [Judge of the London Consistory Court] in
1844 (*Roy. Com. Divorce, 1853*, vol. 1. *Minutes of Evidence*, 45)

1. The Early History of the Private Separation Deed, 1650–1760

A. ORIGINS C.1650

Informal private separation agreements sprang up in the 1650s as a response to the administrative chaos during the Interregnum. This sort of *ad hoc* improvisation was made necessary by the abolition of the old ecclesiastical court system and the failure of the Commonwealth or Protectorate to put anything in its place. The judicial administration of separation and divorce virtually collapsed from about 1644 to 1660, while the law of marriage remained throughout the whole period in a state of confusion.[1]

As a result, the civil magistrates were left to handle matrimonial and sexual problems as best they could. An example of such improvisation is revealed in a letter by a village rector to the Consistory Court of Worcester in 1662, written in reply to a request for a full account of how a couple in the village had come to be separated several years before. He explained that Mrs Packwood had left her husband's house and obstinately refused to return. She had come before a local JP, Mr Townshend, and asked for permission to continue to live separately from her husband. The JP not only had agreed but had settled the financial terms, thus giving a separation agreement the sanction of the law. The rector added that Mrs Packwood still wished to live separately, and was very unwilling to return home. He said that he approved of this arrangement, since she had been a lazy and improvident wife, and he hoped the court would not interfere to force an unwilling couple back together again.

---

[1] K. Wrightson, 'The Nadir of English Illegitimacy in the Seventeenth Century', in P. Laslett, K. Osterveen, and R. M. Smith (eds), *Bastardy and its Comparative History* (Cambridge, Mass., 1980), 184.

What is here revealed is a kind of proto-separation agreement, the work of a local JP improvising as he went along.[2]

It has to be assumed that private separations occurred before 1640, especially among the landed élite, but there are several reasons for believing that formal private separation deeds only began in the 1650s. One is that 1658 is the first date at which a dispute about their legitimacy is known to have been brought before a court of law.[3] In the 1670s and 1680s there occurred a flurry of lawsuits in Chancery to enforce these deeds, which suggests that it is only then that they begin to be widely used.[4] It is surely also significant that examples of private separation deeds were not included in contemporary handbooks for use by attorneys and conveyancers before the eighteenth century, and first appear in quantity in a book about conveyances published in 1770.[5] Because a wife had legally no personality, she was unable to contract with her husband, so these deeds were always between the husband and a trustee for the wife. Since the Court at Chancery handled trusts, it acquired major jurisdiction over disputed deeds, along with the common law and the Church courts.

Another reason for believing that the separation deed was a late seventeenth-century development is that it was not until then that the courts began to wrestle with the question of whether they should enforce a clause in a separation deed by which, in return for an allowance for maintenance, the wife's trustees gave bond to indemnify the husband from responsibility for her debts. There was great initial reluctance by common lawyers to accept such a transfer of financial freedom and responsibility to a wife, since it ran counter to the ancient legal concept that a married woman had no legal personality and lacked powers to borrow, sue, or transact any legal business.[6] Indeed, in his summing-up of a case in 1785 in favour of upholding a separation deed, Lord Mansfield remarked on the relative novelty of this underlying concept: 'In modern days a new mode of proceeding has been introduced, and deeds have been allowed under which a married woman assumes the appearance of a *feme sole* and is to all intents and purposes capacitated to act as such.'[7]

---

[2] HWRO, Worcester CC, b 797.51, BA 2367.

[3] *Whorewood* v. *Whorewood* (1675), *Eng. Rep.* 22: 785–6; (1662), ibid. 21: 556; (1674), ibid. 23: 84; see MacQueen, *Rights and Liabilities*, 326–7.

[4] *Eng. Rep.* 23: 305, 319, 499, 847–8, 916; 25: 1.

[5] See *Wilson* v. *Wilson* (1845), ibid. 60: 420.

[6] These early cases are summarized in notes to *Bolton* v. *Prentice* (1745), *Eng. Rep.* 93: 1137–8. The key cases were *Todd* v. *Stokes* (1696), ibid. 91: 1195; *Ferrars* v. *Ferrars* (1682), ibid. 23: 319; *Angier* v. *Angier* (1718), ibid. 24: 222–3; *Dent* v. *Scot* (1647), ibid. 82: 916; *Cragg* v. *Bowman* (1705), ibid. 87: 905.

[7] *Corbett* v. *Poelnitz* (1785), ibid. 99: 943.

The last reason to believe that the separation deeds were not developed before the last half of the seventeenth century is that it was not until the 1730s that standard legal phraseology became common, that tight legal safeguards were built into the deed, and that the language became infused with the repetitive jargon of the conveyancer. We therefore have no reason to disbelieve Lord Mansfield when he declared in 1783, 'within the last century a great change has been introduced into the law relating to married persons by means of trusts; and there is also a system of cases for the protection of the husband against the debts of the wife'.[8]

B. EVOLUTION, 1650–1760

In the late seventeenth and early eighteenth centuries, the concept of contract spread throughout the political and legal system. It was used by Locke to form a basis for monarchical government, and by wealthy laity to formalize a marriage separation by a private deed.[9]

The highly personalized quality of a separation deed in the early stage of its development is well illustrated in the case of the break-up in 1677 of the marriage of Richard Alfrey, gentleman, of Sussex, and his wife, Mary, on grounds of his persistent physical cruelty to her. They had already separated once, and the deed was designed both to lay out the conditions upon which she was willing to return home, and also the terms she would be granted if she decided once more to separate. Several clauses stipulated that if she returned, she was free at any time to go before any Sussex JP and swear the peace against her husband, declaring herself in fear that he would 'wound, maim or beat her'. If and when Mary chose to leave home, she was to be free to live where and with whom she pleased, without molestation or law suit by Richard against either herself or the person or persons with whom she lived. She was to be allowed to remove her jewels, clothes, and 'whatever other thing or things she shall desire'. She was to take with her their youngest child, Richard junior, and keep him until the age of 8, and also the next child (if one were born) until the age of 4. Richard promised to pay her £25 a year for her own maintenance for life, plus £10 a year for maintenance of the son and another £4 a year for the next child. In return for the allowance, Mary agreed to take full responsibility for her own debts as long as she and Richard lived apart and the allowance was paid.

---

[8] *Ringstead* v. *Lady Lanesborough* (1783), ibid. 611.

[9] This chapter was written before I had seen S. Staves, 'Separate Maintenance Contacts', *Eighteenth Century Life* (1987), 11. We are in general agreement about the legal evolution of the separation deed, but disagree about the causes and the significance of the changes.

After signing this document, both parties had afterthoughts, and additional articles were drawn up, mostly to protect Richard. They stipulated that as long as the couple continued to cohabit, Mary was to conduct herself 'as a loving, faithful, obedient wife unto her husband', and should discharge a servant girl named Anne Spafford. Moreover, if they separated again, Richard would be indemnified against responsibility for the maintenance of any illegitimate children to whom Mary might give birth.

It is clear that neither Richard nor Mary nor her trustee, the lawyer who had drafted the document, had a model to which to refer. And it is hardly surprising in view of the many concessions extracted by Mary that no sooner had Richard signed the document than he regretted it. He consulted one of England's leading barristers, Sir John Maynard, as to whether the deed was binding upon him, despite his belief that it was 'against the law of God and man', and asked whether any of the three legal systems, common law, canon law or equity law in Chancery, would help him bar the deed. Finally he asked plaintively, 'what is the best course in law for the husband, either to have the wife to cohabit, or to have his liberty?' Sir John ignored this last question, and scrawled laconically on the bottom of the letter: 'The husband by his deed hath put his finger into a cleft stick, and is bound up by his agreement. I know not how to help him in any particulars. [signed] Maynard.'[10]

Although in this case the clauses were clearly thrown together in haste and disorder, to the subsequent dismay of one of the contracting parties, the Alfrey deed of 1677 contains in embryo many of the conditions which half a century later were to become normal in such documents.[11] By the 1700s, most deeds still mentioned no more than the bare financial terms of a separation allowance in return for indemnity for a wife's debts, although they often also contained provision for the custody and financial maintenance of the children. By the 1730s, however, most of them spelt out the personal, economic, and legal safeguards of the wife with extreme care and detail.[12] An example of this 'standard' separation deed of the

---

[10] East Sussex RO, Dunn MSS 48/10, 53/7/2–4. For the Alfrey family, see W. Berry, *County Genealogies: Pedigrees of the Families in . . . Sussex* (London, 1830), 244–5.

[11] GLRO, DL/C/149, H 1253–4; Hooper and Hooper (1699), Devon RO: DD 39116; Sterry and Sterry (1709), Herts. RO, D/ECd F36; Frederick and Frederick (1714), Surrey RO, 183/28/6.

[12] Seymour and Seymour (1739), Dorset RO, DD/BR/tsk 11; Abergavenny and Abergavenny (1765), East Sussex RO, Abe 1062; Robinson and Robinson (1761), Lincs. CC AO, Misc. Don. 526; Lytton and Lytton (1774), Herts. RO, 574 83B. See also Hurt and Hurt (1766), Lincs. CC AO 1WD2; Mitchell and Mitchell (1782), Herts. RO, 26892; Barttelot and Barttelot (1799), *JH Lords*, 42: 72–3; Comyns and Comyns (1792), Lincs. CC AO, 2 Chat 2/1/2; Southwell and Southwell (1798), Northants. RO, Box 511/8; Esten and Esten (1798), *JH Lords*, 41: 487; Gray

period after about 1770 was printed in 1827 by James Clancy in his legal handbook.[13]

2. The Legality of the Private Separation Deed, 1740–1860

A. THE EIGHTEENTH CENTURY

By the second half of the eighteenth century, conveyancers had thought up language to incorporate several critically important measures. The financial clauses consisted of two parts: the husband gave bond to provide his wife with an annual maintenance allowance, either for as long as they continued separate or as long as she lived. This often included the wife's pin-money, which is sometimes described as 'separate maintenance'.[14] In return, the trustees on behalf of the wife indemnified the husband from any future responsibility for her debts.

There followed three clauses which were of great importance to the wife. The first assured her economic freedom, by empowering her to act financially in all respects as if she were a single woman, capable of making contracts, and of suing and being sued. The second assured her personal freedom, thanks to a bond from the husband not to molest or seize her person, nor to sue her in the ecclesiastical courts for restitution of conjugal rights in order to force her to resume cohabitation with him. The third allowed her to live where and with whom she pleased, the husband giving bond not to molest or sue in any court of law any such person for harbouring her. Fourthly, the couple mutually agreed not to harass each other with litigation.[15] It remained obscure whether this freed the wife to cohabit with (or remarry bigamously) whom she pleased, or whether if she did so her husband was barred from suing her for adultery and her lover from crim. con., but this was clearly the intention.[16] Lastly, many deeds contained a clause which transferred the custody of one or more of the younger children from the father to the mother.

All these clauses made concessions to wives which were in partial or total contradiction with the common law, equity law in Chancery, and canon law in the ecclesiastical courts.[17] The last never recognized the

and Gray (1804), Lincs. CC AO, 2 Chat 1/625; Goode and Goode (1811), Warws. RO, CR 1618/4/97/23; Abell and Abell (1813), Norfolk RO, Y/D 51/1879; Barker and Barker (1824), *Eng. Rep.* 162: 299, n. *a*; *Jee* v. *Thurlow* (1824), ibid. 107: 487–90.

[13] Clancy, app. VII, 629–31.

[14] A. P. W. Malcolmson, *The Pursuit of the Heiress: Aristocratic Marriage in Ireland 1750–1820* (Belfast, 1982), 6.

[15] Shelford, 418–19; MacQueen, *Rights and Liabilities*, 336–7.

[16] Poynter, 220–1; *Eng. Rep.* 22: 26–7. [17] MacQueen, *Rights and Liabilities*, 263, 284–5.

authority of these private agreements to block litigation. As a result, however cleverly they were worded, they could not prevent a husband from suing his wife for separation on grounds of adultery or for restitution of conjugal rights.[18]

The secular courts of England were also very reluctant to enforce these clauses banning litigation. In 1740, for example, Chancery refused to honour such a clause, since it was too explicitly drawn to include sexual freedom. Lord and Lady Vane had agreed to separate, Lord Vane covenanting to bring no legal action for any reason 'against any person with whom she should cohabit', and giving a bond of £20,000 as security. In this case Lord Hardwicke had no hesitation in voiding the agreement as an invitation to adultery and thus contrary to public morality. He angrily declared it 'a shameful clause, and a manifest imposition upon the husband . . . a fraud apparent upon the face of it'.[19]

During most of the eighteenth and nineteenth centuries, the common law courts also normally refused to enforce the financial independence granted to wives in these agreements. The exception was during the tenure by Lord Mansfield of the office of lord chief justice from 1756 to 1788. He laid down that 'where a woman has a separate estate, and acts and receives credit as a single woman, she shall be liable as such', a view with which all the judges of England concurred. Behind such decisions lay Lord Mansfield's belief that the law must keep up to date: 'As the times alter, new customs and new manners arise; these occasion exceptions; and justice and convenience require different applications of these exceptions, within the principle of the general rule.'[20]

As for Chancery, it found itself in the illogical position of refusing to enforce a marital separation, which was the whole purpose of the deed, but assiduously enforcing the means to that end, that is the provisions of the deed by which the husband gave his wife a maintenance allowance to support her in that separation, in return for her trustees indemnifying him from responsibility for her debts.[21]

B. THE CONSERVATIVE REACTION, 1800–1840

In the conservative legal climate of the period 1790 to 1830, a determined effort was made by the common law judges to repudiate over

---

[18] Shelford, 417–19; *Spering* v. *Spering* (1863), *Eng. Rep.* 164: 1225.

[19] *Vane* v. *Vane* (1740), ibid. 27: 586.

[20] *Corbett* v. *Poelnitz* (1785), ibid. 99: 942–3; *Ringstead* v. *Lanesborough* (1783), ibid. 611; Evans, 1: 106–7.

[21] *Elsworthy* v. *Bird* (1825), *Eng. Rep.* 57: 390; Bright, 2: 327–9; *Legard* v. *Johnson* (1797), *Eng. Rep.* 30: 1052–3.

a century of case law in favour of the validity of the separation deed. Lord Chancellor Eldon later recalled: 'I once heard Lord Mansfield say "I never liked law [i.e. common law] so well as when it is like equity"', which to him was stark heresy.[22] Lord Kenyon was equally contemptuous of his famous predecessor. He once declared: 'We must not, by any whimsical conceits supposed to be adapted to the altering fashions of the times, overturn the established law of the land. . . . An action cannot be brought against a married woman.'[23]

One of the first open attacks on Mansfield's opinions occurred in a test case in common law in 1800. Chief Justice Kenyon and all his fellow judges restated the ancient doctrine of 'the incapacity of a married woman to contract or to possess personal property'. They denied that 'a woman may be sued as a *feme sole*, while the relation of marriage subsists', a decision which flew in the face of nearly a century of case law.[24] So angry was Lord Chancellor Eldon that he called these decisions of his predecessors 'impertinent and scandalous'.[25] At the end of his career, he was to claim that he had 'been constantly engaged in a struggle to leave all these matters of separation rather to the ecclesiastical courts', the purpose being to reinstate marriage as an indissoluble contract.[26]

To gain this objective, a general attack was launched upon the validity of all separation deeds made between the husband and trustees for the wife. The opposition, led by Sergeant Onslow, argued that 'it is contrary to the policy of the law and of good morals to enter into any contract which has a direct tendency to loosen the bands of union between husband and wife and facilitate their separation'. But although in his summing up Chief Justice Ellenborough agreed with this principle, he reluctantly pointed out that it was too late: over a century of contrary judicial decisions made it impossible suddenly to invalidate all separation agreements. 'They are now become inveterate in the law. . . . It has been so long established, and by so many decisions, that the Courts will give effect to contracts for separate maintenance, that it cannot now be called in question.'[27] In 1817 it was decided that if they were made via trustees, 'the deeds of separation and appointment are good against all the world', including the husband's creditors.[28] Even so, as late as 1820 Lord Eldon

---

[22] *Westmeath* v. *Salisbury* (1831), ibid. 5: 362.
[23] Evans, 1: 109. See also Campbell, *Lives of the Chief Justices*, 2: 437–43.
[24] *Marshall* v. *Rutton* (1800), *Eng. Rep.* 101: 1539.
[25] *St John* v. *St John* (1803–5), ibid. 32: 1194.
[26] Staves, 'Separate Maintenance Contracts', 95.
[27] *Rodney* v. *Chambers* (1802), *Eng. Rep.* 102: 380–2.
[28] *Worrall* v. *Jacob* (1817), ibid. 36: 103–4.

was still grumbling about finding himself trapped by a long line of pre-cedents into accepting these deeds of separation of marriage.[29]

A particularly thorny question was that of the legal validity of separa-tion deeds which were conditional upon a *future* decision by the wife or her trustees to separate if the husband renewed his cruelty or adultery after a reconciliation. In the middle of the eighteenth century, Lord Chancellor Hardwicke had decided that such future deeds were legally enforceable provided that the decision upon when to separate depended not only on the whim of the wife but also on the consent of her trustees, and in 1805 Lord Ellenborough confirmed this view. In a famous case in 1802, Justice Le Blanc conceded that 'it has been holden that deeds of separation are not illegal. . . . I cannot see how it can be more illegal to contract for separate maintenance in case of future than present separation.'[30]

As might be expected, Lord Eldon took exactly the opposite position.[31] Under prodding by him, the question was finally given a full airing in a general discussion by all the twelve common law judges in the Exchequer Chamber in 1819. They declared void any deed which was contingent upon a future separation.[32] This was a wholly new legal doctrine—so new that it was unknown to an experienced lawyer a year later. The result was to ruin the life of Lady Westmeath who had been assured that her separation deed in the future was valid.[33]

In the early nineteenth century, law lords changed their minds about those clauses prohibiting litigation in their courts, which the church courts had always rejected. Despite nearly two hundred years of case history in their favour, in 1835 Lord Brougham declared: 'the strongest articles of agreement, drawn up and signed with the full acquiescence of husband and wife, will not prevent them suing each other'.[34]

C. THE LIBERAL RESPONSE, 1820–1860

In 1824, the conservative attack on the private separation deed by the law lords generated a liberal backlash. What happened was this. In that year a suit had come before the King's Bench which challenged the legal

---

[29] *Westmeath* v. *Westmeath* (1820), *Eng. Rep.* 37: 801. Eldon's role is well brought out in Roper, 2: 267–84; 3: 270; Shelford, 608–39; and Clancy, 320–39, 346, 350, 369–73, 390–405, 416–17, 439.

[30] *Rodney* v.*Chambers* (1802), *Eng. Rep.* 102: 381–2; *Chambers* v. *Caulfield* (1805), ibid. 1284; Clancy, 421–31.

[31] *St John* v. *St John* (1803–5), *Eng. Rep.* 32: 1194–7; McQueen, *Rights and Liabilities*, 343–4; Roper, 2: 270–1.

[32] *Durant* v. *Titley* (1819), *Eng. Rep.* 146: 1067, 1070–1; see Wharton, 394.

[33] See Stone, *Broken Lives*, Westmeath case.

[34] *Warrender* v. *Warrender* (1835), *Eng. Rep.* 6: 1253; *Wilson* v. *Wilson* (1846–8), ibid. 9: 875–6.

validity of the clause barring suits, and the judges had found themselves forced, very reluctantly, to uphold the clause on grounds of long, if unfortunate, precedents. But they revealed their true feelings by appealing to Parliament to clean up the mess and pass an act declaring once and for all that all private separation deeds were illegal on grounds of public policy.[35]

This open appeal for legislation drove one of England's most thoughtful and learned commentators on the law, Edward Jacob, to publish a reply.[36] He drew attention to the marked difference between the views of Lord Eldon and his brethren on the bench in the early nineteenth century and those of their predecessors in the eighteenth century, who had been sympathetic to the purpose of private deeds of separation. The idea that these deeds were somehow contrary to public morality and therefore to the ends of the law was of relatively recent origin. He pointed out that no law any longer prohibited man and wife from 'living apart' in a state of voluntary separation; and that no question of morality could arise since the temporal courts were extremely careful not to enquire into the reasons for the separation. Even the ecclesiastical courts no longer assumed that couples living apart were necessarily immoral, as had been the case up to the late seventeenth century. It followed that a deed which made such a separation financially possible was neither illegal nor immoral.

There was therefore no reason for regarding private separation deeds as 'in all cases productive of unmixed evil', nor was there any higher claim of public policy which demanded that the only valid separations had to be the product of litigation rather than private agreement. If the persons involved were satisfied, how was the public interest adversely affected? Finally, Jacob pointed out that the wide difference of views of different judges on these questions suggested the folly of hastily abolishing private separations by legislative *fiat*. They were instruments which clearly met a widespread human need, despite the headaches they caused the lawyers.

In the end, the calmer judgments of Jacob and men like him prevailed, and no attempt was made in Parliament to legislate private separations out of existence. In the second third of the nineteenth century, the Court of Chancery also moved to a more liberal position.[37] As a result, the legal textbook writer MacQueen could report with satisfaction that recent

---

[35] *Jee* v. *Thurlow* (1824), ibid. 107: 487–90.

[36] Bright, 2: app. XII, 'Objections to the Legality of Deeds of Separation Considered', by E. Jacob (first published in 1824); MacQueen, *Rights and Liabilities*, 327–8.

[37] *Wilson* v. *Wilson* (1854), *Eng. Rep.* 10: 816–21, 824. See also *Spering* v. *Spering* (1863), ibid. 164: 1255.

judicial decisions actually tended to 'fortify the footing and extend the scope of deeds of separation'.[38] Like Jacob before him, MacQueen regarded the private separation deed as a legal device which performed a socially useful function as 'a family arrangement—a compromise of litigated rights', which should be enforced by the courts since it was in the public interest.[39]

As a result of these twists and turns in the three branches of the law in early nineteenth-century England, the situation regarding the private separation deed was verging on the chaotic. In 1827 a legal textbook writer concluded:

The law upon this subject stands in this very peculiar state, that if there be a covenant by which the husband engages to leave his wife free to reside where she likes, a court of equity will not enforce it, nor will it restrain the husband from violating it; that a court of [common] law will not entertain an action founded on the breach of it, though the very same court would enforce the due observance of it; and that the spiritual court may pronounce a sentence for the restitution of those very rights which the legal tribunal had declared the husband to have renounced beyond the power of revocation. These are difficulties arising from the different remedies which may be given by different jurisdictions upon the same subject matter, which, even supposing the agreement between husband and wife for separation and a separate maintenance to be perfectly valid, must introduce some embarrassment in the administration of the rights springing from such contract.[40]

This confusion arising from conflicting jurisdictions fuelled the growing demand for structural legal reform. The rising tide of complaints about crim. con. actions, Parliamentary divorces and private separation deeds at this time all stem from the same demands of the middle-class Victorian public for morality, order, clarity, and rationality in the legal system.

3. The Popularity of the Private Separation

Despite these contradictions and uncertainties, there can be no doubt that the number of private separations continued to increase by leaps and bounds. As early as 1745, Horace Walpole could report that the three chief landowners and power-brokers of Norfolk—the heads of the families of Walpole of Houghton, Townshend of Raynham and Coke of Holkham—were all privately separated from their wives.[41] But the most

---

[38] MacQueen, *Rights and Liabilities*, 350.
[39] Ibid. 327–8, 329, 344–5, 350; Roper, 2: 270 n. G.
[40] Clancy, 370; he discusses the consequences in 370–5, 397–8.
[41] *Walpole's Correspondence*, 19: 27 n. 22.

obvious proof of the popularity of these private separations is the very extensive coverage given to them by legal textbooks of the 1820s to 1840s.[42] The principal reason for the continued growth in the use of the private separation deed was its convenience as a way of dissolving a broken marriage which did not involve adultery or extreme cruelty, and so could not be terminated in any other way. Among the less affluent, it was also popular as a very cheap way of terminating all marriages, even ones involving adultery.[43] Thus, private separation deeds continued to flourish despite the legal tangles; to the vast majority of clients who had no intention of going to law with each other and were content with the separation agreements they had mutually agreed upon, such obstacles were of little importance.

The Divorce Act of 1857 made little difference to these private separation agreements since it did nothing for the many cases of break-up because of temperamental incompatibility. Conveyancers and attorneys therefore continued to come up with ingenious ways of effecting *de facto* divorce by private agreement. One such device came to the attention of the new Divorce Court in 1859, in the case of a Mr Walton who had signed a deed of separation from his adulterous wife and now sought a divorce. By the deed, Mr Walton had accepted the lover as trustee on behalf of his wife, and the lover had paid the husband a farthing compensation for her infidelity. Lord Campbell indignantly denounced the deed as fraudulent, saying that Walton 'had assigned his wife to the adulterer by deed, and sold her as effectively as if he had exhibited her in a market overt with a rope round her neck'.[44] This was a middle-class separation agreement which certainly came very close indeed to the much-criticized wife-sales of the poor.

4. The Advantages to the Husband

To a husband, the only clear advantages of a judicial separation over a private agreement were that if his wife was proved guilty of adultery, the court would free him from all alimony payments, and that it would also bastardize all of the wife's future children, which a private agreement could not do. The illegitimacy of children born to a privately separated wife could only be established by offering compelling evidence to the Court of Chancery that sexual relations had never been resumed between the original spouses, which was not an easy thing to prove.[45] But

[42] Clancy (1827), 366–439; Shelford (1841), 608–733; Bright (1849), 2: 305–53.
[43] *Roy. Com. Divorce, 1853*, 1: 45.   [44] MacQueen, *Marriage, Divorce, and Legitimacy*, xi.
[45] Poynter, 220–1; *Eng. Rep.* 22: 26–7.

this was not an issue of paramount importance to fathers who had living sons who, under the laws of primogeniture, would inherit the bulk of the property. They could always disinherit by will any later children they regarded as not their own.

The great advantage of a private separation deed over a judicial separation was precisely that it was private, and therefore permitted a parting without the washing of dirty family linen in public, and the consequent embarrassment and disgrace of both sides of the family.[46] It was a device particularly favoured by a husband wishing to part from his wife but unable to prove her guilty of adultery. On the other hand, in a few such cases the husband refused a separation agreement since it committed him to paying his wife a maintenance allowance. This reason was openly expressed by Mr Elwes in 1794 when he was seeking ways to be separated from a wife whom he strongly suspected of adultery. A friend suggested a private separation, but Mr Elwes replied: 'I cannot do that, for that she would not take less than five hundred pounds a year. I will leave her to take her own way, by which I will have her in my power to divorce [separate from] her without allowing any maintenance.'[47] In other words, he preferred to let things stay the way they were, and to go on living with her until he could prove her guilty of adultery, and so could obtain a judicial separation without payment of any alimony or maintenance.

5. The Advantages to the Wife: Financial Freedom

One of the reasons for the success of the private separation deed was that it went a long way towards satisfying the needs of a separated wife for full economic freedom. In the first place, she was granted a maintenance allowance. In the nineteenth century this usually came to about a third of the husband's net income, which was the same as court-ordered alimony after a judicial separation.[48] In the second place, she was enabled to act economically as if she were a single woman, free to contract, buy, or sell, in return for a grant by trustees on her behalf to her husband of an indemnity against any responsibility for future debts incurred by her.[49] This 'valuable consideration' made the clause valid in Chancery and common law.[50]

---

[46] *Parl. Hist.* 35: 316–18.
[47] LPCA, D. 675, 853.   [48] MacQueen, *Rights and Liabilities*, 335.
[49] *Stephens* v. *Olive* (1785), *Eng. Rep.* 29: 52. For an extended discussion of maintenance allowances and their enforcement see Clancy, 397–431.
[50] *Dent* v. *Scott* (1647), *Eng. Rep.* 82: 916; *Gregg* v. *Bowman* (1707), ibid. 87: 905; see *Todd* v. *Stokes* (c. 1690), ibid. 91: 1195; *Arnold* v. *Arnold* (1767), *Trials for Adultery*, 3: 5.

For the private separation document to be legally enforceable, however, the husband was also expected publicly to warn shop-keepers in the vicinity in future not to allow his separated wife credit for goods and then expect him to pay them. After about 1750 it became common practice to insert an advertisement for this purpose in the newspapers, such as the following which appeared in the London *Daily Advertiser* in 1767:

'Whereas Dorothy Arnold, the wife of John Arnold, hath agreed to lie separate and apart from me, and I do allow her a separate maintenance, this is to caution all persons not to give her any credit on my account, as I will not pay any debts she shall contract.

John Arnold, Watchmaker in Devereux Court'

It therefore seems likely that an important cause of the spread of these agreements in the last half of the eighteenth century was the willingness of the Court of Chancery to enforce the financial terms swiftly and cheaply, so long as trustees were involved. In a test case heard in 1718, the chancellor decided that the court had such powers since the articles had merely been intended 'to save the expense of a sentence in a Spiritual Court'.[51]

A more debateable issue raised by the financial clauses of these private separation deeds was whether common law could or would uphold the clauses which protected the business and earnings of the separated wife from seizure by her husband. Without these clauses, a wife remained financially at the mercy of her husband. He retained the right to all his wife's earnings during her life, 'every farthing she makes by her labour being his, because she is his wife, though separated'. All future legacies to her became the property of her husband, who was free to use the profits but not the capital. Any income she drew from real estate also remained his.[52] There are many cases on record of an estranged husband swooping down, sometimes years or decades after the separation, seizing and selling all his wife's goods and chattels, taking all her savings, and disappearing again. And he was legally within his rights to do so.[53] Sometimes the common law would protect a wife's earnings and property, and sometimes it would not. Chancery was more active in this area, and in 1737 declared that a wife was immune to the pillage of her business earnings by virtue of a prior separation agreement.[54]

---

[51] *Angier* v. *Angier* (1718), ibid. 24: 222–3; *Guth* v. *Guth* (1792), ibid. 29: 729–33.
[52] Speech by Lord Lyndhurst in 3 *Hansard*, 142: 410.
[53] See e.g. the Calvert case in Stone, *Broken Lives*.
[54] *Cecil* v. *Juxon* (1737), *Eng. Rep.* 26: 178–9.

A separated wife was also always exposed to the possibility that her husband, by expressing a willingness for a reconciliation, could prosecute her in the ecclesiastical court for 'restitution of conjugal rights', thereby forcing her to resume cohabitation in the same house even if not in the same bed. More often than not, this was merely a clever trick by the husband to free himself of all financial obligation towards his wife and allow him to seize her property and earnings. All he had to do was to rent a small house in some out-of-the-way place and offer his wife free accommodation in it. His expectation and hope was that she would soon get tired of this isolated way of living 'and if she disliked the retreat she would lose her alimony by eloping'. Then her husband would have her financially at his mercy, and could force her to agree to a more modest maintenance allowance or none at all. In 1774, Richard Lytton's lawyer advised him to follow this course, telling him that 'something of the kind has frequently been done, since the wife can claim nothing if the husband's house (and his house is wherever he pleases to live) is open for her'.[55]

6. The Advantages to the Wife: Personal Freedom

A. FREEDOM FROM LEGAL HARASSMENT

Clauses were always inserted in separation deeds by which each spouse promised not to molest or sue the other, particularly over the freedom of each to live with whomsoever he or she wished. Such clauses were inserted despite the repeated denial of their validity by the courts. Their wording was usually cautious and ambiguous, leaving it an open question whether the husband meant to surrender his right to sue his wife if she committed adultery, or merely to allow her to live chastely where and with whom she pleased. By the 1780s, conveyancers had become very skilful at drafting clauses which were as tight as they could be, without being overly explicit. A deed drawn up in 1786, however, went too far. The husband gave bond not to launch 'any suit in law in any court whatsoever' against either his wife Sophia or 'against those Sophia should live or cohabit with'. If any such suit should be launched this 'clause shall be pleaded specially in bar, and shall be agreed to be a full bar, recompense and satisfaction for every such actions and suits'. Nothing could be clearer than that, but Lord Chief Justice Kenyon, in his zeal to punish sexual immorality, declared that the clause was illegal, being against the public interest since it was an invitation to adultery. He

[55] Herts RO, 574. 83. B.

therefore permitted the husband's crim. con. action against his wife's lover to proceed.[56]

If Lord Kenyon took this stern line in King's Bench in the 1780s, so too did Sir John Nichol in the Court of Arches in 1824. He denied that the wording of the deed 'amounts to a letter of licence to the wife to conduct herself howsoever, and to connect herself to whomsoever, she pleases', adding that in any case a clause in a deed prohibiting lawsuits is 'nugatory as to any binding effect on the parties'.[57]

Despite these legal repudiations of it, and despite its apparent violation of the standards of Victorian morality, the clause was still a standard one in the early nineteenth century. When in 1813 the Duke and Duchess of Manchester separated, on the grounds of her alleged adultery with a servant (which she hotly denied), the deed contained such a clause. The duchess later said she had not known of its existence, and had only discovered it when she read the deed carefully for the first time several years later: 'I found it authorized me to live with whom I pleased and that no notice would be taken of it. What a licentious idea! If anything would render vice more horrid in appearance, it was this. I confess I was disgusted.'[58]

On occasion, the clause was inserted in the deed as a trap laid by the husband's lawyers to give the wife a false sense of security, and so to inveigle her into an adultery which would enable her husband to seek a Parliamentary divorce. When in 1816 the Hon. John Augustus Sullivan, then a 17-year-old Eton schoolboy, foolishly allowed himself to be entrapped into a marriage with a woman of low birth, his family extricated him by using exactly these tactics and then suing for divorce on grounds of adultery.[59]

Right to the end, the clause barring litigation continued to have very precarious legal and moral status, and yet it continued to be universally used. The obvious explanation of this paradox is that in the vast majority of cases the clause was honoured because it suited the interests of both parties to do so. Each was left free to set up a new household, the husband with a mistress, the wife with a lover, or in some cases with a bigamously married second husband.

[56] *Barttelot* v. *Hawker* (1790), BL 518 1 12(5), 49, 58; *JH Lords*, 42: 72–3. For an almost identically worded separation deed of 1776 see *Danvers* v. *Danvers*, Northants RO, O. 1958; MacQueen, *Rights and Liabilities*, 336–41.

[57] *Barker* v. *Barker* (1824), *Eng. Rep.* 162: 299 n. *a*, 299–300; *Sullivan* v. *Sullivan* (1824), ibid. 305 n. *a*.

[58] Hunts RO, DDM 10 B/32.

[59] *Crim. Con. Gaz.* 2 (1839), 256; MacQueen, *House of Lords*, 635–8; see also *Barttelot* v. *Hawker* (1799), *JH Lords*, 42: 72–3; MacQueen, *House of Lords*, 588–9; *Elsworthy* v. *Bird* (1825), *Eng. Rep.* 57: 389; Roberts, 79.

B. FREEDOM FROM FORCIBLE SEIZURE AND CONFINEMENT

Another clause inserted in all separation deeds deprived the husband of his right to seize his wife by force, take her home with him against her will, and keep her in confinement. It is easy to forget today that this was then a power inherent in all husbands by virtue of marriage. That separated wives were afraid of seizure and confinement is made clear in their correspondence. Thus in 1771, an adulterous wife, Mrs Draper, wrote anxiously to her estranged husband of a rumour she had heard: 'You design a place of confinement. . . . For God's sake, do not harbour such a thought'.[60] A dramatic example of the sort of thing which might happen occurred during the break-up of the marriage of John and Mary Sayer in 1713. Both were members of the elite, he being a squire with £800 a year income, and she the daughter of an admiral with a marriage portion of £1,000. When she became dissatisfied with John's sexual powers, she deserted him, and began to live a life of reckless promiscuity in London, and the two families became locked in a series of litigious quarrels. John and Mary agreed to a deed of separation, but soon afterwards he successfully sued for relief from its terms, on the grounds of his wife's scandalous behaviour. She took refuge in the Mint in London, a sanctuary area from arrest for debt. When John Sayer discovered where she was, he obtained a warrant 'to take up his wife, she being gone from him without his consent, and living in a loose disorderly manner'. Two constables and six assistants were hired to carry out the arrest in the turbulent and dangerous Mint. The group burst into the house, led by Mr Sayer armed with a drawn sword, but in the ensuing scuffle he was accidentally killed with a sword thrust by his wife's solicitor, who was also her current lover. At the trial, the judge ruled that Mr Sayer 'could justify the action to take up his wife', and that although he appeared to be the aggressor his death was murder, not manslaughter. He therefore sentenced Mrs Sayer's lover to death.[61] This story starkly illuminates the level of violence by a husband which was still regarded as legitimate by a common law judge in order to recover possession of a runaway wife.

Then there was the case of Lady Moore. She had long been separated from her husband, when one day in 1716 her husband accidentally met her riding in a coach, and promptly seized possession of her. By the terms of the marriage, Lady Moore's own estate had been settled on trustees for her private use. But the day after her seizure, she was

[60] *Draper* v. *Draper* (1771), *Trials for Adultery*, 7: 17.
[61] Anon., *A Full Account of the Case of John Sayer, Esq.* (London, 1713), (Bodl. G. Pamph 1851 (5)).

coerced into signing a contract with her husband by which, in return for his releasing her and allowing her to live separately, she paid him £1,000 in cash and settled £200 a year on him for life. Once she had recovered her freedom, she sued in Chancery to be relieved of this agreement, on the grounds that it was based on physical coercion and a threat of life imprisonment. But the Chancery judges were divided; the common law judges decided against her; a jury, after nine hours of deliberation, also decided against her; and she lost her final appeal to the House of Lords.[62]

It took some time for the courts to decide to protect a wife from seizure by her husband if the latter had signed a deed of separation with a clause forbidding molestation.[63] A suit in 1723 made clear the willingness of common law courts to intervene under normal circumstances. Mr and Mrs Lister had signed a separation deed by which the husband promised not to molest his wife with law-suits or the use of force. Two years later he wanted his wife back, so he and his servants waylaid her as she came out of church and hurried her away to a remote place, where she was kept under guard. Her relatives eventually found out where she was imprisoned, and obtained a writ of habeas corpus, by virtue of which she was released and brought before the Court of King's Bench. The judge decreed that if a separated wife squanders her maintenance or uses it to live in adultery, her husband is justified in putting her under restraint 'to preserve his honour and estate'. But in this case no such conditions applied, and the separation deed had been made by mutual consent. He therefore freed the lady and warned her husband not to attempt a seizure again.[64]

But this did not settle the matter, and it was only at the end of the nineteenth century, after a century and a half of legal struggle, that a separated wife was at last more or less safe from physical abduction by her husband. Shelford's law treatise, published in 1844, showed that by then the situation at common law had stabilized along the lines established by Lord Mansfield in 1758.[65] But as late as 1888, a husband kidnapped his estranged wife who refused to live with him, and kept her locked up in the house of a relative while he pursued his legal claims on her in the courts. It was only in 1891, when a husband once again seized

[62] *Moore* v. *Moore* (1721), *Eng. Rep.* 22: 22; for other cases, see Stone, *Broken Lives.*

[63] Roper, 317–24; Clancy, 432–9; Bright, 2: 314–16; A. G. R. Hall, *The Law and Practice in Divorce and Matrimonial Causes* (London 1905), 861–2, 864, 885.

[64] *Rex* v. *Lister* (1723), *Eng. Rep.* 93: 645–6; see also *Rex* v. *Clarkson et al.* (1734), ibid. 625; *Rex* v. *Mary Read* (1758), ibid. 97: 440; *Rex* v. *Brooke and Fladgate* (1766), ibid. 98: 38.

[65] *Rex* v. *Mead* (1758), ibid. 97: 440; Evans, 1: 109–10; Shelford, 667–71; Clancy, 432–9.

his wife by force in the street, that the practice was at last declared to be under all circumstances illegal.[66]

Seizure of a wife is one thing, imprisoning her is another. A wife subjected to such treatment had three remedies open to her, or to her friends and relatives on her behalf. She could ask the JPs to bind her husband over to keep the peace; she could ask Chancery to issue a writ of *supplicavit*, which would secure her release and protect her for a year; and she could ask King's Bench for a writ of habeas corpus, which would compel her temporary release in order to appear before the court.[67] She could also, of course, use the confinement as evidence of cruelty, as the basis upon which to sue for separation in an ecclesiastical court.

None of these remedies was very effective in the eighteenth century, and in 1735 an anonymous woman protested bitterly:

Wives may be made prisoners for life, at the discretion of their domestic governors, whose power ... bears no manner of proportion to that degree of authority which is vested in any other set of men in England. ... No individual, not even the Sovereign himself, can imprison any person for life, at will and pleasure, the Habeas Corpus Act providing for the condemnation or enlargement of the prisoner.[68]

The author cited the case of a man who had for years kept his wife locked up in a garret without adequate clothes, food, or heat, and had often horse-whipped her. When in the end she committed suicide by jumping out of the window, her husband was prosecuted for manslaughter at the Old Bailey, but was acquitted by the all-male jury. The proportion of wives subjected to this treatment may have been very small, but the threat was frequently used by angry husbands, and latent fear of its possible use was always present.

In the early years of the eighteenth century, Chancery was not very much help to wives who found themselves locked up. When in 1718 Mrs Atwood applied to Chancery for a writ of *supplicavit*, she was denied relief. The court ruled that a husband 'has a right by law to the custody of her, and may, if he thinks fit, confine her; but he must not imprison her'.[69] The subtle difference between confine and imprison was left obscure.

Locking up a wife in a remote Irish castle and forgetting about her was

[66] P. Levine, 'Marriage and Feminism in Late Nineteenth Century England', *Journal of British Studies*, 28 (1989), 28; *A Century of Family Law, 1857–1957*, ed. R. H. Graveson and F. E. Crane (London, 1957), 178–80. For the equally unhelpful attitude of the ecclesiastical courts, see P. Fraser, *The Conflict of Laws* (Edinburgh, 1860), 40; MacQueen, *Rights and Liabilities*, 325–30, 338–40.

[67] Roper, 312–17; Clancy, 432–3.

[68] *Hardships of Laws on Wives*, 6, 9, 4.

[69] *Atwood* v. *Atwood* (1718), *Eng. Rep.* 24: 221.

not unknown in the early eighteenth century. For example, in 1744 Lord Bellfield suspected his wife of incestuous adultery with his brother, and locked her up at Gaulston Park, County Westmeath, where she languished until her death thirty years later.[70] In 1768 Mrs Daly was locked up in a house in Galway, after being forcibly removed from Dublin.[71] The mentally unbalanced Lord Ferrers kept his wife imprisoned at Staunton Harold in Leicestershire until the King's Bench with great difficulty forced her release.[72] Again and again, the House of Lords had to interfere to prevent its members from illegally seizing their wives. In 1700 it moved to stop the Earl of Anglesea from arresting his wife as she came and went to the House in pursuit of a private law-suit,[73] while in the same year the Duchess of Norfolk expressed her fear that 'my lord duke would confine the duchess to some house'.[74]

Apart from the home, the other favourite place of imprisonment for a tiresome wife between 1660 and 1774 was a private madhouse. Unlike France, England in the late seventeenth century contained very few public lunatic asylums, the best known being Bedlam in London. To fill the need, there sprang up a large number of privately owned and operated madhouses. Some were expensive, attended by trained doctors, and genuinely devoted to caring for the mentally afflicted, most of whom did not stay very long. Others were squalid private prisons which, as long as the fees were paid, would accept anyone and keep them indefinitely behind bars, regardless of their mental condition or the motives of the person who ordered their confinement.

Thus, in 1691 there came to light an elaborate plot by an adventurer to marry, kidnap, and put into a madhouse a wealthy widow, Mrs Graves, in order to be free to seize her property.[75] Another husband imprisoned his wife in a madhouse as a form of blackmail to force her to agree to a separation in return for her release.[76] In 1770, another wife was put by her husband in a madhouse, where she was chained to the floor for two weeks.[77] In 1744, Mr Head tried to seize his admittedly unstable wife and 'convey her to a madhouse'. When she obtained release by a writ from Chancery, Mr Head told the court that he would take her back home, but 'would shut her up, considering her mad'. Lord Chancellor Hardwicke ruled that the attempt to seize her and lock her up 'was not such an act of cruelty as to be ground for an absolute and perpetual separation', and ordered her to return home.[78]

---

[70] A. P. Malcolmson, *The Pursuit of Heiresses*, 37   [71] Charles Daly case, *JH Lords*, 32: 79.
[72] *Laws Respecting Women*, 56–7; *JH Lords*, 29: 36, 249, 271.   [73] *JH Lords*, 16: 649.
[74] *State Trials*, 13: 1321.   [75] See *Graves* v. *Smith* in Stone, *Uncertain Unions*.
[76] *Eng. Rep.* 97: 741.   [77] *Collett* v. *Collett* in *NCC Trials for Adultery*, 2: 204–6.
[78] *Head* v. *Head* (1744, 1747), *Eng. Rep.* 26: 1115; 27: 863.

It was not until 1774 that Parliament at last passed an act to put a stop to the worst of these abuses.[79] In future, all madhouse-keepers in London and the suburbs had to possess a licence issued by the College of Physicians, and in the countryside by the local JPs. Records had to be kept of all inmates, when they were admitted and when discharged, by whom they were sent, and by whom treated. A madhouse-keeper was forbidden to accept any patients without a doctor's order, and the madhouse itself was to be open to inspection by commissioners. There can be no doubt that the act was long overdue. One of the most terrible fates that could be inflicted upon a wife by a husband was to be confined, sometimes actually in chains, in a private madhouse far from her friends and unknown to them, where she might linger for months or even years. The mere threat of such confinement, which was frequently used by angry husbands in the eighteenth century, was enough to strike terror. In eighteenth-century England, this fear hung over every wife, just as it did until very recently over every political dissident in Russia.

Before 1774, the only safeguard against these abuses was for the friends of the wife confined to the madhouse to discover her whereabouts and obtain a writ of habeas corpus from the King's Bench. The court normally appointed a panel of doctors to inspect her, and if they found her of sound mind she was discharged. Only very occasionally was the husband charged with any crime. In one such case, in 1728, in which the husband repeatedly confined his wife in madhouses, he defended his actions on the grounds that she had been taken in adultery. Her lawyer argued that 'it was certain the husband might justify confining her in his own house, and for the same reason in another person's house, if it was not a madhouse'. But it was argued that there was no reason why it made any difference that the place of confinement was a madhouse. The court decided that 'a man might confine his wife in his own house, for proper reasons', but 'they would never allow of such things as this'.[80]

It is noticeable that, just like examples of forcible seizure, recorded examples of wives imprisoned in their homes or in madhouses die away after the middle of the eighteenth century. The change was one in sentiment, which resulted in a change of both legal practice and individual behaviour. This change was commented upon in a revealing conversation which took place in 1769 between Sarah Lady Bunbury and the considerably older Lady Mary Coke. The former told her friend that although she had taken a lover, she was continuing to live in her

---

[79] 14 G III cap. 49; *Laws Respecting Women*, 76–7.
[80] *Rex* v. *Dr Newton and others* (1728), ibid. 94: 2942.

husband's house since 'her running away from her husband would give him the right to lock her up for the rest of her life'. Lady Mary disagreed, observing that in fact 'she would not be locked up, tho' I remembered when people were locked up for no fault of their own'.[81] There was thus an awareness that times and mores had changed.

C. THE LONELINESS OF THE SEPARATED WIFE

While the husband could keep a mistress with impunity, the slightest sexual slip on the part of his separated wife would allow him to stop payment of the maintenance allowance, and the wife would thereafter be socially humiliated and financially ruined. This remained true from the seventeenth to the early twentieth century, and there was alarming confirmation of this in the testimony of a solicitor before the Royal Commission on Divorce of 1912. He described how a husband could blackmail a wife to agreeing to a deed of separation under threat of (falsely) accusing her in public of adultery. He could then go off to live with his mistress, but still keep a close watch on his wife in order to file for a divorce at the first sign of a sexual lapse.[82]

The loneliness of some of these women, separated under suspicion of adultery but in fact without a lover, was often very acute. The Duchess of Manchester, separated unwillingly from the duke in 1813, was left alone in Richmond House in London while the duke was away in Ireland: 'How melancholy time passed in this large mansion alone. . . . I remained in London fourteen months in this state of solitary misery.'[83] The same personal predicament of a suspect and separated woman was vividly described by Mrs Norton in the middle of the nineteenth century:

Alone. Married to a man's name, but never to know the protection of this nominal husband, nor the joys of family, nor the every-day companionship of a real home. Never to feel or show preference for any friend not of her own sex, though tempted, perhaps, by a feeling nobler than passion—gratitude for generous pity that has lightened the dreary days. To be slandered, tormented, insulted; to find the world and the world's law utterly indifferent to her wrongs or her husband's sin; and through all this to lead a chaste, unspotted, patient, cheerful life; without anger, without bitterness, and with meek respect for those edicts which, with a perverse parody on Scripture, pronounce that it 'is not good for man to be alone,' but extremely good for woman.[84]

---

[81] *Letters and Journals of Lady Mary Coke*, ed. J. A. Home (Edinburgh, 1889–96), 3: 30.
[82] *Roy. Com. Divorce, 1912: Minutes of Evidence*, 1: 159.   [83] Hunts RO, DDM 10 B/32.
[84] J. G. Perkins, *The Life of Mrs Norton* (London, 1909), 191–2.

7. The Problem of Child Custody

A. THEORY

In any marital break-up, the most crucial issue for the wife, apart from maintenance for herself, was custody of the children. This involved three related questions: the allocation of custody and control between the spouses; visiting rights for the spouse deprived of custody; and who was to pay for the maintenance and education of the children. Governing the attitudes of the spouses and the courts were three conflicting concepts of law and morality. The first was the patriarchal view that the father, regardless of his character and behaviour, had an absolute right to entire and untrammelled control over his children until they reached the age of maturity. He could dispose of them in marriage, employ them, educate them or not, just as he thought fit; and if he so chose he could, and often did, cut off all communication, both orally and in writing, between them and their mother. According to the common law courts, visiting rights by the mother, and even her right to communicate by letter, were entirely at the discretion of the father.

The second concept, which spread rapidly in the second half of the eighteenth century, and especially in the nineteenth, was an outgrowth of the increasing concern of mothers with the welfare of their children, expressed most concretely by the rise among the middle and better sort of the practice of maternal breast-feeding instead of resort to wet-nurses. The practice created close mother–child bonding and intensified maternal affection. In 1735 a woman wrote bitterly: 'I can't figure to myself a more afflicting circumstance in human life than to be entirely deprived of my child by the unkindness of my husband.'[85] Thanks to the rise of the cult of domesticity in the period after 1780, motherhood increasingly came to be considered by women as an end in itself, and no longer as merely a biological device for the production of male heirs to property. In consequence the mother–child bond became even closer and more intimate, especially in families where marital relations were strained.[86] Thus the mothers who were most likely to be involved in private separations were also those most likely to be passionately attached to their children, and most distraught by their removal.[87]

Part cause and part consequence of this mother–child bonding was the growth of the idea that mothers were by nature particularly nurturing and attentive to childish needs, and consequently the most suitable

---

[85] Anon., *Hardships of Law on Wives*, 20.
[86] Lewis, 55–6.   [87] Plowden, 2: 246, 338.

custodians of young children, especially girls, but also including boys up to the age of seven. Thus, in a case before the King's Bench in 1804, the lawyers for a mother argued, unsuccessfully, that the court had a right and duty to protect from seizure by their father all children 'of such a tender age, that they cannot without grave danger be separated from the mother'.[88] This idea of the mother as the most suitable natural custodian of young children, superior in this respect to the busy and preoccupied father, was strongly reinforced in the early nineteenth century by the paradigm of the two spheres: the internal domestic sphere under the control of the wife, and the external worldly sphere under the control of the husband.

One principle remained entirely unchanged until the very end of the nineteenth century, however. This was that by committing adultery a woman lost all moral and legal rights as a mother, and was by definition unfit to have custody of her children. A wife convicted, or merely accused, of adultery could be virtually certain that she would never again be permitted to set eyes on her children. The only way for an adulterous wife and mother to keep both her lover and her child was to flee with them to the Continent, where they would be safe. For example, when in 1814 Mrs Taafe eloped abroad with her lover Lord William Fitzgerald and her youngest child, she declared flatly, 'the child shall not be given up'.[89]

Only in the mid-twentieth century did another ethical principle governing the disposal of children of broken marriages come to dominate public attitudes and legal rules. This puts the welfare of the children above all other considerations, and treats both spouses as potentially equally competent at the upbringing of children, depending upon the character and circumstances.

B. THE LAW

The ecclesiastical courts had no jurisdiction whatever over child custody, and never attempted to interfere, leaving the field to common law and equity. The common law courts always gave full patriarchal power to any father, however unworthy, until his children had reached maturity. In law, the age of maturity was 21, but in 1861 a judge remarked without contradiction that 'the common law courts never assisted parents seeking to obtain the custody of their children, those children resisting, after the

---

[88] *De Manneville* v. *De Manneville* (1804), *Eng. Rep.* 32: 763.
[89] *Taafe* v. *Fitzgerald*, RIA/HP, 1102: 12, 35.

age of discretion'. This was defined by another judge as 'after the age of fourteen, or rather, as now seems settled, sixteen years'.[90]

The common law courts paid no attention to the personal conduct of the father in terms of his own adultery or cruelty which might have led to the marital separation.[91] For example, as late as the early nineteenth century, King's Bench refused to interfere in a case where the wife had been forced to leave home because of intolerable cruelty, leaving behind a child aged 6. Although the father was now in gaol and cohabiting with a woman, and the child was in gaol with them, the court refused to give the child to its mother.

Throughout the eighteenth century, however, private deeds of separation normally included clauses allocating custody of one or more of the younger children to the mother. For over half a century, it was generally believed that a father could by these deeds cede to the mother his legal powers over custody and access to the children, so long as she did not commit adultery. For example, some time before 1782, Mr and Mrs Lewis signed a private separation deed by which the husband gave to his wife custody of all four children. It was only later, when Mrs Lewis committed adultery, that her husband sued for judicial separation from bed and board and recovered possession of the children.[92]

But this belief in the legal validity of conceding custody to a wife was rudely shattered by a court decision in 1820, which was part of the general legal reaction led by Lord Eldon. Lord Westmeath had signed a separation deed, giving custody of their only daughter to her mother, but he later seized the child by force while she was visiting him with her governess. When he was obliged by a writ of habeas corpus to produce the child in King's Bench, Lord Eldon declared that the inherent power of a father over his children could not be abrogated by any private agreement he might enter into, and therefore released the child back into the custody of her father.[93] As late as the 1850s a judge reinforced the 1820 sentence, solemnly declaring that it was 'contrary to public policy to allow a husband, though guilty of adultery and cruelty, to transfer to his wife his rights and duties with reference to his children'.[94]

In pursuit of this rigid doctrine of absolute paternal control over children, the common law courts were always ready to use the writ of habeas corpus to force a mother to bring her children before the court, to be

---

[90] *Ryder* v. *Ryder* (1861), *Eng. Rep.* 164: 981–2.

[91] Shelford, 678–90; *De Manneville* v. *De Manneville* (1804), *Eng. Rep.* 102: 1055.

[92] *Lewis* v. *Lewis* (1782), GLRO, DL/C/179; see also *Guth* v. *Guth* (1792), *Eng. Rep.* 29: 729–33.

[93] See Stone, *Broken Lives*, Westmeath case; MacQueen, *Rights and Liabilities*, 351.

[94] MacQueen, *Marriage, Divorce, and Legitimacy*, 166, 277.

handed over to the father as their rightful guardian. Nor would the courts do anything to prevent a forcible seizure of children by the father and his agents, so long as there was no active breach of the peace. Thus, in 1804, Lord Chief Justice Ellenborough, following a rule by Lord Kenyon, defended the action by a separated husband in forcing his way into his wife's house, wrenching an infant from its mother's breast, and carrying it off with him.[95] The result of so rigid an interpretation of the law was to reduce a wife and mother to a condition of abject fear of loss of all access to her children. In 1850, Lord Chancellor Cottenham remarked sympathetically:

A wife is precluded from seeking redress against her husband by the terror of that power which the law gives him of taking her children from her. . . . The torture of the mother will make the wife submit to any injury rather than be parted from her children.[96]

Although the Court of Chancery had the authority to mitigate the rigours of the common law in cases where the child held property in trust, in practice it was very reluctant before the 1830s to interfere with the powers of the father for custody of his children.[97] In 1732 the lord chancellor reiterated the old principle, and declared: 'The father is entitled to the custody of his own children during their infancy, not only as guardian by nurture, but by nature. . . . If he can in any way gain them, he is at liberty to do so, provided no breach of the peace be made in such an attempt.'[98]

A century later, however, attitudes, if not the law itself, were beginning to change. In a case in 1827, the vice-chancellor, a high official in Chancery, made it clear that he believed an overhaul of the rigid law of custody was overdue. He publicly regretted that he could find no legal precedent for interference in a case such as the one before him, saying 'if any could be found, I would most gladly admit it, for, in a moral point of view, I know of no act more harsh or cruel than depriving the mother of proper intercourse with her child'.[99] Things were indeed beginning to change in Chancery, and when in 1831 Mrs Mytton asked for the custody of her five children, it was decreed 'under the directions of the Court of Chancery, the children are to remain with their mother, and to be placed under guardians'.[100] By 1848 the settled view of Chancery was

---

[95] *De Manneville* v. *De Manneville* (1804), *Eng. Rep.* 32: 768; 34: 1057–8; *Rex* v. *De Manneville* (1804), ibid. 102: 1055.

[96] MacQueen, *Marriage, Divorce, and Legitimacy*, 154–5.

[97] Ibid. 159–63; Shelford, 684–91.

[98] *Ex parte* Hopkins (1732), *Eng. Rep.* 24: 1009–10.

[99] *Ball* v. *Ball* (1827), ibid. 57: 703–4.   [100] *Mytton* v. *Mytton* (1831), ibid. 162: 1298.

that, regardless of blame for the separation, the court should make every effort amicably to divide custody of and access to the children between the parents in such a way that they should continue to love and respect both parents, regardless of who was to blame.[101] On the other hand, in 1897 the lord chancellor again pronounced against the legal validity of a clause about custody in a private separation deed, saying: 'I do not think . . . that the bargain between parties, whereby he surrenders his paternal rights, is worth the parchment on which it is engrossed. The law would not give effect to it. Nor is the paternal right capable of being bargained away in any way.'[102] Patriarchalism died hard in the English courts.

C. PRIVATE NEGOTIATIONS

Behind this façade of persistent common law rigidity and Chancery timidity before 1830, private separations always involved delicate prior negotiations between spouses about custody and visiting rights. In the few cases in which we have access to private correspondence, the reality turns out to be very different from the patriarchal absolutism exhibited when cases came before the common law courts. By no means all fathers wanted to be bothered with children, especially if they were intending to cohabit with a mistress. Other fathers did not want the responsibility of looking after children, even if the burden was delegated to a governess. Yet others were persuaded by the rising tide of sentiment about maternal love and nurturing that mothers made the best custodians of young children.

In addition to these theoretical considerations, there was also a very practical problem: children can be expensive to clothe, feed, and educate, besides often being a nuisance around the house. Not every man or woman, especially among the poor, was anxious to take on the burden of child support, and some of the great custody battles among the well-to-do were concerned as much with which parent was going to pay for upkeep as they were with which parent would obtain custody and control. As the emotional stakes of the mother in custody and access rose in the late eighteenth century, so did the opportunities for emotional and financial blackmail by the husband. In these private negotiations, there is therefore a secret complexity of motives and a wide variety of outcomes.

When Mr Heatley sued his adulterous wife for separation on grounds

---

[101] *De Manneville* v. *De Manneville* (1804), *Eng. Rep.* 34: 1057; 32: 764; MacQueen, *Rights and Liabilities*, 351–4; id., *Marriage, Divorce, and Legitimacy*, 174–5.
[102] Roberts, 93.

of her adultery, he ejected her from the house and kept her baby, which was still at wet-nurse. It was above all this separation from her infant that caused most anguish to Mrs Heatley. She wrote timidly to her husband: 'I have one favour to beg of you ... to see my poor child once more, once more—think what I suffer from parting from you both.' When he agreed, she expressed her 'thanks, ten thousand thanks, for the pleasure you gave me in seeing my sweet boy'. This success emboldened her to try again, asking 'let me once more see my dear babe, let me once more press him to my bosom'. She reminded her husband that 'the loss I feel in my child, nothing but a mother that loves as I do can tell'. There is no doubting her sincerity, but it did her no good.[103]

Fairly extensive correspondence has survived about the negotiations in 1774 over the custody of the 1-year-old daughter of Richard and Elizabeth Lytton of Knebworth, descendants of an old but somewhat impoverished landed family. During negotiations for a separation, Richard wrote firmly to his wife:

With respect to the child, my determination is to take care of her myself, but in such a way as to give you the least pain possible. Pursuant to this plan, I shall leave her with you till I have found a proper place to send her to; as soon as I have, I shall inform you of it and you shall have access to her, but nobody else without my special permission. But she is not on any account to be removed from where I shall place [her], not even for the shortest time.

After further negotiations, Elizabeth was granted custody of the daughter for one full year before she had to hand her over to her father. Thereafter the father planned that the child would be 'solely under my direction during her minority'.

This was, however, far from the end of the story, for at the end of the year Elizabeth refused to give up the child, since she strongly opposed her husband's plan to send her to school. Richard had the mother and her trustees who had signed the agreement brought before Lord Mansfield in King's Bench by a writ of habeas corpus for the recovery of the child. Instead of handing over the child to her father, which by common law usage he should have done, Lord Mansfield apparently ordered that she be sent to school for a year. This merely heated up the dispute: Richard tried to have the girl removed to his home at Knebworth, but Elizabeth retorted with accusations that he 'was rascal enough to commit the education of his daughter to a harlot'—presumably, the woman with whom he was living. The little girl apparently remained in school for some years, while the parents fought for her allegiance. Richard accused

---

[103] *Heatley* v. *Heatley* (1770), *Trials for Adultery*, 7: 61, 65, 72, 74, 85.

Elizabeth and her family of visiting her frequently, 'trying to poison her mind with respect of me'. He complained bitterly that he was merely trying to defend 'my just right of having full possession of my child, a right which every father has in every country, and has possessed in every age ... which right is in my case fortified over and over again with repeated legal sanctions of the very strongest kind'.

Year after year the battle continued, Richard complaining that the child was 'bred up in principles utterly repugnant to my own' and 'taught to hate her father as the most odious person possible'. He concluded: 'I had not the remotest suspicion of it being possible to interpret the Rule of the Court [for the child to go to school for a year] as a surrender of my paternal rights over my child ... and [I] consequently acknowledge no jurisdiction whatever of the Court of King's Bench over my child.' Richard Lytton was legally in the right, and Lord Mansfield's rule of court was highly unusual, reflecting his idiosyncratic view of his legal power and his limited respect for precedent. Richard Lytton was sticking to the ancient common law rule of patriarchy, whereas Lord Mansfield was acting in what he thought was in the best interests of all parties, including the mother and child. In doing so he was responding to the diminishing role accorded by public opinion to the claims of absolute patriarchal power.

In the end, Richard Lytton seems to have won. In 1781 he removed the child from the school to which she had been sent by her mother, took her home to Knebworth, and denied his wife access to her. The mother obtained a writ of habeas corpus from King's Bench, and asked Lord Mansfield to allow her access to the child, according to the articles of separation. This time, Lord Mansfield adopted the standard line that 'the Court cannot at any age take a child from the father'. But he decided that the father was bound by the articles of separation to allow Elizabeth Lytton access to her child, which was some concession to the rights of a mother.[104]

Examination of this and other cases of family breakdowns demonstrates how crucial the question of child custody could be in negotiations for private separation.[105] The mother was often frantic to keep one or more of her children, especially the girls and the babies, and some husbands seem to have recognized that, despite their absolute legal authority, an innocent mother had some moral claims. There were clearly wide possibilities for the father to suggest a trade-off between a reduc-

---

[104] Herts RO, 574. 83. B; This judgment only survives as cited in a later case in 1804, *Eng. Rep.* 102: 1055.

[105] *Evans* v. *Evans* (1789), LPCA, D.693.

tion in the size of the allowance to the mother and concessions to her over child custody.

By the early 1800s, educated public opinion was becoming more and more convinced of the injustice of absolute paternal control of child custody, which was being clung to so obstinately by common law judges. This can be seen in the increasingly intricate negotiations over child custody in cases of private separation. Very young infants and girls were now often allocated to the mother, and reasonable visiting rules for both spouses were conceded. Even custody was now often shared, the object being to 'give both parents a fair intercourse with them', and to instil in the children 'affectionate regard for the character and person of both'. In 1848 the lord chancellor argued that 'nothing could be more injurious to children than their being brought up with a bad opinion of either one or other of their parents'.[106] It was the alleged use by the wife of her visiting rights to her daughter to poison her mind against him which had so enraged Mr Lytton.

By the early nineteenth century, this issue of child custody loomed larger and larger, and the plight of the privately separated wife became merged with that of the wife separated by judicial decree. The judges in the ecclesiastical courts were soon affected by these new sentiments, and did their best to support them. Although powerless to control child custody, the church courts did determine the size of alimony, and by the 1820s they were openly using this authority to manipulate child custody on behalf of the mother. The court defended this delicate financial blackmail on the increasingly familiar grounds that: 'the welfare of the child would probably best be served under her maternal care'. The judges in the ecclesiastical courts were here displaying a totally different moral view of justice between husband and wife concerning child custody than that still upheld by the judges in the common law courts.[107]

In Chancery, the turning point came in 1827, arising out of a decision by Lord Chancellor Eldon, of all people. In that year, Mrs Pole sued her wealthy husband, Wellesley Pole, for separation on grounds of his continuing and scandalous adultery with a Mrs Bligh. She also sued in Chancery for the custody of her daughter and two sons, on the grounds that their father was manifestly unfit to have charge of them. Eldon was a great conservative stickler for the old rules, but he was deeply shocked at the evidence about Pole's continued adultery and his curious ideas about the bringing up of children. He therefore twisted the law to fit the circumstances, declaring that 'I should deserve to be hunted out of

---

[106] MacQueen, *Rights and Liabilities*, 352.
[107] *Kempe* v. *Kempe* (1828), *Eng. Rep.* 162: 669.

society if I were to hesitate one moment whether I should permit these children to go to a father who had the slightest connection with so abandoned and infamous a woman as Mrs Bligh has proved herself to be'[108] (Plate 16).

The rising tide of opinion in the 1830s in favour of the rights of mothers in child custody disputes finally resulted in a major change in the statute law in 1839. The key influence behind the legislation was the persuasive pleadings of Caroline Norton, a well-born and well-educated woman whose husband had publicly accused her of adultery and had abducted their three children. Although she was acquitted, he refused to return the children to her. His own counsel later described her husband's behaviour as 'obviously making the love of a mother for her offspring a means of barter and bargain', in order to make her accept a reduction in the size of her maintenance allowance. At the time, she referred to 'those dear children, the loss of whose pattering steps and sweet occasional voices made the silence of [my] new home intolerable as the anguish of death'. Years later, in 1855, she recalled 'what I suffered respecting those children, God knows . . . what I endured . . . of pain, exasperation, helplessness, and despair, under the evil law which suffered any man, for vengeance or for interest, to take baby children from the mother.'[109]

Under the persuasive influence of Mrs Norton, in 1837 Sergeant Talfourd introduced his Child Custody Bill, only to see it rejected by the Lords. Reintroduced in 1839, it finally passed the Lords, thanks to the active support of Mrs Norton's other influential friend, Lord Lyndhurst. The purpose of the act was to relieve grossly ill-treated wives from the fear that if they sued for separation, they would have their children taken from them and would never see them again. This act once and for all stripped traditional unlimited patriarchal authority from the father, and its successful passage through a legislature consisting of elite males is an indication of the change of opinion in upper-class circles. The act made it possible for the Court of Chancery to transfer legal custody of all children under the age of 7 to the mother, on the grounds that she was best suited to take care of children of such a tender age. Only after the age of 7 could the father claim his legal right of custody. Second, it made provision for visitation rights by the other spouse at all times, on the grounds that children should be brought up with an affectionate respect for both parents.

[108] *The Annual Register* (1827), 293–313.

[109] Perkins, *The Life of Mrs Norton*, 120; C. Norton, *A Letter to the Queen on Lord Chancellor Cranworth's Marriage and Divorce Bill* (London, 1855), 68–9; see also *Letters of Caroline Norton to Lord Melbourne*, ed. J. O. Hoge and C. Olney (Ohio State University Press, 1974).

On the other hand, wives who had been proven by an ecclesiastical court or in a crim. con. case to have committed adultery were specifically excluded from the benefits of the bill, and so continued to be deprived of further access to their children. If anything, the act raised the penalties for female adultery even higher than they had been before, indicating that belief in the double standard of sexual morality was still strong in the minds of the legislators.[110]

The child custody issue arose again during the lengthy debates over the Divorce Reform Act of 1857. Members of Parliament told many horror stories about the plight of mothers at marital separation; about the father who tore an infant from the breast of its mother, in order to force the latter to make a new disposition of her property in his favour; about the child taken from its mother and given into the hands of an unknown governess; about three little girls removed from their mother and placed in the care of their father's mistress.

The attorney-general claimed in rebuttal that by now 'generally speaking, the Court of Chancery would give the custody of the children to the innocent parent', which was roughly true.[111] But nothing had changed in the common law courts. In 1857 Lord Justice Turner repeated once more the stock common law position that any private separation deed by which the father relinquished custody of his children was against 'the settled law and policy of the country'.[112]

Although the new secular Divorce Court set up in 1857 was given very broad and ill-defined powers to allocate custody and order access, it entered this mine-field with caution. In practice it seems to have been most active in giving custody of the children under 14 of separated or divorced parents to the mother, provided that she was the innocent party.[113] If she were guilty of adultery, however, the court persisted in denying her both custody and access. In 1862 a judge refused to grant the wife even access to her children, observing: 'It will probably have a salutory effect on the interests of public morality that it should be known that a woman, if guilty of adultery, will forfeit, as far as this court is concerned, all right to the custody of or access to her children.' The

---

[110] 2–3 Vict. C. 54; MacQueen, *Marriage, Divorce and Legitimacy*, 154–5.

[111] 3 *Hansard*, 147: 1268–9, 1750.

[112] *Hope* v. *Hope* (1857), *Eng. Rep.* 44: 577; see *Vansittart* v. *Vansittart* (1858), ibid. 70: 26–31; in this last case, the father considered his children a burden, and 'it is rather for his benefit that they are to be handed over to his wife'—an argument the court still refused to accept.

[113] *Eng. Rep.* 167: 636; *Boyd* v. *Boyd and Collins* (1859), ibid. 861; *Ryder* v. *Ryder* (1861), ibid. 981; *Clout* v. *Clout and Hollebone* (1861), ibid. 1047; *Thompson* v. *Thompson and Sturnfells* (1861), ibid. 1052; W. E. Browning, *The Practice and Procedure of the Court for Divorce and Matrimonial Causes* (London, 1862), 91–4.

battle for equal rights between husbands and wives was clearly far from over.[114]

It was only in 1873 that the double standard was officially removed as a criterion in the granting of child custody: a new act empowered the Divorce Court to give a mother custody of the children up to the age of 14, even if she was guilty of adultery. In 1881 the court was empowered to allocate custody as it thought fit, and in 1925 it was instructed by another act to make the welfare of the child the paramount considera-tion.[115] Thus, between 1830 and 1881, the principle governing child custody had moved from the absolute right of control by the father to the nurturing rights of the mother, provided that she was not an adulteress; and in the early twentieth century it shifted priority from the rights of either parent to the welfare of the children.

D. LEGITIMACY

The last issue which often loomed large in disputes over private separa-tion was that of the legitimacy of children conceived and born after physical separation of the spouses had taken place. This might be no trivial matter, since upon its resolution might depend the inheritance of huge properties and noble titles. For example, a couple had separated in 1785, but when in 1791 the wife gave birth to a child in her lover's house, she remarked 'it is a pity it is a girl, and that such an estate [meaning her husband's] should be lost'.[116]

The assumption of the law was that when separations were private, a child conceived after separation was legitimate unless proved otherwise. This put the onus on the husband of proving that he could not have had access to his wife in the eight or nine months before the birth. But it took the opposite position in the case of couples after a judicial separation, when a child conceived by the wife was assumed to be illegitimate unless proved otherwise. For a hitherto childless couple, this was a great incent-ive to a husband to obtain a judicial separation rather than a private one, if at all possible, since otherwise any future child would be his legal heir.[117]

---

[114] *Seddon* v. *Seddon and Doyle* (1862), *Eng. Rep.* 164: 1147.

[115] Holcombe, 53–4.

[116] *Hodges* v. *Hodges* (1795), *Eng. Rep.* 162: 1102 n. *a*. For other examples in which this issue became critical, see the Beaufort and Grafton cases in Stone, *Broken Lives*.

[117] Shelford, 680, 708–33; Poynter, 220–2; *Eng. Rep.* 22: 26–7.

8. Conclusion

Private deeds of separation developed in the mid- to late seventeenth century to meet a growing need of incompatible but non-adulterous couples somehow to break free from an insupportable cohabitation. The procedure clearly became increasingly common among the middling sort and the elite, especially in the last half of the eighteenth century. By then, the standard clauses devised by conveyancers made a private separation deed tantamount to a divorce, granting total economic and sexual freedom for both parties. This development was stimulated by the increasing use of the concept of contract in society, the notable erosion of the patriarchal principle in marriage, and the persistent encroachment of equity and common law upon areas of jurisdiction previously left to canon law.

Between 1790 and 1830, an attempt was made by lords Kenyon and Eldon and others not merely to reduce the scope of private separation deeds, but even to abolish them altogether. However, their efforts generated a backlash. Other conservatives were reluctant to overturn a century of case law, and reformers were anxious to meet a clear public need. As a result, private separation deeds were still flourishing when the new Divorce Court was set up in 1857, and even afterwards they continued to serve a useful purpose. In 1908 it was estimated that there were still 2,000 private separations a year, compared with a mere 100 judicial separations. A further 6,600 magistrates' orders for separation with maintenance were also issued to the poor every year, but these were mostly temporary, and the couples usually came together again. The extent of private separation was estimated at 28 a year per 100,000 population, which was very small by modern standards, but five times higher than that of such other European countries as France, Austria, or Norway.[118]

During the eighteenth and nineteenth centuries, the chief defect of the private deed of separation was the shaky legal status of some of its clauses, and the consequent difficulty of enforcement if they were challenged in the courts. The ecclesiastical courts never recognized the validity of these deeds. The common law courts first accepted them in the eighteenth century and then tried to reject some of their clauses in the early nineteenth. Chancery accepted the financial clauses, but denied the validity of clauses which banned litigation and gave the appearance of encouraging adulterous liaisons.

[118] *Roy. Com. Divorce, 1912*, 2: 217.

The fact that the deeds continued to increase in numbers and popularity despite these legal obstacles suggests that in most cases they were satisfactory to both parties and were never challenged in court. They performed the same function for the middling and better sort as the public wife-sale did for a much smaller number of the poor. It was a form of quasi-legal collusive self-divorce, which in practice opened the way to the formation of a new adulterous or bigamous household by the husband, and sometimes—but probably much less frequently—by the wife. It was a popular institution which flourished in the margins of the law, but was totally reliant upon the legal skills of conveyancers in drafting the deeds in such a way as to survive the hostility to them of many distinguished judges. It was the most informal, but the most commonly used and most convenient legal option available to the victims of marital discord. It is a remarkable example of how an officially non-divorcing society could devise its own quasi-legal instruments to cope with the fact of irremediable marital breakdowns.

❧ VIII ❧

Judicial Separation

Law! What law can search into the remote abyss of Nature, what
evidence can prove the unaccountable disaffections of wedlock? Can
a jury sum up the endless aversions that are rooted in our souls, or
can a bench give judgement upon antipathies?

G. Farquhar, *The Beaux-Stratagem* (1707), III/iii

1. Introduction

Suits for judicial separation in the ecclesiastical courts served three
purposes. Most suits launched by a wife were in reality blackmail devices
to improve the financial terms of a separation which had already physically taken place. At issue above all else was the size of the alimony to be
paid by the husband. Most suits brought by a husband, whether contested or not, were in order to obtain a separation from an adulterous
wife without having to pay her alimony. Uncontested or nominally contested suits brought by a husband were usually part of a collusive
arrangement by which both parties conspired together to prepare the
ground for a parliamentary divorce.

A. THE ECCLESIASTICAL COURTS

In the first instance these suits usually began in one of the twenty-six
Consistory Courts attached to each diocese, each of which was run by a
group of professional civil lawyers, headed by a chancellor, who acted as
a delegate of his bishop. If dissatisfied with the sentence, the loser in a
case could appeal the sentence to one of two higher courts, situated in
London and York, of which the Court of Arches served the Province of
Canterbury.

Beyond the Court of Arches, it was always possible, but very expensive, to appeal to the High Court of Delegates, an *ad hoc* body appointed
for each occasion by the lord chancellor, and consisting of three eminent
common law judges and three young and inexperienced canon lawyers.[1]

[1] G. I. O. Duncan, *The High Court of Delegates* (Cambridge, 1971), 34, 162–9; *Report on
Ecclesiastical Courts, 1831 (PP 1831–2)*, 24: 76, 148.

These appeals were a favourite device of obstinate wives, since their husbands were obliged to foot a large part of the legal bill for both sides, and their temporary court-ordered alimony continued to be paid so long as the suit was not finally settled. But appeals to this level were rare, only eleven matrimonial cases being heard by the delegates from all England and Wales in the thirty years in the middle of the eighteenth century, and only twenty-one in the thirty years 1800–30. In only six of the twenty-one cases was the decision of the lower court overthrown.[2]

Beyond the Court of Delegates lay the remote possibility of yet another appeal court, the Commission of Review. Requests for a commission were rarely sought, and even more rarely granted, and it was in practice 'an application to the indulgence of the Crown'. It could only hear appeals over cases where there was clear prescriptive evidence of an error in law; or an important question in law the answer to which was doubtful and needed to be settled; or a gross miscarriage of justice. If any of these situations arose, the lord chancellor would recommend that the Crown appoint a special commission to hear the case.[3]

B. THE NUMBER OF LITIGANTS

As has been seen, in the vast majority of cases of broken marriages, the couples managed to separate without the expense and publicity of litigation in open court. Only the tiny minority who could not agree on terms came before a court, and very large numbers of the suits initiated were settled privately or dropped before they came to sentence, since their true purpose had always been blackmail rather than victory. Those who fought their legal battles to a finish at huge cost were only a minority of those who went to law, who were themselves only a minority of those who separated, who were again only an infinitely tiny minority of all married couples. Thus, between 1660 and 1830 the Consistory Court of the huge diocese of York only heard about three or four cases a year. Excluding the Court of Arches, in all England and Wales in the late 1820s fewer than fifty matrimonial suits a year were begun.[4] Between 1845 and 1850, only fifty-four matrimonial cases a year reached sentence in all courts, a tenth of which were merely preliminaries to prepare the way for a Parliamentary divorce.[5] Since the number of marriages a year in the first

[2] *Report on Ecclesiastical Courts, 1831*, 20: 360; Till, 161.
[3] *Dew* v. *Clarke* (1828), *Eng. Rep.* 38: 989. For the Westmeath case, see also Stone, *Broken Lives.*
[4] Till, 10, 71, 84, 244, 299; *Return of Matrimonial Suits (PP 1844)*, 38: 156–7; 3 *Hansard*, 14/ 7: 1164; *PP 1831–2*, 24: 567.
[5] *Roy. Com. Divorce, 1853*, 1: 29.

half of the nineteenth century was over 100,000, this means that only about one marriage in 3,000 ever ended up in a court.

Apart from their rarity at any period, the second most striking feature of the statistics on matrimonial suits is the near collapse of activity in the provincial Consistory Courts during the end of the seventeenth and early eighteenth centuries, the reasons for which have already been explained.[6] Another important reason for the permanent decline of matrimonial litigation in these provincial courts was the attraction of more and more of this specialized business to the London court, which by the 1820s was handling between one-half and two-thirds of all the cases in the Province of Canterbury.[7] In 1854 the lord chancellor remarked that separation suits 'are very few. The great bulk of these causes are here in London and they are only eleven a year. In the country, they are hardly ever heard of.'[8] One reason for this concentration of business upon London in the early nineteenth century was a legal loophole which allowed litigants, by taking up residence in London for twenty-one days, to qualify to sue in the London court. This was an attractive option since

suitors in heavy and important cases preferred to have their case tried in the Consistory Court of London, not only for the advantage of having it heard before an experienced judge and in a Court remarkable for the rapidity of its proceedings, but also to enable them to have it conducted by the London proctors and members of the Doctors' Commons Bar, instead of its being tried in the country diocesan courts, where they had no such advantages.[9]

Yet another reason was that the court, in its desire to attract litigants, went out of its way to make things easy. The mid-nineteenth-century legal text-book writer, MacQueen, believed that this facility enticed couples into the court, instead of directing them to processes of arbitration and conciliation:

Under the existing law and practice, a husband who chooses to quarrel with his wife, or a wife who chooses to quarrel with her husband, let the grounds be ever so slight, has only to draw up a short petition, make an affidavit, and walk into Doctors' Commons where the legislature has established an office for the uncontrolled issue of matrimonial citations. The moment a citation is issued, litigation becomes inevitable; the husband and wife prepare for combat. Friends, relations, and peradventure witnesses, share in the humiliation.[10]

In 1854, Lord Brougham described the London Consistory Court in

---

[6] See above, 41–3, and Fig. 1.8.   [7] *PP 1831–2*, 24: 567; *PP 1844*, 38: 156–7.

[8] 2 *Hansard*, 134: 942; *PP 1831–2*, 24: 567.

[9] H. S. Giffard, Earl of Halsbury (ed.), *The Laws of England.* 2nd edn. (London, 1933), 11: 600 n. *b*.

[10] MacQueen, *Marriage, Divorce and Legitimacy*, v.

Doctors' Commons as 'the great central jurisdiction where the bulk [of separation cases] arise'.[11] But according to Charles Dickens, not the most reliable of witnesses, it was not exactly a busy hive of activity. Four years earlier, he had made a visitor to Doctors' Commons observe: 'altogether, I have never, on any occasion, made one at such a cosy, dozy, old-fashioned, time-forgotten, sleepy-headed little family-party.'[12] One illustration of the court in session in 1825 suggests that it was neither cosy nor dozy (Plate 4). The number of matrimonial cases coming before the Court of Arches fell dramatically after the 1660s, but rose again after 1810 (Fig. 1.2, Table 1.1). As a result by the early nineteenth century matrimonial cases were the mainstay of the business of the court (Fig. 1.3, Table 1.1).

C. TYPES OF LITIGANTS

As has already been explained, in the late seventeenth century, the poor could still afford to go to court, and in the London Consistory Court between 1671 and 1705 over a fifth of the plaintiffs were drawn from the most impoverished and socially insignificant class: servants, sailors, etc. A century later, between 1760 and 1805, the poor had almost entirely vanished from the London court, and the litigants were now largely drawn from the upper levels of the middling sort, well-to-do professionals, and the landed elite.

In the Court of Arches, the rise in the quality and wealth of litigants in matrimonial cases from the late seventeenth to the mid-eighteenth centuries is even more apparent. By the late eighteenth century, fighting a matrimonial case to the finish through the appeal process had become a luxury open only to the rich. Nor was expense the only deterrent to litigation in the Court of Arches in the mid-eighteenth century. Publicity in the newspapers had made such litigation much less attractive, and one victim, writing in 1733, warned bitterly that anyone who appealed a matrimonial case up to the Court of Arches 'must expect to have as much filth as a scavenger's cart will hold emptied upon him'.[13]

D. THE SEX RATIO OF PLAINTIFFS

Between 1660 and 1857, the sex ratio of plaintiffs in matrimonial cases in the London Consistory Court changed erratically. In the late seventeenth

---

[11] 3 *Hansard*, 34: 12.

[12] C. Dickens, *David Copperfield*, ch. 23; see G. D. Squibb, *Doctor's Commons* (Oxford, 1977).

[13] J. Goole, *The Contract Violated, or the Hasty Marriage* (London, 1733), 63.

century, the court was predominantly used by women, over 60 per cent of all plaintiffs being female. By the late eighteenth century, however, only a minority of plaintiffs were female. Inspection shows that this change was largely due to the decline in suits by women—usually pregnant—desperately trying to prove a contract or clandestine marriage; and by the growth of separation suits, most of them brought by husbands because of their wives' adultery (Table 1.8).[14] Whereas in the late seventeenth century there were only about seventeen cases a year of such suits, by the late eighteenth century the number had risen to fifty. It is also noticeable that, at all times, suits by husbands far more commonly resulted in a favourable sentence than those initiated by wives, many of which tended to peter out. Either wives were more willing to settle out of court than husbands, or the court was less willing to grant them separations, or perhaps both. The shift in the early nineteenth century back to a majority of female plaintiffs is consequently hard to explain.

E. COSTS OF LITIGATION

Evidence about the cost of litigation in the ecclesiastical courts comes from three sources. The first is the assessments by the court itself of costs incurred by the wife, which the husband had to pay. Surviving assessments in the court records suggest that the bill presented by the proctor was normally scaled down by a quarter to a third.[15] The bill of costs included the strictly legal fees in the court, but not all the many out-of-pocket expenses like hiring detectives and preparing witnesses.[16] So small was the proportion of taxed costs to full costs that it was claimed in 1791 that if a creditor sued for his debt and recovered both the debt and taxed costs, 'he will in general be a loser of considerably more', since the untaxed costs would still exceed the debt.[17]

The second source of evidence is public gossip and the claims of the litigants themselves about what a suit or a series of suits had cost them. These estimates tended to be as exaggerated as the assessed costs were understated. Finally, there are a series of statements made in the first half of the nineteenth century by knowledgeable judges, lawyers, and legal writers before parliamentary committees about the average true

[14] GLRO, London CC, *passim*.

[15] Some of these bills of costs are to be found in the records of cases in the Court of Arches. Many others were presented to Parliament in Parliamentary divorce cases, which have been extensively analysed by Anderson. His conclusions are vitiated, however, by his failure to realize how greatly assessed costs underestimated the full expenses of litigation.

[16] For a list of approved fees, see J. Merrifield, *The Law of Attorneys* (London, 1830), app., 11–72.   [17] F. Hargrave, *Collectanea Juridica* (London, 1791), 1: 477.

costs of litigation. These statements were often made under oath, the speakers knew what they were talking about, and there is no good reason to reject their fairly unanimous conclusions.

In 1844 Dr Lushington, the judge of the London Consistory Court, declared that the minimum cost of an unopposed suit in his court was £50, while a strongly contested suit could run up to £800. Other expert witnesses put the range at between £100 and over £1,000. An appeal to the Court of Arches was reckoned to cost between £165 and £400 for both sides, while a Parliamentary divorce was said to cost the husband at least £400.[18]

There is evidence to support such estimates, and particularly the wide variation in costs between uncontested and contested suits. The cost of an impotence case which wound its way through the courts in 1840–1, uncontested in the Consistory Court and the Court of Arches but contested on appeal to the Judicial Committee of the Privy Council, was assessed at no less than £1,200.[19] One of the most bitterly fought suits for aristocratic adultery, that brought by Lord Ellenborough against his wife in 1830, was generally believed in legal circles to have cost him £5,000.[20]

These enormous costs were explained by the fact that matrimonial suits were especially difficult and expensive. There was often no direct visual evidence of any act of adultery, so that the case for reasonable probability had to be built up from the testimony of a large number of witnesses. Secondly, in seriously contested cases, the litigants were usually extremely bitter, and they and their witnesses had a tendency to bias, prevarication, exaggeration, and even lies.[21] Moreover the guilty wife had every incentive to delay and to appeal. In the mid-nineteenth century, a leading legal expert observed that 'the rules of Doctors' Commons enable a wife to ruin her husband. . . . For although her case may be wholly groundless, she can have her costs paid *de diem in diem*. She may ask a commission to examine witnesses in Italy, although there are no witnesses in Italy.' He claimed that this actually happened once, and that the futile trip of the commissioners to Italy cost her husband £450. It was commonly believed in legal circles that some of the longest and most bitterly contested cases of separation for adultery were prolonged by the wife merely out of spite.[22]

There can be no doubt that legal costs generally were rising, despite

---

[18] *Roy. Com. Divorce, 1853.* 1: 27, 33, 39, 58–9, 75; *Law Review* 1: (1844–5), 367.
[19] *Roy. Com. Divorce, 1853*, 1: 59.
[20] *Law Review*, 1 (1844–5), 367.   [21] *PP 1831–2*, 24: 69–71.
[22] MacQueen, *Marriage, Divorce, and Legitimacy*, 222; for an example of such litigation see the Middleton case in Stone, *Broken Lives*.

the otherwise widespread price stability between 1660 and 1760. One reason was that clerks and copyists were paid by the page, and gradually they realized that fewer words to a page would increase their income. Since the documentation in hotly contested suits involving many long depositions could run to up to five thousand pages, such strategies increased costs.[23] This also accounts for the difference between the densely packed legal sheets of the late seventeenth century and the half-empty pages of the early nineteenth, with their broad margins, large spaces between each word, and wide gaps between each line.

Another reason for the high and rising expense of litigation was the increasing elaboration of the pre-trial activities by local attorneys. A rare close-up view of what might be involved is provided by a detailed bill of costs by a Shropshire attorney for a legal process which began with negotiations for a private separation deed in 1788 and ended with preparations for a suit for separation in the Court of Arches in 1791.[24] The Corbets were a rich, landed couple who separated because of the husband's cruelty and adultery. The bill presented by Mrs Corbet's Shrewsbury attorney, Mr Chambre, begins with the cost of drafting the private separation agreement. Naturally, he charged a per diem for the days he spent on horseback, riding to and fro to consult Mrs Corbet, Mr Corbet, and her proposed trustee, all of whom lived a day's ride from each other. He also had to travel to London to take expert advice about the exact wording of the deed. After the draft deed had been completed, he discovered that Mr Corbet was still balking at the size of the maintenance allowance to his wife, so that he was obliged to seek out and interview potential witnesses for a possible law-suit for separation. This involved long, and often futile, journeys all over the country, which took many days of work and cost about £55. Often he would ride all day, only to find his quarry absent. He even had to travel as far as Buscot Park in Berkshire in order to interview the Corbets' ex-butler, who was now in service there.[25] On his return to Shrewsbury, Chambre spent two days with Mrs Corbet going over the evidence of the various witnesses. Some potential witnesses, such as a surgeon, were afraid of incurring the wrath of Mr Corbet, and refused to testify voluntarily; this entailed further expense to obtain from the court a compulsory order (which cost 2s. 6d.) and to have it served (which cost another £1. 11s. 6d.).

The depositions were duly copied out (£1. 13s. 4d.) and sent to Dr

---

[23] *Roy. Com. Divorce, 1853*, 1: 58; see the Middleton case in Stone, *Broken Lives*.

[24] *Corbet* v. *Corbet* (1788–91), Salop RO, 731/225; LPCA, B.18/55; E.44/44; Ee. 11, fo. 74; Eee.16, fos. 126–34.

[25] For life in Buscot Park a few years later, see the Loveden case in Stone, *Broken Lives*.

Scott in London for his opinion on them (two guineas). Finally Mr Chambre had to go to London himself for three weeks to consult proctors and court officials to find out 'what kind of evidence would be absolutely necessary to obtain a divorce [i.e. separation] and procure a proper alimony for Mrs Corbet, and likewise to have the libel properly settled for this purpose'. Since Mr Chambre charged two guineas a day for his time, the cost of the trip came to £44. Finally, a commission was appointed by the Court of Arches to hear Mrs Corbet's witnesses locally, for which she had to pay, via Mr Chambre. The commission of three gentlemen spent fifteen days on the job, based at Oswestry. Mr Chambre's expenses and those of the witnesses and the commission's clerk amounted to about £90. More money was spent in searching parish registers for evidence of the baptism of illegitimate children fathered by Mr Corbet, so as to prove his adultery.

At this point, Mr Corbet seemed to be willing to come to terms and to agree to the private deed of separation. The seven-page separation deed was therefore duly engrossed on parchment and sealed, at a cost of twelve guineas. But at the last minute Mr Corbet did not appear in Shrewsbury at the meeting arranged to sign it, the negotiations collapsed, and the whole affair was turned over to a London proctor, with instructions to start a suit for separation in the Court of Arches. Mr Chambre's total bill came to £448. 19s. 6d., not a penny of which could Mrs Corbet recover as part of her assessed costs by the Court of Arches.

What this document shows very clearly is how much legal time was spent in travelling by horseback or by chaise or coach from place to place to talk to the principals and the trustees, to interrogate witnesses, to prepare deeds, and to consult professional legal experts in London, to say nothing of the cost of a local commission to take written depositions for witnesses for presentation to the court. It was the slowness of transport and communications which ran up the attorney's bill, since the time of a professional man such as Mr Chambre was not cheap. It is small wonder that by the 1790s the litigants in the Consistory Courts were confined to the upper ranges of the middling sort and above, and those who appealed up to the Court of Arches to an even more limited class of wealthy businessmen, professionals, and landed elite.

2. Types of Suits

As has been seen, the great bulk of all matrimonial suits in the Middle Ages concerned disputes over the validity of marriage, and only about one in ten involved the separation of a legally married couple. It was only in the late eighteenth century that separation suits came to predominate[26] (Table 1.3, Fig. 1.4), and only in the nineteenth that they comprised over 90 per cent of all matrimonial litigation.

A. NULLITY

There were four types of matrimonial suits open to litigants in ecclesiastical courts. The first were nullity suits, which challenged the legal validity of the marriage itself. Among those which were void in themselves were unions which involved incest, which usually meant marriage with a deceased wife's sister, or with a niece or nephew; or an incapacitating state of mind or body—such as lunacy or male impotence (and, very rarely, female frigidity, or physical deformation of the vagina)—which prevented the essential purpose of marriage, namely sexual intercourse.

The most common reason in the late seventeenth and early eighteenth centuries for declaring a marriage intrinsically void was bigamy arising from a previous marriage. Only in 1603 was bigamy first made a penal offence, as part of a general tightening up of the laws governing marriage and divorce at that time. The act followed custom in exempting persons whose spouses had been overseas or absent without news for seven years or more. More remarkable was that it also exempted those who had been previously judicially separated from bed and board. The church courts, however, continued to treat second marriages under these circumstances as bigamous, and so null and void.[27]

Marriages voidable by litigation fell into a different category. The kidnapping and marriage of an heiress by the use of force had long since been made a criminal offence, and the church courts made such a marriage voidable in law, especially if the victim was under the age of consent. In 1776 this old doctrine was reaffirmed on appeal from the Court of Arches to the Court of Delegates in a case where a guardian abducted his 13-year-old ward, took her off to the Continent, and married her. The Delegates eventually nullified the marriage.[28]

In the sixteenth century, the great bulk of litigation about the nullity of marriage had been caused by pre-contracts. But as litigants slowly realized the hopelessness of their cases in the face of a strict legal policy, the number of suits to void church marriages on these grounds went down sharply between 1660 and 1760. In the London Consistory Court

[26] Helmholtz, 74–5; Houlbrooke, *Church Courts*, 96 (Table 1); Ingram, *Church Courts, Sex, and Marriage*, 171, 181–2, 185–6, 189–94, 205–9, 216.
[27] Poynter, 144. [28] *Harford* v. *Morris* (1776), *Eng. Rep.* 161: 792–7.

they declined from a seventh of all matrimonial cases in the period 1670–99 to none in the 1750s (Table 1.8).

After the passage of the 1753 Marriage Act, however, nullity cases rose again sharply, for a quite different reason. This act declared null and void any marriage of a minor under 21 made without the written consent of parent or guardian. As a result, by the 1770s nearly three-quarters of all nullity suits were being brought on the grounds that one of the spouses had been under age at the time of marriage (Table 1.8).

B. JACTITATION

A suit for 'jactitation' was brought by a man or woman seeking to obtain a court order forbidding the defendant from ever again publicly making a claim to a marriage. This action was fairly widely used in the seventeenth century, when contract marriages were very common and not infrequently repudiated. In the 1660s and 1670s it comprised 14 per cent of all matrimonial cases in the Court of Arches (Table 1.3). By the early eighteenth century, the virtual disappearance of the contract marriage greatly reduced the need for this particular action, but it was still used up to 1753 to bar claims to a clandestine marriage, proof of which was 'always precarious and sometimes impossible'.[29] But the shutting down of the clandestine marriage business by the act of that year more or less put an end to actions for jactitation. Finally, the public rejection by a common law court of an erroneous sentence of jactitation in the famous Duchess of Kingston case in 1776 cast doubts upon the value of the suit. It fell into almost complete disuse thereafter, so much so that it was alleged that there was only one such suit brought between 1776 and 1820—and that failed.[30]

C. SEPARATION FROM BED AND BOARD

The two other types of matrimonial suits were both concerned with establishing a case for claims to a larger or smaller maintenance allowance for the wife, after a separation had already physically taken place. The commonest of such suits was for separation from bed and board, with a bond not to remarry in the lifetime of the other spouse. This was granted on three grounds only: adultery, life-threatening cruelty, or a combination of both.

Nothing was said in the canon law about separation on grounds of

---

[29] Poynter, 264–7.
[30] *Walton* v. *Rider* (1752), *Eng. Rep.* 161: 7; *Hawke* v. *Corri* (1819), ibid. 743–7.

desertion or abandonment, although in practice we have seen that the common law courts refused to prosecute for bigamy those who married after an absence of a spouse without news for seven years or more.[31] When such spouses reappeared, however, the church courts tended to restore to the first husband his former rights over his wife's property and person.

Nor was anything said in canon law about homosexuality as a cause for separation, and two test cases, each brought by a wife against an elite husband accused of sodomy or attempted sodomy with a boy, caused great embarrassment to the courts. In both cases—one in 1793, which was fought up to the Court of Delegates, and another in 1824—the penal offence of actual sodomy had been declared not proven in the common law court, and the husband had only been convicted of attempted sodomy or persuasion to consent to it. In both cases, a court of appeal eventually decided that this reduced offence was the equivalent of marital cruelty.[32] The cautious approach to these two cases by the common law courts, and the uncertainty shown by the church courts about whether or not they constituted legal cruelty, are in striking contrast to the brutal attitudes of juries and mobs towards convicted homosexuals in eighteenth-century London.

If the husband sued his wife for separation on the grounds of her adultery and he won, the court would not allocate alimony to her, and she was consequently left penniless. If she had also eloped, by medieval law she even lost her common law right to dower (a third of her husband's property for life as a widow).[33] On the other hand, an adulteress retained her claims to her widow's jointure, because the marriage was still intact, and therefore the marriage settlement was still in force. She also retained any property settled on trustees for her separate use, and perhaps any pin money, although this last was sometimes disputed.[34] A wife was legally free to sue her husband for his adultery, and a few did so. But these cases are relatively rare, and the wives usually only won when there were aggravating circumstances, such as the replacement of the wife by the mistress as head of the household, or the infection of the wife with venereal disease. Even as late as 1985, 42 per cent of all divorces initiated by the husband were on grounds of adultery, but only 23 per cent of those initiated by the wife.[35] This suggests that even today most men and women still accept the moral validity of the double standard, even if not as whole-heartedly as they did two or three centuries ago.

The 1857 Divorce Act radically altered the function of suits for

[31] Godolphin, 494.   [32] *Mogg* v. *Mogg* (1824), *Eng. Rep.* 162: 301, 252 n. *c.*
[33] Shelford, 420.   [34] See above, 160–2.   [35] *Social Trends,* 17 (1987), 50.

separation. In 1860, a legal commentator remarked that judicial separation, now awarded by the new secular Divorce Court, had become primarily 'the wife's remedy rather than the husband's'. He pointed out that it was rarely worth the husband's while to contest his wife's suit, since he still kept the income from her property unless it had been settled upon trustees for her own use.[36] Judicial separation lingered on until the twentieth century, but it was increasingly overshadowed by the prodigious rise in the number of divorces.

The last question to be addressed is the practical consequences of this system of judicial separation without permission to remarry. What happened to the husband and wife after the case was over? In 1844, Dr Lushington, the judge of the London Consistory Court, was asked by a Parliamentary committee whether separation from bed and board led to 'profligacy on the part of the husband', to which his terse reply was: 'No doubt it universally does', thus echoing the objections to the system by all the Protestant Reformers of the sixteenth century except some of the Elizabethan bishops.[37]

A considerable number of judicially separated wives seem to have been only too happy to be freed from the tyranny of husbands and settle down to a life of contented independence and chastity. But many others—how many we do not know—found celibacy and loneliness hard to bear, and sooner or later entered into adulterous or bigamous relationships with other men. In consequence those who had been the innocent parties and were thus receiving alimony ran grave danger of losing it if their husbands chose to sue them. On the other hand, wives who had been separated because of their own adultery obtained no alimony, and unless they were helped by their former lovers (or their family) they might fall into destitution. The incentive of women in this last situation to cohabit with the old or a new lover was therefore very strong indeed. It is thus very likely that after judicial separation most husbands and many wives entered into new adulterous or bigamous relationships.

D. RESTITUTION OF CONJUGAL RIGHTS

The last type of matrimonial suit available from the church courts was one for 'restitution of conjugal rights', by which was meant cohabitation in the same house, not sexual intercourse. This suit could be used both to make and to break a marriage. Thus, a wife could use it as a means of

[36] MacQueen, *Marriage, Divorce, and Legitimacy*, 274–8; W. Ernst, *A Treatise of Marriages and Divorce* (London, 1879), 203–6.
[37] *Roy. Com. Divorce, 1853*, 1: 37.

claiming the validity of a contract or clandestine marriage or one allegedly performed not in conformity to the 1753 act. Most commonly, however, it was a tactic employed by a deserted wife to force her husband to pay her a maintenance allowance. If she won, the court ordered the husband to let her back into his house—not necessarily into his bed. When he refused, the court would award her separation and alimony. Or if the wife had thrown herself on the parish and asked for poor relief because of the refusal of her husband to support her, he ran the risk, in case she won, of being prosecuted by the Overseers of the Poor for criminal neglect.[38]

The suit could also be used by separating or separated couples as a tactical manoeuvre against each other. An abandoned husband could sue to obtain a court order obliging his separated wife to return to the home. If she refused to obey the court, the husband was, as we have seen, legally entitled to seize his wife by force. Her only effective defence was to come to terms with him about the finances of a private separation deed, or to sue him for separation for a marital offence. Finally, since the church courts did not recognize the legal validity of a private separation deed, this suit was the easiest way for either husband or wife to overthrow its terms.

3. Procedure

The procedure used in the ecclesiastical courts in the eighteenth century was identical to that prescribed by medieval canon law and radically different from that employed by the common law courts, which depended on oral testimony and cross-examination in open court. Canon law depended upon private written documents and private interrogation of witnesses by professional examiners; it was decided by a judge and not a jury; and the rules of evidence concerning proof were different.

A. LAUNCHING A SUIT

A plaintiff wishing to start a suit in an ecclesiastical court had first to hire a proctor, a professional lawyer who specialized in civil law and was licenced to practice in these courts. His first step was to register a citation in court to summon the defendant, which was cheap and quick, and was often enough to bring the defendant to terms. There then followed a struggle to oblige the defendant to appoint a proctor and prepare a

---

[38] Poynter, 241–4; 3 *Hansard*, 147 (1857), 1236.

defence, the only real weapons open to the court to enforce its will being the now rather empty threat of excommunication. After a delay of ten to forty days, it was possible to issue a writ to the Court of Chancery, which would in turn issue a writ to the sheriff to arrest the delinquent and imprison him until he agreed to co-operate. But this was a slow, clumsy, and expensive procedure, and court officials from the sixteenth to the nineteenth centuries were extremely reluctant to use it, especially against poor men unable to pay the substantial fees involved. Thus, over the three years 1827 to 1829, all the ecclesiastical courts in England imprisoned only sixty-eight persons for contumacy.[39]

The first major step was for the plaintiff to give the court a written 'Libel' drawn up by his proctor and containing the gist of his or her accusations against the defendant. This 'Libel' was a convenient preliminary, 'enabling the parties to take the opinion of the Court in a very summary way'.[40] It might be accompanied by supporting 'Exhibits', that is, documents such as love letters. Its contents might well go beyond what later could be proved by the depositions of witnesses. If the defendant decided to contest the case, he or she appeared in person to make an Answer, on oath, which was written down by a short-hand clerk. The plaintiff offered a rebuttal of the facts and arguments of the defendant in a written Responsive Allegation, and the latter replied with an Allegation in Rejoinder. Supplementary Allegations were somewhat reluctantly allowed, but only if they added more facts and arguments.

The court then interrogated the witnesses named by both sides, either in London or, if they were in the country, through commissioners appointed for the purpose. Recalcitrant witnesses could be forced to appear by a 'Compulsory'. The witnesses were twice examined in private, first in order to make their depositions, and later to reply to written Interrogatories supplied by the other side—all of which were written down by a notary. But at no point was there any oral cross-examination, although it was argued that the examiners in practice used their discretion about this if they had any reason to suspect evasion or perjury.

Husbands and wives accused of adultery could refuse to answer direct questions on that subject, since they might be liable to incriminate themselves. On the other hand, an Interrogatory by the defendant was allowed to turn into a fishing expedition. In the late seventeenth century, it was common to ask witnesses on oath about their religious practices, particularly when and where they had last taken holy communion, the hope being to cast doubt on their credibility if they replied 'never'. They might

[39] *PP 1831–2*, 24: 568–71; Wharton, 410; Houlbrooke, *Church Courts*, 50.
[40] Wharton, 413.

be interrogated on oath about their politics and their loyalty to the regime; about their place of residence and their occupations for many years back; and even about their net worth. The wife was allowed to make wild guesses about the income of her husband, in order to force him to state the truth on oath, so as to form the basis for an award of permanent alimony in case she won the case. It is striking how little most wives knew about the finances of their husbands.

Finally, a day was appointed for the hearing. The format of the hearing was that the two proctors spoke for their clients, and the judge then delivered the sentence in open court. After 1752, the sentence was accompanied by a declaration of the judge's reasoning. Unfortunately, the speeches by the judges were not recorded in the files of the court, and the few which survive in newspaper accounts or in law reports were those which seemed to make some innovation in case law. Worse still, since the files in the Court of Arches contain draft sentences submitted by both proctors, it is sometimes impossible to know which of the two the judge favoured.

In the middle of the nineteenth century, it was claimed that an uncontested suit took on the average two to five months, and a contested one up to two years, the average being a year and a half. In fact, an undefended case took between four and nine months, a time which had not changed since the early eighteenth century.[41] One of the longest cases on record was a nullity case on grounds of insanity, which occupied fifty-six court days and required forty-one witnesses, the written record amounting to three thousand folio pages.[42] During all this time the wife was awarded a small alimony out of her husband's income, to enable her to live modestly according to her station, while her husband also had to pay the assessed legal costs of both his wife and himself.

B. THE RULES OF EVIDENCE

Canon law courts worked to different rules of evidence than did the common law courts: canon law demanded two witnesses to every act, while common law was satisfied with one. Canon law also excluded the testimony of the principal participants, the husband, wife, and lover, on the grounds that they were hopelessly biased witnesses and unlikely to tell the truth. Unlike the common law, canon law accepted as evidence documents whose authorship was established by a comparison of hand-

---

[41] *Roy. Com. Divorce, 1853*, 1: 29–31, 38.
[42] *Smith* v. *Morris* (1819), LPCA, H.285/1–28; *PP 1831–2*, 24: 69.

writings by someone with personal knowledge of the individual concerned.[43]

These differences could lead to different verdicts in different courts. For example, in 1842 Herbert Williams and a maid caught his wife in bed with another man. He sued the lover for crim. con. in King's Bench, and on the basis of his and the maid's testimony was awarded £500 damages. But when he sued in an ecclesiastical court for separation on grounds of adultery, his suit was rejected since there was only one valid witness (the maid), his own testimony being unacceptable to the court.[44] On the other hand, the church courts accepted as valid proof circumstantial evidence 'such as would lead the guarded discretion of a reasonable and just man to the conclusion'. The argument was that if adultery could only be proved by visual evidence of the sexual act itself, very few adulterers and seducers would ever be convicted.[45]

C. THE LEGAL DEFINITION OF CRUELTY

One of the two marital offences, adultery, is clear enough: it means sexual intercourse by a spouse with a third party. No such simple definition can be offered for cruelty, however. Cruelty was almost exclusively confined to husbands, who were not merely physically the stronger of the two sexes but also possessed considerable legal authority to torment and even physically chastise a wife. In canon law before the late eighteenth century, only physical cruelty was taken into account, and that had to be unjustified, extreme and repeated: not one, but many episodes of brutal random violence which posed a threat to life or limb.

The causes of marital cruelty were and are very numerous. Modern studies indicate that a great deal of domestic violence is still going on at all social levels. In the eighteenth century, just as today, violence on the part of husbands was closely correlated with alcoholism, and it is rare to find a case in which it does not play some part. But it seems to have been an exacerbating factor rather than the root cause. Some husbands were obsessive personalities imbued with traditional values of patriarchal power, and furiously resentful of any challenge to their absolute authority. Others were simply cold, distant, and angry, locked up in their own mental hell. Many were social misfits or failures, who took out their frustrations on their wives. In consequence the records are full of examples of beating, starving, locking up, expulsion from the marital bed or from the home in the middle of the night, the threat or actuality of

---

[43] *Eng. Rep.* 32: 438.   [44] *Evans* v. *Evans* (1844), *ibid.* 163: 1000–3.
[45] Shelford, 405–6; see the Loveden Case in Stone, *Broken Lives*.

imprisonment in the home or in a madhouse, repeated infections with venereal disease, and so on.

In the eighteenth and early nineteenth centuries, however, some husbands were cruel with a rational purpose. They were deliberate schemers who tormented their wives in order to extract something from them—either to drive them to surrender property and money or to force them to leave the house. An example of this came before the Court of Arches in 1825, when a husband was proved to have practised systematic cruelty against his wife, in order to force her to surrender her pin-money and sell some of her property, which had been vested in trustees for her separate use. The court described deliberate cruelties inflicted for a pecuniary purpose as 'acts of a deeper malignity' and granted the wife a separation.[46]

In the eighteenth century, domestic cruelty often took bizarre and extreme forms bordering on madness. Such acts were provoked by the bitter fact that the marriage was indissoluble, and that, for better or for worse, the couple were linked together for life. The only escape for a husband from a hated wife who was not adulterous was by private separation, but that would severely reduce his income since he would be obliged to give her a generous maintenance allowance. An alternative was to make a wife's life so miserable that she would leave the house, thus putting herself legally in the wrong.

Even more striking than the ferocity of some husbands is the passive endurance of so many abused wives in the eighteenth century. For years, even decades, they put up with severe verbal and physical abuse, total severance of all contacts with their relatives, loss of control over their children, and often infection from venereal disease. They were held back by the knowledge that desertion of the home would involve a total loss of all contact with their children, and often dire poverty in the absence of any alternative place of permanent refuge with relatives or friends. Added to this, there was a powerful culture of female submission, and a sense of fear, guilt, and helplessness, amounting in some cases to masochism. Some hoped that their persistent acquiescence in face of gross abuse would in the end soften the hearts of their husbands. It rarely did.

An extreme example of this passivity occurred in a case in Somerset in 1679. A wealthy yeoman farmer was so jealous of his wife that, besides beating her regularly, he put on her 'an iron that came around her waist, and there was fastened another iron behind, which came down between her legs, and was fastened with a lock upon one side of her belly'. This

---

[46] *Hanham* v. *Hanham* (1825), Plowden, 2: 205; see also a similar case in Chancery, *Lambert* v. *Lambert* (1767), *Eng. Rep.* 1: 764–9.

chastity belt, 'being so broad, had written deep strokes into her flesh and wrung her so cruelly that she could scarcely go at all'. In between pregnancies, when she grew too big to keep it on, she wore it for over two years. When a female friend urged her to get it taken off, she refused, saying 'I will undergo that and more if I might make my husband any way the better.' Only after enduring it for three years did she finally sue her husband for separation.[47] This was an unusual case, since most wives trapped in these very bad marriages may have left home several times under intolerable provocation, only to return again and again in hopes, usually dashed, of better treatment in the future.

One such long-suffering woman tormented by an irrationally jealous and cruel husband in the early nineteenth century was the second wife of John Mytton, a very rich but eccentric Shropshire squire. Mytton's interests were limited to fox-hunting, horse-racing, shooting, drinking, and womanizing. His wife, Caroline, put up with him for ten years, after nearly leaving him within the first two weeks of marriage. He kept her almost constantly pregnant and as constantly abused her and tormented her with his jealousy, his cruel practical jokes, and his neglect. On the second day after their marriage he deserted her completely and settled down to an extended drinking bout. He was so jealous of her that he virtually confined her to the house. He often beat her so badly that she was forced to wear dresses with long sleeves and high collars to cover up the bruises. She and her children all lived in unremitting terror because of his bizarre and violent sense of humour. For example, he had bought a bear from a travelling salesman, which he would occasionally release to roam freely about the house, until one day it savaged a servant so badly that it had to be killed.

By 1830, thanks to his prodigal extravagance he faced financial ruin, crushed by debts of over £35,000. By then Caroline had had enough. She managed to get herself and the five children out of the house and flee from his creditors to the house of her brother. Once safely there with her children, she started a law-suit for separation from bed and board, confident that the evidence of his misconduct towards the children would persuade Chancery to give her custody of them. So crushed was he by the separation from Caroline that he wrote her a series of passionate letters urging reconciliation; when this did not work, he tried to kidnap her by force from her brother's house. A ferocious battle ensued, and eight men were injured before the constables could get a pair of handcuffs on him.

John Mytton was clearly more than a little mad, as well as a man of

---

[47] *Bullock* v. *Bullock* (1679), LPCA, D.302. 32, 65–7, 75–6, 95.

immense physical strength, and his behaviour was at the extreme end of the range of husbandly misconduct. But he was a popular squire in the county, picked as sheriff, an MP for Shrewsbury, and the subject of a eulogistic biography as an eccentric racing man. What is even more remarkable is that for ten long years his wife put up with his cruelty, his wholly unreasonable jealousy, his utter neglect of her, and his repeated whoring with the lowest of prostitutes.[48]

Stories such as this prove on the one hand that, wives were infinitely more submissive in the past, thanks to the strength of patriarchal values; and on the other that the legal and practical authority of husbands to ill-treat, punish, or confine them was very much greater than is the case today. As late as 1782, a judge declared that, if he had good cause, a husband might legally beat his wife with a stick no thicker than his thumb.[49]

It would be a mistake, however, to think that a battered wife had no redress. Even in the eighteenth century there were limits on husbandly powers, and when in 1737 a jealousy-crazed husband sewed up his wife's labia before leaving to work five miles from home, he soon found himself before the Leicester Assizes on a charge of assault.[50] In fact, many wives today are in one respect more exposed than in earlier times to marital violence, since they live in houses without servants, and without a tradition of neighbourly intervention in other people's affairs. In the eighteenth century, family violence among the poor was often kept in check by the intervention of neighbours, and among the middling sort and the rich by the intervention of domestic servants.

In addition to this constant, if limited, protection from neighbours and servants, a battered wife in the eighteenth century had several legal options. For one thing she could bring her husband before a JP, who would make him give bond to keep the peace. This was a procedure which might be effective in reducing actual violence, but would hardly help to smooth domestic relations. Moreover if a husband was gaoled for mistreatment of his wife and children, they might well starve in consequence, or be thrown on to the parish for poor relief.[51] By the late eighteenth century, a rich wife with her own separate estate could also appeal to the Court of Chancery for protection from her husband's cruelty by asking for a writ of *supplicavit*, and a few women did just that.[52]

---

[48] Nimrod, *A Memoir of the Life of John Mytton* (London, 1837; repr. 1903); LPCA, H. 458/ 1–39; Virginia Woolf, *The Common Reader*, two vols., 3rd edn. (London, 1945), 2: 126–31.
[49] M. D. Pagelow, *Family Violence* (New York, 1984); Stone, *FSM* pl. 29.
[50] *Gent's Mag.* (1737), 250.
[51] *Hardships of Laws on Wives*, 19, 32; *Laws Respecting Women*, 54–5.
[52] Shelford, 424; *Lambert* v. *Lambert* (1767), *Eng. Rep.* 1: 764–7.

Lastly, a battered wife could sue her husband in an ecclesiastical court for separation on grounds of cruelty. In the late seventeenth century, the ecclesiastical courts still took a narrow line on the definition of cruelty, rarely enquiring too closely about extenuating circumstances. As a result, the church courts sometimes found themselves at odds with the secular authorities, who were more concerned to probe what lay behind the brutality and to find explanations for it.

This conflict of values becomes very clear in a case in 1672 of a young Cambridge couple of the middling sort, John and Anne Disbrow.[53] The two-year-old marriage had been disturbed by an ugly legal battle between the two sets of parents over payment of Anne's full marriage portion. The immediate reason for the final episode of physical violence was the wife's refusal to go to bed with her husband that night. There followed a savage beating which left Anne with her eyes, nose, head, and breast badly swollen and bruised. She was also spitting blood, suggesting that a broken rib had penetrated her lungs. But she was well enough to go to the Mayor of Cambridge the same day in order to obtain a warrant to bring John before the court on a charge of assault and battery.

The case was heard at the Quarter Sessions six weeks later. On the one hand, the bench was shocked by the extreme brutality of John's behaviour. On the other, it was disturbed that Anne had sided with her parents against her husband, and had threatened to leave him and return to them. The recorder observed: 'I know where the fault lies, I am assured it is in the old ones', by which he meant the parents of both parties. As a result, the bench dismissed the case, and ordered Anne's parents to submit the dispute over the portion to arbitration. In the eyes of the justices, Anne had betrayed her wifely obligations by siding with her family against her husband (and perhaps by refusing her sexual services); and her family had violated the norms of society by refusing to submit to arbitration the dispute over the portion. In the eyes of the justices, and presumably those of the community, these faults balanced John's unquestionably brutal assault upon Anne.

Anne defied the JPs, flatly refused to return to her husband, and began a suit in the ecclesiastical court for separation on grounds of cruelty. In these courts, the complex issues of motivation which had attracted the attention of the justices were not relevant: all that counted was the hard facts. Since physical cruelty was clearly proved in this case, the court decreed a separation. This meant that John lost a wife, and thus her assistance in his goldsmith's shop; he was barred from ever remarrying; and, unless his wife committed adultery, he would be burdened with

[53] LPCA, D.602. 71, 76, 80–98, 104–7, 143, 149–50, 156–60.

alimony payments to her for the rest of her life. He thus paid very dearly for his outbreak of ungovernable fury, an outburst the JPs were willing to condone. The narrowly pragmatic application of a harsh ecclesiastical law thus occasionally favoured wives against husbands more than contemporary public opinion did.

Normally, however, this was not the case, and in 1755 and again in 1813 the courts accepted evidence of a wife's bad temper as a bar to a cruelty suit against her husband. In the former case, the judge declared that 'a wife is not entitled to a divorce [i.e. separation] for cruelty, unless it appears that she is a person of good temper and has always behaved well and dutifully to her husband'.[54]

Under a smoke-screen of judicial conservatism, the courts in the nineteenth century began to adapt the rules to conform to changing public opinion concerning the claims of women for more equitable treatment from the courts. On the other hand, the traditional legal definition of cruelty was eloquently, if ambiguously, restated by Sir William Scott in a famous and much quoted judgment on a case in 1790: 'What is cruelty?', he asked, and continued:

It is the duty of Courts, and consequently the inclination of Courts, to keep the rule extremely strict. The causes must be grave and weighty, and such as shew an absolute impossibility that the duties of the married life can be discharged. In a state of personal danger no duties can be discharged; for the duty of self-preservation must take place before the duties of marriage ... What merely wounds the mental feelings is in few cases to be admitted where they are not accompanied with bodily injury, either actual or menaced. Mere austerity of temper, petulance of manners, rudeness of language, a want of civil attention and accommodation, even occasional sallies of passion, if they do not threaten bodily harm, do not amount to legal cruelty; they are high moral offences in the marriage-state undoubtedly, not innocent surely in any state of life, but still they are not that cruelty against which the law can relieve ...

The Courts ... cannot make men virtuous; and, as the happiness of the world depends upon its virtue, there may be much unhappiness in it which human laws cannot undertake to remove. Still less is it cruelty where it wounds not the natural feelings, but the acquired feelings arising from particular rank and situations ... of course the denial of little indulgences and particular accommodations, which the delicacy of the world is apt to number among its necessaries, is not cruelty. It may, to be sure, be a harsh thing to refuse the use of a carriage or the use of a servant; it may in many cases be extremely unhandsome, extremely disgraceful to the character of the husband; but the Ecclesiastical Court does not look to such matters; the great ends of marriage may very well be carried on without them ...

[54] *Taylor* v. *Taylor* (1755), *Eng. Rep.* 161: 303; *Waring* v. *Waring* (1813), ibid. 161: 699–704.

These are negative descriptions of cruelty; they shew only what is not cruelty, and are yet perhaps the safest definitions which can be given under the infinite variety of possible cases that may come before the Court . . . The danger of life, limb or health is usually inserted as the ground upon which the Court has proceeded to a separation . . . I have heard no one case cited in which the Court has granted a divorce [i.e. separation] without proof given of a reasonable apprehension of bodily hurt. I say an apprehension, because assuredly the Court is not to wait till the hurt is actually done; but the apprehension must be reasonable; it must not be an apprehension arising merely from an exquisite and diseased sensibility of mind.[55]

This statement by Sir William Scott was a meticulously careful redefinition of the traditional legal meaning of cruelty, as modified by case law after about 1750. It stood the test of time for about thirty years, being too lax to please conservatives and too tight to satisfy liberals. Some conservative judges even launched a rearguard action to try to stem the slow tide of change. Thus, in 1835, Judge Joseph Phillimore was confronted with a case in which a husband normally stationed on the West Coast of Africa had given his wife a venereal disease on three occasions in three years, each time he had returned home. Finally informed by a doctor that this was what was wrong with her, Mrs Belcher refused to sleep with her husband any more. Negotiations between them broke down, and Mr Belcher launched a suit for restitution of conjugal rights, to which Mrs Belcher responded with a counter-suit for separation on grounds of cruelty.

In his judgment on the case, Judge Phillimore came to some remarkable conclusions. He argued that communication of a venereal disease by a husband to his wife was only cruelty under two conditions: first if it was deliberately intended; and second if it was the result of an act of adultery after the marriage. In this case Mrs Belcher had fallen ill the first time immediately after her honeymoon, which proved that the infection had been contracted by sexual activity *before* marriage. The judge ruled that 'accidental and involuntary communication of the venereal disease, contracted before marriage and wholly unconnected with marital infidelity, cannot of itself constitute cruelty, in the legal acceptance of the term'. Consequently he ordered that Mrs Belcher must take the consequences of making a bad choice of a husband, and renew cohabitation with him. He could not order her into his bed, but since marital rape was not recognized as a legal offence at the time, there was nothing to stop Belcher from taking his wife by force.[56]

[55] *Evans* v. *Evans* (1790), *Eng. Rep.* 161: 467–8; Shelford, 425.
[56] *A Report of the Judgement by Joseph Phillimore in the Cause of* Belcher *v.* Belcher (London, 1835), 1–66.

But this was an extreme case of judicial conservatism in the interpretation of legal cruelty, and was never quoted as a precedent. From the 1830s onward, more liberal judges, such as Dr Stephen Lushington, were using the ambiguities of Sir William Scott's definition in 1790 to grant separations for mental as well as physical suffering.[57] By the early nineteenth century, one or two physical confrontations, or even mere threats of violence, would suffice for a separation, and by the middle of the century the infliction of mental stress and a justified fear of physical cruelty were enough.[58] In 1850 Lord Brougham flatly denied that legal cruelty 'required either actual injury to the person, or threat of such injury'.[59] By 1879, over twenty years after the new secular Divorce Court had taken over from the old ecclesiastical courts, the definition of legal cruelty had been modified still further. In a handbook of that date it was said that 'constant repetition of insulting and degrading language and conduct' was sufficient, since it breaks down the health of both mind and body and renders life almost unbearable. In 1897 a legal authority declared that 'from the meaning of pain inflicted on the body, it [cruelty] has in recent years attained meaning that includes pain inflicted on the mind. Coldness and neglect may now almost of themselves constitute such cruelty as, coupled with misconduct, will give right of a divorce [i.e. separation].[60]

On the other hand, in conformity with the class-ridden views of even the most liberal of Victorians, judges continued to believe that blows meant quite different things in different classes, a supposition in which they may well have been right. In 1841, the author of a legal handbook cited a recent case in which the judge had argued that the use of violence in upper-class families was to be taken more seriously than violence among the lower classes, among whom 'blows sometimes pass between married couples who are in the main very happy and have no desire to part'.[61] A legal writer nearly forty years later, in 1879, echoed this belief: 'A blow endured between persons of the lower conditions of life and in the highest stations of life bear very different aspects.'[62] As a corollary to this belief, it was argued that high aristocratic rank should be taken as an aggravation of the offence, for example in the Westmeath case.[63]

[57] Biggs, 22–9.

[58] *Report on . . .* Belcher *v.* Belcher, 21–6; *Collett* v. *Collett* (1838), *Eng. Rep.* 163: 237–41; see also *Ciocci* v. *Ciocci* (1853), ibid. 164: 70–88.

[59] MacQueen, *Marriage, Divorce, and Legitimacy*, 290; Shelford, 429–33; Wharton, 467–70; Biggs, 29–38; see also *Leete* v. *Leete, Eng. Rep.* 164: 1119.

[60] J. E. G. de Montgomery, 'The Changing Status of a Married Woman', *Law Quarterly Review*, 13 (1897), 191–2.   [61] Shelford, 426–8.

[62] Ernst, *Marriages and Divorce*, 75–6, 88, 92.

[63] See the Westmeath case in Stone, *Broken Lives.*

The new, broad, legal definition of cruelty, taken to include mere mental cruelty, was also accepted by the Royal Commission on Divorce of 1912. It was clearly acting under pressure from public opinion, for Sir Bargrave Dean, a judge of the Divorce Court who supported the older and stricter definition, grumbled that nowadays 'a jury will not listen to you'. The key agent of change in the nineteenth century was thus not the judges themselves, but public opinion, enforced after 1857 by the juries.[64]

D. LEGAL DEFENCES

The first and most obvious defence in a contested separation suit was to deny the facts of the accusations of adultery or cruelty or both. For this strategy to work, the key tactic was to assemble as large an army as possible of servant witnesses who had been in a position to know. Failing this, there were four alternative arguments which could be used, any one of which, if proved, would suffice to bar the suit.

i. Condonation

The pardon of a marital offence by the other spouse, and the subsequent resumption of cohabitation and sexual relations, would normally suffice to wipe out any charge based on prior marital behaviour, whether it was adultery or cruelty or both. In 1794 Sir William Scott ruled that: 'the wife's unwilling acquiescence in a return to live in the same house, but without connubial cohabitation, does not amount to a complete forgiveness'. But in 1799 he changed his mind and declared that 'the general presumption is, that a husband and wife living together in the same house do live on terms of matrimonial cohabitation, but particular circumstances may repel this presumption'.[65] Exactly what constituted legal condonation was therefore still not clear in the early nineteenth century. When in 1820 Lady Westmeath, under pressure from her family, reluctantly allowed her separated husband to occupy a room in her house—but not her bed—she had been assured by her lawyer that this arrangement could never be interpreted as condonation, and thus act as a bar to any future suit against her husband for all his previous cruelties and acts of adultery.[66] The advice turned out to be wrong.

As soon as a husband discovered his wife's adultery, it was therefore vital that he should expel her from the house as soon as possible, in order

---

[64] *Roy. Com. Divorce, 1912*, 1: 71; 2: 51.

[65] *Worsley* v. *Worsley* (1730), *Eng. Rep.* 162: 735; *D'Aguilar* v. *D'Aguilar* (1794), ibid. 748; *Beeby* v. *Beeby* (1799), ibid. 757 n. *a*; 758; *Durant* v. *Durant* (1809), ibid. 746.

[66] See the Westmeath case in Stone, *Broken Lives*.

to block any possible charge of condonation by proving that sexual relations had been broken off. This was usually a formal and public procedure, a good example being the solemn expulsion of Lady Clavering from her husband's town house in London in 1734.[67] When he was informed that his wife had been caught red-handed committing adultery with the groom, Walter Gremley, Sir Francis Clavering took the news coolly and proceeded to lay his plans carefully. First, he removed himself from the house and went to visit his legal adviser, returning a few days later accompanied by two close friends, Mr Capper and Mr Smith; young Francis Capper, his lawyer; and his accountant Mr Bowles. First they all assembled in the front parlour; then, Bowles, Smith, and the lawyer retired to the back parlour and summoned Gremley. Bowles paid him his wages, and served him with a process from King's Bench in an action for damages for crim. con. Leaving Gremley behind, they then returned to the front parlour and summoned Lady Clavering. Smith then announced to her, on Sir Francis's behalf and in his presence: 'You have defiled your husband's bed with Wally, for which he will be turned out at the back door, and you must go out at the fore door.'

At first she laughed, but when she realized that he was serious she began to whimper and cry. She shouted to Gremley, who was still in the back parlour: 'Wally, confess nothing,' asserted her innocence, and asked for some linen to take with her. Sir Francis ordered some brought, and said he would send some of her clothes the next day. Smith offered her ten guineas, but she still had her dignity and refused to take them except from Sir Francis's hands, which was done. She then asked for a servant, but was refused on the grounds that 'they are my servants, none of them yours now'. She asked Sir Francis to provide her with lodging, but he again refused, saying 'No, you may go where you will.' Asked by Smith whether she would leave in a coach or a chair she chose the latter, and one was summoned. While they were waiting, she suddenly jumped to her feet and tried to run upstairs, and was with difficulty restrained by Mr Smith holding on to her stays. There followed another struggle as she was forcibly pushed into the chair. The ritual had been formal enough, but the result was a distinctly undignified exit for the wife of a baronet. Her performance had failed to match the occasion.

ii. Collusion

Collusion was a secret agreement between spouses to conceal, invent, or create facts in order to smooth the path through a crim. con. action and a suit for separation for adultery to a Parliamentary divorce, so as to allow

[67] LPCA, D.427, 519–25, 580.

all parties to remarry. It was a perversion of the legal system which was stimulated by the growth of Parliamentary divorces in the late eighteenth century, although it may well have existed from the very beginning of the procedure in 1700.[68] By 1800, collusion had spread through all three legal processes, and as a result by 1850 nearly all cases of separation and divorce went uncontested.[69]

The judge in the London Consistory Court, Dr Lushington, explained to the Royal Commission on Divorce of 1853 just how collusion might work. A wife was often in a position to block a separation suit brought on grounds of her own adultery by bringing forward evidence of her husband's adultery. In order to facilitate the divorce that would free her to marry her lover, and in order to save him from paying huge damages in a crim. con suit she would normally agree with her husband to remain silent about his infidelities and let the suit, action and bill go uncontested. It was an arrangement which often suited all parties.

Dr Lushington explained that it was almost impossible for the canon law courts to detect this sort of collusion if cleverly managed: 'They bring forward an *ex-parte* case, charging the wife with adultery, and if she does not interrogate witnesses, how is it possible but that the court must pronounce a sentence of separation?' Even harder to detect were the common cases in which wives appeared in court 'as if for the purpose of resisting', but in fact merely allowed the prosecution witnesses to appear and carefully omitted to summon key witnesses in their own defence.[70]

Dr Lushington took a surprisingly tolerant view of this perversion of the law. He said that ecclesiastical court judges tolerated collusion, asking 'why, if the wife has already committed the greatest possible offence against her husband, by violating his bed, should she add to it by increasing the expense of the remedy' by contesting the suit?[71] Parliament was a much better watchdog against collusion than either King's Bench in a crim. con. action, where the wife was not allowed to present her case, or the church courts in a separation suit, where written interrogatories were the rule, uncontested suits could not be investigated, and other witnesses could not be called.

iii. Connivance

If it could be proved that the other spouse knew all about and positively encouraged the marital offence of adultery, this would suffice to bar the suit.[72] But what conduct constituted connivance? Did gross neglect and studied indifference provide adequate proof of it? Did passive

---

[68] See below, 308–22.   [69] 2 *Hansard*, 134: 12, 941.
[70] *Roy. Com. Divorce, 1853*, 1: 46.   [71] Ibid. 46–7.   [72] Shelford, 416, 449–58.

acquiescence count as connivance, or only active encouragement of the act of adultery? This was tested in a case which came before the London Consistory Court in 1792. Full evidence of the wife's adultery was provided, but she accused her husband of grossly neglecting her. She claimed that he was cool and cruel, that he did not go with her to parties, but allowed her lover to pick her up at the house and take her out in the evenings; that her lover was well known to be 'gay, lewd, and debauched, and his general character was such that no married man in his neighbourhood would permit him to visit or associate with the females of his family'; and that the lover had been introduced to her by her husband, and had been encouraged to consort with her. Moreover, her husband had frequently seen them kissing and in 'amorous attitudes' while at the harpsichord, but had never once remonstrated with her.

On the other hand, stupidity was not enough: 'there must be intention'. Most telling was the interview the husband had with his wife's mother. Warned by her to stop the intimacy of his wife with a man with such a bad reputation as the lover, he coolly replied: 'I must not affront my best customer.' The court ruled that 'if a man sees what a reasonable man could not see without alarm . . . he must be supposed to see and mean the consequences'. But it finally decided that although the husband had behaved imprudently and had contributed to the disgrace of his family, he had not acted with a deliberate intention of encouraging his wife to commit adultery. He was therefore granted his separation.[73] Since the court demanded such high standards of proof, it is hardly surprising that there are only a few very flagrant cases on record in which such a defence of connivance succeeded.[74] When the suit by the husband was not for separation but for monetary damages from his wife's lover, connivance became even more scandalous.[75]

iv. Recrimination

A far more effective and more common defence of a wife accused of adultery was the plea of recrimination, that is, that her husband had also committed adultery (cruelty would not suffice), so that the two marital offences cancelled each other out.[76] This was a plea admitted as a bar by the ecclesiastical courts in England, but not in Scotland. If proved, the only possible rebuttal was that the husband's adultery had already been condoned by the wife by her continuing to cohabit and sleep with him. In

---

[73] *Moorson* v. *Moorson* (1792), *Eng. Rep.* 162: 1090–1, 1097, 1100, 1101 n. *b*.

[74] *Rix* v. *Rix* (1777), ibid. 1085–6; *Timings* v. *Timings* (1792), ibid. 1086–9; *Crewe* v. *Crewe* (1800), ibid. 1106.

[75] See below, pp. 279–82.   [76] Shelford, 400.

view of the importance of marriage to a wife, and the casual attitude taken by society to male infidelity, condonation by a wife, as has been seen, was very common, even normal.

But if the wife could prove that her husband had continued to commit adultery after her condonation, his suit for separation from her in an ecclesiastical court was barred, although he might still successfully sue her lover for crim. con. at common law and even obtain a Parliamentary divorce on grounds of her adultery. But if the husband actually sued for separation and lost, he would be unable to petition for a Parliamentary divorce; he would be obliged to maintain her and also her children, who would have a claim to inherit his property; and he would continue to be responsible for paying her debts.[77]

E. ALIMONY

After a successful suit by a wife against her husband for separation on grounds of adultery or cruelty, the court customarily awarded her permanent alimony. The amount varied according to the degree of turpitude of the husband, his net income, the size of the portion and estate brought to him on his marriage with his wife, and the cost of child maintenance.

Writers of legal handbooks of the early nineteenth century declared that the temporary alimony during a trial was small—only a fifth or less of the joint income—since the wife was expected to live in a modest way while the litigation was in progress. There is some little evidence to suggest that in the late seventeenth and early eighteenth centuries, awards of permanent alimony to judicially separated wives were also quite small. In 1734, an angry woman complained that the church courts would only leave the wife with 'a small pittance, with which she may keep herself from disease and want. If she brought the whole that her husband possesses, she may be assigned a fourth or fifth part.'[78] But by the early nineteenth century, writers of legal handbooks said that permanent alimony was normally between a third and a half of the joint net income—an observation supported by the fragmentary data about actual cases of that period.[79] If this is true, then the increased generosity of the courts over alimony is one aspect of the general movement of this period to redress the balance of justice between the sexes, which can be seen in so many aspects of matrimonial law and practice.

[77] Shelford, 439–44; *Forster* v. *Forster* (1790), *Eng. Rep.* 161: 504–6, 509; *Beeby* v. *Beeby* (1799), ibid. 162: 755–9; *Proctor* v. *Proctor* (1819), ibid. 161: 747–51; *Astley* v. *Astley* (1828), ibid. 162: 728–31.

[78] *Hardships of Laws on Wives*, 16.

[79] Bright, 2: 359; Wharton, 434; *Roy. Com. Divorce, 1853*, 1: 2.

4. Servants and masters

In disputed matrimonial suits, the eye-witnesses who deposed always included kin, friends, and neighbours, summoned either to testify to events or as character witnesses. In the eighteenth century, among the poor and the middling sort, neighbours in villages and urban areas were usually prepared to take action if they suspected the presence of morally reprehensible marital behaviour. Noisy public 'charivaris' took place to shame cuckolded husbands, wife-beating husbands, termagant wives, marriages between old men and young girls, and other violations of accepted social norms. Individual neighbours also did not hesitate to intervene. Thus, one day in 1703, when a Mr Austin was savagely beating his wife, a saddler entered the room. Mr Austin: 'God damn you what makes you here?' The saddler: 'Because you shall not beat your wife.'[80] Thanks to such neighbourly surveillance, in some cases a whole community found itself on the witness stand, especially in cases involving members of the elite.

A. THE ABSENCE OF PRIVACY

Since the only two causes for judicial separation were adultery or life-threatening cruelty, servants were always the most crucial witnesses: they alone were in a position to testify about what exactly had gone on in the relative privacy of the home. Houses of the elite might be isolated and large, but there were always servants about, whose duties involved the constant possibility of their intrusion into their employers' privacy. In the early modern period, domestic servants were employed by the top 30 per cent of the population, and therefore by virtually all litigants in separation suits after 1700.[81] In the nineteenth century, the number of households with servants was still very large. In the tiny Devonshire village of Colyton in 1851, only day labourers and the poor were without servants—domestic, agricultural, or proto-industrial—living in their households.[82]

Servants, therefore, were key witnesses to all domestic dramas. Servants of both sexes played other roles, from protector, confidant, messenger, or conspirator, to spy or delator. They not only dominated the proceedings in the courtroom but acted as the chorus, judging, com-

[80] LPCA. D.75. 98.
[81] P. Laslett and R. Wall (eds), *Household and Family in Past Time* (Cambridge, 1972), Table 4. 13.
[82] R. Wall, 'Work, Welfare, and the Family: An Illustration of the Adaptive Family Economy', in L. Bonfield, R. M. Smith and K. Wrightson (eds), *The World We Have Gained* (Oxford, 1986), Table 10. 1 and pp. 289–90.

menting on, and explaining events. In real life they served the same functions as they did in literature from Ben Jonson's *The Alchemist* to Fielding's *Tom Jones*.

They knew everything because they were always either present or within earshot. Employers were culturally trained to be helpless, and to rely for all their physical needs—even dressing and undressing—upon servants, who therefore had to be constantly in attendance or within call. In the seventeenth and eighteenth centuries, it was normal for the valet to sleep in a closet adjoining the bedroom of his master, and the waiting-maid in a closet adjoining that of her mistress. At Erdigg in 1732 it was said in praise of the architectural plan that the bedrooms 'have the convenience of dressing-rooms and rooms for servants' attached to them.[83] It was not until the late eighteenth century that the growing desire for privacy and improved technology led to the removal of all the servants' bedrooms to a separate attic floor, linked to those of their employers merely by a bell and a bell-wire.

An endless succession of servants were constantly entering bedrooms and private apartments. They came in the morning, some to open the shutters and light the fires, others to bring the breakfast or help their master and mistress to dress. Later they would remove the slops from the close-stools and chamber pots, make the feather beds, and clean the rooms. In the afternoon they came back to bring tea and more fuel for the fires. In the evening they came in again to close the shutters, light the candles, and replenish the fires. Late at night they brought up warming pans to warm the beds, and returned a little later to help their master and mistress to undress. All through the day they carried messages to and fro. There was thus no moment in the day or night when servants were not coming and going in the private apartments at unpredictable times. Their ubiquity was taken entirely for granted by employers, who in the main ignored their servants except when giving an order or asking them a question. The striking exceptions were the close attachments which often developed between an employee and a personal attendant—valet or lady's maid—who often became friend, confidante, and sometimes the essential go-between in an adulterous liaison.

The only occasions when this lack of privacy became irksome, and even dangerous, was when the employer had something to hide. Adultery in the home was peculiarly difficult. If a pair of adulterous lovers did not lock the doors, they risked being caught *in flagrante delicto* by a servant coming into the room on a routine chore (Plate 17). If they locked the

[83] J. M. Waterson, *The Servants' Hall* (New York, 1980), 28.

doors, or gave strict instructions that no servant was to enter until summoned by the bell, this would immediately arouse the suspicions of the household. Nor was a liaison out of doors much easier to carry on undetected. On any visit, whether to a shop, a private house, or the theatre, a gentleman was usually accompanied by his valet, a lady always by her maid. Both were driven in a coach by a coachman, or if on horseback were accompanied by a groom.

Moreover, during a husband's absence it was usual for a wife to take her maid to bed with her, for warmth, as a protection against possible rape, and as proof of her innocence. This being the case, there was no way a man could enter the private rooms of a lady without the active complicity of her waiting-maid, probably also of a footman to admit him secretly to the house and smuggle him out again, and possibly of the coachman if the liaison took place elsewhere. All these servants had to be rewarded handsomely for their help and their secrecy, and like all blackmailers, they were liable eventually to become arrogant and excessively demanding. Servants, especially in large houses, had plenty of time on their hands, and most of them were intensely inquisitive.

Only a minority were reluctant to get mixed up in the whole dirty business. One explained that 'I did not like to be concerned in a matter of this sort'; another told the court that he had deliberately kept out of the way to avoid knowing anything.[84] More common was the behaviour of servants who stood on tables in the room below to listen to the creaking of a bed;[85] who carefully inspected the bed-linen or the sofa cover or the carpet for tell-tale signs of sexual activity; who examined the feather bed for the imprint of two bodies; and who found it exciting to sit up all night in the dark on the stairs in order to see who slipped quietly at dead of night into whose bedroom.

The internal lay-out and construction of eighteenth century houses also made privacy very difficult, if not impossible. For one thing, corridors were still a rare novelty before the late eighteenth century, and most rooms were built *en suite*. To enter one room, one had therefore to pass through others. Moreover many of the internal partitions were far from sound-proof, being made of thin lathe and plaster, or simply deal wainscotting. Keys were still very clumsy, and key-holes consequently large, which often provided the inquisitive with a good viewpoint. This was particularly the case in London houses, where 'the bedroom doors are almost invariably placed upon the staircase fronting the bed, and the keyhole commands an ample prospect of all the rites dedicated to Venus.

---

[84] RIA/HP, 804. 33–4; LPCA, D.350–1. 617.
[85] See the Loveden case in Stone, *Broken Lives*.

Many discoveries have been made, and not a few trials for crim. con. ensued, in consequence of a peep through a key-hole.'[86] There are indeed dozens, if not hundreds, of cases in the eighteenth century where the witnesses were servants testifying to what they had seen through keyholes (Plate 18).

If the keyhole was obstructed, and the wainscotting was still tight, many inquisitive servants had no scruples about boring holes through the latter in order to get a view of the room.[87] In a 1782 suit, an embarrassed witness confessed that he was induced 'from an instigation of ridiculous curiosity to bore holes in the wainscot of her bedchamber—the apertures are still visible'. In another case, a witness testified that 'I bored holes through the wainscot and could see them very plainly.' As was said about another case in 1772, 'a wanton curiosity, not principle, is the actuating motive' of the servants who spied on their employers.[88]

A classic example of this curiosity was the action taken in 1770 by Earl Grosvenor's butler to expose the adultery of Lady Grosvenor with one of the royal brothers, the Duke of Cumberland, at the White Hart Inn in St Albans. While Lady Grosvenor was at supper, he bored two holes in the door to her bedroom. Later in the evening, after she and her lover had retired, the butler and his brother took turns in peering through the holes. They were unable to see the bed, but heard enough to justify breaking open the door with a poker; and having done so, they caught Lady Grosvenor and the Duke *in flagrante delicto*. Since it involved one of the royal brothers, the subsequent crim. con. trial was the sensation of the year. The butler was a star witness, and was well rewarded for his trouble.[89]

Even if direct visual evidence of the act of adultery was not available, it was still virtually impossible in the eighteenth century to conceal the fact that sexual activity had taken place. There is no doubt that from the moment servants suspected adultery, they were constantly on the watch. In a savage satire written in the 1730s, Swift suggested to a chambermaid: 'Get your favourite footman to help you in making your lady's bed; and, if you serve a young couple, the footman and you as you are turning up the bedclothes, will make the prettiest observations in the world, which, whispered about, will be very entertaining to the whole family and get among the neighbourhood.'[90] This prurient search by maidservants

---

[86] *T & C Mag.* (1785) 17: 179.

[87] Evidence of the deliberate drilling of holes in the wainscotting is too common to be worth footnoting; there must be 50–100 examples.

[88] *T & C Mag.* (1783), 15: 178; *Crim. Con. Gaz.* 2: 77; *Trials for Adultery at Doctors' Commons*, 7: 16. [89] Ibid. 6: 66–9.

[90] J. Swift, *Directions to Servants* (1745–written *c.* 1731–42) in *Prose Works of Jonathan Swift*, ed. H. Davis (Oxford, 1959), 52–3.

making the beds was evidently very common, and was produced as evidence again and again in court cases. It was often the way in which the guilt of adulterous wives was finally proved in open court.

B. THE REPUTATION OF THE SERVANTS

Servants in the eighteenth century were generally regarded by their employers as lazy, gossipy, inquisitive, venal, and frequently also as alcoholic, promiscuous, and treacherous. Although male servants were only rarely the lovers of their mistresses, if only because it was too dangerous, the maids were frequently the sexual prey of their masters (Plate 20). Swift's advice to a waiting maid in a great household was nothing if not practical in its cynical assumption of the bartering of sexual favours for money:

My Lord may probably like you . . . but never allow the smallest liberty, not even the squeezing of your hand, unless he put a guinea into it . . . Five guineas for handling your breast is a cheap pennyworth. But never allow him the last favour under a hundred guineas, or a settlement of twenty pounds a year for life . . . If you happen to be with child by my lord, you must take up with the chaplain.

Above all, Swift advised a maid to stay away from the son of the house: 'after ten thousand promises, you will get nothing from him but a big belly, or a clap, or probably both together'.[91] His advice to a waiting-woman who served 'a lady who is a little disposed to gallantries' was equally cynical. She should pursue three objectives: to please her lady, to prevent suspicion by the husband, and to 'make it most for your own advantage'.[92]

Another line of criticism levelled against servants, especially those in London and in the service of the leisured classes, was that they aped all the vices of their superiors. A favourable sociological interpretation of their behaviour would be that they absorbed city and elite culture and manners, and were important agents in passing them out into the country and down through the social system. By doing so, they stimulated that active consumerism which became so characteristic a feature of this age of so-called 'luxury'. A less favourable interpretation, laying emphasis on external behaviour, was offered by David Garrick in 1775:

A servant lives up to his eyes in clover; they have wages and board wages, and nothing to do, but to grow fat and saucy—they are as happy as their master, they play for ever at cards, swear like emperors, drink like fishes and go a-wenching

[91] Ibid. 52–8.　　　　　[92] Ibid. 59.

with as much ease and tranquillity as if they were going to a sermon. Oh! 'tis a fine life![93]

Whichever way one chooses to look at eighteenth-century servants, they were not regarded as the most reliable of persons to whom to trust your life and your honour in a legal conflict where their testimony was crucial.

C. THE LIVES OF SERVANTS

An examination of the many life histories which servant witnesses in a separation suit were obliged to recount on oath to the court makes several things clear beyond possibility of dispute. One is that a very high proportion of servants in London or the other big cities had been born and bred in the country, and had come to London to earn a living for a few years before entering the marriage market with some financial savings. It is therefore not surprising that in most families they did not stay long. The traditional long-term loyal retainer, who devotedly served a single family for decades and in return was taken care of in old age, was by the eighteenth century very hard to find. Great aristocratic households with fifty servants or more certainly possessed their own status hierarchies below stairs, thanks to which they could offer an extensive promotion ladder for long service. As a result, the senior servants in a great house often served in that one family for all their active lives, and were pensioned off with leases of farms at low rent. But these were a tiny minority at the topmost level of the servant class, and almost all were men.

One such household was that of the Cadogans in the last decade of the eighteenth century. When Lady Cadogan was prosecuted for adultery in 1794, some twenty-three servants gave evidence in court, eleven of whom had served the Cadogans for between fourteen and twenty-five years, and all but two for more than four. But this does not seem to have made much difference to their behaviour and attitudes. The eighteen years of faithful service by Lady Cadogan's waiting maid clearly encouraged her to throw in her lot with her mistress, and actively to cover up the adultery. More striking is the fact that long service did not stop the other servants from concealing their knowledge of the adultery from their master for at least a year. One maid was so upset by her discovery that she cried, but she did nothing to warn her master. Even on oath in the witness box, the other servants were very evasive, most of them denying having seen anything improper, or even having heard gossip below stairs, which was manifestly untrue. To judge by this example, length of service does not seem to have created much loyalty towards a master.[94]

[93] 'Bon Ton' in D. Garrick, *Three Farces* (New Haven, 1925), 126.   [94] LPCA, D.350–1.

The Cadogans were the exception to the rule, even among the aristocracy, in the long duration of service in their household. Smaller households, comprising two to ten servants, formed the vast majority, and these saw a very rapid turnover of domestic staff: a servant would remain with an employer on the average for only two to four years.[95] As early as 1700, Congreve had been satirizing this high speed of turnover. While paying a call on his aunt, Sir Wilford Witwood meets a saucy footman and asks him: 'How long hast thou lived with thy lady, fellow, ha?', to which the footman replies: 'A week, sir; longer than anybody in the house, except my lady's woman.'[96]

One reason for the high turn-over which characterized the employment careers of most domestic servants was that, as transportation improved, the upper classes became increasingly peripatetic, favouring the excitement of mobility over the convenience of a large retinue. The yearly round now changed to include regular winter seasons in London, Bath, and Tunbridge Wells, and even occasional long trips abroad. This made service even in a great house a volatile and insecure form of employment. If they were going abroad, or even to London for the season, employers did not hesitate to dismiss most or all their staff and shut up their house. At most, only a handful would be left as a skeleton staff. The speed of turnover of servants in England in the first half of the eighteenth century, especially in great houses, was further accelerated by the fact that only a proportion of their income came from their employers. The rest came from tips called 'vails', levied upon all visitors to the house, including even persons coming only for a meal. The result was to increase the greed of the servants and to reduce the control over them of their masters. The solution was to eliminate 'vails' and raise wages, which in the 1760s was often accomplished by local agreements among the landed gentlemen of a county. This increased the economic power of the master over the servants, but it also emphasized the purely cash nexus between them, and did nothing to slow down servant mobility.[97]

It is surprising to discover that servants did indeed not hesitate to give notice if they thought themselves ill-treated by their master or mistress, just as their employers were equally ready to dismiss them if they thought

---

[95] The same high turnover existed in France: J. P. Gutton, *Domestiques et serviteurs dans la France de l'ancien régime* (Paris, 1981), 83–6; S. C. Maza, *Servants and Masters in Eighteenth-Century France* (Princeton, 1983), 76; C. Fairchilds, *Domestic Enemies: Servants and their Masters in Old Regime France* (Baltimore, 1984), 69–70. For England, see J. J. Hecht, *The Domestic Servant Class in Eighteenth-Century England* (London, 1956), and Waterson, *The Servants' Hall*.

[96] W. Congreve, *The Way of the World* (1700), III/iii.

[97] See Hecht, *The Domestic Servant Class*, 158–68; *Gent's Mag.* 34 (1764), 449.

they showed insubordination or rudeness. Indeed, servants in the eighteenth century displayed every sign of almost truculent independence and an astonishingly strong sense of self-worth, especially in view of the high economic and psychological costs of moving rapidly from job to job, and the strong probability of being let go without a reference. In 1707, nearly twenty years after the Glorious Revolution, Steele displayed on the stage an exasperated mistress declaring that 'the English are so saucy with their liberty—I'll have all my lower servants French. There cannot be a good footman born outside an absolute monarchy.'[98] In 1760, the *Gentleman's Magazine* lamented that 'servants very rarely continue long in any place; for if they are not dismissed for being detected in ill conduct or any other fault, they are ever ready to quit them'.[99]

This sturdy independence displayed by servants was the bane of the existence of the employer class, and often led to angry confrontations followed by resignations or dismissals. For example, Lady Clavering's butler later deposed that one day in about 1733, Lady Clavering, 'being in a passion, flung a pair of breakfast tongs at my face, and they stuck in my wig, and I pulled them out and threw them on the floor, and she bid me pick them up, and I told her I would not'.[100] Thus, when a marriage broke up and witnesses were being sought to give evidence about marital offences, there was nearly always a pool of disgruntled ex-servants seeking revenge for old grievances.

The many life histories of servants in court records make it clear that most of those who were dismissed or resigned took several months to find fresh employment, especially if they could not produce satisfactory letters of reference from their previous employers. Just how they kept alive during these periods of short-term unemployment is less certain. Some claimed that they lived on their savings. Many returned home to their parents or were given shelter by a relative. Women earned a little money by taking in washing or acting as sempstresses or mantua-makers. Although they never admitted it, one has to assume that at least some of these women also took to casual prostitution while between employment, if only because it was so much better paid than other temporary occupations. It was certainly widely believed that in London the occupations of female servant and prostitute were closely linked. An anonymous tract of 1749 asserted that

the town being overstocked with harlots is entirely owing to those numbers of women-servants incessantly pouring into it from all corners of the universe. . . .

---

[98] R. Steele, *The Tender Husband* (London, 1705), III/i.
[99] *Gent's Mag.* 30 (1760), 77.   [100] LPCA, D.427. 599.

Many of them are . . . running from place to place, from bawdy-house to service and from service to bawdy-house again . . . so that, in effect, they neither make good whores, good wives, or good servants.[101]

This was, of course, a satirical comment and must not be taken too seriously. It presented an exaggerated picture of the London scene, and there is little doubt that most female servants up from the country went into service in the hope of saving money with a view to marriage. How many succeeded in this ambition in so highly mobile and sexually hazardous an occupation is another matter.

One such girl testified in a separation case in 1717.[102] Catherine Smith had been born in Epsom thirty years before the trial, and had begun her working life rather well, as a servant to the Duke of Ormonde in St James's Street. From there it was downhill all the way. From the Duke she passed into service of the middling sort, successively with Mr Husk, a 'figure-maker' near Hyde Park Corner, Mrs Hull in Piccadilly, and Mrs Brook in Parton Square. But this was her last even mildly respectable and stable job. She then passed into service with several women lodged in different places, too many for her to remember, and ended up two years before the trial as servant in Mrs Whitty's bawdy-house. At about the same time she married a gunsmith in Wood Street, but the alliance did them no good since they soon found themselves arrested for debt and in Marshalsea Prison. On their release, she returned to Mrs Whitty, where she rather implausibly claimed that her work was confined to showing clients up to their rooms, fetching women when they wanted one, and bringing them breakfast in bed. This is the story of one young woman who came up to London from the country to go into service in order to better herself, but who failed. There were probably thousands, maybe tens of thousands like her, all trace of whom has disappeared from the historical record, the failures and drop-outs in the great migration into London which was turning it into the largest metropolis in the Western world.

A good example of this drifting population, forever on the move from employer to unemployment to employer, is provided by the autobiographies of those who served the various members of the Calvert family in their several establishments in the first decade of the eighteenth century.[103] Of the nineteen servants who testified in the trial in 1709, only two had been with the couple for as long as five years, and these were both coachmen, whose known skill, reliability and sobriety was of critical

---

[101] Anon., *Satan's Harvest or The Present State of Whorecraft* . . . (London, 1749), 3–5.
[102] LPCA, D.362.   [103] For the story of the Calverts, see Stone, *Broken Lives*.

importance. Two servants had served for four years, and six more for between two and three years. Thus, half of all the servants had been with the Calverts for less than two years, some of them only for a matter of months, and not a single one had lasted for the full ten years from the marriage in 1699 to the trial in 1709, and few even to the first separation in 1705. These domestic servants lived in a cold, unfriendly, insecure, and marginal world. Even if they were married, and both husband and wife were working, they often were scarcely making a living on their combined income, and were regularly separated by their employment for months or years on end. Very few of these married couples in the records were ever in continuous employment with one employer for more than a few years.

5. Servants in Court

A. SERVANTS AS OBSERVERS

Physical cruelty by the husband towards his wife could not be concealed from the servants, for the sounds of blows and screams were inevitably heard in nearby rooms in the house. Nor could the sight of bruises easily be concealed. In such cases all the female servants, and most of the male, nearly always sided with the victim, and there are countless stories of servants intervening actively to protect a wife from gross physical abuse by her husband. Only very occasionally did the servants join in the abuse and mistreatment of the wife, clearly enjoying the opportunity of openly humiliating a social superior.[104]

Adultery aroused much more complicated responses. Sexuality was a particularly troubling problem for servants, who were almost all either unmarried as a condition of their employment, or married but separated by the obligation to live in. They were mostly young and were constantly thrown into close proximity with fellow servants of the opposite sex. Many of them were actively seeking a spouse. The pressures were made worse since the segregation by sex of the servants' sleeping quarters was a thing of the future, which only developed in the Victorian period.[105] Women servants were consequently exposed to constant flirtation, court-ship, sexual harassment, seduction or near-rape, not only by their fellow-servants but also by the master of the house, his friends, and his adolescent sons. Houses with six or more servants therefore tended to be

[104] Stone: *Broken Lives.*
[105] M. Girouard, *The Victorian Country House* (Oxford, 1971), 122–3; Waterson, *The Servants' Hall*, 28.

hotbeds of sexual intrigue, and the larger the house the greater were the opportunities (and dangers), and the more absorbing the gossip. Downstairs was as much a sexual pressure-cooker as Upstairs sometimes was.

Adultery by the master of the house did little to disturb the equanimity of the servants. It was treated as normal and to be expected, a subject for amused comment but not a matter which raised moral problems. No one thought of informing the wife. Elite male adultery only caused trouble and anxiety below stairs when the woman seduced was one of the maidservants in the house. This aroused feelings of sexual and social jealousy, and friction developed with the favoured servant if she seemed to be profiting from her liaison in terms of money and power within the strict household hierarchy.[106]

But whenever the servants either suspected or knew that the mistress of the house was committing adultery, they were thrown into a state of great moral confusion, since it was not clear where their duty lay. The situation called into question the validity of the traditional ideology of paternalism, loyalty, and fidelity. What was the moral obligation of servants who detected their master's wife in adultery? Should they warn her to stop, and themselves keep silent, thus saving the marriage and preserving the household? Or should they tell their master and bring the whole household down in ruins? Or should they look after their own best interests, and sell the information to the highest bidder: to the mistress to keep their mouths shut, or to their master to reveal the truth?

The servants were thus faced with a morally ambiguous, personally dangerous, and financially risky choice. If they played their cards well, they might be able to sell their information, or their silence, for a great deal of money and some promotion. They might also be able to pay off old scores and take revenge for past slights. But if they played their cards badly, they could easily find themselves dismissed for impertinence, out of a job and without a reference.

Adultery by the mistress of the house therefore struck a very sensitive nerve among many servants. At least before 1790, few of them expressed strong moral disapproval of wifely adultery on principle, or felt that it had at all cost to be exposed and punished. The majority seem to have found adultery an intriguing subject for endless below-stairs gossip. What did shock them, however, was the seduction of a wife by a lover who took advantage of the friendship and hospitality of her husband.

It was the wife's waiting maid who faced the most acute moral dilemma. Apart from the lover, she was usually the person in the world

---

[106] See the Middleton case in Stone, *Broken Lives*.

most intimate with her mistress, who after all lived apart from her mother and whose adultery proved that she no longer loved her husband. When asked by her mistress to conspire to facilitate a sexual liaison, what was a maid expected to do? The evidence seems to indicate that in most cases in the seventeenth and eighteenth centuries, she put her duty to her mistress first and that to her master second. But by the early nineteenth century, the general rise in moral sensitivity had filtered down through the social hierarchy, and servants were often much less willing actively to cover up wifely adultery.[107]

By committing adultery, the mistress of the house inevitably put herself at the mercy of her waiting woman, since the liaison could only be carried on with the latter's active assistance. Once she had confided in her maid, from that day on she was exposed to the possibility of blackmail or delation. As David Garrick made Melissa lament in 1741, 'we discover our weakness to our servants, make them our confidants, put 'em upon equality with us, and so they become our advisers'.[108] In 1778, another commentator observed:

The misfortune is that servants are domestic spies . . . A woman of fashion, who yields to the impulses of her passions, must live a very disagreeable life with her waiting-maid, if she does not condescend to wink at all the impertinence or even insolence of her Abigail . . . Her fate is determined, her reputation is in her domestic's hands, and she [the maid] can dispose of it at pleasure.[109]

This was true enough, but the moral duty of the maid was not so clear. For example, the position of the lady's maid in the household of Lord Cadogan in 1794–6 was clearly a peculiarly difficult one. She had been with Lady Cadogan for eighteen years, first as nurse-maid, then as lady's maid; but on the other hand, Lord Cadogan had, as a mark of gratitude for her services, given her a bond to pay her £30 a year for life. Faced with this clash of obligations, female solidarity and eighteen years of friendship drove her to side with her mistress, and eventually to accompany her after she had been exposed and expelled from the house.[110]

The vast difference in the financial resources at the disposal of employers and servants inevitably opened the door to large-scale bribery by the former or blackmail by the latter. The motive behind a good deal of the espionage carried out by servants in cases of wifely adultery was to store up information for potential profit later on. By the last half of the

---

[107] See the Loveden case in Stone, *Broken Lives*.
[108] 'The Lying Valet' (1741), in D. Garrick, *Three Farces*, 21.
[109] *T & C Mag.* (1778), 10: 234.
[110] *Cadogan v. Cadogan* (1796), LPCA, D.350–1. 1272–5.

eighteenth century, most of the higher servants were literate, and a number of them made careful written notes of the times, days, and places when they saw or heard anything suspicious. They clearly kept these notes either for possible use when testifying in court some time in the future when the scandal broke, or else for money in return for withholding the evidence. It must have been common knowledge among servants that they could expect to receive from their mistress anything up to the equivalent of a year's wages in a single day in order to buy their silence, and that their master might be willing to pay even more to get them to testify in court about what they had seen.

Some servants went to extraordinary lengths to keep these written records with which to threaten their employers. When in 1796 Mr Elwes began to suspect his wife of infidelity, he instructed his postilion to 'watch the conduct of his mistress closely, and to take notice of every person that came to her, and to what places she went, and to keep a book in which he might make his memorandums of what passed'. The book, or part of it, in which the postilion noted every movement of his mistress, day by tedious day, is preserved. It was indeed produced in court, but whether thanks to bribery or out of conviction, the postilion was now a witness for the defence. His book revealed nothing incriminating, and he swore that Mr Elwes had instructed him to set a trap for Mrs Elwes, to make overtures to her, and then to lure her to an assignation in a bagnio, where they might be discovered together.[111]

Servants were therefore willing, or unwilling, to testify for a wide variety of reasons: duty, loyalty, affection, spite, revenge, greed, or even pure curiosity. A maidservant in a remote village in Devonshire was motivated to testify by no more than the desire for a free trip to a city. She confided to a friend that 'she would make herself in evidence in the case, that she might have the pleasure of seeing Exeter without being at any expenses'.[112]

Others felt strongly that appearing to give evidence against a former employer was a serious moral betrayal. At the trial of the Duchess of Norfolk in 1700, one servant criticized another who had appeared in court to support the prosecution by the duke of his master Sir John Germain, the duchess's lover. He expressed his surprise that 'a man that had got his bread under his master should appear here against him in so ungrateful a thing. . . . I should think myself ungrateful to eat a gentleman's bread seven years and do him all the spite I could.' On the other hand, he admitted that 'I would not speak an untruth for all the masters

---

[111] *Elwes* v. *Elwes* (1796), LPCA, D.675. 1034–1125, 914, 1173.
[112] LPCA, D.127. 503.

in the world.'[113] Here was an expression of the traditional ethic of the bond of loyalty between master and servant. If he was put on the witness stand under oath, his duty was to tell the truth. But his loyalty to his master should lead him to go into hiding and refuse all financial offers from his master's enemy to appear in court against him. This was a concept of loyalty which was slowly but surely eroded in the course of the eighteenth century.

To supplement the information supplied by servants, more and more employers in the eighteenth century were turning to semi-professional detectives. These could easily be hired in London, and were probably drawn from that small army of bailiffs who prowled the London streets, looking for debtors to arrest. They were hired to locate servants dismissed by husbands or wives contemplating separation litigation; to investigate the lives and backgrounds of servants so as to check their reliability or to discredit their testimony; and to search for evidence of adultery beyond the view of the servants. For example, in 1770 Lady Grosvenor, herself exposed to litigation for her affair with the Duke of Cumberland, hired detectives to track down her husband's many adulteries. She instructed them 'to go about into bawdy houses and other places to search and procure witnesses ... they were authorized to offer or promise any person they could find ... that they should be handsomely rewarded'.[114] It is not surprising that a great deal of information, not all of it strictly truthful, could be assembled by the use of professional detectives and the offer of large rewards.

B. SERVANTS AS DELATORS

The critical question which bothered servants most was if and when and how to inform their master of his wife's adultery. Was it prudent to watch and wait, hoping that the affair would blow over and the marriage be saved? This would probably be in the best interests of all parties. But how long should servants wait after they had convincing proof before informing their master? None acted immediately, some waited months, many others for several years.

One reason for what may at first sight seem like excessive procrastination was that reporting to a husband the adultery of his wife was often a dangerous undertaking. Servants ran the risk that their story would be rejected by an over-trusting husband, unwilling to believe that his wife was unfaithful. In that case, the servant would be accused of acting

---

[113] *State Trials*, 13: 1304–5.
[114] *Grosvenor v. Grosvenor* (1770), *Trials for Adultery*, 6: 177–8.

merely from malice, and be discharged on the spot in disgrace without a reference.[115] Another reason for delay was that the livelihood of servants depended on continuing employment in service with their master, and any break-up of the marriage was quite likely to lead to a reorganization of the household, a severe reduction of the staff, and possibly the closing up of the house altogether. Thirdly, if they did have to seek other employment, servants were heavily dependent on a good reference from their former master. He might well be angry with a servant who knew of such adultery and had failed to tell him earlier. Moreover, prospective employers might not be very anxious to hire someone with a reputation as a domestic spy and teller of tales. There was therefore always a fear that there might be some truth in the suggestion that delation rarely paid. In 1777 the adulterous Mrs Harris gave her maid a petticoat and a guinea and told her 'not to tell tales, as servants never get anything by it'.[116]

The most serious problem which faced a servant with the knowledge of his mistress's infidelity and who wished, for whatever reason, to inform her husband, was how to avoid the odium of being the bearer of bad news. As a result, all servants took great care to pass the information to an intermediary, a member of the family or a family friend, who in turn could convey it to the husband. Even relatives were often fearful of telling what they knew. In 1818 Mr Taafe's brother did not tell him of his wife's infidelity because 'I did not choose on such a painful occasion to be the first person to let him hear of such a horrible thing.' In this case, it was alleged that the situation had gone on for years without anyone telling Mr Taafe, a story which the House of Lords chose not to believe.[117]

There is no doubt that telling a husband about his wife's infidelity could sometimes be a very traumatic experience for the informant. When in 1784 a family friend told Mr Nisbet, he promptly fainted. Other husbands became hysterical or fell into fits.[118] In the Barttelot divorce case in 1798, a servant explained that he did not tell his master since 'it is very dangerous to communicate such things'. He was right, for when Mr Barttelot was told, 'he was like a madman . . . he was going to shoot himself'.[119] When reproached in 1789 for not informing his master Mr Dodwell of his mistress's adultery with Mr Bate, a servant explained that he was 'very apprehensive of mischief in consequence of any discovery, and that [Mr Dodwell] might resolve on some desperate act which might be fatal to Mr Bate or both of them'.[120] In short, he was afraid of provok-

[115] See e.g. the Middleton case in Stone, *Broken Lives*.
[116] *JH Lords*, 35: 58; *Crim. Con. Gaz.* 2: 37.
[117] *JH Lords*, 52: 296–7.   [118] Ibid. 37: 40.
[119] Ibid. 42: 57.   [120] *Dodwell* v. *Dodwell* (1789), LPCA, D.611. 242.

ing a duel. In another case, a servant confessed that 'I did not inform Sir James, for I knew his temper. I was afraid he would take a pistol and shoot me.'[121] When in 1779 the Marquis of Carmarthen upbraided his valet for not informing him about his wife's adultery earlier, the latter replied calmly: 'You know, my lord, you turned away two of your servants before upon a similar occasion, for having been too busy in prying into your family affairs, and acquainting you with misfortunes which might have reached your knowledge soon enough without troubling their heads with them.'[122]

C. SERVANTS AS WITNESSES

It was upon the sworn testimony of servants that the sentence in a trial for separation on grounds of adultery would usually turn. In consequence, their services suddenly came into high demand from both sides as soon as a law-suit became likely, and the search began for credible witnesses. Employers were very conscious of how much they were at the mercy of venal servants. Their predicament was very well put by the adulterous Duchess of Norfolk, the evidence against whom at her trial in 1700 came entirely from bribed ex-servants of her lover, Sir John Germain:

Masters are already too much in the power of their servants, and if they charge their masters with adultery, felony, or even treason, it is not easily in the power of the master to defend himself against downright swearing: servants having those opportunities of the knowledge of times and places and company, which cannot easily be denied or avoided, and which others have not; whereupon they may frame and build false evidence; and many times are of ill principles and desperate fortunes, and of tempers very revengeful; so that whoever turns away a servant, he is in his power for his estate, honour, and even life itself.[123]

One hundred and fifty years later, in 1853, the writer of a well-known legal handbook reiterated the warning offered by the Duchess of Norfolk: 'the testimony of discarded domestics should be received with great caution, and the most sifting; otherwise our position is fearful, our tables and beds would be surrounded with snares, and our comforts converted into instruments of terror and alarm'.[124] The hysterical language reveals something of the nightmare fears of the employer class lest they find themselves at the mercy of their venal inferiors. This was a situation which became even worse in the course of the eighteenth century, as servants were increasingly obtained from impersonal and often corrupt

[121] *Crim. Con. Gaz.* 1: 53.
[122] *T & C Mag.* 11: 10. [123] *State Trials*, 13: 1343. [124] Wharton, 439.

employment agencies, instead of by word of mouth from relatives and friends. Erskine observed in 1789 that it would be foolish to put much trust in the evidence of 'gossiping servants, whom nobody knows, taken from advertising offices where every vice and corruption prevails'.[125]

Because of the high turnover in servants, whenever a marriage broke up there were usually some recently discharged servants with old scores to settle. This is why at the first hint of a law-suit, the husband and wife each initiated an intensive search to locate these former servants. Once found, they were quickly re-employed, and bribed either into silence, or into revealing the truth, or on occasion into direct perjury. These generalizations can best be exemplified by an examination of the servants who testified on both sides in the 1709 divorce case of Leonard and Charlotte Calvert, that we have already considered.[126]

Leonard Calvert began assembling evidence for a lawsuit as early as the spring of 1708, when he tracked down and interviewed Maria Holt, the maidservant who had kept the Knightsbridge lodgings which his wife Charlotte and one of her several lovers had visited from time to time over the previous six months for adulterous nights without disturbance. Soon after he had obtained this vital testimony, Leonard engaged the girl as a maid in his own house, to make sure that she would be available as a witness when he needed her. Later he had even greater success, obtaining the testimony of two disgruntled Irish ex-servants, who gave vital testimony about Charlotte's liaisons with two of her lovers and about her two illegitimate children. Both were said to be being 'provided for' by Leonard while the trial was in progress.[127]

But two could play at this game of tracking down and securing the services of disgruntled ex-servants, and Charlotte's lawyers soon had private investigators hot on the trail of witnesses to the equally numerous infidelities of her husband Leonard. Their best find was a 16-year-old girl, Anne Peters, who had been the maid-of-all-work at a house near London where Leonard and his mistress had spent the summer of 1709. In September of that year she suddenly disappeared from the house, leaving her clothes behind her, departing on the excuse of going for a short ride with a friend. A week later she resurfaced in Charlotte's employment as a maid in her home in Stratton Street. Charlotte's agents had clearly bribed the girl to leave Leonard's service and enter hers.[128]

---

[125] *Crim. Con. Gaz.* 1: 70; there is a satirical Rowlandson drawing dating to about 1800–5, of a servants' Register Office with a strong emphasis on potential sexual qualifications, in J. Riely, *Rowlandson Drawings from the Paul Mellon Collection* (New Haven, 1978), no. 78, pl. xii; J. Reid, *The Register Office* (London, 1761), was a popular two-act farce.

[126] See the the Calvert case in Stone, *Broken Lives*.

[127] LPCA, D.356. 314, 319, 320, 400–7, 425, 454, 466.   [128] Ibid. 763–70, 962, 987.

Charlotte also tracked down another vital witness, Sarah Gaines, a charwoman who had worked at a house in Richmond while Leonard and his mistress had lived there during the summer of 1708. When she gave her testimony in court, she too was safe in employment in Charlotte's house in Stratton Street, where she had spent the last couple of weeks.

Bribery was also freely used, as well as food and lodging. Mary Shrubb, who had been the living-in servant at the Stratton Street house, admitted that Charlotte had paid her one month's wages to give testimony. An old man in whose company Leonard Calvert had visited a prostitute admitted that Charlotte had promised to get a keeper's place in a royal park for his son (presumably through her father, the Earl of Lichfield) in reward for his agreeing to testify.[129]

Both sides clearly employed semi-professional agents, and both managed without much difficulty to locate the midwives who had delivered the illegitimate children of both Leonard's mistress and Charlotte. Neither Charlotte nor Leonard succeeded in covering their tracks sufficiently carefully to escape discovery. They had both, and particularly Leonard, been reasonably discreet and prudent while in London, but they had assumed—wrongly, as it turned out—that they could relax their precautions in houses in the country around London which they rented for the summer months. The suburban villages in which these were located turned out to be small, inquisitive, gossipy societies, and everyone at Banstead apparently knew that the woman living with Leonard Calvert was his mistress. The maids who plumped up the feather beds each morning always knew who was sleeping in whose bed, and only if these female servants could be silenced by money or loyalty was reasonable security possible.

D. CONCLUSION

Between 1660 and 1860, servants thus lived in closely symbiotic relationship with their masters and mistresses. Neither could exist without the other, but the internal tensions between the two were always great. Theoretically they were held together by a web of life-long devoted loyalty on the one side and paternal protection on the other. The practice was rather different. For one thing, there was rapid mobility of this labour force from one employer to another. For another, many of them were no down-trodden lackeys, bullied and exploited by their masters and mistresses. They were self-confident and ambitious human beings

---

[129] LPCA, D.356. 810, 899, 782.

who did not hesitate to disobey orders, to stop an enraged husband from beating up his wife, or to give instant notice if they felt themselves abused or mistreated. In any case, for most of them service was not a lifetime occupation, but a liminal period between the parental home and marriage, while the necessary capital was accumulated with which to start a business—a public house, a livery stable, a millinery shop—where the skills learnt in service could be used. As a result, there is not much evidence of paternalism on the part of employers, or of loyalty on the part of servants. It certainly still existed, especially among the upper servants in great houses, but it could rarely be relied upon in a moment of crisis.

In families where there was adultery or suspected adultery by the wife, or persistent and violent cruelty by the husband, the servants inevitably played a critical role. In most cases their interference, or lack of it, and their decisions about when to speak and when to remain silent, were decisive in damping down marital friction or in bringing matters to a head. Some servants were always no more than a Greek chorus, watching and commenting passively upon events. But whether from motives of principle or profit, many others would become involved as key actors in the unfolding drama of a marital break-up.

It should be noted, however, that after the middle of the eighteenth century, the demand for privacy increased among the elite and the middling sort; and accordingly, employers installed bell-wires and dumb waiters and carved out corridors in an effort to create for themselves larger areas of private space. Accompanying this change was another, for which the reasons remain rather more obscure: servants now became identified as domestic enemies rather than domestic allies or co-conspirators. In consequence their evidence in court became less useful, for now they saw and heard less than before. Thus, the Loveden case, in the first decade of the nineteenth century, is one of the very first on record in which a lady in a great house tried—unsuccessfully, as it turned out—to conduct an adulterous liaison without the co-operation of her waiting maid, who in fact was now attempting to trap her. Such loyalty as still existed was that between the upper male servants, especially the valet, and the master of the house, who was the person who paid the wages.[130] The loyalty of some of the female servants was now also to their employer, the husband, rather than to the mistress whom they served. It is significant that throughout the eighteenth century there was a steady decline in the proportion of rich employers who left in their wills

---

[130] See the Loveden case in Stone, *Broken Lives.* According to C. Fairchilds, the identical change occurred in the last third of the 18th century in France; *Domestic Enemies*, 12–19; 47–54, 124–6; Maza, *Servants and Masters*, 247–53.

bequests to servants, either collectively or selectively by name. Monetary values, casual employment, and impersonal market relationships increasingly characterized domestic service in the very late eighteenth and early nineteenth centuries.

⚙ IX ⚙

The Action for Criminal Conversation

All other injuries, when put in the scale of . . . the crime of adultery
. . . are as nothing. Is there any other private wrong which produces
so many public consequences? The sanctity of marriage, of a contract which is the very foundation of the social world, is violated—
religious and moral duties made a sport of—the peace and happiness of families utterly broken up—the protection of daughters
destroyed, and their character, though innocent, disparaged in
opinion by their mother's dishonour.

Thomas Erskine in the House of Commons, 1800 (Parl. Hist. 35: 311)

The verdict of a jury . . . is a pure nothing. It does not in one case
out of twenty elucidate the real facts of the case.

Dr Stephen Lushington, Judge of the London Consistory Court, in the House
of Commons, 1830 (2 Hansard, 23: 1385)

1. The Nature of the Action

The outward appearance (but not, as we shall see, what was by then the
latent function) of a crim. con. action was well described by a foreign
visitor, L. Simond, a Franco-American gentleman who spent two years
in England in 1810–11. He wrote:

This criminal conversation is not prosecuted *criminally*, but produces only a civil
suit for the recovery of damages, estimated in money. The jury determines the
amount of these damages, by the degree of union and conjugal happiness existing before the criminal conversation which destroyed it, and by the rank and
fortune of the parties. The smallest appearance of negligence or connivance on
the part of the husband deprives him of all remedy against the seducer, who owes
him nothing, if he only took what was of no value to him, and which he guarded
so ill. I have heard of £10,000 Sterling awarded in some cases, which is certainly
rather dear for a *conversation*! The husband pockets this money without shame,
because he has the laugh on his side, and in the world ridicule alone produces
shame. A divorce is generally granted by act of Parliament in these cases; and
marriage as generally takes place between the lovers. The publicity which such

prosecutions necessarily occasion, and all the details and proofs of the intrigue, are highly indelicate and scandalous. The testimony, for instance, of servants, of young chambermaids, who are brought into open court to tell, in the face of the public, all they have seen, heard or guessed at, is another sort of prostitution more indecent than the first. Morals are far from being purified by this process; but the substantial infringement is prevented. This sort of chastity resembles the probity of certain persons who are sufficiently honest not to be hanged.[1]

In the sixteenth and seventeenth centuries, cases of adultery and fornication had been reported to the church courts by the churchwardens of the parish in which they took place, and by court officials called apparitors. If found guilty, delinquents were made to stand in a white sheet holding a candle before a congregation on a Sunday, or before a crowd in the market-place on market-day, and publicly to confess the sin of fornication or adultery or pre-nuptial conception. At the same period, the local JPs were also empowered to punish adultery and fornication by fines, the stocks, and whipping.

In the late seventeenth and early eighteenth centuries, however, the church courts in England went into a startling decline. By the early eighteenth century, they were no longer in a position to enforce upon a recalcitrant population the old moral code by means of officially initiated prosecutions and the infliction of shame punishments. To make matters worse, the traditional use of private informers fell into disrepute, Defoe remarking that 'a rogue and an informer are synonymous in the vulgar acceptation'.[2] At just the same time, the JPs became noticeably less enthusiastic about punishing adultery for its own sake. Up to 1746, adultery was still occasionally prosecuted as a misdemeanour, but thereafter it disappeared from secular court records. The main concern of JPs was now not morality but money, to keep down the burden upon the soaring poor rates by identifying the putative father of an illegitimate child and forcing him to pay for its upkeep.[3]

To fill the growing legal gap left by the decline of the church courts, attempts were made to enforce morality in the period 1690 to 1730 by private Societies for the Reformation of Manners. Encouraged by royal proclamations for 'preventing and punishing Immorality and Prophaneness', the main targets of these societies were Sabbath-breakers, blasphemers, swearers, and prostitutes, and their main supporters were dissenters and low churchmen. They flourished for a while and claimed

---

[1] [L. Simond], *A Journal of a Tour and Residence in Great Britain during the Years 1810 and 1811 by a French Traveller . . .* (New York, 1815), i: 34.

[2] E. J. Bristow, *Vice and Vigilance: Purity Movements in Britain since 1700* (London, 1977), 13.

[3] 3 *Hansard*, 147: 1854.

to have won a hundred thousand convictions, mostly of prostitutes. But their long-term effect on society was small, and they died away in the 1720s, when Mandeville launched a utilitarian defence of prostitution as a prime safeguard for the chastity of respectable women.[4] All this activity is testimony to the anxiety felt during the 1690s about the apparent deterioration of morality since 1660, but it did nothing to affect the problems of adultery and divorce in high places.

This silent decriminalization of adultery made England almost unique in Europe, and set it off sharply from the other part of Britain, namely Scotland, where adultery remained a criminal offence. Part cause, part consequence of this decline in the enforcement of moral controls at the local level was the entry into the field of the central common law courts. In the late seventeenth century, the two superior courts of common law, the King's Bench and Common Pleas, extended the range of the action of trespass, which had previously been used as a remedy for mayhem, battery, or wounding. It was now made to cover an action by a husband for damages against the seducer of his wife, the seduction being described as a 'criminal conversation', despite the fact that it was neither criminal nor a conversation in the usual sense of the word. Trespass could be prosecuted by a civil suit at the county assizes, but whether this was done on any scale in the seventeenth century for actions of criminal conversation is unknown, since the records have now virtually all disappeared.[5]

The setting of the action was predominantly not in Common Pleas but in King's Bench, especially in the period 1760 to 1820 when this court virtually monopolized common law business.[6] The court was set up in the south-east angle of Westminster Hall, entirely exposed to all the other activity going on there. In 1760, however, a partition was built in the corner to create a room into which crowded judge, jury, plaintiff, defendant, counsel, stenographers, and curious spectators (End papers and Plate 20). On other occasions, the chief justice sitting alone tried crim. con. actions in the Guildhall in the evenings, where he dealt with cases of misdemeanour in Westminster and Middlesex. Here he had his own separate courtroom.[7]

---

[4] T. Isaacs, 'The Anglican Hierarchy and the Reformation of Manners 1688–1738', *Journal of Ecclesiastical History*, 33 (1982); Bristow, *Vice and Vigilance*, 2–21.

[5] J. S. Cockburn, *A History of English Assizes, 1558–1714* (Cambridge, 1972), 139.

[6] Brougham attributed this near-monopoly of King's Bench to the exceptional speed and efficiency of Lord Chief Justice Mansfield; in fact it persisted long after his day, so that when legal reform at last began in 1828, the discrepancy still persisted; *Works of Henry Lord Brougham* (Edinburgh, 1872), 3: 198; *Speeches of Lord Brougham* (London, 1838), 2: 330–7.

[7] E. Foss, *Memories of Westminster Hall* (Boston, 1874), 84–7; J. C. Oldham, Unpublished Legal Papers of Lord Mansfield, 160. (I owe a sight of this unpublished MS to the kindness of Professor Oldham of Georgetown University Law Center.)

The action was carried on exclusively between the two men: the husband and the wife's alleged lover. The wife, as one whose legal personality was absorbed into that of her husband, was not permitted to play any part in it; she was denied the opportunity to call witnesses or testify in her own defence. Moreover, neither the plaintiff nor the defendant was allowed to testify in person in court.[8] In the minority of suits which were contested, the trial therefore consisted of speeches by the barristers on both sides, and the oral testimony and answers in cross-examination of sworn witnesses. At the conclusion of the proceedings, the judge directed the jury about the law and about the criteria to be used in assessing the damages.

The jury either acquitted the defendant, which rarely happened, or awarded the plaintiff damages and costs, which often amounted to very large sums indeed. The crucial decision-making process took astonishingly little time. A verdict which might destroy a man's career, reduce him to a pauper, or cast him indefinitely into exile or a debtors' prison was normally made in a matter of minutes. Even in the most complicated and bitterly contested of cases, the jury rarely took more than 'a short time' or 'a few minutes' to make up its mind on a figure, and in all but a handful of cases the longest time taken was half an hour. In some cases, the jury never left the box, but merely whispered briefly among themselves. For example, they 'instantaneously' awarded £700 in 1790, and £5,000 in 1802. When in 1815 they took an hour to reduce damages from the £30,000 claimed to £15,000, this was regarded as unusual. It is clear, however, that the time taken increased significantly during the early nineteenth century, presumably because the jurymen began taking their duties more seriously.[9]

This speed of judgment, which nowadays would seem irresponsible, aroused no criticism whatever at the time. Indeed, similar speed was normal even in deciding cases involving capital punishment. The rapidity of decision-making in crim. con. cases was no doubt facilitated by the fact that in London these cases were tried by a 'special jury of gentlemen of fortune'—twenty-four men selected from freeholders of substance, knights, and urban gentry. The same jurymen, usually substantial merchants in the City, often served in many trials, and so gained experience. These special juries were originally used since they were thought to be more sensitive to the value of honour to a gentleman than were ordinary

---

[8] These restrictions were not lifted until 1869, by 32–33 Vic. cap. 68. s. 2.

[9] *Barttelot* v. *Hooker* (1790), (BL. 518 1 12(5)); *Lingham* v. *Hunt* (1802), *Lond. Chron.* (1802), 92: 103; *Lord Rosebery* v. *Sir Henry Mildmay* (1815), *The Times*, 12 Dec. 1814: 3.

jurymen, who were drawn from the lower ranks of the middling sort. In 1661, Justice Hyde had remarked that a trial before an ordinary jury was 'a disparagement to many a burger, much less should such therefore be judges of differences between gentlemen and their wives'.[10]

For reasons which will be described later, many actions, and indeed by the 1790s a large majority, went uncontested. In these cases the plaintiff won his suit in King's Bench by default, and the assessment of damages was delegated to a sheriff's jury at the local assizes. The jury used was often that of Middlesex, since most of the litigants had a residence in London, but it might also be assembled out of London at the assizes of the county where the plaintiff resided. The damages awarded by the jury, however unreasonably excessive or trivial, could not be altered on appeal. In an appeal against excessive damages in a crim. con. case in 1758, Lord Mansfield refused a retrial, even though the jury had awarded £500 damages against a clerk earning only £50 a year. His reason was that 'the jury are the proper judge of damages in an action founded upon a tort, and only they can judge the particular circumstances of the case'.[11] This refusal by the judges to intervene, even in cases of the most blatantly unjust of sentences, prevailed until the early nineteenth century. In 1805, however, Lord Ellenborough for the first time allowed the possibility of an appeal against excessive damages, if there was evidence of undue motivation or gross error. This was a decision which was made against a background of rising indignation in judicial and lay circles at the arbitrariness and irresponsibility of juries.[12]

Once the damages had been awarded, payment of them and the assessed costs were enforced in the same way as for any other debt. A warrant was issued and the defendant arrested and thrown into prison. His moveable goods, such as furniture, would be distrained and sold, but his real estate could not be touched. The defendant therefore had four options. He could pay the damages and costs in full; he could come to terms with the plaintiff (if he had not already secretly done so); he could go to prison and live off the income of his real estate; or he could sell all his goods or convey them in trust to others, and flee the country

---

[10] *Manby* v. *Scott* (1661), *Eng. Rep.* 83: 980–1, 1036, 1045; D. Hay, 'The Class Composition of the Palladium of Liberty: Trial Jurors in the Eighteenth Century', in J. S. Cockburn and T. A. Green (eds.) *Twelve Good Men and True* (Princeton, 1988), 318, 344, 353–4. J. C. Oldham, 'Origins of the Special Jury', *University of Chicago Law Review*, 50 (1983), 137–221; id., 'Special Juries in England: Nineteenth-Century Usage and Reform', *Journal of Legal History*, Sept. 1987; I owe these references to David Sugarman.

[11] J. Sayer, *The Law of Damages* (London, 1770), 212–14; *Laws Respecting Women*, 317; *Wilford* v. *Berkeley* (1758), *Eng. Rep.* 97: 472.

[12] *Leverington* v. *Edwards* (1786), *Crim. Con. Gaz.* 1: 141; *Duberley* v. *Gunning* (1789), *Lond. Chron.* (1792), 1: 443; *Chambers* v. *Caulfield* (1805), *Eng. Rep.* 102: 1285.

either before, during, or immediately after the trial. He could then live in exile off the proceeds of the sale of his goods and the income of his real estate. By 1800, Calais and Boulogne were said to be full of fugitives from crim. con. actions.

It was never quite clear what effect, if any, these verdicts at common law had upon suits for separation on grounds of wifely adultery in ecclesiastical courts and upon private bills of divorce in Parliament. As a matter of principle, church courts 'take no cognizance of a verdict obtained in the common law courts by any of the parties to their suits'. But they were particularly sceptical about the verdicts in crim. con. actions, partly because so many were undefended cases, and partly because, as Sir William Scott, later Lord Stowell, put it in 1794 'how can that be evidence against the party, which has passed in a suit to which she was not party?'[13]

A verdict in a crim. con. action was also by no means decisive in influencing the passage or rejection of a bill of divorce in Parliament. Although the Lords were not entirely confident about the capacity of juries to detect collusion, they none the less in 1809 ordered that every bill of divorce should be accompanied by a transcript of a previous trial for crim. con. But this did not mean that Parliament always accepted the verdict. In 1809, Colonel Powlett obtained a sentence of separation in an ecclesiastical court, and was awarded £3,000 in a crim. con. suit, but his divorce bill was rejected by Parliament on the grounds that the evidence for his wife's adultery with the defendant, Viscount Sackville, appeared to be collusive—Mrs Powlett having tipped off her husband to the fact that the servants could provide evidence against her.[14] There were also other cases in which the jury in a crim. con. action awarded only nominal damages or none at all, in spite of which the divorce bill passed smoothly through Parliament.[15] Thus in 1814, George Green was awarded a farthing's damages in King's Bench, but granted a full divorce by Parliament.[16]

2. The Principles of the Action

A. INTRODUCTION

There were several principles which underlay the action. The first was

[13] *Middleton* v. *Rose* (1795), Poynter, 199–200; *Elwes* v. *Elwes* (1794), *Eng. Rep.* 163: 327; *Evans* v. *Evans* (1844), ibid: 1002; see also Dr Stephen Lushington in *Phillips* v. *Phillips* (1844), ibid. 163: 997.
[14] MacQueen, *House of Lords*, 490, 605, 624; *JH Lords*, 14: 152, 304, 329; Roberts, 22.
[15] MacQueen, *House of Lords*, 491, 640, 644.
[16] George H. Green (1814), *JH Lords*, 49: 749, 778, 780, 878.

that the common law should and could provide facilities for litigants to obtain monetary damages for any tort, even when it did not involve physical violence or financial loss. There can be little doubt that one motive of the common law judges was to attact more business to their courts. But it was one thing to set up the legal machinery, and another to persuade the public to use it.

B. MALE HONOUR AND THE DUEL

The shift from violence to the law was of course a by-product of the growth of the nation-state in the sixteenth and early seventeenth centuries. In the process, the aristocracy and squirearchy had slowly been weaned from their earlier irresponsible and unregulated use of violence and persuaded to settle their disputes by other means: first by ritualized duelling, and then by litigation in the royal courts—by 'wars in Westminster Hall'.[17] It was not until the late seventeenth century that the state began exerting its full power to place curbs upon the duel, by prosecuting for manslaughter those duellists who killed their opponents.[18]

In addition to this pressure from the state, the critical change which made possible the rise of the crim. con. action was a very slow and very hesitant redefinition of male honour, a process which began in the late seventeenth century. In the early years most of the litigants were members of the social elite—squires, baronets, and peers. In such a society, a man's honour was defined in terms of sexual potency and bravery, and shame by cuckoldry and cowardice; honour in a woman was defined by sexual purity, and shame by adultery.[19] In consequence, the injured husband had been accustomed to resorting to murder, open violence, or a challenge to a duel in order to obtain satisfaction for the seduction of his wife. The code of honour of the duel thus fed straight into this ideology.[20]

The first to raise the moral issue of duelling or litigation over injured male honour were the late seventeenth-century playwrights, some of whom suggested satirically that the crim. con. action was developed in part in order to protect peaceable or timid cuckolds from being killed in

[17] L. Stone, *The Crisis of the Aristocracy, 1558–1641* (Oxford, 1965), ch. v.

[18] See G. Farquhar, *The Beaux-Stratagem* (1707), III/iii.

[19] J. Pitt-Rivers, 'The Moral Foundations of the Family', in his *The Fate of Schechem or the Politics of Sex* (Cambridge, 1977), 23; see also id., 'Honour and Social Status', in J. G. Peristiany (ed.), *Honour and Shame* (London, 1966); J. Schneider, 'Of Vigilance and Virgins: Honor, Shame, and Access to Resources in Mediterranean Societies', *Ethnology*, 10 (1971); D. D. Gilmore (ed.), *Honor and Shame and the Unity of the Mediterranean* (Washington, 1987).

[20] Stone, *Crisis of the Aristocracy*, 242–50; V. G. Kiernan. *The Duel in European History: Honour and the Reign of Aristocracy* (Oxford, 1988).

duels by truculent seducers of their wives. The spirit of bourgeois prudence and calculation was seen to be triumphing over the spirit of chivalry and the readiness to risk and take life in defence of honour. Thus, when pointedly reminded by his wife's lover that the latter wore a sword, Vanbrugh's Sir John Brute protested feebly in 1697: 'Wear a sword, Sir?—And what of that, Sir?—He comes to my house; eats my meat; lies with my wife; dishonours my family; gets a bastard to inherit my estate. And when I ask a civil account of all this, "Sir," says he, "I wear a sword." '[21]

A perfect example of the confusion of values caused by this drive to suppress duelling in the 1690s is the case of Sir Thomas Aston, who became convinced that his wife had committed adultery with a number of gentlemen. One of these he challenged, fought, and killed. He challenged a second, but before the fight began the defendant called a halt and swore to Sir Thomas that he had not slept with his wife. The duel was abandoned, and the combatants adjourned to a nearby tavern, where they spent the night drinking together. Sir Thomas met a third putative lover in the street, drew his sword and challenged him to do the same. The man promptly threw himself on the ground and refused to get up, despite kicking and prodding with the tip of his sword by Sir Thomas. He claimed that the new government policy against duelling made it too dangerous.[22] Thus, one man, behaving according to the old rules of honour of the European aristocracy, accepted a challenge and died; while another, behaving according to the new rules laid down by church and state, threw himself on the ground and lived. The latter clearly shared the standard of ethics of the influential non-juring clergyman, Jeremy Collier, who in 1698 wrote a pamphlet against duelling in which he described duellists as 'murtherers by *principle*'.[23]

It is difficult to imagine clearer evidence of the beginning of a shift from an honour and shame society to a commercial society than this evolution of litigation as an acceptable alternative to previous standard modes of revenge for cuckoldry by physical assault or a duel. After all, trading injured honour for monetary damages is a commercial transaction, taking place in a legal market. There can be little doubt that the commercialization of honour was much on men's minds in the late seventeenth and early eighteenth centuries. For example, at the height of

[21] *The Provoked Wife* (1697), v/i; for an example in real life, see *T & C Mag.* 4: 122; see also *Friendship in Fashion* (1678), in *Works of Thomas Otway*, ed. J. C. Ghosh (Oxford, 1932), 1: 423–4.

[22] Claydon House, Verney MSS; I owe this reference to Susan Whyman.

[23] J. Collier, 'Of Duelling', in his *Essays upon Several Occasions* (London, 1698), quoted in Kiernan, 172; H. Fielding, *Jonathan Wild* (Everyman edn.), 156–7.

the South Sea Bubble in 1720–1, an entrepreneur was said to have been offering to insure clients for the 'female chastity' of their wives or prospective wives.[24]

The evidence suggests that after about 1670, the culture of litigation began slowly to be accepted in elite circles as an acceptable alternative to the still-flourishing culture of *machismo*. This shift from the duel to the lawsuit decisively transferred the whip-hand from the wife's seducer to the injured husband. The latter now ran no risk of mortal injury, and was in a position to extract large monetary compensation from the former. Thus when in 1794 a seducer offered 'to give the satisfaction of a gentleman', he was turned down by the husband, who sued for crim. con. and won damages of £5,000.[25] For this to happen, there must have taken place a major revolution in concepts of how male honour could and should be satisfied. Part cause and part consequence of this shift in mental attitudes was the transfer of control of a seduction case from the individuals concerned to common law judges and juries.

But if unregulated personal violence was largely suppressed by 1700, the code of the duel lived on, since so much of aristocratic honour depended on it.[26] Indeed, it actually revived among some members of the army officer class who came to maturity during the endless wars of the late eighteenth and early nineteenth centuries, when a high proportion of the landed elite saw service in the army. This militarization of the landed classes resulted in a curious mixture of moral codes: crim. con. cases flourished as never before, but there was also a concurrent rise in the number of known cases of challenges issued by army officers, even if the challenger now ran the risk of being cashiered, and was liable to be condemned as 'a damned fool'.[27]

For example, in 1814 Sir Henry Mildmay fell passionately in love with his sister-in-law Countess Rosebery, and her husband became sufficiently alarmed both to forbid him access to the house, and ostentatiously to cut him in the street. Sir Henry then devised a plan for a reconciliation with the suspicious husband. His idea was to provoke Lord Rosebery to 'call him out'—that is, challenge him to a duel. He would first let the latter fire at him—apparently assuming that he would not shoot to kill, or would miss—and then he himself would deliberately fire into the air. By doing so he calculated that he would oblige Lord Rosebery 'by the

[24] Cornelius Walford, *The Insurance Cyclopaedia* (London, 1871–80), 3: 203; J. Francis, *Annals, Anecdotes and Legends: A Chronicle of Life Assurance* (London, 1853), 82; W. Maitland, *The History and Survey of London* (London, 1756), 1: 527–9. I owe these references to G. Clark.
[25] *Biscoe* v. *Gordon, NC Trials for Adultery* (1797), 1: 54.
[26] Ibid., *passim*.
[27] *Crim. Con. Gaz.* 2: 291; see also V. Alfieri, *Autobiography* (1949), quoted in Kiernan, 130.

etiquette among men of honour, to bow to him and notice him in the street', which would perhaps lead to a reconciliation and a renewal of access to the house. Nothing came of the scheme, so Sir Henry smuggled himself into Lady Rosebery's bedroom, armed with a brace of loaded pistols and disguised with a beard and the dress of a sailor, and was caught *in flagrante delicto*. He was prosecuted for crim. con. and fined the huge sum of £15,000. Unable to pay such damages, he was forced to flee the country with Lady Rosebery to avoid either financial ruin or arrest for debt.[28] It is clear that what wounded Sir Henry most was being cut in the street, and the actions of both himself in planning a duel and Lord Rosebery in suing for damages show how the two moral codes ran side by side in the early years of the nineteenth century. But in this case the code of the duel was only a pipe-dream, and the reality was crim. con. damages of £15,000.

This competition of conflicting values survived into the early nineteenth century. In 1823, for example Captain Johnstone sued Lord Brudenell for crim. con. and won £1,000. Annoyed, Lord Brudenell challenged Johnstone to a duel, which the latter refused on the ground that his lordship had already given him the fullest satisfaction for the injury by relieving him of having to live with his wife any more.[29]

What seems to have happened was a shift of violated honour from the husband to the wife.[30] After 1700 there appears to be no record in England of a husband murdering his wife's lover on the spot: the *crime passionnel* simply withered away (at a time when it was still flourishing in the Mediterranean basin). This is not to say that many husbands were not shattered by the news of their wife's infidelity. In 1769 Mr Heatley went into convulsions when informed that his wife had infected him with venereal disease. William Middleton of Stockeld Park was so broken in spirit by the proofs of his wife's infidelity that he was never the same man again.[31] By and large, however, what is so striking is the contrast between the relative calm and sometimes even calculating greed with which many a husband greeted the news of his wife's infidelity, and the ferocious passion sometimes unleashed by news of similar behaviour on the part of a mistress. According to Horace Walpole, when in 1749 Sir Francis

[28] *The Annual Register . . . for the year 1815* (London, 1816), 283–6; *The Times*, 12 Dec. 1814: 3. For a case when a duel was threatened by a husband as late as 1830, see the Ellenborough case (2 *Hansard*, 23: 445, 455).

[29] C. Woodham-Smith, *The Reason Why* (London, 1982), 13.

[30] I owe this suggestion to Simon Newman. See also R. M. Bloch, 'The Gendered Meaning of Virtue in Revolutionary America', *Signs: Journal of Women in Culture and Society*, 13 (1987).

[31] *NCC Trials for Adultery* (1780), 2: 214, 217; for the Middleton case, see Stone, *Broken Lives*.

Blake-Delaval of Seaton Delaval was informed that his mistress, a German singer, was in bed with an Italian eunuch, he seized his horse-whip and rushed off with one of his chair-men to surprise them. On arrival, Delaval had the chair-man first hold down the woman while he horse-whipped her, and then hold down the eunuch while he sodomized him. In the same spirit, in 1779, Lord Clanwilliam, on hearing that his favourite mistress was in bed with a younger man, had the latter seized and held down by four servants while he personally castrated him, from which operation the man died the next day.[32]

Satirists liked to portray violent physical assault when a husband caught his wife in bed with another man in the eighteenth century (Plate 21), but in fact the evidence for such confrontations is virtually negligible. Only one such act of brutal revenge is reported against the lover of an adulterous wife. This occurred in 1751, when a man in Newport was said to have caught a shopkeeper making love to his wife in a barn, and to have castrated him, with the assistance of others.[33] The most common reaction was a cold-blooded calculation of the damages to be collected from crim. con. litigation, for, as Henry Fielding cynically remarked:

> While juries value virtue at their rate,
> Each wife is (when discovered) an estate.[34]

Only occasionally were milder forms of revenge resorted to, and they were by members of the middling sort. For example, in 1751 a dealer from Banbury caught a man in bed with his wife, 'on which he got assistance and took them out of bed, and tying their arms together set them before a large fire, and had tea, coffee and punch provided; then he went to invite his neighbours, to whom he exposed his wife and her gallant for some hours to their extraordinary mortification, while the husband appeared perfectly contented'.[35]

C. PROPERTY

Once this shift in concepts of male honour had begun to take place, the way was open for the elevation in the eighteenth century of the idea of property to a central position in political ideology and legal practice. Taken in its broader sense, property was made to cover almost everything from the right to vote to the holding of an office, and it was only a

[32] *Walpole's Correspondence*, 20: 41; 24: 544.
[33] *Gent's Mag.* 21 (1751), 183.
[34] Quoted in A. G. J. Hall, *The Law and Practice of Divorce and Matrimonial Causes* (London, 1905), 208.   [35] *Gent's Mag.* 21 (1751), 136.

small extension to include a wife's body in the capacious definition. Although marriage was widely regarded as a holy state based on mutual affection, there was nevertheless nothing odd or shocking to eighteenth-century sensibility in Judge Kelyng's description in 1756 of sexual intercourse with someone else's wife as 'the highest invasion of property'; or in the assertion in 1789 that 'a man's wife may be deemed no less his property than his money'.[36]

On the other hand, a wife did not acquire a similar property right over the body of her husband, despite the mutual exchange of vows at the wedding ceremony. As an indignant woman protested in 1735, a hundred years before such views became common:

Our law gives the husband the entire disposal of his wife's person, but she does not seem to retain any property in his. He may recover damages on any man who shall invade his property in her, but she cannot recover damages from any woman who shall invade her property in him.[37]

As late as 1878, a feminist was complaining that 'the notion that a man's wife is his PROPERTY, in the sense in which a horse is his property . . . is the fatal root of incalculable evil and misery'.[38]

The conventional defence of this inequity was given by a lawyer for a plaintiff in a case in 1803: 'casual revelry and immorality in the husband is not supposed to cast an indelible disgrace upon the wife, and cannot be productive of defrauding the children or his wife by introducing a spurious offspring, which the infidelity of the wife may lead to'.[39] Many cases suggest that this fear was a reality; thus, in 1770, Lady Compton, pregnant by a lover, boasted that the child in her womb 'would inherit Sir Walter Compton's estate, in spite of the world'.[40]

Modern critics of the double sexual standard have focused on its undeniable injustice, but they have failed to take into sufficient consideration the huge economic, legal, and moral consequences of the biological fact that a woman can become pregnant from a sexual encounter, but a man cannot. Anxiety about the legitimacy of heirs, and the consequent enshrinement in English custom and law of the double sexual standard, was a by-product of the system of direct patrilineal descent to male heirs of the body. If England had been a matrilineal society in which

[36] J. M. Beattie, *Crime and the Courts in England, 1660–1800* (Princeton, 1986), 95; *T & C Mag.* (1789), 21: 24; see also H. Fielding, *Amelia* (Everyman edn.), 2: 172–3.

[37] *Hardships of Laws on Wives*, 15; see also *The Lady's Last Stake*, in C. Cibber, *Dramatic Works* (London, 1777), 2: 216.

[38] P. Levine, ' "So Few Prizes and So Many Blanks": Marriage and Feminism in Later Nineteenth-Century England', *Journal of British Studies*, 28 (1989), 165–6.

[39] *Pentland* v. *Crick* (1803), RIA/HP, 849. 9.

[40] *Compton* v. *Compton* (1770), LPCA, D.461. 145.

property descended to the children of the mother regardless of who was the father, it is doubtful whether there would ever have developed to their fullest extent either the double standard or the assertion by husbands of an absolute sexual monopoly over the bodies of their wives. These two values were functional necessities for the prevailing system of property descent. This is true even if the root of the desire by males for a monopoly control over the body of a woman—especially that of a wife—may well be biologically rather than culturally determined. Adultery by a wife is usually taken as a reflection upon her husband's sexual powers, and thus represents a severe blow to his self-esteem.[41] Consequently, wifely chastity is prized by males for its own sake, as well as being necessary for the control and transmission of property in the blood line.

These fears of inheritance by spurious children were only very slowly undermined in middling and elite circles during the late eighteenth and early nineteenth centuries by the countervailing ideologies of affective individualism and legal equality between the sexes. There was also a growing moral reluctance by wives to pass off illegitimate children as heirs to their husbands' estates. When in 1769 Lady Sarah Bunbury eloped, taking her illegitimate baby with her and explaining as she did so that 'her conscience would not allow her to impose a child upon her husband', Princess Amelia made the perceptive comment that such an attitude was 'quite new'.[42]

D. FEMALE PURITY

It has been suggested that another possible contributing factor in the rise of the crim. con. suit was a growing concern about female virginity and purity. It is true that two of the three legal actions which were developed in the late seventeenth century—the seduction suit for damages, and the breach of promise suit for damages—were designed to offer greater protection to young women who had been seduced and abandoned. But the third action, the crim. con. suit, was expressly designed to benefit the husband, and was grossly unjust to the wife. Moreover, these legal actions were all developed by the 1670s and therefore could not have been inspired by the new concern, which only developed in the 1740s, about the protection against seduction of innocent virgins from respectable homes, as expressed most successfully in literature by Richardson's best-selling *Pamela*.

---

[41] This problem has been discussed with great sensitivity by K. V. Thomas, 'The Double Standard', *Journal of the History of Ideas*, 20 (1959); for the biological genetic explanation, see D. Symons, *The Evolution of Human Sexuality* (Oxford, 1979).

[42] *Letters and Journals of Lady Mary Coke*, ed. J. A. Home (Edinburgh, 1889–96), 3: 28.

The adoption by some of the aristocracy of the crim. con. action after the 1690s was one piece of evidence of a drive to reinforce male contractual control over female chastity, another being the reluctant acceptance by Parliament of responsibility for granting divorce for female adultery. It is noticeable that a Parliamentary divorce act at this period always included formal bastardization of illegitimate children and was specifically granted in order to allow the man to remarry in order to beget legitimate heirs to title and property. Whig theories of contract and the sanctity of property provided support for this reinforcement of male patriarchy, although they also supplied the intellectual foundations upon which criticism of this patriarchy could build.[43]

3. The Early History of the Action, 1620–1760

A. THE PRE-HISTORY, 1620–1692

Resort to the crim. con. action by members of the elite was preceded by a lengthy period of a century or more during which husbands from the middling sort had negotiated privately with their wives' lovers for financial compensation, as an alternative to exposing them to discipline for sin imposed by an ecclesiastical court. So psychologically wounding was the publicity of these shame punishments that most lovers were willing to compound with the husband to buy his silence. The husband exhibited very little anger or jealousy in these cases, but merely an avaricious zeal to secure the maximum economic advantage from his wife's transgression.

A typical example occurred in the Lichfield area in 1701 when a tailor found a man called Mounteney in bed with his wife. He threatened to sue Mounteney at common law, and brought in his attorney to negotiate with him. He started with a demand for £10, but was prepared to come down to £5 'for the injury he received'. The money had been paid and the two men had become 'very intimate' by the time the ecclesiastical officials heard about it and sued Mounteney for adultery. The latter told a friend: 'I have fucked a woman in Duffield and they are going to put me into the court for it,' despite the fact that both he and his new friend the tailor were now denying that any impropriety had taken place or that any compensation had been exacted.[44]

---

[43] M. Astell, *Some Reflections upon Marriage*, 4th edn. (London, 1730), 106.

[44] *Office* v. *Mounteney* (1701), Lichfield JRO, LCC, B/C/5 (1701); see also *Office* v. *Barker*, ibid. (1707 and 1708); *Eng. Rep.* 25: 7; 24: 128–9; *Office* v. *Hulme* (1707), Lichfield JRO, LCC, B/C/5 (1708).

This kind of out-of-court bargaining seems to have gone on after as well as before a crim. con. trial and sentence, for in 1720 a seducer who had £500 awarded against him negotiated the amount down to 200 guineas.[45] Moreover the possibility of gaining money from a wife's seduction inevitably tempted a few husbands to attempt a little blackmail, by encouraging their wives into amateur prostitution. In Staffordshire in 1707, a labourer, Thomas Lawson, accused a much richer man (and a former employer) Thomas Alderley, of seducing his wife. Alderley first gave bonds to pay Lawson £5 in compensation, but when he learned that two other men in the village were also paying hush-money to Lawson for having had dealings with Mrs Lawson, the three seducers conspired to get the bonds returned and burnt. This they achieved by means of a counter-threat of having Lawson drafted and sent off to France as a soldier if he did not comply.[46]

Higher up the social and economic scale, a rich and influential lover often found it easy to buy off a husband from a more humble rank. Thus, when in 1769 the Earl of Halifax ran off with the wife of a customs officer, the latter took no overt action, but soon found himself promoted to a lucrative post in the West Indies, where he made a fortune. It is hard not to suspect a private arrangement between the husband and the lover.[47] A more open transaction occurred a year later when Lord Delorain ran off with the wife of a poor man, who first threatened a crim. con. suit and then agreed to surrender all claims to his wife for £200. They met in a tavern to sign an agreement drawn up by an attorney. Lord Delorain put down the £200 and the husband took his wife by the hand and gave her to his lordship. The wife remarked crossly: 'Can you part with me so easily?', to which her husband replied: 'I would part with all the sex for half the money.'[48] Even if some of these stories are exaggerated, they show how the patronage system, which flourished in eighteenth-century England became inextricably entangled with the legal process of extorting compensation for a wife's adultery, since it could be used to obtain large payments or rewards without the publicity of a lawsuit.

It is against this context of a widely accepted system of barter and financial compensation for the seduction of a wife that the slow emergence of the crim. con. action in the late seventeenth century has to

---

[45] GLRO, London CC, DC/C/323.
[46] Lichfield JRO, LCC, B/C/5 (1708), *Office* v. *Mott, Mott and Alderley*.
[47] *T & C Mag.* 1: 225–7. For another case which was settled out of court for £200, see ibid. 2: 626.
[48] Ibid. 2: 625; see also ibid. 22: 532–3; 24: 532; *Morrison* v. *Meagher* (1805), RIA/HP, 894.

be set. Late seventeenth-century playwrights made a point of satirizing how members of the money-grubbing middling sort hastened to exploit the opportunities offered by the new action. In a 1673 play, a cuckolded London citizen says to another: 'I'll pass it by for once. But I'll not fail to sue Cuff upon an action of assault and battery. . . . I have known a man recover 4 to 500 li. in such a case, and his wife not one jot the worse.' His friend agreed that 'if we order our business wisely, and impanel a good substantial jury, of all married men, they'll give us vast damages'.[49] When in 1686 a joiner, Peter Ilee, took another man's wife off to an inn in Knightsbridge for two nights, her husband sued him for crim. con. and was awarded £67 damages 'for trespassing on his wife's body'. Thus, the action was evidently well known and used by the small business class of London by the 1680s.[50]

B. THE ERA OF STAGNATION, 1692–1760

The culture of litigation only very slowly replaced the culture of the duel, as was proved by the fact that the crim. con. action brought in 1692 by the Duke of Norfolk, the premier duke in England, failed to stimulate a rush to the law-courts by cuckolded husbands of the upper classes. The crim. con. action was very little used for the next forty years, only fourteen cases being known between 1692 and 1730 (Fig. 9.1, Table 9.1). One reason for hanging back was the sense that adultery was immoral, and should be punished in a more straightforward way. It was probably the Norfolk case which inspired an attempt in 1699 by the House of Lords to make adultery a misdemeanour punishable by common law.[51] The bill was rejected by the majority on the grounds that it would turn their own servants into spies and informers for profit, and might put a dangerous weapon into the hands of the party in power with which to disgrace families of the opposition. Pragmatism and politics thus triumphed over the reformation of manners.

A more important reason for the rarity of crim. con. cases before the late 1730s was that other options were still open to a cuckolded husband. In the first place local authorities, both ecclesiastical courts, and Quarter Sessions and Assizes, were still prosecuting and punishing adulterers,

---

[49] T. Shadwell, *Epsom Wells* (1673), v/i, quoted in Alleman, 139; *Lewknor v. Freeman, Eng. Rep.* 24: 51; LPCA, D.128: 101–3, 154–5.

[50] *Ilee v. Ilee* (1686), GLRO, London CC, DL/C/211, fos. 246–9.

[51] Lambeth Palace MSS 641, 497–9. I owe this reference to David Hayton. See also 4 *Camden Society*, 34 (1987); *Camden Misc.* 29: 375.

[52] *Gardner v. Nott*, Worcester CC, 794. 052 B. A. 2102/11(1); *Eaves v. Eaves* (1730), Lichfield CC; *Mathews v. Mathews* (1738), Worcester CC, 797. 51. B. A. 2637; 3 *Hansard*, 145: 1854; LPCA, D.470, 42, 56.

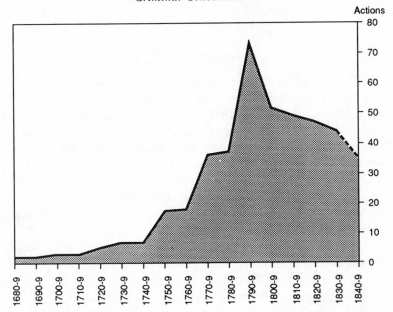

FIGURE 9.1   Recorded Criminal Conversation Actions 1680–1849 [Table 9.1]

although at a rapidly diminishing rate.[52] In the second place, many cuckolded husbands among the middling sort often continued to find it more profitable and less embarrassing to pursue the traditional strategy of exercising threats of litigation and exposure as blackmail to obtain private cash payments from a wife's lover.

Another reason for the relative rarity of the crim. con. action before 1760 was its high cost in legal fees and travel expenses. The fact that crim. con. suits could only be heard in London, at the Courts of King's Bench or Common Pleas, inevitably meant that they were peculiarly expensive.[53] In consequence, the plaintiff cuckolds in these suits were mostly men of means, predominantly from the leisured classes but also including well-to-do businessmen, some clergy, and the military.[54] Among husbands from the middling sort, only Londoners could afford the expense, since they had few transport costs.

Finally, it seems likely that many potential plaintiffs in the early eighteenth century were still ashamed of washing their dirty linen in public and exposing their cuckoldry to the world. The development of the action therefore depended to a considerable extent upon it being stripped of much of its novelty and the accompanying sense of shame as it became more well known, thanks to the publicity devoted to it.

[53] Anderson, 437, Table IV.   [54] Wolfram, 167–73.

247

4. Publicity and the Press

A. THE CAUSES OF PUBLICITY

In the last half of the eighteenth century, crim. con. trials began to attract more and more attention from the press, a process facilitated by three developments. In the first place, in the 1750s striking improvements were made in the techniques of stenography.[55] By the mid-eighteenth century, professional law reporters were advertising their services in legal publications,[56] and could make a good living, some catering to the legal profession seeking case law, and others to the general public seeking sensational trial evidence. By the late eighteenth century some of them had acquired high status and high salaries, and a few went on to become judges.

The second development was the enormous expansion of the numbers of newspapers and new books and pamphlets published, which occurred from 1740 onwards.[57] There was an avid search by booksellers for interesting copy, and enterprising reporters soon found a juicy vein of material in the law-courts. As was observed in 1884, 'it has long been considered a practicable scheme for any barrister and bookseller who unite together with a view to notoriety or profit, to add to the existing list of Law Reports. . . . It is a good channel to professional notoriety.'[58] At the same time there was an equally dramatic explosion in the satirical caricature print-trade, which also found rich copy in the reports of crim. con. actions.

Lastly, there occurred a shift of sensibilities among the English elite, and even in some official quarters, away from regarding illicit sex as basically sinful and shameful to treating it as an interesting and amusing aspect of life. The very language of extra-marital sexual relations was softened in the late seventeenth century, a love affair becoming an 'intrigue' and adultery an act of 'gallantry'. The collapse of the moral controls of the church courts, the decline of Puritanism, the expiration of

[55] T. Skelton, *A Tutor to Tachygraphy* (London, 1642), and *Tachygraphy* (London, 1647); T. Gurney, *Brachygraphy* (London, 1750); S. Taylor, *An Essay . . . of Stenography* (London, 1786); I. Pitman, *Stenographic Shorthand* (London, 1837); see P. A. Pickering, 'Class without Words: Symbolic Communication in the Chartist Movement', *Past and Present*, 112 (1986), 148–9.

[56] For example, in 1743 there appeared the notice that 'Trials at law, etc, are taken in shorthand by N. Fromenteel at the Two Black Boys within Whitechapel Bars', *OB Proc.* (1743–4), 84.

[57] R. S. Crane and F. B. Kaye, *A Census of British Newspapers and Periodicals, 1620–1800* (Chapel Hill, 1927); G. A. Cranfield, *A Handlist of English Provincial Newspapers and Periodicals, 1700–1760* (Cambridge, 1952); C. J. Mitchell, 'The Spread and Fluctuation of Eighteenth-Century Printing', *Studies on Voltaire and the Eighteenth Century*, 230 (1985), 305–21.

[58] W. T. S. Daniel, *The History and Origin of the Law Reports* (London, 1884), 8–9.

the licensing laws, and the general secularization of thought in the eighteenth century all facilitated the publication not only of pure pornography such as *Fanny Hill*, but also of full transcripts of detailed evidence produced in trials for crim. con.

B. TYPES OF PUBLICATIONS

The reporting of detailed accounts of adultery, whether in suits for separation in the ecclesiastical courts, crim. con. actions in the common law courts, or divorce cases before Parliament, was only part of a much wider explosion of reporting of legal cases in the eighteenth century. This began tentatively in about 1670 with summary accounts of London criminal trials in the *Old Bailey Proceedings*, which slowly evolved from brief abstracts of the trials to selective verbatim transcripts. After the 1750s, the stress on sensationalism in accounts of criminal trials became less prominent, and the legal and moral aspects were given greater emphasis. The genre became a kind of didactic fiction drawn from real life, a substitute for the novel. One publisher explained that 'these little stories will afford the curious not only instruction but an agreeable amusement. . . . They may be considered as a collection of dramatic pieces.'[59] Accounts of individual cases of trials for adultery began in about 1690, collections of the more sensational items in about 1750, and by the 1770s the genre had grown from a trickle to a flood. In 1780 there was issued a seven-volume collection of *Trials for Adultery . . . at Doctors' Commons*, the full testimony of witnesses being 'taken in shorthand by a civilian [i.e. a civil lawyer]'.

The publications concerned with crim. con. trials fall into three categories, each catering for a rather different audience. The notes taken down for publication in law reports focus on the speeches of the counsels for the plaintiff and the defendant, and more especially on the directions given by the judge to the jury. They were published as separate pamphlets, often later reprinted in collections of the decisions of famous judges, while summaries of them appeared in the more serious newspapers. The appointment by the judges after 1785 of official reporters who held a monopoly for the purpose of legal citation led to a marked increase in the quality and quantity of this genre.[60]

[59] M. Harris, 'Trials and Criminal Biographies: A Case Study in Distribution', in R. Myers and M. Harris (eds.), *Sale and Distribution of Books from 1700* (Oxford, 1982).

[60] Campbell, *Lives of the Chief Justices*, 2: 396; C. G. Moran, *The Heralds of the Law* (London, 1948), 16, 36–8; W. S. Holdsworth, *A History of English Law* (London, 1903–72), 6: 555, 559; 12: 116–17, 130–46; 13: 424–8; 15: 248–57; Daniel, *History and Origin*; most of these reports were republished in *Eng. Rep.*

The second and smallest category of publications were articles which were written or paid for by the plaintiff or the defendant. These were planted in newspapers or periodicals, or were issued as privately printed pamphlets, and were intended to offer a highly partisan presentation of the affair in order to sway public opinion in their favour. Thus in 1793, Mr Middleton and his family arranged to have published in the *Bon Ton Magazine* a racy description of the alleged adultery of his wife, only to have it suppressed by an injunction from the lord chief justice after a formal protest by the defence.[61] These private tracts were printed in very small numbers, but they were widely read at the time, at least one being distributed freely not only to the London newspapers but also to the London clubs for perusal by their members.[62]

The third, and by far the largest, category was stenographic records of the trials, which focused mainly upon their human interest and on the detailed evidence of adultery supplied by witnesses testifying to looking through key-holes, listening to creaking beds, inspecting bed-linen, etc.[63] These appeared both as pamphlets and as reports in newspapers and periodicals. In addition to these individual pamphlets on single trials, again and again the more sensational cases were gathered together and published in book form, often in many volumes (Plates 22 and 23).[64]

All these publications were hawked about the streets and sold by booksellers, some of whom seem to have specialized in this material. Thus in 1800, when Lord Auckland was trying to push a bill through Parliament to prevent an adulterous wife from marrying her lover after a divorce, the result of his victory was prematurely celebrated by the poetaster 'Peter Pindar':

---

[61] See Stone, *Broken Lives*, The Middleton case. For another case, see *Campbell* v. *Hooke* (1793); *Lond. Chron.* (1793), 1: 202; *Bon Ton Mag.* 2: 453; *Major Hooke's Defence* (London, 1793), (Bodl. Cw. UK. 690. C. 187).

[62] See Stone, *Broken Lives*, The Westmeath case.

[63] P. Wagner, 'The Pornographer in the Courtroom: Trial Reports about Cases of Sexual Crimes and Delinquencies as a Genre of Eighteenth-Century Erotics', in P.-G. Boucé (ed.), *Sexuality in Eighteenth-Century Britain* (Manchester, 1982), 120–40.

[64] *Cases of Impotency as Debated in England*, 2 vols. (London, 1715); *Cases of Divorce for Several Causes* (London, 1715, 1723); B. Ochino, *Cases of Polygamy, Concubinage, Adultery, Divorce, etc.* (repr. London, 1732); *Cases of Impotency and Virginity* (London, 1732); *A Collection of the most remarkable and Interesting Trials for Adultery*, 2 vols. (London, 1756); *Adultery Anatomised*, 2 vols. (London, 1761); *Trials for Adultery or the History of Divorces, being select Trials at Doctors' Commons from the year 1760 to the Present Time*, 7 vols. (London, 1779–80); *A New and Complete Collection of Trials for Adultery, etc.*, 2 vols. (London, 1780); *A New Collection of Trials for Adultery or a General View of Modern Gallantry and Divorce from the year 1780 to the middle of the year 1797*, 2 vols. (London, 1796 [sic]); F. Plowden, *Crim. Con. Biography*, 12 vols. (London, 1838–9); *Crim. Con. Gazette*, 2 vols. (London, 1838–9); *Crim. Con. Actions and Trials* (London, n.d.).

And last of all, no catering Mr Hogg [a bookseller]
To suit salacious tastes with prurient prog.
No more shall hawkers gallop on,
Roaring away 'CRIM. CON., CRIM. CON'.[65]

It is interesting to note that in France before the Revolution there was
an identical explosion of publications about sensational trials, including
over seventy for adultery and bigamy. Thanks to the efforts of the cen-
sors, however, there are no records of eye-witness testimony, and no
detailed descriptions of sexual activity. The general tone is one of moral
satisfaction at the detection and punishment of wickedness.[66] In the
American colonies, however, the report of the peculiarly scandalous
Grosvenor *v.* Cumberland crim. con. trial was pirated in Philadelphia in
1770, and in 1798 there was published in Boston *The Cuckold's Chronicle,
being select Trials for Adultery, Incest, Imbecility, Ravishment and etc.*[67]

C. THE MOTIVES OF THE READERS

This material clearly circulated widely among the general reading public
eager for sexual titillation, and especially among the elite, such as Horace
Walpole, who were avid for gossip about the sex lives of their friends and
acquaintances.[68] A pamphlet reporting on the first prominent crim. con.
case, that of the Duke of Norfolk and John Germain in 1692, set the tone
for future publications by including a detailed and highly lubricious description by a maidservant of Germain practising *coitus interruptus* with the
duchess.[69] Advertisements for these trial pamphlets emphasized their
sensational aspects. Thus in 1782 one of them stated that it had 'all the
interesting scenes fully, minutely and circumstantially displayed' and was
'teeming with such extraordinary incidents as to awake the curiosity of
the most incurious reader'. The pamphlets were clearly designed for a

---

[65] Peter Pindar [John Wolcot], *Lord Auckland's Triumph, or the Death of Crim. Con.* (London,
1800), 29.
[66] H.-J. Lüsebrink, 'Les Crimes sexuels dans les "causes célèbres" ', *Le XVIIIᵉᵐᵉ siècle*, 12
(1980), 153–5.
[67] C. Evans, *American Bibliography, 1639–1800* (Chicago, 1903–59).
[68] P. Wagner, 'Trial Reports as a Genre of Eighteenth-Century Erotica?' *British Journal of
Eighteenth-Century Studies*, 5 (1983). See *Walpole's Correspondence, passim.*
[69] *The Trial between the Duke of Norfolk . . . and John Jermaine in an Action of Trespass* (London,
n.d.); *State Trials* 12: 928–48; the maid deposed that 'she saw Mr Germain's y[ard] come from
the Duchess, reeking, slimy and limber, casting his s[perm] about the room' (*Further Depositions
. . . in the Affair of the Duke and Duchess of Norfolk* (London, 1692), 16 (quoted in Trumbach, 156
n. 116; it is doubtful whether an uneducated servant girl would without prompting have used
such vivid and obscene language.

wealthy and sophisticated market, being 'elegantly printed on superfine paper' and priced at two shillings and sixpence each.[70]

During the last quarter of the eighteenth century, there sprang up a number of magazines which were designed to be read by members of either sex without embarrassment and with some confidence in the accuracy of the reporting. The prime example of these elite scandal periodicals was the monthly *Town and Country Magazine*, which specialized in describing the extra-marital affairs of well-known persons in London society, and had a 'prodigious sale' between 1769 and 1790. Others were frankly coarse and sensationalist, and cannot be trusted not to have invented and embroidered to heighten the effect. A classic example of this genre was the *Bon Ton Magazine* which flourished between 1791 and 1796.[71] At the bottom end of the market came the openly pornographic publications, like the *Rangers Magazine*.[72]

But there was more to these reports of cases than mere sexual titillation. There was intense interest in the human drama of the narrative, the discrepancies in the evidence, the moral and factual differences between the testimony of the witnesses on the two sides, the rhetorical feats of the rival counsels, and, at the climax, the always unpredictable assessment of the damages by the jury. Crim. con. reportage thus served all the purposes of a modern TV sitcom. It was ostensibly designed as a morality play to expose and castigate the vices of the rich, but in fact it was deliberately couched in immoral terms.

Quite apart from the flood of newspaper reports and pamphlets, there is ample evidence in correspondence about the rising public interest in the more sensational of these cases. This rise closely paralleled the rise in the circulation of novels, which dealt, in a more discreet and moralistic way, with much the same themes of love, marriage, sex, and money. In 1786, a magazine commented that a recent trial 'is at present the topic of conversation in all the polite circles'.[73] Three years later an even more sensational trial lasted from 9 a.m. till 2 p.m. 'to the great entertainment of a crowded court'.[74] By this time the publishers and editors of journals were eagerly looking for copy, so that in a Dublin court-room in 1804 it was observed, with satisfaction, that 'a famous note-taker has been sent here'.[75] Later on in the century, in the 1830s, there appeared a specialized journal, the *Crim. Con. Gazette*, exclusively devoted to the publication of past and recent cases, while an enterprising author put together

---

[70] Advertisement in *The Trial of Lady Mary Bayntun* (London, n.d. [1782]).
[71] H. Bleakley, 'A Bibliography of Forgotten Magazines', 12 *Notes and Queries* (1916), pt. 2, pp. 143–5. [72] *The Rangers Magazine* (London, 1795).
[73] *Fawkener* v. *Townshend* (1786), *T & C Mag.* 18: 345.
[74] *Duberley* v. *Gunning* (1789), *Bon Ton Mag.* 1: 483. [75] RIA/HP, 872. 80.

a large collection of abstracts of the most sensational cases over the previous hundred years.[76] In 1820, at the height of the sensational trial for adultery of Queen Caroline, Leigh Hunt wrote 'You may look upon the British public as constantly occupied in reading trials for adultery.'[77]

D. THE CONSEQUENCES OF THE PUBLICITY

This tide of publicity had two completely opposite results. One was to disseminate among the public at large knowledge about separation suits, crim. con. actions, and Parliamentary bills of divorce. By making such actions better known and more commonplace, it made them more morally acceptable, and therefore directly stimulated the surge of litigation. For example, the huge and sustained publicity given to three peculiarly sensational cases between 1715 and 1738 must have helped to prepare the way for the great increase of crim. con. cases after the middle of the century.[78]

There was also a rather sinister symbiotic relationship between the publicity given to crim. con. actions and the making of the fame and fortune of some of the greatest lawyers of the century. In the third highly publicized case, that of *Cibber* v. *Sloper* in 1738, the young counsel for the defence, William Murray, later Lord Mansfield, made so brilliantly blistering an attack upon the character of the plaintiff that he became famous overnight. He later reported that 'henceforth business poured in upon me from all quarters', and his annual income from his practice rose suddenly 'from hundreds to thousands'.[79]

A generation later, the prosecution (or very occasionally the defence) in crim. con. suits was virtually monopolized for nearly thirty years by Thomas Erskine, later lord chancellor. It was this which first made him rich and famous, and the editor of his works observed that 'none of the speeches of Lord Erskine when at the bar excited a greater interest, or were attended with a greater success, than those (and they were most numerous) in cases of adultery'.[80] Thus, two of the most distinguished

[76] *Crim. Con. Gaz;* Plowden.
[77] *Correspondence of Leigh Hunt* (London, 1862), 1: 157. I owe this quotation to Thomas Laqueur.
[78] *Dormer* v. *Jones* (1715); *Lord Abergavenny* v. *Lyddell* (1730); and *Cibber* v. *Sloper* (1738).
[79] *Cibber* v. *Sloper* (1738); Campbell, *Lives of the Chief Justices*, 2: 341–3; M. Nash, *The Provoked Wife: The Life and Times of Susannah Cibber* (New York, 1977), 137–63; *Adultery Anatomised*, 1: 109–52; F. Truelove, *The Comforts of Matrimony, exemplified in the memorable . . . action brought by Theo. C. against S. Esq. for criminal conversation with the Plaintiff's Wife* (London, 1739).
[80] *Speeches of Lord Erskine*, ed. J. Ridgway (London, 1847), 4: 279; J. Campbell, *Lives of the Lords Chancellors and Keepers of the Great Seal of England* (London, 1846), 6: 530.

lawyers of eighteenth-century England, lords Mansfield and Erskine, who are today remembered for their contributions respectively to English jurisprudence and English liberties, owed their careers and their fortunes to the huge publicity which surrounded the more sensational crim. con. cases.

If one result of all this publicity was to disseminate knowledge of the crim. con. action and stimulate litigation, the other was the exact opposite, to act as a deterrent to potential litigants. This fear of publicity had arisen in the late seventeenth century over cases of separation in ecclesiastical courts, although at that time knowledge was confined to those who took the trouble to attend in court. In 1688 Lord Halifax advised his daughter that 'the causes of separation are now so very coarse, that few [wives] are confident enough to buy their liberty at the price of having their modesty so exposed'.[81] The much greater publicity now given to a crim. con. action threatened the reputation of all parties in the suit. The husband was exposed to the world as a cuckold; the wife was branded as a whore, without a chance to defend herself; and the lover was often revealed as a treacherous friend of the husband. The withering blast of publicity engendered by these suits was certainly a major inducement to many unhappy couples to take the path of private separation rather than that of public litigation.[82]

An early warning of what was in store for a wife involved in a crim. con. suit was issued by Congreve in 1700. In *The Way of the World*, Mrs Marwood points out to Lady Wishfort the frightening publicity already surrounding such suits. She told Lady Wishfort that not only would she have 'her name prostituted in a public court', 'and then to have my young revellers of the Temple take notes ... and after talk it over again in Commons', but also 'it must after this be consigned by the short-hand writers to the public press; and from thence be transferred to the hands, nay into the throats and lungs of the hawkers. . . . And this you must hear 'till you are stunn'd; nay you must hear nothing else for some days.'[83] If in 1700 the publicity and malicious gossip lasted some days, by 1800 it was liable to last some weeks. A good example of the kind of humiliation experienced by the victim of a crim. con. suit is the case of *Peter* v. *Hancock* in 1824. A London grocer, John Hancock, had been so foolish as to fall in love with the lonely wife of a naval lieutenant, as a result of which he found himself not only mulcted £5,000 damages for crim. con.

[81] Marquis of Halifax, *The Lady's New Year's Gift, or Advice to a Daughter*, in H. C. Foxcroft, *Life and Letters of Sir George Savile Bart.*, 1st Marquis of Halifax (London, 1898), 2: 394–5.

[82] See Stone, *Broken Lives*, The Westmeath case.

[83] W. Congreve, *The Way of the World*, quoted in Alleman, 123.

but also held up to ridicule in the press and in prints (Plate 24). One of the latter was divided into two panels, the left labelled 'Moments of prattle and pleasure,' the right 'Moments of parting with treasure.' In between was the cautionary poem:

> When a grocer forgets his ledger and debts,
> Leaving Figs, Tea and Sugar behind him,
> To imitate Ton and practise Crim Con,
> A man of Five Thousand you'll find him.[84]

Two centuries later, nothing much had changed. Witnesses before the Royal Commission on Divorce in 1912 testified that the fear of publicity in the newspapers still deterred many men and women from suing for divorce (and damages). Moreover, unscrupulous husbands still used the threat of a suit for damages as 'an elaborate blackmailing machinery'. One of the judges on the divorce court estimated that 20 per cent of all cases before the court involved some form of blackmail, and were dropped after the money was paid by the alleged co-respondent to the husband, in order to avoid publicity. The result was 'an extremely lucrative living' for some 'husband–criminals'.[85]

It would thus appear that there were significant changes over time in the effect of publicity on litigation. In the first half of the eighteenth century, the chief effect of the blaze of publicity was to deter potential litigants. By the second half of the century familiarity had bred contempt, and publicity stimulated use of the action. Later still, in the nineteenth century, it mainly again served to frighten off potential litigants.

5. The Apogee of the Action

A. THE EVIDENCE OF GROWTH

Beginning in 1770, there was a dramatic explosion of recorded crim, con. cases, which peaked in the thirty years from 1790 to 1829 (Fig. 9.1, Table 9.1). It should be emphasized that the crim. con. action was almost entirely confined to England. It was illegal in Scotland, and in Ireland it was said in 1804 to be 'novel in this country', and in 1816 to be still 'very rare'.[86] Nor was it common in the colonies. Only three cases are recorded

---

[84] Captain Peter, RN v. John Hancock, in Dorothy George (ed.), *Satirical Prints in the British Museum*, no. 14706.

[85] *Roy. Com. Divorce, 1912*, 3: 20.

[86] RIA/HP, 872 (*Massey v. Marquis of Headfort*); ibid. 1102 (*Hinds v. Middleton*), 4; ibid. 1085 (*Guthrie v. Sterne*), 4.

in Massachusetts, in the whole of the eighteenth century;[87] in India the first recorded action occurred in 1819.[88]

The magnitude of the explosion of actions displayed in Fig. 9.1 may well be something of an illusion caused by a spurt in publications at just that period. On the other hand, the recorded numbers are at all times far below the reality, since only the more interesting and dramatic cases involving heavy damages or persons of social prominence were widely reported. What has survived is evidence about the more sensational of a large number of routine cases, routinely handled. Thus, Lord Mansfield's trial notes record twenty crim. con. cases which went to a jury. Of these twenty, seven resulted in damages of £20 or less, ten of between £100 and £500, and only three of over £2,000. It is those small awards of under £100 awarded to persons in relatively humble positions in the world which tended to go unrecorded.[89] On the other hand, it is fairly certain that the rise in the graph in the late eighteenth and early nineteenth centuries is not purely an illusion created by changes in the quality of record-keeping. It also depicts—probably inadequately—a reality which requires an explanation.

B. THE CAUSES OF GROWTH

There are two possible reasons for the rise in the number of crim. con. cases. One is that it reflects a real increase in wifely adultery in respectable circles; another is that it reflects no more than changes in habits of litigation.

i. A Rise in Wifely Adultery?

Lamentations at the exceptional sexual turpitude of the age are a common theme at all times and places, but they recurred with peculiar intensity between 1660 and 1820. During this period there was a widespread and growing conviction, first that sexual immorality was on the increase; second that this depravity was particularly prevalent among the elite of high title and great wealth; and third that it was the wives who were mostly to blame. As early as 1700, an anonymous writer observed that "Twas in the late reigns [of Charles II and James II] that this abominable iniquity came to be so epidemic an English vice'. In 1739 another writer asked why cuckoldry was 'so frequent among us of late years', and also

---

[87] N. Cott, 'Divorce and the Changing Status of Women in Eighteenth-Century Massachusetts', 3 *William and Mary Quarterly*, 33 (1976), 600 n. 44.

[88] 1 G IV, cap. 101; MacQueen, *House of Lords*, 547, 796–9.

[89] I owe this information to Professor J. C. Oldham, who is editing Lord Mansfield's trial notes for publication.

suggested that such sexual excesses had been one cause for the fall of Rome. Similar laments appeared in print every decade from the 1780s to the 1820s.[90] Although there would appear to be an association between these anti-vice campaigns and periods of intense warfare, such as that between 1776 and 1815, which aroused fears that sexual excess would impair military bravery, all that one can safely conclude is that there was a continuity of lamentation throughout the eighteenth century over the degeneracy of the age.

The theme of a rising tide of female adultery among the quality, imperfectly held in check by crim. con. actions, also runs through the literature of the mid- and late eighteenth century. As early as 1742, one of Henry Fielding's characters in a play observed that 'virtuous women and gentlemen's wives come so cheap, that no man will go to the price of a lady of the town'; to which another replies: 'I thought Westminster Hall would have given them a surfeit of their virtuous women; but I see nothing will do, though a jury of cuckolds were to give never such swinging damages.'[91]

It would be false to conclude, however, that the belief in moral decline was held by most, or even a majority, of knowledgeable and influential persons. The prolonged debates in Parliament over anti-adultery bills in 1771, 1779, 1800, and 1809 show that the only group consistently to take this position were the bishops and the more conservative peers. Their opponents, such as Lord Mulgrave, pointed out that 'the calculation of the number of divorces is not of itself a proof of the deterioration of morals, for it remains to be proved that adultery is more frequent and public manners more depraved'. Even the lawyers were split, the Whig Lord Erskine being a pessimist and the Tory Lord Eldon an optimist.[92] The pessimists may have formed the majority among those who voted in the House of Lords, but they were clearly a minority, even if a substantial one, in the House of Commons.[93]

It was also widely believed in the eighteenth century that this alleged spread of sexual depravity was especially marked in elite circles in England. In 1772, a fashionable London magazine published a story about the life-style of Lord and Lady Percy, to support the allegation that the current nobility were morally degenerate. Lord Percy was said to be virtually impotent, as a result of excessive masturbation at school and

---

[90] *Conjugium Languens*, 19; Philogamus, 1, 5; Anon. [Francis Douglas], *Reflections on Celibacy and Marriage* (London, 1771), 60; *Bon Ton Mag.* 3: 39–40; *Preventing Marriages Founded on Adultery*, 3; *Crim. Con. Gaz.* 1 (1838), 4; Sibbit, 4.

[91] H. Fielding, *Miss Lucy in Town* (1742), I/i; see also *The Universal Gallant* (1735) and *The Wedding Day* (1743).   [92] *Parl. Hist.*, 35: 264, 310.

[93] Ibid. 304, 306; for the statistics of cases in the London CC, see Table 1.8.

excessive haunting of brothels in youth. As for Lady Percy, she was a notoriously promiscuous adulteress, but her husband refused to divorce her because this would allow her to marry one of her lovers. So they remained together, 'in a state of married separation, her ladyship pursuing her innocent gallantries, while his lordship is enraptured by every new face in King's Place, Pall Mall'.[94] True or false, such stories helped to build up the image of an effete and promiscuous aristocracy. This particular story had some truth to it, for seven years later, in 1779, Lord Percy sued his wife for adultery, and obtained a Parliamentary divorce.

The cause of this degeneracy was usually ascribed to that standard eighteenth-century scapegoat, the growth of idleness and luxury.[95] In 1811, a foreigner commented on the crowds of upper-class women who attended Dr Davy's scientific lectures at the Royal Institution. When told by a husband that 'it keeps them out of harm's way', he commented acidly: 'considering the great number of prosecutions for crim. con. recorded in the newspapers, one would think that no preservative is to be neglected'. On the other hand, he also observed that 'upon the whole . . . there is more conjugal fidelity in England than in most other countries, and these *crim. con.* prosecutions calumniate the higher ranks of society'.[96]

There is no doubt that a large proportion—perhaps a half—of the recorded litigants in crim. con. suits were drawn from the ranks of the leisured, landed elite—esquires and above. But the idea of an indolent and degenerate aristocracy indulging in widespread adultery and wife-swapping is largely fantasy. The total number of holders of heritable titles in 1800—that is, peers and baronets of England, Scotland, or Ireland, and those holding courtesy titles including that of 'Honourable' (many of them heirs to a title)—was 1,203.[97] A sampling indicates that on the average each individual held a real or courtesy title for about thirty-five years, which means that the pool of holders of titles over the sixty-year period 1770 to 1830 was about 2,050. Only 79 out of these 2,050 men of title, or less than 4 per cent, were involved in crim. con. actions or Parliamentary divorces, either as plaintiffs or defendants. This is not a negligible figure, and it is undoubtedly very much higher than the proportion in other classes of the society. But if one assumes that the amount of litigation bears some relation to that of real adultery, the

---

[94] *T & C Mag.* 4: 513.

[95] *Preventing Marriages Founded on Adultery*, 4; *Bon Ton Mag.* 3: 39–40.

[96] L. Simond, *op. cit.* 1: 33, 34.

[97] J. Cannon, *Aristocratic Century: The Peerage of Eighteenth-Century England* (Cambridge, 1984), 32.

figures offer little support for the extravagant claims that a tide of marital infidelity was engulfing the British aristocracy.

We may conclude that the wide publicity given to notorious crim. con. cases concerning members of the titled elite gave a distorted picture of the adulterous behaviour of wives of this rank. Of course, this tells us nothing about the sexual habits of their husbands. We can be sure that they were much more sexually promiscuous than their wives, but possibly no more so than one or two hundred years before, or indeed after. Between 1769 and 1790, the *Town and Country Magazine* published well-informed accounts of the irregular sex lives of some 260 prominent and often titled men, most of whom were married men supporting mistresses.[98] But such men expected their wives to remain faithful, as was on the whole the case so long as the marriages held together and there were no separations.

These data do not alter the possibility, even probability, that wifely adultery was indeed on the increase in elite circles, and there are several reasons why this might have been the case. One is that the growing protection of the property of elite married women by the use of trust deeds offered some cushion against the financial penalties for marital infidelity, and so encouraged more female adultery. On the other hand, below this economically fairly elevated group of women, perhaps the richest 10 per cent, these provisions were unknown, and nothing had changed between 1660 and 1860 to improve the financial prospects of poorer wives in the event of marital separation or divorce for adultery.

What can hardly be doubted is the influence of the rise of affective individualism, the ideal of the companionate marriage, and romanticism, all of which increasingly took hold in upper and upper middle-class circles in the middle and late eighteenth century.[99] Critics now tended to put a good deal of the blame for wifely adultery on 'the abuse of parental authority', which forced some romantically inclined women into loveless marriages in defiance of these changes in ideology.[100] It was also widely believed that the reading of romantic novels was raising to unrealistic levels the expectations by women of personal happiness in marriage. More women were demanding more from marriage than ever before, and if they did not find the love, sexual satisfaction, friendship, and companionship they had anticipated, they were more apt to look for it elsewhere, and so to be more tempted into adultery. The solution, it was

---

[98] *T & C Mag.* (London, 1769–93), vols. 1–24.

[99] Stone, *FSM*, chs. 6–8; Trumbach; Lewis, ch. 1.

[100] For example, Anon., *Letters on Love, Marriage and Adultery* (London, 1789), 57–62, 85–7, 96.

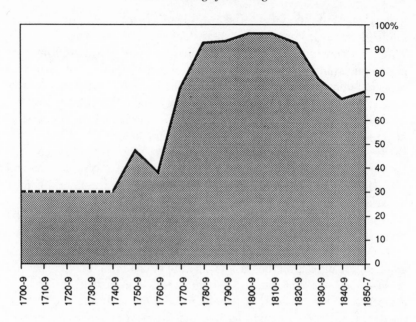

FIGURE 9.2 Parliamentary Divorces Preceded by Criminal Conversation Actions 1700–1857 [Table 9.2]

believed, was marriage based on 'the well-grounded affection, the deserved approbation and heart-felt attachment of the best and tenderest of friends'.[101] But this was easier said than achieved.

ii. A Rise in Litigation?

Another explanation for the rise in crim. con. actions after 1770 is that it was to some extent an accidental by-product of a concurrent rise in Parliamentary divorces. Success of a bill for a Parliamentary divorce came increasingly to depend on both a previous sentence of separation in an ecclesiastical court, and a previous award of substantial damages by a jury in a crim. con. action at common law (Fig. 9.2, Table 9.2). Between 1780 and 1830, about 95 per cent of all petitions for divorce were accompanied by evidence of a crim. con. action, largely because of the formal demand for such evidence from Parliament.[102]

As a result, an increasingly common motive of the plaintiff in bringing

[101] See Lewis.

[102] House of Commons Standing Order, 10 June 1773; House of Lords Standing Order 141 (see Anderson, Table III and nn. 5, 7; Wolfram, 160, Table 2, and 170, Table 4); after 1830, however, the proportion dropped to about 75% apparently because of the growing number of defendants who fled the country before they could be sued.

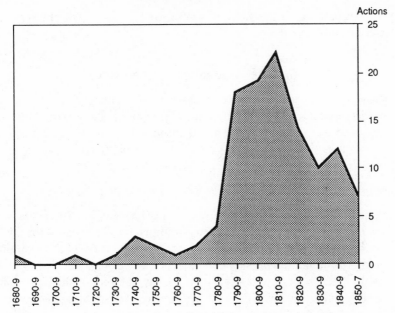

FIGURE 9.3   Damages over £2,000 in Criminal Conversation Actions 1680–1857
[Table 9.3]

a crim. con. action after 1780 was not to recover damages but to facilitate a Parliamentary divorce.[103] In 1857, Lord Chancellor Cranworth told the House of Lords that he believed that 'those actions had hitherto been mainly, if not entirely, in consequence of the rule laid down by their lordships that without a verdict in such an action, a divorce could not be granted'.[104] Although the number of crim. con. actions were always about double the number of petitions for divorce, this discrepancy could easily be explained: 'there are many actions for crim. con. tried which are not followed up by applications for divorce, the verdicts in some cases being against the plaintiff, in others only nominal damages are given, and in many the parties are not possessed of the means to enable them to apply for a divorce'.[105]

Another probable cause for the rise in the number of crim. con. cases was the dramatic increase in the size of damages awarded by juries in the decades between 1780 and 1830, when the number of awards over £2,000 rose precipitously (Fig. 9.3, Table 9.3). Many aggrieved husbands must have been tempted to go to court rather than settle on a

103 For full details of collusion, see below, 282–4.
104 3 *Hansard*, 142: 1975–6.   105 Ibid. 147: 1160.

private separation, in the hope of winning one of these rich prizes in the lottery of jury awards.

6. The Assessment of Damages

In assessing damages in crim. con. cases, juries in the period 1660–1857 exercised considerable independence of judgment. They carried out the same careful evaluations of the moral merits and demerits of plaintiff and defendant as they did in their verdicts in criminal trials.[106]

A. THE STATUS AND WEALTH OF THE PLAINTIFF

In the assessment of damages, juries clearly regarded the status and wealth of the plaintiff as the most important factor. The reason for this is first the significance in the crim. con. action of the concept of reparation for injured honour; and second the very close connection believed to exist between honour and status in a society like that of the eighteenth century, still based on hierarchy, deference, and snobbery. Moreover, the well-born were thought to have more tender feelings than the vulgar, and therefore to need greater compensation. In 1794, Thomas Erskine, trying to plead for the defendant seducer, admitted: 'I readily agree that an injury of this nature is more severely felt by a man of sensibility and honourable birth than it can be by a person of a different description.'[107] In 1804, Baron Smith instructed the jury to pay attention to the rank of the plaintiff, due to the greater 'delicacy of sentiment and punctilio of honour engendered by the refined habits which belong to opulence and distinction'. Baron Smith also added the further argument that men of high rank were more open to public scorn as cuckolds, and therefore deserved more compensation.[108] In 1796, Chief Baron Yelverton angrily rejected the subversive notion 'that men of high rank, of high honour, of splendid situation, had no feelings to be wounded, had no honour to be injured, had no domestic comforts to be sacrificed'. He confidently asserted that 'the higher the rank and honour' of the husband, 'the more ample should be the reparation'.[109]

The proof that Baron Yelverton expressed the values of the juries is that fifteen out of the twenty-four awards of damages over £10,000 went

---

[106] T. A. Green, *Verdict According to Conscience: Perspectives on the English Criminal Trial Jury, 1200–1800* (Chicago, 1985), 283–4, 288, 304, 307, 346–9, 353, 369, 380–3.

[107] *Lord Cadogan v. Rev. W. H. Cowper* (1796), NC *Trials for Adultery* (1797), 1.

[108] *Massey v. Marquis of Headfort* (1804), RIA/HP, 872 (1) 89.

[109] *Westmeath v. Bradshaw* (1796), NC *Trials for Adultery* (1797), 1: 37–8; Anon., *Trial of the Hon. Augustus Cavendish Bradshaw* (Exeter, 1796), 44 (Oxford Law Lib. CW E.U. 690 D. 685).

to men of title. If the cut-off point is put at £5,000, a third were awarded to men of title, another third to esquires, and the last third to rich professional and business men. At the other end of the social and economic scale, a butcher, a trimming-maker, a veterinarian, and a cabinet-maker were all awarded damages of less than £100.[110]

There was thus a broad correlation of status and income of the plaintiffs with size of damages. But there were so many exceptions due to considerations of morality and propriety that it is impossible to predict the size of the damages awarded merely from the rank and wealth of the plaintiff. Too many ethical and social variables were involved to make possible any confident guess about how much a jury was likely to award.[111]

B. 'LOSS OF COMFORT AND SOCIETY'

The action began in the late seventeenth century in order to provide financial recompense for injury to honour and pollution of blood in a patrilinear society, reinforced by the early eighteenth-century idea that a wife's body was the property of her husband. Up to about 1760, a most important consideration was whether or not the wife already had given birth, or was about to give birth, to an illegitimate child, who under the conditions of the settlement of the family estates might inherit property, name, and title.[112] Thus in 1740, when Sir William Morice sued Lord Augustus Fitzroy, he asked for damages to cover the huge expense of litigation 'to get rid of her spurious issue from inheriting his estate'. Similarly, in 1796 Lord Valentia claimed that he was childless and now found himself with 'a child he could hardly call his own and another he certainly could not'.[113] In yet another case, in 1802, a man discovered that his wife had been carrying on an adulterous liaison for no less than five years, as a result of which he had no idea which or how many of his children were his, and which were fathered by his wife's lover. In this case the jury awarded very large damages indeed—£7,000.[114]

After about 1750, however, as the concept of affective individualism slowly began to erode that of property as the linch-pin of marriage, the

---

[110] Wolfram, Table 5 and p. 172.

[111] For a different view, see S. Staves, 'Money for Honour: Damages for Criminal Conversation', *Studies in Eighteenth-Century Culture*, 11: 280–1.

[112] See Stone, *Broken Lives*, The Beaufort case.

[113] *Morice* v. *Fitzroy* (1742), (BL, 518. c. 22, 48).

[114] *Markham* v. *Faucett* (1802), *Speeches of Lord Erskine*, 4: 286; *Webster* v. *Lord Holland* (1797), *Crim. Con. Gaz.* 1: 381–2; *Lond. Chron.* (1797), 1: 181. See also *Walford* v. *Cooke* (1789), (BL, 518. C. 18(4).) 8, 15, 47.

core of the action began to shift to 'the loss of the comfort and society of his wife'. By this was meant deprivation of her sexual, maternal, economic, and social services.[115] The value of all this clearly turned on the terms upon which the couple had lived before the act of adultery, the argument being that the greater the happiness before the adultery, the larger should be the financial compensation for its loss.[116]

As a result of this shift in moral perceptions, attention was drawn to the question of whether the marriage had been arranged by parents or friends, or whether it had been a love-match based on mutual choice. Though rarely mentioned in the first half of the century, by the 1790s great stress was being placed upon this question both by the prosecution and the defence counsel. In a well-publicized case in 1793–4, of an arranged marriage, *Howard* v. *Bingham*, Thomas Erskine used all his histrionic talents in a brilliant speech, on this occasion for the defence. Elizabeth Pierrepont, he argued, 'was dragged a victim to the marriage bed, without having the least love or attachment to Mr Howard'. Working himself up, he referred to Elizabeth as a young woman

whose affections were irretrievably bestowed upon and pledged to my honourable and unfortunate client. You must behold her given up to the plaintiff by the infatuation of parents, and stretched upon this bridal bed as upon a rack—torn from the arms of a beloved and impassioned youth, himself of noble birth, only to secure the honours of a higher title: a legal victim on the altar of Heraldry.

He described the marriage as 'the legal prostitution of parental choice in the teeth of affection'.[117] Even the austere Lord Chief Justice Kenyon was moved by this emotional appeal, and for once failed to ask the jury for heavy damages. Half a century later, Lord Brougham wrote of Erskine that 'one or two of his speeches upon seduction, especially that for the defendant in *Howard* v. *Bingham*, are of exquisite beauty'.[118]

That these sentimental arguments were now powerful ones with a jury is shown by the identical rhetoric employed in the equally well-publicized case in 1796 of adultery following a marriage by free choice, *Westmeath* v. *Bradshaw*. The solicitor-general, who was counsel for the plaintiff, emphasized at some length that the match was 'purely the result of love to the lady', reciprocated by her, and that no 'compulsion of parental authority' had been used on her. The jury responded by awarding damages of £10,000.[119]

[115] Defined in 1794 by Thomas Erskine in sentimental and emotional terms in *Howard* v. *Bingham*, in *Speeches of Lord Erskine*, ed. J. Ridgway (London, 1847), 4: 308–9.
[116] Anderson, 425–6. [117] *Speeches of Lord Erskine*, 310, 312.
[118] *Works of Henry Lord Brougham* (Edinburgh, 1872), 3: 319–20.
[119] *NC Trials for Adultery* (1797), 1: 3–4; *Trial of Augustus Cavendish Bradshaw*, 52.

Other aggravating or mitigating circumstances were the personal qualitities of the wife. For example, in 1796 Lord Westmeath's counsel pointed out that Lady Westmeath was 'of most respectable family and connexions, polished education, high accomplishments and great beauty of person'.[120] Another consideration was the degree to which the wife had been a faithful, diligent, and competent household manager. If she possessed all these qualities, and had run the household efficiently, then her loss was all the more severely felt and deserved greater compensation. And finally there was the question of the number of children, especially under the age of 7, who would henceforth be deprived of maternal care, since it was unthinkable that an adulterous mother could be permitted to continue to take charge of her children. These were not critical factors in assessing damages, but they were always mentioned by counsel as matters which should be taken into consideration by the jury.[121]

Conversely, the counsel for the defence tried, where possible, to impugn the wife's ancestry and upbringing. Thus, when in 1757 Captain Gambier found himself on trial for adultery with the wife of Admiral Knowles, his defence counsel stressed that the admiral's wife was no more than the daughter of an inn-keeper or keeper of a cook-shop. The argument seemed to have had some effect, since the damages awarded were only a relatively modest £1,000.[122]

Counsel now also talked more freely about sexual pleasure, or the absence of it. Erskine in 1794 exclaimed that 'nothing, certainly, is more delightful to the human fancy than the possession of a beautiful woman in the prime of health and youthful passion'.[123] Or, as the 23-year-old Francis Seymour put it more crudely in 1835: 'conceive the delight of having a wife to do this, instead of being obliged, as one now is, to go running after every dirty housemaid ... *pour passer le temps*'.[124] Conversely, if the wife was old and ugly, 'a matron of no personal beauty or attractions', the defence counsel went out of his way to draw attention to these mitigating circumstances.[125]

C. THE MORAL RESPONSIBILITY OF THE HUSBAND

i. *Quarrels or Neglect*

Once marital happiness before the adultery began to overshadow other

[120] *NC Trials for Adultery* (1797), 1: 3.
[121] *Knowles* v. *Gambier* (1757), *Crim. Con. Gaz.* 2: 53–4; *Lindon* v. *Mallock* (1826), ibid. 283.
[122] *Knowles* v. *Gambier* (1757), *NCC Trials for Adultery* (1780), 1: 135.
[123] *Speeches of Lord Erskine*, 4: 309.   [124] Quoted in Lewis, 37.
[125] Erskine for the defence in *Cecil* v. *Sneyd* (1791), BL, 518.1.12(5). 27.

considerations, lurking behind every suit for crim. con. lay the question of the responsibility of the plaintiff in driving his wife into the arms of another man. Sir William Scott, later Lord Stowell, who was the most distinguished civil lawyer in early nineteenth-century England, was sure that in ninety-nine cases out of a hundred the blame for a wife's adultery lay first with the husband for his neglect, cruelty, or adultery; then with the wife for her lack of moral courage to resist temptation; and last of all with her lover, the defendant in a crim. con. action.[126] This was an opinion supported by other experienced lawyers and judges at this time, for example Lord Erskine, who had been counsel, almost invariably for the plaintiff husband, in every major crim. con. action for thirty years.[127]

In consequence of these changed moral perceptions, after about 1770 the amount of the damages could be seriously reduced by evidence of quarrels, alienation, or indifference.[128] In 1769 use of evidence about a prior separation of beds was attempted without success: the jury 'went out shamed sick to her husband—by a separate bed in his own house', but none the less awarded him £2,000 damages. Twenty years later, however, the result was very different. In 1788 the defendant's counsel, the ubiquitous Erskine, used his usual rhetoric to sway the jury: 'he would not sleep in the same bed with her, as if she had been seized with some loathesome disorder. She was obliged to lie in a solitary bed without the consolation, without the friendship, and without the society of her husband, who was snoring, by himself, in the opposite side of the house.' So moving was this appeal to pity for a neglected wife in the new age of the companionate marriage that the jury awarded the derisory damages of one shilling.[129]

ii. Prior Private Separation

In the first half of the eighteenth century, judges tended to the view that even after a formal separation the husband was still entitled to some compensation for his loss of honour by the seduction of his wife, over whom he retained certain inalienable rights.[130] In 1769, several years after he had insisted upon a private separation because of his wife's intolerable temper, the Duke of Grafton was successful in his suit for damages against her lover, Lord Ossory.[131]

---

[126] 2 *Hansard*, 24: 1285.   [127] See below, pp. 273–7.

[128] For a few examples of the use of the unhappy marriage argument, see *Lond. Chron.* (1789), 1: 7; *Crim. Con. Gaz.* 1: 53–4, 93–4.

[129] J. C. Oldham, Unpublished Legal Papers of Lord Mansfield. I am indebted to Professor Oldham, for permission to use this quotation; *Lond. Chron.* (1789), 1: 7.

[130] *Morice* v. *Fitzroy* (1742), *Trial of Lord Augustus Fitzroy* (London, 1742), BL, 518. c. 22. In 1742 Morice was awarded £5,000, despite evidence of earlier quarrels and a decision to separate.   [131] See Stone, *Broken Lives*, the Grafton case.

By 1790, as reparation for 'loss of comfort and society' took priority over loss of honour, the question was asked whether a prior private separation deed did not actually bar a later suit for crim. con.[132] After a period of uncertainty, the King's Bench finally decided in 1805 that the husband could still sue for damages for the disgrace brought on his name, for the danger of spurious children inheriting his estate, and for the residual claims he still had on his wife's society and assistance. This allowed the suit to go forward, but in the eyes of juries a prior separation deed now severely mitigated the size of the damages awarded.[133]

The size of the potential damages tempted some husbands who had long before abandoned or separated themselves from their wives, suddenly to start suing their wives' lovers for crim. con. In cases in 1794, 1804, and 1807, respectively, one husband asked for damages of £10,000 and two for £5,000; the award in each case was £100; another in 1818 asked for £10,000 and got 6d.[134] These cases contrasted sharply with normal cases, in which juries tended to give half what was asked.

iii. Prior Adultery by the Husband

In both the ecclesiastical courts and in Parliament, evidence of adultery by a husband automatically disqualified him from any legal right to sue for either separation or divorce. At common law, however, during the late seventeenth and eighteenth centuries, adultery by the husband was treated as no more than strongly mitigating circumstances in the assessment of damages, but not as an absolute bar to the action.[135] The common law courts still had not fallen into line with the church courts or Parliament when the action was finally abolished by Parliament in 1857.

D. THE MORAL TURPITUDE OF THE ADULTEROUS COUPLE

The prior relationship between the two men—the husband and his wife's lover—could also seriously influence the size of the damages awarded. If the lover was a bare acquaintance of the husband, then no breach of

---

[132] *Parkes* v. *Cresswick* (1825), *Crim. Con. Gaz.* 2: 139: Sullivan case (1825), MacQueen, *House of Lords*, 638; *Graham* v. *Wright* (1827), ibid. 644; *Cherer* v. *Marriot* (1827), Plowden, 2: 316; *Chamberlayne* v. *Broomfield* (1812), *The Speeches of Lord Brougham* (Philadelphia, 1841), 2: 294 n. *.

[133] *Weedon* v. *Timbrell* (1793), *Eng. Rep.* 101: 199–201; *Chambers* v. *Caulfield* (1805), ibid. 102: 1280–5.

[134] *Elwes* v. *Harvet* (1794); *Gillespey* v. *Leeder* (1807), LPCA, D.830. 87–95; *Nugent* v. *Norrie* (1818), RIA/HT, Box 399; *Parkes* v. *Cresswick* (1825), *Crim. Con. Gaz.* 2: 139; *Bloxham* v. *Goddard* (1804); Plowden, 2: 98–100.

[135] Shelford, 439–44; *Stuart* v. *Blandford* (1801), *Lond. Chron.* (1801), 1: 509; *Astley* v. *Garth*, Plowden, 2: 237–40; *Crim. Con. Gaz.* 1: 45–6.

friendship and hospitality had taken place. If, on the other hand, he had been an old family friend on regular dining terms and free to stay the night whenever he chose, then the breach of faith was regarded on all sides as very serious. If the lover was a close male friend of the husband, adultery was regarded as a double betrayal, first of the spousal relationship and second of male bonding.[136]

A famous crim. con. action which turned upon the issue of betrayal of this personal bond of male friendship was one initiated by Lord Abergavenny in 1730 against Mr Lyddell. On catching Lyddell in bed with Lady Abergavenny, Matthews the house-steward reproached him for his treachery: 'For you, Sir, to come so frequently in such a show of friendship, and to wrong his lordship after such a manner as you have done, is a crime for which you can make no satisfaction.' Overcome with remorse, Lyddell replied: 'I am a vile wretch. For God's sake do not speak to me.' Lady Abergavenny cried, 'Dear Matthews, do not ruin me! Do not ruin me!' and went into shock. Twenty-six days later she was dead. It is hardly surprising that the report of this case was constantly reprinted for over a century, since it was such a gripping moral epic of sin, guilt, repentance, and punishment. The early death of the lady seemed like divine retribution, and Mr Lyddell's immediate sense of shame and humiliation came long before his later financial ruin, brought about by the award of damages to the staggering amount of £10,000.[137] Nor did this repugnance at a betrayal of a male friendship change over time. For example, in 1815 a lawyer for the prosecution in a crim. con. case reminded the jury that 'the breach of friendship enhances the guilt'.[138]

Perhaps even more morally objectionable to the eighteenth-century mind than betrayal by a friend was betrayal by one who was also an associate. Cases where the husband and his wife's seducer were bound together in loyalty as fellow-officers in the same regiment nearly always resulted in the award of especially heavy damages. When in 1789 Captain Sykes seduced the wife of Captain Parslow, the jury awarded dam-

---

[136] For cases in which the counsel for the plaintiff laid special stress on the breach of friendship by the defendant, see e.g. *Baring* v. *Webster* (1822), *Beresford* v. *Bective* (1816), *Duberley* v. *Gunning* (1789), *Crim. Con. Gaz.* 2: 207–8; 1: 61, 77–8. For other examples of the use of the breach of friendship argument by counsel, in crim. con. cases, see *Lond. Chron.* (1800), 1: 524; (1802), 426; *NC Trials for Adultery* (1797), 1: 3, 5; *Crim. Con. Gaz.* 1: 21–2, 45, 70, 77; 2: 126, 283; *T & C Mag.* 18 (1786), 345.

[137] *Letters of Lady Mary Wortley Montagu*, ed. R. Halsband (Oxford, 1965–7), 2: 295 n. 3; *Abergavenny* v. *Liddell* (1730), *Trials for Adultery at Doctors' Commons* 7: 13; *NCC Trials for Adultery* (1780), 1: 29–38; *A Collection of Most Remarkable and Interesting Trials for Adultery*, 2: 94; Plowden, 1: 26–36; *Crim. Con. Gaz.* 2: 13–14; *Crim. Con. A & T*, 89–94.

[138] *Lord Rosebery* v. *Sir Henry Mildmay*, *The Times*, 12 Dec. 1814: 2.

ages of £10,000, the full amount asked for.[139] One reason was that seduction of the wife of a brother officer was regarded as a grossly immoral betrayal of male bonding.[140]

But perhaps equal in infamy was betrayal by a relative.[141] If the relative was a close one, the infamy became so much the greater. Erskine, pleading for the plaintiff against a defendant who was both cousin and business partner, called it, with characteristic hyperbole, 'the most shocking instance of depravity that ever entered the human mind'.[142] The same mentality was shown by the jury in the action of Viscount Bellfield against his brother Mr Rochfort in 1740, in which the viscount was awarded the totally unprecedented damages of £20,000, which in the end put his brother in gaol for the rest of his natural life.[143] Similar moral outrage was expressed by both judge and jury in 1793, in a case in which an uncle and guardian had seduced and then eloped with his nephew's wife during the latter's absence in India. Even the counsel for the defendant had to admit that it was 'a very aggravated case'.[144]

The motives of the seducer also counted for something in the assessment of damages. Counsels for the defence would if possible make the argument that the adultery was the product of an unpremeditated, sudden, overwhelming gust of sexual passion, which temporarily turned the heads of the lovers, and of which they later bitterly repented. Counsel for the plaintiff, on the other hand, stressed where possible the premeditated nature of the seduction. Thus it told against Captain Sykes, when sued by Captain Parslow for crim. con. with the latter's wife, that he had remarked to a friend some months before: 'I should like to debauch that woman'[145] (Plate 25).

Where and how the seduction took place was also not without its importance. Only in a minority of cases were the wife and her lover willing to break the taboo of violating the marriage-bed itself, an act which was regarded as a serious sexual insult to the husband. When this happened, much was often made of it at the trial. For example, in 1815 the counsel for the prosecution, in a case where the seducer was found in the wife's own bed, urged that 'the jury should consider the place where this outrage was committed'.[146]

[139] *Parslow* v. *Sykes* (1791), *NC Trials for Adultery* (1797), 1: 36, 40, 44; *Westmeath* v. *Bradshaw*, ibid. 1: 10.
[140] *Lindon* v. *Mallock* (1826), *Crim. Con. Gaz.* 2: 283.
[141] *Smith* v. *Smith* (1803), ibid. 2: 224.
[142] *Boddington* v. *Boddington* (1797), ibid. 2: 78.   [143] Ibid. 2: 61.
[144] *Campbell* v. *Hooke* (1793), ibid. 1: 118.
[145] *NC Trials for Adultery* (1797), 1: 3, 14.
[146] See Loveden case in Stone, *Broken Lives*; *Lord Rosebery* v. *Sir Henry Mildmay* (1815), *The Times*, 12 May 1815: 3.

Largely as a result of this taboo, by far the largest number of recorded acts of adultery, of which there are several hundred, took place in the home, but rarely in the bedroom. They occurred in the drawing-room or the dining-room, on the carpet, or on two chairs, or most commonly on a sofa. Away from home, the most favoured places were a secluded spot in the countryside, at a bagnio or a hotel (Plate 26) or while riding in a coach. Unlike the modern, windowed automobile, the eighteenth-century coach was ideally suited for an assignation. With the blinds drawn down, it was entirely private, while, as an eighteenth-century magazine delicately put it, 'the undulating motion of the coach, with the pretty little occasional jolts, contribute greatly to enhance the pleasure of the critical moment, if all matters are rightly placed'.[147] Coaches were such common places for sexual activity that in 1698 a bill before Parliament against 'vice and prophaneness' contained a clause specifically prohibiting 'unlawful commerce between men and women' in hackney coaches.[148] It was alleged in 1838 that the coach commissioners, who licensed hackney coaches in London, were so disturbed by the immoral use to which the amenities of their coaches were being put, that they 'seriously intended at one time to pass an order for doing away with coach blinds and coach cushions altogether'.[149]

E. THE STATUS OF THE DEFENDANT

The extent to which the rank and wealth of the defendant was to be taken into consideration was more controversial. At the top of the scale there was general agreement that rich noblemen should be made to pay heavily for theirs acts of gallantry, especially with married women of genteel birth. In 1770, Wedderburn, counsel for Earl Grosvenor who was suing a royal brother, the Duke of Cumberland, gave the argument an egalitarian and populist flavour by claiming that 'severe damages would teach that the laws of England in the hands of an English jury were superior to the most elevated degree of rank'. Lord Mansfield, who presided, incurred much criticism as pandering to the Crown when he instructed the jury that they 'were not to be governed in estimating their damages by the rank or fortune of the defendant; but to pronounce the damages that the plaintiff ought to receive'.[150] This was a position which later judges did

---

[147] *Harris's List of Covent Garden Ladies: Or a Man of Pleasure's Kalender for the Year 1788* (London, 1788), 110.

[148] J. Oldmixon, *The History of England*, London (1735), 175. I owe this reference to David Hayton.　　　　[149] *Crim. Con. Gaz.* 1: 81.

[150] *Grosvenor* v. *Cumberland* (1770); *NCC Trials for Adultery* (1780), 2: 46–127; Plowden, 1: 240, 264; *T & C Mag.* 2 (1770), 368; Evans, 2: 359.

not support, and in 1796 Chief Baron Yelverton restated the traditional position: 'The more exalted the culprit, because the less excusable the crime, the higher should be the punishment.'[151] This partly explains why such very large damages were so often awarded against titled defendants.[152]

The one glaring exception to this rough correlation between the size of the damages and the rank of the defendant were occasions when the latter was of utterly contemptible status, a poor servant who had become the lover of a rich and well-born woman. In cases such as these, judges and juries combined to levy savage damages in order to compensate not only for the breach of trust between servant and master, but more especially for the threat to social hierarchy involved in so grossly unequal a pairing. According to the values of the age, it was legitimate, indeed so common as to be normal, for a gentleman to take his maidservant to bed with him. But it was outrageous that his wife should do the same with a low-born male servant.

The first such case was the action of *Dormer* v. *Jones*, in 1715. John Dormer was a rich squire of good family, well educated and with good manners, who had married a woman of great beauty but humble origins. Mrs Dormer, whom today we would classify as a masochist, fell hopelessly in love with Thomas Jones, the stable groom, 'a short thickset squat fellow' who was 'rude, insolent, ungrateful and cruel'. He treated Mrs Dormer abominably, beating her with his fist, spitting on her publicly in church, and boasting that 'Mr Dormer is a cuckold. I have lain with his wife several times.' Mrs Dormer conceived and gave birth to a child by Tom Jones. To the eighteenth-century mind this was a particularly atrocious case, involving a subversion of the hierarchy of ranks, and the physical and psychological abuse of an upper-class woman by a servant and a man of no account. An indignant jury assessed damages against Jones at the huge sum of £5,000, the clear intention being to imprison him for debt for the rest of his life. But Jones had the wit to skip out of the court-room just before the verdict, and take refuge in the sanctuary of the Mint, whence he later escaped, never to be heard of

---

[151] *Trial of Augustus Cavendish Bradshaw*, 44.

[152] *Morice* v. *Lord Fitzroy* (1740), *Crim. Con. Gaz.* 2: 109; *Elliott* v. *Viscount Valentia* (1775), *Peerage*, 12: ii. 209 n. *d*.; *Foley* v. *Earl of Peterborough* (1785), BL, 518. 1. 12(2). 27; *Dunnage* v. *Turton* (1797), *Crim. Con. Gaz.* 2: 78; *Poulett* v. *Lord Sackville* (1798), ibid. 1: 101–2; *Massey* v. *Marquis of Headfort* (1804), RIA/HP, 872 (1); *Lord Glancurry* v. *Sir John Piers, Bt.* (1807), ibid. 918; *Wellesley* v. *Lord Paget* (1810), *Crim. Con. Gaz.* 2: 102; *Sir William Abdy* v. *Lord Charles Bentinck, JH Lords*, 50: 620; *Lord George Beresford* v. *the Earl of Bective* (1816), *Crim. Con. Gaz.* 1: 61–2; *Taafe* v. *Lord William Fitzgerald* (1816), RIA/HP, 1102; *Bell* v. *Marquis of Anglesea* (1840), MacQueen, *Marriage, Divorce and Legitimacy*, 132–3.

again.[153] He was lucky, since other servants in his position all ended up in prison.

So intense was the taboo against upper-class women sleeping with lower-class servants that there are only 11 such cases on record among about 500 crim. con. trials and divorce petitions between 1692 and 1857.[154] Of course, there were plenty of rumours, and no doubt plenty of cases, which never became public knowledge.[155] Most of these episodes of cross-class adultery involved outdoor rather than indoor servants, affairs with whom would be more easy to conceal.[156]

The intense indignation demonstrated by litigants, judges, jury, and the public in general at the breach of trust between master and servant, and at the breach of the rules of social rank endogamy, outweighed the strong probability that in the initial stages of these affairs, the servants must in most cases have been the seduced rather than the seducers of their mistresses (Plate 27). These servants were so far below their superiors in rank, power, and wealth that they could not possibly have dared to make the first move, except perhaps very tentatively by the use of body-language.

F. THE CAPACITY OF THE DEFENDANT TO PAY

One of the most vexed questions concerning the award of damages in crim. con. actions was whether or not the jury should take into consideration the defendant's poverty. On the one hand, one could argue that being poor should not create immunity from punishment for the seduction of a married woman nor diminish the just compensation due to the husband. On the other hand, there was the fact that according to the English law of debt, inability to pay would lead to arrest, which might in some cases result in imprisonment for life in a debtors' gaol. Should a jury in a civil suit *de facto* condemn a man to life imprisonment?

During the eighteenth century, judges and juries remained uncertain how to settle this question. In the case in 1730 of *Lord Abergavenny* v. *Mr Lyddell*, the plaintiff's counsel argued that the latter's financial situation was irrelevant: 'It is but reasonable, if a person destroys the happiness of

---

[153] *Dormer* v. *Jones* (1715), *Collection of Trials*, 84–90; *NCC Trials for Adultery* (1780), 1: 91–7; Plowden, 1: 71–5; *Crim. Con. Gaz.* 2: 101; *Cases of Divorce for Several Causes* (London, 1715), 47–57; *Crim. Con. A & T*, 85–8.

[154] The cases were: *Dormer* v. *Jones* (1715); *Clavering* v. *Gremley* (1738); *Ennever* v. *? [a cowman]* (1753); *Morgan* v. *Hall* (1754); *Larking* v. *Juson* (1792); *Wilmot* v. *Washbourne* (1793); *Middleton* v. *Rose* (1794); *Fowler* v. *Hodges* (1807); *?* v. *McCarthy* (c.1800s); *Gregson* v. *Theaker* (1809); *Talbot* v. *? [a groom]* (1852).

[155] See e.g. *Bon Ton Mag.* 3 (1793), 355.

[156] See Stone, *Broken Lives*, The Middleton case.

another, his happiness ought to be disturbed as long as he lives,' so that there was need for 'a retribution for life for an injury for life'. This was a doctrine not about civil damages, but about sheer vengeance, but it was accepted by the jury, who awarded damages of £10,000, which were clearly intended to put Lyddell in prison for life.[157]

This verdict did not set a precedent, for the normal rough correlation of a defendant's rank and income to the damages awarded against him indicates that the judges and juries did tend to take capacity to pay into consideration. Thus in the case of Admiral Knowles *v.* Captain Gambier, a friend of the latter testified that: 'I fear, after all, that he will be thrown into gaol for debt . . . [and] lie there and rot until he dies, for he has lost his captainship and is now over head and ears in debt.' The defence counsel made much of this plea of poverty, and after twenty minutes' consideration the jury brought in damages of £1,000, which were heavily scaled down from the £10,000 demanded—presumably in part in order to adjust them to Gambier's limited capacity to pay.[158]

7. The Moral Panic of the 1790s

A. LORD KENYON AND THOMAS ERSKINE

In 1788, Lord Kenyon was appointed lord chief justice, and promptly inaugurated a reign of terror in King's Bench against adulterers (Plate 28). By 1791, a London elite magazine was ruefully commenting that nowadays 'adultery is not one of the cheapest amusements that might be thought of'. A story began to circulate about a sexual adventurer who deliberately avoided married women and sought a widow, who 'had no partner in her person who could plead the loss of her affections . . . and obtain a verdict with excessive damages'.[159] Lord Kenyon was described by Wraxall in unforgettable terms: 'Irascible in his temper, like his countrymen the Welsh, destitute of all refinement in dress or external deportment, parsimonious even in a degree approaching to avarice, he never the less more than balanced these defects of deportment and character by strict morality, probity, and integrity.'[160] Kenyon came to

---

[157] *Trials for Adultery at Doctors' Commons*, 7: 23; *Crim. Con. Gaz.* 2: 14. What makes this verdict all the more unjust is that since Lady Abergavenny died 26 days after the discovery, her husband only lost a month of her company and services; moreover, it appears that this was by no means the first of her adulteries (*Letters of Lady Mary Wortley Montagu*, ed. R. Halsband), (Oxford, 1965), 2: 295 n. 3).

[158] Plowden, 1: 101; *Trials for Adultery at Doctors' Commons*, 6: 58.

[159] *T & C Mag.* 23 (1791), 293; 24 (1792), 100.

[160] *The Historical and the Posthumous Memoirs of Sir Nathaniel William Wraxall 1772–1784*, ed. H. B. Wheatley (London, 1884), 2: 265.

crim. con. actions with four powerful convictions. The first was a visceral horror of sexual irregularity, which led him to believe that it was a vice of such enormity as to threaten the very fabric of society. The second was that moral turpitude was spreading, but that it could be curbed by the award of punitive damages on an unprecedented scale. The third was that the income of the defendant was totally irrelevant to the size of the damages. The fourth and last was that in crim. con. actions, judges and juries had a responsibility not merely to recompense the plaintiff in a private suit, but to set an example to the nation by the infliction of exemplary punishment upon the defendant. It did not bother him that this converted a private civil action into a public criminal one. In a series of increasingly extreme pronouncements in open court, Lord Kenyon laid down the new doctrine, the most obvious result of which was a massive rise in the number of very large damages awarded (Fig. 9.3, Table 9.3).

Lord Kenyon used fire-and-brimstone rhetoric in his directions to the jury, being encouraged by the skilful pandering to his moral foibles of the usual counsel for the plaintiff, the great rhetorician Thomas Erskine. Kenyon 'admired and loved him fervently', and for thirteen years, from 1789 to 1802, they together dominated the court-room.[161] In an action in 1789, Kenyon told the jury that 'when a man, in a case like this, cannot pay with his purse, he must pay with his person'—the first recorded use of a slogan which he and Erskine were to toss back and forth to each other repeatedly in the future. Kenyon once concluded his directions to the jury with the words: 'the preservation of the morals of society, independent of the injury Mr W[alford] has sustained, calls for very exemplary damages. . . . To you, gentlemen of the jury, is committed the protection of the peace of families.' Responding to the exhortation, the jury awarded damages of £3,500.[162]

In the suit of *Parslow* v. *Sykes* in the same year, Erskine, 'in a speech equal to any we ever heard in that court', seized on Lord Kenyon's rhetoric and threw it back at him. He told the jury that if the defendant 'be unable to pay with his purse let him make what acknowledgement he can in the captivity of his person'. It was useless for the defence counsel to protest that this doctrine could only apply to criminal proceedings and not to civil cases like crim. con.; or to point out that deliberately to condemn a man to 'a perpetual imprisonment would be in diametrical opposition to one of the most wise maxims of the laws of England: "no man shall be charged with the payment of a sum which is beyond his

---

[161] *Works of Lord Brougham* (Edinburgh, 1872), 3: 321.
[162] *Walford* v. *Cooke* (1789); *The Trial of Mr Cooke* (London, 1789), BL, 518. C 18(4), 41–9; *T & C Mag.* 21 (1789), 340.

capacity to pay" '. Lord Kenyon brushed these objections aside with an impassioned appeal to the jury: 'God forbid that in this civilized country, such a monster should be suffered to commit these crimes with impunity.' The jury was out for only a few minutes before awarding damages of £10,000, exactly what the plaintiff had requested. In fact, this savage verdict did not cause the ruin of the defendant, for Captain Sykes was lucky enough to have an enormously rich nabob as a father. Indeed he made a joke out of the damages, for he 'ever after called her *Dear* Mrs Parslow, having a right, he said, to use the word after he had paid £10,000 for her' (Plate 25).[163]

For less opulent defendants, however, the results of this severity could be catastrophic. In 1794, Lord Cadogan was awarded £2,000 damages for crim. con. against an impoverished old family dependant and friend, the Revd William Henry Cooper. After the verdict in King's Bench, Lord Cadogan instructed his steward to have Lady Cadogan and the Revd Cooper closely watched to see where they went. The steward soon found that on the day the verdict was given, Lady Cadogan had slipped secretly out of her father's house, where she had lived during the trial, and had fled in a chaise with her lover and two maids to Herefordshire. They had stayed for a night at Abergavenny, being easily identified since Lady Cadogan was carrying two bull-finches in a cage. They then rented a house in the suburbs of the town, where they were seen walking arm-in-arm. But the idyll did not last long, for two months later Lord Cadogan's solicitor brought down a writ from King's Bench. The steward got a warrant from the under-sheriff, and Cooper was arrested and imprisoned in Monmouth Gaol, with orders not to release him until he paid the £2,000 damages. Unless Lady Cadogan was able to pay his fine, the Revd Cooper was likely to have languished in Monmouth Gaol for a very long time, perhaps for years.[164]

As time went on, the language used by Kenyon and Erskine in the court-room became more and more reckless. In a case in 1792, they vied with each other in pouring abuse upon the elderly defendant General Gunning (who certainly deserved much of it). In his opening speech for the plaintiff, Erskine, ever the consummate actor, began to read to the jury a pathetic letter from the errant wife to her husband about the children: 'Take care, my dear James, of our offspring. Teach them not to

[163] *Parslow* v. *Sykes* (1789); *The Trial of Captain Sykes*, (BL, 1132. q. 102), 11, 17, 19–22; *NC Trials for Adultery*, (1797) 1: 12, 27–8, 36, 40, 44–6; T. Brasbridge, *The Fruits of Experience* (London, 1824), 202; see also *Moorson* v. *Clark* (1791), *Lond. Chron.* (1791), 1: 574; *Barttelot* v. *Hawker* (1790); *The Trial of Samuel Hawker* (BL, 518. 1. 12(5)).

[164] LPCA, D. 350–1. 1735–75.

despise their mother and . . .'—at this point, overcome by his own histrionics, he broke down and began weeping in open court. He nearly fainted and could not continue (Plate 29). In his summing up, Kenyon described Gunning as 'that hoary, detestable, abandoned, and degraded lecher' who had 'broken through every social and religious obligation'. The jury was urged by Erskine, who had recovered sufficiently to make a concluding speech lasting one-and-a-half hours, to 'guard your families from the growing debaucheries of the age', and duly responded by awarding damages of £5,000.[165] In 1794, Lord Kenyon overstepped his legal authority as judge by recommending to the jury an actual figure for damages. He suggested £10,000, but the jury ignored him and gave £5,000.[166]

In the face of this barrage of moralistic invective, it was in vain for Sergeant Bearcroft, speaking for the defence, to make the valid legal point that the jury 'have no power to give vindictive damages . . . Vengeance . . . belongs in another jurisdiction . . . To punish the defendant criminally for any crime or offense . . . the common law has no such jurisdiction.'[167]

By 1793, however, Kenyon was beginning to despair since instead of slackening off, the number of crim. con. actions was rising fast—tenfold he alleged. Instead of curbing adultery, his great crusade seemed to be having precisely the opposite effect, and by 1799 he was so desperate that he remarked of a defendant seducer, 'I could wish the law would punish capitally.'[168] It did not cross his mind that the huge damages he was encouraging might actually be stimulating husbands to bring suit.

It was just as well that Lord Kenyon was no longer alive when in 1820 his old friend and ally in the great moral crusade, Thomas (now Lord) Erskine, whose wife had died in 1805, made a fool of himself. Threatened with a breach of promise suit by a young girl to whom he had written love-letters, he decided to run off to Gretna Green to make a hasty clandestine marriage with his housekeeper and long-time mistress. In order to throw the girl and his own son off the scent, he travelled to Scotland 'disguised in female clothes with a large Leghorn bonnet and veil' (Plate 30). 'It is a melancholy proof of dotage,' remarked Lady Wil-

[165] *Duberley* v. *Gunning* (1792); *NC Trials for Adultery* (1797), 1: 7, 17–18; *Crim. Con. Gaz.* 1: 78.

[166] *Biscoe* v. *Gordon* (1794); *NC Trials for Adultery* (1797), 1: 62.

[167] *Barttelot* v. *Hawker* (1790), (BL. 518. 1. 12(5)), 37; *Martin* v. *Petrie* (1791) *Lond. Chron.* (1791), 2: 603; *Ricketts* v. *Taylor* (1798), *ibid.* (1798), 1: 178; *Vassall* v. *Holland* (1796), *Crim. Con. Gaz.* 1: 38: *Lord Valentia* v. *Gawler* (1796), *NC Trials for Adultery* (1797), 1: 14. See also *Dunnage* v. *Turton* (1797), *Crim. Con. Gaz.* 2: 78; *Campbell* v. *Addison* (1799), *Lond. Chron.* (1799), 1: 198.

[168] *Campbell* v. *Addison* (1799), *Lond. Chron.* (1799), 1: 198.

liams-Wynn.[169] It was certainly a come-down for the terror of male seducers in the 1790s.

B. FEAR OF THE FRENCH REVOLUTION

The idea that luxury and sexual licence went together and that both threatened the security of the nation was nothing new, but it aroused especial anxiety in the late eighteenth century. In the 1780s Gibbon had cited it as a cause of the decline and fall of Rome, and fundamentalist popular preachers had long dwelt on this theme. For example, in 1772 Thomas Pollen had thundered 'as virtue has dropped, so vice has reared its head. . . . Where luxury has gained ground, there effeminacy has done the same. . . . Where lasciviousness reigns, there flows in a torrent of debauchery, to the destruction of private families and to the insult of public laws.'[170] By 1792, these hysterical anxieties about moral decay were reinforced in upper-class circles by the fear spread by the news from France of the September massacres, the execution of the king and the outbreak of the Terror, which some read as punishment for the sexual and financial depravity of the pre-Revolution French court and aristocracy. 'Let the aristocracy of England, which trembles so much for itself, take heed of its own security,' thundered Thomas Erskine in 1793.[171]

Others associated sexual libertinism with the excesses of the French Revolution itself, and in 1796 Chief Baron Yelverton urged a jury to 'check and deter the progress of crime in this country', which had grown so much 'in another Kingdom [France], and whose vices we are apt to borrow'. In the House of Lords, the Bishop of Rochester talked about the current 'prophanation of marriage' in France and associated it with violent insubordination and anarchy, while Lord Auckland incoherently characterized the new French divorce laws as 'approximating the system of legalized prostitution and profligacy'.[172]

In the 1790s many commentators were worried about the broader social consequences of an outbreak of elite sexual promiscuity. They were afraid lest 'a prevalence of vice among the great' would 'set an

---

[169] *Correspondence of Charlotte Greville, Lady Williams-Wynn*, ed. R. Leighton (London, 1920), 234; J. Farington, *The Farington Diary*, ed. J. Greig (London, 1922–8), 8: 268.

[170] T. Pollen, *The Fatal Consequence of Adultery to Monarchies as well as Families* (London, 1772).

[171] *Speeches of Lord Erskine*, 313.

[172] *Parl. Hist.* 34: 1557, 1560; 35: 251. For an even more apocalyptic vision of England's moral depravity, see A. Sibbitt, *Thoughts on the Frequency of Divorces in Modern Times* (London, 1800), 1–20; see also Anon., *Thoughts on the Propriety of Preventing Marriages founded on Adultery* (London, 1800), 1–5.

example of depravity to the humble-born'. Lord Kenyon told a jury: 'if adultery is to be treated as a mere refined morality, what a lesson is read by the superior ranks of society to those who are to be governed and to be obedient to the laws. The next step is that there is no God—no religion.'[173] In the House of Lords, the Bishop of Llandaff argued that the growth of adultery was caused by 'the total extinction of the internal monitor of shame', and resulted in 'misfortunes to the state'. The Bishop of Rochester claimed that divorces caused by female adultery 'sapped the morality and manners of the people' and warned that 'our country . . . if once it is sunk in dissoluteness and abandoned immorality, will soon fall an easy prey to corruption and slavery'. Lord Loughborough, the lord chancellor, saw in it a threat to 'the welfare of the nation in its nearest interests', and Thomas Erskine, that master of forensic eloquence, asked rhetorically 'would it not be the height of folly to say that national prosperity was not deeply affected by this crime'—though he failed to explain why.[174]

As a result of this atmosphere of war-time paranoia, it was possible for Lord Kenyon over a period of thirteen years to turn a private civil suit for personal damages into a public criminal suit to punish vice and set an example to society. It should be noted that a normal response of a society under stress is a strenuous attempt to create order in a disorderly world by the imposition of rigid codes of moral conduct.[175] Its technical name among anthropologists is 'pollution behaviour'.

8. The Results of the Moral Panic

A. THE RUIN OF DEFENDANTS

The first result of the dramatic rise in the size of crim. con. damages was exactly what was intended by judges and jurymen: it added the seduction of married women to the list of ways by which a man could lose a fortune.[176] The numbers of men who were ruined and perhaps ended up in gaol was clearly limited by the number of actions, but their fall was sensational and caused a great deal of gossip and anxiety. There can be little doubt that the fear of prosecution must have had a chilling effect

---

[173] *Westmeath* v. *Bradshaw* (1796), *NC Trials for Adultery*, (1797), 1: 47; *Taylor* v. *Birchwood*, *Lond. Chron.* (1800), 1: 523; see also Peter Pindar [John Wolcot], *Lord Auckland's Triumph, or the Death of Crim. Con.* (London, 1800), 6–7; *Crim. Con. Gaz.* (1838–9). 1: 5.

[174] *Parl. Hist.* 20: 592, 594, 596–7; 34: 1556; 35: 311; *JH Lords*, 35: 624, 687.

[175] M. T. Douglas, *Purity and Danger: An Analysis of Concepts of Pollution and Taboo* (London, 1970).

[176] See J. L. Allingham, *The Marriage Promise* (London, 1803).

upon some would-be seducers (Plate 31). It is significant that a popular wife-sale in 1775 was accompanied by a document 'drawn up by way of indemnification from bringing an action for crim. con.'.[177]

B. ENTRAPMENT AND CONNIVANCE

It soon became clear, however, that the rise in the number and size of damages awarded was also having unexpected and most unwelcome results. One was that on occasion the husband and the alleged lover might be tempted to conspire together to frame the wife in order to allow the former to obtain a divorce and remarry. A very experienced barrister who specialized in crim. con. cases said in 1789 that this was 'a common trick'.[178] It was made all the easier because of the rules governing crim. con. actions in King's Bench, which both denied the wife the right to appear in her own defence and permitted verdicts based on no more than circumstantial evidence. Lord Kenyon in the 1790s laid it down in his instructions to the jurymen 'that "where the parties have been traced to a place of privacy, and closetted for a given time . . . the parties must have so retired for the indulgence of an illicit passion" . . . and directed them in all instances to find their verdict accordingly'.[179] Under these rules of evidence, it is hardly surprising that there were very few acquittals in crim. con. cases.

In 1794 there occurred an example of the way in which in a crim. con. case a wife could be made the victim of a collusive agreement behind her back between the husband and her supposed lover. The defendant had assembled a group of witnesses on his behalf in order to offset the one witness against him, but he never called on them to testify in court. The reason was that the husband had made a last-minute agreement with him 'to the great injury of the character and hurt of mind of the wife'. The deal was that the defendant would not produce his witnesses in court, and would allow the jury to convict him and award damages. In return the husband would pay all his legal expenses, and would not receive the damages awarded; or if he did receive them would secretly pay them back.[180]

More serious was the incentive to the husband deliberately to set a trap for his wife.[181] The most notorious example of a suit by a husband seeking to exploit the action for profit was that launched in 1836 by Mr

[177] *St James's Chronicle*, 25 Feb. 1775: 3 (quoted in Menafee, 217).
[178] *Parslow v. Sykes*, 1789, BL, 1132. g. 102. 18.   [179] *Crim. Con. Gaz.* 1: 4.
[180] *Elwes v. Harvey* (1796), *Eng. Rep.* 161: 555 n. *; LPCA, D. 675. 500–10.
[181] *Parl. Hist.* 35: 278, 319, 322; *Massey v. Marquis of Headfort* (1804), RIA/HP, 872 (1) 28. See also *Bon Ton Mag.* 1 (1791), 329.

George Norton against the prime minister, Lord Melbourne. The trial inevitably had strong political overtones, the Tories hoping and suspecting guilt and the Whigs stoutly maintaining innocence. The defence counsel showed that Mr Norton had many times walked his wife to Melbourne's door in Downing Street and had left her there, thus proving either that he did not seriously suspect his wife of adultery, or that he had connived at it in return for the lucrative government job given him by Melbourne.

No plausible evidence was produced in court to suggest that the relationship was more than what both Melbourne and Mrs Norton to the end of their lives claimed it to have been—the platonic attraction of a busy politician in his late fifties and separated from his wife to an intelligent and beautiful married woman in her late twenties. On the other hand, Melbourne had a reputation as an adulterer, and Caroline Norton evidently knew all about his flagellant tastes, joking about them in her letters to him. At the time, Lord Malmesbury commented that, if true, the verdict of acquittal indicated that 'Melbourne had had more opportunities than any man ever had before, and made no use of them.'[182]

Some husbands and wives were tempted to conspire together to lure a wealthy man, catch him in the act of seduction, sue him for crim. con., and then quietly share the damages between them. The novelists had long anticipated such a development. In 1751, Fielding in *Amelia* has Mr Trent rent his wife to a lord in return for a promise of promotion to office, which was not fulfilled. He then, with two witnesses, catches them in bed, and exerts blackmail by threatening a crim. con. action. When challenged to a duel by the lord, he refuses to fight, explaining frankly: 'My Lord, it would be the highest imprudence in me to kill a man who is now become so considerably my debtor.'[183] This one, admittedly sardonic, sentence of Fielding's epitomizes the perceived shift in concepts of honour from the early seventeenth to the mid-eighteenth centuries.

There were two notorious cases in the eighteenth century which drew public attention to the problem of connivance between spouses in a wife's adultery. In 1737–8, the actor–playwright Theophilus Cibber and his wife established a ménage à trois with Mr William Sloper: every evening Mrs Cibber undressed in the marital bedroom, and then retired across the hall to the bedroom of the lodger, who paid for the rent and

---

[182] J. G. Perkins, *The Life of Mrs Norton* (London, 1909), 88–95; H. M. Hyde, *A Tangled Web: Sex Scandals in British Politics and Society* (London, 1986), 63–9; *The Letters of Caroline Norton to Lord Melbourne*, ed. J. O'Hoge and C. Olney (Ohio State University Press, 1974), 157–8; J. H. Harris, Lord Malmesbury, *Memoirs of an Ex-Minister* (London, 1884).

[183] H. Fielding, *Amelia* (Everyman edn.), 236–8.

full maintenance for all three. Eventually, however, Cibber became greedy, and sued the lodger for £5,000 damages for crim. con., described as an attack on 'his peace of mind, his happiness, and his hopes of posterity'. But the story came out in court, and the defence counsel, William Murray, tore Cibber's case to shreds: 'He takes his money, lets him maintain his family, resigns his wife to him, and then comes to court for justice, for reparations in damages.' He concluded that 'there is no denomination in coin small enough to give in damages'. The jury duly awarded Cibber a nominal £10, and he became a public laughing stock. In no way abashed, Cibber tried again the next year, bringing an action in King's Bench against the lodger for damages of £10,000 for 'detaining' his wife. This time the jury awarded him £500, but by now Mrs Cibber, her lover and their child had all disappeared.[184]

Six years before, in 1732, literature had anticipated life. In *The Modern Husband*, Fielding had portrayed an anti-hero, Mr Modern, a man ruined by the South Sea Bubble and looking for a way to recoup his losses and avoid arrest for debt. Lord Richly had been showing an interest in Mrs Modern, and she in him. Mr Modern warns her brutally: 'Your person is mine; I bought it lawfully in the church, and unless I am to profit by the disposal, I shall keep it all for my own use.' When his wife asks him what he wants her to do, he replies: 'Suffer me to discover you together; by which means we may make our fortunes easy all at once. One good discovery at Westminster Hall will be of greater service than [Lord Richly's] utmost generosity.' When Mrs Modern protests: 'But then, my reputation . . .' her husband brushes aside this trivial consideration: 'Pooh, you will have enough to gild it; never fear your reputation while you are rich.' A detached observer of the scene comments cynically: 'It is a stock-jobbing age, everything has its price. Marriage is a traffic throughout; as most of us bargain to be husbands, some of us bargain to be cuckolds.'[185]

The second notorious case of husband and wifely connivance occurred in 1782, when Colonel Sir Richard Worseley, the controller of the royal household, sued Mr G. M. Bissett for £20,000 for eloping with his wife, Seymour. At the trial, it came out that Worseley, who seems to have had the sexual tastes of King Candaules, had raised Bissett up on

[184] F. Truelove, *The Comforts of Matrimony, exemplified in the memorable Case and Tryal lately brought by T. C. against W. S. esq. for crim. con. with the Plaintiff's Wife* (London, 1739); see also M. Nash, *The Provoked Wife* (New York, 1977), 142–6, 160–2; H. Fielding, 'Juvenal's Sixth Satire Modernized in Burlesque Verse', in L. Stephen (ed.), *The Works of Henry Fielding*, (London, 1882), 12: 309.

[185] H. Fielding, *The Modern Husband* (1732), I/iv; IV/i; II/viii; see also T. Smollett, *Ferdinand Count Fathom* (1743), chs. 36–7.

his shoulders so that the latter could peer through an upper window and see Lady Worseley naked as she washed herself (Plate 32).[186]

C. COLLUSION

Collusion was a far more more common threat to the integrity of the crim. con. system than connivance. By the 1790s, it was a well-known and openly admitted fact that in an increasing number of cases, indeed the great majority, the case itself was collusive. By pre-arrangement, the damages were first paid by the defendant to the plaintiff, who then secretly returned all or part of them back to him. This procedure developed primarily because of a common desire by the husband, his wife, and her lover to obtain an uncontested divorce so as to allow all three to remarry. Having lost faith in the religious grounds for the indissolubility of marriage, members of the landed elite and professional people no longer felt any moral scruples about thus conspiring to obtain a divorce by mutual consent. As a cuckolded husband suing for damages in 1811 observed with unusual frankness: 'I am not in want of money, but of a divorce.'[187]

To achieve this end, the husband first entered into an agreement with his wife that she would not oppose a separation suit in the ecclesiastical court or a divorce bill in Parliament on grounds of recrimination—that is, by producing in court or Parliament evidence of this own adultery, which was usually available. In some cases it was the wife who threatened her husband in order to force him into acquiescence. Thus in 1809 Mrs Chambers, who was seeking a divorce in order to marry her lover Caulfield, wrote to her husband: 'If you will give up the damages against Caulfield, I will give up my defence in the Ecclesiastical Court—I have proofs against you [about his adulteries] which shall be brought forward before the court and before the world unless you comply.'[188] In other cases, the husband took the initiative to persuade his wife. The carrot used to obtain her consent was a promise of a handsome life annuity, and the knowledge that after the marriage she would be free to marry her lover; the stick was a threat that unless she complied, her husband would ruin her lover by exacting every penny of damages. Based on these prior

---

[186] Anon., *Memoirs of Sir Finical Whimsey and his Lady* (London, 1782); LPCA, D.2324; *The Trial of Sir Richard Worseley v. Captain G. M. Bissett*, BL, 518. 1. 12(1); *Walpole's Correspondence*, 25: 227–8, 245. For similar cases, see *Gordon* v. *Mathews* (1793), *Lond. Chron.* (1793), 1: 202: Gordon claimed £20,000 but got nothing; other cases include: *Norton* v. *Parsons* (1795) ibid. (1795), 1: 171; *Allen* v. *Hodges* (1796), *The Register of the Times*, 1 (1795), 55.
[187] *Defries* v. *Holden*, GLRO, London CC, DL/C/189.
[188] *Chambers* v. *Caulfield* (1809), *Eng. Rep.* 161: 613.

agreements, the two uncontested suits, in King's Bench and an ecclesiastical court, and an uncontested bill of divorce in Parliament, would all go forward, the three parties being very careful to conceal all traces of their double collusion. After the divorce act was passed, the money was returned by the lover to the husband, the ex-wife married the lover, and the husband found himself another wife. In practice, the result was a divorce by mutual consent for the purpose of starting two new legal households.

Apart from gaining the freedom to remarry, a second great benefit of collusion was the huge savings in taxed legal costs from an undefended suit, which might amount to between £200 to £500 (Table 9.5). The true savings in costs would certainly be much larger, in view of the fact that in the most hotly contested and expensive suits in the ecclesiastical courts, the taxed costs were sometimes little more than half of what was claimed, and what was claimed was only a portion of the total.[189]

Collusion in crim. con. cases in King's Bench certainly existed by 1768, when the Duke of Grafton and Viscount Bolingbroke both entered into agreements with their wives and the latters' lovers not to collect the damages, in order to obtain agreement to conceal their own adulteries and so procure Parliamentary divorces.[190] Over the next fifty years, some forty cases of collusion are definitely known or strongly suspected, and there must have been dozens of others which went undetected.

In the debate in Parliament in 1800, Lord Eldon claimed that nine out of ten cases of crim. con. were 'founded in the most infamous collusion'. He went on to complain that 'As the law stands, it is a farce and a mockery, most of the cases being previously settled in some room in the City, and juries are called to give exemplary damages, which damages are never paid to, nor expected by, the injured husband.'[191] Half a century later, in 1857, the same point—that collusion in crim. con. actions was a normal procedure—was reiterated by the home secretary, Sir George Grey, and by Lord Lyndhurst, both of whom were in a position to know the truth.[192] So disturbed did Parliament become about the situation that after 1809 the House of Lords demanded proof that damages had been paid. Attorneys and bankers were summoned to testify that they had actually received the money.[193] But this did little to help detect collusion, because, as a witness to a Parliamentary commission observed half a century later in 1852, 'If the parties are anxious to collude, what is to

---

[189] Anderson, 437–9.
[190] See Stone, *Broken Lives*, the Grafton case.
[191] *Parl. Hist.* 35: 237, 252, 280.　　　[192] 3 *Hansard.* 147: 1983; 145: 781–2.
[193] MacQueen, *House of Lords*, 493.

prevent the plaintiff from receiving the damages with his right hand, and then as soon as the bill of divorce has passed, returning them with his left?'[194]

This collusion, which spread like a cancer through the whole crim. con. and Parliamentary divorce process after 1770, provides a classic example of how unintended consequences arise at least in part from changes introduced for totally different purposes—in this case, an increase in the size of damages in crim. con. cases in order to punish sexual immorality. As Lord Kenyon discovered to his dismay, there were social, cultural, and psychological forces at work which would convert his drive for moral reformation by repression into a fraudulent means of facilitating marital separation, or occasionally into a tool for the criminal entrapment of unwary wives or their wealthy male admirers.

Heavy damages remained overtly functional merely for the handful of husbands who were not only determined to secure for themselves the money awarded to them, but also actually succeeded in doing so. They were now covertly functional for the very much larger number of husbands, wives, and lovers who had no qualms about conspiring to use the action to obtain a divorce by mutual consent, but who did have strong moral scruples about making money out of the wife's shame. In this respect there was a clear revival—or re-emergence into the open—of that sense of honour which until 1692 had prevented members of the landed elite from using the crim. con. action at all. After 1780, they increasingly used the action, but more and more of them secretly refused to touch the money. Thus by making a crim. con. action a necessary prelude to a Parliamentary divorce, Parliament assured the survival of the empty shell of the former until the latter was legislated out of existence.

D. FLIGHT

Another wholly unanticipated result of the imposition of huge punitive damages in crim. con. actions, far in excess of the capacity of the defendant to pay, was evasive action taken by defendants in that minority of cases in which, for motives of greed or revenge, the plaintiff was determined to enforce collection of the damages. Increasingly, lovers thus threatened did not wait for the trial, but sold their possessions and took refuge in exile abroad, frequently taking the plaintiffs' wives with them. In 1792 it was observed that 'the culprit prefers a residence in some other country rather than pay a sum which would reduce him

---

[194] *Roy. Com. Divorce, 1853.* 1: 18 n. 9; see also the remarks of Dr Lushington, an ecclesiastical court official, in 1830 (2 *Hansard,* 23: 1385).

almost to penury'.[195] Most fled to Scotland or the Continent. Some went to the East or West Indies or America, and one as far as South Africa.[196] Any exile, however remote, was better than rotting for life in a debtors' prison in London. For example, when in 1815 Lord Rosebery was awarded £15,000 damages against his brother-in-law Sir Henry Mild-may, the latter fled (with Lady Rosebery) to the Continent with a chariot and piles of clothes and furniture, leaving nothing behind but some £2,000 worth of furniture in his house. In order to avoid arrest for the unpaid £15,000 damages, and because the subsequent marriage of the adulterous couple in Stuttgart, after the Parliamentary divorce, was incestuous by English law, they could never return to England. They remained in exile until they died, many years later. Similarly in 1816, when Sir William Abdy was awarded £7,000 damages for crim. con. against Lord Charles Bentinck, he found that he could not collect a penny, since Lord Charles had sold all his goods and fled to Paris.[197]

E. CONCLUSION

During a debate in the House of Lords in 1800, the master of the rolls denounced 'the vindictive damages to the husband' that had recently been awarded. The result, he claimed, was first that the husband 'might now sell his wife's honour for a piece of money'. Second, 'husbands often connived at the misconduct of their wives in the hope of being enriched by the damages they were likely to receive'. Third, 'it very frequently happened that the damages are not exacted and the adulterer escaped unpunished'; and fourth, '[Parliamentary] divorces were granted when they ought to have been refused', as when 'the husband intimidated the wife from disclosing his misconduct, by threatening to act harshly to her paramour' by exacting large damages.[198] A more damning indictment of the practical consequences of the crim. con. action could hardly be imagined.

Because of these unintended and very unwelcome consequences of Lord Kenyon's habit of frequently awarding very large damages in crim. con. actions, his judicial colleagues felt obliged to challenge him.[199] But it

---

[195] *T & C Mag.* 24 (1792), 484.

[196] *2 Hansard*, 23 (1830), 1385.

[197] *The Times*, 12 Dec. 1814: 3; *JH Lords*, 50: 205. See also *Abdy* v. *Bentinck* (1816), *The Annual Register . . . for the year 1815* (London, 1816), 283–6; *JH Lords*, 50: 620; H. M. Hyde, *A Tangled Web: Sex Scandals in British Politics and Society* (London, 1986), 45–9.

[198] *Parl. Hist.* 35: 319, 322, 325.

[199] Campbell, *Lives of the Chief Justices*, 4: 74; *Fowler* v. *Hodgson* (1807), *Crim. Con. Gaz.* 1: 94; for the last known statement of the Kenyon doctrine, see *Massey* v. *Marquis of Headfort* (1804) RIA/HP, 872(1). 86–8.

took the dramatist and MP, R. B. Sheridan, to put him in his place during a debate in the House of Commons in 1800: 'A learned gentleman has talked of exemplary damages being given. To talk of exemplary damages in civil actions is talking exemplary nonsense. Who told juries that they were to be the *custodes morum?* The man who stated this doctrine was responsible for the effect it produced.'[200]

Despite this onslaught, the moral panic whipped up by Kenyon did not begin to subside until about 1820, when judges began to direct juries to adjust the damages to the capacity of the defendants to pay, and so to keep them out of prison.[201] As a result, after about 1830 the era of exorbitant damages slowly died away (Fig. 9.3, Table 9.3), and in 1838 Parliament passed a law limiting imprisonment for inability to pay damages to two years. [202] Thus, both lawyers and politicans were being affected by the new climate of penal reform.

9. The Moral Reaction

A. MORAL SCRUPLES ABOUT TAKING DAMAGES

The first clear evidence of a moral reaction against the crim. con. procedure was the growing reluctance of plaintiffs to accept such tainted money as damages. During the debate in the House of Lords over the adultery bill in 1800, the Duke of Clarence referred to 'the pretty generally known fact that the husband who, by suing for pecuniary damages, obtained a verdict, was considered not a very honourable man if, when he received them, he put them in his own pocket, instead of returning them to the purse of the defendant'. Nine years later, Lord Auckland referred to damages in crim. con. cases as money 'which in many cases the injured husband is ashamed to receive'. This growing repugnance at trading honour for cash appears again and again in statements by counsel for the plaintiff between the 1790s and the 1850s.[203]

---

[200] *Parl. Hist.* 35: 325; for similar complaints by C. W. Wynn in the House of Commons in the 1830s, see 2 *Hansard*, 24: 1284.

[201] *Lord Beresford* v. *Earl Bective* (1816), *Crim. Con. Gaz.* 1: 63; *Baring* v. *Webster* (1822), ibid. 2: 207–8; *Swetenham* v. *MacNaghton* (1823), ibid. 62. See also *Flight* v. *Willat* (1823), Anon., *A Familiar Compendium of the Law of Husband and Wife* (London, 1831), 41–3; MacQueen, *House of Lords*, 495, 657; *Taylor* v. *Boyle* (1838), *Crim. Con. Gaz.* 2: 283–4; *Close* v. *Parker* (1838), ibid. 1: 21–2; the plaintiff had asked for £3,000 from a man earning at most £300 a year. The defence counsel had described this as 'absurd', and the jury awarded £350.

[202] 1–2 Vict. cap. 110, para. 78.

[203] *Parl. Hist.* 20: 229; 1 *Hansard*, 14: 326. To cite only two examples among many, see *Hodges* v. *Wyndham* (1791), *NC Trials for Adultery* (1797), 1: 4; *Close* v. *Parker* (1838), *Crim. Con. Gaz.* 1: 21–2; *Foley* v. *Peterborough* (1785), (BL, 578. 1. 12), 4.

In other words, there was developing a system of principled collusion, not as a blackmail bargain between husband and lover, but as an honourable solution to a dishonourable necessity, in order to obtain a divorce. Such well-informed judges as lords Thurlow, Eldon, and Kenyon admitted that this form of principled collusion was very common. Once a wife's body ceased to be regarded as a part of her husband's property, and once frustrated domestic happiness rather than injury to masculine honour became the prime stated cause for financial reparation, the moral foundation of the crim. con. action crumbled to dust. Erskine, who for over twenty years had made a handsome living from acting as prosecuting counsel in crim. con. cases, now underwent a change of heart. He remarked in the House of Commons that 'the man who could consider any sum as a satisfaction for such an injury deserved no damages at all'.[204]

The clearest statement from a litigant of this moral revulsion came in 1805, when the Revd J. Moore was seeking a divorce from Parliament because of the adultery of his wife. He was closely interrogated about the payment of the £1,000 damages awarded to him for crim. con., which he frankly admitted he had not claimed. When asked why not, he replied: 'because it is not consistent with my principles to take damages ... because I do not wish that either I or my children should put money taken from such a source into our pockets'. But he decided that 'there was nothing dishonourable in taking the amount of what expenses I might be put to here'.[205]

The moral panic which had been expressed in such exaggerated and illegal forms by Lord Kenyon now created a quite different response among both the public at large and the legislators. Evangelical religion was spreading among the elite, as was Methodism among the lower middle class. Both religious movements were highly moralistic in their content and their effect upon adherents. Many now wanted to modify or abolish the crim. con. action itself, although few wanted to allow seducers of married women to go unpunished, since it was believed that this was both morally objectionable and a threat to the social fabric of the family.

The obvious solution was to make adultery a criminal act, subject to punishment by fine or imprisonment. This proposal was first introduced into Parliament in 1800 by Lord Auckland as a bill 'for the purpose of doing away with the action for criminal conversation'. Despite the fact that Auckland's idea of suitable punishment for adultery was two or three

[204] *Parl. Hist.* 35: 229, 234, 252; see also ibid. 278, 326.
[205] *Moore v. Durnford* (1805), *JH Lords*, 45: 213.

years in solitary confinement, in the wave of moral reformism it was supported by Lord Eldon, most of the law lords, the bishops, and many peers. Despite the support in the House of Commons of the master of the rolls, Sir William Scott, Pitt himself, Windham, and Wilberforce, the bill failed. But the idea did not die,[206] and was extensively discussed again during the debates in Parliament over the first Divorce Act in 1857.

B. LEGAL JUSTICE FOR WOMEN

During the eighteenth century, especially the latter half, protests by women about unequal legal treatment and the double sexual standard had been steadily increasing in volume and intellectual coherence.[207] Recognition of the strength of the argument in influential male circles was strikingly displayed in the opposition in the House of Commons to all four bills introduced between 1771 and 1809 to forbid a wife divorced for adultery from marrying her lover. In 1779 Charles James Fox objected not only that such a ban would ruin these women's lives, but that it was unjust to lay all the, punishment on the woman and let the man go scot-free. He also argued that since women were entirely unrepresented in Parliament, they were therefore entitled to 'the most tender treatment'.[208] In 1800, support for this position that a ban on remarriage with a lover was unfair to women was widespread in the House of Lords.[209]

As a result of the slow growth of this attitude, by the 1830s it was becoming quite common to argue that the whole legal procedure of crim. con. was grossly unjust to women. More and more thoughtful men and women began to realize that in a crim. con. suit, a wife could be falsely charged by a husband anxious only to be rid of her, or falsely blamed for enticement, or falsely accused of previous promiscuity by a lover anxious to mitigate the damages awarded against him. In all these circumstances, she was legally helpless to make known her side of the case. Nor in a suit at common law was it open to her to bring before the court evidence of her husband's prior adulteries, cruelty, or indifference to her, as was the case in the church courts or Parliament. In 1824 a canon law handbook asked, 'how can that be evidence against a party which had passed in a suit to which she was not party?'[210]

In 1809, Erskine admitted that 'much of his knowledge could not come

---

[206] Plowden, 1: 316.

[207] A. Browne, *The Eighteenth-Century Feminist Mind* (London, 1987), pt. 2; K. L. M. Rogers, *Feminism in Eighteenth-Century England* (Brighton, 1982).

[208] *Parl. Hist.* 20: 599; see also 17: 185.

[209] *Ibid.* 20: 593, 595, 597–600; 35: 228, 230, 236–7, 241, 255, 262, 278–9, 282, 302–3, 307, 323–4.   [210] Poynter, 200.

before the court' since the wife's story could not be presented to it.[211] For example, in 1836, during the suit of *Norton* v. *Lord Melbourne*, Mrs Norton had been obliged to sit helplessly by while discharged servants told lies about her in court which, given an opportunity, she could easily have disproved. She wrote bitterly to a friend: 'a woman is made a helpless wretch by these laws of men, or she would be allowed a defence, a counsel, in such an hour. . . . To go for nothing in a trial which decides one's fate for life is very hard.'[212] In 1855, shortly before the abolition of the crim. con. action, there was a flurry of pamphlets, articles, and speeches denouncing it because of its unfairness to women.[213]

In the House of Lords these pleas for justice for wives were supported by an unusual alliance of four great legal luminaries: Lord Brougham, Lord Campbell, the aged Lord Lyndhurst, and Lord St Leonards, the last of whom castigated the crim. con. action as 'a disgrace to the country . . . a stigma on the law of England'.[214] In the debate over the Divorce Act in 1857, Lord Lyndhurst concluded eloquently:

The woman has everything at stake—her character, her fair fame, her home, the society of her children, her position in the world, all her future prospects of happiness; and yet . . . though she has such a stake in the result, she is not allowed to take any part whatever in the action. Can anything be more scandalous and more inconsistent with the principles of justice?[215]

C. THE IDEAL OF VICTORIAN DOMESTICITY

At the same time as influential male legislators were realizing the need for greater justice for women, public opinion was moving towards a new ideal of Victorian domesticity.[216] There was a shifting of the balance away from the traditional view of women as property, and towards the concept of marriage as a contract for the development of mutual comfort and domestic happiness. Lord Kenyon's stress on the moral turpitude associated with acts of seduction and adultery struck a strong chord in the new moralism of middle-class judges and juries. As a result, in their directions to juries about the criteria upon which to assess damages, judges began changing the balance of factors to be taken into account. Less

---

[211] 1 *Hansard*, 14: 332–3.

[212] Perkins, *The Life of Mrs Norton* (n. 182 above), 95–6.

[213] Anon., *Remarks upon the Law of Marriage and Divorce Suggested by the Hon. Mrs Norton's Letter to the Queen* (London, 1855), 6–10 (Bodl. G Pamph. 2429); *Law Review*, 23 (1855–6), 85–6.

[214] C. Norton, *A Letter to the Queen on Lord Chancellor Cranworth's Marriage and Divorce Bill* (London, 1855), 10–11. [215] 3 *Hansard*, 145: 782; 147: 1646; 142: 422.

[216] W. E. Houghton, *The Victorian Frame of Mind* (New Haven, 1957), 348–93.

emphasis was given to status and wealth, and more to moral qualities: a wife's chastity, probity, devotion as a mother to her children and as a friend and companion to her husband, as well as her educational accomplishments, her physical beauty, and her competence as a household manager. Moreover the lover was now pilloried more as a home-wrecker and a destroyer of domestic bliss, and less as a trespasser upon private property.

One straw in the wind was a significant change in the arguments used in defence of the double standard of sexual morality, by which husbands could take mistresses with impunity whereas wives were subject to moral obloquy and economic ruin, and their lovers to heavy damage in a crim. con. suit. Right through the eighteenth century, the standard defence had been that a wife's infidelity involved a threat to property since she might introduce a bastard child as inheritor of the estate. In 1803 an Irish lawyer abandoned this ancient defence and tried a new one, based on the theory that the effect of sexual transgression upon marital sentiment and affection was quite different in the two sexes:

The consequences resulting from the infidelity of a husband and wife are very different. It is the nature of man that he may have a connexion with other women, besides his wife, and yet have a sincere affection for her; but a married woman never yet made a sacrifice of virtue without, at the same time, making a sacrifice of every sentiment of honour, decency and decorum, which are guardians of connubial felicity and domestic happiness.[217]

The double standard now rested on a theory about a fundamental difference between male and female sexual psychology: a man commits adultery as an act of pure sensuality, for instantaneous physical gratification; a woman commits adultery only as a by-product of a deep emotional commitment. An MP in 1857 tersely quoted a French aphorism that for men adultery is 'a surprise of the senses', but for women 'a surprise of the heart'.[218] Although plausible, this is obviously a much weaker argument than that based on property rights and fear of inheritance by spurious children.

10. The Abolition of the Action in 1857

A. THE OPPOSITION TO CRIM. CON.

Moral revulsion to the crim. con. action had been building up for half a century when in 1857 the first divorce bill was introduced into Parlia-

---

[217] *Pentland* v. *Clarke*, RIA/HP, 849. 57.   [218] 3 *Hansard*, 147: 1274, 1558.

*Anne Buckley discovers Mr. Mully and Mrs. Worgan with Mrs. Worgan's Coats half up,
and Mr. Mully endeavouring to Conceal that his Breeches are down.*

17. Adultery Interrupted

18. Curiosity, 1817

19. A Master and his Maid, *c.* 1788

20. Court of King's Bench, by T. Rowlandson, 1808

21. Adultery Discovered, by T. Rowlandson, c. 1800

A
NEW AND COMPLETE COLLECTION
OF

Trials for Adultery:
OR
A GENERAL HISTORY OF
MODERN

GALLANTRY and DIVORCES.

CONTAINING

All the moſt remarkable TRIALS heard and determined in the *Courts* of *Doctors' Commons*, the *King's Bench*, &c. &c. for

ADULTERY,		CRUELTY,
FORNICATION,		INCEST,

AND OTHER
CRIMINAL CONVERSATION, IMPOTENCY, &c.

From the Year 1780 *to the Middle of the Year* 1797.

TOGETHER WITH
The SUBSTANCE of the EVIDENCE on each Cauſe, and the CORRESPONDENCE between the AMOROUS PARTIES.

INCLUDING ALSO
The moſt remarkable *Trials* for *Adultery*, &c. in *Wales, Ireland*, and *Scotland*, during the ſaid Period. Being a Work comprehending ſelect Reports of the Court of Doctors' Commons, &c. and which will include a Complete Hiſtory of the Private Lives, Intrigues, and Amours, of many Characters in the moſt elevated Spheres of Life ;—as every Scene and Tranſaction, however Ridiculous, Whimſical, or Extraordinary, will be fairly repreſented, as becomes a Faithful Hiſtorian, who is determined not to ſacrifice Truth at the Shrine of Guilt and Folly.

Interſperſed with ſome of the moſt remarkable and curious Trials for CRIM. CON. &c. *prior to the above Period.*

The Whole taken in Short Hand, from the *Records* of the *Courts* of *Doctors' Commons*, the *King's Bench*, &c. and arranged for Publication, with Reflections upon the numerous Caſes,

By a CIVILIAN of DOCTORS COMMONS.

EMBELLISHED with an ELEGANT SET of PLATES, Repreſenting the moſt ſtriking Scenes deſcribed in the Work, whether Humorous, Ridiculous, Whimſical, or Amorous.

VOL. I.

LONDON:

Printed, for the Proprietors, by J. GILL ;—Sold at the Shops of PARSONS and HOGG, in *Paternoſter-Row ;* and may be had of all the Bookſellers, Newſcarriers, &c. in every Part of Great Britain and Ireland.

1796.

22. *Trials for Adultery* (London, 1780): Title page

PREFACE.

THE great Defire which Readers of every Defcription entertain for well-reported Cafes of ADULTERY, FORNICÁ-TION, SEDUCTION, and all Kinds of CRIMINAL CONVERSATION, and the uncommon Avidity with which former Accounts of the kind have always been received, together with the Benefits likely to accrue to the Public, by laying before them authentic Relations of the *heavy Damages*, and other fatal Confequences unavoidably attendant on *illicit Amours*, have induced the Editor hereof to felect and procure from the Records of the Courts, the moft remarkable Trials of this Nature, from the Year 1780 to the prefent Time, including genuine Narratives of ILLEGAL ELOPEMENTS, UNEQUAL MARRIAGES, CALEDONIAN EXCURSIONS, PRIVATE INTRIGUES, AMOURS, &c. with faithful Copies of the feveral Exhibits, LOVE LETTERS, SONNETS, &c. which are, on thefe Occafions, the general *Telegraphs* of Love from one Party to another.

A Publication of this Kind will, it is prefumed, afford no lefs Improvement than Entertainment. Accounts of Vices,

1   A 2   the

23. *Trials for Adultery* (London, 1780): Preface

24. *Lt Peter RN v. J. Hancock, Grocer, for Crim. Con.*, 1824

25. Mrs Parslow and Captain Sykes, 1789

Miss Roberts sitting naked in L.d Grosvenor's lap at the Hotel in Leicester fields.

26. Adultery in a Hotel: Lord Grosvenor and a Prostitute, 1770

27. Adultery of Caroline Lady Harrington and her Footman, 1778

28. Lord Chief Justice Kenyon, by John Opie

A Legal Faint i,e, a Feint.

29. Thomas Erskine, Barrister, Fainting at his own Eloquence, 1791

30. Lord Erskine's Marriage to Sarah Buck at Gretna Green, 1820

31. The Danger of Crim. Con. Damages, 1797

Sir Richard Worse—than—sly,
Exposing his Wifes Bottom; O fye!

32. Sir Richard Worseley and Mr G. M. Bissett, 1782

ment. It is hardly surprising, therefore, that a good deal of time and rhetoric was spent on an ultimately successful effort to insert a clause abolishing the action. Lord Chancellor Cranworth introduced the subject into the House of Lords with the admission that 'the feelings of mankind revolted at the notion of a husband making a sort of profit from his wife's disgrace and his own dishonour'. Lord Lansdowne declared: 'these proceedings are founded on the monstrous assumption that the affection of a wife is to be treated as the loss of an ordinary chattel, and is to be compensated in pounds, shillings and pence'.[219] The aged Lord Lyndhurst, in his youth no mean rake himself, asked rhetorically, 'What common measure is there between the wounded feelings, the affliction, the domestic misery, occasioned by a violation of the sanctity of marriage, and the pounds, shillings and pence of a tradesman's ledger?' Lord St Leonards expressed his belief that 'many persons would rather touch a scorpion than the money which is awarded as damages in compensation for their dishonour'.[220]

Similar expressions of shame and disgust about the crim. con. action were also used in the House of Commons.[221] Outside Parliament, the *Westminster Review* agreed that it was disgraceful that a crim. con. action should treat the seduction of a wife just like damage to any other piece of property.[222] Thus, what had seemed perfectly reasonable to all in the eighteenth century had by the 1850s become 'monstrous', 'abominable', and 'odious'. The reason for this passionate sense of shame about crim. con. stemmed from the fact that it confused the external world of commerce and the market-place with the private world of Victorian domesticity and love, two spheres which the public mind was coming increasingly to view as entirely separate.[223] As a result, the old undemocratic, unsentimental, half-mercantile, half-patriarchal view of female chastity had become abhorrent to the respectable sectors of the Victorian public, the lawyers, and the legislators. The Victorians had finally come to believe that wives were also entitled to a share of the world's virtue and honour, and that neither should be traded for money.

By the 1850s the great law lords were particularly upset about the crim. con. action because of the withering criticism it received from their continental colleagues. The future lord chancellor, Lord Campbell, spoke for them all when in 1857 he said bitterly in the House of Lords: 'I

---

[219] Ibid., 145: 491; 142: 1974.
[220] Ibid. 145: 782–3; 147: 2031; see also the Bishops of Lincoln and Oxford, ibid. 145: 537; 143: 231.
[221] Ibid. 147: 723, 1745; see also Ibid. 1838, 2051, 2052.
[222] Anon, 'The English Law of Divorce', *The Westminster Review*, 65 (April 1856).
[223] Houghton, *The Victorian Frame of Mind*, 348–93.

am ashamed of it. I have been taunted with it by foreigners, and have blushed when I was obliged to confess that such was the law of the land.'[224] Lord Lansdowne told the House: 'There is no other country in the world where such actions are brought. On the Continent, they are looked upon with feelings of disgust and horror; and it is wondered at that a civilized country like this should maintain a law of this description.'[225] In the Commons, the attorney-general and other members joined in the chorus of denunciation.[226] Indeed, the two things which foreign jurists seem to have known was that English husbands did not hesitate either to put their wives up for auction in a cattle market, with halters round their necks, or to make a financial profit from the adultery of their wives. Both confirmed the continental stereotype of the English as a nation of shop-keepers.[227] These charges were devastating to a political elite which was just beginning to assume the high calling of taking up the White Man's burden to bring civilization, Christianity, and morality to backward, heathen peoples.

The second charge levelled against the crim. con. action in 1857 was its adverse effect upon public morals because of the publicity which surrounded the more sensational cases. The peers in the House of Lords were particularly sensitive to this issue, since in the previous year the Talbot divorce bill had dragged on for three days, during which 'most indecent details were given, which were subsequently printed and circulated throughout this country and indeed throughout Europe'.[228] A journalist complained that in these trials the 'foulest of French novelists might have learned something from the innuendoes gratuitously thrown out on either side'.[229] In the Commons, an MP observed that 'there is nothing more pernicious to public morals than the publication of the proceedings in actions of criminal conversation'. The Bishop of Lincoln pointed out that, now that Parliament had just passed a strict Obscene Publications Act, 'the reports in the newspapers are the only authorized immoral publications'.[230]

The third objection to the crim. con. action was the known fact that the vast majority of these actions were collusive, in order to obtain an uncontested divorce, so that they were useless for the discovery of truth. And the last was that by excluding the wife from the trial altogether,

---

[224] 3 *Hansard*, 145: 513.
[225] Ibid. 142: 1970, 1974; see also comments by Lord St Leonards in 1854 (ibid. 134: 23).
[226] Ibid. 147: 723, 756, 765, 871, 1745, 1838.
[227] Ibid. 142: 1977; 144: 714; 145: 926–7.
[228] Ibid. 145: 781; for details of the Talbot case, see *Crim. Con. A & T.* 11–25.
[229] Anon., 'The Last of Criminal Conversation', *Saturday Review*, 3 (1857), 590.
[230] 3 *Hansard*, 142: 1975; 145: 537; 147: 1755, 1758, 1759.

grave injustice was often done to her, a point repeatedly brought up by the aged Lord Lyndhurst under the prodding of his friend Caroline Norton.[231]

One of the very few open defenders of the crim. con. action in Parliament was Lord Wensleydale. He raised all the old arguments in its favour: that it offered a legal remedy for a real injury; that it was silly to call it disgraceful to take damages for the loss of a wife's services because of her adultery, since this was no different from taking damages for libel, slander, seduction, or breach of promise—all provided monetary compensation for psychic wounds. He went on to argue that it was only very rarely that the husband and the lover conspired to traduce a wife in open court. He pointed out that a husband suffered real financial losses from a divorce: in the upper classes, he lost the use of his wife's estate; in the lower classes he lost the use of her earnings; in all classes he lost her services as manager of his household and supervisor of the education of his children. Finally, he expressed his belief that the action was a deterrent to male seducers of married women, and therefore helped to reduce adultery. Lord Chancellor Cranworth added the telling point that the crim. con. action could not be as offensive to public opinion as the opponents of it made out, since the juries in such actions continued to award substantial damages, even if not as large as in former times.[232]

In his defence of crim. con., Lord Wensleydale represented only a minority opinion, and in 1857 the only obstacle to the abolition of the action was the lack of consensus on what to put in its place. As Lord Cranworth warned: 'If you abolish an action for criminal conversation, what do you propose as a substitute? That is the real practical difficulty.' The most serious problem with abolishing the action outright was that this would leave a poor husband without any money to help pay for his legal costs in obtaining a divorce.[233] Lord Brougham agreed that for the poor, the loss of a wife caused real economic hardship which deserved some economic compensation through damages.[234] It was pointed out how often poor families were dependent upon a wife's income for support, an income which was lost if the wife was persuaded to elope.[235]

In the House of Commons, some MPs argued that the crim. con. action also offered the poor man his only remedy against a rich man who

---

[231] Ibid. 142: 409, 1970; 145: 783–4.
[232] 3 *Hansard*, 146: 230–1, 922–4; 145: 919–20. [233] Ibid. 145: 919.
[234] Ibid. 146: 208. [235] Ibid. 1869; 147: 1833, 1835.

had seduced his wife. Mr Adams reported the case of a woman who worked in a factory to support her sick husband and their children. The overseer threatened to take away her job if she did not give in to his sexual demands. With her family's interests at heart, she reluctantly allowed herself to be seduced by the overseer. Her husband did not want to separate from her or divorce her, but he did want some compensation for the injury he had suffered.[236]

It was thus widely felt that there ought to be some punishment for the seducers of wives, who if the crim. con. action were abolished would get off scot-free. Turning adultery—here defined as the seduction of a married woman—into a criminal misdemeanour punishable by fine or imprisonment was seriously discussed. But the exclusion of husbands from prosecution equally with wives disturbed the consciences of the more pious Christians, like William Gladstone, who believed that the double sexual standard should be removed from the law. On the other hand, the alternative of making men liable to criminal prosecution for adultery was even less acceptable. Others objected strongly to the confusion of sin with crime, and to the imposition of yet another jury trial. In the face of all these objections, the proposal was abandoned.[237]

C. COMPROMISE

The result of this tug of war was an awkward compromise. After discussing and rejecting various alternatives, an amendment abolishing the crim. con. action passed in the House of Lords by a vote of 78 to 46.[238] But in response to objections about the hardship to poor husbands, and the need to punish seducers of married women, the House of Commons added another clause which in practice revived it, but under another name and in a much less objectionable form. The suit for damages against the 'co-respondent' was now incorporated as an option into the new suit against the wife for divorce, but the distribution of the damages was placed under the strict control of the court. Henceforth, the judge divided the damages between provision for the now motherless children, maintenance for the ex-wife, and compensation for the ex-husband, especially for his legal costs.[239]

The new system solved the two problems of compensating a poor husband and punishing the seducer of a married woman. But it failed entirely to keep the sordid details of divorce proceedings out of the

---

[236] 3 *Hansard*, 1869; 146: 209.
[237] Ibid. 145: 831, 929; 147: 393, 1268, 1274, 1644, 1741–2, 1747.
[238] Ibid. 147: 1833–5.   [239] Ibid. 2052.

newspapers. In 1859, two years after the act came into force, Queen Victoria wrote an anguished letter of protest to Lord Chancellor Campbell, asking for a curb to be placed on publication of items 'of so scandalous a character that it makes it almost impossible for a paper to be trusted in the hands of a young lady or boy. None of the worst French novels . . . can be as bad . . . and its effect must be most pernicious to the public morals of the country.'[240] Despite the queen's letter, and the attorney-general's lurid description of how 'crowds congregate there [in court] for the purpose of hearing details which would give gratification to depraved and diseased minds', Lord Campbell's proposed bill to conduct court hearings in private was defeated in the House of Lords by 131 to 23.[241]

As a result, in 1909 the newspapers were still printing the details of adultery cases, and the public was still eager to read them. During the testimony presented to the Royal Commission on Divorce of 1912, Sir George H. Lewis, a judge in the Divorce Court, remarked 'I think they are spicy reading: a great many people take up the paper and the first thing they do is to turn up and read about the Divorce Court.'[242] In 1909, respectable papers like the *Times*, the *Daily Telegraph*, and the *Daily Mail* devoted to divorce cases some 82 to 126 columns of print every year, while one Sunday paper, *The Umpire*, printed no fewer than 238.[243] It was not until 1926 that Parliament, spurred into action by the wide publicity given to all the details about a peculiarly scabrous divorce case (*Russell* v. *Russell*), at last passed legislation restricting the publication of such materials in the newspapers.[244] The *News of the World* and the *Sun* of the 1980s thus belong to an old English tradition.

As a footnote to the history of the crim. con. action, it should be noted that the action for damages for adultery instituted in 1857 was not finally eliminated from the statute book until 1970.[245]

11. Conclusion

A. STAGES OF EVOLUTION OF THE ACTION

When all is said and done, the principal forces at work behind the rise and fall of the crim. con. action between the 1690s and 1857 were deep

---

[240] *Roy. Com. Divorce, 1912*, 1: 146; *Letters of Queen Victoria*, ed. A. C. Benson and Viscount Esher (London, 1907), 3: 482.

[241] *Roy. Com. Divorce, 1912*, 1: 148–56. [242] Ibid. 2: 75. [243] Ibid. 1: 146.

[244] The Regulation of Reports Act, which at last brought English law in conformity with that in Scotland; Hyde (n. 182 above), *A Tangled Web*, 164.

[245] Law Reform (Miscellaneous Provisions) Act 1970, cap. 33, sect. 5, cited in J. H. Baker,

changes in the values and sensibilities of the elite and the middling sort which affected litigants, lawyers, and reporters alike. There were no simple shifts from one moral code to another, but rather a babble of conflicting voices. Predominance in the debate shifted in a series of overlapping stages involving competition and conflict between divergent codes of ethics. For example, as late as 1748, over half a century after the crim. con. action for damages was fully in place, there still survived the ancient custom by which Ash Wednesday was 'the day people go to church to curse them who lie with other men's wives'.[246]

In the end, however, clearly identifiable changes in the predominant moral code did occur. Between 1600 and 1860 it is possible to discern four distinct phases in the evolution of educated elite public opinion over the way to treat adultery by a married woman. In elite circles, where honour was held in particularly high esteem, before about 1670 it was morally acceptable to avenge the insult by personal violence, whether spontaneous and untrammelled or ritualized as a duel. The lower classes, however, either used threats of public litigation in order to blackmail the seducer into paying a sum of money in compensation, or prosecuted him for adultery in the ecclesiastical or lay local courts.

The second phase began in about 1670, when the common law courts of King's Bench and Common Pleas devised the new action for crim. con. and provided monetary damages for the loss of male honour incurred through the seduction of a wife. In consequence, even its limited use symbolized the beginnings of a shift among at any rate some members of the landed elite from a code based on honour and shame to one based on the legal property right by a husband in the body of his wife, and his moral right to monetary compensation for any trespass upon it.

This shift from honour to money can be paralleled in other spheres of life, for example in electoral politics. Before the 1670s, the prime objective of a Parliamentary candidate was to avoid the loss of honour by defeat in an election, and bribing of electors was minimal. As a result, there were few publicly contested elections, and the electors were rewarded by no more than lavish gifts of food and drink. After the 1670s the rage of party dramatically increased the number of contested elections, and thus of losers, while bribery of the electorate with cash became commonplace. Thus, here also, honour began to give way to money, although both were to remain in competition for a very long while.[247] The two codes vied with

An Introduction to English Legal History, 2nd edn. (London, 1979), 383; S. Cretney, 'Law Reform (Miscellaneous Provisions) Act 1970', *Modern Law Review*, 33 (1970), 540–1.

[246] *Copley v. Copley* (1748), LPCA, D. 478. 233.

[247] M. Kishlansky, *Parliamentary Selection: Social and Political Choice in Early Modern England* (New York, 1986).

one another for over a century, until in the early nineteenth century both came under severe attack as equally immoral and un-Christian.

The third phase began in about 1770, when two simultaneous and related developments began to take place. The number of actions shot up, in large part because a successful crim. con. action became a necessary prerequisite to a Parliamentary divorce, the numbers of which were also increasing. Second, the motives behind crim. con. actions and Parliamentary divorces were also changing in the last half of the eighteenth century. Emphasis shifted from the preservation of patrilineal property rights to the loss of 'the comforts of matrimony', caused by separation without remarriage. These changes in legal arguments show how concern for companionship was tending to drive out cruder claims about property.[248]

The fourth phase, which is visible by 1800, overlapped with and built upon the third, and took the form of a many-faceted moral reaction against the crim. con. action. The critical change was that the acceptance of money for a wife's dishonour became so totally unacceptable in the propertied classes that most plaintiffs secretly either failed to collect or promptly returned the damages awarded to them. This procedure involved acceptance of deliberate collusion between the husband and his wife's lover in order to deceive the court. This was made possible by a decline in the ethical authority of the Anglican church, so that by the late eighteenth century there had arisen considerable scepticism among the elite about the religious foundations of the principle of the indissolubility of marriage.

The abolition of the crim. con. action in 1857 was preceded by the almost total withdrawal after 1830 of the titled aristocracy and baronetage from this form of litigation, presumably under the influence of Evangelical religion (Table 9.4). It was therefore hardly surprising that the House of Lords should have taken the lead in killing it. The abolition was also helped by revulsion of the law lords at the blatant collusion in so many cases, by the acid criticism of their continental colleagues, and by the growing demand among both educated women and lawyers for greater legal equality between the sexes.

B. SOCIETY AND THE LAW

There can be no doubt that the crim. con. action began in the late seventeenth century because of a desire by the common lawyers to extend their

---

[248] See below, 327–8.

capacity to offer a remedy for any tort. The crim. con. action allowed the common law courts to compete with the ecclesiastical courts in punishing adultery, and thus to capture at least a small share of the litigation concerning marital affairs. This legal rivalry was undoubtedly always present, and was occasionally expressed in the debates in Parliament in the middle of the nineteenth century. It might therefore seem plausible to attribute some part of the late seventeenth-century invention of the crim. con. action to a desire by the common lawyers to increase their business, especially since the action turned out to be even less capable of eliciting the truth and preventing collusion than the much-criticized canon law procedure.

On the other hand, the common law judges in the late seventeenth century moved very slowly and cautiously into the crim. con. business. They never directly challenged the authority of an ecclesiastical court by issuing an injunction against it.[249] At an early stage they expressed grave doubts about the wisdom of exposing matrimonial differences in open court, they deliberately restricted juries to the better sort, and in general showed little sign of aggressively seeking to expand the use of the action.

Whatever their motives and their degree of enthusiasm, or lack of it, there can be no doubt that the invention of the crim. con. action by the common lawyers changed public perceptions and sensibilities. If there had been no crim. con. action available, the Duke of Norfolk in 1692 and other nobles who later followed his example would not have been tempted to turn their wives' shame and their own dishonour into something to be compensated in a courtroom by the award of monetary damages. The mere fact of the shift from the duel to the courtroom is symbolic of a shift of elite mental attitudes about honour. This remains true, even though the principal motive of the duke and many others after him was to improve their chances for a Parliamentary divorce, rather than to be revenged upon a seducer, and even though the duel in England survived well into the nineteenth century. To a significant extent, therefore, the law itself helped to mould opinion and mentality, while the judges' public directions to the juries moulded moral sentiments.

It is not surprising that there was a close relationship between the lawyers and the elite they served. Ostensibly the courts as institutions lived a life of their own, indifferent to the waves and eddies of public opinion which washed over and around them, although a few of the

---

[249] This point was made by the Bishop of Rochester in a debate in the House of Lords in 1800 (*Parl. Hist.* 35: 284).

judges, such as Lord Mansfield, were activists who openly stated their belief that it was the duty of a judge to modify case law to meet changing societal needs and values. In fact, of course, the judges and lawyers who operated the system were members of a wider society to which they were bound by a common university experience, a reading of the same newspapers and periodicals, and a shared sociability in London clubs and fashionable drawing-rooms, all of which exposed them to the same contemporary values.

The crim. con. action was a legal device which was twisted to suit the needs of the key participants in the process: the elite males who were the plaintiffs, the barristers, and the judges who staffed the courts. The action could also even be used to satisfy occasional popular outbursts of moral rectitude, as during the 1790s. In the first stage, from 1690 to about 1770, the crim. con. action gave elite husbands a powerful weapon with which to enforce the sexual fidelity of their wives and to punish any men who poached on this particular piece of domestic property. It also made it easier for those plaintiffs who wanted to start new families to obtain a Parliamentary divorce. In the second stage, after about 1770, collusion became normal, and the action allowed the most adulterous of husbands to circumvent the law in order to obtain a divorce, so that all three members of the sexual triangle could happily remarry. Meanwhile, morality was upheld, seducers of married women were ostensibly punished, and a number of common lawyers, barristers, attorneys, and solicitors became rich and famous for their roles in these highly publicized court dramas. The fact that what was revealed in court often bore little relation to the real situation was a positive advantage to all concerned, except those with strong views about the evils of collusion to defraud the law. These radical changes in the latent functions of the action, made to satisfy the leading participants, are enough to explain why it survived until 1857. But no one can argue that this was the most functional and economical way to achieve the desired ends.

When it came to the abolition of the action as part of the 1854–7 divorce bills, the role of a struggle between two different legal cultures of civil and common law, represented by two different sections of the legal profession, is clear beyond all possibility of a doubt. The original purpose of the bills was to remove so much jurisdiction from the ecclesiastical courts that to all intents and purposes they would be obliged to shut down. The divorce bill transferred all matrimonial business to a new common law/equity court, and a concurrent bill designed to go with it removed to a new probate court all business concerning wills. The common lawyers regarded the civil law and the ecclesiastical courts as grossly inefficient at establishing the truth, very slow in coming to final judgment, and very expensive. Their motives were thus a mixture of high-minded zeal for reform and a shrewd eye for self interest. It was the law lords who took the lead in persuading the House of Lords to abolish the crim. con. action, on the grounds that it was something which brought discredit upon their profession and made them ashamed to meet their continental colleagues. The obvious way to reduce costs and make the law more accessible to the poor would have been to set up decentralized local courts to handle both divorce and the new procedure for suing a co-respondent for damages, rather than to concentrate all business in a single High Court in London. One is tempted to attribute this centralization at least in part to a desire by the London bar to obtain some compensation for what it had lost by the setting up of County Courts.[250] Lawyers' self-interest thus played a more prominent role in circumstances surrounding the abolition of crim. con. than in its creation.

The wealthy laity were also well satisfied with the change. Thanks to the new law it was now easier and cheaper for a few hundred of them to obtain divorces without passing through the squalid procedure of the crim. con. action. The third interest group, the clergy and laity who stood for middle-class Victorian morality, and who were well represented in the House of Commons, were also satisfied by the continued punishment of the seducer by a new system of damages, now fully controlled by the court itself. The story of the rise, transformation and abolition of the crim. con. action therefore lends support to an interpretation of the latent function of the law as an institutional structure based on concepts of justice, but moulded and twisted by changes in secular morality and conflicts of legal cultures, as well as by the selfish interests of both clients and lawyers.[251]

[250] I owe this suggestion to Professor David Sugarman.

[251] This section on the role of the law and lawyers owes much to perceptive criticism by Professor Owen Fiss. The conclusions, however, are my own.

❧ X ❧

Parliamentary Divorce

1. Establishing the Rules

A. INTRODUCTION

Protestant theologians at the Reformation had rejected the idea that marriage was a sacrament, and had pointed out that the Roman Catholic practice of separation from bed and board had no justification in the Bible and was a later accretion. They strongly opposed it, since it deprived both parties of the essence of marriage, namely, sexual relations and companionship, and thus acted as a positive incentive to irregular cohabitation and adultery. This was a position taken, among others, by Luther, Calvin, Becon, Tyndale, Hooper, Bucer, and Zwingli.[1]

After the dust had settled by the late sixteenth century, England stood out as the only Protestant country without some form of legalized divorce. Elsewhere, divorces were available to plaintiffs who were victims of one or more of three marital offences: wifely adultery, wilful desertion for a period of years, and life-threatening cruelty. The reasons why England was the exception lie partly in the tortuous and zig-zag path by which it moved from the Catholic into the Protestant camp; partly in disputes among English Protestants about which new divorce code to adopt; and perhaps also in understandable psychological sensitivities about marriage of one strong-willed spinster sovereign, Queen Elizabeth.[2]

B. THE PERIOD OF UNCERTAINTY, 1534–1597

The stirring of change began with one of the first Reformation statutes, the Act in Restraint of Appeals of 1534, which ordered the establishment of a commission of thirty-two persons, appointed by the king, to revise the canon law. For various reasons, Henry VIII procrastinated, and no commissioners were appointed until 1546. They worked fast and soon produced a draft for the king's approval, but he did not sign it for fear of

[1] Howard, 2: 73–7.
[2] The most scholarly and reliable account of what happened is to be found in Dibdin and Healey.

the opposition of the Catholic conservatives at home, such as Bishop Gardiner, and of his new Catholic ally abroad, the Emperor Charles V.

After Henry's death in 1547, the accession to the throne of the boy-king Edward VI, and the seizure of power by a radical Protestant faction, Parliament asked for the appointment of a new commission. In 1550 a bill was passed to this effect, and eight commissioners were named a year later, including Archbishop Cranmer and two foreign theologians, Peter Martyr and John A. Lasko. A draft, known as the *Reformatio Legum Ecclesiasticarum*, was prepared by Cranmer and others, but both the Catholics and the Duke of Northumberland, a radical Protestant, strongly objected to it on many grounds, and nothing was done before the death of Edward and the accession of Mary in 1553.[3] Catholics particularly objected to the clauses which proposed a regular system of divorce on grounds of adultery, long desertion, lasting cruelty, or mortal enmity, a proposal which they denounced as 'more than licentious'. There was also lay opposition to the draconian clauses which proposed to punish adultery with life imprisonment or transportation, as well as forfeiture of fortune. Finally, the canon lawyers were naturally opposed to the clause proposing the abolition of separation from bed and board, as administered for so long by the church courts. In one way or another, the *Reformatio* was a hopelessly impractical and unpopular document, the work of a small minority of Protestant zealots.

When Elizabeth came to the throne in 1558 and a group of moderate Protestants seized power, the old commission of thirty-two was revived by statute, but nothing was done about it due to opposition from Catholic peers in the House of Lords. In 1566, the more radical Protestants made a second attempt to revive the *Reformatio*, but only managed to push it through the Lower House of Convocation by the very close vote of 59 to 58. It then died. In 1571 a last attempt was made to impose this radical reshaping of the church and canon law upon convocation and Parliament. The *Reformatio* itself was printed for the first time by John Foxe the martyrologist, and a copy was presented to the House of Commons, which set up a commission of twenty-two to consider it and consult with the bishops. Under its terms, divorce was to be made available on grounds of adultery, desertion, deadly hostility, or incest, but remarriage was to be allowed only to the innocent party. The canon law procedure of separation from bed and board was to be abolished as a mere popish innovation. But the document as a whole was far too radical to be acceptable to the pragmatic Protestant moderates such as Lord Burghley,

---

[3] W. K. Jordan, *Edward VI: The Threshold of Power* (London, 1970), 357–61.

Elizabeth herself, and most of the bishops. So the *Reformatio* died in committee, and divorce reform along with it.

Thus England failed to reform its divorce laws because of the historical accident that the proposal was embedded in a radical recasting of all of canon law, much of which was unacceptable to the moderate Protestant faction in power after 1558. No attempt seems to have been made to push for divorce reform alone, separate from the other radical clauses concerning ceremonial, dress, church organization, punishment of heresy with death, and a purely symbolic interpretation of the Eucharist.[4] After 1571, there is no further mention of the *Reformatio* until 1640, when it was twice reprinted at the beginning of the English Revolution, presumably as a blueprint for a radical reformation of the church. The definitive edition, which included the original draft of 1552 and the revised version of 1571, was published in 1850, just in time to be used as a precedent by the proponents of the first Divorce Act of 1857.[5]

During the late sixteenth and seventeenth centuries, there were intermittent proposals made by influential theologians for some limited system of legalized divorce in England. All these reformers relied on Christ's words as reported in the New Testament, and were willing to accept adultery by the wife as sufficient cause. In the reign of Elizabeth, Henry Smith had declared that 'the disease of marriage is adultery, and the medicine thereof is divorcement'. Far fewer were willing to include adultery by the husband, but that minority included Jeremy Taylor and bishops Joseph Hall and John Cosin.[6]

While these theological debates were in progress, what was happening in practice? The question has been obscured by the anomalous case of the first Marquis of Northampton, who was a very powerful political figure, the brother of Henry VIII's revered widow and a close ally of Protector Somerset. In 1547 he obtained a judicial separation from bed and board from his wife on the grounds of her adultery. After he had succeeded in forcing through Parliament a private act to bastardize his wife's children by her lover, he asked Cranmer whether he could now remarry. In response, Cranmer, with his usual scholarly caution, set up a commission to consider the question. But while the commission was still deliberating, Northampton became impatient and married again without waiting for an answer. Eventually the commission decided that an act of female adultery in itself dissolved a marriage, and that the traditional

---

[4] J. E. Neale, *Elizabeth I and her Parliaments, 1559–1581* (London, 1953), 63–4, 89, 194, 197.

[5] *The Reformation of the Ecclesiastical Laws as Attempted in the Reigns of King Henry VIII, King Edward VI, and Queen Elizabeth*, ed. E. Cardwell (Oxford, 1850).

[6] Howard, 2: 73; Cardwell, *Reformation of the Ecclesiastical Laws*, 49–58.

remedy of the church courts (separation from bed and board without permission to remarry) was illegal. But these findings were never ratified, and in 1552 Northampton, presumably advised by his lawyers, found it prudent to push a private act through Parliament confirming the validity of his second marriage. A year later, when Mary came to the throne and the Catholics returned to power, Northampton's divorce bill was repealed by Parliament.[7] Except for its complaisant acquiescence in legitimating the turbulent matrimonial affairs of Henry VIII, this was the first occasion on which Parliament had passed judgment on the divorce proceedings of a private individual. It was not a very auspicious beginning.

What actually took place during the reign of Elizabeth is obscure. It is often alleged that ecclesiastical courts were granting to men with adulterous wives divorces *a vinculo*, that is, with permission to remarry. But despite intensive searches of surviving Consistory Court records, no evidence for this has ever been uncovered. Moreover in 1596, Francis Clarke, who had practised for thirty-six years as senior proctor in Doctors' Commons, expressly stated that no such sentence had ever been issued by an ecclesiastical court. He declared that the church courts had followed the law and confined themselves to the traditional sentences of separation from bed and board and had forbidden *all* remarriages.[8]

It seems clear, however, that during the reign of Elizabeth, many innocent parties among the laity had been interpreting these sentences of separation from bed and board as *de facto* grants of permission to remarry, just as had Northampton before them. A critical test case occurred in 1572. Seven years earlier, a wealthy squire and Somerset JP, John Stawell, had obtained a sentence of separation from bed and board for the adultery of his wife with a servant. Seven years later, he asked permission of the Bishop of Bath and Wells to remarry, although his wife was still alive, and although he acknowledged that 'the common law and the laws of the realm' were against him. He argued that he could not be expected to be reconciled to a wife who had committed adultery with a servant, but that he needed to beget a male heir to his large estates. The apprehensive bishop passed the appeal on to the Archbishop of Canterbury, Matthew Parker, who in the end reluctantly issued a licence to marry. One reason for this odd decision was that Stawell's proposed second wife was the sister of an influential courtier, Sir Edward Dyer,

---

[7] *Parl. Hist.* 35: 265–6.

[8] F. Clarke, *Praxis in Curii Ecclesiasticis* (London, 1596; repr. Dublin, 1666), quoted in full by Gladstone in 3 *Hansard*, 147: 849; Cardwell, *Reformation of the Ecclesiastical Laws*, 49–58; W. H. Hale, *A Series of Precedents . . . in . . . Criminal Causes from 1475 to 1640* (London, 1847), *passim*; Dibdin and Healey, 48–54.

who persuaded the Earl of Leicester and Lord Burghley to exercise heavy pressure on the archbishop. Even so, the marriage was of dubious legality, and Stawell and Dyer found it prudent to pay the first wife £600 not to launch a suit to contest it in the ecclesiastical courts. The marriage was not recognized at common law, so that when in 1604 Stawell died, his first wife successfully claimed her dower. It was altogether an ambiguous affair.[9]

There is reason to believe, however, that this view that a husband legally separated because of his wife's adultery could remarry was not uncommon in Elizabethan England. It also appears that those who took the traditional position were liable to be accused of popish sympathies. Thus, an anonymous complaint was made in the 1580s against President Swale of Caius College, Cambridge—a notoriously Catholic college in a Protestant university. It was reported that he had argued in a public discussion in the college chapel with the fellows and scholars that 'it was not lawful for those that are divorced for adultery to marry again, neither for the guiltless party nor the guilty, the which position is maintained only of papists and such like'.[10]

C. FIXING THE RULES, 1597–1603

It was not until the last years of the reign of Elizabeth, between 1597 and 1603, that a series of legal actions were taken, under the leadership of Archbishop Whitgift and the queen, to make it clear that divorce with remarriage was not available in Protestant England. They were no doubt inspired by the desire on the one hand for order in the church and on the other once and for all to crush the radical ideas of some extreme Protestant sectaries. In 1597, a revised set of canons were embodied in a set of ecclesiastical constitutions in Latin, and were re-enacted as canons in English by Convocation in 1603–4.[11] The old separation from bed and board was retained, but a new rule was introduced that obliged both parties in the separation in future to give a bond of £100 not to remarry during the lifetime of his or her spouse. This was ambiguous, since the canon did not explicitly say that such a remarriage was either invalid or adulterous. Indeed, making a second marriage subject to a financial penalty almost implied that it was illegal but binding, and thus put it in much the same position as clandestine marriage. Unlike that of a clandestine marriage, however, the validity of the second marriage itself was also in doubt.

[9] Dibdin and Healey, 82–92, 152–3.
[10] BL, Harleian MSS, 7031 fo. 129 v; I owe this reference to Victor Morgan.
[11] *Synodalia*, ed. E. Cardwell (Oxford, 1842), 154–5, 307–8.

Second, a test case at common law was staged in the Star Chamber, the Rye *v.* Foljambe case. Foljambe had remarried after a judicial separation and was litigating about the property of his new wife. Archbishop Whitgift, supported by a conference of 'sage divines and civilians', testified that the marriage was illegal in canon law, and therefore that Foljambe had no claim in common law on his alleged wife's property. Foljambe argued that he had been assured by 'diverse divines and civilians of great account and learning' that his two previous marriages had been fully dissolved by judicial separations, but he failed to produce any of them to testify on his behalf. No doubt they were intimidated by Archbishop Whitgift and the great lay lords in the Star Chamber. So Foljambe lost his case, but whether his third marriage was ever declared null and void is not known.[12]

Third, in 1603 Parliament passed an act which for the first time made bigamy a felony, although it allowed benefit of clergy so that the punishment would be not hanging but branding on the thumb. Moreover much of its bite was removed by a very peculiar clause which exempted from the provisions of the act those who were 'divorced by sentence of the ecclesiastical court'—meaning those judicially separated from bed and board.[13] Nevertheless, taken together, these steps show evidence of a concerted official drive against divorce followed by remarriage, a position reinforced by an official sermon at St Paul's Cross and the publication in 1601 of a tract by Lancelot Andrewes, the Dean of Westminster, entitled *A Discourse written against Second Marriage after Sentence of Divorce with a Former Match, the Party then living*, and another by the Bishop of Oxford.[14] Finally, Richard Hooker's great work, *Of the Laws of Ecclesiasticall Politie*, which at last defined the legal and theological positions of the Church of England, declared marriage to be indissoluble, except for nullities.[15]

The many legal statements made and the positive legal steps taken between 1597 and 1603 evidently marked a deliberate attempt by the dominant faction in the clerical and lay establishment to make it clear that the English church and state would not adopt some version of the divorce laws which were universally in force in the Protestant countries of Scotland and continental Europe. On the other hand, the calculated ambiguity of the wording of the canons and the Bigamy Act suggests that there was still a great deal of opposition in both clerical and lay circles to

---

[12] *Rye* v. *Foljambe* (1598) *Eng. Rep.* 72: 838.   [13] 1 JI cap. 1.

[14] *Works by Lancelot Andrewes*, ed. J. P. Wilson and J. Bliss (Oxford, 1841–54), 11: 106–10; *Law Review*, 1 (1844–5), 356–62; Dibdin and Healey, 30–4.

[15] R. Hooker, *Of the Lawes of Ecclesiasticall Politie* (London, 1594–7).

shutting off all avenues to divorce and remarriage, so that the possibility was left open of further change in the future.

It seems unlikely that practice by the laity tamely followed these prescriptions by the government, many influential clergy, and Parliament. There can be little doubt that many private separations which amounted to self-divorces continued to take place among the lower orders. In 1640, Daniel Rogers complained about 'the separation of such in the country of all sorts, as depart from their yoke-fellows, abandoning each other by law, or lawless divorces'.[16] The landed elite, however, had to be much more careful since property was involved, as Stawell and Foljambe had discovered.

It is indicative of the uncertainty which still surrounded the issue that an ambitious young clergyman named William Laud nearly ruined his career before it had even begun. In 1605, he was imprudent enough to marry his patron, Charles Blount Earl of Devonshire, to the latter's mistress, Lady Rich, who only a month before had been separated from bed and board by an ecclesiastical court at the suit of her husband Lord Rich, on the grounds of her adulterous connection with Blount. This rash act on Laud's part suggests that the principle of the indissolubility of marriage was not yet fully accepted, even by noblemen and conservative clergy. King James, however, was furious when he heard of the matter. Laud had remarried not only a separated spouse but a guilty one; and according to the attorney-general Sir Edward Coke, such a bigamous marriage was unlawful and void in common law, but not felonious. To confuse the situation even more, after the Earl of Devonshire's death a year later in 1606, the College of Arms refused to allow the alleged second countess to impale her arms with those of her husband during the funeral pageantry in Westminster Abbey, 'which brings into question the lawfulness of the marriage'.[17]

From the Middle Ages to 1857 there was no formal change at all in the official doctrine and practice of the canon law as enforced in the ecclesiastical courts about separation, divorce, and remarriage. But as Sir Lewis Dibdin was to put it in 1912, in the late sixteenth century 'there was a widespread relaxation of opinion with regard to divorce' by a separated man, and 'a general slipping away from old convictions' about the indissolubility of marriage.[18] It is certain, however, that these bigamous marriages carried with them no rights over property at com-

---

[16] D. Rogers, *Matrimonial Honour* (London, 1640), 131, quoted by Ingram, 147.

[17] P. Heylyn, *Cyprianus Anglicus, or the History of the Life and Death of Archbishop Laud* (London, 1688), 53–4; *Les Reportes del cases in camera stellata, 1593–1609*, ed. W. P. Baildon (London, 1894), 444; Dibdin and Healey, 74.

[18] *Roy. Com. Divorce, 1912; Minutes of Evidence* 3: 58.

mon law, and the Devonshire–Rich marriage proves how uncertain their legal status was in the eyes of the heralds.

On the other hand, far into the seventeenth century, theological opinion remained divided on the subject of remarriage by the innocent party in a separation from bed and board.[19] In 1610 Bunny admitted that many were 'ready to take fast hold of so plausible a liberty' and pointed the finger at four members of the elite 'who had so gotten divorce and were married again'.[20] One may safely conclude, therefore, that despite the tightening of the official legal screws in 1597–1603, the practice of remarriage by a husband after a judicial separation for a wife's adultery still occurred occasionally—or possibly quite frequently—in the first half of the seventeenth century, with the cautious blessing of at least a few highly respected church dignitaries and theologians.

D. THE INTERREGNUM, 1642–1660

The 1640s and 1650s were a period of disorganization and institutional chaos in the church. The ecclesiastical courts ceased to function in the early 1640s, and in 1646 church control over marriage was abolished, authority being shifted in theory to secular authorities. But the bulk of the population seems either to have found ways to be married clandestinely by the old rituals of the Church of England, or were married by non-conformist clergy of their own religious persuasion, or reverted to marriages by verbal contract.[21] As a result of this confusion, when the ecclesiastical courts were restored in 1660 they found themselves faced with an unprecedented torrent of petitions for separation which had been pent up for over a decade.[22]

2. Creating the exceptions: 1670–1750

Such a situation satisfied neither the lay aristocracy, still mindful of the precedent set by the Marquis of Northampton's divorce Act of 1552, nor many of the Whig clergy, who favoured the adoption of some kind of limited full divorce rules similar to those in force not only in other Protestant countries on the continent, but also in the sister nation of Scotland.

---

[19] Dibdin and Healey, 44.

[20] J. Rainolds, *A Defence of the Judgment of the Reformed Churches* (London, 1610); E. Bunny, *Of Divorce for Adultery, and Marrying Again* (London, 1610).

[21] Howard, 2.

[22] LPCA, *passim*; see above, Fig. 1.1.

A. THE ROOS CASE, 1670

The case of John Lord Roos in 1670 first drew attention to the power of Parliament to legalize a full divorce by a private act. John had been a younger son, but was now the heir to the great estates of the Manners, earls of Rutland. In 1658 he had married Anne Pierrepont, the daughter and co-heiress of the Marquis of Dorchester, who had brought with her the huge portion of £10,000. Soon after the marriage she had a great quarrel with her husband and mother-in-law over whether or not she should wear tight stays in the early stages of pregnancy. To punish her, John's mother, who seems to have dominated her son, carried him off, along with most of the servants, to Belvoir Castle for the Christmas festivities, leaving the new bride all alone in the country house of Haddon, with no more than four maids and one male servant to attend her. It must have been an eerie and melancholy experience for the young bride to spend a month cooped up alone in the middle of winter in this huge, rambling, medieval, fortified house.

Thereafter the marriage went steadily downhill. Occasionally Anne would excite John sexually, for example by dressing up as a boy in a suit of his clothes. This transvestite act he clearly regarded as provocative, for he objected strongly when she did it once again in his absence. According to Anne, John developed into an alcoholic, drinking day after day for weeks on end with male companions until they passed out. Once he vomited all over her fine damask bed and sheets, which she claimed had cost £200. Since he habitually came to bed so late, and by that time was usually too drunk for sex, they took to sleeping in different rooms.

In June 1659, ten months after the marriage, Anne gave birth to a female child, who died shortly thereafter. By this time Anne's quarrels with her husband and her mother-in-law had become so frequent and so bitter that she finally fled back to her father, the Marquis of Dorchester. She carried with her not only another unborn child in her womb but also all her plate and jewels, alleged to be worth £5,000. Following a formal reconciliation, she returned to Haddon, but her father kept the plate and jewels. John and his mother were furious at this loss, and at the latter's instigation John swore that he would never again go to bed with his wife between the sheets until the jewels were returned.

By January 1661 Dorchester had sold the jewels, and Roos was still bound by his oath until he got them back. John's version of what happened next is that he stuck to his oath and never renewed sexual relations with his wife after November 1659. Anne's version is that John came to her in private and pointed out that 'he could be as kind to her and perform the actions of a husband as well out of the bed as in it'. They therefore circumvented his oath by having sexual relations on the bed, rather than inside it. This alleged episode became the crux of the story, when two months later Anne was visibly pregnant. John accused her of committing adultery, claiming that he had not slept with her since he swore his oath eighteen months before. Anne did not help her case by allegedly saying during a quarrel with her husband: 'A better man than you got it. I will make you father it in this world, and let me answer it in the world to come.' She then left the room singing 'Cuckolds all in a row'.[23] She also allegedly excused her conduct to a friend on the grounds that 'my husband gives his mind so much to drinking and hunting that he is not fit to perform the duty of a husband to a wife, and one may as soon raise a house as raise him'.[24]

During the next seven months before the new birth, John locked Anne up in one room, attended by a single maid-servant and denied the use of pen and ink. The object was to make sure that Anne did not substitute a false male infant in case of a miscarriage, a stillbirth, or the birth of a female baby, for if the child was a male he could lay claim to the Manners inheritance. While Anne lay in the agony of her confinement in September 1661, the midwife was ordered to cross-question her about who was the father 'as if she was a whore' and to withhold assistance until she confessed. But she confessed nothing, and gave birth to a son. John had the infant removed from her two days later, and allegedly tried to get a shepherd to 'put a brand mark (such as he used to mark his sheep withall) upon some part of the body of the child'. This may be an invention, but he certainly had the child baptised 'Ignotus'—on the grounds that no one knew the name of his father—and refused to allow the mother to see him.

In December 1661 the Marquis of Dorchester, who still believed in his daughter's innocence, used his influence at court to have Anne released and sent to London, where the Privy Council, attended by Charles II in person, heard the evidence on both sides. They concluded that Anne was probably guilty of adultery, but that since it could not be proved, Roos should make a private separation agreement, with provision for Anne's future maintenance. But no settlement was reached, and Anne soon became pregnant yet again, giving birth once more in April 1663. This time there was ample proof of her sexual promiscuity with many lovers, and John produced enough evidence to obtain a separation

---

[23] This song was later bowdlerized into the nursery rhyme: 'Mary, Mary, quite contrary', where the line appears as 'pretty maids all in a row'; see I. and J. Opie, *Oxford Dictionary of Nursery Rhymes* (Oxford, 1952), 301.   [24] LPCA, Bbb.48; Eee.1. fos. 4, 329.

in the Court of Arches. Lady Anne's conduct was now so patently scandalous that even her father, the Marquis of Dorchester, was convinced of her guilt. This separation did not help John much, however, since unless he could convince a common law court to declare the boy Ignotus illegitimate, he might one day inherit the title of Earl of Rutland and the estates of the Manners family.[25] So, early in 1663 Roos introduced a bill into the House of Lords 'for illegitimating of a child called Ignotus born of the body of Anne Lady Roos'. While the bill was pending, Anne gave birth yet again, so a new bill was introduced and unanimously passed in 1664, bastardizing all her children born since 1659.[26]

In 1670, Lord Roos asked Parliament not exactly for a divorce, but for an enabling act to allow him to remarry, in spite of having given bond not to do so when he had obtained a separation from bed and board in an ecclesiastical court. According to contemporary reports, Charles II strongly supported the bill, since he was contemplating using it as a precedent to divorce his queen, Catherine of Braganza, so as to be free to remarry and beget a legitimate male heir to the throne. His brother, James Duke of York was opposed to the bill, since the king's project, if successful, would deprive him of the succession to the English throne. The issue thus became a political one 'it being considered, as the test of the question, whether Charles II was to be divorced from his queen or not', as a learned civilian summed it up in 1830. Charles was said to have attended the lengthy sessions in the House of Lords incognito, hearing with amusement all the scabrous details of Lady Roos's many sexual exploits, and commenting that it was 'better than a play'.[27]

Whether the Roos Act can be regarded as the first exception made by act of Parliament to the rule of the indissolubility of marriage is technically moot, since what was asked for, and granted, was not the dissolution of a first marriage but permission to contract a second one. But during the debate the post-Reformation official principle of the indissolubility of marriage was questioned in a lengthy and learned speech by John Cosin, Bishop of Durham.[28] This was a powerful and well-argued case, and was to be quoted again and again, as late as during the passage of the first Divorce Act in 1857.[29]

[25] LPCA, E1.124, 269–70; E2.37, 139–45; Ee.2, fo. 90–123; Eee.1, 320–404, 605–16, 700–3; Eee.2, fos. 90–123.

[26] *JH Lords*, 11: 433; 12: 15, 71, 95, 110; HMC, Rutland MSS 2. 8.

[27] 2 *Hansard*, 24: 1266; G. Burnet, *History of His Own Time* (London, 1734), 2: 126–7; 1: 262; HMC Rutland MSS 2: 11, 14, 17, 19; 22 ch. II, 14.

[28] *State Trials*, 13: 1332–8; see below, pp. 347–8.

[29] See e.g. *Abstract of Bishop Cosin's Arguments proving that Adultery works a Dissolution of the Marriage* (London, n.d.), BL, 816 m 18 (16).

But the rhetoric of Bishop Cosin was not sufficient to convince Parliament or the convocation of the clergy to draft new legislation. Many clergy and laity were convinced that divorce was against the will of God. Clerical conservatives were always afraid that such a move might undermine the monopoly of jurisdiction of the church courts over marital breakdown through their control of separation from bed and board; and some parish clergy were afraid of finding themselves forced to conduct second marriages they regarded as bigamous.

In consequence, the only result of Bishop Cosin's speech was to encourage the anomalous and illogical practice begun in the Roos case of passing private acts of Parliament for the divorce with remarriage of individual elite males. It was also paradoxical that liberal Whig ideology about marriage as a dissoluble contract resulted in practice in a strengthening of male control over female sexuality. In the 1690s, Whig political radicalism about the dissolubility of the contract between king and people and moral radicalism about the dissolubility of the contract between man and wife came together, despite Locke's attempt to keep them separate.[30] In about 1688, Gilbert Burnet, one of the most active of the radical Whig supporters of the Glorious Revolution and a future bishop, had published a tract advancing the view that adultery can dissolve the marriage contract.[31] This Whig ideology helped to institutionalize Parliamentary divorce for wifely adultery in cases in which the patrilineal descent of property was endangered by the adultery of a wife and the production of spurious children. It was thus the transmission of property—not justice, equity, the need to follow the sayings of Christ, or a desire to bring England into line with other Protestant countries like Scotland—which drove Parliament, step by step, into the practice of making these rare and grudging exceptions.

In the 1680s the issue of divorce became politically charged because of the reaffirmation by Robert Filmer and others of the theory that royal power by Divine Right was not merely analogous to but closely dependant upon the power of a father in a family. This drove Locke to launch a lengthy attack on patriarchal power in the family. He argued that the function of marriage was merely to keep the household together until the children were grown up and capable of fending for themselves. Thereafter, he implied, the marriage contract could be broken since it had served its purpose. Furthermore, if a contract of marriage between husband and wife could be broken, so too could a contract between a

---

[30] J. Locke, *Two Treatises of Government*, ed. P. Laslett (Cambridge, 1967), 1: chs. 7–11; 2: ch. 6.

[31] G. Burnet, *An Enquiry into the Measures of Submission* (London, 1688).

king and his people. This had been the Republican position worked out in the 1640s, which Locke revived and refined upon in the 1680s in order to deal with the arguments of Filmer. Locke's family is based on a purely voluntary contract, whose force and duration is derived from natural law rather than the Scriptures.

B. THE NORFOLK CASE, 1692–1700

Just as in the Roos case in 1670, political issues were again very much involved in the second major Parliamentary divorce case, that of the Duke of Norfolk in the 1690s. The connection between the arguments for divorce and those for the contract theory of monarchy was well brought out in a satirical poem about the first Norfolk divorce bill of 1692, in which the Whig Archbishop Tillotson is portrayed talking to his ally the Whig Bishop Burnet of Salisbury:

> A virtuous wise lord, that is troubled in mind
> How to get rid on's wife and a new portion find,
> By my pious advice a divorce has designed,
>   Which nobody can deny.
>
>   . . .
>
> Our master and dame[32] we shall please in the thing,
> And ourselves justify; for spouse, bishop, and king
> All used to be made with the help of a ring,
>   Which nobody can deny.
>
> Parting kings and their crowns, abdication we call;
> For supplying full sees, we new bishops install;
> Yet both's but divorcing, when all comes to all,
>   Which nobody can deny.[33]

In this poem, the forced abdication from the throne of James II, the forced deprivation of their sees of bishops who would not swear allegiance to William and Mary, and the forced divorce of the adulterous wife of a rich nobleman, are, if only for the purpose of satire, all linked together as parts of a single coherent legal principle, that contracts can be broken if one party breaches the conditions.

The case of the Duke of Norfolk was in many ways very similar to that of Lord Roos, except that the stakes were higher—not only were the Howards a richer and more ancient family than the Manners, but theirs

---

[32] William III and Mary II.
[33] *Poems on Affairs of State: Augustan Satirical Verse, 1660–1714*, gen. ed. G. de F. de Lord, [1688–97], vol. 5 (New Haven, 1971), ed. W. J. Cameron, 319–20; I owe this reference to Rachel Weil.

was the premier dukedom of England, whereas the Manners were mere earls. There were also political issues involved, now compounded by matters of religion. The duke was a Protestant supporter of the Glorious Revolution, whereas the duchess was a Catholic Jacobite, as were all the nearest heirs to the title and estates should the duke die without a legitimate son of his own. So if Norfolk could not free himself to remarry and beget an heir, the title and estates would pass to a papist.

As in the Roos case, the marriage had been arranged for money and property rather than for love, and it was appropriate that it should have been shattered by disputes over money and property—the extravagance of the duchess and the desire of the duke to sell land to clear debts. It was widely alleged that the break-up of the marriage in 1685 had been encouraged or contrived by the duke's brother, Lord Thomas Howard, whose eldest son stood to inherit the title and estates if there were no offspring of the marriage. The argument of the duchess's counsel against the bill concluded with the words: 'because she will not divorce herself from her estate is the best reason can be given for this bill of divorce.'[34] This may have been true at the beginning, but by 1685 the duchess had become the mistress of a Dutch soldier and gambler, John Germain, who was reputed to be an illegitimate son of William II of Orange.[35] By now the duke was also publicly carrying on his own amours, so that both parties were notorious for adultery.

In 1691 an early coup by the first Society for the Reformation of Manners in London was the arrest and fining of the Duke for 'breaking the Sabbath by gambling'.[36] Undeterred by this experience, in 1692 the duke introduced a bill into the House of Lords, the preamble of which explained that 'Henry Duke of Norfolk hath no issue, nor can have any probable expectation of posterity to succeed him in his honours, dignities and estate unless the said marriage be declared void by authority of Parliament, and the said duke be enabled to marry any other woman'.[37] If the explanation was reasonable, the case was weak, since Norfolk had not yet even sought, much less obtained, a separation from bed and board from a church court, the reason being that his own sexual behaviour exposed him to the counter-charge of recrimination, that is that he too was an adulterer. This failure to seek a legal separation from the church courts made Norfolk's case different from that of Northampton or Roos, and turned many of the bishops against him. Moreover, the factual evidence of the duchess's adultery was not strong, largely because

---

[34] Northants RO, SS 4331.　　[35] *DNB*, *sub* Sir John Germain.
[36] D. W. R. Bahlman, *The Moral Revolution of 1688* (New Haven, 1957), 19.
[37] *State Trials*, 12: 886–7.

Germain had had the two key witnesses (two of his personal servants) smuggled off to Holland.[38] Politics also played an important part, since at that time a majority of the bench of bishops had been appointed by the Stuarts before 1688. They, along with the Tory and crypto-Jacobite peers, now rallied solidly behind the Catholic duchess to oppose the bill, leaving as its supporters only the Whig peers and new Whig bishops, such as Bishop Burnet and Archbishop Tillotson. Not surprisingly, the bill was finally defeated.[39]

The duke's next step was to try to strengthen his case by bringing a crim. con. suit in King's Bench against Germain, claiming £10,000 damages. Although Germain's counsel argued that all the evidence was seven years old, and so beyond the six-year limit in such cases, the jury perversely voted him guilty, but awarded the duke only a contemptible £66, presumably because of his own disreputable sexual conduct.[40]

Hoping to exploit this distinctly ambiguous victory, Norfolk presented another divorce bill to the House of Lords, but was again defeated— though by only six votes.[41] His refusal even to attempt to obtain a separation from bed and board from an ecclesiastical court told heavily against him, for it was hard to rebut the argument of the duchess and her lawyers that if Parliament passed a bill of divorce, and an ecclesiastical court later rejected a separation from bed and board, the former would look rather foolish.[42] Bishop Burnet probably expressed the general feeling when he commented that although the duchess was undoubtedly guilty, the duke was 'notoriously a very vicious man'. The extent of this moral opprobrium was made clear a few years later, when the duke openly brought his mistress, Mrs Lane, down with him to the festivities connected with the assizes at Norwich, where he had a palace. He threw a great ball, but the Dean of Norwich reported that 'no one would come to it . . . All that have any regard to their reputations think it scandalous to accept his invitations.' He commented indignantly that the Duke 'carrieth himself here as cattle use to do, without shame or modesty'.[43]

In 1700, the Duke of Norfolk for a third time introduced into Parliament a bill for divorce.[44] By now he had secured possession of the two key witnesses who had been sent to Holland to stop their mouths during the hearings on the 1692 bill. They had switched sides, perhaps because

---

[38] Ibid. 891–948.

[39] G. Burnet, *History of His Own Time*, 2: 127; MacQueen, *House of Lords*, 562–70; Luttrell, 2: 337–8, 341–2, 347–50, 356, 361–2.

[40] *State Trials*, 12: 928–48; HMC, Portland MSS, 3: 508; Luttrell, 2: 439, 623–5.

[41] Luttrell, 2: 652; 3: 2. [42] Northants RO, SS 4331.

[43] MacQueen, *House of Lords*, 570–2; *Letters of Humphrey Prideaux*, 2 Camden Soc. 15 (1875), 184. [44] *State Trials*, 13: 1283–332; Luttrell, 4: 614–16, 620–1.

the duchess and Germain also wanted a divorce in order to get married, perhaps because the duke was offering the larger bribes. On this occasion the duke's counsel laid great stress on the religious issue. The bill was 'a means to preserve the inheritance of so great an office and honours to persons of the true religion', and the duke's objective was to put him out of 'danger of being succeeded by Sir John Germain's issue, or deprive him of the expectation of leaving his honours, offices and estates to a protestant heir'.[45]

Fortified by these appeals to their religious prejudices, the Lords finally passed the bill into law after a three-hour debate which lasted till midnight.[46] A minority entered a protest. They objected that this was the first bill of divorce in English history to pass through Parliament without a prior sentence of separation from bed and board in an ecclesiastical court; that only five or six bills in the last six hundred years had been passed to dissolve one marriage and validate a second one; and that in the previous cases the husband had himself been innocent of adultery, which could hardly be said of the Duke of Norfolk. The duke's reply to this criticism was an unabashed defence of the double sexual standard on the traditional grounds of the problem of bastardy: 'a man by his folly brings no spurious issue to inherit the land of his wife, but a woman deprives her husband of any legitimate issue'. The rebuttal was offered by Sir Thomas Powys: 'I doubt it happens oftentimes to them that go abroad, that they bring home that to their wives which sticks longer by them than their children'—by which he meant venereal disease.[47]

Thus the duke at last obtained his divorce from Parliament, but as things turned out it was Sir John Germain who was the real beneficiary. In the first place, the Lords made Norfolk return the £10,000 marriage portion he had received in 1677. Secondly he died soon after in 1701, before he had had time to remarry—let alone to beget heirs—so that the purpose of the Act was frustrated and the dukedom and estates passed into Catholic hands, where they have remained ever since. The duchess promptly remarried her lover of fifteen years, but she too was dead four years later, leaving to Germain the great house at Drayton and most of the Mordaunt property which had come to her on her father's death in 1697. It is possible that the duchess and Germain had been collusively acquiescent in the 1700 divorce bill, since they stood to gain so much from it. If so, William III presumably threw his weight behind the bill in order to promote the fortunes of his half-brother, just as Charles had

<hr>

[45] *State Trials*, 13: 1328, 1332; Northants RO, SS 4332–7.
[46] Luttrell, 4: 621–7.
[47] *State Trials*, 13: 1343, 1357, 1362.

done, for other reasons, for Lord Roos. All we know is that, just as Charles II had attended the Lords incognito during the Roos bill, so William III attended incognito to hear the testimony of the witnesses for the first Norfolk bill.[48] Norfolk's skilful exploitation of anti-Catholic sentiment also certainly helped to stifle opposition, so that both politics and religion played important roles in the final outcome.

C. OTHER CASES IN THE 1690s

During the 1690s, the long-drawn-out Norfolk case was far from being the only example of Parliamentary interference in matrimonial affairs. What makes that decade so unique is not only the precedent this case set for the granting of full divorce with remarriage in cases of wifely adultery, but also the readiness with which Parliament also accepted a swarm of miscellaneous cases. The most straightforward one, which most nearly approximated to the Roos–Norfolk model, was the divorce granted to the Earl of Macclesfield in 1698, which some regard as the first real Parliamentary divorce after that of Northampton in 1552. The Countess of Macclesfield had for years lived with Earl Rivers, by whom she had two children. But her husband had not launched a crim. con. action as Norfolk had in 1692, nor had any decision been arrived at in the separation suit he had begun in the Court of Arches. Moreover, the countess had fought back, claiming that she had saved her husband's life during the reign of King James, and that it was he who turned her out of doors in the first place, rather than she who had eloped with Lord Rivers. She petitioned Parliament, asking for a refund of her marriage portion (as was to be granted to the Duchess of Norfolk two years later). This was the first case in which there was a strong suspicion of collusion. It was suspected that the opposition of the countess was not serious, and that there was an agreement between her and her husband to contrive a divorce so as to allow her to marry Earl Rivers. In the end the bill passed, the marriage portion was returned—and the countess married a Colonel Brett.[49]

Other cases which came before Parliament in this decade were far removed from the relatively simple model set by Roos, Norfolk, and Macclesfield, men of high rank and great wealth who needed to remarry and to bastardize illegitimate children in order to preserve patrilineal descent of title and property. There was, for example, the case of the

---

[48] Luttrell, 2: 344.
[49] MacQueen, *House of Lords*, 574–6; LPCA, E.12/34–41, 89; Eee.8, fos. 415–44, 447–77, 514–20, 524–6; *JH Lords*, 16: 195, 197, 224, 235.

Countess of Anglesea, who was suing her husband in an ecclesiastical court for separation from bed and board on grounds of cruelty. She appealed for help from Parliament since her husband was claiming his privilege as a peer and thus could not be forced by the court to settle a maintenance allowance upon her. She asked Parliament either to compel her husband to waive his privilege of freedom from arrest, or else to allow her to introduce a bill in Parliament for separation (*not* divorce) on grounds of cruelty.

The Lords first tried to arbitrate a settlement and persuade the countess to return home, but without success. They then voted to allow her to introduce her bill, but found themselves obliged to give her a safe-conduct so that 'the Earl of Anglesea will not seize his Lady in her passage to or from this House'. The countess appeared and swore that her life would be in danger if she returned home, so that, slowly and reluctantly, both Lords and Commons were grudgingly pushed into passing the bill. For the first and almost the last time, Parliament was persuaded to intervene directly in a marital dispute about cruelty and the settlement of maintenance on a wife, because a husband insisted in blocking suits in lower courts by claiming the privilege of a peer.[50]

Another case of a marital dispute with which Parliament allowed itself to become involved in the 1690s arose from a petition from a Mr Lewknor, whose wife had deserted him many years before and had lived in adultery with a Mr Montagu, producing a number of children. He had obtained a sentence of separation from an ecclesiastical court and was now seeking a full divorce with permission to remarry. This time Parliament adopted a fairly tough position. It agreed to bastardize the illegitimate children, but refused either to grant a full divorce or to allow Lewknor to tamper with the provisions for Mrs Lewknor in the marriage settlement. Two of the three objects of a divorce bill were thus rejected, and the only action taken was, significantly enough, to protect the rights of property inheritance. This might have set a model for future legislation in cases when there was a legitimate heir to inherit, but in fact it proved to be a unique decision which was never repeated.[51] In this same decade, Parliament also allowed itself to become involved in three cases of annulment of the forcible or fraudulent marriage of a child heiress, which should have been left to the ecclesiastical courts.[52]

---

[50] *JH Lords*, 16: 607, 609, 611, 613, 630, 640, 649, 652, 654, 657–9, 664, 705; *JH Commons*, 13: 511. The only similar case was that of Countess Ferrers in 1757, which was finally rejected (*JH Lords*, 29: 36, 50, 71, 76–9, 98, 108, 119, 249–50, 271–5, 280, 289–96, 325, 329, 332, 381).

[51] *State Trials*, 13: 1347; Northants RO, SS 4331.

[52] Mrs Wharton case (1690), *State Trials*, 13: 1349; *JH Lords*, 14: 583, 591; *JH Commons*, 10: 493; Northants RO, SS 4331; *Knight* v. *Goodinge* (1700), *State Trials*, 13: 1357; *JH Lords* 16:

D. THE DEBATE ABOUT PARLIAMENTARY DIVORCE, 1690–1700

It seems clear that for a decade during the 1690s Parliament came close to taking on a quite new role as a court of equity over matrimonial affairs. Persons of both sexes with a wide variety of marital grievances were being allowed to petition for bills in Parliament. The principles behind the voting in both Houses were as unclear as were the procedures, and the decisions taken were erratic, inconsistent, and arbitrary.

The playwrights were quick to point out that Parliament was making itself ridiculous. In a turn-of-the-century play in which a woman allows her friends to take a vote on which suitor she should marry, one of them observes: 'This is extremely new, but I don't know why it should not be brought into a custom to marry, as well as to divorce, by vote.' In another play of the same period, a citizen who suspects his wife of adultery is made to proclaim that he will 'petition the House o' Commons to prove me a cuckold, and be divorc'd by Act of Parliament'.[53]

These interventions by Parliament in matrimonial affairs, which culminated in the final passage into law of Norfolk's divorce in 1700, gave rise to a flurry of anonymous pamphleteering, all arguing in favour of creating a regular judicial system of divorce and remarriage of the innocent husband in the case of wifely adultery. It was urged that 'where the sin (adultery) is, the punishment (divorce) ought to follow it, without injury to conscience'.[54]

The author of a pamphlet published in 1700 proposed two solutions to prevent bastards from inheriting titles and estates and so dispossessing legitimate heirs. These were to be the subject of continued debate for another century or more. The first was to make adultery a misdemeanour, punishable like any other crime, a bill for which had been proposed in Parliament and defeated the year before. The second was 'to render divorces less chargeable and difficult than they now are', restricted as they were to the slow, expensive, and difficult process of getting a private act through Parliament. The author rightly pointed out that Parliament did not sit regularly, that costs were exorbitant, and that the delays in the case of Roos and Norfolk were respectively five and eight years. So he asked 'why should not some more easy method be thought

146; *JH Commons*, 11: 753, 770–3; Clifford *A History of Private Bill Legislation*, 1: 427–31; Monke case, Northants RO, SS 4331.

[53] Mrs Trotter, *Love at a Loss* (1701), V/iii; Baker, *An Act at Oxford* (1704), IV; both quoted in Alleman, 137–8.

[54] Anon., *A Treatise Concerning Adultery and Divorce* (London, 1700); *Conjugum Languens*, 21–3; T. Morer, *Two Cases, The First of Adultery and Divorce* (London, 1702).

of than now is practiced for relieving the parties injured and oppressed?'
This was a question which was not to be solved until 1857.[55]

It is no accident that it was in 1699 that the first attempt was made to
turn female adultery into a statutory offence, just at the time when the
crim. con. action was beginning to be used by a few of the aristocracy as a
means of punishing male seducers of wives and clearing the way for
Parliamentary divorces. Sir John Phillips introduced into the House of
Commons a bill to impose a fine of £100 on every wife convicted of
committing adultery. But as William Cowper, the future Whig lord
chancellor, was quick to point out, this was a bill 'which 'tis plain would
most affect the person most injured'—that is, the husband, since he was
legally responsible for his wife's debts. In the end, only a few moralistic
Presbyterians supported the bill, which was 'publicly ridiculed' by the
younger MPs. Objections against the whole plan of turning female
adultery into a criminal misdemeanour were that it would expose the elite
to blackmail by informers, predominantly their own servants; that it
might be used as a tool in the hands of some future arbitrary government,
in order to disgrace the families of political opponents; that it would give
wide publicity to obscene evidence; and that it would encroach upon the
jurisdiction of the ecclesiastical courts. The bill died, and the crim. con.
action therefore survived instead as the only means of punishing the
seducers of married women and thereby curbing the production of
bastard children to inherit great estates and titles.[56]

The Lords were clearly disturbed about their increasing involvement
in resolving matrimonial affairs, and after about 1702 there was a policy
decision, presumably by Lord Chancellor Cowper, that in future there
would be very strict procedural rules concerning Parliamentary divorce
bills.[57] After the Norfolk case in 1700, Parliament resolutely refused to
consider any bills except ones for divorce by childless males of rank and
wealth who had already been separated from bed and board by an
ecclesiastical court and whose inheritance was threatened by illegitimate
children produced by an adulterous wife. Of the thirteen successful petitioners from 1700 to 1749, six held titles and another three the rank of
esquire, and all but two were childless.[58] Each bill normally included the
argument that the petitioner 'hath no issue nor hope of any'.[59] The three
purposes of the bills were: to bastardize the illegitimate children of the
wife; to free the husband to remarry and beget a legitimate heir to inherit

[55] *Conjugum Languens*, 14, 16, 26–8.
[56] *Camden Misc.* 29, *Camden Soc.* 34 (1987), 352, 373–5.
[57] See the recent articles by Anderson and Wolfram on the history of Parliamentary Divorce
from 1700 to 1857, based respectively on studies of the petitions and acts.
[58] Wolfram, 163, 175.   [59] Ibid. 175, app. 1A.

the property and title; and to rearrange the marriage settlement in order to provide for maintenance for the wife. During this half-century, the object of granting Parliamentary divorces was thus exclusively the preservation of the patrilineal descent of property in the legitimate male blood line.

Other signs of the new restrictive policy are that although two female petitioners had sought relief from Parliament in the 1690s, such petitioners disappeared from the record during the eighteenth century, as did bills to annul child marriages or forced marriages. There was a famous test case in 1715 which once and for all declared this latter option closed. Back in 1700, Mary Forester, aged 13, had been married by arrangement of parents and guardians to Sir George Downing, Bt., a boy aged 15 whom she had never seen before. They were formally and publicly made to lie in a bed together for an hour, as a token of consummation, after which Sir George left for a three-year grand tour of Europe while Mary went back to her parents. When Sir George returned, he refused either to see his wife or to consummate the marriage, and she expressed equal indifference to him, refusing even to use the name of Lady Downing. By 1715 they thoroughly disliked each other, as shown by mutual 'disgusts and aversions', and they jointly appealed to Parliament to annul the sham of a marriage they had been forced into as mere children fifteen years before. Their counsel asked: 'I would fain know how much a divorce is worth, above sixpence, without leave to marry again, if the injured party pleases.' He also wanted to know why a marriage contract was indissoluble when all other contracts could be dissolved if done by mutual consent and without harm to third parties. The church admitted that in this case, although there was verbal acquiescence there was neither 'consent of understanding nor consummation'. Counsel argued that if 'the verbal contract is the thing itself', then the result is 'no end of absurdities'.

On the other hand, at the time of their marriage both children had been above the age of consent (12 for girls and 14 for boys), the ceremony had been carried out according to the canonical rules of the English church, and there was no adultery or cruelty charged against either party. The case was dismissed, but only after a three-hour debate and by a very close vote of 19 to 17.[60] This case aroused bitter feelings at the time and a lawyer protested that the law about the age of consent was ridiculous: 'it seems senseless and unreasonable to give our children the

---

[60] Anon., *The Councillor's Plea for the Divorce of Sir G. D. and Mrs Forester* (London, 1715), 2, 4, 9, 14–18, 31; Anon., *Cases of Divorce for Several Causes* (London, 1715), 2; *The Case of George Downing and Mary Forester* (London, 1715), 3–6; *JH Lords*, 20: 41, 45.

power of disposing of their persons for ever at an age when we will not let them dispose of five shillings without direction or advice'.[61] It was a case which stirred up a good deal of anti-clerical agitation, but the defeat of the bill was evidence of the narrowing of the Parliamentary avenue of escape from an impossible marriage.

Between 1700 and 1749, there was only one apparent exception to the rule that all successful petitioners must be men of large properties and titles. Closer inspection, however, shows that it too conformed to the stereotype. This was a divorce bill submitted in 1701 to Parliament by plain Ralph Box, a citizen of London, a member of the Grocers' Company, and a druggist by occupation. This puzzling anomaly of a mere druggist among all these men of landed wealth and titles is explained by the fact that he was the son of Sir Ralph Box, one of the richest business-men in late seventeenth-century London, also a druggist and member of the Grocers' Company. As the son of a knight, Ralph Box was certainly a gentleman, and his marriage with a landed wife promoted his upward mobility into the elite.[62] His tragedy was that he was unable to hold on to either his wife's person or her truly enormous marriage portion of £4,000, which was the kind of sum an earl might expect with his bride at this period. Mr Box had prepared the ground for divorce very carefully, being the first husband to appear before Parliament with both a success-ful crim. con. suit for damages against his wife's lover, and an uncon-tested sentence for separation from the Court of Arches. His only mistake was that he had promised his wife to return to her £3,000 of her £4,000 marriage portion if she agreed not to oppose the separation suit or the divorce bill. The Committee of the Lords approved the bill and proposed giving Mrs Box £3,000, but this last was defeated in the full House, which substituted an annuity of no more than £100 for life. Mrs Box protested that she had been double-crossed, but her plea was rejec-ted and the bill was passed.[63]

3. The Reshaping of the Procedure, 1750–1830

A. THE STANDARDIZATION OF THE RULES

During the course of the late eighteenth and early nineteenth centuries, the procedural rules for moving a divorce bill through Parliament slowly

---

[61] *The Councillor's Plea*, 4; see also Salmon, 147–52, 158–9.

[62] I owe this information to Gary De Krey.

[63] *JH Lords*, 16: 602, 648, 649; MacQueen, *House of Lords*, 538. With the passage of the Box bill, the stage was set for future developments of the Private Divorce Bill in the late 18th

became standardized, as a result partly of decisions in particular cases which served as precedents, and partly of a deliberate effort to regularize the procedure and tighten up the rules of evidence by Standing Orders. In consequence, the character of the proceedings became more judicial than legislative, and in 1868 Lord Westbury observed that 'in fact, the House acted as a Court of Justice'.[64]

The main burden of the investigation by the Committee in the House of Lords fell on the law lords, headed by the lord chancellor. It became normal for the second reading of the bill to take the form of a full trial, with personal testimony of witnesses and cross-examination of them and of the petitioner. If it survived the Committee of the Lords and a third reading, the bill went to the House of Commons, where it was examined by a Select Committee on Divorce Bills made up of nine members. A majority of these were laymen, but they also included all current and former law officers of the Crown. Among them was a member known as 'the Ladies' friend', whose special duty was to see that 'some suitable but moderate provision' was made for the maintenance of the wife. Since the wife did not get her marriage portion back, this often amounted to the jointure or annuity assured to the wife on the death of the husband by the terms of the marriage settlement.[65] After acceptance by the Commons, the bill was returned to the House of Lords, rarely with amendments, and in due course became law.[66]

By 1810 the basic requirements for the successful passage of a divorce bill were clear. The first was plausible, if often only circumstantial, evidence of the wife's adultery, testified to by two or more witnesses. The second was evidence of good marital relations prior to the adultery. The Lords tried to make sure that there was no signs of extreme prior negligence, neglect, separation of beds, or formal separation.[67] The third was the absence of evidence of any act of adultery or cruelty by the husband which could have driven the wife to adultery. By Standing Orders adopted in 1798 and 1809, the House of Lords also insisted on proof of a successful outcome to an ecclesiastical court suit for separation and a

century. Only one lone protest seems to have been raised throughout the century against the principle of passing a handful of individual bills, rather than reforming the divorce laws for all citizens along the lines advocated by Bishop Cosin and the Protestant theologians of other countries. Anon., *Considerations upon the Institution of Marriage by a Gentleman* (London, 1739).

[64] Roberts, 6.
[65] For example, *Percy v. Percy* (1779), *JH Lords*, 35: 529, 537, 548–9, 637.
[66] Roberts, 5–6, 68, 73, 114. For details of the procedure over private bills, see S. Lambert, *Bills and Acts: Legislative Procedure in Eighteenth-Century England* (Cambridge, 1971), 86–9; *Roy. Com. Divorce, 1853*, 1: 15.
[67] *JH Lords*, 52: 209.

common law action for crim. con., or a plausible explanation why none was possible.[68]

The last requirement was that there should be no evidence of joint collusion between husband and wife in organizing the divorce proceedings, either by arranging for the earlier crim. con. action or ecclesiastical court suit to go undefended, or by not enforcing payment of damages. But obstinate and cunning collusion over these matters in order to obtain a divorce by mutual consent was almost impossible to ferret out, and in 1854 the former lord chancellor, Lord St Leonards, observed that 'nothing is so difficult as to get at the facts in applications for divorce', especially since both sides are determined 'to conceal everything that can be concealed'.[69] Two years later, just before the end, Lord Chancellor Cranworth had to admit that in practice the passage of a divorce bill was virtually automatic if it had been preceded by a successful separation suit and crim. con. action.[70]

This may have been true then, but there had been some striking exceptions to this rule in the previous hundred years. There had been at least five occasions on which a jury in a crim. con. suit in King's Bench had either acquitted the defendant or awarded the plaintiff derisory damages but Parliament had granted him a divorce.[71] There had been six cases in which the ecclesiastical court had granted a separation but Parliament rejected a divorce, almost always on grounds of suspected collusion.[72]

The standardized divorce act of the early nineteenth century contained a number of clauses. First of all, it dissolved the marriage and freed the innocent husband to remarry. The draft bill in the House of Lords always included a clause prohibiting the guilty wife from marrying her lover, a clause which was routinely later struck out (except when the marriage would be incestuous). That part of a Standing Order of the Lords in 1809 was thus a dead letter, and by custom the guilty wife was left free to marry whomsoever she chose, who was normally her lover. After 1700 the husband always kept his wife's marriage portion, but in return he was expected to make provision for a life annuity to be settled on her for maintenance, despite her guilt.[73]

---

[68] MacQueen, *House of Lords*, 791; Wolfram, 170, Table 4. In debates over the Lord Ellenborough divorce bill in 1830, it was said that it was one of the first cases for decades in which there had been neither a prior crim. con. action nor an explanation why not (2 *Hansard*, 23: 1130, 1132, 1136).

[69] 3 *Hansard*, 134: 22.   [70] Ibid. 142: 403.

[71] MacQueen, *House of Lords*, 491, 500.

[72] Haynes in 1762; Chisim in 1769; Lewis in 1783; Esten in 1797; Hoare in 1802; and Woodcock in 1802; *JH Lords, passim*; MacQueen, *House of Lords*, 582, 585, 588, 600, 601.

[73] For details of the financial arrangements, see below, 345.

B. THE RISE IN NUMBERS

After 1750, the number of divorce bills and the proportion which became Acts both rose sharply (Fig. 10.1, Table 10.1). During the 1780s and 1790s, the number of bills rose from 20 to 41 per decade, and the 12 petitions for divorce received in 1799 (10 of which were successful) were the highest number ever handled in a single year, before or after. This

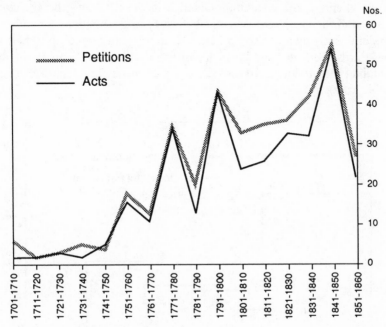

FIGURE 10.1   Parliamentary Divorce Petitions and Acts 1700–1857 [Table 10.1]

growth in the number of divorce petitions put increasing pressure on the House of Lords, which was estimated to have spent forty hours in 1799 on the examination of witnesses and the amendment of petitions for private divorces. This situation induced the poet Cowper to weigh in with a tactless rebuke to the House of Lords:

> ... senates seem
> Conven'd for purposes of empire less
> Than to relieve th'adultress from her bond ...
> Men were too nice in honour in those days,
> And judg'd offenders well. But now, yes now,
> ... sinners of either sex
> Transgress what laws they may.

325

The poem, quoted in the House of Lords by Lord Auckland, infuriated Lord Mulgrave, who called it 'a gross and criminal misrepresentation of this House of Parliament'.[74]

C. THE CHANGES IN SOCIAL COMPOSITION

The causes of this rise are to be found in the changing social composition of the clientele, the changing objectives of the laity, and the changing attitude of the law lords. Whereas before 1750 the petitioners had been predominantly men of title and landed squires, after 1760 up to half or two-thirds seem to have been drawn from the richer elements of the middling sort, to judge from some rather unsatisfactory data (Fig. 10.2, Table 10.2).

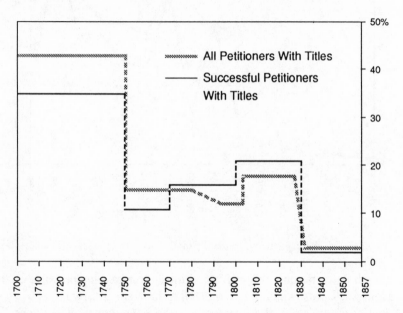

FIGURE 10.2   Social Status and Parliamentary Divorce 1700–1857 [Table 10.2]

Thus, Parliamentary divorce certainly began in the late seventeenth century as a privilege intended to be largely reserved by the aristocracy for the aristocracy, in order to assure patrilinear descent in the legitimate male line of large properties and ancient titles. It is a striking fact that 85 per cent of the successful petitioners before 1749 were childless, and so

[74] *Parl. Hist.* 35: 246, 255.

were desperately in need of an heir. But by the late eighteenth century it had become a privilege reserved for the rich, regardless of status or source of income.[75] And after the scandalous Ellenborough divorce bill in 1830, the titular aristocracy virtually dropped out altogether, presumably under the moralizing influence of Evangelical religion, coupled with a fear of violent revolution if they did not present a more responsible image to the public.

Contemporaries were well aware of these changes. In a debate in the House of Commons in 1830, a leading official in Doctors' Commons, Dr Lushington, commented that 'from an exclusive privilege for rank and station, divorce bills have become the remedy for the evils attendant on matrimony adopted by the middle classes, by all who can command the pecuniary means and have any reason for calling on the House to interpose its authority'.[76]

Among the petitioners there were also a handful of persons following fairly lowly occupations. In the late eighteenth century there were a butcher, a farmer, a French dentist, a coach-founder, a trimming-maker, a master mariner, and a riding master. In the early nineteenth century there were a veterinary officer in a regiment, a cabinet-maker, a piano-maker, a flour factor, a slate merchant, a linen-draper, a schoolmaster, a commercial traveller, and an oil-cooper.[77] It should be noted, however, that all of these must have been men in very comfortable circumstances, since they were able to afford the several hundred pounds needed in order to obtain a divorce.

4. Changes in Purpose and Function, 1750–1857

A. FROM THE PROTECTION OF PROPERTY TO THE PURSUIT OF HAPPINESS

The sharp rise in the number of petitioners for a Parliamentary divorce in the second half of the eighteenth century and the broadening of their social composition were both caused by a complete change in the moral justification for the granting of exceptions to the rule of the indissolubility of marriage. Before 1750 these exceptions had been exclusively

[75] Anderson, 433–4.
[76] 2 *Hansard*, 24: 1268. Both Anderson (419–22) and Wolfram (164, Table 3) agree on the rise in the number of petitioners from the upper middling sort after about 1750 to a fairly stable plateau, which Anderson puts at a half and Wolfram at a third. Both sets of figures are too low, since they include within 'upper classes' persons calling themselves 'gentleman', which by the late 18th and 19th century had become a largely meaningless social category.
[77] Wolfram, 165.

intended to protect patrilinear legitimate descent of honours, titles, and great estates. An essential element of each bill was therefore a clause bastardizing children conceived a year or more after a separation, or during a husband's absence abroad. These clauses begin to die away after about 1765. After 1829, only one bill passed which included a bastardization clause, although the preamble to several others contained accusations of bastardy, two of which specified the name of the alleged father. These preambles, however, had no legal standing.[78] There thus occurred a complete reversal, by which a clause which had been standard practice before 1760 had become all but unknown after 1830.

There were two reasons for this change. The essential one was the shift of the function of a Parliamentary divorce from the protection of property to the pursuit of happiness, defined as getting rid of an adulterous wife in order to remarry. The second reason for the change was a technical one concerning standards of proof. Before disinheriting a child, the House of Lords became increasingly concerned with the need for 'very strict proof of non-access' by the husband, and became very reluctant to deprive a child of its legitimacy before it was old enough to defend itself. In 1829 the House of Lords was told that 'that clause has not of late been introduced into bills of this nature, there being no person in attendance to watch the interests of the child; that that must be left until the child should be of age to defend itself'.[79]

B. THE RISE OF CONNIVANCE AND COLLUSION

Along with this change of purpose, it was inevitable that the incidence of connivance and collusion should grow by leaps and bounds, just as it did in separation suits and crim. con. actions.

i. Connivance

A flagrant case of connivance came to light in 1783 when Andrew Bayntun introduced into Parliament his bill for divorce from his wife, Lady Maria Coventry. She had already manifested her partiality towards Jack Cooper when her husband took the latter aside and urged him on, saying: 'I have this one further favour to beg of you, Jack, that you will go to bed with Lady Maria and allow some of my servants to come in and see you in that situation, in order that I may obtain my divorce with as little

---

[78] MacQueen, *House of Lords*, 650; Roberts, 29–31; Wharton, 474, 484; Anderson, 422; Daniel Haynes (1829), *JH Lords*, 61: 218. The one later exception was Edmund Heathcote (1851); *JH Lords*, 83: 24, 59, 61, 63, 71.
[79] Roberts, 30; Wharton, 484; *JH Lords*, 61: 218.

trouble and expense as possible.' He promised to pay all Lady Maria's debts up to that day; to return her marriage portion; and to continue to be Jack's friend and patron.

After Lady Maria had duly bedded and then eloped with Cooper, Bayntun proposed to launch an undefended crim. con. action against the latter. But Cooper could not be absolutely sure that Bayntun was not planning to double-cross him. He was afraid lest, after having obtained hard evidence of the adultery, and having sued Jack for huge damages— rumours of £10,000 were floating about—Bayntun might be secretly planning to enforce payment. However, in the end things seem to have arranged themselves, and the law case passed off smoothly. But in Parliament the plot was exposed, owing to the testimony of a servant about the conversation which he claimed to have overheard.[80]

ii. Collusion

Not many eighteenth-century husbands were willing to encourage their wives to commit adultery, however much they might have wanted to be rid of them. But by the late eighteenth century, confidence was waning in the truth of the claims of most Anglican divines that marriage was an indissoluble contract according to the word of God. If this were true, why did the bishops regularly vote for Parliamentary divorces? Enlightenment ideas, and the knowledge that other Protestant countries accepted divorce further undermined acceptance of the official position. As a result, although few were yet ready to demand a change in the divorce law, many of the upper middling sort and the landed elite saw nothing immoral about entering into collusive agreements about the handling of the legal proceedings in order to obtain a divorce by mutual consent. By the late eighteenth century, although various lords chancellors, especially Thurlow, Eldon, and Brougham, did all in their power to detect and repress it, many canon lawyers, attorneys, and laity looked upon such legal collusion as a morally neutral arrangement to achieve a mutually satisfactory legal end.

In 1800, the Bishop of Rochester accurately described the sort of behaviour which was encouraged by the existing law. By his account, it said to persons wanting a divorce:

Nothing [is] so easy as for all of you to have your several wishes. . . . The lady must make no defence; she must kindly supply the husband with the proofs of her own shame; the lover must not defend the action of damages; he may find his account in suffering judgment to go by default. Great damages may be given; but

[80] Bayntun case (1783), *JH Lords*, 36: 636–8, 648, 653, 671, 676–7. Oddly enough Bayntun obtained his divorce, presumably because the Lords did not believe the servant.

if the husband is opulent, every shilling may be remitted. However that may be, if you can amongst you defray the charges, a divorce will be obtained, and you will all be at liberty.[81]

It is clear that some such prior agreement, sometimes actually put in writing, was often made between husband, wife, and lover, a document Lord Auckland denounced as 'a contract founded in turpitude'.[82]

In the debate on the Ellenborough divorce bill in 1830, Lord Radnor hypothesized in the House of Lords about how things had been arranged in much the same manner:

Suppose two profligate persons—their Lordships will see that my hypothesis requires they should be profligate—were to make this agreement between themselves, 'You go your way, and I will go mine: please yourself, and I will please myself'; suppose two such persons agreed to shut their eyes to each other's conduct and to remain silent, the husband reserving to himself the right of coming here for a divorce, if the lady should happen to prove with child. Does not this supposed case come up precisely to that now before us?

It is significant of the level of cynicism in the Lords, and the degree of political pressure exerted, that the second Lord Ellenborough obtained his divorce, despite the very substantial evidence of collusion, and the fact that he had obtained neither a separation in an ecclesiastical court nor damages for crim. con. in a common law court.[83]

Contemporaries observed that most bills in Parliament after about 1780 went undefended, and that most of them no longer contained details of the maintenance settlement of the wife. They concluded from these two facts that a collusive deal had already been struck. In return for the prior settlement of a satisfactory annuity, the wife had agreed not to oppose the divorce and to keep secret any knowledge she might have about her husband's adulteries, any separation that might have occurred before her own adultery, and any complaints she might have about his neglect or cruelty.[84]

From 1750 onward, blatant examples of collusive petitions to Parliament for divorce became increasingly frequent. In 1754 the wife of a petitioner destroyed her husband's case by producing before the Lords a written agreement for collusion between him, herself, and her mother.[85] In another case in 1779, it soon became obvious that there was collusion when it came out that the cost of the divorce was being paid for by the wife's father in order to allow her to marry her lover, by whom she had

---

[81] *Parl. Hist.* 35: 295.
[82] Ibid. 35: 242; see also Lord Eldon, ibid. 35: 233.
[83] 1 *Hansard*, 23: 439.   [84] Anderson, 422.
[85] Moreau case (1755), *JH Lords*, 28: 313–14; MacQueen, *House of Lords*, 578–80.

already had two children. In a similar case a few years later, the petitioner's solicitor refused to swear under oath that he was not being paid by the wife's father.[86]

In 1808, another petitioner, Mr Bland, used both the carrot and the stick to persuade his wife not to defend either an ecclesiastical court suit for separation or a divorce bill in Parliament. He agreed to pay her some money that had been left her by an uncle, in return for her withdrawing her defence, and allegedly also threatened her that 'unless the defence was withdrawn it would be fatal' to her lover, whom he was suing for crim. con.[87]

Untypical only in that the collusion was so obvious that it was detected was the Gooch divorce bill, introduced into the House of Lords in 1781.[88] The Gooches privately agreed to separate in 1778, and Mrs Gooch went off to France. Three years later Mr Gooch obtained a judicial separation in the London Consistory Court on grounds of his wife's adultery with a number of French officers, the key witness being Mrs Gooch's French maid. But when Mr Gooch petitioned Parliament for a divorce, Lord Chancellor Thurlow, who chaired the committee on the bill in the House of Lords, became extremely suspicious. He did not much like the way Mr Gooch had allowed his wife to wander about all alone in the garrison towns of France. He was suspicious of the evidence of the French maid, whose wages were being paid by Mr Gooch both when she observed the adulteries of her mistress and when she testified about them. He was even more suspicious of Mrs Gooch's reaction when informed by her husband's attorney that two witnesses to her adulteries were needed for a Parliamentary bill. She promptly hired another servant as a cook to join her in France, got into bed with a French officer, rang the bell to summon the cook up into the bedroom, and told her to take a good look and remember what she had seen, since she would be needed as a witness.

It was perfectly clear that Mrs Gooch had deliberately provided the evidence against herself in order to obtain a divorce. What was not clear, however, was whether her husband and her attorney also knew about it. At the first reading of the bill, Lord Thurlow expressed his strong reservations, while agreeing that it would be hard on Mr Gooch if he should be deprived of his divorce because of the unsolicited contrivances of his wife. Convinced that the evidence of collusion was overwhelming,

---

[86] Chism case (1779), *JH Lords*, 35: 561–2, 570; MacQueen, *House of Lords*, 582–3; Downes case (1782), *JH Lords*, 36: 433–4.

[87] Bland case (1808), *JH Lords*, 46: 597; see also MacQueen, *House of Lords*, 593.

[88] *Parl. Hist.* 21: 1207–22.

Thurlow worked himself up into a rage, declaring that because of this practice of collusion

the manner and grounds of procuring divorces in this House ... frequently approaches to the ludicrous, if not the downright ridiculous, and in every sense might be well deemed unbecoming the dignity, gravity and justice of this House, and in fine are a disgrace to the legislature itself, which should never, upon any account, be put in situations tending to excite levity and ridicule.[89]

Thus between 1750 and 1800, the whole character and purpose of a Parliamentary divorce was being adapted to suit the changing social needs, sensibilities, and moral values of the petitioners and their wives. Less and less emphasis was being laid on the legitimate descent of property, and more and more on considerations of personal happiness and matrimonial comfort. And changing views about the theological and ethical propriety of divorce and remarriage meant that the great majority of bills were collusive.

iii. The Reaction: Lord Loughborough's Rules of 1798

It was inevitable that the rising tide of petitions for divorce and the rapid spread of collusion should have led to attempts to curb them both. It was not only conservatives like Lords Chancellors Thurlow and Eldon, but easy-going men like Lord Chancellor Loughborough and moralistic lawyers like Lords Kenyon and Erskine, who were appalled by a development which, when coupled with the concurrent rise of crim. con. cases, was taken to indicate a general rise in upper-class adultery. This assumed rise—whether true or false—was not only offensive to Evangelical and Methodist morality, but was also thought to be a threat to the very fabric of the nation, as we have seen in the arguments about crim. con. damages.

During the 1790s frequent allusions were made in speeches in both Houses to the results of the introduction in France in 1792 of legalized divorce with remarriage, on grounds of mutual incompatibility. As in England, separation from bed and board by an ecclesiastical court had previously been a remedy rarely used; overnight the new legislation opened the floodgates, and unhappy French couples, who would otherwise either have continued to live together or who had already separated by private agreement, now rushed to divorce. Between 1792 and 1801, there was one divorce for every eight marriages, three-quarters of them being instituted by wives. Put another way, 6 per cent of marriages performed in 1793 had been dissolved ten years later, and one

---

[89] *Parl. Hist.* 21: 1207–22.

may surmise that if the laws had remained, the total proportion of dis-solutions would have reached 10 per cent or more of all marriages.[90]

It was this experience which led fearful conservatives in England to try to make divorce even harder to obtain than it had been before, since they feared that so high a rate of dissolutions would undermine the fabric of society.[91] The result was two attempts to reduce the rising tide of Parliamentary divorces, the first by tightening up the procedure in Parliament, the second by punishing female adultery.

The first concrete attempt to turn back the tide of divorce petitions to the House of Lords was the introduction by the lord chancellor in 1798 of new set of Standing Orders, known as Lord Loughborough's Rules. Their purpose was to try to make sure that in future every effort was made to detect and reject suits in which the husband and wife were colluding to conceal unwelcome facts from the House in order to obtain divorces by mutual consent. The second purpose was to enable the House to discover whether the couple had in fact been separated long before the alleged adultery of the wife which formed the factual basis for the divorce. Earlier in the century such prior separations had not been held to be absolute bars to divorce acts. For example, in 1746 a husband who had been separated for three years caught his wife in bed with another man in a bagnio and successfully used the evidence to obtain a divorce.[92] In 1757 and 1779, the fact that the adultery by a wife had taken place nine years after a formal private separation did not prevent the successful passage of a divorce bill.[93] In 1798, however, the Lords rejec-ted a bill of divorce by a man whose wife had become the mistress of the Duke of Hamilton some five years after a deed of separation which had given her freedom to live where and with whom she pleased, and had barred him from instituting any suit against her for doing so.[94]

The first of the Standing Orders of 1798 demanded that an official copy of proceedings for separation in an ecclesiastical court be provided to the House with every bill of divorce. The House had long before demanded a copy of proceedings in a crim. con. action, and in 1831 it also asked for a copy of notes by the judge.[95] The second Standing Order

---

[90] R. Phillips, 'Women and Family Breakdown in Eighteenth Century France: Rouen 1740–1800', *Social History*, 2 (1976); id., *Family Breakdown in Late Eighteenth Century France: Divorces in Rouen 1792–1803* (Oxford, 1980); D. Dessertine, *Divorcer à Lyon sous la révolution et l'empire* (Lyon, 1981).　　　　　　　　　　　[91] *Parl. Hist.* 35: 251.

[92] Morris case (1747), *JH Lords*, 27: 96–7, 101, 107, 138.

[93] Wentworth case (1758), ibid. 29: 217–18; Lord Percy case (1779), ibid. 35: 548.

[94] Esten bill (1797), ibid. 41: 485–7; MacQueen, *House of Lords*, 588. But see also Twistleton Act, which passed in 1798, *JH Lords*, 41: 540–2, 549.

[95] 3 *Hansard*, 4: 921–2.

was more far-reaching. It ordered that every petitioner must present himself at the bar of the House, to be cross-examined about possible collusion and prior separation.[96]

In the hands of an energetic and intelligent lord chancellor, these Standing Orders offered a formidable weapon. Even before their passage, Lord Thurlow, lord chancellor from 1778 to 1792, had shown that it was possible, by relentlessly harassing petitioners, both to drive down the numbers applying and to increase the proportion of bills which were rejected (Fig. 10.3, Table 10.3). Whereas in the fourteen years before he took office, all 37 petitioners for divorce had been successful, during Thurlow's chancellorship the success rate fell to 25 out of 32.[97]

In 1801 Lord Eldon succeeded Lord Loughborough in the office of lord chancellor; he was to hold it for over a quarter of a century, until 1827. Using to the full the new powers of investigation offered by the Standing Orders of 1798, Eldon by fierce cross-examination almost single-handedly succeeded for at least his first twenty years in office in frightening off petitioners, and greatly increasing the number of bills

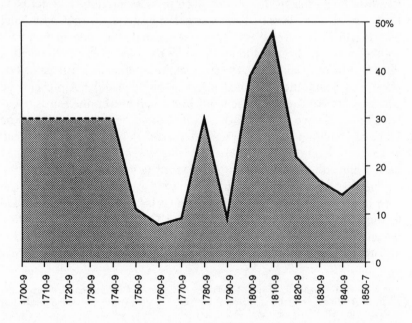

FIGURE 10.3   Proportion of Parliamentary Divorce Petitions Withdrawn or Rejected
1700–1857 [Table 10.3]

[96] Standing Orders nos. 175–8 in Roberts, 110. The 1798 orders are printed in full in *JH Lords*, 41: 517. For the 1809 Standing Orders, see 1 *Hansard*, 14: 326–35; 612–15.
[97] Anderson, 425.

which were abandoned, withdrawn, or rejected. By the 1820s, however, it is clear from the figures that Lord Eldon's efforts were failing. The number of petitioners for divorce was once more on the increase, as was the proportion succeeding in getting their bills turned into acts (Figs. 10.1 and 10.4, Tables 10.1 and 10.4). Remarks thrown out during debates in the House of Commons in 1830 in the aftermath of the patently collusive divorce of Lord Ellenborough and his wife explain what had happened. The critical Standing Order, that the petitioner submit himself to personal cross-examination about possible collusion 'has been dispensed with, because it would be a painful thing to those who had friends, and are well known, to submit to a public examination on such a subject. The Standing Orders, then, are perfectly nugatory as a protection against collusion.'[98]

In the end, therefore, the changed religious and moral attitudes towards divorce, and the social pressures of that clubby institution the House of Lords, were too much even for Lord Eldon, and political and family influence triumphed over legal justice. But Eldon was not solely responsible for the success up to 1820 in holding back the mounting demand for full divorce and in exposing at least some of the collusive actions of couples seeking divorce by mutual consent. He had been supported for twenty years in his draconian policy by the conservative majority in the House of Lords, which after about 1820 began to lose control. As the Whigs increased in numbers, so did the numbers of petitioners for divorce, to reach the unprecedented height of fifty-five per decade in the 1840s.

iv. The Reaction: The Anti-Adultery Bills, 1771–1809

The second effort to choke off the numbers of petitioners for divorce, which was even less successful, was the introduction of legislation to bar the divorced wife from marrying her lover. Four times between 1771 and 1809, bills were introduced into Parliament to achieve this objective, the most serious of which was proposed by Lord Auckland in 1809.[99]

The arguments used on the two sides provide an interesting insight into attitudes at the turn of the century towards adultery, divorce, and the legal position of women. Some of those in favour of the bill employed the same hysterical rhetoric about the threat of moral degeneracy sapping the moral fibre of the nation, and the danger of contamination from France,

---

[98] 2 *Hansard*, 134: 1265, 1272, 1286.
[99] *Parl. Hist.* 17: 185–6; 20: 591–601; 34: 1554–62; 35: 235–326; 1 *Hansard*, 14: 326–35, 612–15; see the premature encomium on the mover of one of these bills in Peter Pindar [John Wolcot], *Lord Auckland's Triumph, or the Death of Crim. Con.* (London, 1800).

as was being used by Lords Kenyon and Erskine to increase the damages awarded in crim. con. actions.[100] A more concrete motive behind these bills was a sense of moral outrage that adultery should be rewarded. Pamphleteers such as Thomas Pollen complained that 'our modern fine gentlemen look upon this crime [adultery] as mere gallantry, and though guilty of it never so often, would still pass as men of honour'. He lamented that 'the statute laws against immorality have lost their edge, which has been blasted by informations laid by low and hungry evidence, for the sake of rewards only; by which means informers are looked upon as infamous and rendered in a manner useless.'[101] Lord Auckland, who lobbied for thirty years for the passage of such a bill, denounced the whole system of Parliamentary divorces as 'a code of adultery for the privileged classes' and hoped to use the measure to place a curb upon it. The proponents of all four bills talked a great deal about the rising tide of immorality among the rich, the contamination of blood, and the threat to property resulting in 'the corruption of her offspring and her family and consequently of society'. Many pointed out, not entirely accurately, that the punishment for adultery by a wife was now nominal in England since shame was dead.[102]

The central moral question posed by the supporters of the bill was why an adulterous wife should be allowed to benefit from her own crime. This was something which was permitted only in England. In Scotland, the guilty party in a divorce for adultery was theoretically forbidden to marry anyone during the lifetime of his or her former spouse.[103] Proponents of these bills argued that, by removing from the wife contemplating adultery any hope of subsequent marriage with her lover, her incentive to succumb would be severely reduced, and in consequence there would be a sharp drop in the amount of female adultery in high society.

Another argument was that the bills would reduce collusion, by depriving wives of the incentive to participate in the private conspiracies of silence which lay behind so many divorce petitions.[104] The first bill in 1771 was in fact provoked by the scandalously collusive divorce in 1769 of the then prime minister, the Duke of Grafton, who for several years had been ostentatiously living with a famous courtesan, no hint of which notorious fact was allowed to emerge during the hearings in the House of Lords. Immediately after the divorce, his ex-wife married her lover, and

[100] See above, 273–8, 479–86.
[101] Pollen, *The Fatal Consequences of Adultery*, 72–3, 266–7, 272–4, 285–7.
[102] *Parl. Hist.* 20: 592, 586, 599; 35: 226.
[103] 3 *Hansard*, 147: 1763.
[104] *Parl. Hist.* 35: 237; 34: 1557; 35: 234, 252, 275, 295, 319; 1 *Hansard*, 14: 327.

the duke pensioned off his mistress and married for a second time. This was well known to be a blatantly collusive affair in which all parties conspired to keep out of the courts official knowledge of the duke's own adultery or the duchess's intention to marry her lover.[105] In the same year, Lord Bolingbroke had also divorced his wife by an identical collusive arrangement, so that the business was becoming a public scandal. George III appealed to Lord Chancellor Camden to do something 'that might be likely to prevent the very bad conduct among the ladies, of which there had been so many instances lately'.[106]

These arguments were apparently quite persuasive, and four times they induced a small majority of the House of Lords to vote in favour of these bills.[107] Ultimately, however, it was two counter-arguments that proved the most persuasive. The first was that the measure would do nothing to reduce the amount of wifely adultery. A wife, it was argued, does not commit adultery after a careful cost–benefit analysis, with the possibility of a second marriage with her lover acting as a powerful factor in her calculations. Rather, she commonly acts in a fit of romantic or sexual passion, without regard for short-term consequences, let alone the long-term. Charles James Fox, not surprisingly, was very eloquent on this subject, on which he no doubt considered himself something of an expert. It was also pointed out that the moral condition of Catholic countries, where there was no possibility of divorce and remarriage, did not support the argument. Rightly or wrongly, all Englishmen were convinced that in Rome, Naples, Spain, Austria, and France, female adultery in elite circles was normal and taken for granted: every lady had her *cicisbeo*. This led some opponents to suggest that a more effective way to deter wifely adultery in England would be to make marriage between the wife and her lover compulsory rather than forbidden. This would be enough, they suggested, to frighten off a great many sexual adventurers.[108]

The second argument, which became the decisive one, was that such a bill, even if it worked as intended, would be intolerably unfair to women. It would punish them with extreme severity, by depriving them of any chance of rehabilitation into the world of respectable married couples, while it left their lovers entirely unpunished. Several speakers pointed

---

[105] *JH Lords*, 33: 82, 104, 110, 114, 116; for the Grafton case see Stone, *Broken Lives*.

[106] *Letters and Journals of Lady Mary Coke*, ed. J. A. Home (Edinburgh, 1889–96), 3: 52–3.

[107] In 1800 the vote was 77 to 69 in a full House, after an exhaustive debate; in 1809 it was 28 to 12 (*Parl. Hist.* 35: 300; 1 *Hansard*, 14: 335).

[108] *Parl. Hist.* 17: 185; 20: 596, 598, 599; 35: 255–7, 276–7, 282, 294, 302, 314. For one example among many, see Lady Montagu's comments on Austria in *Selected Letters of Lady Mary Wortley Montagu*, ed. R. Halsband (London, 1986), 84–5.

out, without contradiction, that all these remarriages, which would in future be prohibited, had so far proved to be happy, respectable, and stable, and had produced a fine crop of legitimate children. If these ex-wives were now to be deprived of the opportunity to marry their seducers, they would be forced instead into concubinage or prostitution, since no one else was likely to marry them. It was for this reason that in 1800 Lord Mulgrave sardonically suggested that the title of the bill should be changed from 'An Act for the more effectual Prevention of Adultery' to 'An Act for the more effectual Promotion of Adultery and for the better Propagation of Bastardy'.[109]

Again and again, men in opposition to the bill in both the Lords and the Commons returned to this point that it involved 'a merciless punishment upon the unfortunate female', while leaving both her probably adulterous husband and her definitely guilty seducer to go scot-free. Many observed that in most cases wives were driven to adultery in the first place by the prior neglect, indifference, cruelty, or adultery of their husbands. The wide diffusion of this sentiment in both Houses in the year 1800 comes as a surprise to the historian accustomed to believe that men at that time were uniformly neglectful of women's claims to more equal treatment under the law.[110]

It was in response to these objections about gender inequity that Lord Auckland redrafted his bill during the debate in 1800 so as to introduce a quite new concept: a plan to criminalize all acts of adultery by either sex, making it subject to punishment by fine or imprisonment. But this did not go down at all well with a body of men, most of whom must have either already committed adultery at one time or another, or recognized that they might very well do so one day. Their anxiety is hardly surprising in view of the fact that Lord Auckland's idea of a suitable punishment was of such disproportionate ferocity.[111] Even so, the amended bill passed in the House of Lords, but it was defeated on the second reading in the House of Commons.[112]

These four anti-adultery bills gave rise to debates which took up a great deal of parliamentary time, aroused great public interest, and generated considerable passion. In 1800, Lord Chief Justice Keynon added fuel to the flames by publicly insinuating, in some comment to a jury in a crim. con. case, that those peers who opposed the bill, and particularly Lord Carlisle, were themselves guilty of sexual promiscuity.

[109] *Parl. Hist.* 35: 255, 278, 300–1.
[110] Ibid. 17: 185; 20: 593, 595, 597–600; 35: 228, 230, 236–7, 241, 249, 256, 258–9, 262, 277–9, 282, 299, 302–3, 307, 309, 313, 319, 323–4; 1 *Hansard*, 14: 330.
[111] Ibid. 14: 326–7.
[112] *Parl. Hist.* 35: 236, 275, 325; 3 *Hansard*, 142: 411; 147: 1744.

When his remarks were published in a newspaper, Lord Carlisle was furious and complained in the House of breach of privilege. Pitt asked George III to help him and the government in opposing this proceeding, which was being actively supported by the Prince of Wales and the two royal brothers, the dukes of Clarence and Cumberland, none of whom, to say the least, had unsullied reputations when it came to women. There may therefore have been some basis of truth in Kenyon's suggestion that the opponents of the anti-adultery bill were mostly themselves adulterers. In his diary, he summed up the outcome of the affair with typical acerbity: 'that puppy and adulterous profligate the Earl of Carlisle was to bring on his motion . . . against me for breach of privilege in alluding to his infamous speech on the Bill against adultery, but he withdrew his motion'.[113]

Frustrated by the defeat of all four bills, the conservative majority in the House of Lords in 1809 agreed instead upon a new Standing Order of the House, which prescribed that in future all bills for divorce should include a clause which forbade marriage by the adulterous wife with her lover. The House of Commons objected strongly, and thereafter it became standard routine for the Lords Committee to insert such clauses, and for the House at large to strike them out before voting on the bills.[114] Even this was not the end of the idea of forbidding the guilty party to marry her lover; Bishop Wilberforce of Oxford added such a clause in the course of the passage of the first Divorce bill in 1856, but it was defeated in both Houses thanks to opposition supported by the prime minister, Lord Palmerston.[115] On this stale and sour note, the eighty-year struggle to pass a bill forbidding the marriage of divorced wives to their lovers finally petered out.

5. Divorced and Remarried Wives, 1750–1857

A. INTRODUCTION

Wives from the upper classes who had committed adultery were often tormented with guilt and shame. When caught in adultery, a wife commonly exclaimed in horror that she was 'a ruined woman'—which in most cases turned out to be true. Many adulterous wives were rejected and abandoned by their lovers as soon as the first transport of sexual

---

[113] Lord Kenyon's Diary, 10 June 1800 (Kenyon MSS), quoted in *The Later Correspondence of George III*, ed. A. Aspinall (Cambridge, 1967), 3: no. 2165 n. 1.

[114] 1 *Hansard*, 14: 335, 612–15; MacQueen, *House of Lords*, 509–11.

[115] 1 *Hansard*, 143: 251, 308–9, 710; 147: 1760–6; see *Roy. Com. Divorce, 1912*, 1: 141.

passion had worn off. Only those whose husbands also wanted a divorce in order themselves to remarry, and whose lovers were willing to marry them, could look forward to a happy resolution of the affair. The despair that overtook many married women caught in adultery was therefore only too well founded, since they might well have to face total separation from all their children, severe financial hardship, loneliness, and social ostracism.

B. SEPARATION FROM CHILDREN

An abnormally high proportion of those couples who obtained a Parliamentary divorce were childless (Fig. 10.4, Table 10.4). When there were children, however, the most painful consequence of divorce for an adulterous wife, whether remarried or not, was her total separation from them. As with judicial separations, however badly a father might have behaved, after divorce he had a perfectly legal right in common law not only to keep all the children, however young, but also to cut their mother off from all access to or communication with them. In 1735 a woman wrote: 'I can't figure to myself a more afflictive circumstance in human life than to be entirely deprived of my child by the unkindness of my husband.'[116]

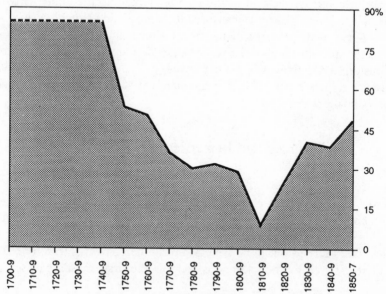

FIGURE 10.4 Proportion of Successful Petitioners for Parliamentary Divorce with No Known Living Issue 1700–1857 [Table 10.4]

[116] *Hardships of Law on Wives*, 21.

A case in point is the Duchess of Grafton, who was deprived of her children after her divorce and remarriage in 1769, and only saw her beloved son again on her death-bed, forty years later.[117] Worse still was the lot of the Countess of Westmeath in the 1820s and 1830s, whose husband kidnapped her only surviving child, Rosa, and forbade all access or correspondence. When she tried to get in touch with Rosa again, she found that her husband had turned the child's mind against her.[118] In the case of Lady Rosebery in 1815, the prosecuting lawyers for her husband turned the situation around by using 'the pitiable situation of the children in having their mother torn from them' as an argument for supporting her husband's claim to compensation. Indeed, when Lady Rosebery was discovered in the act of adultery, she became hysterical and tried to force her way out of the room saying 'I will see my children. Nobody shall prevent me.' But she was physically restrained, and told that she could never again set eyes on the children without their father's permission.[119]

One or two desperate mothers are on record as trying to retain a child by concealing its existence from the father. For example, in 1799 Elizabeth Lady Webster fled to Italy with her lover, Lord Holland, whom she subsequently married. In order to prevent Sir Godfrey Webster from laying hands on her little daughter, she pretended the child had died in Italy, going to the length of staging a mock funeral with an empty coffin. She later explained that 'the certainty of losing all my children was agonizing, and I resolved to keep one in my possession, and I chose that one who from her age and sex required the tenderness of a mother'. It was only three years later that she repented and returned the child to Webster, as a result of which she did not see her daughter again until the latter was grown-up and married.[120]

C. SOCIAL OSTRACISM

It is fairly clear that in the eighteenth century, kept mistresses, if equipped with a good education and the genteel graces, were able to build a social life for themselves without too much difficulty. Thus, the notorious courtesan Nancy Parsons presided for several years over a well-attended table in her capacity as official mistress of the prime minister, the Duke of Grafton. It is also notable that the 240-odd stories of titled men and their mistresses published in the *Town and Country*

---

[117] See the Grafton case in Stone, *Broken Lives*.
[118] See the Westmeath case, ibid. [119] *The Times*, 12 Dec. 1814: 2–3.
[120] Quoted in Lewis, 43; for other examples, see *Trials for Adultery at Doctors' Commons*, 7: 59, 60, 65, 72, 78; Shadwell bill (1796), *JH Lords*, 40: 609; Charles Christie bill (1815), ibid. 50: 246.

Magazine in the 1770s and 1780s make little or no mention of social ostracism.[121] On the other hand, these women had to live with the constant fear that their lovers might one day get tired of them and abandon them, as the Duke of Grafton eventually did with Nancy Parsons, although in this case with an annuity.

The situation of divorced wives who had legally remarried their lovers was clearly very different from that of semi-permanent mistresses. The former had moral and social rights associated with their legal status as wives, but whether these were the same as those of other wives is very uncertain. The mere fact of divorce hit them hard. Inevitably, those whose first husband possessed a title, but whose second did not, lost status and dignity after the divorce. Duchesses in particular had to endure the ignominy of no longer being addressed as 'your Grace'. Although she was to marry her lover, an Irish earl, this loss was something which the Duchess of Grafton took very hard in 1769. Indeed, it was mentioned by the duke's lawyer as something worthy of compensation.[122] In the light of this it is significant that she had had herself painted holding a ducal coronet.

An intractable problem for the historian is to discover the attitude of society at different periods towards a divorced and remarried wife. Was she happily reintegrated into a familiar circle of friends and acquaintances? Or was her name eliminated from invitation lists, was she denied admission to Court, was she cut in public, was she rarely visited, was she exiled into the countryside or abroad? The evidence is too sparse and too diverse to provide any firm conclusion on this matter, especially since it is likely that conditions varied not only from period to period, but also from class to class, and even from family to family within the same class. It seems quite likely that in the early nineteenth century, as the ideal of the companionate marriage and the cult of domesticity took hold, the attitude of high society towards divorced and remarried women became more severe than it had been in the more easy-going days of the eighteenth century. It is equally likely, although the evidence is largely lacking, that attitudes among the aristocracy and the leisured, landed classes were more tolerant than those among upper professional and business people, the only two groups below the elite who could also afford the luxury of a divorce and remarriage.

It is also probable that treatment of divorced and remarried wives varied from person to person. Horace Walpole, for example, remained a close friend of the divorced and remarried ex-Duchess of Grafton, now Lady Ossory, gossipped with her about new adulteresses among their

---

121 See the Grafton case in Stone, *Broken Lives*; *T & C Mag.*, *passim*.
122 Suffolk RO, HA 513/4/89.

acquaintances, but denied that he 'confound[ed] ... yourself with women who brave the public censure or level themselves to the most abandoned of their sex'.[123] On the other hand, Dr Johnson was one of those who took a brutally simplistic attitude towards divorced women. In 1773 Boswell presented the case of a wife, recently divorced by her husband for adultery, after having suffered abominable ill-treatment by him over a long period which had entirely alienated her affections. Her seducer had 'gained her heart whilst thus unhappily situated'. Dr Johnson brushed aside all these excuses with the savage remark: 'the woman's a whore, and there's an end on't'.[124]

During the debates in Parliament in 1779 and 1800 over bills to prevent divorced wives from remarrying their lovers, two distinct views were put forward about their social integration. The conservatives, who were seeking to bar remarriage, claimed that by this means delinquent wives went scot-free, since they were readily accepted again into high society. The Bishop of Llandaff claimed that, thanks to remarriage with her lover, 'a woman might now enjoy as many conveniences of rank and situation after a compelled dismission from her husband as after a separation from him by the hand of Providence [i.e. his death]'.[125] In 1800, an anonymous commentator deplored 'the frequency of intermarriage between the adulteress and the person with whom the offence has been committed; and her restoration in consequence of that event to society'. He alleged that in many cases the women 'have, in a great measure, regained the countenance of the world'. Lord Auckland even claimed that remarried adulteresses formed a sect of persons 'the elegance of whose manners and whose attractive habits of life would be well calculated to fascinate and corrupt the pure mind of others'.[126]

Lord Mulgrave, on the other hand, described divorced and remarried women as living in the 'poor, degraded, and secluded separation which he [the seducer] could offer to her wounded reputation'. He stressed 'that exclusion from the gay circles of general society which her former conduct has incurred', and described her as 'driven from the protection of her family, from the society of her friends, and deprived of the notice and estimation of her whole circle of acquaintance'. The Earl of Malmesbury took the same view in 1857, saying that 'the public showed their feelings by turning their back upon the guilty woman'.[127]

The fragmentary surviving evidence provides support for both views.

---

123 *Walpole's Correspondence*, 32: 78–9, quoted by Trumbach, 160.
124 J. Boswell, *Life of Johnson*, ed. A. Birrell (London, 1896), 3: 102.
125 *Parl. Hist.* 20: 592; 35: 250.
126 *Preventing Marriages Founded on Adultery*, 4, 10; *Parl. Hist.* 35: 250.
127 *Parl. Hist.* 35: 256–9; 3 *Hansard*, 146: 202.

On the one hand, the future Marchioness of Anglesea's divorce from Wellesley and her remarriage with her lover, Lord Paget, did not stand in the way of her new husband being made lord lieutenant of Ireland twenty years later in 1828, and her thus becoming the highest-ranking woman in Dublin society. On the other hand, she was snubbed by the wife of the Irish under-secretary, who refused to receive her.[128] Similarly, Lady Holland's divorce from Sir Godfrey Webster and her remarriage to her lover Lord Holland did not prevent her from establishing the most successful and fashionable Whig salon in London. On the other hand, a strict moralist such as Coke of Holkham would not invite her to his country seat, and wrote: 'She is not a woman I approve of at all.' However, he did accept her invitations to Holland House.[129] Of the separated Countess of Derby who lived with her lover, Lady Sarah Lennox commented that 'the lessening of her visiting list is her only misfortune'.[130] These stories point to substantial social and moral reintegration of some divorced wives into high society in the period 1780–1820, but also to their constant risk of exposure to occasional obloquy and ostracism.[131]

Was partial social rehabilitation still possible in the more prudish atmosphere of the early nineteenth century? It would seem that it was, for it was observed about the Ellenborough divorce bill in 1830 that 'Lady Ellenborough's friends' wanted the bill to pass 'in order that she might be restored, in some measure, to society, by her union with the party with whom the crime had been committed'. Although he was an ecclesiastical court judge, Dr Lushington made it clear that he favoured collusive divorce and remarriage in order to permit an adulterous wife to regain at any rate some degree of respectability.[132]

One may conclude from this very mixed bag of scattered evidence that some divorced and remarried aristocratic wives were successfully reintegrated and accepted by most of high society, although shunned by some and gossiped about by most. Others, however, were forced to live lonely and isolated lives in the countryside or abroad, and did not attempt to be seen in London society. What happened to divorced wives from lower down the social scale, among the rich professional and business classes, is entirely unknown. It seems likely that they found it much harder both to persuade their lovers to marry them, and to find a niche for themselves in society if they succeeded.

[128] Marquis of Anglesea, *One Leg: The Life and Letters of Henry William Paget 1768–1854* (London, 1961), 356.

[129] Lewis, 41–2.

[130] Trumbach, 159.

[131] For flight abroad, see above, 284–5.

[132] 2 *Hansard*, 24: 1279.

D. FINANCIAL POSITION

After 1700, it became customary to allow the husband to keep his former wife's marriage portion, but to secure to her an annuity adjusted both to her situation in life and to the size of her marriage portion. The divorce bill of Mr Loveden in 1811 provided a test case which challenged this Parliamentary custom. He was so outraged by the size of the allowance awarded to his wife by the Commons—£400 a year—that he preferred to let his divorce bill be defeated in the Lords rather than agree to it. His objection was that it amounted to subsidizing her adultery, since at the time of the passage of the bill she was living with her lover.[133] After this, it became standard practice for this matter to be resolved by a deed of settlement drawn up before the submission of the bill to Parliament.[134]

At first sight, this grant to an ex-wife of an annuity for life without strings appears as an act of generosity, especially if the wife was proposing to cohabit with or marry her lover. On the other hand, it has to be remembered that by the terms of a divorce bill, the wife forfeited claim to a return of her marriage portion, and also to her pin-money and her widow's jointure according to the terms of the marriage settlement. Moreover, the wife usually had friends in Parliament who could exercise political pressure on her behalf, while her husband was often desperate to obtain a divorce and willing to settle on any reasonable terms in order to be rid of her.[135] But the arrangement had many critics, and Lord Thurlow represented a large body of opinion when in the 1780s he declared that a maintenance grant to a divorced wife was 'an encouragement of immorality'.[136] In 1815, *The Times* protested against Earl Rosebery offering his incestuously adulterous and eloped wife a maintenance of £200 a year, in addition to her own £300 a year, in order to ease the passage of his divorce bill through Parliament. *The Times* asked: 'Is it fitting in a moral and Christian country that a pecuniary premium should be given for adultery?' The answer of Parliament seemed to be that it was.[137]

The obvious solution to this moral dilemma was to make the maintenance annuity conditional on living chastely or unmarried, a stipulation which in 1833 a legal commentator declared to be now standard practice. And indeed the first Divorce Act of 1857 laid down that maintenance for the ex-wife should only last as long as she remained 'chaste and alone'.[138]

---

[133] See the Loveden case in Stone, *Broken Lives*.
[134] Ibid, 2 *Hansard*, 23: 1128–9, 1138.
[135] MacQueen, *Marriage, Divorce and Legitimacy*, 145–7.   [136] Ibid. 146.
[137] *JH Lords*, 50: 205; *Annual Register . . . for 1815*, 283–6.
[138] Wharton, 478; Roberts, 37, 104–5.

It would appear, therefore, that this change in the terms of the grant to the divorced wife from an unconditional life annuity to one dependent on her remaining chaste and unmarried took place some time between 1811 and 1830, as a result of moral protests about rewarding adultery.

6. Conclusion

Parliamentary divorces began in the 1690s as a series of individual exceptions to the principle of the indissolubility of marriage, each one made in the interest of the patrilineal descent of property in a particular family. It ended as a convenient collusive agreement between a rich husband and his wife for a divorce by mutual consent in order to remarry, the objective now being the pursuit of happiness and the replacement of lost marital comfort. The provision of such an escape hatch exclusively confined to a handful of wealthy males, was clearly indefensible on grounds of theology, morality, or logic, and the major puzzle is why it lasted as long as it did, until 1857. Long before that time there had been growing rumblings of discontent, with protests arising not only from women and political radicals but also from leading civil and common lawyers and from politicians sensitive to growing external pressures for change.

❧ XI ❧

Divorce Reform Proposals,
1604–1850

Between the Reformation in the 1530s and the Divorce Act of 1857, the laws governing separation and divorce were those which had come down unaltered from the Middle Ages. This legal situation, which was unique in the non-Catholic Christian world, may be described as 'Protestant reactionary'. After 1604 it was virtually identical to the Catholic position, tempered only by some ambiguities in the wording of the canons and acts of Parliament.[1]

1. Reform Proposals from 1604 to 1800

Throughout the two-and-a-half centuries from 1604 to 1857 there were repeated proposals for change, beginning with those made by some highly respected clergy in the seventeenth century such as bishops Hall, Burnet, and Cosin. Their position may be described as 'Protestant conservative', namely that England should grant full divorce for wifely adultery, with permission to remarry restricted to the innocent husband. Some of these conservatives also proposed freedom of remarriage for the guilty wife, while others wanted to include cruelty and wilful desertion for a period of years among the legitimate grounds for divorce.

The best known and most cogently argued public statement of the 'Protestant conservative' legal position in the late seventeenth century came in the speech of Bishop Cosin of Durham, a former Laudian and a staunch Royalist, in the House of Lords in 1666 over the Roos divorce bill.[2] The bishop pointed out, correctly, the ambiguity of the evidence concerning what Christ really thought about divorce, as recorded in the Gospels. In the most lengthy version of Christ's views, recorded by Matthew, he seemed to concede that divorce was permissible on grounds of the adultery of a wife. Cosin also reaffirmed the old charge that separation from bed and board without dissolution of the marriage was merely a later popish invention, with no basis in the Gospels and unknown to the

---

[1] See above, ch. x/1/c.   [2] *State Trials*, 13: 1332–8.

Greek Orthodox church. He quoted Erasmus as saying that bed and board—that is, sexual relations and social companionship—were the very essence of marriage, and that the bond was broken by either adultery or malicious desertion. He referred to the peculiar ambiguity of both the canons of 1604 and the Bigamy Act of the previous year, neither of which quite closed the door to the possibility of a full divorce and remarriage. He pointed out that the current position of the Church of England was contrary to the *Reformatio*, which had been drafted by Cranmer; was at variance with the practice of all other Protestant churches in Europe; and had been overridden once by the Northampton Divorce Act of 1552. He concluded that a marriage contract 'does not extend even to tolerating adultery, or malicious desertion, which according to God's ordinance dissolves the marriage. . . . By adultery the very essence of the contract is directly violated.' He also cited bishops Jeremy Taylor and Joseph Hall, both eminent and highly respected divines and theologians of the 1630s, as supporters of his views.[3]

As for the counter-arguments, Bishop Cosin dismissed them all, on the grounds that the current system of divorce simply made things worse, not better. The husband was left uncertain of the paternity of his wife's children; the danger of unhappy spouses killing each other in desperation was increased; and adulterous concubinage was made more likely rather than less by blocking remarriage even to the innocent party in a suit for adultery. This speech by Bishop Cosin offered a powerful and well argued case, and it became the standard source for arguments in favour of the 'Protestant conservative' position, being quoted by Lord Lyndhurst in the House of Lords as late as 1856.[4]

The third possible position, the 'Protestant radical' one, was adopted by one or two Puritans and Dissenters, who demanded full divorce on grounds which included irreconcilable incompatibility and mutual hatred. This was argued most forcefully in the mid-seventeenth century by John Milton, based on the ideas of Martin Bucer published a century before.[5] Milton found few allies over the next two centuries. One of them was John Salmon, who in 1724 published a pamphlet in which he

[3] Jeremy Taylor, *Ductor Dubitantium* (London, 1660), 1: 191; Joseph Hall, *Works*, ed. P. Hall (Oxford, 1837–9), 7: 473–4.

[4] 3 *Hansard*, 142: 416; for an earlier use, see *Abstract of Bishop Cosin's Arguments proving that Adultery works a Dissolution of the Marriage* (London, n.d.), BL, 816 m 18 (16); for another attack on the *status quo* stimulated by the Roos case, see Anon., *The Case for Divorce and Remarriage occasioned by the late Act of Parliament for the Divorce of Lord Rosse* (London, 1673), 44–5.

[5] M. Bucer, *De regno Christi*, translated by Milton in 'The Judgement of Martin Bucer'; Milton's own views are given in his 'Doctrine and Description of Divorce', 'Telechordon', and 'Colasterion'. See *Complete Prose Works of John Milton*, ed. John Wolfe (New Haven, 1953), 2: 416, 222, 586, 719.

declared that the dogma that marriage was an indissoluble sacrament was merely a product of 'the superstition and corruption of the Papal See'.[6] He cited Montaigne as arguing that the Romans of antiquity 'kept their wives the better because they might part with them if they would', and reminded his readers that many peoples, for example, Islamic Arabs and Jews, had very liberal divorce laws.[7] He quoted Milton as arguing that 'the main benefits of conjugal society . . . are solace and peace', so that 'indisposition, unfitness, or contrariety of mind . . . is a greater reason of divorce than natural frigidity'. Consequently, 'if mutual affection causeth matrimony, with good reason the contrary inclination, by mutual consent, should dissolve it'.[8]

Salmon also claimed that, at the time of writing in 1724, it was 'held by some to be a great absurdity to forbid people to marry who are divorced [i.e. separated] even for adultery. Do they, say these gentlemen, really acknowledge that the calls of Nature in some are irresistible, and if people so separated are not permitted to marry they will certainly do worse . . . ? What is this but to drive men to despair, or to compel them to be wicked?"[9]

An equally radical position was adopted in 1739 by George Booth, Earl of Warrington, who was a Dissenter and therefore not attached to the traditions of the Church of England. He stated the Dissenting position—that marriage is a purely secular contract between two persons, God being only a witness and not a party to the contract. He pointed out that polygamy was widely practised in the Old Testament; that divorce for mere dislike was accepted in Jewish law; and that Christ was very ambiguous on the subject. He concluded that the marriage bond could be dissolved for adultery, desertion, cruelty, and even for psychological damage to peace of mind. Like Milton, he urged freedom from 'a bondage uncomfortable, and perhaps unsupportable to Humane Nature'. So if 'we find ourselves linked to a mere animated vegetable', there is 'nothing for the affection to fix on but bare sensuality', which is 'a prophanation of that Holy ordinance' of marriage. He rejected the ecclesiastical court separation from bed and board as a direct incitement to extra-marital sexual relations, and Parliamentary divorce as a lottery unjustly reserved for a few special cases among the rich. He therefore recommended a liberalization of the English divorce law by granting full divorce for female adultery, bringing it into harmony with those of other

---

[6] Salmon, 118.   [7] Ibid.
[8] Ibid. 125, 147. Salmon correctly pointed to the recent *Downing* v. *Forrester* suit (see above, 321) as a typical example of the break-up of a marriage because of a total incompatibility of tempers.   [9] Ibid. 161–2.

Protestant countries, including Scotland.[10] This was a restatement of the position first advanced by Cranmer in the 1550s and intermittently revived thereafter, but they seem to have had little influence on public opinion.

Thus, during the seventeenth and eighteenth centuries, there continued to be criticism not only of the concept of the indissolubility of marriage, which after 1666 was *de facto* breached by the Roos Divorce Act, but also the standard canon law procedure of granting legal separation from bed and board without permission to remarry. Both criticisms were destined to have a long life, but to judge by the results they were supported only by a small minority. But as the detractors of the legal system of divorce between 1698 and 1857—if system it could be called—were quick to point out, the bishops found themselves in a logically untenable position. Whereas in convocation they resolutely upheld the indissolubility of marriage as a sacred bond based on the words of Christ and canon law, when sitting in the House of Lords they regularly voted for the passage of private divorce acts for a handful of rich and privileged individuals who had already given bond before an ecclesiastical court that they would not remarry in the lifetime of their spouses.

2. Opposition to Reform, 1604–1800

It is natural to ask why it was that reform of the divorce law had to wait until the 1850s. One reason was the enormous respect for the law and the constitution as it existed in 1688, any tampering with which was thought to be liable to open the floodgates of revolution. Another was the near-sanctity accorded to the rights of property and male primogeniture. Evidence of the power of this ideology was starkly revealed in the only major reform of the period, the Marriage Act of 1753, which significantly strengthened legal supports for these values. A third was the catastrophic effects on reform of the French Revolution, the fears engendered by which held up all serious change in any field from 1792 to 1828. As Sir Samuel Romilly observed bitterly in 1808:

If any person be desirous of having an adequate idea of the mischievous effects which have been produced in this country by the French Revolution and all its attendant horrors, he should attempt some legislative reform on humane and liberal principles. He will then find, not only what a stupid dread of innovation, but what a savage spirit it has infused into the minds of many of his countrymen.[11]

---

[10] G. Booth, Earl of Warrington, *Considerations upon the Institution of Marriage* (London, 1739), 42, 48, 79–80, 90–1, 103, 111.
[11] S. Romilly, *Memoirs of the Life of Sir Samuel Romilly* (London, 1840), 2: 247.

As a result, up to the 1830s the political nation remained fearful of legal change over divorce, while the public at large were entirely indifferent to the matter. Even when willing to move, the elite were unable to agree on what to put in place of the existing courts and the existing law. The religious arguments against change were based on the belief that Christ's disjointed and confusing recorded remarks on the subject can only be interpreted as forbidding divorce for any cause. Consequently, most Anglican theologians regarded marriage as indissoluble—sacred in the eyes of God, even if no longer a sacrament of the Church.

Some of the secular arguments against change do not seem very persuasive to modern eyes. There was contrary evidence from Scotland, just across the border, to prove that the granting of cheap divorces on grounds of both adultery or desertion did not in practice open the floodgates to a tidal wave of family dissolutions. Moreover, it was widely believed that in Catholic countries, where there was no official divorce at all, there had developed a custom of tolerated mass adultery, at any rate among the elite.[12]

Despite these counter-examples, fear of social chaos because of serial polygamy through legalized divorce bulked large in nearly all the secular arguments against change right up to the nineteenth century. Less common was the argument that the strength of the nation depended on population growth, that this growth depended on marital intercourse, and that therefore easy divorce should be prohibited. Equally important, if rarely mentioned, was the vested interest of judges, officials, proctors, and civil lawyers in the preservation of the expensive and clumsy machinery of the ecclesiastical courts.

By far the most persuasive case against making divorce too easily accessible was made by the sceptic David Hume in 1724. First of all, he defined marriage as based on friendship, not on the ephemeral passions of romantic love or sensual lust. He first cited the opposite argument, so well put by Milton:

Nothing can be more cruel than to preserve by violence a union, which at first was made by mutual love, and is now in effect dissolved by mutual hatred. . . . The heart of man delights in liberty: the very image of constraint is grievous to it. . . . In vain you tell me, that I had my choice of the person, with whom I would conjoin myself. I had my choice, 'tis true, of my prison; but this is but a small comfort, since it must still be a prison.

Against this powerful appeal to affective individualism, Hume advanced four practical arguments:

[12] This theory had a long life. For a late example, see Anon., *A Plea for an Alteration in the Divorce Laws* (London, 1831), 11–12.

First, what must become of the children upon the separation of the parents? Must they be committed to the care of a step-mother; and instead of the fond care and concern of a mother, feel all the indifference or hatred of a stranger or an enemy? . . . Shall we seek to multiply these inconveniencies, by multiplying divorces, and putting it in the power of parents, upon every caprice, to render their posterity miserable?

Secondly, if it be true, on the one hand, that the heart of man naturally delights in liberty, and hates every thing to which it is confined; 'tis also true, on the other hand, that the heart of man naturally submits to necessity, and soon loses an inclination, when there appears an absolute impossibility of satisfying it. These principles of human nature, you'll say, are contradictory: But what is man but a heap of contradictions! . . .

In the *third* place we must consider that nothing is more dangerous than to unite two persons so closely in all their interests and concerns as man and wife, without rendering the union entire and total. The least possibility of a separate interest must be the source of endless quarrels and jealousies. What Dr Parnell calls 'The little pilf'ring temper of a wife,' will be doubly ruinous; and the husband's selfishness, being accompanied with more power, may be still more dangerous.

Fourthly Hume argued that the constraint of a more or less indissoluble marriage forces a couple together, while knowledge that divorce is available on demand drives them apart. He pointed out that the authors of romances pursue the tangled story of the pair of lovers only up to the moment of marriage, and hastily end the story before the really hard part begins of actually living together in harmony, offering the reader no more than the vague and implausible claim that the hero and heroine 'lived happily ever after'.

Hume concluded:

We need not, therefore, be afraid of drawing the marriage-knot the closest possible. The friendship between the persons, where it is solid and sincere, will rather gain by it; and where it is wavering and uncertain, this is the best expedient for fixing it. How many frivolous quarrels and disgusts are there, which people of common prudence endeavour to forget when they lie under a necessity of passing their lives together; but which would soon inflame into the most deadly hatred, were they pursued to the utmost under the prospect of an easy separation?[13]

Similar arguments in favour of the status quo were advanced in the early nineteenth century by that most learned but conservative of ecclesiastical lawyers, William Scott, Lord Stowell, who was quoted in

[13] D. Hume, 'Of Polygamy and Divorces', in his *Essays: Moral and Political* (London, 1742), 2: 187–91.

1853 by Lord Chancellor Cranworth during a debate in the House of Lords over divorce:

Though in particular cases the repugnance of the law to dissolve the obligations of marriage may operate with great severity upon individuals, yet it must be carefully remembered that the general happiness of the married life is secured by its indissolubility. When people understand that they must live together, except for a very few reasons known to the law, they learn to soften by mutual accommodation that yoke which they know they cannot shake off, and they become good husbands and good wives—from the necessity of remaining husbands and wives—for necessity is a powerful master in teaching the duties of life.

Lord Cranworth went on to argue that if divorce for cruelty or desertion were permitted, husbands who tired of their wives would have only to beat them up or desert them in order to obtain a divorce and be free to marry again. He made the same argument with respect to granting wives the right to divorce their husbands for adultery: since the husband loses nothing in public respect or social status by adultery, he has only to do it in order to get his wife to divorce him. The wife, on the other hand, 'loses her station in society' by her adultery, and is therefore much more reluctant to commit it.[14]

Thus, in the middle of the nineteenth century, all the old secular arguments were still being trotted out, but now under the banner of protecting women from exploitation by men. They were arguments which seem far-fetched today, but at the time they carried considerable weight and cogency. It is striking, for example, how little public pressure there was from women about the reform of the divorce laws. They were, rightly, much more concerned with the reform of the laws concerning married women's property.

3. Rising Demands, 1800–1850

A. SOCIAL CHANGES

In the early nineteenth century, there were four powerful cultural influences at work in society at large which tended to support a change in the law of divorce. The first was the growing acceptance of secular control over all aspects of life. That this included matrimonial affairs was first clearly enunciated in the Marriage Act of 1753, and powerfully reinforced by the introduction of secular marriage by public registrars in 1836. Since more and more members of the political nation were adopting secular attitudes towards divorce, the opinions of the Anglican

[14] 3 *Hansard*, 134: 5–6.

bishops, even if unanimous, could no longer dictate policy, despite their privileged access to the forum of the House of Lords. This secular tendency continued to grow and find expression in legislation in Victorian England, at the same time that religious feelings were becoming more intense, and theological debate more alive and acrimonious.

One result of these secular and pragmatic attitudes underlying active piety was that the ecclesiastical courts fell into considerable disrepute. It was not only that the common lawyers regarded their procedure of written deposition based on answers to written interrogatories as far less successful in elucidating truth than oral cross-examination by a skilled counsel in open court. There was also the growing feeling, first expressed at the Reformation, that the only remedy for a failed marriage offered by the church courts, namely separation from bed and board, was a highly unsatisfactory, even immoral solution to a difficult situation.

The second trend was the general acceptance of the Benthamite demand for a thorough overhaul of the legal system in order to create a single integrated structure. An early result was the setting up in 1824 of a commission to investigate the ecclesiastical courts and make recommendations about their reform. This revealed a situation which aroused the indignation of many common lawyers, who came to the conclusion that the church courts were grossly inefficient and should be stripped of their jurisdiction over what were now regarded as secular affairs, such as the probate of wills, and marriage, separation, and divorce.

The third was a recognition that it was morally indefensible to maintain any longer the ancient inequities of some aspects of the double sexual standard. These included the absence of legal protection for the property rights of abandoned or separated wives; the denial to separated or divorced women of custody of, or even free access to, their children; the denial to wives of legal rights to Parliamentary divorce; and the total exclusion of wives from the crim. con. action.[15] The first statute to recognize one of these injustices was the Infant Custody Act of 1839.

B. THE EXCLUSION OF ALL BUT THE RICH

There was also a growing recognition that more of the middling sort were entitled to a share in privileges hitherto reserved for the rich. Having been granted access to the vote in 1832, how much longer would they have to wait to be granted access to divorce? As things stood, a lot of money was needed in order to obtain a parliamentary divorce, and in the

---

[15] See above, 288–9.

late eighteenth and nineteenth centuries every knowledgeable contemporary commentator was convinced that only the rich could afford
one. During the debates in the Lords over anti-adultery bills in 1800 and
1809, Lord Auckland declared that 'the opulent class of adulterers and
adulteresses . . . by the expensive nature of the proceedings, are alone
implicated in divorce bills'.[16]

A major cause of the high cost of a Parliamentary divorce was that it
involved three distinct legal cases: one for separation in the ecclesiastical
courts; one for damages for crim. con. in the common law courts; and
one for divorce in Parliament. In 1846 a civil lawyer claimed that the
average cost of a contested separation suit was £1,700, while that of an
appeal up to the Judicial Committee of the Privy Council, which had just
replaced the Court of Delegates, might run to another £580.[17] In 1857
Patrick Fraser estimated that an unopposed crim. con. action cost £120
and an opposed one £300 to £500.[18]

In 1844, it was explained that 'the House of Lords . . . is beyond
comparison the most expensive tribunal in the Kingdom'. Counsel
charged double the standard fees, as well as 10 guineas a day for
attendance and 5 guineas for each consultation. The attorneys' fees were
also proportionately high, while the litigant also had to pay the heavy
expenses of having all the documentation printed.[19]

There are two difficulties about testing the truth of these estimates.
One is the enormous differences in costs between one suit and another,
especially between defended and undefended cases. The other is that
almost the only hard evidence is the costs taxed by the courts, and no one
seems to know quite what relation they bore to the real total costs. These
last included not only the legal fees of the court officials and the lawyers,
and the expenses of the witnesses, which were taxed at about 70 per cent,
but also the potentially enormous additional expenses incurred in hiring
detectives, tracking down witnesses, interrogating them, and preparing
them for their depositions—to say nothing of probable bribes and *dou-
ceurs*. As a result, there was often a very large discrepancy between
private claims about the full expenses of a divorce case and the officially
taxed fees.[20] A hotly contested case, like that of Lord Ellenborough in

---

[16] *Parl. Hist.* 35: 248; See also L—— McN——, *Chaste Thoughts on Adultery* (London,
*c.*1789), 4.

[17] *Roy. Com. Divorce, 1853*, 2: 27, 28, 58, 212, 403, 407, 419, 447, 455, 467; *Law Review*, 1
(1844–5), 367.

[18] Shelford, 377; Wharton, 451; P. Fraser, *A Treatise on Husband and Wife according to the Law
of Scotland* (Edinburgh, 1857), 4.

[19] *Law Review*, 1 (1844), 340.

[20] For a list of allowable taxed fees, see J. Merrifield, *The Law of Attorneys* (London, 1830),
app. 11–14; *Roy. Com. Divorce, 1912: Minutes of Evidence*, 1. 38–9; Lord Brougham, *Speeches*

1830, was said in informed legal circles to have cost him £5,000, and the cost of many other contested cases were said to run to £2,000.[21]

By the time the end of Parliamentary divorces was approaching in the 1840s and 1850s, costs seem to have sky-rocketed. For example, in 1850 a Mr Hartley introduced an uncontested divorce bill into the House of Lords. He had first been put to 'very large expense' for a year's search by detectives for proof of his wife's adultery. The unopposed suit for separation in an ecclesiastical court had cost him another £400 in legal fees, and his costs in the crim. con. action in King's Bench were taxed at £695. On the other hand, these latter costs were charged to the defendant lover, and the husband obtained £4,000 damages, £2,500 of which had already been spent in three months on the legal costs of the bill of divorce in Parliament. Lord Chancellor Brougham was outraged by these figures, and went out of his way to draw attention to 'the enormous amount of expense which parties are put to in cases of this sort, in consequence of the present system', which, he concluded, 'really amounts to a denial of justice'. He estimated that the whole of the £4,695 in damages and taxed costs which Mr Hartley obtained from his crim. con. action would probably have been spent by the time his divorce bill was finally passed, a situation he described as 'monstrous'.[22]

In 1849 the legal writer MacQueen summed up informed opinion when he wrote ominously: 'Justice is denied to the bulk of the Queen's subjects; whose long submission to this state of things is a conspicuous proof of the patient qualities which distinguish the English nation'.[23] The question which troubled many of England's rulers in the 1840s and 1850s was how long this patience would last if nothing was done to remedy so obvious an injustice. What they did not fully realize, however, was that there was in fact no great pent-up demand by tens of thousands, or even thousands, of middle-class couples urgently demanding cheaper divorce.

One may conclude that Parliamentary divorce was the privilege of a plutocracy, composed half of members of the landed elite and half of rich professionals and businessmen, legal costs being the determining factor in this restriction of access. Proof that this was so is the abrupt jump in the number of divorce Acts passed each year, from about four to over a hundred, immediately after the passage of the 1857 Divorce Act. The reason for this jump can only be the substantial reduction of costs

---

(London, 1838), 2: 475–6. Anderson (438–44) and Wolfram (166–72) argue, unconvincingly, that the costs were significantly less than was claimed by contemporaries.

[21] MacQueen, *House of Lords*, 367 n. 6.   [22] *The Times*, 8 Mar. 1850: 6.
[23] MacQueen, *Rights and Liabilities*, 234.

brought about by the act, even if it still left divorce out of reach of the bulk of the population. But the fact that for another fifty years divorces were still only counted in hundreds a year demonstrates the weakness of the demand by the middle class.

C. THE REVOLT OF THE LAWYERS

During the first half of the nineteenth century, factors specific to the law itself increased the political pressure for divorce reform. One motive driving the law lords and lawyers to demand change was growing friction between the two very different divorce laws of England and Scotland, a friction which was exacerbated by a series of difficult test cases which embarrassed and exasperated leading lawyers on both sides of the Scottish border. Scotland was a Presbyterian country with its own laws and law-courts, and ever since the late sixteenth century divorces had been granted by the Commissary Court in Edinburgh.

There were many important differences between the two countries in the laws governing divorce. Whereas in England the sole ground for full divorce by Act of Parliament was female adultery, in Scotland after 1573 it could be granted by the Commissary Court for adultery by husband or wife, as well as for desertion for four or more years. Whereas in England the law of recrimination applied, according to which the husband's sexual behaviour prior to the adultery was taken into account, there was no such law in Scotland. Whereas in England Parliamentary divorce was very expensive, and so restricted to the rich, in Scotland divorce was cheap, and so accessible to the middling sort; despite this facility, between 1836 and 1841 the numbers divorcing were only nineteen a year, over 40 per cent of the plaintiffs being wives, and most of them from fairly humble ranks.[24] Whereas in England the guilty party in a Parliamentary divorce was allowed to marry the person with whom the adultery had been committed, in Scotland such a marriage by the guilty was theoretically forbidden (although in practice this must have been a normal occurrence since the court never included in the sentence of divorce the name of the wife's paramour). Whereas in England separation from bed and board was the only remedy offered by the church courts, in Scotland it was almost unheard of, there being only two cases in the six years 1836–41.[25]

---

[24] 3 *Hansard*, 142: 420–1; 145: 534; 147: 392, 868; MacQueen, *Marriage, Divorce and Legitimacy*, 28–30.

[25] Lord Guthrie, 'The History of Divorce in Scotland', *Scottish History Review*, 8 (1911), 39–52; Wharton, 486–8; MacQueen, *Marriage, Divorce and Legitimacy*, 28–9; Poynter, 178–9.

So long as the English stayed in England and the Scots in Scotland, these gross legal discrepancies did not matter very much. But by the late eighteenth century when migration to and fro across the border had become common practice, the two sets of laws came into sharp conflict. The situation was greatly exacerbated by the fact that after 1753 the two countries were also practising two diametrically opposed laws of marriage: Scotland still accepted as binding both contract and clandestine marriages, whereas England after 1753 treated both as null and void. Problems consequently arose if an Englishman who was contracted in marriage in Scotland then married another woman in church in England. By Scottish law his second church marriage was void and bigamous, but by English law his first contract marriage was void. Thus, a man might have two legal wives, one in each country, each of whom could sue him if he crossed the border.[26]

After about 1810, divorce began to raise special difficulties between Scottish and English judicatures. The key question was whether the Scottish court was empowered to divorce an English couple married in England, but who had been domiciled in Scotland for the requisite forty days, or whose act of adultery or desertion had taken place in Scotland.[27] This issue was raised in 1811 by Mrs Teush when she was denied her divorce by the English Parliament for the adultery of her husband who was then living in Scotland. Thwarted in England, she petitioned for full divorce in the Edinburgh Court and won.[28]

The courts were caught on the horns of a dilemma. If domicile was the decisive test of jurisdiction, one Scottish commissary rightfully foresaw that couples wishing for divorce would in future shop around for the country with the most permissive divorce laws, which would probably lead them from England to Scotland, and from Scotland to some state in America.[29] On the other hand, if the place of marriage was decisive, serious injustice might be done to unwary individuals. Thus in 1812 an Englishman, Mr Lolly, who had been married in England, divorced in Scotland, and married again in England, found himself treated as a lawfully married man in Scotland but arrested and tried as a bigamous felon in England. His appeal against the sentence of transportation for seven

---

[26] In 1811 the two national jurisdictions came into bitter conflict over the case of *Dalrymple* v. *Dalrymple*. See Wharton, 488–9 and J. Dodson, *A Report on the Judgement . . . by Sir William Scott . . . in the Cause of* Dalrymple v. Dalrymple (London, 1811). The judgment, giving priority to a Scottish contract marriage over an English church marriage, was overthrown in 1844 by two other test cases, *Regina* v. *Millis* and *Catherwood* v. *Caslon*; see 'Marriage de Jure and de Facto', *Law Review*, 2 (1845), 126–52.

[27] J. Fergusson, *Reports on Some Recent Decisions by the Consistory Court of Scotland in Actions of Divorce* (Edinburgh, 1817), 9–16, 277–301.

[28] See below, 360; Fergusson, *Reports*, 23–39.

[29] Fergusson, *Reports*, 284.

years was heard by the twelve judges of England, who agreed unanimously that no foreign court could dissolve an English marriage; Lolly was therefore guilty, and the sentence should be carried out. The unfortunate Lolly was confined for some months in the hulks awaiting transportation, until common sense prevailed, and he was pardoned by the Home Office and released. This decision put English divorce law in conflict with those of every other Protestant country, including the United States. After about 1830, however, the Lolly doctrine of the indissolubility of an English marriage except by an act of the English Parliament was slowly undermined in a series of case judgments.[30]

In 1841 a commentator summed up the chaotic condition of the laws of marriage and divorce in Britain. Britain, he said, was

a country where the inhabitants were, on one bank of a fordable river, allowed to marry at twelve or fourteen years old by merely pronouncing five or six words, while on the other side of the stream, they could not marry under twenty-one, without the consent of their parents, and in neither case without religious ceremonies; . . . yet if the latter class walked across the river they might validly marry at any age and without consent; . . . on the northern bank of the same river, the marriage contracted there might be dissolved by sentence of the courts of justice for various reasons, but on the southern the contract was indissoluble; . . . Though a marriage contracted in the south could not be dissolved in the north, nevertheless, if the parties to the southern contract chose to have it dissolved, the northern courts would do so, and then they might marry again there, but if they came and married south of the river, they would be guilty of felony; . . . the same person is a bastard in one part of the country and legitimate in another, nay, a bastard in the same part when he claims landed property and legitimate when he claims personal effects.[31]

In 1860 nothing had changed; thus, the conflict of laws in reference to cases of divorce had been a matter of controversy for more than half a century.[32] This prolonged Anglo-Scottish battle over law and jurisdiction gave an added incentive to the lawyers to support the passage of the 1857 Divorce Act.

Conflict of laws with Ireland posed less of a problem. The Irish Parliament had hardly ventured into the divorce business before it acquired independence in 1782. Before 1779 only two bills had been passed, after approval of the English Privy Council; in the short eighteen-year life of the independent Irish Parliament, from 1782 to the Union in 1800, there were only nine petitions for bills of divorce, of which one was rejected.[33]

---

[30] *Law Review*, 1 (1844), 365; see also *Conway* v. *Beazley* and *Warrender* v. *Warrender* (Fergusson, *Reports*, 14–22).   [31] *Speeches of Henry Brougham* (Philadelphia, 1841), 2: 290.

[32] P. Fraser, *The Conflict of Laws in Cases of Divorce* (Edinburgh, 1860), 5.

[33] *Parl. Hist.* 20: 598; *Austin* v. *Mitchell* (Roberts, 9c).

In addition to these powerful reasons why legislators and lawyers should press for divorce law reform, there was one other consideration which has already been discussed, namely, the growing repugnance at the scandals associated with actions for crim. con., and the widespread use of collusion in Parliamentary divorces.[34] One leading lawyer in England who regarded collusion with equanimity was Dr Stephen Lushington, a judge of the London Consistory Court, who in 1830 and 1853 testified that in his opinion the word 'collusion' should be limited to active connivance in adultery.[35]

D. THE EXCLUSION OF WIVES AS PETITIONERS

Between 1700 and 1800, no wife even attempted to break the male monopoly of Parliamentary divorce.[36] In 1801, however, a Mrs Addison made the first try. She introduced a bill for divorce from her husband on the grounds of his incestuous adultery with her married sister. She won the unexpected support of two lords chancellors: the current holder, Lord Rosslyn; and his predecessor, the conservative Lord Thurlow, who was so appalled by the idea of sexual relations with a sister-in-law that he urged the passage of the bill, with a special clause to transfer custody of the children from the husband to the wife. Despite opposition from Lord Eldon and the Duke of Clarence, the future William IV, support from such eminently respectable legal quarters persuaded Parliament to break all precedents and to pass the first divorce bill submitted by a woman.[37] Encouraged by this example, four years later Mrs Teush tried to widen the narrow breach in the exclusive male monopoly of divorce. But by English law this was a run-of-the-mill case of male adultery, compounded by a persistent refusal to pay alimony, with no hint of incest or other unnatural practices, and her petition was therefore rejected in committee by a vote of 10 to 3.[38]

Over the next forty years, five more women introduced into Parliament bills of divorce, all of which were rejected or dropped. The one who came closest to success was Mrs Moffat, a woman with many aristrocratic connections, who in 1832 tried to obtain release from a marriage to a wholly impossible husband. Mr Moffat had been unfaithful

---

[34] See above, 286–8, 329–32.
[35] 2 *Hansard*, 24: 1278–9; *Roy. Com. Divorce, 1853*, 1: 46.
[36] For a general survey of this question, see *Law Review*, 1 (1844), 371–4; 8 (1848), 348–9; Roberts, 33.
[37] *JH Lords*, 43: 55, 75–8, 101–4, 190, 219, 220, 290, 319, 333; MacQueen, *House of Lords*, 475–8, 517, 594–8; J. Campbell, *Lives of the Lords Chancellors* (London, 1846), 5: 473–6.
[38] *JH Lords*, 45: 246, 296, 320; *Law Review*, 1 (1844), 372–3. See above 358.

to her on their wedding night, had debauched all the maidservants in the house, had given his wife venereal disease, and was constantly drunk. Mrs Moffat had fled back to her father and obtained a separation from bed and board. At the time of the bill, Mr Moffat was in the King's Bench prison, living there with a woman who maintained them both from her earnings as a common prostitute in Drury Lane.

This case, which was merely a peculiarly aggravated example of male adultery and alcoholism, attracted the sympathy and support of the conservative Lord Eldon, who had for so many years kept the lid on Parliamentary divorces. He took the radical position that under these extreme circumstances a woman had as good a right to divorce as a man, and disagreed with the conventional view that a husband was free to treat a wife 'as he thought proper'. In a reversal of roles, it was the liberal lord chancellor, Lord Brougham, who pointed out that access to divorce by act of Parliament had traditionally been restricted to husbands, except when there were peculiarly aggravating circumstances like incest. Mrs Moffat's bill was defeated and never became law.[39] This must have been the case a legal commentator had in mind when he remarked that

it is not many years since an attempt was made to show favour towards the family of an individual connected with many peers, by passing a divorce bill, contrary to all precedent and practice at the suit of his wife. Upon a division, the attempt was frustrated by a very narrow margin, in a House much more full than is ever found to assist at judicial proceedings.[40]

In the debate over the divorce bill in the House of Commons, one MP observed that 'we all know the influences that have been brought to bear in many individual instances'. This ostentatious political log-rolling helped to undermine the moral foundations for divorce by act of Parliament.[41]

Despite the defeat of Mrs Moffat's bill, what is remarkable is that by the 1830s and 1840s, after a century of precedents to the contrary, lawyers as distinguished and as conservative as lords Stowell, Erskine, and Eldon, and the leading civil lawyer, Dr Lushington, were all now convinced that access to divorce should be granted to both husband and wife. Where they disagreed was whether the access should be equal, or should be heavily weighted in favour of the husband.[42] Most of the Lords took the second view, and when in 1848 a Mrs Dawson was 'foolish enough to introduce a bill of divorce based merely on her husband's

---

[39] *JH Lords*, 64: app. III c; MacQueen, *House of Lords*, 658–9.
[40] *Speeches of Henry Brougham* (Philadelphia, 1841), 2: 295.
[41] 3 *Hansard*, 147: 1763.   [42] *Law Review*, 1 (1844), 374.

adultery and cruelty, the latter exemplified by whipping her with a small riding whip and a hair-brush, her petition was greeted by loud laughter among the Lords, and rejected.[43]

In the thirty years from 1827 and 1857, only three petitions for divorce by wives were successful. One was another case of incestuous adultery with the wife's sister, following the precedent of Mrs Addison, and the others were cases of bigamous adultery.[44] Thus by 1857, Parliament had by a series of precedents set up guidelines that established that divorce bills would only be granted to wives if the husband's adultery was accompanied by criminal circumstances, such as incest or bigamy.

Before the 1857 Divorce Bill, therefore, only the smallest of cracks had been opened in the wall of traditional belief in the double sexual standard, as a result of which wives were virtually denied access to Parliamentary divorce. On the other hand, the fact that more and more distinguished lawyers, including some very conservative ones, were publicly conceding that this situation was unjust was proof that educated opinion was beginning to shift in favour of somewhat greater equality for women before the law. In 1844, the liberal *Law Review* claimed with some justice that 'the tendency of public sentiment in the country has become at last favourable to the wife's claims of absolute release from her fetters', on grounds of 'long-continued, flagrant, and systematic adulteries'.[45] But this was overstating the case, and equal access to divorce on grounds of adultery by either sex did not become the law of the land until 1923.

E. WOMEN'S DEMAND FOR LEGAL JUSTICE

It is hardly surprising that another lobby for divorce reform, apart from the lawyers, was composed of upper-middle-class women. But these women were more concerned with the protection of their property as wives than with equal access to divorce, which was to most of them a secondary consideration. They were protesting vigorously the injustice of their legal impotence as married women due to the merging of their legal personality with that of their husband. This meant that so long as they

[43] MacQueen, *Marriage, Divorce and Legitimacy*, 43; Clifford, 1: 416–18; *JH Lords*, 80: 209–10.

[44] Louisa Turton case (1831), *JH Lords*, 63: 781–9, 824–7, 959; Anne Battersby case (1840), ibid. 72: 75, 86, 132, 137, 437, app. 316–21; Georgina Hall case (1850), ibid. 82: 305, 382, 417, 423, 473.

[45] *Law Review*, 1 (1844), 370; this was opposed by R. Phillimore *Thoughts on the Law of Divorce in England* (London, 1844), 23.

remained married, even though officially separated from bed and board, they were unable to sue or make a contract.[46]

It should be emphasized that the most prominent and influential of these women agitating for legal justice were very far from being 'feminist' in the modern sense of the word. For example, one of the most important was Caroline Norton, who not merely bullied and persuaded men in 1839 to alter the law on custody of small children in favour of mothers, but also helped substantially to alter the Divorce Bill of 1857.[47] But Caroline Norton was no flaming radical. In 1838 she publicly declared in a letter to *The Times*: 'The natural position of woman is inferiority to man. Amen! That is a thing of God's appointing, not of man's devising. I believe it sincerely, as part of my religion. I never pretended to the wild and ridiculous doctrine of equality.' In 1854, she again publicly proclaimed that 'the wild and stupid theories advanced by a few women, of "equal rights" and "equal intelligence" are not the opinions of their sex. I for one (with millions more) believe in the natural superiority of man, as I do in the existence of a God.' Mrs Gaskell also believed that men were superior to women in intelligence, the latter being 'at best angelic geese'.[48]

All that these women wanted, and which between 1835 and 1885 they succeeded in obtaining, was access to the courts for all wives, legal protection for their property, right to child custody, and a limited right, in extreme cases, to full divorce. It was the sheer moderation and justice of these demands, and the fact that they were advanced by women like Caroline Norton, who moved in the same social circles as the legislators of both Houses, which slowly convinced an increasing number of the leading lawyers of the age that some change was long overdue.

It was only very late in the day, in 1869, that John Stuart Mill came to the aid of the women's legal rights movement with a powerful pamphlet about the justice of power-sharing in marriage. He singled out wives as peculiarly discriminated against by the English legal system: 'There is never any want of women who complain of ill-usage by their husbands', but 'wives . . . hardly dare avail themselves of the laws made for their protection'.[49]

[46] For typical but rather mild pamphlet written by a woman, see Anon., *A Plea for an Alteration in the Divorce Laws* (London, 1831).

[47] For further discussion of the role of Mrs Norton, see below, 373-4.

[48] J. G. Perkins, *The Life of Mrs Norton* (London, 1909), 149; C. Norton, *English Laws for Women in the Nineteenth Century* (London, 1854), 165 (quoted by M. L. Poovey, *Uneven Developments: the Ideological World of Gender in mid-Victorian England* (Chicago, 1988). I am very grateful to Professor Poovey for allowing me to see a typescript of her book before publication; *Letters of Mrs Gaskell*, ed. J. A. V. Chapple and A. Pollard (Cambridge, Mass., 1967), 808 (quoted by L. Holcombe, *Wives and Property* (Toronto, 1983), 72).

[49] J. S. Mill, *The Subjection of Women*, ed. W. R. Carr (Cambridge, Mass., 1970).

4. The Debates Over the Ellenborough Divorce and Dr Phillimore's Bill, 1830

In 1830, the second Lord Ellenborough introduced into the House of Lords a bill for his divorce from his wife. This was so scandalous in its collusive nature that it generated a full discussion of the need to remove divorce from the jurisdiction of Parliament and make it accessible to a wider section of the population than a mere handful of the very rich. The general debate stimulated by this private bill reveals how confused and divided the governing classes still were in their attitudes towards divorce.[50]

In response to the sense of outrage generated by the scandal of the success of the Ellenborough divorce, a month later, Dr Phillimore, a conservative civil lawyer, introduced into the House of Commons a bill to transfer control of divorce from Parliament to the ecclesiastical courts. He argued that the current situation was indefensible. It was unique in Europe, discriminated unjustly between rich and poor, and was based on mass collusion to push through undefended bills in order to obtain divorce by mutual consent. Parliament was incapable of resisting 'the torrent which threatens to bear down all morality and virtue', he said. 'Does not the House feel itself degraded by every divorce bill? It is either a mere mockery of legislation, to which nobody attends, or else the House is made the instrument for covering the guilty connivance of two parties'—for example Lord and Lady Ellenborough. Phillimore was no radical, however. He merely wished to improve the procedure and shift the burden from Parliament to the ecclesiastical courts. He was opposed to making any alteration in the basic rules of the game, which was that marriage should be indissoluble, not on theological grounds, but in the interest of social stability; and he believed that divorce should be permitted only for female adultery.[51]

The solicitor-general was tormented by uncertainty. On the one hand, he defended Parliamentary divorce on the now outdated grounds that it was intended 'in the first instance to secure the descent of property in high and mighty families'. He also expressed his strong belief that 'it is desirable to throw impediments in the way of divorces', rather than 'to render it easier for persons of every rank to obtain that relief'. He was therefore opposed to 'appointing a separate court to give cheap divorce to the people'. On the other hand he freely admitted that 'under the present system, there is one law for the rich and another for the poor', and

---

[50] 2 *Hansard*, 23: 1386–7; 24: 1276–81.   [51] Ibid. 24: 1260–3.

declared that 'this consideration is so revolting to me, that I could not uphold such a system, if I did not conscientiously believe that by extending the remedy, the legislation would only increase the mischief'.[52]

Mr C. W. Wynn, the Whig secretary at war, was more strongly opposed to the *de facto* reservation of divorce to the rich through the procedure of the Parliamentary bill. He asked rhetorically: 'Is not the clergyman, the professional man, or the shopkeeper, as well entitled to the remedy as the great landed proprietor?' In fact, as we have seen, the members of the upper middle class already had access to divorce—but only if they were rich enough to pay for it. Mr Wynn also pointed to a rise in cases of bigamy, and alleged that most of the defendants were husbands 'whose wives had quitted them or eloped'. These men were therefore now punished by transportation, merely 'because they wished to enjoy the comfort and satisfaction of domestic society', but were unable to afford a Parliamentary divorce.[53]

A more radical position was advanced by the Whig secretary of the treasury, Mr Spring-Rice. He claimed to represent 'the unanimous feeling of the country', that cases should be removed from Parliament to a new tribunal which could handle them cheaply and expeditiously and on other grounds than the single cause of female adultery. Joseph Hume joined him in protesting that the government was dragging its feet despite 'one universal exclamation against the mode of procedure . . . this great practical evil'.[54]

Both moderate Whigs and radicals were thus willing and anxious for change, but it was the extreme reactionary position which ultimately won the day on this occasion, thanks to the conservatism of the House of Lords. The case against change was laid out by the arch-Tory, Sir Charles Wetherell. To vote for the bill, he argued,

would be letting in a wild, latudinarian, and mischievous principle, not recognized hitherto by any country in the world. . . . It would follow as a necessary consequence that the lower classes, whose morals are more corrupt and whose principles on these subjects are more lax than those of the higher classes, will be continually applying for divorces, while the facility of obtaining them, at a small expense, will increase the immorality of adultery, and indeed give encouragement to the commission of that offence.[55]

In his opposition to all change, Sir Charles was expressing a minority view. The majority was troubled, and willing to abolish the Parliamentary divorce system, provided that a conservative substitute could be found. In

[52] Ibid. 1275–6.   [53] Ibid. 1283.
[54] Ibid. 23: 1376, 1397, 1399; 24: 1272–4.   [55] Ibid. 24: 1269.

1830, the majority still agreed with Dr Phillimore when he pronounced that 'experience shows the happiness of the married life is best promoted by considering marriage, generally speaking, as an indissoluble contract'.[56] But Dr Phillimore's proposed solution—to transfer jurisdiction to the thoroughly discredited and distrusted ecclesiastical courts—was totally unacceptable to the laity, and his bill was soundly defeated.[57]

5. Conclusion

It was the secularization of control over matrimonial affairs, starting with Parliamentary control over the law of marriage in 1753, which slowly opened the way to a liberalization of English laws of divorce. After 1832, the principle of extending political privilege further down the social system to the ranks of the middling sort had been accepted, and by the 1840s the time had come to extend sexual privilege, including the power to divorce an adulterous wife, to those hitherto quite unable to afford the lengthy procedures involved in a parliamentary divorce.

In 1839, the *Crim. Con. Gazette*—not normally given to philosophical insight or moral posturing—summed up the situation in a nutshell:

A man with a very large sum of money may get a divorce from the Houses of Parliament and may marry again. A man with a smaller but considerable sum of money may get from the Ecclesiastical Courts a half divorce which relieves him merely from his wife's debts but does not enable him to enter into another matrimonial connection. A man with no money, or an insufficient income, can have no divorce at all.

The *Gazette* went on to point out that Prussia had over three thousand divorces a year, and England only two or three. The difference, it argued, was made up by 'undivorced but miserable couples, and by an extensive system of infidelity, concubinage and prostitution. . . . Certain classes have, moreover, their sale of wives.'[58] This was not a situation of which mid-Victorian lawyers and legislators were proud.

The second issue that bothered many thoughtful men in the early Victorian period was the injustice of allowing husbands to divorce wives for adultery, but not *vice versa*. Thus in 1842 the legal writer MacQueen thought that public opinion, while still tolerant of occasional male adultery, was coming round to the opinion that a wife was entitled to divorce for the systematic, persistent, and flagrant adultery of her

---

[56] 2 *Hansard*, 23: 1363, 442.
[57] Ibid. 24: 1293–4.
[58] *Crim. Con. Gaz.* 2: 75.

husband.[59] As a result of these shifts in basic attitudes, and a recognition of specific legal deficiences and injustices, by 1850 reform of the divorce law had at last become part of the official agenda.

[59] MacQueen, *House of Lords*, 481–2, 370–1.

❧ XII ❧

The Passage of the Divorce Reform Act, 1850–1857

1. Preliminary Skirmishes

By the 1840s there were strong feelings in the legal profession that something had to be done about the chaotic distribution of separation and divorce proceedings over various courts in England.[1] This was just the sort of legal disorder which attracted the attention of Benthamite reformers, who were anxious to produce a unified, equitable, and coherent court structure. Their solution was to take authority over separations away from the church courts and authority over divorces away from Parliament in order to place both under a new secular High Court.

As we have seen, there were growing complaints after 1830 that the high cost of Parliamentary divorce created one matrimonial law for the rich and another for the poor. This issue was brought to public attention in 1845 by a brilliantly sarcastic sentence upon a hapless bigamist issued by Justice Maule, several versions of which were widely circulated at the time and for decades to come:

Prisoner at the bar, you have been convicted before me of what the law regards as a very grave and serious offence: that of going through the marriage ceremony a second time while your wife was still alive. You plead in mitigation of your conduct that she was given to dissipation and drunkenness, that she proved herself a curse to your household while she remained mistress of it, and that she had latterly deserted you; but I am not permitted to recognise any such plea. . . . Another of your irrational excuses is that your wife had committed adultery, and so you thought you were relieved from treating her with any further consideration—but you were mistaken. The law in its wisdom points out a means by which you might rid yourself from further association with a woman who had dishonoured you; but you did not think proper to adopt it. I will tell you what that process is. You ought first to have brought an action against your wife's seducer, if you could have discovered him; that might have cost you money, and you say you are a poor working man, but that is not the fault of the law. You would then

[1] *Roy. Com. Divorce, 1853,* 2: 30–8.

be obliged to prove by evidence your wife's criminality in a Court of Justice, and thus obtain a verdict with damages against the defendant, who was not unlikely to turn out a pauper. But so jealous is the law (which you ought to be aware is the perfection of reason) of the sanctity of the marriage tie, that in accomplishing all this you would only have fulfilled the lighter portion of your duty. You must then have gone, with your verdict in your hand, and petitioned the House of Lords for a divorce. It would cost you perhaps five or six hundred pounds, and you do not seem to be worth as many pence. But it is the boast of the law that it is impartial, and makes no difference between the rich and the poor. The wealthiest man in the kingdom would have had to pay no less than that sum for the same luxury; so that you would have no reason to complain. You would, of course, have to prove your case over again, and at the end of a year, or possibly two, you might obtain a divorce which would enable you legally to do what you have thought proper to do without it. You have thus wilfully rejected the boon the legislature offered you, and it is my duty to pass upon you such a sentence as I think your offence deserves, and that sentence is, that you be imprisoned for one day; and in as much as the present assizes are three days old, the result is that you will be immediately discharged.[2]

The first constructive step forward towards reform was the setting up in 1850 of a Royal Commission on Divorce, chaired by Lord Campbell. In its three-volume report of 1853, it proposed no change whatever in the law concerning separation and divorce, but recommended a major reconstruction of the courts.[3] The prime objective was to destroy the fifty local ecclesiastical courts by transferring to two new secular courts virtually all their non-clerical business, that is the probate of wills and matrimonial affairs. One MP openly called the probate bill 'a sister measure, upon which this divorce bill in some degree depends'.

When he first introduced the divorce bill into the House of Lords in 1854, Lord Chancellor Cranworth specifically rejected the idea of changing the law to allow the wife to be able to sue for divorce on grounds of her husband's adultery, just as the husband could sue on grounds of that of his wife. He argued that it was harsh to punish a husband who was merely 'a little profligate'—an off-hand reference to the double standard which would have passed unnoticed in the eighteenth century, but now aroused indignant comment in the press.[4]

---

[2] *Regina* v. *Hall*, 1845. There are various versions of this much quoted speech, of which this is the most elaborate, and possibly embroidered by other hands. *The Times*, 3 Apr. 1845; 3 *Hansard*, 134: 14–15; ibid. 142: 1985; see also W. E. H. Lecky, *Democracy and Liberty* (London, 1896), 2: 166–7. It was still quoted in O. R. McGregor, *The History of Divorce in England* (London, 1957), 15–17, from which this extract is taken.

[3] *Roy. Com. Divorce, 1853*, vol. 1.

[4] 3 *Hansard*, 134: 7; 142: 406; M. L. Shanley, ' "One Must Ride Behind": Married Women's Rights and the Divorce Act of 1857,' *Victorian Studies*, 25 (1981–2), 364–5.

By her own adultery, however, a wife 'loses her station in society', and commits a crime which her husband cannot be expected to condone. He therefore recommended that wives could only divorce their husbands if the latter committed adultery aggravated by incest or bigamy, which had been the standard procedure in Parliament for half a century.

What the 1854 bill proposed was to remove two of the current three legal actions from the existing courts—separation from bed and board from the ecclesiastical courts, and divorce from Parliament—and to turn them both over to the Court of Chancery which already dealt with child custody when trust property was at issue. The crim. con. action was retained in King's Bench or Common Pleas, but in future it was to come *after* judicial separation or divorce, not before. The bill was thus little more than an open power play by the common and equity lawyers to capture full control of all matrimonial litigation. The bill did nothing whatever to reduce costs or abolish crim. con. actions. Indeed, by forcing all litigants to come to London, the proposal would have increased rather than reduced costs, leaving the great bulk of the population even more deprived of access to judicial separation than they had been before.

In defence of this very limited bill, it was argued, correctly, that there were no signs of public agitation for 'a cheap tribunal for granting divorces'. Lord Redesdale stated that 'there have been no petitions in favour of an alteration nor the least expression of a desire for a cheap tribunal for granting divorces', while Gladstone claimed that the labouring classes were 'unanimously opposed'.[5] Moreover, separations from bed and board, half of which were now heard by the London Consistory Court, only amounted to about twenty a year, while there were only three or four Parliamentary divorces a year. Demand was clearly minimal.[6] Such opposition as was raised against the bill was moderate in tone and content, and led by law lords. Lord St Leonards protested against crim. con. being allowed to continue, and regretted that so little effort was being made to bring English law into line with that of Scotland. He also pointed out that it was impractical to put more litigation into Chancery, which was already clogged with excess of business. The lord chancellor then withdrew the bill, but merely in order to amalgamate it with the parallel bill to remove probate of wills from the ecclesiastical courts. To him, the basic object was still no more than the transfer of business from the church courts and Parliament to some other common law or equity tribunal.[7]

---

[5] 3 *Hansard*, 134: 20; 145: 1406; 147: 758, 827–8, 870.

[6] *Roy. Com. Divorce, 1853*, 1: 29–31.

[7] 3 *Hansard*, 134: 22–5, 936–7, 1436.

2. The Debate Over the Divorce Bill, 1856–1857

A. GOVERNMENT OBJECTIVES

When in May 1856 Lord Chancellor Cranworth reintroduced into Parliament a divorce bill, it was clear that he and the Palmerston government were still exclusively concerned with abolishing the jurisdiction of Parliament and the church courts. The attorney-general argued forcibly that 'the country would be benefitted by the abolition of the prolix, extortionate, and extravagant system' of canon law applied by the church courts.[8] No compensation was offered to officials working in the church courts for the loss of their business, a callousness defended on the grounds that 'this divorce business is confined in a few hands'.[9]

The government also argued that the bill 'would bring divorce, which heretofore had been a privilege within the reach of the rich man only, home to the doors of the humblest classes'.[10] This was a fraudulent claim, for neither the government nor its opponents had any desire to make either divorce or judicial separation accessible to the poor. In Macaulay's blunt words, it was 'a claptrap observation'.[11] Gladstone and others pointed out that the new court and its procedures 'will apply to only an infinitesimal part of the population'—someone estimated only thirty thousand families. As a result, it was prophesied that the poor would be forced to continue the old practice of self-divorce. Parted from their wives, they 'find a new companion and often commit bigamy . . . not so much for the satisfaction of the man as for the woman'.[12]

In fact, there was great ambivalence in Parliament about granting access to divorce to the poor. One MP prophesied that easy access would turn out to be 'one of the greatest social curses that this country has ever been visited with', which did not deter him from denouncing the hypocrisy of the government in 'deluding the people with regard to this measure'.[13] In the upper House, Lord Redesdale, a conservative, accurately summed up the opinion of virtually the entire Lords, when he said that 'it was felt to be a dangerous step to throw open the power of divorce to the whole society'. The reactionary Bishop Wilberforce of Oxford warned that 'equal justice to the poor would be purchased at the price of the introduction of unlimited pollution', and even the Whig Lord John Russell admitted that he was not in favour of 'giving greater facilities for divorce'.[14]

[8] Ibid. 142: 401–8. [9] Ibid. 147: 1196, 1237, 1852. [10] Ibid. 147: 1975.
[11] Ibid. 1182; see also 758, 1048, 1191. [12] Ibid. 1989. [13] Ibid. 1173, 854.
[14] Ibid. 146: 228; see also ibid. 142: 1980: 145: 514; 147: 871, 1173.

One MP pointed out that under the new proposals, a poor man would be obliged to hire both a local attorney and a London attorney, and to travel with all his witnesses to London to give evidence at a series of trials. The total cost of all this would be far beyond his means.[15] Late in the prolonged debate, Palmerston at last revealed that this was precisely what the government intended. Knowing that judicial separations merely led to either concubinage or bigamy, he wanted to reduce them as far as possible by making them more expensive.[16] This was the reason why the government consistently opposed the many attempts to allow separations to be granted in future by local secular tribunals such as the new County Courts.

In reality, the government had four objectives. The first was purely administrative, to concentrate all matrimonial litigation in a new secular High Court in London, so as to put an end to the jurisdiction over these matters of the church courts and Parliament. The other three objectives were substantive. One was to make full divorce rather easier and cheaper, and therefore rather more accessible to the upper middle class; another to make judicial separation more expensive, and therefore rarer; and an unspoken third was to keep judicial separation and divorce wholly inaccessible to the lower middle class and the poor. The hypocrisy of the vague talk of equality of access for all was exposed by many critics during the course of the debates.[17]

B. OUTSIDE PRESSURE GROUPS

In view of the way the bill was drafted, it is hardly surprising that it could be alleged by an MP, with some plausibility, that Parliament had received ninety thousand petitions against the bill—from both left and right. The poor had nothing to gain by the bill, and were in any case confused by the technical terms, being naturally unable to understand the use of the same word 'divorce' to mean two entirely different legal conditions: full divorce with the right to remarry; and separation without the right to remarry. This verbal ambiguity was only finally cleared up in the course of the debate in 1857, when the lord chancellor agreed that in future the former would be called 'divorce' and the latter 'judicial separation'.[18]

It is hard to detect much sign of political pressure being brought to bear from those members of the middle class who before the act could obtain legal separations from bed and board but had been unable to afford a Parliamentary divorce. Immediately after the act was passed,

---

[15] 3 *Hansard*, 147: 1979–81.   [16] Ibid. 1194.
[17] Ibid. 1161–4, 1168–70, 1191–3.   [18] Ibid. 145: 1406–7.

only about a hundred of them a year transferred from the judicially separated category to the divorced category. These thwarted would-be divorcees who stood to gain from the bill were thus few in number, and so far as can be seen they played little or no part in influencing the extensive Parliamentary debates during 1854, 1856, and 1857.

There were, however, three influential upper-middle-class groups who agitated actively, and with considerable success, to convert the bill from a purely administrative reorganization of the courts to a significant change in the laws governing divorce. The first was led by Mrs Caroline Norton.[19] Having, as we have seen, succeeded in 1839 in helping to push through Parliament the Infant Custody Act, her prime interest was now to obtain legal protection of the property and earnings of separated women (like herself) against seizure by their husbands. Her mouthpiece in Parliament was Lord Lyndhurst, a highly respected elder statesman and her intimate friend.

There were two other extra-Parliamentary influences on the side of reform. One was a group of impeccably respectable upper-middle-class women organized by Miss Barbara Leigh Smith Bodichon—a group which carefully kept its distance from the morally dubious Caroline Norton. The other was a group of Whig lawyers organized into the Law Amendment Society, founded and chaired by Lord Brougham since 1844. These two groups worked closely together, and it was they who in 1856 drafted a carefully worded petition to Parliament about the Married Women's Property Law.[20]

On the conservative side there were ranged against the bill many pious Christians, led by Gladstone, who were convinced that all divorce was against the words of Christ. Aligned with them were large numbers of parish clergy, who were appalled at the (in fact unlikely) prospect of being obliged by law to perform the marriage service over adulterous divorcees. They were a well-organized body which quickly mobilized up to ten thousand clerical signatures to a petition against this alleged threat to their consciences.[21] Secondly, some sixteen thousand housewives were said to have petitioned the queen against any expansion of the facilities for divorce or separation, being fearful that it would be exploited by husbands in order to get rid of their wives, leaving them penniless and lonely in their old age.[22]

---

[19] C. Norton, *A Letter to the Queen on Lord Cranworth's Marriage and Divorce Bill* (London, 1855), 8–9; see J. G. Perkins, *The Life of Mrs Norton* (London, 1909), 248–9.
[20] Holcombe, 85–6, app. I; Shanley, 'One Must Ride Behind', 358–63.
[21] 3 *Hansard*, 147: 380, 758, 870, 1028–30.
[22] Ibid. 827, 1028, 1031.

It is today widely believed that divorce was forced on to the political agenda in the middle of the nineteenth century by major changes in the economic conditions of the labouring poor. The argument runs that a strain was put on the working-class family system by the growth in the number of wives earning a wage in factories outside the home. Coupled with the alienating effects of rapid urbanization and demographic growth, this created pressure to provide some security for married women's property, and greater access to divorce when marriage broke down, as it now more frequently did. However, there is nothing in the Parliamentary debates of the 1850s which shows the slightest awareness of these problems. To virtually all legislators, the poor were seen as a threatening, immoral, dissolute mass of people to whom it would be extremely dangerous to extend the facility of easy divorce, or to offer protection of married women's earnings outside control by their husbands. Either concession might, it was argued, undermine what elements of stability existed in working-class families. In any case, there was no evidence at all that the poor were demanding divorce. As late as May 1857, the House of Commons 'had not received a single petition on the subject', and there were many voices raised against it. An ardent supporter of equality of property rights for women, Sir Erskine Perry, was right to argue that 'no popular demand has arisen on the subject. . . . We certainly have no reason to believe that the people of England desire that the facilities of divorce which exist in some Protestant countries, so much to the corruption of morals therein, should be introduced into England.'[23]

C. THE DRIVE FOR WOMEN'S LEGAL RIGHTS

The most eloquent and influential spokesman in Parliament for the legal rights of women was Caroline Norton's friend, the ex-lord chancellor Lyndhurst. Although now 84 years old and confined to a wheel-chair, he still retained his full energy and mental vigour, and was happy to take up the cudgels in the House of Lords to remedy 'the system of hardship and cruelty as regards to women'. He began by drawing attention to the appalling plight of a separated wife (such as Caroline Norton) whose earnings and property could be seized by her husband at any moment, and went on to denounce the injustice of totally excluding a wife from a crim. con. action. He asked: 'Is that fair? Is that honest? Can it be vindicated upon any principle of justice, of mercy, or of common humanity?' He then turned to a more sensitive aspect of legal discrimination against

[23] 3 *Hansard*, 145: 267.

women, with respect to equal access to divorce. He quoted three lords chancellor, Thurlow, Eldon, and Brougham, in favour of sexual equality of access to the law. At present, he concluded, 'men make the laws and women are the victims'.[24]

In three brilliant speeches, Lyndhurst succeeded in turning the main thrust of the divorce bill away from a mere procedural shift of litigation from church courts and Parliament to common law courts, and refocused it upon significant changes in the law of divorce itself. A whole new battle was now joined about three issues critical to women: the legal protection of married or separated women's property; the ability of women to defend themselves in a crim. con. action; and legal access to divorce for women on equal terms with men.[25]

Protection of married women's property and equal access to divorce for men and women were the two most delicate and dangerous issues on the agenda of the women's reform movement in mid-Victorian England. The demand for equal access to divorce on grounds of adultery by either husband or wife struck at the very foundation of the double sexual standard. The demand for the placing of a married woman's property under her own control struck at the heart of the economic aspects of a marriage contract, and threatened the strategic manipulation of marriage to advance family property interests. It also created a dual economic interest between husband and wife, which over a century before Hume had declared to be a threat to marital harmony.[26] In fact, the top 10 per cent of society, including almost all those represented in Parliament, were already marrying under the settlement arrangement, by which the wife kept control over her own property through trustees. But the idea of extending by statute this privilege to the bottom 90 per cent of the population struck terror into the hearts of most of the legislators. It seemed to threaten the Victorian ideology of the two spheres—the one the warm, domestic world of women, represented by the wife at the fireside, and the other the harsh outside world of men, struggling daily in the market place under the banners of economic competition and possessive individualism. It is no wonder, therefore, that these two bombshells thrown into the divorce bill legislative process should have generated prolonged and fierce debate. In the end, some significant concessions were made on both issues, but the last redoubts remained intact:

[24] Ibid. 142: 408–25; 145: 496–58, 779–85.
[25] Shanley, 'One Must Ride Behind', 358–61; Perkins, *Mrs Norton*, 248–51. See also a penetrating survey by M. L. Poovey, *Uneven Developments: The Ideological World of Gender in Mid-Victorian England* (Chicago, 1988).
[26] See above, 351–2.

married women's property was not secured until 1882, and equal access to divorce only in 1923.

To go some way to satisfying these demands, the House of Lords Select Committee in 1856 produced a draft which tacked some of Lord Lyndhurst's proposals over women's legal rights on to the original, purely procedural, bill. By a unanimous vote, it recommended the reform most dear to the heart of Mrs Norton, that is, the protection of the property and earnings of *separated* wives from seizure by their husband. The draft gave these women financial security and freedom to make contracts and generally to be treated in law as if they were unmarried women. It also recommended a major enlargement of the grounds upon which wives could sue their husbands for divorce: before, it had been merely adultery aggravated by bigamy or incest; now it was to include adultery aggravated by cruelty. But in handling the crim. con. action, the committee was evasive. It expressed its distaste for the action, but rejected total abolition for lack of an alternative, so that an action for damages remained as an option.[27] These compromise proposals, which included some very large concessions to wives, were only grudgingly accepted by the government.

In achieving this significant but limited victory for women's legal rights on two fronts—access to divorce and security of property for separated wives—Lyndhurst may in one vital respect unintentionally have further diminished the very dim prospects of more radical change on the second. Soon after he had introduced into the House of Lords his own amendment for the protection of the property of separated wives, Sir Erskine Perry introduced into the House of Commons a more far-reaching measure.

This bill had been drafted by the Law Amendment Society headed by Lord Brougham, and was based on suggestions made by the committee of upper middle-class women which had been started by Miss Barbara Leigh Smith Bodichon back in 1854.[28] The ladies had collected on a petition some twenty-five thousand signatures, including those of 'the most distinguished names in literature, science, and art, and belonging to the most influential classes in society'.[29] They had also collected many examples of appalling injustice done to married, separated, and deserted wives. There was the married woman whose husband went bankrupt and whom she supported in comfort for many years by her successful millinery business. When he died, he bequeathed all her property and the

---

[27] *3 Hansard*, 142: 1969–71.

[28] Holcombe, ch. IV: 86; *3 Hansard*, 145: 266–75; see C. A. Lacey (ed.) *Barbara Leigh Smith Bodichon and the Langham Place Group* (London, 1987).   [29] *3 Hansard*, 145: 167.

business to his illegitimate children, leaving his widow penniless. There was the deserted wife whose husband went off to Australia with another woman. For years she supported herself by running a school, until at last her husband, having failed in Australia, returned to England and seized all her property, including the school. And there was the separated French milliner who came to London and established a flourishing business. Hearing of her success, 'her husband suddenly came over, pounced upon her earnings, sold her stock in trade, carried off the proceeds, collected the debts, and returned with her entire fortune to Paris'.[30]

To put an end to these horrors, Sir Erskine Perry's Married Women's Property Bill proposed making all married women, whether living with their husbands, separated, or deserted, responsible for their own property, their own debts, and their own torts, capable of making contracts, and able to dispose of their property in life and by will. But the bill was opposed by the government and the great majority of both Houses, on the grounds that it was likely to lead to separation of economic interests in a single household and thus to 'a corruption of morals'. The proposal consequently died.

All that was left of it were two more modest proposals, one by Lord Lyndhurst, which protected the property of *separated* wives, and the other by Lord St Leonards, which protected that of *deserted* wives. Although these amendments left untouched the husband's full control over the property of his wife among normal cohabiting married couples, they succeeded in salvaging something from the wreckage, and at least the most egregiously ill-treated wives were henceforth protected.[31] The bill passed, despite opposition from the *Saturday Review*.[32]

Women were far from lacking male support in this battle, which was the reason for their partial success. Mr Drummond told the House of Commons that 'the laws of England were more severe against the woman than were those of any other country in Europe'. Citing another radical who had asserted that 'adultery is in itself a dissolution of marriage', he faced his fellow MPs with the awkward logical consequences: 'If that is so, how many men in this House are married?' Gladstone told his colleagues that by legislating different grounds for access to divorce to men and women they were defying the basic tenets of Christianity and merely exemplifying 'the assertion of the superiority of our position in the creation'.[33] Since this was what most of his colleagues believed, Gladstone's

---

[30] Ibid. 142: 1274–7; 144: 608–9, 614–17; Holcombe, 66.
[31] Holcombe, 101–2; 3 *Hansard*, 144: 619; 145: 266–75; 146: 1520–3.
[32] Anon., 'Marriage Law Reform', *Saturday Review*, 3 (14 Feb. 1857).
[33] 3 *Hansard*, 147: 1267–8; 1271–4.

gibe did not cut very deep. But even in the conservative House of Lords, there were peers, like lords Lyndhurst and Brougham, who felt very strongly about the injustice of the legal inequality of wives, and agreed with Lord Lansdowne when he said he would rank England among 'the least civilized and most barbarous states. Certainly she occupies a condition which is inferior to that which prevails in any other modern country,' and inferior to that which prevailed in Rome.[34]

But modern feminist values should not be read back into the mid-Victorian period. For example, while Gladstone believed that the Christian religion demanded total equality of treatment of men and women, Mrs Norton believed that the Christian religion dictated the absolute superiority of men over women. As a result, while Gladstone was demanding full legal equality between the sexes, Mrs Norton was only asking for just protection of her rights from her natural superiors, men. If Caroline Norton was as much under the spell of the ideology of the double standard as any man in England, it is hardly surprising that its legal consequences took a very long time indeed to be altogether removed from the statute book.[35] Sir Erskine Perry was equally ambivalent in his attitudes. While introducing proposals to create a full legal separation of property rights of husbands and wives, he went out of his way to assert that he 'was advocate of no speculative or theoretic reform' and to deny that he entertained 'any novel or theoretical notions on the position which women ought to occupy in society'.[36]

D. THE BATTLE OVER THE BILL, 1857

The great mystery about the passage of the Divorce Act is why the prime minister, Lord Palmerston, pursued it so relentlessly throughout the months of June, July, and August 1857. He did so although it meant keeping Parliament in session for an unprecedented time into the summer, forcing members to endure the burden of debating from noon to two in the morning every day in the broiling heat of one of the hottest summers in living memory, and ignoring the daily attrition of members drifting back to the cool and peace of their country seats.[37] It is hard to see why Palmerston, who thereafter showed no signs of interest in domestic reforms, should have invested so much energy and political capital in forcing through a bill which was very substantially different from the one that his government had introduced, and which had so little

---

[34] 3 *Hansard*, 142: 1972–3.
[35] For Gladstone, see ibid. 147: 1271–4; for Mrs Norton, see above, 373–4.
[36] 3 *Hansard*, 145: 267; Holcombe, 66.   [37] 3 *Hansard*, 147: 1021.

popular support behind it. One can only suppose that he was tired of the endless debates, which had gone on since 1850, and was anxious to get the matter over and done with once and for all. He also probably wanted to demonstrate his power over Parliament, was not averse to the virtual destruction of the ecclesiastical courts, and was urged on by the law lords. But it was not a popular bill in either House, and probably would not have passed if the opposition had not melted away into the countryside while the government kept its placemen severely in hand.

During these long, hot months, an intense battle raged over the contents of the bill. First, there was strong opposition, as we have seen, to giving married women control over their property so long as they were living in a normal married condition and were not either separated or deserted. Second, there was even greater opposition to extending the grounds upon which wives could sue for divorce. This opposition was based on what Christ was recorded to have said in the New Testament, on the danger of admitting spurious progeny into families, and on instinctive support for traditional male property rights over the bodies of wives.

Although Gladstone was totally opposed in principle to divorce, he supported Lyndhurst in opposing any discrimination of any kind between wives and husbands in terms of access to it. So strongly did he feel about this that he tentatively suggested that in future perhaps there should be two marriage and divorce systems in England, one for Christians and one for non-Christians. The latter already had access to civil marriage by the act of 1836. So perhaps they should now have access to civil divorce, as proposed by the bill, followed by civil remarriage. The Christian sector of the population could be left to continue in its old ways, with Christian marriage but without any divorce at all. This was an interesting idea, but one that was unacceptable in an age in which Christians wanted divorce almost as much as did non-Christians.[38] In any case, Lyndhurst and Gladstone's extreme demands for full gender equality in access to divorce had little support in either House, a motion for it in the House of Lords being defeated by 71 to 20.[39]

Once these demands for total equality of access to divorce had been defeated, there was still no consensus on the additional marital crimes, in addition to the basic one of adultery, which had to be present to enable a wife to sue for divorce. The list varied from draft to draft. Incest and bigamy had long been agreed to be sufficient aggravating factors. At one time or another there was added adultery within the marital home, cruelty, rape, sodomy, bestiality, wilful desertion for a period of years,

[38] Ibid. 389–94, 1271–8.   [39] Ibid. 145: 812–14.

and involuntary desertion because of transportation or penal servitude. There was particular objection to adding wilful desertion, since it was feared that this would open the way to collusive divorce by mutual consent, as widely practised, it was alleged, in Prussia. A motion by Lord Lyndhurst to add wilful desertion was defeated 97 to 8 in the Lords, but it was approved by the Commons, and in the end survived. [40] Adultery in the marital home, however, was firmly removed by the Lords, who argued that it would be too easy for a wife seeking a divorce to entrap her husband by hiring a pretty maid and observing the consequences. In view of the apparently high rate of seduction of maidservants in great houses at this period, the Lords were exercising prudent self-interest by deleting this clause. [41]

A third great source of contention was the old question whether or not to prohibit the remarriage of the guilty wife and her lover, as proposed yet again by Bishop Wilberforce. After a seven-and-a-half-hour debate in the House of Lords, the bishops voted for it 13 to 2. But the House of Lords as a whole rejected the amendment by the narrow margin of 53 to 47, on the usual grounds that in theory it would create a kind of 'penal celibacy' applicable only to women, which in practice would drive the couple into concubinage. The proposal was soundly defeated in the Commons by 110 to 50. [42]

A fourth issue which gave rise to lengthy debate concerned the crim. con. action. Everyone disliked it and was ashamed of it, and the House of Lords, urged on by Lord Lyndhurst, voted to abolish it altogether. But the House of Commons felt very strongly that there had to be some machinery to punish the seducers of married women, and to provide injured husbands with at least their legal costs in obtaining a divorce. The Lords at one stage proposed to make adultery with a married women a criminal misdemeanour punishable by a fine of up to £500, but this was rejected by the Commons without too much discussion. [43] On the other hand, as Mr Butt put it, 'the action for criminal conversation has been the scourge of adultery . . . and very few persons would be willing to abolish this action without some substitute being provided for it'.

As a result, after endless amendments it was at the last minute decided by the Commons to incorporate into a divorce suit before a judge in the new court the option of a suit for damages assessed by a jury. The damages would in future be paid to the judge and divided by him, at his discretion, between the maintenance of the wife, the endowment of the children, and the payment of legal costs and reparations to the husband.

[40] 3 *Hansard*, 815–17; 147: 722.　　[41] Ibid. 147: 2016
[42] Ibid. 145: 819–30, 1760–6.　　[43] Ibid. 147: 723, 1836–9, 2016–17.

By perpetuating trial by jury to assess damages for the offence of adultery, however, this clause preserved the odious principle of monetary compensation for a wife's adultery, and involved the airing in open court of obscene materials for publication in the newspapers.[44]

A fifth running battle was fought over judicial separation—the legal replacement for the old ecclesiastical court separation from bed and board, but now stripped of the bond to remain chaste and not to remarry in the lifetime of the spouse. The contentious issue was whether or not it was desirable to make this judicial separation available to the lower middle class by giving jurisdiction to some lay local courts, either the old assizes or the new county courts. This was hotly contested, first because there was no agreement over the issue of principle, whether it was desirable to continue to grant judicial separations; secondly whether it was in the best interests of society to put such an option at the disposal of the population at large, including the relatively poor; and thirdly whether any existing local courts were capable of handling this new burden. In the end, both Houses abandoned the proposal as impracticable and unwise.[45]

A sixth source of disagreement was nominally over procedure, but in reality raised the basic issue of the relations of church and state. If the bill passed, so as to allow both innocent and guilty to remarry, then, if numbers grew as feared, many clergymen might be forced against their consciences to remarry adulterous divorcees. As we have seen, Gladstone whipped up a great public campaign over this red herring. In vain a government spokesman pointed out that parish clergy had for centuries married pregnant girls and buried suicides and the unbaptized dead without raising moral objections, and were now jibbing at something which they had long tolerated even if over the last century-and-a-half the number of remarriages of an adulterous wife with her lover had not exceeded a hundred in all. But in view of the scale and passion of the protest, the attorney-general judged that it was prudent to execute a tactical withdrawal. He therefore reluctantly agreed to allow a clergyman to refuse to marry an adulterous couple on grounds of conscience, but not to forbid the use of his church for the same purpose by another clergyman.[46]

The fight over these issues continued throughout July and into the fourth week in August 1857, at which time the rump of peers and MPs still left in London finally gave in, from sheer exhaustion. It was said that by the end seven-eighths of the MPs had already left, and that the

---

[44] Ibid. 145: 779–85, 918–30, 1097–1100; 147: 1833–43, 1978–81.
[45] Ibid. 145: 499–500, 508–9; 147: 1243–57, 1260–7, 1845–51, 1976, 2015, 2027–30, 2041–3. [46] Ibid. 147: 380, 850, 1768–832.

government was getting its way thanks to the presence of a solid block of a hundred placemen in the House of Commons whom it was forcing to stay in London until the bill was passed.[47] This rump rejected some of the key amendments proposed by the Lords and sent the bill back for approval. In late August in a very thin House,the peers in weariness and frustration finally accepted the amended bill by the narrow margin of 46 to 44.[48]

As a result of this prolonged struggle, it was calculated that 59 of the 73 clauses in the bill were either new or had been altered; five had been deleted and twenty-one added by the House of Commons.[49] In other words, the final draft bore very little relation to the bill first introduced by the government two years before. It had started as a mere tidying up of judicial institutions, designed primarily to remove jurisdiction from the ecclesiastical courts. But it had been highjacked by the reformers on its way through Parliament and turned into a vehicle for the first significant change of the English divorce law since the sixteenth century. As such it was a landmark act. But what did it achieve, and what did it imply for the future?

[47] 3 *Hansard*, 1993–4.   [48] Ibid. 2036.   [49] Ibid. 2035.

❧ XIII ❧

Epilogue: The Century of Divorce Law Reform, 1857–1987

1. The Effects of the Act of 1857

A. CONSERVATIVE MORAL ATTITUDES

Despite notable exceptions, which have been given careful attention, the predominant morality which was on display in the debates on the 1857 bill in both Houses was not one of liberalism but of nervously defensive conservatism. The principal object of the act was to reduce the amount of unregulated adultery, and by improving the legal position of wives to shore up the family from the threats that surrounded it. Much time was spent in debating reactionary old proposals, dating back to the late seventeenth century, to make adultery a criminal offence punishable by fine or imprisonment and to forbid the guilty wife in a divorce suit from marrying her lover. The universally condemned crim. con. action for damages from a wife's lover was abolished, but at the last moment a much modified and more acceptable way of punishing the seducer was introduced, retaining the concept of damages, but having them distributed between wife, children, and husband at the discretion of the judge. The refusal to allow local secular courts to administer judicial separations left the lower middle class worse off than before in terms of access to the law, since they now had to go to London to get it. As for the much-touted aim of making full divorce equally accessible to rich and poor, it was never even attempted, and in reality was strongly opposed by the great majority.

Furthermore, the old and much-criticized separation from bed and board was retained, although it was declining in popularity, and was now only administered by the new High Court in London. The theological dogma about the indissolubility of marriage was still widely accepted among clergy and pious laymen like Gladstone, and was reinforced by the purely secular argument that 'the permanence of the nuptial tie is all but universally admitted to be of advantage to the state', as the Archbishop of York put it in 1912. And so, although it was now little used, this early medieval canon law invention survived in England right up to the mid-twentieth century (Table 13.1).[1] This was despite the fact that everyone was aware that these separations almost inevitably led to new adulterous connections, especially by the husband, who tended to engage a housekeeper who soon became his mistress or *de facto* second wife.

Another important conclusion which emerges very clearly from the debates over the bill is that these upper-class male Victorian legislators had grave doubts whether their own sex could be trusted to make responsible use of any relaxation of the strict laws of divorce. In the 1850s, the dangerous sex was not female but male. The report of the Royal Commission on Divorce of 1853 argued that the laws against divorce were designed 'chiefly to protect children from the inconstancy of parents, and next to guard women from the inconstancy of husbands' who if free to do so would obtain a divorce 'as soon as they were tired of their wives'.[2] Thus, it was widely believed that many husbands were only tied to their families by legal constraints. If divorce were to be made easy and respectable, it was feared that it would lead to the growth of a society based on serial polygamy, since this was the arrangement most suited to the promiscuous sexual appetites of the human male. It was alleged that in Prussia, where there was what for the time was an extraordinarily high divorce rate, running at 57 per 100,000 population, the result was that wives were 'bought, sold, or exchanged'.[3] It was fantasies such as these which caused Gladstone to oppose the bill because 'I believe [it] would lead to the degradation of woman'.[4]

Women seem to have shared this belief in the naturally promiscuous tendencies of men. It was this belief in the double sexual standard that explains why middle-class women's movements in the nineteenth century concentrated their attention upon ameliorating conditions within marriage, especially by giving wives control over their own property, rather than upon extending the scope and scale of opportunities for divorce. In any case, in a society where few middle-class women were educated for a career, and where few careers were open to them, the consequences of a divorce at the will of a husband could be even worse than those of a bad marriage.

In fact, the statistics for divorce over the half-century after 1857 do not support this belief in the natural promiscuity of men. Despite the modest cheapening of the legal process, no tide of male petitioners for divorce in order to marry new wives swept through the narrow channel which had

[1] *Roy. Com. Divorce, 1912,* 1: 172.   [2] *Roy. Com. Divorce, 1853,* 1: 12.
[3] *3 Hansard,* 147: 770, 759–60.   [4] Ibid. 393.

been partly opened. Although the number of successful divorces increased from 141 in 1861 to 580 in 1911, this growth was barely twice as fast as that of the population (Fig. 13.1, Table 13.1). The major change caused by the 1857 Divorce Act was that thereafter a steady 40 to 45 per cent of the petitioners were now wives (Fig. 13.2, Table 13.2). The obvious, and probably correct, explanation of this change is that a number of very unhappy wives were at last free to obtain full divorces and to remarry, which by law they could not do before the passage of the act.

A corollary of the distrust of the human male was an even more pronounced distrust of the poor, whose sexual behaviour was generally believed to be deplorable. Gladstone and Bishop Wilberforce were among the very few to speak well of the morals of the poor. Although Gladstone believed that England was outstanding for the extent of prostitution and pre-nuptial conceptions, he found it remarkable how 'a great and deplorable laxity with respect to chastity before marriage should be coupled with extraordinary strictness in the observance of the marriage vow'. Bishop Wilberforce, who spoke eloquently of 'the hitherto blessed purity of English life', also admitted that pre-nuptial conceptions were common, but agreed that there was a very strong sense of shame among

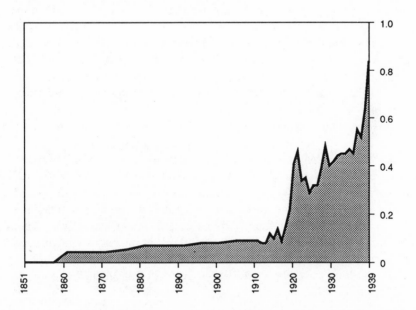

FIGURE 13.1   Divorce Rate per 1,000 Married Couples (England and Wales) 1851–1939 [Table 13.1]

385

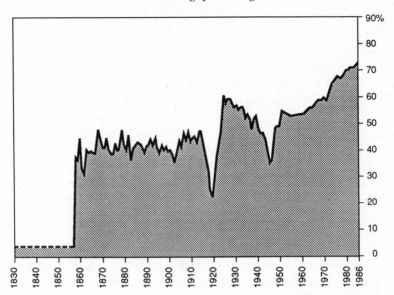

FIGURE 13.2   Proportion of Divorce Decrees Awarded to Wives (England and Wales) 1830–1986 [Table 13.2]

married women about adultery.[5] However, these were minority views; the vast majority of legislators remained strongly hostile to any move towards granting the poor easier access to divorce. This explains why the act of 1857 did nothing to relieve the plight of the brutalized, abandoned, or separated wives of the lower middle class or the poor. Since both legal separation and divorce were now only obtainable in London, the high cost of transportation and lodging meant that they were to all intents and purposes 'absolutely debarred from it'.

The huge numbers who were excluded by poverty from both divorce and judicial separation only became apparent after the passage in 1878 and 1886 of two Maintenance of Wives acts, which allowed a battered or deserted wife to obtain a temporary maintenance order from a local magistrate. The result was an avalanche of applications to the magistrates' courts. In around 1900, some 10,700 wives applied on their own behalf, and it is believed that another 4,000 or so applications were made on behalf of paupers by the Poor Law authorities, making a total of nearly 15,000 (Table 13.3). These numbers should be compared with about 700 applicants for divorce[6] and about 100 for judicial separation at the same date (Table 13.1).

[5]   3 *Hansard*, 853; see also ibid. 142: 1982.
[6]   O. R. McGregor, *Divorce in England, a Centenary Study* (London, 1957), 49 n. 3, 51 n. 3; Rowntree and Carrier, 189–90, 201.

One may safely conclude that there was not much enthusiasm in the public at large or the political nation for any further easing of the divorce laws, at any rate before 1920. Many MPs argued, probably correctly, that the women of England were suspicious of any relaxation of the laws. Divorce was still largely out of the reach or even imagination of the poor before about 1918, when some legal aid became available (Table 13.2). The Church of England remained solidly opposed to any relaxation of the grounds for divorce, presenting a monolithic front which only began to crumble in the early 1920s. Rich men had little personal incentive to press for divorce law reform, since by collusive agreement with their wives they were nearly always able to obtain divorce, although admittedly by the degrading process of faking adultery.

It seems that before the 1920s there were only two groups who were enthusiastically in favour of divorce reform. One was the ardent liberals, distressed at the sufferings of those who were either trapped in a hopelessly miserable marriage, or had established a stable second illegal union which they were unable to legitimize. The other was the judges, who experienced at first hand the anomalies, injustices, and absurdities of the laws they were supposed to administer.

B. THE NUMBER OF DIVORCES, 1858–1900

There can be little doubt that the increase in the number of divorces between 1858 and 1914 represented no more than a shift of legal categories, and does not signify much, if any, increase in marital breakdowns. Within three years of the passage of the 1857 Divorce Act, the number of divorces granted had risen from about 4 a year to about 150, and by 1914 it was up to over 800 (Fig. 13.1, Table 13.1). Thus as a result of the 1857 act, several hundred middle-class men and women were moved every year from the categories of the eloped, the deserted, the privately separated, or the judicially separated to the category of the divorced. This change in legal status had real effects, since it enabled these men and women to remarry instead of living in solitude, concubinage, or bigamy. But the number of people involved remained statistically minute. As long as there were under a thousand divorces a year in a population of about forty million, England still remained basically a non-divorcing society.[7]

One undeniable achievement of the 1857 act was the reduction in the proportion of judicial separations relative to divorces. Before the act the ratio of judicial separations from bed and board to full divorces had been

[7] Wolfram, appendix 2A; A. Horstman, *Victorian Divorce* (New York, 1985), 101.

about 5 or more to 1. By the 1880s, this ratio was inverted and there were almost three divorces for every judicial separation, nine-tenths of the latter being sought by wives in order to obtain maintenance (Table 13.1).

C. THE BENEFITS TO WOMEN

The debates over the Divorce Act led to greater public awareness of the problems of wives, and as a result they were the main beneficiaries. Those with property who were privately separated or deserted were now protected from the economic exploitation of rapacious husbands. The situation of judicially separated or divorced wives was also improved by the 1857 act in two important ways. In the first place, the new court was given authority to award child custody to either parent as it saw fit, and to guarantee visiting rights. No longer did a husband, however promiscuous, venereally diseased, brutal, or drunken, automatically have legal possession of all the children. Secondly, in the new trial for damages by the husband against the alleged seducer of his wife, the latter was now entitled to appear, to be represented by counsel, and to bring witnesses in defence of her good name.

There were also very significant changes in the grounds upon which women could petition for a divorce, the importance of which is demonstrated by the rise in the proportion of women petitioners (Fig. 13.2; Table 13.2). The list of aggravating circumstances was now extended to the very common ones of desertion for two years and cruelty, the definition of which last was at just this time being broadened by judicial interpretation to include mental cruelty. This still did not give wives full legal equality with their husbands, who could divorce them for adultery alone. The criticism of the 1857 act by modern feminist historians is therefore fully justified on grounds of the moral principle that any form of inequality between the sexes before the law is unjust. Gladstone and Lord John Manners did indeed protest at the time that the act 'gave a fresh sanction to the inequality of the sexes in the eye of the law'.[8] But it has to be remembered that although there was a small but growing minority which held these more advanced ideas, 1857 was a time when belief in the moral and practical propriety of the double sexual standard was widely shared by both sexes.

D. CONCLUSION

Looking back on the 1857 Divorce Act from the perspective of 1990, it is clear that in itself it started no immediate great revolution in the family; it

[8] 3 *Hansard*, 147: 1992–3.   [9] Horstman, *Victorian Divorce*, 169.

is impossible to agree with the claim of one modern scholar that it was 'the most successful piece of legislation in the nineteenth century'.[9] It was a botched and bungled job, cobbled together over months of wrangling by a dwindling band of weary legislators engaged in debate for up to twelve hours a day in the broiling heat. It is hardly surprising that it was a far from perfect draft, and that some clauses are obscure or contradictory. The miracle is that it should have remained for so long the law of the land, largely unaltered for eighty years.

On the other hand, by making divorce rather cheaper than it had been, it acknowledged—in principle, if not in practice—the injustice of having one law for the rich and another for the poor; it once and for all took control over matrimonial affairs from the hands of the church, and by doing so openly rejected the theological principle of the indissolubility of marriage. It also grudgingly recognized the principle that it was unjust to deny married women any standing in common law, and did something to soften the rigidities of the double sexual standard. Even if the 1857 act itself achieved only modest changes, the Parliamentary debates of 1856 and 1857 were clearly a major event in English history, since they set precedents for the changing attitudes towards divorce for the next century right up to 1960. In the course of the debate, suggestions were made which were not to become law for another eighty years—for example, about extending the cause of divorce to include desertion, and about setting up cheap, local divorce courts.

In 1897, a legal commentator could observe with satisfaction that:

woman was born in chains and, behold, now on every side she is free. . . . The alteration in status to which I allude has taken place, almost in its entirety, during the reign of our gracious Queen Victoria. . . . The Victorian epoch may claim with justice the gratitude of enfranchised womanhood; a gratitude, moreover, that will at least be leavened by a lively sense of favours to come.[10]

As proof of this complaisant proposition, the author could cite a list of significant changes. In terms of physical control by the husband over the wife, as late as 1832 Bacon's *Abridgement of the Law* still instructed its readers that 'the husband hath by law the power and dominion over the wife, and may beat her, but not in a violent or cruel manner'. In the Cochrane case in 1840, Judge Coleridge upheld a husband's right to confine his wife to prevent her from eloping. In 1891, however, a judge in another case reversed the ruling in the Cochrane case, while an act of Parliament in 1884 ended the powers of the Matrimonial Causes Court to use the threat of imprisonment to force a wife to cohabit with her

[10] J. E. G. de Montgomery, 'The Changing Status of a Married Woman', *Law Quarterly Review* 13 (1897), 187.

husband. Battered wives of the poor were protected by another act of 1895 which empowered magistrates to grant them both maintenance and custody of children up to the age of 16. As a result, by the end of the century, legal support for the physical control of husbands over wives had finally been ended.[11]

But the most important change, affecting the largest number of women, was that wives at last were granted full control over their own property. The Married Women's Property Acts of 1870, 1874, and 1882 had far more influence on the lives of far more women than the Divorce Act of 1857, which was limited to putting full divorce with right to remarry within the financial reach of the upper middle class.[12]

There was also a revolution in attitudes towards child custody in cases of separation and divorce. For centuries, common law had given no rights whatsoever to the wife, however atrocious the circumstances, although Chancery could, and sometimes rather timidly did, interfere in the case of children who possessed property in trust. But not until Sergeant Talfourd's Act in 1839 was the first real breach made in this last bastion of absolute patriarchal power, by removing the presumption of custody of very young children under the age of 7 from the father to the mother. In 1857, the new Matrimonial Causes Court was empowered to allocate custody of children in divorce cases, a power which it exercised with extreme conservatism. But in 1873 another act enabled Chancery to award custody as it saw fit, and by 1886 it had become morally accepted that it was only right to grant custody of young children to their mother.[13] It is uncertain to what extent these reforms were the result of growing pressure from emancipated women, or of broader changes in social attitudes affecting upper-class male legislators. Both features seem to have been present.

2. Divorce Law Reform, 1906–1923

A. REFORMIST MORAL ATTITUDES

There were three trends which were to continue to erode opposition to divorce law reform far into the twentieth century. The first was the progressive secularization of society and the consequent weakening of the power of the Church of England and a division of opinions within it.

[11] De Montgomery, 'Changing Status', 188–90; 47–8 Vict. Cap. 68; 58–9 Vict. Cap. 39.
[12] For the story about the prolonged late Victorian struggle over Married Women's Property bills, see Holcombe; M. L. Shanley, ' "One Must Ride Behind": Married Women's Rights and the Divorce Bill of 1857', *Victorian Studies*, 25 (1981–2), 364–5: M. L. Poovey, *Uneven Developments: The Ideological World of Gender in Mid-Victorian England* (Chicago, 1988) ch. 3.
[13] De Montgomery, 'Changing Status', 190–7.

The contrast between 1857 and 1912 is startling. In the former year the main opposition to the divorce bill, led by Gladstone and Bishop Wilberforce, was inspired by religious scruples derived from the sayings of Christ on the subject. In the Royal Commission on Divorce of the latter year, however, the ancient canon law practice of judicial separation as a substitute for divorce was denounced as

one of the most corrupting devices ever imposed by serious natures on blindness and credulity. It was tolerated only because men believed, as a part of their religion, that dissolution would be an offence against God. . . . As the fruits of compromise we have this ill-begotten monster of divorce *a mensa et thoro*, made up of pious doctrine and worldly stupidity . . . an unnatural and unsatisfactory remedy.

Some witnesses pointed out that legal separation from bed and board was unknown in the Scriptures or the early church, and was no more than an invention of celibate male canonists of the Western church in the early middle ages. Others described its practical consequences as 'a most odious form of punishment . . . hanging up people between heaven and earth—neither married nor unmarried'. Thus, in the late nineteenth and early twentieth century, a legal position widely accepted as conforming to religious truth and public policy, and devoutly practised for nearly a thousand years, quite suddenly came to be regarded as something unnatural and immoral and an intolerable cause of widespread personal misery.[14]

How does the historian explain this remarkable change in educated public opinion between the 1850s and the early 1900s? The obvious answer is the erosion of the old religious and political beliefs by the advancing tide of secularism and individualism. The problem of divorce and remarriage began to be seen in purely secular terms, and the interests of the happiness of the individual to take priority over the alleged stability of society and the interests of the state. The obvious weakness of such an argument is the tenuous thread which binds two vague impersonal forces, secularism and individualism, to a particular shift in opinion on the specific matter of the desirability and legitimacy of separation from bed and board as the normal solution to a disastrously failed marriage. On the other hand, it it impossible to read the rhetoric of legislators and witnesses in the 1850s and the 1900s without being convinced that a great shift in view-point had taken place in that half-century. Nor is this an isolated case of such a shift, which can be found changing long-standing attitudes on a wide variety of issues in just this period. Demands

[14] *Roy. Com. Divorce, 1912,* 1: 91; 2: 79, 51, 62.

for greater equality of rights between the sexes and for legalized access to birth-control are two examples among many.

The second stimulus to demands for reform of the divorce laws was the persistent and growing exasperation of the Law Lords at the outrageous, absurd, and scandalous forms of collusion forced upon litigants by the existing law. However conservative they might be, they became convinced by day-to-day experience in court that almost any change had to be for the better. Between 1857 and 1923, couples who agreed on divorce were able to obtain collusive divorces only by an elaborate legal procedure. If the wife had not committed adultery, it was necessary for her to prove that her husband had done so, and had also committed one other marital offence. If the husband had long since left home to live with another woman, the adultery charge was easy: the wife sued her husband for restitution of conjugal rights, won her case, and wrote him an affectionate letter, inviting him to return to the conjugal home within fourteen days. The husband either refused or did not reply, and the wife then launched an uncontested suit for separation with maintenance on grounds of adultery plus desertion.[15] If the husband had *not* committed adultery, however, but the couple wished to divorce, an even more scandalous and ludicrous form of collusion was practised, which involved the performance by the husband of a duly witnessed fake adultery.

The third stimulus for change was the growing movement for female equality of rights and opportunities, not only in law, but also in voting, education, access to professional occupations, and in the work-place. John Stuart Mill and William Gladstone had been early advocates of the cause of sexual equality before the law, and by the late nineteenth century they were supported not only by liberal thought but also by activist organizations of middle-class women. As for the wives of the working class, they remained as suspicious of divorce as they were of the vote.[16]

B. THE ROYAL COMMISSION OF 1912

During the late nineteenth century, divorce reform was hampered by a series of accidents and miscalculations, bitter divisions in public opinion, suspicion or downright hostility by many women's organizations, direct opposition by the clergy of the Church of England, and the lack of full support by any political party. As a result, demand for reform did not

[15] 5 *Parl. Debates: Lords* (1937) 105: 745, 780.
[16] B. Harrison, *Separate Spheres: The Opposition to Women's Suffrage in Britain* (London, 1978).

begin in earnest until 1906. In that year, the president of the Probate, Admiralty, and Divorce Division of the High Court publicly denounced the divorce laws as administered by his court as 'full of inconsistencies, anomalies, and inequalities, almost amounting to absurdities'.[17] Prompted by this onslaught, in 1909 the government appointed a Royal Commission on Divorce, under the chairmanship of a distinguished judge, Lord Gorell. This was, of course, the standard English way of avoiding involvement in a politically unrewarding topic. The investigation was long and thorough, hundreds of witnesses were heard, and a far-reaching, three-volume report was published in 1912. Unfortunately, the commissioners were split. A Majority Report advocated reform of the legal machinery for processing divorce and offered reasons to justify it.[18] A Minority Report, signed by three members, opposed all the important proposals on the grounds that they would make divorce easier; that this would merely create more divorces; and that any extension of the causes for divorce beyond female adultery was against the express words of Christ.[19]

The Majority Report was a remarkable document for its day. It set out three principles. The first was that there should be equality of access to divorce between both rich and poor and men and women. Over this there was ostensibly not much dispute. The second was that divorce should be regarded as merely a legal mopping-up operation after the spiritual death of a marriage. The third was that in any society there is no necessary correlation between the number of divorces and the level of sexual immorality. It was argued that the laws may be constricted to grant divorce to only a minority, or expanded to cover all whose marriages have failed, without in any way affecting the amount of illicit sex and concubinage.

To cheapen the cost of divorce so as to make it accessible to the poor, the Majority Report recommended setting up a series of decentralized divorce courts around the country. It also proposed to provide equality of access to divorce for husbands and wives by granting it to the latter merely on the grounds of adultery by the husband, rather than of adultery combined with another matrimonial offence. Thirdly, it proposed expanding the grounds for divorce to include more than adultery, the only statistically important new cause being desertion for three years. These proposals set the agenda for a debate which was to last, on and off, for another sixty years.

[17] 5 *Parl. Debates: Lords* (1937) 105: 843.
[18] *Roy. Com. Divorce 1912*, 1: 1–170.
[19] Ibid. 1: 171–85.

C. THE DIVORCE LAW REFORM BILL, 1918–1923

Because the commission was split, and because the political nation became diverted first by a major constitutional crisis, and then by the outbreak of the First World War, nothing was done until 1918 to implement the reforms proposed by the 1912 commission. By then the country was just beginning to realize with alarm the full scale of the increase in marital breakdowns caused by the four years of mass mobilization for war.

The divorce rate per 1,000 married couples, after rising very slowly between 1858 and 1913, jumped sixfold between the last pre-war year, 1913, and the post-war peak in 1921 (Fig. 13.1, Table 13.1). This striking increase in divorces must have reflected a real and massive increase in marital breakdowns in the years immediately following the war. There are three possible reasons for the huge post-war rush to divorce. The sharp but short-lived change in the sex ratio of petitioners, from about 55 per cent husbands before the war to about 75 per cent immediately after it, in 1920–2 (Fig. 13.2, Table 13.2), strongly suggests that large numbers of lonely wives had committed adultery and set up new households during the long absences of their husbands at the front. When their husbands were demobilized and returned home, they discovered what had happened and started divorce proceedings. The second probability is that many hasty and juvenile war marriages quickly fell apart when the couple at last had to face the realities of daily cohabitation. The third is that a number of soldiers had undergone such stress in battle that they were psychologically disturbed and found it impossible to return to the routine of domestic life. Some husbands may also have fallen in love with nurses and other women, and wanted a divorce. But the very high proportion of post-war divorces initiated by husbands suggests that the infidelity of wives during wartime was probably the crucial factor. Of course, this is not to deny that a much larger proportion of husbands had committed war-time adultery overseas, whether with prostitutes or other women as proved by the mass distribution of condoms to soldiers. But this behaviour was much more easily concealed.[20]

In an attempt to facilitate divorces for these huge numbers of broken marriages Lord Buckmaster, a law lord, introduced a private bill into the House of Lords to add desertion to adultery as a valid cause for divorce. Surprisingly, he lost by only ten votes, despite the horrified opposition of the archbishops and bishops.[21] In 1920, as the post-war divorce rate was

[20] J. Haskey, 'Secular Changes in Divorce in England and Wales by Class of Decree: A Socio-Legal Analysis', *Biology and Society*, 3 (1986).

[21] 5 *Parl. Debates: Lords* (1920), 39: 342.

nearing its peak (Fig. 13.1, Table 13.1), Lord Buckmaster tried once more. This time he proposed not only to add desertion as a cause for divorce, but also to set up local divorce courts in order to provide the poor with inexpensive access to the judicial machinery. The House of Lords debated the bill almost non-stop for over three months, and finally passed it by a vote of 154 to 107, despite the passionate objections of the bishops to any extension of the causes for divorce beyond adultery. But it was a Pyrrhic victory, for a nervous government then quietly allowed the bill to die.

The next year, in 1921, the second Lord Gorell tried again, this time on more modest lines, dropping the controversial suggestion of including desertion as a matrimonial offence. He asked a Parliament which had recently granted women equal access to the vote now to grant them equal access to divorce, and also to provide easier access for the poor. But the hopes for easy passage of the bill were wrecked, because Lord Buckmaster insisted on adding an amendment which extended the causes of divorce to desertion, in accordance with the Majority Report recommendation of 1912. The 1920 vote had already proved that the laity, even in the House of Lords, was no longer intimidated by a united front of bishops. Now, in 1921, the church itself was beginning to speak with many voices. Outside the House of Lords, the influential Dean Inge of St Paul's had declared that desertion as grounds for divorce was in conformity with Christianity. Inside the House, the Bishop of Durham supported the addition of desertion as a cause for divorce, arguing that marriage laws should shift under the influence of 'modern conditions, social and intellectual'. 'We live in a time of revolutionary change, nowhere more far-reaching than in the region of sexual morality'. He also expressed his belief that 'the number of divorces is a most untrustworthy index of social morality'.[22]

The desertion clause was accepted by the Lords on a narrow vote of 66 to 48, with all fifteen bishops and archbishops present voting against it—and almost as many absentees. On the basis of a vague promise by Lord Birkenhead that this time the government would make time for the Commons to debate the bill, its proponents thought that they at last smelt victory. But in the end the government failed to abide by Lord Birkenhead's half-promise, and the bill was allowed once again to die.

Finally, in 1923 another private bill was introduced into the House of Commons, designed to save something from the wreckage of the 1912 report. Its object was to achieve one thing only—that is, equality of

[22] Ibid. (1921), 44: 487; 45: 91.

access by wives to divorce on the grounds of the adultery of their husbands. This bill was said to be 'practically universally demanded by the women of this country' who, it will be remembered, had recently been granted the vote. Afraid of offending this large new constituency, most of the opponents of the bill ran for political cover, and it easily passed both Houses and became law.[23]

There was a good deal of hypocrisy and humbug spoken during the debate. The few opponents of the bill stuck to the traditional position that a single act of adultery by a husband on a drunken spree away from home did not have the same social and psychological significance for a stable marriage as an act of adultery by a wife—a position which in their hearts was probably shared by virtually all the members of both Houses. They also pointed out that although the proponents of the bill all expressed their virtuous horror at creating a situation of divorce by mutual consent, in practice the bill would make collusive divorce even commoner than before, since wives would now have to prove only one matrimonial offence instead of two.[24]

D. THE RESULTS OF THE ACT OF 1923

This was just the time when the influence and cohesion of the church was declining; when the sexual revolution was beginning; when the number of married women in the work force outside the home was on the increase; when fertility was declining sharply, thus freeing wives for activities other than child-rearing; when adult mortality had been declining for fifty years, thus extending the probable duration of a marriage long after the maturity and marriage of the children; and when the powerful ideology of individualism and the pursuit of personal happiness was becoming increasingly widespread. All these long-term trends contributed to the likelihood of a rising demand for divorce, especially by wives. It is hardly surprising, therefore, that after the 1923 act there was a big jump in the proportion of women petitioners, from 39 per cent in 1923 to 63 per cent in 1925 (Fig. 13.2, Table 13.2).[25]

But the First World War had a long-term as well as a short-term effect on the divorce rate. After the immediate post-war peak, the rates fell back, but only to a new plateau four times above that of the pre-war years (Figs. 13.1, 13.3). This indicates that numbers of the lower middle classes who had previously rested content with mere desertion for the

[23] 5 *Parl. Debates: Commons* (1923), 160: 2356–81.
[24] Ibid. (1923), 160: 2368–9, 2383.
[25] Rowntree and Carrier, 201.

husband and a maintenance order from a magistrate for the wife now shifted over into the category of the legally divorced. The conclusion is reinforced by the fact that between 1900 and 1930 the ratio of petitions for divorce or judicial separation to applications for maintenance orders issued by a magistrate rose from about 7 per cent to 55 per cent.[26]

It therefore seems plausible to argue that what was really happening up to the 1930s was predominantly a shift of categories, as an increasing number of the lower middle class whose marriages had broken up were able to obtain a divorce, thanks to legal aid. The scale of divorce had not yet become large enough to disrupt family life, since there were still fewer than four thousand divorces a year, giving a rate per thousand married couples of under 0.5 (Fig. 13.1, Table 13.1). The growth of divorces in England was held back by the cost and complexity of litigation, which remained substantially unchanged from 1857 to 1937, and a persistent sense of moral shame, which was given wide public expression in the royal abdication episode. Whether the law did anything to either stimulate or stabilize the number of broken marriages, however, is another matter. The hypothetical answer is probably not, given that marital breakdown was being stimulated by so many different trends in society.

3. The Divorce Reform Act of 1937

A. THE NEED FOR REFORM

Between 1923 and 1936, the question of reform of the divorce laws was allowed to slumber. The laws themselves remained virtually unaltered since 1857, until the pressure for reform was revived by the energy and persistence of a back-bench MP, Mr A. P. Herbert.[27] By now, however, England's social, sexual, and religious cultures were much altered, and, although still relatively only a trickle, the divorce rate had been rising sharply between 1925 and 1937.

Behind these figures there lay a story of collusion and duplicity even more scandalous than that which had prevailed up to 1923. By allowing a wife to divorce a husband because of a single act of adultery, Parliament had in practice made it easy for the rich to divorce by mutual consent. The way it was done was for the husband to provide his wife with the evidence of his adultery by a procedure known as a 'hotel bill case'. A woman was hired for a free trip for a week-end to an expensive seaside

---

[26] Ibid. 190.
[27] For a brilliant and witty description of his battle see A. P. Herbert, *The Ayes Have It: The Story of the Marriage Bill* (London, 1937).

hotel, with no duties to perform except to be seen in bed with the husband for a few minutes before breakfast, having spent the night either drinking and playing cards or sleeping in separate beds. Divorce was then obtained on evidence either of the hotel bill, helpfully sent by the husband to the wife, or of testimony from the chambermaids 'opportunely arriving with the morning coffee when the couple were still in bed'. Mr. A. P. Herbert thus begins his 1934 novel with the words: 'So here he was at last, travelling down to Brighton with a strange young woman in a first-class carriage.'[28] These proceedings were made to appear still more ludicrous in Evelyn Waugh's novel of the same year, *A Handful of Dust*, by the simple expedient of having the woman suffer from a severe head-cold and insist on bring her 8-year-old daughter with her.[29]

B. THE PASSAGE OF THE ACT

In Parliament, Herbert used such stories as evidence that 'we are rapidly reaching a situation in which no stigma whatever will attach to a public confession of adultery'.[30] His bill followed the recommendations of the Majority Report of the Royal Commission of 1912 to expand the causes for divorce beyond mere adultery. The main additions were desertion for three years and cruelty, but Herbert also threw in habitual drunkenness and incurable insanity. He argued that this expansion of the legal causes for divorce was surely preferable to the current situation of divorce by mutual consent through deliberate and sordid collusion. In order to diminish this collusion, he agreed to shift the burden of proof of innocence on to the petitioner for divorce. He also proposed to phase out judicial separations—which were now down to about a hundred a year—on the old grounds that they merely encouraged illicit cohabitation. Finally, he repeated the argument of 1857 that still in 1937 'divorce is a luxury, or vice, of the rich and does not really concern the poor'.[31]

By granting a time-lag of five years after marriage before either spouse could be granted a divorce, Herbert satisfied conservative opinion, which was reluctant to encourage easy divorce in the first years of marriage. The clause succeeded in winning over many moderates, but in practice it was a concession of only minor importance, since at that time less than 14 per cent of all divorces occurred in the first five years.

---

[28] Herbert, *Holy Deadlock* (New York, 1934), 1.
[29] E. Waugh, *A Handful of Dust* (London, 1934), 128–45.
[30] 5 *Parl. Debates: Commons* (1936–7), 317: 2083–4.
[31] Ibid., 317: 2089.

Herbert's main opponents were large numbers of married women, both elite and working class, who were on the whole by no means dissatisfied with the status quo. As Herbert himself remarked bitterly in 1934: 'No wonder the women of England were said to be solid in defence of the divorce laws. Those laws were the most powerful instruments ever invented for the extraction by the female of ease and comfort and money from the male. They were never defended upon that ground, but that was the truth of it.'[32] In 1937 he admitted that one of his most active opponents was the 500,000-strong Mothers' Union.[33] On the other hand he had the support of the lord chief justice, most of the law lords, and almost all the members of the legal profession, who were disgusted with having to take part in these endless charades of collusive divorce. He even won the active assistance of the king's proctor, whose unpleasant duty it was to block occasional divorces because of collusion, evidence of which had usually been brought to his reluctant attention by a malicious anonymous letter.[34]

On this occasion the church spoke with two voices. Herbert's bill won the guarded neutrality of the archbishops of Canterbury and York and the active support of a number of bishops, but an equal number remained opposed and an even larger number abstained. The Archbishop of Canterbury hopelessly confused his followers by explaining that he was going to abstain on the vote, since as a statesman he believed that the bill provided a 'timely and valuable remedy' for many abuses, yet as a clergyman he could not support any bill in favour of divorce since it was contrary to the words of Christ (or at least to some of them).[35]

Not only had the Church of England lost most of its influence over sexual and marital affairs, but its leadership was now split, and its troops were largely silent. Some of the bishops were actively in favour of reform, the Bishop of Durham assuring the House of Lords that in his opinion the bill was in conformity with Christian doctrine. Herbert skilfully contrasted this situation with that in the 1920s, when all but a handful of churchmen were still strongly opposed to any extension of the causes for divorce beyond adultery.[36]

But Herbert found it prudent to buy off another and larger group of strong opponents of the bill, namely the Anglican parish clergy. They were expressly exempted in the bill from any obligation to conduct in their churches any marriages of divorced persons. As late as 1979, the

---

[32] Herbert, *Holy Deadlock*, 341–2.
[33] Id., *The Ayes Have It*, 74, 116, 147.   [34] Ibid., 62, 103, 106.
[35] 5 *Parl. Debates: Lords* (1937), 105: 744–6, 782.
[36] 5 *Parl. Debates: Commons* (1936–7), 317: 2080, 2102.

clergy of the Church of England still felt so strongly on this subject that at a time when 47 per cent of all first marriages were being celebrated in their churches, this was true of only 1 per cent of marriages involving divorced persons.[37]

Among other opponents of the bill, according to Herbert, were members from strongly Catholic constituencies who feared punishment at the polls. There were also the cynics who favoured the status quo on the grounds that the rich could always get divorced by collusive fake adulteries in a hotel, while it was dangerous to society to grant easy access to divorce to the poor.[38] Even principled opponents of the bill stuck to largely pragmatic arguments, realizing that voicing theological concerns now had little effect, even in the House of Lords.[39]

The most radical speech in the Lords was that of Lord Dawson of Penn, a distinguished and fashionable physician, who pointed out that a massive shift of public opinion had taken place between 1920 and 1937. It was now generally believed that in cases where the true purpose and function of a marriage—that is, love and companionship—had irretrievably withered away, there remained only the bare legal husk, and the sooner that was shed the better. He argued that laws which are not in accord with public sentiment, like those on divorce, are always systematically circumvented, in this case by squalid collusion. He ascribed the rapid rise in the number of divorces, so many of them now initiated by women, to the sexual revolution, as a result of which wives were now demanding 'a sex-satisfied life' and asking for divorce if they did not get it. The result, he concluded, was that although there was a rise in the number of petitions for divorce, successful marriages were happier than before, and 'the home and the family stand fast'.[40] Those in favour of the bill repeatedly cited the example of Scotland, where divorce had been granted for adultery or desertion since the late sixteenth century, and yet still only affected less than 2.5 per cent of marriages.[41]

Thanks to strenuous lobbying, skilful concessions to buy off potential opponents, and astute manœuvring in Parliament, in 1937 the Herbert divorce law reform bill won the warm endorsement of the law lords, the press, and the House of Commons, apparently reflecting the general support of public opinion. The amended bill easily passed both Houses, and was described by a leading supporter in the Lords as 'the most far-

[37] J. Haskey, 'The Proportion of Marriages ending in Divorce', *Population Trends*, 27 (1981), 6; id., 'Trends in Marriage: Church, Chapel, and Civil Ceremonies', ibid. 22 (1980), 19, 20, 27.
[38] Herbert, *The Ayes Have It*, 66–80.
[39] 5 *Parl. Debates: Lords* (1937), 105: 770–9, 818–19.
[40] Ibid. 824–6.　　　　　　　　　　　　　　[41] Ibid. 831.

reaching and most important bill of a domestic character which has been introduced into this House for a generation'. The recommendations of the majority of the 1912 Royal Commission had at last become law, a quarter of a century later.[42]

C. THE EFFECTS OF THE ACT

The preamble to the act, written by A. P. Herbert, stated that its object was to offer true support for marriage; protection for children; the removal of hardship for the unhappily married; the reduction of illicit unions; the elimination of unseemly litigation; the relief of consciences of the clergy; and the restoration of due respect for the law.[43]

What happened in practice? The act certainly removed road-blocks in the way of divorce and remarriage by many couples trapped in intolerably miserable unions. This is proved by the sudden increase in the number of divorces granted from 4,900 in 1937 to 8,200 in 1939 (Table 13.1). That the act was responsible is proved by the fact that of the causes for divorce cited by women petitioners in 1950 (the first year for which data are available), over 50 per cent were the new ones of desertion and cruelty rather than adultery (Table 13.4). The act apparently put an end to the grotesque charade of the 'hotel bill' adultery cases, but it can have had done nothing whatever to reduce collusion in that 90 per cent of all petitions which were now undefended. In the short run, it is unlikely to have affected the stability of marriage one way or another.

The long-term effects of the act are unknown, since the lives of most English men and women were soon afterwards seriously disrupted by the Second World War, after which, just as after the First World War, the number of divorce decrees rocketed—in this case, from about eight thousand a year in 1939 to about sixty thousand in 1947. And just as after the First World War, two-thirds of these immediately post-war divorces were initiated by husbands, which suggests that the prime cause was war-time wifely infidelity (Fig. 13.2, Tables 13.1 and 13.2).

4. The Divorce Reform Act of 1969

A. THE ROYAL COMMISSION OF 1956

After the passage of the 1937 bill, the pressure for divorce law reform eased off, especially in the light of the gigantic increase in the divorce

---

[42] Ibid. 567; 1 Ed. VIII and 1 G. VI cap. 57. For the text, see Herbert, *The Ayes Have It*, 227–40.   [43] Ibid. 66.

rate briefly stimulated by the Second World War, which far exceeded the wildest fears of the conservatives. But after reaching a dramatic peak in 1947, the numbers sank again rapidly, first to 31,000 in 1950, and then to a low of 23,000 in 1958 (Table 13.1). Even so, the divorce rate per married couples was still two and a half times higher than it had been before the war, so that once again war caused a long-term shift as well as a short-term reaction (Fig. 13.3, Table 13.1). This structural change was undoubtedly also greatly stimulated by the Labour government, which in 1948 started making legal aid for divorce proceedings widely available to the poor. As a result, the proportion of divorce petitions supported by legal aid shot up from a fifth to over a half (Table 13.2), and the proportion of manual labourers among petitioners rose to 58 per cent.[44] For the first time in English history, divorce had been thrown open to the poor, with the results so much feared by the political nation ever since 1857.

In 1956, yet another Royal Commission on Marriage and Divorce produced its report. It surveyed the changes in divorce in the first half of the twentieth century and rightly identified the two world wars as each causing huge and permanent leaps in the annual number of divorces. Other adventitious causes of the rise of divorces in the twentieth century

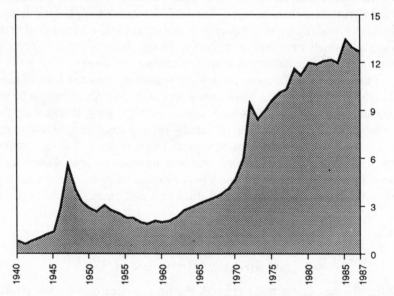

FIGURE 13.3   Divorce Rate per 1,000 Married Couples (England and Wales) 1940–1987 [Table 13.1]

[44] Rowntree and Carrier, 202, 222.

were the 1937 act, which added desertion for three years and cruelty to the list of causes for divorce, and above all the extension in 1948 of financial aid for the poor to support the legal costs of divorce.

The report also identified some general trends in the culture which were driving up divorce rates all over the Western world. These included a housing shortage, which forced an increasing number of married couples to live with a parent or parent-in-law, leading inevitably to frictions caused by lack of privacy and too close cohabitation. A significant decline in the age of marriage was also a factor in the 1960s, since teenage marriages were almost twice as likely to break up as those contracted at a later age.[45] There were probably various reasons for this. Some juvenile marriages were the forced result of pre-nuptial conceptions; an abnormal number were made by the poor and the uneducated, who might be expected to make worse choices than the better-off and better-educated. In any case, youthful marriages tend to be based on the passions of romantic love or lust, both of which are both ephemeral and uncontrolled by the wisdom of experience. The report suggests that the emancipation of women may have played a part in the growth of divorce, since it led wives to demand greater equality in power with their husbands and the sharing of chores in the home, thereby increasing friction with those husbands who still believed in the traditional deferential and subservient role of wives as mothers and domestic servants. And finally, as more women entered the labour force, they were less afraid that divorce would mean financial disaster.

Attitudes towards sexuality were changing: freer sexual practices were greatly stimulated by the invention of penicillin and greater knowledge and acceptance of birth-control devices. Huge numbers of women were thus relieved of many of their ancient fears of venereal disease or pregnancy. The introduction of the Pill in 1960 was to complete this mental shift. These new attitudes and new technologies did more than undermine the previous mild inhibitions on pre-marital sexual activity. They may also have caused a breakdown of the ancient public moral stigma upon extra-marital affairs by wives. Evidence to support this hypothesis is that between 1950 and 1970, the proportion of all divorces granted to men which were on the declared grounds of their wives' adultery rose from 48 per cent to 70 per cent (Fig. 13.4, Table 13.4).[46]

The commission also identified what may perhaps be the most important influence of all in driving up the divorce rate, namely the idealization of the individual pursuit of self-gratification and personal pleasure at the

---

[45] *Social Trends*, 9 (1979), 51.   [46] Ibid. 17 (1987), 50.

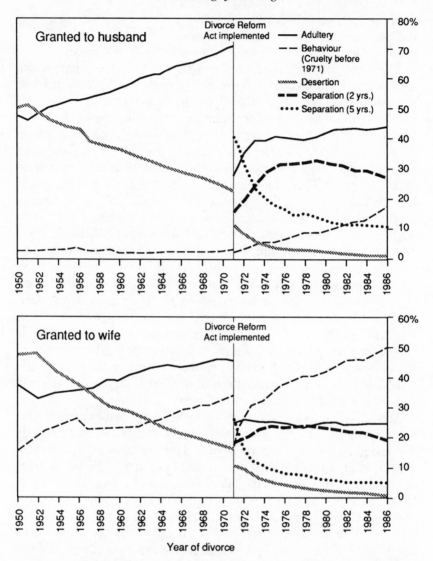

FIGURE 13.4 Declared Grounds for Divorce Decrees (England and Wales) 1950–1986 [Table 13.4]

expense of a sense of reciprocal obligations and duties towards helpless dependants, such as children, and/or to society as a whole. The commission ended its introductory section on a high moral note, calling for more marriage counselling and the inculcation into the young of a greater sense of responsibility to the community and a greater sense of duty to protect the children from the psychological effects of a broken marriage.[47]

To deal with this new situation, some members of the commission proposed what they claimed to be an entirely new basis for granting divorce. Until now, divorce had always been a legal response to a specific marital fault, whether it be adultery, cruelty, or desertion. It was now proposed that in future it be regarded as no more than legal recognition of an irremediable matrimonial breakdown. Without even a mention of possible religious or moral objections, this segment of the commission put forward a plan by which in practice divorce would be available on demand if mutually desired by both spouses; and also available, even against the wishes of one spouse, after a delay of seven years.

These proposals were bitterly opposed by the rest of the commission as unfair to the other spouse and the children; contrary to the interests of the state in encouraging stable marriages; and contrary to the interests of the community, which would have to provide the numerous female and child victims with financial aid through public assistance. The committee split in two, voting nine to nine on its own proposals. But, for better or worse, it left behind it the germ of an idea, as well as a precedent for treating divorce as a purely secular issue, to be discussed on purely secular and pragmatic grounds.[48] It also put forward the idea that quite a high level of divorce—if regarded as the burial of 'dead' marriages in order to create 'live' ones—was actually a sign of health in the concept of the family, rather than a harbinger of social disintegration.

The commission also drew attention to some important developments which had occurred over the previous century. Although the law had not changed since 1857, judicial interpretation had substantially modified practice in two ways. Recrimination—that is, the counter-accusation of the defendant that the plaintiff was also guilty of adultery, had been left to the discretion of the court by the 1857 act. After about 1900, however, the court routinely granted divorce to all petitioners, even if they themselves were adulterous, except in the most flagrant cases. Secondly, the legal definition of cruelty had been substantially softened by case law, especially after 1890.[49] The commission also pointed out that by a series of acts passed between 1878 and 1895, Parliament had empowered magistrates to grant separation maintenance and child custody for a wide set of matrimonial faults. This had facilitated a flood of temporary separations among the poor (Table 13.3).[50]

---

[47] *Roy. Com. Divorce 1956*, 8–11. [48] Ibid. 8–16.
[49] Biggs, 172–6. [50] *Roy. Com. Divorce 1956*, 261–2.

B. THE DEBATE IN 1968–1969

In view of the deadlock among the members of the Royal Commission of 1956, it is hardly surprising that its proposals were allowed to slumber for another twelve years. But by the mid-1960s, the national mood had changed drastically from what it had been even a decade before. As a result, two separate bodies were set up to consider the problem of divorce. One was appointed by the Archbishop of Canterbury; it consisted of clerical and lay members of the Church of England, and was known as the Archbishop's Group. The other was composed of distinguished judges and lawyers and was known as the Law Commission. In 1966 each issued a report, respectively entitled *Putting Asunder* and *The Field of Choice*.[51] Both were optimistic and radical documents, in striking contrast to the timid Royal Commission Report of 1956. They pointed out that since 93 per cent of all divorce cases were undefended, divorce by mutual consent was already standard practice. They therefore came to the revolutionary conclusion that divorce should be considered as no more than a legal remedy for 'irretrievable matrimonial breakdown'. A year later, the two groups issued a joint statement proposing this radical change, and over the next two years the new principle of 'irremediable marital breakdown' as a sufficient cause for divorce was duly accepted by the General Assembly of the Church of England, the Methodist Conference, and the Presbyterian General Assembly of Scotland. The former Christian lobby against divorce was thus effectively silenced or converted. The clergy wanted to turn a divorce proceeding away from its adversarial tradition, and make it more like a coroner's enquiry about a corpse, the corpse being the marriage. The lawyers supported the change, but they remained deeply sceptical that a judge would have the time to undertake such a delicate investigation of just what had killed a marriage. The future was to prove them right.

As a result of all this pressure, in 1969—just as the great waves of sexual liberation and radical life-styles were breaking over the West—a bill was introduced into the House of Commons, by a back-bencher, Mr L. Abse, to convert this new idea of no-fault divorce into the law of the land.[52] Abandoning the ancient principle of matrimonial fault, there was now to be substituted the principle, first enunciated back in the 1640s by

[51] [R. C. Mortimer], *Putting Asunder: A Divorce Law For Contemporary Society* (London, 1966); The Law Commission, *Reform of the Grounds of Divorce: The Field of Choice* (London, 1967); for summaries of both publications, see *Modern Law Review*, 30 (1967), 72–6, 180–6.

[52] 5 *Parl. Debates: Commons*, (1967–8), 758: 810–902; (1968–9), 774: 2035–55; (1968–9), 784: 1874–2072.

John Milton, that the only just ground for a divorce was as relief from the irremediable breakdown of a marital relationship.

Mr Abse set out the theoretical and sociological arguments in favour of the bill, claiming that it did no more than reflect changes occurring in society—notably, the greater equality of the sexes in marriage, and the rise of the nuclear family as greater geographical mobility caused greater physical separation from relatives. He argued that there were two principal defects in the current law of divorce. First, it terminated dead marriages by funnelling all cases directly into contestatory litigation. This procedure positively discouraged attempts at reconciliation and merely created bitterness and humiliation. He also pointed out that the government spent £4 million a year on legal fees for divorce suits for the poor, but only £4,200 a year on marriage guidance councils. Second, the current law left 250,000 men and women living in stable but illegitimate second unions, one of whose partners was trapped in a marriage from which there was no escape, since the other (innocent) spouse refused a divorce. The bill would allow these illegal couples to be officially married, and so to legitimize their estimated 200,000 children.[53] The proponents of the bill therefore concluded that it would strengthen rather than undermine both family life and the institution of marriage.

The practical proposals to implement this new principle were as conservative as the idea itself was radical. Evidence that the marriage was irretrievably shattered was provided by the same old matrimonial faults, adultery and cruelty. The latter had recently been redefined by the law lords as no more than 'grave and weighty conduct making a continuation of cohabitation intolerable, which has caused or is likely to cause injury to health'—meaning, physical, mental, and emotional health. This broad definition of cruelty was now expanded still further in the bill to cover any behaviour because of which the petitioner 'cannot reasonably be expected to live with the respondent'.[54] As critics warned at the time, this clause was so vaguely worded that it opened the way to divorce on demand, and indeed a few years later 'behaviour' had become the most common declared cause for divorce put forward by petitioning wives (Fig. 13.4, Table 13.4). Other proofs of 'irretrievable breakdown' were in future to be a two-year separation followed by a mutual agreement to divorce; or a five-year separation followed by a desire for divorce expressed by one of the two spouses, even if opposed by the other. To aid reconciliation, there was provision for the judge to impose a delay of up to six months, if he thought that it might do some good.[55]

[53] Ibid. (1967–8), 758: 858, 861, 895–902, 2038; (1968–9), 784: 2070.
[54] Ibid (1967–8), 758: 892; (1968–9), 784: 1904, 1913.   [55] Ibid. (1967–8), 758: 810–18.

Despite the support of the church and the law, the bill was not without its critics. For one thing, it was by no means clear that women's organizations supported the bill. Some, like the Married Women's Association, the Mothers' Union, and the Family Law Association—all conservative bodies—were clearly against it. They were opposed on the usual grounds that any liberalization of the divorce laws would make it easier for middle-aged husbands to trade in their ageing wives for sexually more attractive young girls.[56] Statistically, it is clear that divorced men remarry much more frequently than do divorced women. What remains unclear is the degree to which this discrepancy between the sexes in the post-divorce marriage market is due to deliberate choice—more women than men wishing to remain single—or to the relatively greater attractiveness of divorced men, since they possess more power and wealth to compensate for their age. It was also argued that women are always the main sufferers in either separation or divorce, because of the extreme difficulty in making husbands pay maintenance or alimony. Many of the working poor simply cannot afford to support two households. In 1968, former husbands only paid £3 million a year to support their ex-wives, to whom welfare services paid another £32 million, of which a mere £2 million was recovered from delinquent husbands.

Finally, opponents of the bill argued—as had been argued in the 1850s—that every time divorce is made easier or cheaper, divorce rates rise. They were also afraid that the concurrent reduction in the minimum age for marriage without parental consent to 18 'will send the divorce figures soaring', since young marriages are those most likely to break down. They pointed out that more divorces inevitably lead to more abandoned and impoverished wives and more single-parent children. They were especially concerned about the effects of an increase in the divorce rate upon young children, whose interests were not represented in or out of Parliament. They claimed, without any hard evidence one way or the other, that 'easy divorces are a disaster for the children'.[57] Despite this opposition, at eleven o'clock in the morning after an all-night debate, the bill finally passed the second reading in a much reduced House of Commons by a vote of 91 to 58.[58]

In the House of Lords, the bishops were notable mostly for their silence during the debate. Possible explanations are that the tide of lay opinion was too strong for them, that they knew that few peers cared very much any more what they thought, that they were too absorbed with

[56] 5 *Parl. Debates: Commons*, (1967–8), 758: 826, 838, 849, 2052.
[57] Ibid. (1968–9), 774: 2044–55; 784: 1885.
[58] Ibid. (1968–9), 784: 2019.

diocesan business, or that they knew that the Archbishop of Canterbury favoured the bill. What is striking about this debate was the contrast with those in 1857 and 1937: this time, no speaker so much as mentioned the old theological arguments about the sanctity of marriage according to the words of Christ.

The most profound question was asked by Mr Quentin Hogg (now Lord Hailsham). He expressed his fears about the rising tide of divorce. No one seemed to know just how many marriages already ended in divorce, but one suggestion was 10 per cent. Hogg questioned the wisdom of making divorce even easier than it was already, but based his argument on the liberal premise that priority should be given to the pursuit of individual self-fulfilment. It was known that the divorce rate had risen nearly tenfold in the previous thirty-five years (Fig. 13.3, Table 13.1). Hogg asked: 'Are we sure how much human happiness has increased during those thirty-five years? Would anyone care to dogmatize?' There was an uneasy silence, for nobody really knew. Despite this uncertainty, Mr Abse confidently prophesied that in future there would be more, not fewer, stable, legitimate and happy households. On that optimistic note the debate ended and the bill passed, to become law on 1 January 1971.[59]

Secular society, with the blessing of the leaders of the church, had launched itself upon the unknown waters of no-fault divorce on demand for all, at precisely the moment when a cultural and social hurricane was beginning to blow through Western society.

5. The Divorce Revolution 1960–1987

A. FACTS

In the twenty-seven years between 1960 and 1987, the number of divorces per annum in England and Wales has multiplied sixfold, from 24,000 to 151,000. As a result, the rate of divorce per annum per 1,000 married couples has also risen sixfold, from 2.0 to 12.6 (Fig. 13.3, Table 13.1). Up to 1960, the increase in the divorce rate can to a large extent be interpreted as a shift of legal categories among those whose marriages had broken down. Between 1900 and 1957 the divorce rate increased twentyfold, but the increase of applications to magistrates for temporary maintenance orders, judicial separations, and divorces, if all lumped together, increased only fivefold. This suggests that there was indeed a significant real increase in marital break-downs, but not on the scale

[59] Ibid. 2070–2; ibid. 788 (1968–9), 719.

suggested by the figures for legal divorce alone (Tables 13.1 and 13.3).[60] It is impossible to deny that after 1960 a shift of legal categories from the divorced or separated to the divorced was also occurring, since now for the first time the privately separated were almost all getting divorced. But it is hard to avoid the conclusion that this recent massive increase in legal divorce must also reflect a very substantial increase in marital breakdowns.

Statistically speaking, marriage has today in many ways merely reverted to a pattern which existed before the sharp decline in adult mortality in the late nineteenth and early twentieth centuries. The difference is that whereas in the early nineteenth century the driving force was a high adult mortality rate, today it is a high divorce rate. Thus the proportion of marital dissolutions by death or divorce in England and Wales at early stages in marriage was much the same for the cohort marrying in 1826 as for that marrying in 1980. What happened was that as adult mortality fell after about 1870, the duration of marriages rose for a while, until the trend was reversed by the rise in divorces. Thus the duration of marriage of the cohorts marrying between 1920 and 1950, when death rates of young adults had dropped precipitously and divorce had not yet taken on a major role, were historically quite different from those before and after. During those thirty years, fewer than 20 per cent were broken by death or divorce after twenty years, compared with over 30 per cent (by death) for the 1826 marriage cohort and 30 per cent (mostly by divorce) for the 1980 marriage cohort (Table 13.5).[61] By these calculations even the explosion of the divorce rate since 1960 has done no more than cut the duration of marriage back to its traditional level by compensating for a prior fall in mortality. On the other hand, it would be rash to claim that the psychological effects of the termination of a marriage by divorce, that is by an act of will, bear a close resemblance to its termination by the inexorable accident of death.

B. CAUSES

Historians, demographers, and sociologists have done their best to provide a satisfactory explanation for the soaring rates of marital breakdown in England in particular and the West in general in the late twentieth century, as reflected in the statistics of legal divorce. But so far the result has been a cacophony of voices.

[60] Rowntree and Carrier, 190; McGregor, *Divorce in England*, 54.

[61] M. Anderson, 'What is New about the Modern Family: An Historical Perspective', *Office of Population Censuses and Surveys*, Occasional Paper 71 (1983), 4 and Fig. 2. I owe this reference to Mr John Haskey.

Four statistical trends and three sets of political events are of critical importance. One trend is that, for unknown reasons, divorces are increasingly taking place early, within four years of marriage, the proportion rising from 11 per cent to 27 per cent between 1961 and 1985 (Table 13.6). A second trend is the rise between 1961 and 1986, from 9 per cent to 33 per cent, in the proportion of all marriages which were remarriages of the divorced. This also inevitably raised the divorce rate, since such remarriages are much more likely to end in divorce than are first marriages (Fig. 13.5, Table 13.7). A third trend is a decline in the age at first marriage, which between 1931 and 1971 fell by three years, as

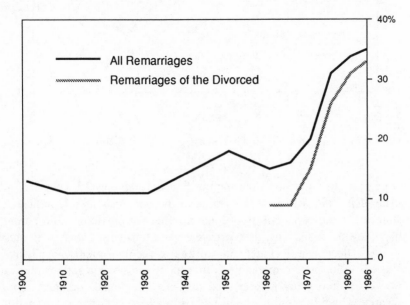

FIGURE 13.5   Remarriages as a Proportion of All Marriages (Great Britain) 1901–1986 [Table 13.7]

a result of which marriages by teenagers rose from 14 per cent to 28 per cent of all marriages (Fig. 13.6, Table 13.8).[62] This has inevitably raised the divorce rate, since, presumably because of emotional immaturity, these marriages are twice as likely to end in divorce as marriages made between the ages of 20 and 24. The fourth trend is the massive entry into the divorce market of the unskilled, who have taken to divorce on such a

[62] J. Haskey, 'Marital Status before Marriage and Age at Marriage: Their Influence on the Chances of Divorce', *Population Trends*, 32 (1983), 11, 14; id., 'The Proportion of Marriages ending in Divorce', ibid. 27 (1982), Fig. 3; *Registrar General's Statistical Review of England and Wales for 1967*, pt. iii (London, 1971), 22.

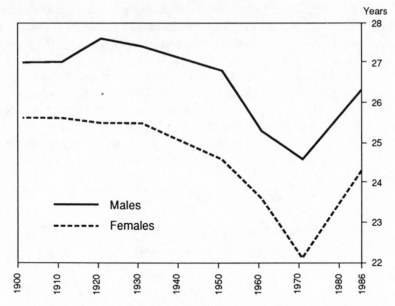

FIGURE 13.6 Average Age at First Marriage (Great Britain) 1901–1986 [Table 13.8]

large scale that in 1966 they for the first time comprised a third of all male plaintiffs.[63] Much of this influx of the poor may merely indicate a shift into the divorce courts of huge numbers of previously unrecorded breakdowns, desertions, and private separations, but some of it must surely reflect a real change in working-class matrimonial behaviour. What is even more remarkable is that today the divorce rate of manual workers is four times greater than that of professional couples.[64] Thus divorce, which for centuries had been a privilege exclusively confined to the rich, has now become a legal device most commonly used by the poor.

One political cause is the impact of two world wars, each of which had the short-term effect of a sudden post-war explosion of divorces, mostly initiated by husbands against adulterous wives; and the long-term effect of raising divorce rates permanently by a factor of four or five. The second is the progressive easing of the laws governing divorce, first in 1937 and then in 1969, each of which triggered off a growth spurt of divorces. For example, wives were quick to realise the potential of the act of 1969 to obtain immediate divorce by use of the new grounds of

[63] *Registrar General's Statistical Review of England and Wales for 1967*, pt. iii (London, 1971), Table C15. [64] *Social Trends*, 15 (1985), 39.

'intolerable behaviour'; by 1984 nearly half of all women petitioners were citing this cause (Fig. 13.4, Table 13.4). With over 150,000 cases to be processed every year, no judge has the time to investigate 'behaviour', and since most suits are uncontested he has no evidence about the case except the bare statement of the petitioner. The result, therefore, is not a careful evaluation of the reasons for the breakdown of the marriage, but merely a swift and cheap administrative procedure to churn out hundreds of thousands of no-fault divorces on demand.

The third political cause, which may have been more important in the long run than either of the other two, is the granting by Parliament of legal aid to the poor. Thanks to increasingly generous grants of legal aid, first in 1914, then in 1920, in 1949, and again in 1960, the working class has at last obtained access to the divorce market. These measures, which passed almost without debate, were more effective in widening the pool of potential petitioners for divorce than the divorce reform acts which led to such passionate and prolonged debates in 1923, 1937, and 1969.[65] The reason for the discrepancy is that the latter, unlike the former, involved highly controversial issues of morality and public policy.

Behind all this recent legislation facilitating divorce, there lies a pent-up demand causing the relentless rise in divorce rates. This demand must be linked to changes in mental attitudes towards religion, marriage, personal happiness and self-fulfilment, and sexual pleasure. But the extreme difficulty of establishing these linkages is highlighted by the recent discovery that in America there is a clear inverse correlation between pre-marital cohabitation, or 'trial marriage', and later marital stability: those whose marriages were preceded by a period of cohabitation are *more* likely to divorce quickly than those who did not live together before marriage.[66] If confirmed by other studies, this finding flies in the face of all previous assumptions that trial marriages reduce the prospects of divorce in the future. But what does the finding mean? It could be that those who cohabit before marriage have higher expectations of marital happiness, and are therefore less willing to put up with what they get in terms of personal intimacy, friendship, and love. In other words, their happiness threshold is higher than that of others. Alternatively, it could mean that those who cohabit before marriage take the marriage bond less seriously than others, and are more inclined to regard it as a conditional contract, easily entered into and easily broken. The rapid rise in pre-marital cohabitation in the last thirty years may indicate

[65] Rowntree and Carrier, 213; McGregor, *Divorce in England*, 31–2.
[66] *New York Times*, 9 June 1989: A1, 28.

a reduced respect for marriage as an institution. If this is so, the level of happiness does not enter into the picture.

To find a more adequate explanation of what has happened, one is forced to fall back on broader psychological and economic generalities. At the personal level of perceptions and grievances, divorcing wives in Cleveland, Ohio—which may or may not be a typical area—complained of physical, mental, or verbal cruelty, quarrels about money, drinking, neglect of home and family, and absence of love. Divorcing husbands, by contrast, complained about parents-in-law and unsatisfactory sex.[67] These perceptions, however, may have concealed more basic realities, just as court claims are likely to be tailored to fit the criteria of the divorce law. The key to personal motivation must surely lie in the increasingly pervasive ideologies of individualism, the pursuit of personal happiness, and the expectation of relatively speedy gratification. The combination of modern technology, the rise of consumerism, and unparalleled affluence have made redundant the older need for deferred gratification, without which life in the not so distant past would have been intolerable, and which was inculcated by the practical problems of day-to-day life, as well as by religion, school, family, and kin. This new demand of instant gratification of individual desires tends to erode the sense of obligation and responsibility both within the family and in society at large, and in consequence leads to a rise in the divorce rate.

To move from the particular to the general, it is arguable that the expectation of sexual and emotional fulfilment from marriage has recently risen to quite unrealistic levels. Although hard to document, there appears to be more stress on rights and less on duties. As a result, many marriages which would have been regarded as tolerable in the past are today seen as unendurable. No clearer proof of the revolution in marital expectations is available than the steady erosion over 150 years of the legal definition of marital cruelty from violence which threatened life or health to mere 'intolerable behaviour' as defined by the offended party. One can also argue that this rise in expectations is faithfully reflected in the divorce law reforms of 1937 and especially 1969. It was this ideology which induced bishops, law lords, and legislators to recommend widening the acceptable causes of dissolving a marriage to a point where no-fault divorce becomes the rule.

The decline of the influence of parents and kin has removed much of the support system which in the past held together many moderately

---

[67] R. Phillips, *Putting Asunder: A History of Divorce in Western Society* (Cambrige, 1988), 584–5.

unsatisfactory marriages. But this is a change which should not be exaggerated, since the car, the plane, and the telephone have gone a long way to compensate for greater geographical separation. Thirdly, the egalitarian ideology of feminism has had a major impact, in that it has drawn attention to the gross injustice to women of unequal opportunities for jobs. The result of this pressure has been an opening of doors to married women, who have poured into the labour market on a large scale. These ideas have radically transformed the personal relationships of males and females in marriage and the relative allocation of economic responsibilities and powers within the family unit. Beneficial though this has been in many ways, it has put modern marriage under greater stress than ever before.

Fourthly, there has been removed the ancient moral stigma that for centuries lay upon marital breakdown, and especially upon a public divorce. One reason is that now that it has become so extremely common, familiarity has led not to contempt but to public indifference: divorce is thus sociologically reinforcing, like any other habit. Another factor that has undoubtedly been important in lifting the moral stigma against divorce is the decline of the influence of the church and religion in an increasingly secularized society. This decline was clearly responsible for the abandonment by 1960 by British legislators of any reference to Christian doctrine when arguing about reforms in the divorce laws. Moreover, if one seeks to explain why England today has so very high a divorce rate by European standards, one of the most likely explanations must surely be the marginal level of current English religious belief and practice, as evidenced by very low church attendance and the rising proportion of marriages which take place in a civil Registry Office (Fig. 5.1, Table 5.1).

Economic changes have also played their part in stimulating divorce. In the past, the family was an integrated economic unit which was very hard to break up. Child care and home maintenance was left to wives, who performed these and other functions which played a large part in holding the family together. The economic interdependence of husband and wife in the past is a major reason why marital breakdown was relatively so rare.

Today, many of these functions, which formerly chained the wife among the poor within the family home but at the same time increased her sense of responsibility for those she cared for, are now largely performed by others. Much of the preparation, processing, and cooking of food has been transferred to the market, epitomized by the rise of the take-away; and the cleaning of clothes, dishes, and space has been revolutionized by machines.[68] Much of the burden of child-minding is handled by schools, day-care centres, and baby-sitters. Thus, technology has both reduced the demand for work in the home and increased the opportunities and incentives for work outside it.[69] It is no accident that the divorce rate has risen concurrently with the influx of married women into the labour market. This has occurred since family planning and a higher expectation of life have together radically altered the lives of working-class women. An Englishwoman born in 1951 could expect to complete child-bearing at 28 and live for another fifty-two years. Not surprisingly, having had her children, she has gone out to work.[70] As a result, so many wives are now more or less economically self-sufficient that they are at last freed—or think they are freed—from the traditional fear of economic destitution arising from divorce.

It is thus changes in social, religious, and moral values, which seem to have been permanently affected by two world wars, together with the by-products of modern medical and contraceptive technologies, the rise of service economies, and the opening of the labour market to married women, that have affected not only courting, marriage, marital conduct, and the functions performed by the family, but also marital breakdown and the laws which govern the granting of legal divorce.

C. CONSEQUENCES

During the debates of 1856–7, an MP prophesied:

If we increase the facilities for divorce, we will have, in the course of time, an enormous number of increased divorces. If we once pass this law, we can never go back, but must continue on the same course, however terrible the evils which will flow from it.[71]

In the long run, he turned out to be right in his prophecy, in the sense that divorce rates have now soared to levels far beyond his worst imaginings.

It is projected that if the level of divorces continues at its present rate, whereas 1 in 10 marriages of the 1950s ended in divorce, the proportion of those of the 1970s ending in divorce will be 1 in 3 (Fig. 13.7, Table

[68] C. Hardyment, *From Mangle to Microwave: The Mechanization of Household Work* (Cambridge, 1988).

[69] For a moving description of the realities of the lives of working-class women before 1920 and the reasons for their indifference to access to the vote (or the divorce court), see B. Harrison, 'Class and Gender in British Labour History', *Past and Present*, 124 (1989).

[70] M. Anderson, 'The Emergence of the Modern Life Cycle in Britain', *Social History*, 10 (1985), 73–4.

[71] 3 *Hansard*, 146: 756.

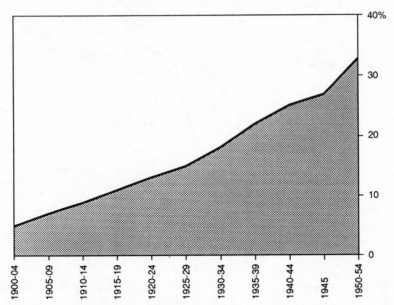

FIGURE 13.7   Proportion of First Marriages Ending in Divorce (England and Wales) by Male Birth Cohort 1900–1954 [Table 13.9]

13.9).[72] This means that England and Wales today has the highest divorce rate of any country in the European Community (Fig. 13.8, Table 13.10).[73]

The consequences of a third of all marriages ending in divorce are unpredictable, since the change is too recent and the sociological evidence is too thin. Some will conclude that not only an important stabilizing factor has been lost to society, but also that there will be adverse effects on the minds, morals, and happiness of large numbers of both lonely adults and one-parent children. This may be true, but it is essential to bear in mind that statistically similar social conditions existed in the past, although then driven by mortality rather than conscious choice.[74]

There is emerging a little evidence to suggest that some of the worst predictions of the pessimists with regard to the social and economic consequences of divorce on demand may perhaps now be coming true. It

[72] Haskey, 'The Proportion of Marriages ending in Divorce', 5.
[73] *Social Trends*, 13 (1983), 32; ibid. 18 (1988), 43.
[74] R. Schoen and J. Bas, 'Twentieth Century Cohort Marriage and Divorce in England and Wales', *Population Studies*, 38 (1984), 443; S. C. Watkins *et al.* 'The Demographic Foundations of Family Change', *American Sociological Review*, 57 (1987), 341.

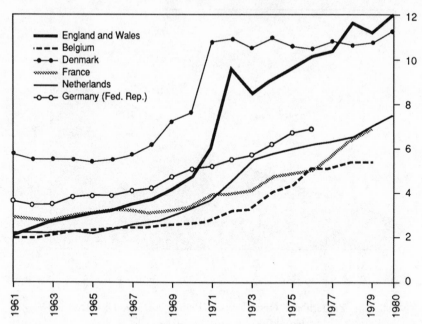

FIGURE 13.8   International Comparisons: Divorce Rates per 1,000 Married Couples
1961–1985 [Table 13.10]

was expected that the proportion of illegitimate to all live births would decrease after the 1969 act made it possible for marriage to replace cohabitation for couples previously unable to divorce and remarry. Instead it has rocketed from eight per cent in 1971 to 21 per cent in 1986. Although part of this rise may be accounted for by the decline in the number of legitimate births, there can be no doubt that despite this being an era of easy contraception and easy marriage or remarriage, illegitimate births are running at a much higher rate than ever before in recorded history (Fig. 13.9, Table 13.11).[75]

Moreover, the proportion of all divorced couples with children under 11 has risen from one third to two thirds, so that in the one year 1980 112,000 children under 11 years of age experienced the trauma of parental divorce (Fig. 13.10, Table 13.12).[76] The psychological consequences of such ruptures for spouses and children are still a matter of debate. It is not yet possible to be certain whether or not the sudden

[75] B. Werner, 'Recent Trends in Illegitimate Births and Extra-marital Conceptions', *Population Trends*, 30 (1982), 9–10; *Social Trends*, 18 (1988), 46–7.
[76] *Social Trends*, 16 (1986), 40.

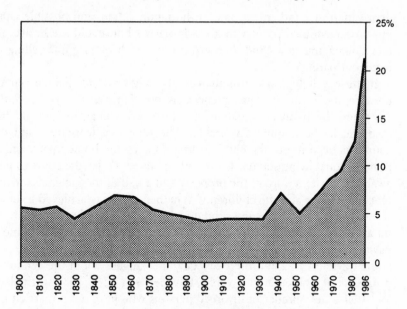

FIGURE 13.9   Illegitimate Births as a Proportion of All Births (England and Wales)
1800–1986 [Table 13.11]

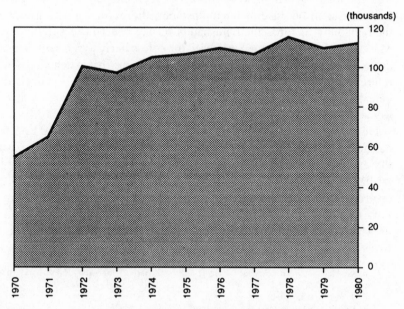

FIGURE 13.10   Total Children under 11 Years of Divorcing Couples (England and
Wales) 1970–1980 [Table 13.12]

deprivation of a father, the sale of the family home, and possible lapse into unaccustomed poverty in a single-parent household are or are not more damaging to a child than growing up with bitterly quarrelling or negligent parents.[77]

If the psychological consequences of a high rate of divorce remain obscure, the economic consequences are now fairly clear. Ever since the 1857 act, the financial situation of a divorced woman in England has theoretically been quite favourable. The object of legislators and the court has been to put the children first, to keep the home intact, and to provide equal living standards for both spouses. Today the court usually awards the wife a third of the property and a half of the income as maintenance for her and the children.[78] Whether all this is achieved in practice, however, is another question, to which at present there seems to be no answer. It is notoriously difficult to extract full and regular alimony payments from an ex-husband who is either unable or unwilling to pay, so that even in England there are gloomy statistics about the economic prospects of women after divorce. Between 1951 and 1986 in England and Wales the number of divorced persons who have not remarried has risen tenfold, from 200,000 to 2.2 million, although of course many will remarry later (Fig. 13.11, Table 13.13). Sixty per cent of these were women, many of whom were forced to seek support from the public welfare system because of unemployment, the burden of children, and their inability to force their husbands to pay court-ordered alimony.[79] Moreover, divorced women are three times less likely to remarry than are divorced men.[80] It is therefore hardly surprising that when in 1986 a referendum about the introduction of divorce into Ireland was decisively defeated, largely by the women's vote, an opponent remarked that 'a woman voting for divorce is like a turkey voting for Christmas'.[81]

Despite these facts, a striking feature of twentieth-century England has been the predominance of wives among petitioners for divorce, with the exception of the two brief post-war episodes of divorce mainly by husbands. By the 1980s the proportion of wives among petitioners for divorce had risen to over 70 per cent (Fig. 13.2, Table 13.2).[82] There is thus in England a wide discrepancy between the apparent economic drawbacks of divorce for many women and the huge predominance of wives as petitioners for divorce.

[77] L. C. Halem, *Divorce Reform: Changing Legal and Social Perspectives*, (New York, 1980), 167–93.

[78] Ibid. 85, 88, 96, 196–9, 201–3.

[79] R. Leete, 'Changing Marital Composition', *Population Trends*, 10 (1977), 18.

[80] *Social Trends*, 16 (986), 37.   [81] Phillips, *Putting Asunder*, 580.

[82] Haskey, *op. cit. Biology and Society*, 3 (1986), 65, 68.

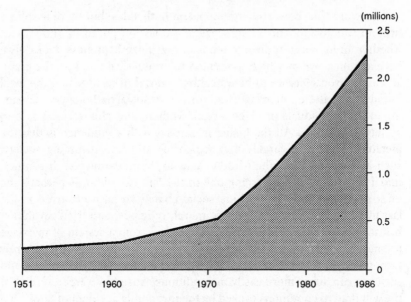

FIGURE 13.11   Number of Divorced Persons Not Remarried (England and Wales)
1951–1986 [Table 13.13]

On the positive side, there can be no doubt that, as a result of this divorce revolution, a whole mass of unworkable laws governing marriage have been swept away. Collusive agreements to commit perjury in court are no longer necessary. The principle first adumbrated by Milton, that a marriage without love or respect is dead and should be legally buried as soon as practicable, has become the law of the land. This has brought to millions of unhappily married couples the opportunity to remarry and start again. It has offered freedom to many tens of thousands of women who were subjected to various forms of cruelty by their husbands.[83] It has reduced from tens of thousands to virtually none the number of couples forced to live in concubinage since they could not obtain a divorce. The hundreds of thousands of couples who now live in concubinage do so from choice and not from compulsion. The poor now have equal access to the divorce court with the rich, as do wives with husbands, thereby doing away at last with two ancient injustices. Nor is there any doubt that lamentations over the collapse of the family in England are exaggerated, based on a failure to realize that in the past death was as important a cause of the premature dissolution of marriage as divorce is today.

[83] For the slow broadening of the concept of cruelty, see Biggs, 22–50.

There are thus powerful arguments on both sides, but there is still no firm answer to Quentin Hogg's nagging question posed in 1969 about whether an increase in divorce tends to maximize happiness. Nor do we have any measure by which to identify the numerical point on the graph at which divorce ceases to be a healthy removal of dead wood, the legal burial of a shattered marriage, and turns into social pathology as damaging to the individuals involved—men, women, and children—as it is to society as a whole. All the historian can say with confidence is that the metamorphosis of a largely non-separating and non-divorcing society, such as England from the Middle Ages to the mid-nineteenth century, into a separating and divorcing one in the late twentieth, is perhaps the most profound and far-reaching social change to have occurred in the last five hundred years. A gigantic moral, religious, and legal revolution has accompanied and made possible the shift from a system of marriage prematurely terminated by death to a system of marriage prematurely terminated by choice. It is an open question whether individuals and societies can adapt more easily to conditions caused by a free exercise of the will than to conditions caused by the inexorable accident of fate. That the divorce reformers of the nineteenth and twentieth centuries meant well is beyond dispute. But the results have clearly not altogether measured up to their expectations, and it is very uncertain whether the benefits of no-fault divorce on demand, as introduced in 1971, have outweighed its drawbacks. This is something which only time will tell.

Appendix

A List of Pamphlets Concerning the Marriage Act of 1753

H. Gally, *Some Considerations upon Clandestine Marriages* (London, 1750); A. Keith, *Observations on the Acts for Preventing Clandestine Marriages* (London, 1753); Anon. [Marsh?], *A Letter to the Public . . . Upon the Subject of the Act of Parliament for the better Preventing of Clandestine Marriages* (London, 1753); 'A Freeholder', *Considerations on the Bill for Preventing Clandestine Marriages* (London, 1753); Anon., *Reasons against the Clandestine Marriage Bill in the House of Commons* (London, 1753); J. Shebbeare, *The Marriage Act*, 2 vols. (London, 1754); H. Stebbing, *An Enquiry into the Force and Operation of the Annulling Clause in a late Act for the better preventing of Clandestine Marriages with Respect to Conscience* (London, 1754); Anon., *An humble and serious Representation of some great Hazards and Difficulties . . . in the Execution of the late Act for preventing Clandestine Marriages* (London, 1754); 'A Gentleman of the Temple', *Some Considerations on the Act to prevent Clandestine Marriages* (London, 1754); 'A Country Clergyman' [H. Dodwell], *A Letter to the Author of Some Considerations on the Act to prevent Clandestine Marriages* (London, 1755); H. Stebbing, *A Dissertation on the Power of States to deny civil Protection to the Marriages of Minors made without the Consent of their Parents or Guardians* (London, 1955); J. Sayer, *A Vindication of the Power of Society to annull the Marriages of Minors* (London, c.1755); J. Tunstall, DD, *A Vindication of the Power of States to prohibit Clandestine Marriages under the pain of absolute Nullity* (London, 1755); id., *Marriage in Society Stated* (London, 1755); N. Forster, *Remarks on the Rev. D. Stebbing's Dissertation on the Power of States to deny civil Protection to the Marriage of Minors* (London, 1755); Sir Tanfield Leman, *Matrimony Analysed* (London, 1755); Anon., *Some Observations on two Pamphlets concerning Clandestine Marriages* (London, 1755); H. Stebbing, *Review of the Principles of Enquiry . . .* (London, 1755); id., article in the *Monthly Review*, nos. 12 and 13 (London, 1755); Anon., *Reflections on the Repeal of the Marriage Act, now under consideration of Parliament* (London, 1764); Anon., *An Essay on the late Act to prevent Clandestine Marriages* (London, 1769); M. Madan, *Thelyphthora, or a Treatise on Female Ruin . . . including an examination of the Marriage Act*, 2nd edn., 3 vols. (London, 1781).

Tables

TABLE 1.1. *Court of Arches: All Cases and Matrimonial Cases, 1660–1849*

	All types of cases	Matrimonial cases	
	Total	No.	% of total
1660–9	2,330	204	9
70–9	1,915	174	9
80–9	1,220	70	6
90–9	755	76	10
1700–9	735	83	11
10–19	640	63	10
20–9	450	34	8
30–9	515	47	9
40–9	305	23	8
50–9	250	27	11
60–9	235	17	7
70–9	210	33	16
80–9	195	32	16
90–9	160	46	29
1800–9	135	53	39
10–19	185	96	52
20–9	170	72	42
30–9	165	70	42
40–9	200	85	42

Source: Based on a 20% sample (Nos. 1–1,100 and 9,000–10,100).

TABLE 1.2. *Court of Arches: Proportion of Matrimonial Cases Reaching Sentence, 1660–1745*

	No.	% of matrimonial cases
1660–99	524	39
1700–45	245	42

Source: This does not mean that the Court actually issued a sentence, but rather that the penultimate stage in the case had been reached, and that the two lawyers had submitted draft sentences on behalf of their clients, from which the judge would select one. Unfortunately, these draft sentences—sometimes two of them—are bound up with those actually issued, which makes counting the latter virtually impossible.

TABLE 1.3. *Court of Arches: Types of Cases, 1660–1849*

	Marriage						Separation							Nullity (not Pre-Contract)	Total
	Restitution of Conjugal Rights	Jactitation	Espousals, Contracts, Nullity for Pre-Contracts	Clandestine Marriage	Total	%	Adultery	Cruelty	Misc.	Adultery and Cruelty	Restitution of Conjugal Rights	Total	%		
1660–9	44	29	43	1	117	57	30	29	8	6	0	73	36	14	204
70–9	27	26	45	2	100	57	20	30	6	7	0	63	36	11	174
80–9	11	7	14	1	33	47	4	19	4	2	0	29	41	8	70
90–9	11	11	18	1	41	54	8	15	3	5	0	31	41	4	76
1700–9	12	8	15	4	39	46	10	18	5	6	0	39	47	5	83
10–19	24	8	4	1	37	45	8	15	1	2	0	26	41	0	63
20–9	11	1	2	2	16	47	4	3	0	7	0	14	41	4	34
30–9	5	4	11	3	23	49	11	8	1	3	0	23	49	1	47
40–9	3	2	6	0	11	48	5	5	0	0	0	10	43	2	23
50–9	2	5	2	0	9	39	9	5	2	1	0	17	63	1	27
60–9	0	2	1	0	3	17	9	2	2	0	0	13	76	1	17
70–9	0	2	3	0	5	15	9	2	0	4	6	21	63	7	33
80–9	0	0	0	0	0	0	14	3	0	5	3	25	78	7	32
90–9	0	2	0	0	2	4	28	4	0	3	3	38	83	6	46
1800–9	0	0	0	2	2	5	24	3	2	2	9	40	75	11	53
10–19	0	0	1	0	3	3	33	8	2	13	14	70	74	21	94
20–9	0	0	2	0	2	3	35	6	2	7	11	61	85	9	72
30–9	0	0	0	3	3	4	29	8	1	12	13	63	86	7	73
40–9	0	0	0	2	2	2	40	7	2	15	15	79	91	6	87
	150	107	167	24	448		331	190	41	99	74	735		125	1,308

Notes: From 1770 to 1849, Nullities are mostly cases of under-age marriage voided under the 1753 Act.

From 1770 to 1849, Restitution of Conjugal Rights was a suit by wives as a preliminary to suing for separation with maintenance on grounds of desertion.

TABLE 1.4. *Court of Arches: Proportion of Separation Cases in Process Books, 1660–1849*

	All separation cases		Separation cases in Process Books		% in Process Books
1660–9	73	136	2	3	2
70–9	63		1		
80–9	29	99	4	12	12
90–9	31		4		
1700–9	39		4		
10–19	26	206	8	62	30
20–9	14		6		
30–9	23		11		
40–9	10		2		
50–9	17		4		
60–9	13		1		
70–9	15		3		
80–9	22		5		
90–9	35		16		
1800–9	31		6		
10–19	56	220	1	18	8
20–9	50		2		
30–9	50		12		
40–9	64		3		

TABLE 1.5. *Office Prosecutions in Chester and Lichfield Consistory Courts, 1660–1779*

	Chester CC	Lichfield CC
1660–9	20	2
70–9	64	2
80–9	37	19
90–9	45	24
1700–9	10	11
10–19	8	0
20–9	24	1
30–9	3	6
40–9	2	2
50–9	2	0
60–9	0	1
70–9	0	0
Total	215	68
Of which Clandestine Marriage	66%	77%

TABLE 1.6. *Court of Arches: Social Status of Plaintiffs, 1660–1819*

The poor	Titled and very rich	Esquire and rich	Professional and merchant	Middling sort	Small tradesman, artisan, or husbandman	Total	
	(%)	(%)	(%)	(%)	(%)	(%)	(No.)
1660–99	0	28	19	38	3	12	58
1700–79	1	28	16	36	13	6	136
1780–1819	2	52	23	19	4	0	48
							242

Source: Process Books only.

TABLE 1.7. *Matrimonial Cases in Chester, Lichfield, and Exeter Consistory Courts, 1660–1799*

	Chester CC	Lichfield CC	Exeter CC
1660–9	54	7	17
70–9	80	8	11
80–9	59	24	10
90–9	68	27	13
1700–9	19	25	18
10–19	26	11	14
20–9	38	11	16
30–9	0	18	5
40–9	0	15	5
50–9	0	7	3
60–9	0	4	2
70–9	0	6	2
80–9	4	10	0
90–9	2	14	2

TABLE 1.8. *The London Consistory Court: Numbers, Types of Cases, and the Sex-ratio of Plaintiffs 1670–1857*

	Sex of plaintiffs				Separation cases				Nullity				
	Male	Female	Total	% Female	Adultery	Cruelty	Adultery and Cruelty	Total	Bigamy	Incest	Under Age	Impotence etc.	Total
1670–99	86	134	220	64	47	32	10	89	38	10	0	0	48
1701–20	113	160	273	58	54	43	27	124	38	2	0	7	47
1726–35 / 1746–55	76	110	187	59	49	16	25	90	20	1	0	0	21
1770–99	146	70	216	32	130	7	16	153	9	9	40	0	58
1840–57	47	61	108	56	186	20	23	229	4	1	26	0	33

	Restitution of Conjugal Rights	Jactitation	Contract	Official case	Total
1670–99	20	18	29	0	230
1701–20	49	42	15	22	307
1726–35 / 1746–55	43	32	1	0	187
1770–99	7	6	0	0	216
1840–57	35	0	0	0	297

Note: These statistics are confined to cases which were not merely entered in the Act Books and promptly dropped, but which proceeded at least to the stage of the production of a libel—that is, a bill of charges. It is not at all clear that the sets of statistics for the various decades are strictly comparable one to another. For lack of space, unknowns have been omitted, except in the totals.

TABLE 5.1. Proportion of First Marriages in Civil Registry Offices (England and Wales), 1841–1978

	%
1841	3
1851	4
1861	7
1871	10
1881	13
1891	14
1901	18
1904	18
1914	25
1924	25
1934	28
1952	31
1962	30
1972	49
1978	57

Sources: Registrar General's Statistical Review of England and Wales for 1967, Pt. III (London, 1971), 15; J. Haskey, 'Trends in Marriage: Church, Chapel and Civil Ceremonies', *Population Trends*, 22 (1980); G. Rowntree and N. H. Carrier, 'The Resort to Divorce in England and Wales 1858–1957', *Population Studies*, 11 (1957), 195; J. Haskey, 'Trends in Marriage and Divorce in England and Wales 1837–1987', *Population Trends*, 48 (1987), 13.

TABLE 6.1. Recorded Wife-Sales, 1730–1919

Decade	No.
1730–9	3
40–9	4
50–9	2
60–9	10
70–9	13
80–9	18
90–9	31
1800–9	32
10–19	46
20–9	49
30–9	51
40–9	23
50–9	17
60–9	12
70–9	14
80–9	14
90–9	10
1900–9	9
10–19	2

Source: S. P. Menafee, *Wives for Sale* (Oxford, 1981).

TABLE 9.1. *Recorded Criminal Conversation Actions, 1680–1849*

Decade	No.
1680–9	2
90–9	2
1700–9	3
10–19	3
20–9	5
30–9	7
40–9	7
50–9	17
60–9	18
70–9	36
80–9	37
90–9	73
1800–9	52
10–19	49
20–9	47
30–9	44
40–9	c.35

TABLE 9.2. *Parliamentary Divorces Preceded by Criminal Conversation Actions, 1700–1857*

	Parliamentary divorces[a]	Criminal conversation actions	%
1700–49	14	4	30
50–9	15	7	47
60–9	13	5	38
70–9	34	25	73
80–9	12	11	92
90–9	43	39	93
1800–9	23	22	96
10–19	27	26	96
20–9	25	23	92
30–9	35	27	77
40–9	55	38	76
50–7	29	21	72

[a] Wolfson, App. 1A. There are rather smaller figures, but the identical trends, in Anderson, Table III, and Wolfson, Table 4. These depend exclusively on statements before the House of Lords, and are therefore very incomplete.

TABLE 9.3. *Damages over £2,000 in Criminal Conversation Actions, 1680–1857*

Decade	£2,000–2,999	£3,000–4,999	£5,000–9,999	£10,000 +	Total
1680–9			1		1
90–9					0
1700–9					0
10–19			1		1
20–9					0
30–9				1	1
40–9	1		1	1	3
50–9	2				2
60–9	1				1
70–9				2	2
80–9	2	1	1		4
90–9	4	5	5	4	18
1800–9	3	4	4	8	19
10–19	7	5	4	6	22
20–9	4	3	7		14
30–9	5	4		1	10
40–9	5	3	3	1	12
50–7	4	3			7
Total	38	28	27	24	117

TABLE 9.4. *Men of Title Involved in Criminal Conversation Actions and Parliamentary Divorces, 1700–1857*

A. *Men of Title Involved in Criminal Conversation Actions*

Date	Total actions	Men of title			Total plaintiffs & defendants	% of men of title
		Plaintiffs	Defendants	Total		
1700–49	23	6	7	13	46	28
1750–69	29	2	4	6	58	10
1770–89	68	10	9	19	136	14
1790–1809	124	14	14	28	248	11
1810–29	96	17	14	31	192	16
1830–57	c.80+	2	5	7	c.160	4
1700–1857	c.420	51	53	104	c.840	

B. *Men of Title Granted Parliamentary Divorces*

Date	Total	Titled	%
1700–49	14	6	43
1750–69	28	3	11
1770–1829	163	30	18
1830–57	118	2	2
Total	323	41	

Note: These figures include all men holding titles of peer or baronet, or the courtesy title of 'Honourable'.

Source: Wolfson, 166, Table 3, and App. III.

TABLE 9.5. *Recorded Taxed Costs in Criminal Conversation Actions, 1821–1857*

	£1–74	£75–99	£100–49	£150–99	£200–99	£300–499	£500+	Total suits
1821–40	7	2	8	11	11	6	6	51
1840–57	10	2	7	6	7	8	8	48

Sources: Calculated from Anderson, Tables III–V. This sample is taken from actions which preceded Parliamentary divorces. The costs are likely to be on the low side since almost all crim. con. actions leading to Parliamentary divorce were undefended. Moreover, to estimate real costs, there would need to be added up to 50% or more, depending on the distance travelled and the number of witnesses produced.

TABLE 10.1. *Parliamentary Divorce Petitions and Acts,*
1700–1857

Petitions				Acts	
Decade	Great Britain	India	Total	Decade	No.
1701–10	6	0	6	1700–9	2
11–20	2[a]	0	2	10–19	2
21–30	3	0	3	20–9	3
31–40	5	0	5	30–9	2
41–50	4	0	4	40–9	5
51–60	18	0	18	50–9	16
61–70	13	0	13	60–9	11
71–80	35	0	35	70–9	34
81–90	20	0	20	80–9	13
91–1800	41	2	43	90–9	43
1801–10	31[b]	2	33	1800–9	24
11–20	34	1	35	10–19	26
21–30	28	8	36	20–9	33
31–40	33[c]	9	42	30–9	32
41–50	43[d]	12	55	40–9	54
51–7	22	5	27	50–7	22
Total	338	39	377		322

[a] One woman—rejected.
[b] Two women—one accepted.
[c] Three women—one accepted.
[d] Two women—rejected.

Source: Anderson, 415, Table I; 418 n. 17; Wolfram, App. 1A. See also *PP 1857*, Session 2, *Accounts and Papers*, 42, 121.

Tables

TABLE 10.2. *Social Status and Parliamentary Divorce, 1700–1857*

A. *All Petitioners*

	Total petitioners	Peers & barts.	Landed gentry	% titled
1700–49	20	7	8	35
1750–80	66	10	11	15
1793–1803	51	6	11	12
1803–27	73	13	0	18
1831–57	124	4	28	3

Source: Anderson, 417, 419, 428, 432, 436, for husbands only.

B. *Successful Petitioners*

	Total acts	Peers & barts.	Esquires	% titled	% titled and esquires
1700–49	14	6	3	43	64
1750–69	28	3	12	11	54
1770–99	88	14	34	16	54
1800–29	75	16	36	21	69
1830–57	118	2	67	2	58

Note: These figures for men of title include successful petitioners *and* defendants. For husbands only, see Wolfram, Table 3.

TABLE 10.3. *Proportion of Petitions for Parliamentary Divorce Withdrawn or Rejected, 1700–1857*

	Total petitioners (including women)	Withdrawn or rejected	%	Lord Chancellor
1700–50	20	6	30	
1750–9	18	2	11	
60–9	13	1	8	
70–9	35	3	9	
80–9	20	6	30	Lord Thurlow (hostile)
90–9	43	4	9	
1800–9	33	13	39	Lord Eldon (hostile)
10–19	35	17	48	
20–9	36	8	22	
30–9	42	7	17	
40–9	55	8	14	Lord Lyndhurst (permissive)
50–7	27	5	18	

Source: Anderson, 415, Table 1.

433

TABLE 10.4. *Proportion of Successful Petitioners for Parliamentary Divorce with No Known Living Issue, 1700–1857*

	Known petitioners	Without living issue	%
1700–49	13	11	85
50–9	15	8	53
60–9	4	2	50
70–9	22	8	36
80–9	10	3	30
90–9	34	11	32
1800–9	17	5	29
10–19	23	2	9
20–9	20	5	25
30–9	35	14	40
40–9	47	18	38
50–7	25	12	48

Source: Wolfram, 175, Table 7.

TABLE 13.1. *Divorce Decrees, Divorce Rate per 1,000 Married Couples, and Petitions for Judicial Separation (England and Wales), 1851–1987*

	Divorce decrees[a]	Divorce rate per 1,000 married couples	Petitions for judicial separation[b]
1851	4	0.0001	
1857	4	0.0001	
1861	141	0.04	49
1866			64
1871	161	0.04	86
1876	208	0.05	136
1881	311	0.07	119
1886	325	0.07	133
1891	369	0.07	110
1896	459	0.08	110
1901	477	0.08	89
1906	546	0.09	92
1911	580	0.09	58
1912	587	0.08	
1913	577	0.08	
1914	856	0.12	
1915	680	0.10	
1916	990	0.14	68
1917	700	0.09	
1918	1,100	0.15	
1919	1,600	0.22	
1920	3,100	0.41	120
1921	3,500	0.46	
1922	2,600	0.34	
1923	2,700	0.35	115
1924	2,300	0.29	
1925	2,600	0.32	
1926	2,600	0.32	
1927	3,200	0.39	
1928	4,000	0.48	
1929	3,400	0.40	
1930	3,600	0.42	
1931	3,800	0.44	
1932	3,900	0.45	
1933	4,000	0.45	
1934	4,300	0.47	
1935	4,100	0.45	
1936	5,100	0.55	96
1937	4,900	0.52	
1938	6,200	0.64	99
1939	8,200	0.84	
1940	7,800	0.79	101
1941	6,400	0.63	101
1942	7,700	0.75	102
1943	10,000	0.98	103
1944	12,300	1.2	104
1945	15,600	1.4	105
1946	29,800	2.8	106
1947	60,300	5.6	107
1948	43,700	4.0	108

TABLE 13.1. (*Cont.*)

	Divorce decrees[a]	Divorce rate per 1,000 married couples	Petitions for judicial separation[b]
1949	34,900	3.2	109
1950	31,000	2.8	83
1951	29,000	2.6	
1952	34,000	3.0	
1953	30,000	2.7	
1954	28,000	2.5	
1955	27,000	2.3	
1956	26,000	2.3	
1957	24,000	2.0	
1958	23,000	1.9	
1959	24,000	2.1	
1960	24,000	2.0	
1961	25,000	2.1	128[c]
1962	29,000	2.4	
1963	32,000	2.7	
1964	35,000	2.9	
1965	38,000	3.1	
1966	39,000	3.3	99[c]
1967	43,000	3.5	
1968	46,000	3.7	
1969	51,000	4.1	119[c]
1970	58,000	4.7	90[c]
1971	74,000	6.0	94[c]
1972	119,000	9.4	
1973	106,000	8.4	
1974	113,000	9.0	
1975	120,000	9.6	
1976	127,000	10.1	
1977	129,000	10.3	
1978	144,000	11.6	
1979	139,000	11.2	
1980	148,000	12.0	
1981	146,000	11.9	
1982	147,000	12.1	
1983	147,000	12.2	
1984	145,000	12.0	
1985	160,000	13.4	
1986	154,000	12.9	
1987	151,000	12.6	

[a] *Social Trends*, 1 (1970), 57; 6 (1975), 57; 10 (1980), 84; 11 (1981), 34; 14 (1984), 36; 18 (1988), 43. I owe the data from 1851 to 1931 and from 1950 to 1987 to the kindness of Dr J. Haskey. The data for 1936 to 1950 were derived by multiplying by 1.5 the divorce rate per 1,000 married women aged 20–49, taken from *Registrar General's Statistical Review of England and Wales* for 1961, Pt. III (London, 1964), 45. Tests show that this provides reasonably accurate figures.

[b] *Royal Commission on Divorce* 1956 (PP 1955–6), 22, 355.

[c] *Social Trends*, 4 (1974), 79.

TABLE 13.2. *Proportion of Successful Divorce Petitions Filed by Wives, and Proportion of Petitions Supported by Legal Aid (England and Wales), 1830–1986*

Period	% of successful divorce petitions filed by wives[a]	% of divorce petitions supported by legal aid[b]		
		Husbands	Wives	Total
1830–57	4 (all failed)	32	21	2
1861–5	38			0
1866–70	43			0
1871–5	40[c]			0
1876–80	44[c]			
1881–5	41[c]			
1886–90	42[c]			
1891–5	42[c]			
1896–1901	40[c]			
1901–5	41			
1906–10	46			
1911–15	43			6
1916–17	39			
1918	33			38
1919	26			41
1920	23			41
1921				22
1922	29			28
1923	39			26
1925	63			26
1930	56			35[d]
1935	57			39
1938	50			35
1939	54			42
1940	55			34
1945	37 ⎫			20
1946	39 ⎬ est.			
1947	50 ⎪			
1948	51 ⎭			
1949	51			
1950	51			25
1951–5	55	42	70	58[e]
1952	57			
1953	56			
1954	56			48
1955	55			
1956	54			
1957	54			
1958	54			
1959	55			
1960	55			
1961	58			
1962	56			
1963	56			
1964	57			
1965	57			

TABLE 13.2. (*cont.*)

Period	% of successful divorce petitions filed by wives[a]	% of divorce petitions supported by legal aid[b]		
		Husbands	Wives	Total
1966–70		44	78	65[f]
1966	58			
1967	60			
1968	61			
1969	60			
1970	61			
1971–6		32	70	57
1971	59			
1972	62			
1973	65			
1974	66			
1975	68			
1976	69	27	69	57
1977	69			
1978	69			
1979	69			
1980	70			
1981	70			
1982	71			
1983	71			
1984	71[b]			
1985	72[b]			
1986	73			

[a] Figures for 1901–6 kindly supplied by Dr J. C. Haskey. J. C. Haskey, 'Secular Changes in Divorce in England and Wales by Class of Decree: A Socio-Legal Analysis', *Biology and Society*, 3 (1986), 62; J. C. Haskey, 'Trends in Marriage and Divorce in England and Wales', *Population Studies*, 48 (1987), 17. G. Rowntree and N. H. Carrier, 'The Resort to Divorce in England and Wales 1838–1957', *Population Studies*, 11 (1957–8), 201. O. R. McGregor, *Divorce in England*, Tables VI, VII, pp. 40–1. *Roy. Com. Div. 1912*, 27, App. III, Table 1. *Social Trends*, 18 (1988), 43.

[b] C. S. Gibson and A. Beer, 'The Effect of Legal Aid on Divorce in England and Wales', *Family Law*, 1 (1971); C. S. Gibson, 'Divorce and the Recourse to Legal Aid', *Modern Law Review* 43 (1980), 613; *Population Trends*, 44 (1986), 9.

[c] All Petitions, successful or unsuccessful.

[d] Introduction of Poor Persons' Rules, 1925.

[e] Passage of the Legal Aid and Advice Act 1949.

[f] More generous conditions under the Legal Aid Act 1960.

Tables

TABLE 13.3. *Maintenance Orders by Magistrates Courts, 1900–1965*

Period	Applications for maintenance	Maintenance granted
1900–4	10,736 + *c.*4,000 = *c.*14,700	
1905–9	11,067 +	
1910–13	10,765 +	
1911–15	7,637 + *c.*4,000 = *c.*11,600	
1919–20	11,087 + *c.*4,000 = *c.*15,000	
1920–4	13,603 +	
1921–5		9,101
1925–9	14,475	
1926–30		10,813
1930–4	14,382	
1934		5,765
1931–5	9,617 + *c.*3,000 = *c.*12,600	
1936–40	10,401 + *c.*5,000 = *c.*15,400	
1941–5	13,418 +	
1946–50		19,208
1950–4	26,835	14,489
1965		(118,000 in force)[a]

[a] *5 Parl. Debates: Lords*, 303 (1696), 322. Of these maintenance orders, 88% were for deserted wives, and only 12% for divorced wives.

Sources: O. R. McGregor, *Divorce in England*, 36, 37, 49, 51; Wolfram App. 2A; *Roy. Com. Divorce 1912*, 1:54, 67; *Roy. Com. Divorce 1956*, 358–9; *Social Trends*, 10 (1980), 84; 11 (1981), 34; 44 (1986), 9; 18 (1988), 43; *Demographic Yearbook* (1968), No. 33; (1982), No. 32; J. Haskey, 'Recent Trends in Divorce in England and Wales: the Effects of Legislative Changes', *Population Trends*, 44 (1986), 9; G. Rowntree and N. H. Carrier, 'The Resort to Divorce in England and Wales 1858–1957', *Population Studies*, 11 (1957–8), 189–90; A. P. Herbert, *The Ayes Have It: the Story of the Marriage Act* (London, 1937).

TABLE 13.4. *Declared Grounds for Divorce Decrees Granted to Husband (England and Wales), 1950–1986*

	Adultery	Behaviour	Desertion	Separation (2 yr.)[a]	Separation (5 yr.)[a]
1950	48%	2.5%	50%		
1951	46	2.5	51		
1952	49	2.5	48		
1953	50	3	46		
1954	51	3	45		
1955	52	3.5	44		
1956	52	4	43		
1957	53	2.5	39		
1958	54	2.5	38		
1959	55	3	37		
1960	56	2	36		
1961	58	2	35		
1962	60	2	34		
1963	61	2	32		
1964	61	2	31		
1965	64	2.5	30		
1966	65	2.5	29		
1967	66	2.5	28		
1968	67	2.5	27		
1969	68	2.5	26		
1970	70	2.5	24		
1971	28	2	11	15%	41%
1972	35	3.5	9	19	32
1973	39	5	7	25	24
1974	39	6	5	28	21
1975	41	6	4	30	18
1976	40	7	3	31	17
1977	40	8	3	31	14
1978	39	9	3	31	15
1979	41	9	2.5	31.5	14
1980	42	9.5	2.5	32	13
1981	43	10.5	2	31.5	12
1982	43	11.5	1.5	31	12
1983	44	12.5	1.5	29.5	11.5
1984	43	13	1	29.5	11
1985	44	15	1	28.5	11
1986	45	17	1	28	11

TABLE 13.4. (Continued) *Declared Grounds for Divorce Decrees Granted to Wife (England and Wales), 1950–1986*

	Adultery	Behaviour	Desertion	Separation (2 yr.)[a]	Separation (5 yr.)[a]
1950	37%	15.5%	47%		
1951	35	18	47.5		
1952	33	21	48		
1953	34	23	44		
1954	35	24	41.5		
1955	35.5	25	39		
1956	36	26	37.5		
1957	36.5	23	30.5		
1958	38	23	32.5		
1959	39	23	30		
1960	39	23.5	29.5		
1961	41	23.5	28.5		
1962	42	23.5	27		
1963	43	25	26		
1964	44.5	26	24		
1965	44	28	22.5		
1966	43	29.5	21.5		
1967	44	30	20		
1968	45	31	19.5		
1969	46	31	18		
1970	47	32.5	17		
1971	25	18	11	18%	26%
1972	26	26	9.5	20	16
1973	25.5	31	7	22	12
1974	25.5	32	6	23	11
1975	25	36	5.5	24	9
1976	24.5	38	4.5	23.5	8
1977	24	39.5	4	24	8
1978	23.5	40.4	3	24	8
1979	24	40.5	2.5	23.5	7
1980	25	42	2	23	6
1981	25	44	1.5	22.5	5.5
1982	24	46	1.5	22	5
1983	24.5	46	1.5	22	5
1984	25	46	1	22	5
1985	25	48	1	20	5
1986	25	50	1	19	5

[a] After 1971, divorce was granted for irretrievable break-down based on adultery or intolerable 'behaviour', or by mutual consent after separation for two years, or by consent of one party only after separation for five years.

Source: This table was read off from Fig. 13.4, published in *Social Trends* 1987) 17. 50; (1988) 18. Table 2.18.

TABLE 13.5. *Average Duration of Marriage and Proportion of Life Spent Married (England and Wales), by Male Birth Cohorts, 1900–1945*

	Male birth cohorts									
	1900–1904	1905–1909	1910–1914	1915–1919	1920–1924	1925–1929	1930–1934	1935–1939	1940–1944	1945
Average duration of marriage (in years)	35.3	35.3	35.5	35.3	35.3	35.0	34.1	32.8	31.6	31.0
Proportion of life spent married (as %)	52	52	53	53	54	54	55	56	56	56

Source: R. Schoen and J. Baj, 'Twentieth Century Cohort Marriage and Divorce in England and Wales', *Population Studies*, 38 (1984), 443.

TABLE 13.6. *Proportion of Divorces by Years of Marriage (Great Britain), 1951–1985*

	0–4	5–9	10–14	15–19	20+
1951	10	32	24	14	20
1961	11	31	23	14	22
1971	13	31	19	13	24
1981	20[a]	30	19	13	19
1985	27[a]	26	17	12	17

[a] Result of 1969 Divorce Reform Act reducing time of separation before divorce to 3 years (in effect after 1971).

Source: Social Trends, 17 (1987), 50.

TABLE 13.7. *Remarriages as a Proportion of all Marriages (Great Britain), 1901–1986*

	All remarriages as a % of all marriages	Remarriages after divorce as a % of all marriages
1901	13	
1911	11	
1921		
1931	11	
1941		
1951	18	
1961	15	9
1966	16	
1971	20	15
1976	31	26
1981	34	31
1986	35	33

Source: Social Trends, 4 (1973), 78; 8 (1977), 54; 18 (1988), 40.

TABLE 13.8. *Average and Median Age at First Marriage (Great Britain), 1901–1986*

	Average		Median	
	Male	Female	Male	Female
1901	27.2	25.6		
1911	27.3	25.6		
1921	27.6	25.5		
1931	27.4	25.5		
1941				
1951	26.8	24.6		
1961	25.3	23.6		
1971	24.6	22.1	23.4	21.1
1981			24.1	21.9
1986	26.3	24.3		

Source: Social Trends 1 (1970), 56; 4 (1973), 78; 13 (1983), 30; 14 (1984), 35; 18 (1988), 41.

TABLE 13.9. *Proportion of First Marriages Ending in Divorce (England and Wales) by Male Birth Cohorts, 1900–1954*

Period of births of male cohorts	% ending in divorce
1900–4	5
1905–9	7
1910–14	9
1915–19	11
1920–4	13
1925–9	15
1930–4	18
1935–9	22
1940–4	25
1945	27
*c.*1950–4	[*c.*33][a]

[a] Estimate by J. Haskey, 'The Proportion of Marriages Ending in Divorce', *Population Trends*, 27 (1982), 5. For a calculation producing lower estimates of the divorce rate from 1911 to 1954, see O. R. McGregor, *Divorce in England* (London, 1957), 38.
Source: R. Schoer and J. Baj, 'Twentieth Century Cohort Marriage and Divorce in England and Wales', *Population Studies*, 38 (1984), Table 1.

TABLE 13.10. *International Comparisons: Divorce Rates per 1,000 Married Couples, 1961–1985*

	England and Wales	Belgium	Denmark	France	Netherlands	Germany (Fed. Rep.)
1961	2.1	2.0	5.8	2.9	2.2	3.6
1962	2.4	2.0	5.5	2.8	2.2	3.4
1963	2.7	2.1	5.5	2.7	2.2	3.5
1964	2.8	2.2	5.5	3.0	2.3	3.8
1965	3.1	2.3	5.4	3.1	2.2	3.9
1966	3.2	2.4	5.5	3.2	2.4	3.9
1967	3.5	2.4	5.7	3.2	2.6	4.1
1968	3.7	2.4	6.2	3.1	2.7	4.2
1969	4.1	2.6	7.2	3.2	3.0	4.7
1970	4.7	2.7	7.2	3.3	3.3	5.1
1971	6.0	2.8	10.8	3.9	3.8	5.2
1972	9.6	3.2	10.9	3.9	4.5	5.5
1973	8.4	3.2	10.5	4.1	5.4	5.7
1974	9.0	4.1	11.0	4.8	5.7	6.2
1975	9.6	4.3	10.6	4.9	6.0	6.7
1976	10.2	5.1	10.5	5.0	6.2	6.9
1977	10.4	5.1	10.8	5.8	6.3	
1978	11.6	5.4	10.7	6.4	6.5	
1979	11.3	5.4	10.8	6.9	7.0	
1980	12.0		11.3		7.5	
1981						
1982						
1983						
1984						
1985	13.4	7.3	12.6	8.1	9.9	8.6

Source: This table was read off Fig. 13.11, taken from *Social Trends*, 13 (1983), 32 and ibid. 18 (1988), 43.

TABLE 13.11. *Illegitimate Births as a Proportion of all Births (England and Wales), 1700–1986*

1700–4	1.8	1861–5	6.4
1710–14	2.0	1871–5	5.2
1720–4	2.0	1881–5	4.8
1730–4	2.7	1891–5	4.2
1740–4	2.9	1901–5	4.0
1750–4	3.1	1911–15	4.3
1760–4	4.0	1921–5	4.2
1770–4	4.3	1931–5	4.3
1780–4	4.9	1941–5	6.8
1790–4	5.0	1951–5	4.8
1800–4	5.3	1961–5	6.9
1810–4	5.1	1968	8.3
1820–4	5.5	1971	8.4
1830–4	4.2	1974	8.8
1845–9	6.8	1981	12
1851–5	6.6	1986	21

Sources: 1700–1834 from a sample of 98 parishes, P. Laslett, K. Oosterveen, and R. M. Smith (eds.), *Bastardy and its Comparative History* (London, 1980), Table 1.1*a*);
  1845–1974: ibid., Table 1.1*b* (Great Britain);
  1968–86: *Social Trends*, 1 (1970), 56; 18 (1988), 46.

TABLE 13.12. *Number of Children under 11 Years of Divorcing Couples (England and Wales), 1970–1980*

1970	55,000
1971	65,000
1972	100,000
1973	97,000
1974	105,000
1975	107,000
1976	110,000
1977	107,000
1978	115,000
1979	110,000
1980	112,000

Source: Social Trends, 16 (1986), 40; 17 (1987), 50.

TABLE 13.13. *Number of Divorced Persons Not Remarried (England and Wales), 1951–1986*

1951	209,000
1961	284,000
1971	517,000
1976	969,000
1981	1,543,000
1986	2,245,000

Source: Social Trends, 76 (1976), 68; 18 (1988), 43.

Index